W9-CGQ-109

Fundamentals of INVESTMENTS

RICHARD A. STEVENSON
EDWARD H. JENNINGS

University of Iowa

Fundamentals of INVESTMENTS

WEST PUBLISHING COMPANY

St. Paul • New York • Boston
Los Angeles • San Francisco

Library of Congress Cataloging in Publication Data

Stevenson, Richard A. 1938–
Fundamentals of investments.

Bibliography, p.
Includes index.
1. Investments. 2. Investment analysis.
1. Jennings, Edward H. 1937– II. Title.
HG4521.S759 332.6'78 72-45320

ISBN 0-8299-0077-2

1st Reprint—1977

Preface

Radical changes have occurred in the field of investments during the past ten to fifteen years. New forms of securities have emerged in response to perceived needs and desires of investors. The structure of the markets in which securities trade has undergone substantial change. Investors are increasingly aware of expected returns in relation to the risks that need to be assumed in seeking the return. Investment performance measurement gives increasing recognition to risk-adjusted performance. The impact of a given investment on the portfolio of the investor continues to receive great attention. Investors show growing interest in the investment potential of nontraditional investment media such as metals, commodity futures, paintings, and antiques.

It is within this complex and changing investment environment that we decided to write this book. The text is designed for the introductory college course in investments. We have attempted to introduce many of the new developments in the field of investments, while retaining enough descriptive material so that the beginning student may become familiar with the various investment alternatives and the investment environment in which they are available. In trying to integrate newer developments with more traditional investment management material, we have attempted to explain the newer developments in a clear and comprehensible manner. We have avoided sophisticated mathematical presentations as far as possible and have assumed only a minimal knowledge of accounting and economics.

The book is divided into five main sections. Chapters 1 to 5 provide basic information with regard to the investment environment. Section II (Chapters 6 to 10) provide an approach to the valuation of equity securities. Chapters 11 to 15 introduce the reader to portfolio theory. Chapters 16 to 24 comprise Section IV, which presents an analysis of investments other than common stock. Chapter 25 presents an integrated approach to personal financial asset planning.

We feel that this book is sufficiently flexible in its construction so that it may be used in a wide variety of investments courses. Indeed, most instructors will probably neither want nor be able to adequately cover all the topics in this book in a quarter or a semester. Chapters 11 to 15 cover the basic portfolio approach and the recent risk-return literature. Even though we decided to introduce the portfolio approach in the middle of the text so that we could consider the portfolio implications of the various types of securities as these securities are discussed, the instructor wishing to skip most of this material will find that Chapters 16 to 25 are written in as self-contained a manner as possible. Hence, students should be able to comprehend with little difficulty both the nature of the investment being considered and its portfolio implications.

The text considers a great variety of possible investments. Chapter 19 includes a discussion of money market funds as well as federal government and municipal securities. Chapter 22 discusses such investment possibilities as commodity futures, art masterpieces, stamps and coins, and gold. The nature, method, and portfolio ramifications of foreign investments are discussed in Chapter 23. Chapter 24 deals with leverage-inherent securities such as warrants and options.

Each chapter has questions at the end. These questions are designed for review purposes as well as to encourage the student to think about situations that may not be covered directly in the text material. For those chapters where problems are feasible, a number of realistic problems are included. These problems should allow the student to obtain a better understanding of the material covered in the chapter. Carefully chosen suggested readings are presented at the end of each chapter.

A large number of individuals provided assistance to the authors in the preparation of this book. Over 100 students at the University of Iowa and approximately 75 at the University of Wisconsin at Oshkosh used portions of the book in draft form and provided much valuable feedback to the authors. We benefited greatly from the critical comments of our professional colleagues. Professors Eugene Drzycimski (University of Wisconsin at Oshkosh), Stanley Jacobs (University of Missouri at Kansas City), Paul Jessup (University of Minnesota), Timothy Johnson (University of Cincinnati), Elton Scott (University of Oklahoma), and David West (University of Missouri at Columbia) read all or portions of the manuscript and their valuable contributions are especially appreciated. A number of graduate students at the University of Iowa assisted in the collection and organization of data and also provided additional feedback from the perspective of the student. We are especially appreciative of the contributions of Barbara Burke, Kathy Edwards, David Spencer, and Martin Strabala. Typing assistance was provided by Ellen Smith, Pam Moenk, and Barbara Stanley. Finally, we would like to acknowledge our debt to our families and to our colleagues at the University of Iowa for encouraging us in this endeavor.

Richard A. Stevenson
Edward H. Jennings

Iowa City, Iowa

Contents

3

Investor Participation in the Markets 31

4

Sources of Investment Information 53

5

The Tax Environment 69

6

Introduction to Risk and Return 85

24

Leverage-Inherent Securities 485

25

Integrated Financial Planning 515

Fundamentals of INVESTMENTS

1

The Affluent Society

The success of individual financial management has become increasingly important in recent decades. Making sound asset management decisions requires development of the knowledge and essential skills to make prudent and financially rewarding investments. Knowledge is needed regarding the nature of the myriad investment alternatives available in today's complex economic environment. Skills are needed to evaluate the potential risk and return associated with an investment decision. Additionally, it is crucial for the investor to know what results have been achieved by past investment decisions.

This chapter examines the factors that have made a person's financial management decisions in the investment area increasingly important over the years. Then, the nature and growth of the asset holdings of individuals are detailed. Following this review of background factors, we present an approach to the investment process. Virtually every investment decision follows the four basic steps we will examine. Finally, the plan of the rest of the book is presented along with a summary of the chapter.

IMPORTANCE OF INVESTMENT DECISIONS

Men and women should be concerned with management of their financial resources for many reasons. Included among these reasons are a longer life expectancy, increasing rates of taxation, high interest rates, high rates of inflation, and larger incomes. Each of these five factors is discussed below.

Life Expectancy

People are living longer now than they were fifty or even twenty-five years ago. Coupled with a trend toward earlier retirements, a longer life expectancy suggests that earnings from employment should be saved and invested so the principal and income will be adequate for a greater number of retirement years. The tabulation below shows statistics for 1940 and 1968 for the average sixteen-year-old male.[1]

	1940	*1968*
Additional life expectancy in years	50.4	52.9
Expected retirement in years	5.6	7.6

Moreover, the life expectancy of females is 7.8 years greater than for males.[2] This means that females are likely to have the responsibility of managing the proceeds of an estate for several years. In addition, the growing participation of females in the labor force may mean more females will be responsible for planning for their own retirement years.

Level of Taxation

Higher levels of taxation over the years at the federal, state, and local levels also make careful financial management necessary. For example, federal personal income taxes took 8.1 percent of total personal income in 1950, but 9.9 percent in 1972.[3] The percentage increase at the state and local level for this period is even more pronounced. With a large percentage of income going for various taxes over the years, before-tax rates of return on investment must be at sufficiently high levels so that after-tax rates of return are satisfactory.

[1]Howard N. Fullerton, "A Table of Expected Working Life for Men, 1968," *Monthly Labor Review*, June 1971, pp. 49–55.

[2]*1974 Statistical Abstract of the United States* (Washington, D.C.: U.S. Government Printing Office, 1974), p. 58. These are life expectancy figures at birth for a female born in 1972.

[3]Calculated by dividing individual income tax, after credits, by personal income.

Level of Interest Rates

A third reason for sound individual practice of financial management is the level of interest rates experienced since the mid-1960s. When a person can earn 8 percent or more on good quality fixed-income investments, the failure to employ investable funds fully in the most efficient manner may mean a substantial loss of income. Throughout this book, we are concerned with determining whether the investor is getting an acceptable return given the risks being taken.

Inflation Rates

Inflation was not an especially significant factor until recent years. While the Consumer Price Index (CPI) increased at an annual compound rate of approximately 1.1 percent from 1950 to 1964, the CPI's annual rate of increase was approximately 5.1 percent from 1965 to 1974. In this latter period, a person needed to achieve higher investment returns in order to compensate for the higher inflation rates. It appears that relatively high levels of inflation will be a continuing problem with which investors must cope.

Growth of Income

One final reason for concern with personal financial management is simply that individuals now have more income to manage than in previous years. One concept of income is per capita disposable personal income. Table 1–1 shows the growth of disposable personal income from 1950 to 1974. Disposable personal income is essentially what people have left after taxes and is often referred to as take-home pay. Expressed in current dollars (not adjusted for changes in the cost of living), per capita disposable personal income increased every year since 1950. Even when adjusted for changes in the cost of living by expressing the annual disposable personal income in terms of 1970 dollars, advances occurred in all years except 1954, 1958, and 1974. In these three years the declines were less than 1 percent, except for 1974.

One additional concept of income shows the favorable past growth in consumer income. Figure 1–1 shows the growth of supernumerary income since 1955 along with projections to 1980 and is expressed in 1970 dollars to adjust for inflation. Supernumerary income is that portion of consumer income which is not needed for the essentials of life and which is available for optional spending or investment. It consists of all income in excess of $15,000 for each family unit.[4]

[4] *A Guide to Consumer Markets, 1973/74*, (New York: The Conference Board, Inc., 1973), p. 144.

TABLE 1-1

U.S. per Capita Disposable Personal Income—1950-74

Year	Current Dollars	1970 Dollars
1950	1,364	2,128
1951	1,469	2,143
1952	1,518	2,170
1953	1,583	2,232
1954	1,585	2,216
1955	1,666	2,321
1956	1,743	2,378
1957	1,801	2,384
1958	1,831	2,367
1959	1,905	2,432
1960	1,938	2,435
1961	1,984	2,468
1962	2,066	2,547
1963	2,139	2,605
1964	2,284	2,748
1965	2,436	2,897
1966	2,605	3,022
1967	2,751	3,108
1968	2,947	3,217
1969	3,117	3,264
1970	3,344	3,344
1971	3,595	3,452
1972	3,807	3,569
1973	4,295	3,782
1974	4,645	3,654

Source: U.S. Department of Commerce, *Business Conditions Digest,* various issues.

The supernumerary income series is a general measure of consumer affluence. Supernumerary income almost tripled as a percentage of personal income between 1955 and 1970. The Department of Commerce estimates that supernumerary income will be 22.6 percent of personal income by 1980.[5] If this projection is reasonably accurate, financial management by individuals will continue to become increasingly important.

GROWTH OF INDIVIDUAL ASSET HOLDINGS

People acquire wealth in many different forms. Table 1-2 lists the major financial assets and liabilities of individuals for 1960 and 1973. Subtracting the liabilities from the assets yields the individual net equity position.

[5] *Ibid.*

FIGURE 1-1

Supernumerary Income as Percentage of Total Income

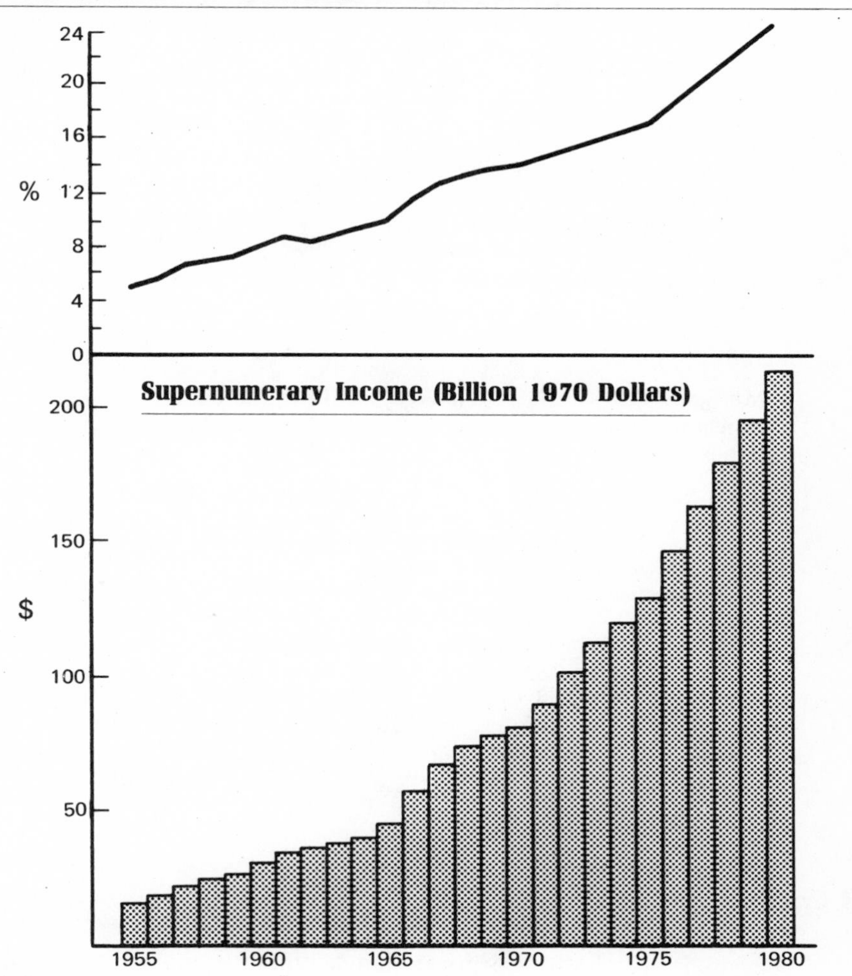

Source: The Conference Board, *A Guide to Consumer Markets, 1973/1974,* p. 144.

During the period from 1960 to 1973, individual net equity rose at a compound annual rate of increase of 6.3 percent. However, a calculation of the rate of increase through 1974 would undoubtedly result in a lower figure because of the pronounced decline in the market value of stocks during 1974. According to a *Business Week* article, the value of stocks owned by individuals fell from $959 billion to $525 billion in the two-year period ending December 1974.[6] The article cites evidence from various

[6]"How Sagging Stocks Depress the Economy," *Business Week,* January 27, 1975, pp. 88–89.

TABLE 1-2

Financial Assets and Liabilities of U.S. Individuals at End of Year

	(Billions of Dollars)		Average Annual Growth Rate 1960–73
	1960	1973	
Financial assets, total	$957	$2,302	7.0%
Currency, demand deposits	65	170	7.7
Savings accounts	165	636	10.9
U.S. government securities	70	105	3.2
Corporate stock (market value)	394	744	5.0
Insurance, pension reserves	176	458	7.6
Other assets	87	189	6.2
Liabilities, total	226	661	8.6
Mortgage debt	146	404	8.1
Consumer credit	56	180	9.4
Other liabilities	24	77	9.4
Net equity	731	1,641	6.3

Notes: Data refer to households, personal trusts, and nonprofit organizations. The numbers may not add because of rounding.

Sources: *Federal Reserve Bulletin,* November 1969, p. A 71.14 and October 1974, p. A 59.20.

business economists that this decline in consumers' wealth influenced their spending decisions. Not only did the decline of about 25 percent in stock prices in 1974 cause the value of individuals' total financial assets to decline, but the decline apparently also had a negative effect on the growth of the economy.

Corporate Stocks

The market value of corporate stock typically makes up about 35 to 40 percent of total U.S. financial assets owned by individuals. Actually, individuals have been net sellers of stock held in their own names for many years. Offsetting this development has been the rapid growth of institutions, such as mutual funds, as a means of channeling investment funds into the stock market. We will discuss the nature and significance of this development at various places throughout the book.

Savings Accounts

Savings accounts were the fastest growing personal financial asset of individuals from 1960 to 1973. Financial institutions have been aggressive in recent years in attempting to attract savings accounts. Not only has the maximum allowable interest payable on regular savings accounts at financial institutions increased since 1960, but even higher rates of return have been offered on money deposited for long periods of time.

Pension Fund Asset Holdings

The rapid post-World War II growth of private and public pension plans has profound implications for financial asset planning. If persons or families experience an increase in their financial security as a result of pension plan participation, other and possibly more risky types of investments may be purchased. Direct investment in either the stock or bond market with the risks entailed becomes more feasible, since one's future financial obligations may be satisfied to a considerable extent with an institutional form of saving.

Private pension plans may be classified as either insured or uninsured. Insured pension plans are administered by a life insurance company. The number of Americans enrolled in insured pension plans reached an estimated 12.4 million at the end of 1972.[7] Private, noninsured pension plans, which are usually administered by the trust department of a commercial bank, covered over 24 million people at year-end 1971.

Approximately 143 million people had Social Security earnings credited to their accounts at year-end 1973. An estimated 116 million people had spent enough time in the system to qualify for some benefits at retirement.[8] Social Security benefits may represent an important part of a person's financial planning. For example, between 1950 and 1974, the average monthly benefit for retired workers rose from $43.86 to $188.21.[9]

Life Insurance in Force

Individual and group life insurance in force in the United States has shown a long-term annual increase virtually without regard to the stage of the business cycle. Figure 1-2 shows the growth of individual and group life insurance in force since 1942.

In recent years, life insurance per family has been about twice as large as annual disposable personal income. This average result in no way implies that a person is adequately insured if life insurance is equal to twice his or her annual take-home pay. The need for insurance must be examined by each individual with consideration given to unique personal circumstances.

[7] *Life Insurance Fact Book, 1974.* New York: Institute of Life Insurance, p. 37.
[8] *Ibid.*, pp. 37–38.
[9] *Social Security Bulletin*, April 1975, p. 56.

FIGURE 1-2

Growth of Individual and Group Life Insurance in Force in the United States—1942-73

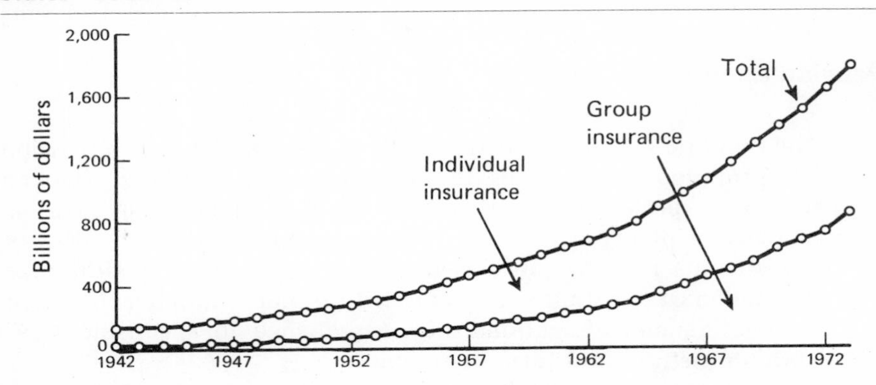

Source: *Life Insurance Fact Book 1973,* p. 24; and *Life Insurance Fact Book 1974,* p. 22.

To the extent that life insurance, in the event of premature death, provides the possibility of an immediate estate and freedom from worry about the needs of beneficiaries, people are able to invest in more risky ventures in pursuit of higher rates of return. In this regard, insurance in force performs in much the same manner as pension fund participation. In the case of a pension fund, one's financial obligations during the retirement years may be satisfied, while life insurance aids in satisfying the financial needs of a beneficiary upon the death of the insured. Similarly, health and disability insurance may provide financial security in the event of illness and help to alleviate the need to make one's investments with health considerations in mind.

A FOUR-STAGE INVESTMENT PROCESS

A Financial Inventory

The investment decision for an individual can be viewed as a four-stage process. The first stage involves making certain one's financial affairs are in order prior to considering other investments. Has enough life insurance been provided to create an immediate estate, if life insurance is needed? Have the needs for accident and disability insurance been carefully examined and satisfied? Has an emergency fund been established? The emergency fund should consist of assets which can be converted into cash quickly and with little loss of principal. Savings accounts are one of the major ways of providing for an emergency fund although credit availability might also be considered.

Forming Beliefs

After an individual has arranged for a logical insurance program and has established an emergency fund, the second stage of the investment process starts. In this stage, the individual forms beliefs regarding the future behavior of the prices of and returns from individual financial assets. This includes personal assets such as the family residence as well as financial assets such as stocks and bonds.

Many questions need to be considered by the investor in this stage. For example, will the price of AT&T common stock increase at a 6 percent rate or at a 12 percent rate, or will it decline? Will the dividend continue at the same rate per share? The primary concern is to determine the expected return on an individual asset and its associated risk. Then, a decision may be made regarding whether the asset's value is greater than its price. The process taking place in this stage is often referred to as security analysis.

Portfolio Planning

The third stage takes the beliefs about the future as given and attempts to determine the combination of assets that will best satisfy the objectives of the investor. These objectives may vary considerably with different types of investors in different economic circumstances and include the growth and safety of principal, liquidity, income, ease of management, and collateral value and tax considerations. Each of these objectives is discussed below.

Safety and Growth of Principal. High-quality investments are often desired so that the principal will remain intact. Many investors equate this objective with the purchase of high-quality corporate bonds and U.S. Treasury securities. While investments of this sort may help keep the dollar value of a portfolio reasonably constant, inflation may reduce the purchasing power of the portfolio. Hence, investors often seek capital growth in the portfolio to keep the portfolio safe in terms of purchasing power. The task of the investor is to balance safety of principal with growth objectives in a manner consistent with his or her personal preferences.

Liquidity. This objective may be very important to some investors and relatively unimportant to others. While almost any portfolio should have the ability to generate cash within a reasonable time period by the sale of portfolio assets at a price reasonably close to their present selling price, such factors as the nature of the investor's wage income become important. For example, a salesman on commission might desire greater liquidity in the portfolio than a teacher with a relatively stable income.

Income. Current income may be sacrificed in favor of growth potential. The need for current income varies greatly, depending upon such factors as the age and wealth of the investor. During an investor's most productive working years, current income may not be very important. Hence, growth often becomes the most important investment objective. For an individual in the retirement years, a portfolio may very well need to be structured to provide a high level of current income.

Ease of Management. The growth of financial institutions specializing in the management of money for individuals is a manifestation of the investor's desire to be relieved of the difficult and often time-consuming tasks of investment management. In essence, the desire for ease of management normally varies inversely with both the investment education of the investor and the other demands upon the time of the individual.

Collateral Value and Tax Considerations. If an investor plans to use securities as collateral against which loans are made, the quality of those securities becomes important. Generally, the higher the quality of the security, the larger the percentage of its value a financial institution will loan. Tax considerations are the subject of Chapter 5.

Feedback

The fourth stage, the feedback step, attempts to measure results and to make any needed corrections. Were the investor's objectives achieved? If not, why not? What should be changed in order to correct the deficiencies? Obviously, this stage overlaps the second and third stages and cannot be examined without considering what decisions were made and what opportunities were available.

Whatever the stage of the investment process, one should recognize that investment decisions are made in a world of uncertainty. Consequently, we cannot and should not expect to be able to develop investment techniques that will always work. Instead, we should be concerned with concepts and applications that will satisfy investment objectives *on the average.* Finding the next IBM or Xerox is a laudable goal but few will succeed. This book may not reveal techniques which will earn millions. Rather, concepts are presented that allow wise investment decisions to be made in the context of one's objectives. Investment performance is examined on the basis of the objectives. If high risk is accepted, performance should be consistent with the performance of other high-risk investment alternatives.

PLAN OF THE BOOK

The subject matter of the book parallels the four-stage fashion outlined above. Chapters 2 to 4 are concerned with the markets where financial assets are traded and sources of information regarding these markets. Chapter 5 discusses the tax environment and its impact on investors. Chapters 6 through 10 examine the security analysis stage. The discussion takes the point of view of the investor in common stock, but this does not imply that other financial assets are unimportant. If the techniques of common stock analysis can be mastered, the analysis of other financial instruments such as bonds, mutual funds, and warrants will seem comparable and less complex. Chapters 11 to 15 discuss the portfolio problem and the performance measurement stage. Chapters 16 through 24 examine specialized types of investments. Chapter 25 attempts to place all the previous material in the context of a lifetime portfolio approach.

The developments in the last ten to fifteen years in the field of investments have been revolutionary. These developments have also been highly complex to many people because of the mathematics involved. This book is written with the philosophy that mathematics and statistics are investment tools designed to improve our decisions. A concept is presented without mathematics if possible. When such a presentation is not possible, the techniques do not go beyond elementary statistics except in certain isolated cases, which are confined to appendices.

The approach taken in this book is that a theory should be practical from the investor's viewpoint. A theory should be positive in the sense that it is applicable to the real world and has the capability of improving investment decisions. A normative theory, which describes what should occur, has no place in the book unless what should occur can occur in practice. The practicality of a given theory is judged using the basic philosophy that the cost of application of the theory should be less than the potential gain from using the approach.

SUMMARY

Not only is investments an exciting and interesting field to study, but proper investment management is becoming increasingly important. Consequently, it is necessary for an individual to integrate all the various aspects of investments into a coordinated financial plan. For example, one must understand the implications of belonging to a private pension plan, of contributing to the Social Security System, of having company-provided life insurance, and of having a whole range of fringe benefits provided by an employer.

Personal financial management also assumes increasing significance in view of the increased number of years a retiree can expect to live. High interest rates coupled with high rates of inflation make it imperative for investors to make sure that investment funds are not idle, but rather are earning the maximum possible return for the risk assumed. As personal incomes have risen, the tax bite by federal, state, and local governments has increased. This means that tax factors often assume an important role in investment decision making.

We discussed the investment decision as a four-stage process. The first stage is the establishment of those elements of a financial program that should be provided before one invests directly in securities. These elements include proper insurance and an emergency fund. We might also include the careful consideration of the ramifications of employer-provided fringe benefits in this stage. The second stage is the formation of beliefs regarding the expected return and risk from an investment alternative. In the third stage, the individual constructs portfolios based upon the investigation of individual securities conducted in stage two. Many questions need to be answered in the portfolio planning stage. What are the investment objectives? What types of assets should be purchased and in what proportions? Which specific assets within a given asset category should be purchased? In the last stage the score is tallied. The investment performance and its possible improvement are the two main considerations.

QUESTIONS

1. Why has the management of personal financial assets become such an important task in recent years?
2. Define supernumerary income. Why do you feel that this concept of income is or is not a good way to measure the affluence of Americans?
3. In addition to the financial assets discussed in this chapter, other forms of assets have important implications in how individuals invest in financial assets. Describe some of these other assets and why they are so important.
4. Inflation since 1965 has been more rapid than in the fifteen years prior to that date.
   a) Describe specific changes that might be expected to occur in the manner in which individuals manage their financial assets as a result of the expectation of continued high rates of inflation.
   b) Might the securities market offer the investor a different form of asset as a result of this inflation?
5. Both public and private pension plan assets have grown rapidly in recent years with the possible exception of 1974.
   a) Of what significance is this institutional arrangement in planning for financial security during retirement years?
   b) Can you think of any problems which could result if an individual relies exclusively on a pension plan for retirement income?
6. What are the four stages in the investment process?

SUGGESTED READINGS

Bauman, W. Scott. *Performance Objectives of Investors.* Occasional Paper Number 2. Charlottesville, Va.: Financial Analysts Research Foundation, 1975, pp. 29–50.

Eilbott, Peter. "Trends in the Value of Individual Stockholdings." *Journal of Business,* July 1974, pp. 339–348.

Freund, William C. "The Historical Role of the Individual Investor in the Corporate Equity Market." *Journal of Contemporary Business,* Winter 1974, pp. 1–12.

Klemkosky, Robert C. and David F. Scott, Jr. "Withdrawal of the Individual Investor From the Equity Markets." *MSU Business Topics,* Spring 1973, pp. 7–14.

Lease, Ronald C., Wilbur G. Lewellen, and Gary C. Schlarbaum. "The Individual Investor: Attributes and Attitudes." *Journal of Finance,* May 1974, pp. 413–433.

Smidt, Seymour. "The Changing Relative Roles of Individuals and Institutions in the Stock Market." *Journal of Contemporary Business,* Winter 1974, pp. 13–23.

*

2

The Capital Markets

The economic strength of the United States is partially the result of strong and efficient capital markets. This chapter describes the capital markets and their importance, noting where changes are being discussed in the financial community. A discussion of the manner in which an individual investor participates in the markets and capital market regulatory activities is presented in the next chapter.

WHAT IS A CAPITAL MARKET?

In a broad sense, capital markets include all financial transactions between a user of funds and a supplier of funds. For example, when we place funds in a local financial institution such as a bank, a savings and loan association, or a credit union, we engage in a capital market transaction in the broad meaning of the term. When we borrow from a financial institution, a capital market transaction is involved. However, for many aspects of this book, we will use a narrower view of capital markets. Much of our discussion of capital markets will be confined to relatively long-term, impersonal financial instruments such as stocks and bonds.

The potential for resale is an important aspect of a capital market transaction for the investor; we will typically limit our discussion of financial transactions to those that would ordinarily be completed *with* the use of a third party such as a broker. If you purchase stock in your brother-in-law's firm, the transaction would not ordinarily be a part of the capital markets discussed here since we are concerned primarily with transactions in the *organized* capital markets.

AGENT AND PRINCIPAL TRANSACTIONS

One of the difficulties in understanding the nature of transactions in the capital markets is that transactions occur in different forms. In addition, these different transactions could be handled by the same party acting in a different capacity each time. Because of these considerations, it is useful to distinguish between an agent transaction and a principal transaction.

An agent transaction occurs when a third party acts only to facilitate the transaction between the two main parties (i.e., the agent's "best effort" is given). For example, a real estate firm typically acts as an agent when bringing the buyer and the seller together so that a transaction can occur. In an agent transaction, the third party *does not have* any capital at risk. The real estate firm does not normally purchase a house from the seller and then attempt to find a buyer for the house.

In a principal transaction, the third party *does have* capital involved in the transaction. If the real estate firm actually purchased the house from the seller and then attempted to find a buyer, the firm would then be a principal in the transaction. In such a case, title to the house has passed from the seller to the real estate firm. The real estate firm now owns the house, has money tied up in the transaction, and is taking the risks associated with the ownership of a house. Of primary concern is the fact that the real estate firm, as a principal in the transaction, may have difficulty finding a buyer for the house and may lose money when the sale is finally made.

WAYS OF CLASSIFYING MARKETS

There are several ways in which capital markets can be classified. Four different ways are examined even though there may be a slight overlap among the different categories. We will divide capital markets into the following classifications: 1) primary and secondary markets; 2) national and regional markets; 3) organized exchanges and the over-the-counter market; and 4) auction and negotiated markets. The specific exchanges and the characteristics of these markets will also be discussed.

Primary and Secondary Markets

A *primary market* is a market in which the users of capital directly obtain funds. The cash involved in the transaction is taken directly into the asset structure of the user firm. *Investment* occurs, in the economist's meaning of the term, since the firm will probably use the funds productively to build a plant, buy machinery, or to increase the sales capacity of the firm. For example, when AT&T issues a *new* stock or bond, the cash goes directly to AT&T to spend as the needs of the business dictate. The new issue transaction occurs in the primary market.

The *secondary market* is confined to transactions involving investors where the ultimate user of funds is not involved. In the secondary market, trades are among investors in previously issued financial instruments. The secondary market might even be described as a market for "used" securities. By far the vast majority of capital market transactions occur in the secondary market. Indeed, the act of raising capital by a corporation is often referred to as an "episodic event," signifying its unusual and infrequent nature.[1]

In spite of the dominance of the secondary market, its purpose and economic function are often misunderstood. What is the economic function of a secondary market if the user of funds is not involved? The following discussion provides a basis for answering this question.

Suppose someone approaches you with an opportunity to purchase the common stock of a firm being formed. After a careful analysis, you conclude that the stock would be a good investment. However, before investing you decide to find out what rights you will have as an owner of the firm. You find out about voting rights, dividends, the right to buy additional shares of stock, and even the liquidation right, but nowhere can you find out how to sell your stock or obtain the return of your initial investment. You realize liquidation of the firm may be the only way "out" and the purchase of the firm's common stock may be a commitment of funds for the life of the firm. When you point out this problem to the firm, you are told that it would be difficult for the firm to agree to return investments to its stockholders on demand. Such a commitment could destroy the continuity of the firm. The end result is that you would probably not invest in the firm even though the opportunity was favorable in every other way.

The problem described is the fundamental reason secondary markets exist in a modern economy. Their existence allows the investor to commit

[1]The majority of new issues are concentrated in a few industries such as utilities.

funds to an enterprise without sacrificing the potential of recovering the investment at some unknown future date (short of liquidating the firm). If the investor requires funds, the common stock can be sold in the secondary market without directly affecting the operation of the firm. The firm can obtain long-term funds while the investor can commit funds for virtually any period of time.

In providing potential liquidity to the investor, the secondary market improves and facilitates the allocation of scarce resources within the economy. Investment in profitable and efficient opportunities is not limited by the potential need that investors might have to liquidate their investments. However, a smoothly functioning secondary market does not imply that one's investment is guaranteed. Factors such as poor management or lack of demand for the firm's products or services would eventually eliminate the firm's appeal to investors and, hence, its ability to attract scarce capital. No additional resources would tend to flow to the corporation. Since expansion is prevented, the firm may eventually be eliminated, freeing resources for more efficient uses. The existence of a secondary market facilitates this process by providing investors with the opportunity to dispose of investments in unsuccessful firms and reinvest in firms with greater potential.

National and Regional Markets

Capital markets may be either national or regional in scope. In fact, some capital markets are even international in scope. National capital markets involve securities issued by the largest, best-known corporations in the country, the federal government, widely held state securities, and investment companies of substantial size. The center for national capital markets is New York City, but several other major cities in the U.S. (such as Chicago and Boston) could also be considered as important in U.S. capital markets.

Many capital markets are only regional in scope. In these markets, the major types of securities traded tend to be those of local companies and debt obligations of the small cities and towns located in the region. The securities of firms originally traded in the regional markets may eventually grow large enough to attract a nationwide following. For example, Winnebago Industries started as a firm that sold common stock only to Iowa residents. The common stock of Winnebago Industries is now traded on the New York Stock Exchange (NYSE), a national market to be described in detail shortly.

Organized Exchanges and the Over-the-Counter Market

Securities trade either on organized exchanges such as the NYSE or in the over-the-counter market. The organized exchanges provide a fixed location at which trading in various securities occurs. This is in contrast to the over-the-counter market, which is not physically located in any one place. Rather, the over-the-counter market is better characterized as a communications network that facilitates the trading of securities not traded on the organized exchanges.[2]

For each stock traded in the over-the-counter market, one or more brokerage firms make a market in the stock. For example, American Express stock trades in the over-the-counter market and the *Wall Street Journal* of September 13, 1974 showed the price of American Express common stock for the previous day was 20¾ bid and 21¼ asked. This representative quotation does not indicate that *every* marketmaker in American Express was willing to buy 100 shares of stock at $20.75 per share and sell 100 shares of stock at $21.25. Consequently, in executing an order for a customer, more than one marketmaker is normally contacted in an attempt to obtain the best price for the customer.[3]

Auction and Negotiated Markets

Capital markets may be referred to as either continuous auction markets or as negotiated markets. In an auction market, prices are determined by the bidding of the market participants. The organized exchanges such as the NYSE and the American Stock Exchange (ASE) are examples of auction markets.

The over-the-counter market is an example of a negotiated market. In a negotiated transaction, market participants agree upon a price without buyers and sellers bidding against each other. For example, most real estate transactions are negotiated transactions between buyer and seller. We will also see negotiated transactions in operation in the securities markets in our discussion of investment banking.

The Exchanges

New York Stock Exchange. We will examine the NYSE in detail since it is an important part of American securities markets and because the operations of other exchanges are similar to that of the NYSE. Our discussion will include the organization of the NYSE, the requirements for membership on the NYSE, the role of the specialist in the execution of transactions, and the listing requirements applied to stocks considered for trading.

The NYSE is by far the largest of the organized exchanges in the United States. In terms of dollar volume, it accounts for about 75 to

[2]New security issues sold in the primary market are considered an over-the-counter transaction.

[3]For certain small over-the-counter issues, there may be only one marketmaker.

80 percent of all organized exchange activity.[4] The dominance of the NYSE is the reason it is called the "Big Board." Stocks of over 1,500 companies are traded on the NYSE.

A membership on the NYSE is represented by one of 1,366 "seats." Most owners of seats on the NYSE are partners in brokerage firms, and most brokerage firms will have several partners who are members. At the end of 1974, there were 508 brokerage firms holding seats on the NYSE.[5]

To obtain a seat on the NYSE, an individual must first find a member willing to sell a seat. In general, the price of a seat closely parallels the volume of trading and price changes of stocks listed on the exchange. In the late 1920s, seats were purchased at prices over $400,000, but were available for $17,000 in 1942. The high was reached in 1968 when a seat was sold for $515,000.[6] On September 11, 1974, a seat sold for $66,000, which is not too surprising considering the decline in stock prices which occurred over the previous months.

Finding a seat for sale is not all that must be done before one can trade on the floor of the NYSE. A prospective member must have approval of the Board of Governors of the NYSE. This group consists of ten directors chosen from member firms, ten chosen from outside the securities industry, and the Chairman of the NYSE. An application is then approved on the basis of the applicant's demonstrated financial strength and reputation within the financial community.

Each listed stock trades at an assigned post on the floor of the NYSE. When an order to buy or sell 100 shares or a multiple of 100 shares is received on the floor of the exchange, the brokerage firm's representative takes that order to the post where the stock is traded. If other brokerage firms' representatives are present at the post with orders to buy or sell that same stock, the auction market will begin and a trade should be executed between two of the brokerage firms' representatives on behalf of their customers. Suppose a sell order arrives at the trading post and there are no orders present to buy the particular stock at a price reasonably close to the price of the last trade, the *specialist* in the stock will participate in the transaction by purchasing the stock to add to his inventory. Each listed stock is assigned by exchange officials to a specialist.

In the role of helping to maintain an orderly market, the specialist acts as a principal by buying when no one else wants to buy and selling

[4]From 1955 to 1974, the percentage varied from 73.8 percent (1968) to 86.5 percent (1962). The 1974 figure was 83.9 percent. The percentages for the number of shares traded are lower because of the higher average price per share on the NYSE relative to other exchanges.

[5]*New York Stock Exchange 1975 Fact Book*, New York: New York Stock Exchange, June, 1974, p. 80.

[6]*Ibid.*, pp. 55 and 80.

when no one else wants to sell. Over the long run, the specialist should make money for providing this economic function by selling shares for more than their purchase price (i.e., money is made on the "spread").

Securities must be listed in order to be traded on the NYSE. Rather stringent requirements must be met for listing. There are requirements dealing with the earnings of the firm, the value of its assets, and the market value of its stock.[7] In addition, there must be at least one million publicly held shares outstanding and these must be owned by at least 2,000 shareholders each owning 100 shares or more. The firm must also demonstrate a national interest in its shares, conduct business in a stable industry with reasonable prospects for expansion, and provide reasonable assurance that the firm will maintain its relative position in the industry. Normally, the NYSE will not list common stock which does not have voting rights. Of course, just because a firm is able to meet the listing requirements does not mean that the firm either is well managed or will be a good investment. Listing is not a guarantee of quality, profitability, or economic efficiency.

The NYSE will occasionally waive certain of the listing requirements when it appears to be in the national interest. For example, in 1964 the Communications Satellite Corporation (Comsat) sold stock for the first time. Normally, only "seasoned" securities are listed on the NYSE, but because of the enormous public interest in this company, the NYSE agreed to begin trading immediately in Comsat stock following its initial sale to the public.

The general listing standards discussed apply to firms when they obtain their initial listing. However, the NYSE reserves the right to review and delist the shares of a corporation at any time. A temporary "delisting" known as a suspension occurs when trading in a given common stock is likely to get out of control because of an injection of very favorable or unfavorable news. Suspensions can be for a few hours or for several weeks. Delisting is much more serious and typically will be considered by the NYSE only when the total market value of the stock falls below $8 million and earnings after taxes are less than an average of $600,000 for the past three years.[8] Delisting will also be considered if the public holds less than 600,000 shares or if there are less than 1,200 remaining shareholders owning at least 100 shares each. However, delisting does not automatically occur when the above conditions are "met," since delisting is a matter which is not undertaken lightly.[9]

[7]For example, listing requirements, effective as of July 15, 1971 require pretax income for the most recent year to be at least $2.5 million, net tangible assets of at least $16 million, and an aggregate market value of publicly held shares of $16 million.

[8]*New York Stock Exchange 1975 Fact Book*, p. 30.

[9]For an interesting article on delisting, see William C. Foster, "Delisting on the Big Board—and How to Avoid It," *Financial Executive*, January 1974, pp. 36–39.

Several advantages to the firm have been suggested as resulting from NYSE listing.[10] First, listing is said to improve the liquidity of shares, making the stock a more attractive investment. In turn, this tends to increase the price of the firm's shares because of greater investor demand. Second, listing improves the collateral value of the shares. Most banks and other financial institutions are likely to loan a greater percentage of the value of the stock on a NYSE security than for a nonlisted security, since good price quotations are available and the stock can be easily sold. Third, by listing its shares, a firm will obtain some publicity benefits. The very act of listing on a national exchange will bring the company's name before the public and various announcements regarding such things as dividends, earnings, and new products will be brought to the public's attention. Of course, bad news as well as good news gets quickly disseminated. Exchange listing also facilitates merger activity since prices are readily determined for the securities of the firms in the merger agreement. Finally, management is accorded a degree of independence by having a diverse group of stockholders as a result of an actively traded common stock listed on the NYSE.

While the advantages to the firm and its stockholders may be numerous, one must be cautious in concluding that stock prices will be higher as a result of listing on the NYSE or any other exchange. Little evidence exists indicating *that listing alone* will increase the price of a common stock.[11] A small firm without a national market for either its stock or its products would probably experience a price increase as a result of listing. However, such a firm is not generally eligible for listing. The firm that is eligible and is trading on the over-the-counter market or on a regional exchange would probably benefit little, since these alternative markets are quite efficient in their ability to provide liquidity for a security of the type eligible for NYSE listing.

The American Stock Exchange and Regional Exchanges. The American Stock Exchange (ASE) is the second largest national securities exchange in the United States. It is often referred to as the "Little Board" in contrast to the NYSE. In terms of dollar volume, the ASE accounted

[10]See "Pros and Cons of Being Listed," *Business Week*, December 10, 1960, pp. 125–126, or John L. O'Donnell, "Case Evidence on the Value of a New York Stock Exchange Listing," *MSU Business Topics*, Summer 1969, pp. 15–21.

[11]The following articles by Anna Merjos appeared in *Barron's* and generally support the contention that listing is valuable: "Going on the Big Board," January 29, 1962; "Loss of Listing," March 4, 1963; "Like Money in the Bank," July 8, 1963; "Up on the Curb," May 1, 1967; and "Going on the Big Board," May 29, 1967. O'Donnell, "Case Evidence on Value of NYSE Listing," concludes that the price of a stock may increase and does not decrease as a result of listing. Richard W. Furst, in his article, "Does Listing Increase the Market Price of Common Stocks?" *Journal of Business*, April 1970, pp. 174–180, examines listing from 1960 to 1965 and concludes that "listing per se does not significantly affect the market prices of common stocks in general."

for approximately 6 percent of trading on registered exchanges in 1973. Its method of trading and form of organization are quite similar to those of the NYSE.

Regional exchanges, such as the Midwest Stock Exchange, the Pacific Stock Exchange, the Philadelphia-Baltimore-Washington Stock Exchange, and the Boston Stock Exchange, trade in securities which are listed on the NYSE, plus stocks in which interest is primarily local. For example, General Motors, a NYSE-listed stock, trades on the Midwest Stock Exchange, as does the common stock of Carson Pirie Scott & Company, a Chicago-based department store chain not listed on the NYSE.

The Third Market

As institutional trading in stocks increased during the 1960s, some financial institutions became increasingly disenchanted with having their transactions executed on the NYSE. Two reasons appear to account for this development. First, until December 1968, no volume discounts existed on the NYSE.[12] It cost 100 times as much in brokerage commissions to have an order of 10,000 shares executed as it did to have a 100-share order executed. Thus, some institutions sought to find an alternative market offering lower transaction costs. Second, there was considerable dissatisfaction with the execution of large trades on the NYSE in terms of the price received. Some institutions felt that the specialist system was not adequate to accommodate the quick purchase or sale of a large number of shares, which was desired by the institutions.[13] It was felt the specialist was undercapitalized to handle the volume generated by institutional trading, and that the specialist was not able to make a fair and orderly market as far as the institutions were concerned.

When an economic need exists, someone is usually ready to fill that need if it can be done at a reasonable profit. Hence, a rationale existed for the development of the third market. Firms such as Weeden & Company were formed to handle institutional transactions in NYSE-listed stocks, but off the floor of the exchange.

The third marketmakers act as principals in that they will buy stock for their own account when it is offered to them by an institution. They

[12]For a history of brokerage commissions during the post-World War II period, see Richard A. Stevenson, "Brokerage Commissions and the Small Shareholder," *Journal of Business Research,* Fall 1973, pp. 193–200.

[13]Ralph and Estell James, "Disputed Role of the Stock Exchange Specialist," *Harvard Business Review,* May–June 1962, pp. 133–138, and Seymour Smidt, "Inadequacies of NYSE Specialist System," *The Commercial and Financial Chronicle,* June 10, 1971, pp. 18–19. Both articles contain good general discussions of the role of the specialist and criticisms of the functioning of the specialist.

will attempt then to resell this stock to other institutions at a higher price as soon as possible. For example, if the last trade of IBM on the NYSE was at $180 per share, a third marketmaker may be willing to buy 10,000 shares from an institution at, say, $178½ "net." This means that the institution will receive a check for $1,785,000, since there is no commission on trades occurring on a "net" basis. The seller must determine if the third marketmaker's quotation of $178½ per share is better than could be realized on the NYSE after deducting commissions. Similar transactions occur on the sell side since the third marketmaker might be willing to sell 10,000 shares of IBM at $181½ "net."

The Fourth Market

The fourth market is similar to the third market except that there is no firm acting as a principal in the transaction. An institution desiring to sell stock can enter the necessary information into a computer under a code name and wait to see if there is a *match*. The computer acts only as an agent. Firms desiring to buy stock can also interrogate the computer to see what is for sale. The two institutions can then get together to work out pricing details. The main drawback is that there may not be anyone willing to buy the firm's stock for a considerable period of time, and this can be unfavorable in a period of rapidly falling prices. In lieu of a computer, an individual could perform the function of bringing buyer and seller together.

INVESTMENT BANKING

Investment banking is the business of either selling long-term financial securities for a customer or helping to arrange for long-term sources of capital from financial institutions such as insurance companies. Investment banking may be viewed as either public or private. Individual investors are concerned primarily with the public investment banking function since this process generates the new securities that become available for public sale. It should be noted that investment bankers sometimes offer for sale large blocks of already outstanding stock. These are known as secondary distributions. The important area of private investment banking deals with the role of the investment banker acting as a liaison between companies needing funds and financial institutions such as insurance companies having loanable funds. The remainder of our discussion deals with public investment banking.

Functions of the Investment Banker

The investment banker may perform several functions in selling new securities. Investment bankers, or underwriters as they are commonly called, perform a marketing function for the issuer of securities by seeking buyers for the securities being offered for sale. To accomplish adequately the marketing of large issues of securities, investment bankers will often form syndicates. There will normally be an originating investment banker having primary responsibility for the issue and syndicate members who have agreed to sell specific quantities of the security being marketed. When the issue is sold (or has failed), the underwriting syndicate is dissolved.

Investment bankers may act either as agents or as principals in any given underwriting. If an investment banker acts as a principal, the investment banker actually purchases the issue from the firm and attempts to resell it. This is a situation which we call the standard form of underwriting. The underwriter has capital at risk and may stand to lose a substantial sum of money if the issue proves to be a poor seller. In the first six months of 1974, underwriters of bond issues had a difficult time because of rapidly changing interest rates. As a result, several bond issues sold very poorly, forcing the underwriters to reduce substantially the selling price. This resulted in large underwriting losses in certain instances. As in most selling endeavors, if the merchandise is selling poorly, a clearance sale is held.

When an investment banker acts only as an agent, the underwriting is called a "best efforts" offering. The investment banker does not take title to the issue as occurs in the standard form of underwriting, but only agrees with the firm issuing the securities to give the best possible effort in marketing the securities. The investment banker in a "best efforts" underwriting does not stand to lose any risk capital. However, some injury to the investment banker's reputation might result if the issue does not sell well. In general, purchase of a "best efforts" underwriting tends to be quite risky for the investor. After all, the investment banker is not even willing to accept the risk of a successful offering.

The investment banker performs two other functions for the firm. The investment banker acts as an advisor to the firm contemplating the sale of securities. As a specialist in capital market activities, the investment banker should be in a position to offer much useful advice to a firm regarding such matters as the form of the proposed issue, the timing of the sale of the issue, the terms which need to be placed on the issue to increase its marketability, and the size of the investment banking syndicate needed.

The investment banker also performs what is known as the origination function by constantly looking for smaller businesses that might benefit from "going public" by selling their common stock to the general public. In this connection, an investment banker may serve as an informal advisor to smaller companies and help nurture them to the point when it appears prudent for them to obtain additional capital by "going public."

Other Types of Investment Banker Offerings

Another method of classifying an underwriting is to determine whether it is negotiated or is the result of a competitive bidding process. In a negotiated underwriting, the issuing firm and the investment banker discuss what the offering should be like and what the terms of the issue should be (including the price). A satisfactory agreement is reached before the offering is made.

In competitive bidding, the firm establishes the terms of the issue except for the price and announces that bids will be accepted up to a deadline set by the firm. The underwriting syndicate offering the best price wins the issue and attempts to resell it at a profit. Competitive bidding is normally used only by those firms required to do so by law or by their regulatory authority. This means that the vast majority of competitively bid offerings are made by firms in the public utility industry and by governmental borrowers.

A trend toward negotiated underwritings has developed as a result of the difficult capital market conditions of 1974.[14] A negotiated offering gives the investment bankers more time to sell the issue than tends to be true for an issue sold under competitive bidding. The investment bankers also have a better opportunity to tailor the terms of the issue to current capital market conditions with a negotiated issue. The major criticism of a negotiated sale is that it may increase the cost of obtaining the needed funds due to the absence of competition among underwriters.

Another form of underwriting is known as standby underwriting. A company required by its corporate bylaws to offer stock to its shareholders under a pre-emptive right provision before offering the stock to the general public will often enter into a standby underwriting agreement with an investment banker. Stock is offered to the current stockholders first so that they may have an opportunity to retain their proportionate ownership of the firm. In a standby underwriting, the investment banker attempts to sell those shares not purchased by the firm's present shareholders.

Exhibit 2-1 shows the front page of a prospectus of what is known as a rights offering. A prospectus is a document describing the nature of the issuing firm and the terms of the issue. In a rights offering, the present shareholders are offered one right for each share of stock they

[14]See Lindley Richert, and Kenneth Bacon, "Underwriters' Plan Could Help Utilities Sell Shares, but Proposal Stirs Concern," *Wall Street Journal,* July 17, 1974, p. 30, and "Utilities: Weak Point in the Energy Future," *Business Week,* January 20, 1975, pp. 46–54.

EXHIBIT 2–1

Front Page of Rights Offering Prospectus

PROSPECTUS

373,641 Shares
UGI Corporation
Common Stock, $4.50 par value

As more fully set forth herein, the Company is offering to the holders of its Common Stock the right to subscribe for additional shares of Common Stock in the ratio of one additional share for each ten shares of Common Stock held of record at the close of business on October 27, 1971.

The Subscription Offer will expire at 5:00 P.M., E.S.T., Monday, November 15, 1971.

In the opinion of Dechert Price & Rhoads, counsel for the Underwriters, the Common Stock offered hereby is exempt from presently existing personal property taxes in Pennsylvania.

THESE SECURITIES HAVE NOT BEEN APPROVED OR DISAPPROVED BY THE SECURITIES AND EXCHANGE COMMISSION NOR HAS THE COMMISSION PASSED UPON THE ACCURACY OR ADEQUACY OF THIS PROSPECTUS. ANY REPRESENTATION TO THE CONTRARY IS A CRIMINAL OFFENSE.

	Subscription Price	Underwriting Commissions(1)(2)		Proceeds to Company(1)(3)	
		Minimum	Maximum	Maximum	Minimum
Per Share	$19	$.19	$.67	$18.81	$18.33
Total	$7,099,179	$70,992	$250,339	$7,028,187	$6,848,840

(1) *See "Underwriting" herein for assumptions on which commissions are computed and for information concerning a contingent payment to the Company.*
(2) *The Company has agreed to indemnify the several Underwriters against certain liabilities, including liabilities under the Securities Act of 1933.*
(3) *Before deducting expenses payable by the Company estimated at $110,000.*

Prior to the expiration of the Subscription Offer, the several Underwriters may offer Common Stock, including shares acquired through the purchase and exercise of Warrants, at prices set from time to time by the Representatives of the Underwriters. Each such price when set will not exceed the greater of the last sale or current asked price of the Common Stock of the Company on the New York Stock Exchange plus the amount of an Exchange commission per share on transactions of 100 shares, and an offering price set in any calendar day will not be increased more than once during such day. After the expiration of the Subscription Offer, the Underwriters may offer Common Stock at a price or prices to be determined, but which it is presently intended will be determined in conformity with the preceding sentence. The Underwriters may thus realize profits or losses independent of the underwriting commissions referred to above. Any Common Stock will be offered by the Underwriters when, as and if issued by the Company and accepted by the Underwriters and subject to their right to reject orders in whole or in part.

The First Boston Corporation   Merrill Lynch, Pierce, Fenner & Smith
Incorporated

The date of this Prospectus is October 27, 1971.

own. In the case of the UGI Corporation offering of Exhibit 2–1, the shareholder can purchase one new UGI share for $19 and ten rights.

The investment banker's compensation in a rights offering normally comes in two parts. The investment banker receives a flat fee in the nature of an insurance premium for all the shares offered. The investment banker also receives a fee for those shares which must eventually be sold by the investment banker. This second fee is essentially a marketing fee.

SUMMARY

The capital markets in a highly developed country such as the United States are complex because they must perform in so many diverse ways for the economy to function properly. The capital markets must function in their role of allocating scarce capital in an efficient manner in order to have a strong economic system. To be sure, the economic system does not always work perfectly, as can be evidenced by the events of the late 1960s when brokerage firms faced a number of problems. These problems included the need to obtain more permanent capital and the need to solve paperwork problems resulting from heavy trading volume.

In viewing the activities of participants in the capital markets, it is useful to distinguish between an agent transaction and a principal transaction. An agent performs a service at the request of the customer and is normally paid a commission for performing that service. An agent has no risk capital tied up in the transaction. A principal in a transaction has money invested in the transaction. Title to the asset passes to the principal along with the risk that goes with ownership.

Investment bankers act as the middlemen between the organizations desiring to issue securities and the investing public. An investment banker can act either as an agent or as a principal. In a "best efforts" underwriting, the investment banker acts only as the issuing firm's agent by providing a marketing service. This is in contrast to the standard form of underwriting where the investment banker acts as a principal and assumes the risk that the issue will be successfully sold. In the marketing of large issues of securities, a single investment banker normally does not have a large enough marketing organization to sell the issue. In addition, it is usually desirable for an investment banker to spread the risk of an unsuccessful sales effort. To accomplish both of these objectives, investment bankers often form syndicates to market large issues of securities.

Capital markets may be classified into primary and secondary markets. Primary markets involve the sale of securities for the first time with the proceeds after underwriting commissions and expenses going to the issuing organization. The proper functioning of the primary market is crucial to the growth and development of the economy. Trading occurs in the secondary market after the securities are sold to the original purchasers. Good secondary markets are necessary before investors will seriously consider participating in many primary market transactions.

QUESTIONS

1. What is the difference between an agent and a principal transaction?
2. In what capital market transactions does the brokerage firm (investment banker) act as a principal?

3. In what ways may capital markets be classified?
4. *a)* What is the role of the specialist on the exchanges?
   b) Why has the role of the specialist been controversial in recent years?
5. In what ways does the execution of a trade on an organized securities exchange such as the New York Stock Exchange differ from a trade execution in the over-the-counter market?
6. Why might a corporation decide not to list its shares on an exchange?
7. What is the nature of a third market transaction?
8. What major functions does an investment banker perform for an organization wishing to sell securities? Are these functions always performed?
9. Why might a public utility firm wish to sell its securities via a negotiated underwriting rather than via competitive bidding?
10. AT&T has typically not used what is known as a standby underwriting in its rights offerings. Why do you suppose AT&T has decided on this course of action?

SUGGESTED READINGS

Baker, Guthrie. "The Martin Report: Blueprint for Constructive Reform." *Financial Analysts Journal,* November–December 1971, pp. 20–22.

Black, Fischer. "Toward a Fully Automated Stock Exchange." *Financial Analysts Journal,* July–August 1971, pp. 29–35ff. (Part I) and November–December 1971, pp. 25–28ff. (Part II).

Davant, James W. "The Martin Report: An Answer to the Critics." *Financial Analysts Journal,* November–December 1971, pp. 14–18ff.

Eiteman, David K. "The S.E.C. Special Study and the Exchange Markets." *Journal of Finance,* May 1966, pp. 311–23.

Farrar, Donald E. "Implications of the Martin Report." *Financial Analysts Journal,* September–October 1971, pp. 14–16ff.

——. "Toward a Central Market System: Wall Street's Slow Retreat into the Future." *Journal of Financial and Quantitative Analysis,* November 1974, pp. 815–27.

Feuerstein, Donald M. "Toward a National System of Securities Exchanges." *Financial Analysts Journal,* May–June 1972, pp. 28–34ff.

——. "Toward a National System of Securities Exchanges: The Third and Fourth Markets." *Financial Analysts Journal,* July–August 1972, pp. 57–59ff.

Freund, William C. "Issues Confronting the Stock Market In a Period of Rising Institutionalization." *Supplement to Journal of Financial and Quantitative Analysis,* March 1972, pp. 1687–90.

Jones, Lawrence D. "Some Contributions of the Institutional Investor Study." *Journal of Finance,* May 1972, pp. 305–17.

Loomis, Carol J. "How the Terrible Two-Tier Market Came to Wall Street." *Fortune,* July 1973, pp. 82–88ff.

Mendelson, Morris. *From Automated Quotes to Automated Trading.* Bulletin nos. 80–82 of New York University, Center for Study of Financial Institutions, March 1972.

Smidt, Seymour. "The Road to an Efficient Stock Market." *Financial Analysts Journal,* September–October 1971, pp. 18–20ff.

Weeden, Donald E. "Competition: Key to Market Structure." *Supplement to Journal of Financial and Quantitative Analysis,* March 1972, pp. 1969–801.

3

Investor Participation in the Markets

Before investing, it is crucial for the investor to appreciate how the securities markets work and how to participate in them. This involves many significant topics such as how to choose a brokerage firm and a broker. The investor should understand what to expect from a brokerage firm and from a broker.

Once an account has been opened at a brokerage firm, the investor should know the different types of orders that may be entered. The manner in which certain orders are executed is important with regard to either the price received when the order is filled or the reason why the order was not filled. In addition, the investor should know the transaction costs associated with an anticipated transaction so a determination of the desirability of the transaction can be made from this viewpoint. This chapter discusses types of orders and brokerage commissions. An examination of the regulatory environments existing at various levels in the securities industry is the final major topic discussed in this chapter.

MARKET MECHANICS

Selecting a Brokerage Firm

Normally, the first step in purchasing securities is to select a brokerage firm. The brokerage firm should be equipped to provide the quality of service desired by the customer. This includes such items as good order execution, research reports and advice, and prompt payment of funds due the investor. The brokerage firm must maintain up-to-date and accurate records of the investor's transactions with the firm. An individual would not tolerate a commercial bank that continually made mistakes in a checking account. Neither should an individual tolerate a brokerage firm that continually made mistakes in executing and accounting for a customer's transactions.

Other factors may also be important in the choice of a brokerage firm. A brokerage firm should have a strong financial position, but this determination is difficult for the average investor. Therefore, the investor should at least determine if the brokerage firm owns a membership on the major exchanges, is a member of the National Association of Securities Dealers, and has its accounts insured by the Securities Investor Protection Corporation. Although these membership considerations do not necessarily provide assurance of financial strength and integrity, they are of help to the investor. Brokerage commissions differ little from one brokerage firm to another, but there are differences that may be important. For example, some firms have minimum dollar charges for stock or bond orders that might make a difference to the small investor. Finally, the investors interested in purchasing new issues of common stock or bonds would need to know the extent to which the particular brokerage firm participates in new issue underwritings. Some of the smaller regional brokerage firms may not participate in nearly as many underwritings as some of the larger national brokerage firms.

Selecting a Broker

It is possible that the selection of a broker will determine the brokerage house handling the account. A broker (also called a registered representative or account executive) may be recommended to an investor by a present or former customer of the broker. Actually, the task of choosing a broker should be somewhat comparable to that of choosing a physician. The physician is concerned with the individual's physical health, while the broker should be concerned with the investor's financial health. If the customer is not satisfied with a broker, it is an easy matter to find another one.

It is important that a customer and a broker have compatible objectives. The broker should know an investor's objectives well enough to assist in planning and implementing the investor's financial objectives. At the very least, the broker should be well informed or be willing to seek the information needed by the investor in making an informed investment decision. Within reason, the broker should make an attempt to keep an investor informed. Of course, the more valuable the customer is to the broker, the better informed the customer will probably be.

The investor should determine what to expect from a broker. Some investors use a broker only for order taking. Other investors expect their broker to give them advice on a variety of investments. If you decide that you want your broker to give you investment advice, there are two critical factors to keep in mind. First, the selection of a broker with objectives compatible to yours is essential. If your broker has a different risk preference than you do, the relationship is unlikely to prove satisfactory. What may happen is that the broker will wind up imposing his or her risk preferences on you, and you will end up with either too conservative or too risky a portfolio. Second, you should realize the broker has the basic conflict of interest inherent in most sales transactions. The broker must sell securities to live and this has the potential of causing complications for the investor. The vast majority of brokers are honest and dependable, but the potential for a conflict of interest is present.

Opening an Account

Prior to entering an order, an investor must open an account with a brokerage firm. This is a relatively simple process, similar to applying for a charge account at a local department store in that the information desired by the brokerage firm and the department store would be approximately the same. The brokerage firm would want to know both personal information (such as name, address, social security number) and certain financial information. Once an account has been opened, the investor is ready to enter orders to buy or sell securities.

Types of Transactions

Several different types of orders are possible. Before discussing types of orders, however, it is necessary to distinguish between a round-lot and an odd-lot transaction. Then, we will examine the following basic types of transactions: 1) market order; 2) limit order; 3) stop order; 4) a short sale order; and 5) a margin account transaction as opposed to a cash account transaction.

Round-lot versus Odd-lot. On the floor of the major exchanges, trading normally occurs only in 100-share multiples known as round-lots.[1] An order to buy or sell 100 shares of AT&T would normally be executed on the floor of the NYSE. An investor desiring to enter an order for less than 100 shares would give the brokerage firm what is known as an odd-lot order. An odd-lot order to purchase 40 shares of AT&T would be transmitted to a special odd-lot dealer. Odd-lot trading is physically located under the floor of the NYSE. An order to buy or sell 140 shares of AT&T would consist of both a round-lot and an odd-lot.

The price for an odd-lot purchase of a stock such as AT&T is the price of the next round-lot trade plus an *odd-lot differential* of 12½ cents per share. In the case of a sale, the odd-lot differential is deducted from the round-lot price. The brokerage commission applying to odd-lot orders is slightly different than for round-lot orders and will be examined shortly.

Market Order. A market order instructs the broker's representative on the floor of the exchange to obtain the best possible price available at the time the order reaches the floor. This may be the price at which the last trade took place in that stock or it may be higher or lower. In addition, the specialist may or may not participate in the trade. Let's look at an example to see what might happen.

If you call your broker regarding an order for AT&T stock, your broker may inform you that the last trade of AT&T common stock was at $42¼. You may also ask your broker to provide you with the specialist's quotation in AT&T. Your broker replies, "$42⅛ bid, $42⅜ asked." This means that the specialist is willing to buy 100 shares at $42.125 per share and willing to sell 100 shares at $42.375 per share. If your broker's representative on the exchange floor can obtain a better price than this by bargaining with the other broker, the specialist will not participate in the transaction.

You decide to place a buy order for 100 shares of AT&T at the market. Your order is transmitted to the floor of the exchange. Your broker's representative goes to the trading post where AT&T is traded. If another broker on the floor has an order to sell at least 100 shares of AT&T at the same time as your order arrives, these two brokers may execute a transaction by auction bidding. Let's assume that they settle on a price of $42¼—identical to the last trade. On the other hand, if no one wants to sell 100 shares of AT&T at a price close to the most recent trade, your broker will buy the 100 shares from the specialist at $42⅜. It normally takes two or three minutes from the time an order is entered for it to reach the trading post where the stock is traded. Prices may have moved up or down in that time—especially in a stock which is being actively traded.

[1]A few inactively traded stocks, especially preferred stocks, trade in ten-share round-lots.

If your order to buy 100 shares of AT&T is executed, an exchange employee at the post marks a special card containing information regarding the trade and feeds it into an optical card reader. Your trade is then reported on the tape showing NYSE transactions.

Limit Order. A limit order restricts the broker in the execution of the order to a specified price. You could have entered an order to buy 100 shares of AT&T at $42 per share. This order would also go to the floor of the exchange. If your broker's representative cannot find anyone willing to sell 100 shares of AT&T at $42, the broker will leave the order with the specialist. One of the specialist's functions is to maintain a book showing all limit orders that could not be filled when they arrived at the trading post. Should the price of AT&T decline from $42¼ as a result of investors' desire to sell AT&T stock, your order to buy 100 shares of AT&T may be filled.[2]

To prevent a conflict of interest, a specialist must fill orders from the book before acting as a principal in the transaction because the specialist is charged with maintaining a fair and orderly market. The specialist would not be doing this if the price dropped sharply on small volume because the only order to buy in the specialist's book was at $39. In this instance, the specialist would be obligated to buy the stock offered for sale to maintain a fair and orderly market.

Limit orders may be valid for varying periods of time depending on the wishes of the customer. Limit orders may be placed on a GTC basis—good till cancelled. They may also be made to expire at the end of the day, the end of the week, and so on. The time dimension of the limit order is up to the investor, but discretion should be used, since market prices may change rapidly as new information becomes available. A limit order may be executed at a price that turns out to be unattractive to the investor simply because the limit order could not be changed in time.

In summary, the basic function of a limit order is to establish a maximum price in a purchase transaction and a minimum price in a sale transaction. When buying the limit order is typically placed below the market. A limit order to sell is typically placed above the market. One may buy the stock for less than the limit or sell for more but not the other way around.

Stop Order. A stop order to sell is entered to attempt to protect a paper profit on a security or to limit the amount of loss on a security. Stop orders to buy are discussed in the next section dealing with short sales. If an investor bought 100 shares of AT&T at $42¼ and the price rose to $49½, the investor might decide to enter the following order: Sell 100 AT&T at $48½ stop. Should the price of AT&T fall to $48½

[2]The order might not be filled at $42 even if the stock trades at $42 since limit orders are filled in chronological order and there may be "stock ahead."

or less, this order would immediately become a market order to be executed at the best price available. If the sale subsequently occurs at $48¼, the investor has realized a profit on the complete transaction. This type of order would be entered if the investor thought AT&T would go up in price, but wanted to protect the profit.

Essentially the same rationale holds if the investor bought 100 shares of AT&T at $42¼ and wanted to limit the amount of potential loss. The investor might place the following order: Sell 100 AT&T at $41 stop. This order would become a market order if AT&T dropped to $41 or below. The investor would suffer a small loss, but may have sold at the beginning of a sustained decline. However, the investor may have been sold out on a minor downward price fluctuation just prior to a major upward movement in the price of AT&T.

Short Sale. In a short sale, stock is sold by the customer hoping the stock will decline in price. The customer does not own the stock being sold short so the brokerage firm must borrow stock in order to make delivery of the shares sold.[3] The brokerage firm will borrow the stock from the account of another customer or perhaps from another brokerage firm.[4] Normally, stock can be borrowed for an indefinite period of time, although the customer must eventually replace the borrowed stock and close out the transaction. At times, it is not possible to enter into a short sale of a security because of the inability of the brokerage firm to find shares available to borrow for the purpose of making delivery.

Suppose an investor visits Disney World and decides to look at the common stock of Disney as a possible investment. Upon investigation, the investor comes to the conclusion that at the existing price of $120 per share for Disney, the stock is substantially overvalued. Naturally, the stock should not be purchased, but it could be sold short in anticipation of a market correction of this perceived overvaluation. The investor's brokerage firm says that Disney stock is available for shorting. An order is entered to sell 100 shares of Disney short at the market. This order can be executed only under certain conditions to be discussed shortly, but let us assume that the order is filled at $120 per share.

The investor must eventually purchase 100 shares of Disney to replace the stock originally borrowed. The investor has strong convictions and waits until Disney is selling for $26 per share to "cover" the short sale. The investor then buys 100 shares of Disney for $2,600. The

[3]The customer can sell short a stock that is owned. This is known as "selling short against the box." See: Theodore F. Whitmarsh, "When to Sell Securities Short Against the Box," *Financial Analysts Journal,* May–June 1972, pp. 80–81ff, for a description of this investment technique.

[4]When a customer opens a margin account, the margin account agreement signed allows the brokerage firm to lend the securities in the account for short sale purposes.

total transaction, excluding commissions and other transaction costs, may be summarized in the following manner:

Sold short 100 Disney at $120	+$12,000
Bought 100 Disney at $26	− 2,600
Net gain on the transaction	+$ 9,400

The Disney transaction produced a fine profit for the investor. However, when the stock was shorted at $120, the potential for loss was virtually unlimited should the stock advance in price. The higher the price of Disney stock, the greater the investor's loss. To alleviate this problem, the investor could have placed a stop buy order. An order to buy 100 shares of Disney at $125 stop would become a market order should Disney sell for $125 or higher. The investor would then have covered the short sale at a small loss.

To prevent investors from selling stock short to drive prices down to abnormally low levels in order to buy the stock back at depressed levels (called a "bear raid"), rules exist regarding the circumstances under which short sales are allowed. A short sale can be made only on a trade where the price of the stock advances or when the last change in price was an advance if the trade on which the short sale takes place is unchanged from the previous transaction. An advance in price is called an *uptick.* Thus, a short sale can occur on an uptick or on a zero plus uptick. A zero plus uptick simply means the situation of no price change on the trade but that the previous change was an uptick.

Margin Account Order. There are two basic methods of settlement of an account. If an investor purchases a security, the investor is normally expected to pay for the purchase on or before the fifth business day following the transaction. Likewise, the brokerage firm is to pay the customer any proceeds from a sale on the fifth business day following the sale. Instead of paying cash for a security, the investor could elect to open a margin account with the brokerage firm and enter a margin account order.

A margin account order is one where the purchaser of the security uses borrowing power. To open a margin account, most brokerage houses require that the investor deposit $2,000 in the account, although some brokerage houses require a higher deposit.[5] To enter a margin account order, the investor need only specify that the transaction is to be made in the margin account previously opened.

If an investor buys 100 shares of AT&T on margin for a total of $4,200, the investor will pay for a portion of the stock and the brokerage firm will borrow the remaining amount from a commercial bank on behalf of the investor. The 100 shares of AT&T stock will remain in the account

[5]The investor could deposit securities having a loan value of $2,000. With a 50 percent initial margin, $4,000 of securities would have a loan value of $2,000.

and will be used as collateral for the loan. How much can the investor borrow? That depends on what the *initial margin* requirement is at the time of the purchase. The Federal Reserve Board sets initial margin requirements as part of its selective credit control authority. The amount of initial margin required has varied from 40 to 100 percent of the amount of the transaction since 1934. If the margin was 60 percent the investor could borrow 40 percent of the amount of the purchase as shown in the following example:

The investor may borrow $1,680 and needs to deposit $2,520 margin. This margin deposit becomes the equity the investor has in the transaction. The amount of equity becomes important should the value of AT&T's common stock decline. For example, the NYSE sets what is known as a *maintenance margin* requirement for NYSE-listed stocks. The investor is required to place additional funds in the account if the equity in the account falls to less than 25 percent of the value of the securities in the account. The request for an additional deposit of funds is known as a *margin call*. While the NYSE maintenance margin requirement is 25 percent, individual brokerage firms often set a higher requirement for their customers to prevent a customer from violating the NYSE maintenance margin requirement.

To see how margin transactions work, let us assume that the common stock of AT&T is the only security in the margin account and begins to decline in price. At a price of $40 for AT&T, we have the following situation:

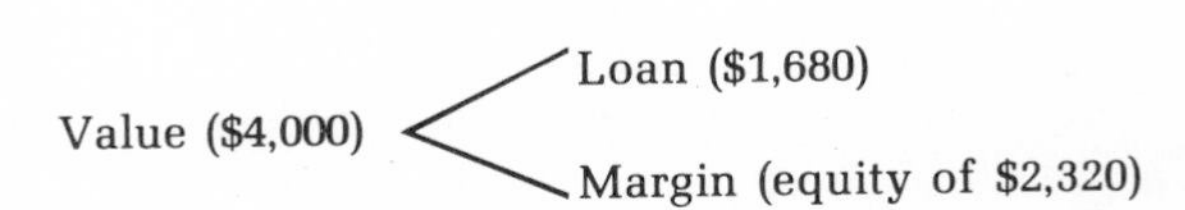

The account shown above with $4,000 worth of securities is known as a *restricted account*, since the equity is now only 58 percent. The customer is not required to put up additional margin, but neither can the customer purchase additional stock on margin without putting up more equity.

At what point will the investor be required to deposit additional margin? This can be calculated fairly easily by allowing the market value of the security in the account to equal x. The investor will be required to deposit additional margin when the equity in the account falls below .25x. Therefore, we have the following situation:

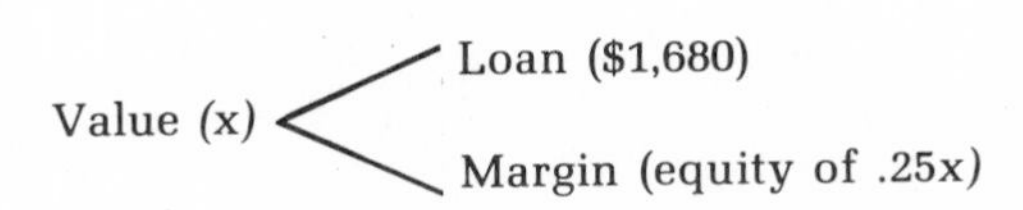

We can solve the following equation:

$$x = \$1,680 + .25x$$
$$.75x = \$1,680$$
$$x = \$2,240$$

If the value of the 100 shares of AT&T falls below $2,240, the customer will receive a margin call requesting the deposit of additional funds. The brokerage firm might require the equity be restored to 30 percent. If the investor does not meet the margin call, securities will be sold to liquidate the loan.

The rules applying to margin accounts are complex and many of the more complicated transactions that could occur have not been mentioned. An investor should make absolutely certain he or she understands the margin rules existing in any individual member firm, as these do tend to differ slightly. In addition, having a broker borrow for the investor from a commercial bank via a margin account is a very impersonal transaction. If a margin call is not satisfied, the investor is sold out. If the investor had borrowed directly from a banker, other considerations might be important, such as the investor's credit rating and the value of his or her business to the bank. Other arrangements with the banker might be made to avoid having to sell a security to liquidate a loan. In fact, the banker may even be willing to make an unsecured loan.

Commission Rates

A *brokerage commission* is the basic fee charged for buying and selling securities as the customer's agent. Many developments have occurred in the commission area in the past few years as institutions have become an increasingly significant factor in the trading of securities. In addition, there is much ferment within the financial community as to what the commission structure should actually be. For example, should institutional traders subsidize small investors? As a result of questions of this kind, the area of commissions has become increasingly complex. Even the small investor has several options available for buying and selling stock that mean different commission charges.

It is first necessary to distinguish between *negotiated commissions* and a *fixed schedule of commission rates.* At the present time, all stock transactions are subject to a commission that is determined jointly by discussions between the customer and the brokerage firm. Prior to May 1, 1975, the commission structure established by the NYSE and approved by the Securities and Exchange Commission (the federal regulatory agency for the securities industry) applied. Exhibit 3-1 shows the minimum commission schedule that applied to stock transactions prior to May 1, 1975. A single round-lot order refers to each individual 100 share

EXHIBIT 3–1

Minimum Commission Rates

Single Round-Lot Orders		Multiple Round-Lot Orders	
Money Involved In the Order	Minimum Commission	Money Involved In the Order	Minimum Commission
$ 100–$ 799	2.0% + $ 6.40	$ 100–$ 2,499	1.3% + $ 12.00
800– 2,499	1.3 + 12.00	2,500– 19,999	0.9 + 22.00
2,500– and above	0.9 + 22.00	20,000– 29,999	0.6 + 82.00
		30,000– 500,000	0.4 + 142.00

Subject to the provision that the minimum commission on single round-lot orders is not to exceed $65.00.

Plus
First to tenth round-lot, $6.00 per round-lot. Eleventh round-lot and over, $4.00 per round-lot.

But in no case shall the minimum commission per round-lot exceed the single round-lot commission. Also, in no case shall the minimum commission for a round-lot plus an odd-lot exceed the commission on the next larger round-lot.

Odd Lot Orders Same as single round-lot rate less $2.00, subject to the provision that the minimum commission on an odd-lot order is not to exceed $65.00.

Effective September 1973, orders up to $5,000 paid a commission of 10 percent more than the above rates. For orders involving $5,000 to $300,000, the commission was increased 15 percent.

Source: New York Stock Exchange.

trade. Multiple round-lot orders involve 200 shares or more in multiples of 100. Odd-lot orders involve orders in the 1 to 99 share range.

While the small investor may theoretically negotiate commissions with the brokerage firm, the commissions actually charged for small transactions have remained the same or are slightly higher than those shown in Exhibit 3–1. Although some differences in commissions exist from brokerage firm to brokerage firm, we will use Exhibit 3–1 as an approximation of the commission structure facing the typical investor.

For the small investor, the commission schedule suggests that the cost of buying and selling stock is not a trivial item. Exhibit 3–2 shows what the one-way commission cost would be for an order of 100, 200, or 500 shares executed at various prices. This dollar cost is translated into a percentage of the money involved in the transaction. For an individual with less than $1,000 to invest, the commission costs tend to be substantial. The transaction costs involved in excessive trading activities tend to make the broker richer and the stockholder poorer. From the point of view of commissions, the investor should plan to hold stocks for a fairly long period of time in order to reduce the impact of commissions.

EXHIBIT 3–2
Commission Costs

Price	100 Shares		200 Shares		500 Shares	
Per Share	Amount	Percentage	Amount	Percentage	Amount	Percentage
$ 5	$18.04	3.61%	$ 40.70	4.07%	$ 81.95	3.28%
10	27.50	2.75	55.00	2.75	111.55	2.23
20	41.80	2.09	77.00	1.93	163.30	1.63
30	53.90	1.80	101.20	1.69	215.05	1.43
40	63.80	1.60	121.90	1.52	266.80	1.33
50	74.75	1.50	142.60	1.43	301.30	1.21
75	74.74	1.00	149.50	1.00	370.30	.99
100	74.74	.75	149.50	.75	373.75	.75

Source: Calculated from Exhibit 3–1.

One of the problems currently facing the financial community is what services the brokerage commission should cover. Should it cover research services and account maintenance fees? Several discount brokerage firms have been established that may not provide the full range of services provided by the typical brokerage firm. If the investor does not need many of the services provided by the typical brokerage firm, a discount brokerage firm provides an alternative at a lower commission cost. For example, an advertisement of Source Securities Corporation appeared in the *Wall Street Journal* of July 24, 1975. This advertisement offered individual investors discounts of from 30 to 75 percent off previous fixed rates provided Source Securities received $250 in commission business.

Another alternative to the standard brokerage commission rates shown in Exhibit 3–1 has been developed by some brokerage firms. Under Merrill Lynch's Sharebuilder Plan, an investor opens a special account at Merrill Lynch. To purchase stock, the investor fills out a brief form and mails it with a check to Merrill Lynch. As soon as Merrill Lynch receives the customer's check, the stock is purchased at the opening of the market on the next business day. Likewise, a stock will be sold under this plan the morning after Merrill Lynch receives the stock. Any stock on the NYSE, ASE, or approximately 550 major over-the-counter stocks may be purchased. In essence, the plan is a pay-in-advance plan.

What does the investor gain from a plan like the Sharebuilder Plan of Merrill Lynch? Merrill Lynch will hold the securities purchased in the customer's account at no charge. The individual with $2,000 (the limit per purchase under this plan) or less to invest gets a break in the form of lower commission costs. Depending on the size of the order, commissions will be reduced from 16 to 25 percent below the rates shown in Exhibit 3–1. The dollar amount sent in purchases both whole and fractional shares for the investor in contrast to a regular order that must be stated in whole shares.

Surely the investor must give up some important advantages under Merrill Lynch's Sharebuilder Plan. It will not be possible to purchase stocks on margin under this plan. Limit orders will not be accepted since each order is executed at the opening the day after the order becomes valid. Customers will receive quarterly rather than monthly statements. Perhaps most importantly, the investor gives up the flexibility of entering an order when the price of a particular stock appears especially attractive. For example, if the investor sees that IBM is trading at $173 and feels that this is an attractive purchase, the investor could enter a market order for ten shares and buy at close to this price. If the investor mails a check for $1,800 to Merrill Lynch, the stock may not be purchased for one or two business days, depending upon the speed of the mails. By that time, IBM's price might have increased to $185.[6]

Bond Trading and Commission Rates

Bonds are traded on both the organized exchanges and in the over-the-counter market. The majority of bonds trade in the over-the-counter market since government bonds are traded in this market along with corporate bond issues. The *Wall Street Journal* reports the daily prices of corporate bonds traded on the NYSE, the ASE, and the Pacific Stock Exchange. Not all corporate bonds are listed on an exchange, but some of the bonds that are listed are actively traded. Bond volume on the NYSE experienced very rapid growth during the 1960s with volume rising from $1.35 billion in 1960 to a record $6.56 billion in 1971. Since 1971, bond volume has declined, with 1974s bond volume at $4.05 billion.[7] In Chapter 17, the important area of corporate bond investing is examined in more detail.

The commission rates for bonds differ from those applying to stocks. In addition, many brokerage firms have specific rules that apply to commissions on corporate bonds with which investors should become familiar before placing an order. In general, the one-way commission per corporate bond is between $2.50 and $10.00, depending upon the number of bonds in the transaction. Some brokerage firms charge $2.50 for the purchase or sale of corporate bonds of short maturity regardless of the number of bonds purchased, while other brokerage firms have

[6]It is possible that IBM's stock might have declined in price.

[7]It is difficult to account for the decline in trading volume given the high interest rates prevailing during the 1972 to 1974 period. Perhaps the volume of new bond underwritings induced investors to purchase new offerings rather than bonds trading on the NYSE. In addition, the growth of both closed-end bond funds and money-market investment companies (see Chapters 19 and 20) might explain some of the decline in corporate bond trading volume on the NYSE. In any event, NYSE bond volume still remains at a relatively high level historically despite the decline from 1971 to 1974.

a specified minimum charge (such as $15) per order. If bonds are purchased in the over-the-counter market rather than on an exchange, the commission may be in the lower part of the range stated above. The bond market is primarily an institutional market and the commissions applicable to institutions tend to be much lower than those stated. The cost of buying government bonds is examined in Chapter 19.

Summary

Commissions are not a trivial part of the cost of investing. Therefore, it is important for the investor to be aware of the nature of the commission structure and the various alternative forms of making investments that carry different commission costs. It may even be desirable to invest indirectly, using an investment company as we will discuss in Chapters 20 and 21.

The subject of commissions has been one of substantial conflict in Wall Street in recent years. Fully negotiated commissions have been in existence since May 1975. For the average investor, however, the change from fixed to negotiated commissions appears to have had little practical impact.

REGULATORY ASPECTS

Regulation of the securities industry occurs at three different levels—at the federal level, at the state level, and by the industry itself. Regulation at the state level started in 1911 in Kansas, and the state laws are known as "blue-sky laws" since they were conceived to prevent an individual from buying a "piece of the blue sky." The dominant regulatory authority at the federal level is the Securities and Exchange Commission (SEC). Self-regulatory activities in the industry are also an important element of the total regulatory environment. These three major areas of regulation will now be discussed. Detailed analysis of specific laws is handled in the section of the text discussing the area being regulated. For example, the federal laws applying to investment companies are discussed in detail in Chapter 21.

State Blue-Sky Laws

The philosophy behind state regulation is characterized by a paternalistic regard for the purchaser of securities. The key words applying to state regulation of securities are *fair, just,* and *equitable.* The administrator of any individual blue-sky law has considerable power to stop the sale of a security within the borders of the state if the sale is not deemed in the best interest of the state's residents.

State security laws generally provide for the following types of regulation:

1. Anti-fraud provisions.
2. Requirements for the registration of dealers and salesmen of securities.
3. Requirements for the registration of nonexempt issues.

Certain types of securities are exempt from the provision requiring that securities sold within the state be registered with the appropriate regulatory agency. Issues of the federal government are exempt in all states as are state and local bonds. Securities issued by public utilities regulated either by the state itself with regard to rates and charges or by a federal or state commission are exempt from registration. In addition, most states exempt securities listed on specific stock exchanges on the presumption that there is adequate disclosure concerning the business activities of these concerns.

If a security is being registered with the SEC under the Federal Securities Act of 1933, it may be registered in a given state under a registration by coordination provision existing in most blue-sky laws. The firm simply files copies of the registration material required by the SEC plus supplementary material required by the state. If the required material has been on file at least ten days, the state registration becomes effective when the federal registration becomes effective. Of course, the state securities regulator can deny the registration of the security in any given state during the period of time prior to the effective date of the federal registration.

All nonexempt securities must become registered in the state in which they will be sold by a procedure known as registration by qualification. The state regulatory agency examines the material supplied to it and either approves or denies the sale. At times, a firm will plan to sell stock only within the borders of one state. This type of offering is known as an *intrastate offering* and may be purchased only by residents of that state. Exhibit 3–3 is a reproduction of the first page of the prospectus of Iowa Steel Mill, Inc., an intrastate offering for Iowa residents only that was made on a "best efforts" basis by the investment banker. The prospectus contains information that should be read carefully by any prospective purchaser to determine the risk of the offering as well as the potential for gain. It should be noted that in the Iowa Steel Mill offering, the investment banker is receiving a 10 percent underwriting commission for marketing efforts only.

EXHIBIT 3-3
Front Page of "Best Efforts" Prospectus

PROSPECTUS

556,875 SHARES

IOWA STEEL MILL, INC.

Common Stock ($1.00 Par Value)

THESE SECURITIES INVOLVE A HIGH DEGREE OF RISK (SEE "RISK FACTORS")

The shares offered hereby are authorized and unissued shares being sold by Iowa Steel Mill, Inc. (the "Company"). Prior to this offering, there has been no public market for the securities offered by this Prospectus and there can be no assurance that there will be a market for the securities after the offering. The offering price per share has been arbitrarily selected by the Company and it bears no relationship to earnings, book value or other recognized criteria of value.

The shares offered hereby are being offered on a best efforts basis. The proceeds will be escrowed with First Trust & Savings Bank of Davenport, Iowa, until a minimum of 306,140 shares are sold. If such minimum number of shares are not sold within six months (which date may be extended) the offering will terminate and all proceeds will be promptly returned to the investors, without interest. See "Escrow of Proceeds". If the 306,140 shares are sold within the period of the escrow, the balance of the shares offered hereby will be offered until sold, or until one year from the date of this Prospectus, whichever event first occurs. The Company will not accept subscriptions for less than 50 shares. Since the offering is on a best efforts basis, there can be no assurance that any shares will be sold or any proceeds derived therefrom.

THESE SECURITIES ARE OFFERED ONLY TO BONA FIDE RESIDENTS OF THE STATE OF IOWA WHO PURCHASE FOR THE PURPOSE OF INVESTMENT AND NOT FOR RESALE.

BECAUSE THESE SECURITIES ARE BELIEVED TO BE EXEMPT FROM REGISTRATION UNDER THE SECURITIES ACT OF 1933, THEY HAVE NOT BEEN REGISTERED WITH THE UNITED STATES SECURITIES AND EXCHANGE COMMISSION, BUT SUCH EXEMPTION, IF AVAILABLE, DOES NOT INDICATE THAT THESE SECURITIES HAVE BEEN EITHER APPROVED OR DISAPPROVED BY THE COMMISSION OR THAT THE COMMISSION HAS CONSIDERED THE ACCURACY OR COMPLETENESS OF THE STATEMENTS IN THIS PROSPECTUS.

THESE SECURITIES HAVE BEEN REGISTERED WITH THE COMMISSIONER OF INSURANCE, STATE OF IOWA, UNDER CHAPTER 502, 1971 CODE OF IOWA. SUCH REGISTRATION DOES NOT, HOWEVER, INDICATE APPROVAL, DISAPPROVAL, RECOMMENDATION OR ENDORSEMENT OF THE SECURITIES BY THE INSURANCE DEPARTMENT OF IOWA, NOR DOES THE DEPARTMENT PASS ON THE ACCURACY OR COMPLETENESS OF ANY STATEMENT MADE HEREIN.

	PRICE TO PUBLIC	UNDERWRITING DISCOUNTS AND COMMISSIONS (1)	PROCEEDS TO COMPANY (2)
Per Share	$ 10.00	$ 1.00	$ 9.00
Total	$5,568,750.00	$556,875.00	$5 011.875.00

(1) For additional underwriting compensation, see paragraph (c) below.

(2) Before deduction of expenses payable by the Company which are estimated at $85,000 ($0.24 per share if minimum number of shares are sold, and $0.15 per share if maximum number of shares are sold), such expenses to include legal, accounting, printing and registration fees. In no event will expenses exceed 5% of the amount of securities actually sold pursuant hereto.

This offer involves:

(a) Special risks concerning the Company. See "Introductory Statement — Risk Factors".

(b) Immediate dilution of the net tangible book value of the stock from the public offering price. See "Introductory Statement — Dilution".

(c) Additional underwriting compensation through reimbursement by the Company of certain expenses of the Underwriter, of which $10,000 has been paid in advance. See "Underwriting".

EMPIRE INVESTMENT CORPORATION
3111 Douglas Avenue
Des Moines, Iowa 50310

The date of this Prospectus is January 9, 1973.

Federal Securities Acts

Starting with the Securities Act of 1933, there have been several significant pieces of federal legislation regarding the securities industry. The regulatory philosophy at the federal level is quite different from that at the state level. Federal law requires fair and adequate disclosure of information concerning the financial condition of the issuing company and of information regarding the management and business of the firm. It has been suggested that the federal government does not care if people invest in a hole in the ground as long as they are not told, without supporting geological data, that it really is a gold mine.

Securities Act of 1933. This important law is sometimes referred to as the "truth-in-securities" act. It requires the registration of new issues of securities except for exempt issues such as those of the U.S. government. Issues offered or sold on behalf of the issuer that do not exceed $500,000 are exempt from most of the provisions of the act.[8] Issues must normally be registered for at least twenty days before they may be offered to the public so that the SEC staff may review the registration material.

The law requires that a prospective purchaser of a security be provided with a prospectus describing the issue and the company. Prior to the effective date of the registration, a prospective purchaser is given what is known as a preliminary prospectus or "red herring." This preliminary prospectus is complete with the possible exception of the price at which the security will be offered. The name "red herring" comes from the fact that a statement is printed in red ink on the face of the prospectus stating that the registration statement has not yet become effective and the security may not be sold nor may offers to buy be accepted until the registration does become effective. The preliminary prospectus gives a prospective buyer a means of deciding whether or not the security being offered for sale would be a desirable investment. If the answer is affirmative, the investor can give the brokerage firm an indication of interest in the security.

Securities Exchange Act of 1934. The Securities Exchange Act of 1934 is the second of the New Deal laws dealing with the securities industry. The act is important for a number of reasons. It established the Securities and Exchange Commission as the federal agency having responsibility for the administration of the various federal laws dealing with the securities industry. The Securities Act of 1933 had given regulatory authority to the Federal Trade Commission.

The 1934 Act is concerned with the manner in which the securities markets work. The SEC is charged with attempting to keep the markets free of manipulative practices. All significant exchanges in the United

[8]These issues are often called Regulation A issues.

States are required to register with the SEC. The SEC is also given authority with regard to many of the general trading practices and policies of the exchanges. From time to time, the SEC has sponsored studies in an attempt to determine if general trading rules and practices need changing.

As a result of this law, insiders are required to file reports concerning their trading activities. Insiders are defined as officers and directors of the firm or any beneficial owner of more than 10 percent of the company's outstanding stock of any registered class. The intent of this provision is to make public the trading activities of parties that may have access to inside or privileged information. It is felt that public disclosure of their activities will act as a deterrent to fraudulent or manipulative trading activities by insiders.

All the provisions of this law will not be discussed since it is a comprehensive act that attempted to deal with the structural ills that many people felt plagued the securities industry during the 1920s and early 1930s. Low margin requirements were believed to be one of these ills since the public could speculate on the price movements of securities with relatively little equity. As a result, the 1934 Act gave the Federal Reserve Board the power to regulate margin requirements.

In summary, this law undoubtedly did much to restore the faith of the American public in the securities industry at a time when it was needed. It is fair to state that this law continues to serve the interests of the American public.

The Investment Company Act of 1940 and 1970 Amendments. The investment company concept suffered a severe blow during the 1930s. The Investment Company Act of 1940 can be viewed as the start of the modern era of investment companies since the legislation helped restore the trust of the American public in the concept of the investment company. This renewed trust aided the tremendous growth investment companies have experienced in the past three decades. The major provisions of the 1940 Act and the 1970 Amendments are discussed in detail in Chapter 21.

The Securities Investor Protection Act of 1970. In the late 1960s, the securities industry started to suffer severe problems, which still have not been completely resolved and probably will not be resolved for many years.[9] Trading volume in stocks expanded rapidly and many brokerage firms found that they were unable to handle the increased volume with their facilities. Many brokerage firms also discovered a tendency to be short of capital, especially in view of the large expenditures that would be required for computers in order to process the blizzard of paperwork

[9]An account of what might have happened is given in "David Ricardo," "The Great 1970 Market Crash," *Financial Analysts Journal*, September–October 1970, pp. 22–27.

the high trading volume was generating. Experienced back office personnel to handle the trading volume also proved difficult to hire.

As a result of these developments, several undesirable events began to occur. Customers were often forced to wait months to receive stock certificates that had previously been delivered in weeks. Bookkeeping problems started to appear in substantial numbers and required much time on the part of both the brokerage firm and the customer to resolve. Dividend checks were sometimes late in arriving, as was payment for securities sold. While some brokerage firms suffered relatively little from these problems, the general crush of back office problems, with the resulting increase in costs, forced many brokerage firms to go bankrupt.

The NYSE had a trust fund to help a bankrupt brokerage firm achieve an orderly liquidation, but there was concern that the trust fund would not be adequate since brokerage firms were failing at a fairly rapid rate. Some market observers feared that there would be a crisis of confidence somewhat similar to the situation in the 1930s. After all, no customer of a brokerage firm wants to be concerned with whether funds in the account at the brokerage firm are safe. It is enough of a problem to attempt to make good investment decisions.

As a result of these events, Congress in late 1970 passed the Securities Investor Protection Act. This law established a government agency, the Securities Investor Protection Corporation (SIPC), to insure brokerage accounts against the failure of a brokerage firm in much the same manner as the Federal Deposit Insurance Corporation insures accounts at commercial banks. The SIPC insures accounts at brokerage firms up to $50,000, including a maximum $20,000 in cash.[10]

Self-Regulatory Activities

Several organizations within the securities industry are concerned with the regulation of the industry. The National Association of Securities Dealers (NASD), the exchanges themselves, and various professional groups such as the Institute of Chartered Financial Analysts are all engaged in self-regulatory activities.

The NASD has a membership of over 4,000 dealers in securities. A code of fair practice has been developed by the NASD and is enforced by a district committee structure. Since no NASD member may transact business with a nonmember except on the same price basis as on a transaction with the general public, the NASD has substantial power over its members. A securities dealer needs to be able to obtain wholesale prices from other NASD members rather than retail prices in order to compete effectively with other dealers.

[10]Some brokerage firms have added privately purchased supplemental insurance coverage of an additional $250,000, bringing the total to $300,000.

The exchanges themselves have considerable authority in the area of trading practices. The exchanges continually monitor the performance of specialists to determine if they are fulfilling the task of maintaining a fair and orderly market. We previously mentioned the fact that a new member to the NYSE must be carefully screened by the Board of Governors of the Exchange. The exchange also has rules regarding the capital requirements of broker-members.

The Institute of Chartered Financial Analysts was established in 1959 and incorporated in 1962. The Institute fosters high standards of education and professional conduct for financial analysts. In addition to sponsoring programs of research, study, and discussion, the Institute administers a series of three examinations leading to the awarding of the professional designation, Chartered Financial Analyst (C.F.A.). The Institute has established a code of ethics and has rigorous procedures for dealing with complaints from the public regarding the professional conduct of a C.F.A.

SUMMARY

There are many ways an investor may place an order for the purchase or sale of a security. Market orders are executed at the best price obtainable. Limit orders specify that the order is to be filled only if certain conditions exist. Margin account orders allow the investor to use borrowing power in the purchase of securities. Investors desiring to place margin account orders should know the general rules regarding margin transactions in addition to the practices and policies of the individual brokerage firm handling the account. Of course, an investor should be aware of the interest rate being charged on the money borrowed in the margin account transaction.

When a broker acts as an agent for a customer, a commission is charged for the services performed. The commission charged an investor for a stock transaction in the $1,000 to $2,000 range is a significant percentage of the value of the transaction. The commission is charged on both the purchase and the sale. The investor should attempt to avoid excessive trading activity in view of the brokerage commission structure. Other means of investing in stock such as using the so-called discount brokerage houses or special investment plans such as Merrill Lynch's Sharebuilder Plan may produce different and possibly lower commissions. While offering lower commissions, Merrill Lynch's plan has restrictive rules regarding investment activity. The commission on bond transactions tends to be a smaller percentage of the value of the trade than for stocks.

Regulation of the securities market occurs at the state level, at the federal level, and as a result of the self-regulatory activities of the market participants. State securities laws are known as blue-sky laws. The philosophy behind these laws is based on whether the proposed offering is in the best interests of the residents of the state. Federal regulation, on the other hand, is based upon the doctrine of fair and full disclosure. Organizations such as the National Association of Securities Dealers, the exchanges, and the Institute of Chartered Financial Analysts are important in the self-regulation of the industry.

QUESTIONS

1. What factors are important in the selection of a brokerage firm?
2. What is the difference between a cash account and a margin account?
3. a) What is the difference between a round-lot transaction and an odd-lot transaction?
   b) Of what significance is this difference to the investor as it relates to 1) commissions and 2) execution of the order?
4. Why would an investor place a limit order rather than a market order?
5. Under what circumstances would an investor use a stop sell order?
6. After analyzing a stock, an investor expects the price of the stock to decline? What action can the investor take?
7. a) Distinguish between an initial margin and a maintenance margin requirement.
   b) Would you agree that the greater the spread between the initial and maintenance margins, the less the risk of getting a margin call?
8. Can generalizations be made regarding the level of brokerage commissions on stocks as opposed to bonds? Is this distinction important to the investor?
9. Why might a new security offering be sold on an intrastate basis rather than on an interstate basis?
10. What is the difference between the regulatory philosophy regarding security sales at the state and federal level?
11. What is the SIPC and why was it established?
12. If an investor is having difficulties with an account at a brokerage firm, either in order execution or record keeping, what can the investor do about it?

PROBLEMS

1. An investor sells short 100 shares of stock at $50 and "covers" the short sale one year later at $35. Ignoring commissions, how much has the investor gained or lost on this transaction? Since short sale transactions are usually made in the margin account, what else would you need to know to calculate a rate of return on this transaction?
2. Henry Joyce has a margin account containing the following securities:

Description	*Cost per Share*	*Current Price per Share*
100 shares Blue Co.	$50	$20
100 shares General Axle	70	90

a) If the initial margin requirement is 60 percent, what is Henry's current equity in the account? Can he purchase additional securities without depositing more cash in the account?

b) If the maintenance margin requirement is 25 percent, when will Henry receive a margin call?

c) If the brokerage firm requires Henry to restore his equity to 30 percent to satisfy the margin call, how much cash will Henry need to deposit?

SUGGESTED READINGS

McEnally, Richard W. and Edward A. Dyl. "The Risk of Selling Short." *Financial Analysts Journal,* November–December 1969, pp. 73–76.

Stevenson, Richard A. "Brokerage Commissions and the Small Shareholder." *Journal of Business Research,* Fall 1973, pp. 193–200.

Van Horne, James C. "New Listings and Their Price Behavior." *Journal of Finance,* September 1970, pp. 783–94.

West, Richard R. and Seha M. Tinic. "Institutionalization: Its Impact on the Provision of Marketability Services and the Individual Investor." *Journal of Contemporary Business,* Winter 1974, pp. 25–48.

——. "Minimum Commission Rates on New York Stock Exchange Transactions." *Bell Journal of Economics and Management Science,* Autumn 1971, pp. 577–605.

Whitmarsh, Theodore F. "When to Sell Securities Short Against the Box." *Financial Analysts Journal,* May–June 1972, pp. 80–81ff.

*

4

Sources of Investment Information

For many people, the critical aspect of an investment decision lies in the information available with which to make wise and thoughtful trade-offs among alternatives. Good investments are often not made simply because the person is unaware of them or did not have sufficient information to determine the risk and potential return. This chapter discusses some of the more important sources of information concerning investment opportunities.

The amount of information available to the investor is enormous. The quality of the information itself and of the investment advice given by investment advisory services varies widely, and we cannot hope to cover all the potential sources of investment information. More important, the cost of obtaining the information may be prohibitive since the cost of obtaining the additional information may be greater than the added return or reduced risk achieved if the information were available.

This chapter discusses only financial information publicly available at a nominal cost or free in libraries available to the typical investor. Consequently, much of our discussion concentrates on information routinely supplied through the financial press. The first section examines the sources of price information available to the investor. This section is brief since later chapters discuss this topic for specific securities. Therefore, only a general discussion is given here and the reader is referred to exhibits in other chapters for specific examples of the reporting of prices. Section two discusses the market indexes, which allow the investor to ascertain how the market is doing. Section three examines some of the investment advisory services and brokerage house reports available, and section four describes various business, academic, and government periodicals. Section five introduces other sources of information, including data available from companies and from the federal government. A summary completes the chapter.

PRICE INFORMATION

Most major daily newspapers include a financial section, which reports the prices of stocks, bonds, and other publicly traded securities. Perhaps the most complete daily report is provided by the *Wall Street Journal*, a national financial newspaper that publishes not only financial news, but also general news of importance to the investor. In addition, it provides opinions of noted financial experts and a daily analysis of the various markets that trade financial instruments. For many investors, the *Wall Street Journal* is required reading.

The New York Stock Exchange price quotations given below for American Can's common and preferred stock are taken from the *Wall Street Journal* of May 19, 1975, and describe transactions that occurred the preceding trading day:

1975			*P-E*	*Sales*				*Net*
High	*Low*	*Stocks Div.*	*Ratio*	*100s*	*High*	*Low*	*Close*	*Chg.*
34½	28	A Can 2.20*a*	6	108	32⅛	31	31¼	−½
23¼	18¾	A Can pf 1.75	—	2	21⅜	21⅜	21⅜	—

Many other newspapers have similar reports. To read these price reports requires knowledge of certain terminology. The first A Can reports transactions in the common shares and the report labeled A Can pf reports transactions in the preferred shares. The first two columns indicate the highest and lowest prices for the calendar year of this report (1975). Thus, we know that from January 2, 1975 to May 16, 1975, American Can common shares sold as high as 34½ and as low as 28 dollars per share. The only exception to the high-low reports comes in the first three months of the year. From January through March of each year, the high-low columns report the highs and lows for both the current year and the previous year. For example, in February 1976 the high-low report will be the highest and lowest prices for 1975 and the first two months of 1976.

Immediately following the name of the company is the annual dividend of the firm. This figure is generally the annual dividend indicated by the last quarterly dividend paid by the firm. For example, the 2.20 noted for American Can indicates that the last quarterly dividend was $.55. There are, of course, many exceptions to this reporting policy, which are indicated by a footnote. Indeed, the small *a* next to the 2.20 for American Can indicates that the dividend is expected to be supplemented by some sort of extra or special dividend. All exceptions are footnoted with the explanations noted at the end of the price report.

The next column is the price-earnings ratio or the ratio of the earnings reported by the firm during the previous twelve months to the closing price of the day. As we shall see in Chapter 10, this ratio is an important analytical tool of investors. However, since an investor is purchasing *future* earning power, the price-earnings ratio given in the *Wall Street Journal* must not be accepted uncritically, since it indicates neither trends in earnings within the past twelve months nor earnings expectations.

The final five columns summarize the trading activity of each security. The column immediately following the price-earnings ratio is the trading volume report on the number of shares that were exchanged on the day in question. The data are reported in hundreds of shares. On May 16, 1975, 10,800 shares of American Can common stock were bought and sold on the floor of the NYSE. This number does not include any transactions that occurred on other exchanges or in the over-the-counter market.

The next three columns report the range of prices of the day's transactions. American Can's common shares traded for a high of 32⅛ and a low of 31. The price of the last transaction of the day is referred to as the closing price. American Can closed at 31¼. The final column reports the change in the closing price from the close of the last day on which American Can's common stock traded. American Can's stock was down ½, indicating that the previous close was 31¾.

In most cases, the price change is as we have just described. However, when a stock goes ex-dividend, the net change is not the difference between the closing prices. When a security goes ex-dividend, anyone purchasing the security does not receive the dividend when it is paid. Suppose a stock closed yesterday at a price of 21. Today the stock goes ex-dividend $.50 per share and the closing price is 20½. For reporting purposes, the financial press would report a net change of 0 and not –½. On the previous day, the stock sold for 21, when the buyer was entitled to the $.50 dividend. On the next day, the dividend was no longer a part of ownership, and ownership represented only $20.50—a decrease in value of $.50. Hence, the financial press reports no change in this situation, since the decline in the closing price was due solely to the ex-dividend date's impact.

Knowing these details, one can determine the activity of virtually any stock on the NYSE. The American Stock Exchange and other exchanges report transactions in the same fashion. However, stocks traded over-the-counter are reported in the manner shown below for the Aceto Chemical price quotation from the *Wall Street Journal* of May 19, 1975.

Stock & Div.	*Sales 100s*	*Bid*	*Asked*	*Net Chg.*
Aceto Chemicl	8	16½	18	−½

The high-low for the year is not reported, nor is the price-earnings ratio. We saw in Chapter 2 that the over-the-counter market is a negotiated market, compared to the auction market system of the organized exchanges. As such, the prices reported for over-the-counter securities are not prices that actually occurred but are representative bid and asked quotations at the close of the trading day. The bid price is the price that dealers are willing to pay and the asked price is the price for which dealers are willing to sell. The net change is the change in the bid price from the previous trading day.

Reports of transactions in bonds follow essentially the same format as that for stocks, with some exceptions. Chapter 17 discusses bonds in detail and Exhibit 17–2 gives some bond quotations. These quotations include the description of the bond, providing its coupon rate and maturity date. The volume, high, low, close, and net change for the day are also reported, just as they are for listed stocks.

The *Wall Street Journal* and several other major dailies also report prices of other financial instruments. These data include the prices of the many and varied bond issues of the federal government, the value of mutual fund shares, price and transaction data for commodities, the prices of stocks sold on some foreign markets, the value of foreign currencies, and the prices of options on common stock that are available to investors. We will not discuss these price quotations now, since they require an explanation of the securities themselves.

MARKET INDEXES

Types of Indexes

In addition to prices, the *Wall Street Journal* and other daily newspapers report other statistics the active investor follows closely. Perhaps the most important of these data are the various market indexes that allow the investor to obtain a summary of daily price and market activity. For example, Figure 15–3 shows the price movements of the Dow-Jones Industrial Average (DJI), a popular and widely used index (or average) of market activity.

As investors, we need to understand the meaning of data such as the DJI. The DJI consists of thirty common stocks, including many large and prominent firms such as Eastman Kodak, Exxon, Sears, and Texaco. These firms do not make up a random sample of NYSE-listed stocks. Although this may suggest the DJI is not representative of the NYSE, it does not necessarily follow that fluctuations in the DJI do not follow those of the market in general. Actually, the DJI appears to be a reasonably good barometer of market activity.

The DJI is not really an average. The average price of a stock is nowhere near the value of the DJI (about 850 in mid-1975). The actual average price of the stocks in the DJI approximates $45. The reason for this difference is the manner in which the DJI is adjusted for stock splits and stock dividends. A stock split is a method used by firms to reduce the per share price of their stock. For example, a two-for-one split means that a stockholder with 100 shares owns 200 shares after the split. The firm simply doubles the shares outstanding. In theory, the price of the share of stock should fall to half its previous price, since nothing has happened to the earning power of the firm. The price may in fact not drop by 50 percent, but it will drop substantially. If nothing is done, the DJI, if it includes that security, will also show a drop. Hence, the split must be taken into account by an adjustment made when calculating the average.

The DJI adjusts for the split by reducing the divisor when the average is figured. When the DJI was first devised in its modern form in 1928, the prices of the thirty securities were summed and the total divided by thirty to obtain the average. By mid-1975, the divisor had declined to 1.598 to reflect splits, stock dividends, and similar capitalization changes that occurred since 1928.

There are three other market indexes published by Dow-Jones: The Dow-Jones Transportation Average (DJT), the Dow-Jones Utility Average (DJU), and the Dow-Jones Composite Average (DJC). As its name implies, the DJT is composed of twenty large firms engaged in air, rail, and truck transportation. The DJU comprises fifteen gas and electric utilities but does not include American Telephone & Telegraph, which is included in the DJI. The DJC consists of the sixty-five stocks included in the DJI, the DJT, and the DJU. Each average has its special use, but when investors refer to the Dow index, they are invariably speaking of the DJI.

As one might expect in a competitive economy, other firms publish market indexes and, without exception, each major index is broader than the Dow-Jones market averages. Another popular market index is the Standard & Poor's 500 stock index, known simply as the S&P index. This index contains 500 common stocks listed on the NYSE and, like the Dow-Jones indexes, the 500 stocks are large and well-known companies.

The S&P index is what is known as a value-weighted index. It is the ratio of the total market value of the 500 securities on the particular day to the total market value of the same securities during the base period, 1941–43. Total market value is the sum of the market price times the number of shares outstanding for each security. This ratio is multiplied by ten in order to make the index roughly comparable to the average price of stocks when the current index was formed in 1957. However, current index values are no longer representative of the average price of a share of stock. The S&P index need not make any explicit adjustments for splits and stock dividends since they will not affect total market value.

Interpreting the S&P index is straightforward. As noted, the base period is 1941–43, when the value of the index was 10. By mid-1975, common stocks had increased in value approximately nine times over the thirty-four years (S&P 500 equal to approximately 90). This increase represents an average annual growth of approximately 6.7 percent. In 1957, the S&P 500 stood at approximately 47. Hence, from 1957 to mid-1975, this index increased at an annual growth rate of 3.7 percent.

Like Dow-Jones, Standard & Poor's publishes an industrial index (S&P 425), a utility index, and a transportation index in addition to indexes for about ninety separate industries. However, the most widely used index is the 500 stock index, which is quite useful since S&P also publishes earnings, dividends, sales, operating income, working capital, and several other financial variables of the companies in the index, all of which can be related directly to the index.

A relative newcomer to the list of market indexes is the NYSE Composite. This index is constructed in nearly the same manner as the S&P index except that it contains all of the securities listed on the NYSE, rather than just 500. The NYSE also reports indexes for groups such as utilities in addition to its composite index. Its base period is December 1965, and the ratio of market values is multiplied by 50 instead of 10. In the base period, the average price was approximately 53. The index in mid-1975 was about 45, which is still quite close to the actual average price. Since December 1965, the average price growth has been close to zero. If a major market movement in either direction occurs, the NYSE index will begin to deviate from the average price of a share of stock as the S&P index has done. However, the NYSE claims that it will adjust the index over time to reflect the average price by "splitting" the index. In other words, if the index grows to 100 and the average price remains at 50, the NYSE expects to split the index by multiplying the ratio of market values by 25 instead of the present constant of 50.

Several other indexes exist, including the New York Times Index, the Value Line Index, Moody's 125, the Dow Over-the-Counter Index, and the NASDAQ OTC Index. The American Stock Exchange also compiles an index, which is the only index of ASE stocks. Its method of construction (average of all price changes in dollars and cents) means that the index has a tendency to go up faster and down slower than more conventional indexes. For this reason, the ASE index is used rather infrequently as a market index. The NYSE, the S&P, and even the DJI are probably superior market guides even for the investor interested in the ASE.[1]

Criticisms of Indexes

Except for the ASE index, we have avoided judgments thus far as to the value of the indexes discussed. But each index may be criticized in specific terms. For example, the DJI is not broad enough and gives too much weight to high-priced stocks. John W. Schultz, writing in *Forbes*, calculated that as of mid-July 1974, four of the thirty DJI stocks accounted for 34 percent of the value of the DJI at that time.[2] These stocks—du Pont, Eastman Kodak, Procter & Gamble, and Sears—were relatively high priced compared to other stocks in the DJI. As a result, the price movements of these four stocks may be especially significant in the movements of the DJI.

To settle these criticisms, a comparison of indexes is necessary. In this context, we discuss three comparisons:

1. The extent to which the indexes move together.
2. The extent to which the volatility of the indexes is similar.
3. The similarity of the rates of return implied by movements in each of the indexes.

On the first point, the evidence seems to indicate that the choice of a particular index for price movements over long periods of time is not crucial. When the movements in the value of a given index are compared with the movements in the value of other indexes, the results are quite similar.[3]

In terms of the volatility of the index, we encounter a similar situation, at least for the more widely used market indexes. The volatility of the DJI, the S&P 500, and the NYSE composite index is roughly comparable.[4] The ASE index typically is more volatile than the DJI, the S&P 500, or the NYSE composite index, suggesting that ASE-listed stocks are more risky than NYSE-listed stocks.

The third criterion, similarity of rate of return, is not so easy to push aside. For example, IBM was dropped from the DJI in 1939 and AT&T was added. One estimate of the impact of this substitution was

[1]See Stephen C. Leuthold and Keith F. Blaich, "Warped Yardstick; The Amex Index Distorts Price Moves Both Up and Down," *Barron's*, September 18, 1972, pp. 9ff.

[2]John W. Schultz, "The Numbers Derby," *Forbes*, August 1, 1974, p. 59.

[3]For a summary of empirical evidence, see James H. Lorie and Mary T. Hamilton, "Stock Market Indexes," in *Modern Developments in Investment Management* ed. James H. Lorie and Richard Brealey (New York: Praeger, 1972), pp. 68–83.

[4]*Ibid.*

that at the end of 1965, the DJI would have been nearly double the actual level if IBM had remained in the index.[5] Other substitutions since 1939 have apparently also served to keep the DJI at a lower level than would be true if the substitutions had not been made.[6] In this sense, the DJI "underestimates" the rates of return available in the market.[7]

INVESTMENT ADVISORY AND BROKERAGE HOUSE SERVICES

The astute investor must evaluate and assimilate information regarding individual firms, and there are literally hundreds of sources of information about these individual companies. For many investors, the quickest and often least expensive source is the broker. Most large brokerage houses offer a wide variety of investment information. The services include providing summary financial data and detailed analyses of companies, industries, and the economy. Most brokers are happy to supply the investor with as much detail as is desired, and the investor should not be shy about asking to be supplied with relevant information. However, the broker eventually expects something in return and hopes for the opportunity to execute transactions. In essence, the size and frequency of trades may influence some brokerage houses regarding the quantity of information supplied. Although some brokerage houses welcome the small investor, others are much less enthusiastic about accepting his or her business.

Several information services that may be valuable are available from private sources. The cost of these services may not be justified given the size of a person's portfolio, but many libraries carry one or more of the more important information services. Three frequently used services are published by Moody's, Standard & Poor's, and Value Line.

Moody's annually publishes a set of massive volumes known as *Moody's Manuals*. These books contain considerable information for literally thousands of firms. The data typically include a brief history of the firm, a description of the business, at least (and frequently more than) two years of financial statements, explanations of the details of the capital structure, and in many cases some analytical work using many of the ratios to be discussed in Chapter 10. Next to the annual report of a company, Moody's is probably the most complete source of readily available information about a company. At the same time, *Moody's Manuals* do not comment on the quality of a particular firm for which information is reported. Subscriptions are also available to *Moody's Bond Survey*,

[5]Robert D. Milne, "The Dow-Jones Industrial Average Re-examined," *Financial Analysts Journal*, November–December 1966, p. 87.

[6]*Ibid.*

[7]See Wyndham Robertson, "The Trouble with the Dow-Jones Average," *Fortune*, March 1972, p. 143, and Frank K. Reilly, "Stock Price Changes by Market Segment," *Financial Analysts Journal*, March–April 1971, pp. 54–59.

Moody's Stock Survey, and the *Handbook of Widely Held Common Stocks*. Each of these publications is informative and makes qualitative judgments about future prospects.

Standard & Poor's publishes *S&P Corporation Records*, which covers much the same material as *Moody's Manuals*. The data are somewhat less complete than Moody's, but still quite acceptable. In fact, the brevity may be an advantage during an investor's initial screening of possible investment opportunities. Standard & Poor's also publishes the *Stock Guide* and the *Bond Guide*, which present summary information on thousands of firms and are useful as a reference to find data for major financial variables. S&P also publishes *The Outlook* and the *Stock Market Encyclopedia*, which are informative and offer opinions on the future prospects of the firms evaluated.

The Value Line Investment Survey is another excellent reference service, but the information here is typically more analytical than strictly informative. *Value Line* reviews more than 1,400 firms quarterly. In addition to a wealth of financial and descriptive information, *Value Line* provides the investor with a quality judgment for each stock reviewed: A numerical ranking from 1 to 5 is assigned to stocks for a) the expected price performance during the next twelve months and b) the stock's rank for safety. *Value Line* also gives estimated price performance for the coming three- to five-year period. Additionally, *Value Line* presents industry data and analysis, special stock recommendations, and an analysis of the economy.

PERIODICALS

Business and Academic Publications

Financial information is not the only information required by the wise investor. A wealth of qualitative information exists and is typically found in one of several daily, weekly, or monthly publications. We previously mentioned the *Wall Street Journal*. It carries financial reports, qualitative business news, general world and national news, and analyses of business and economic conditions. Exhibit 4–1 is the "Abreast of the Market" section from the issue of July 9, 1975. This summary of market conditions and events is worthwhile reading for the investor.

The Dow-Jones Company publishes *Barron's National Business and Financial Weekly*, or simply *Barron's*, in addition to the *Wall Street Journal*. Each week *Barron's* includes an in-depth analysis of three or four companies and industries, which are designed strictly as an analysis of investment possibilities. *Barron's* also contains a good statistical section covering the previous week's market activities including all the organized exchanges, the over-the-counter market, the bond markets, the commodity markets, mutual funds, and general economic information.

EXHIBIT 4–1

"Abreast of the Market" Column

Market Recoups Part of Early Loss As Trading Continues at Slow Pace

By Victor J. Hillery

The stock market continued sliding yesterday morning but came part way back during the afternoon in another slow trading session.

Weakness again was ascribed primarily to recent rises in short-term interest rates following some credit tightening by the Federal Reserve. Yields on new 13-week and 26-week Treasury bills this week soared to the highest levels in over five months.

"The market has exaggerated the interest-rate problem and even if First National City Bank boosts its prime lending rate to 7¼%, this won't indicate that the Fed is going to a policy of constraint," commented Bud Simons, Weeden & Co. research director. Last week, the bank increased its fee ¼-point to 7%. And Robert Stovall, Reynolds Securities Inc. vice president, said part of the pullback was "a delayed seasonal weakness that normally comes in May or June."

The Dow Jones industrial average, which retreated 10.71 points Monday, tumbled another 6.34 points in yesterday's first hour. After a slow and uncertain rebound during the remainder of the session, the indicator finished at 857.79, off 3.29 points. The utility average also ended lower, but the transportation index gained.

New York Stock Exchange losers led better than two-to-one early in the day but their margin later narrowed; at the close, 799 stocks were down and 622 up.

Abreast of the Market

In the early stage of a stock market recovery, the major influence on prices is the trend in short-term interest rates, said Reynolds' Mr. Stovall, but "in the next phase longer-term interest rates are a greater influence." Don H. Straszheim, Investors Diversified Services Inc. economist, looks for the rates on new issues of double-A-rated utility bonds to average about 9.2% in the third quarter and 9% in the fourth quarter.

Consumer Spending Cited

Mr. Straszheim also asserted that it is "normal in the recovery phase from a recessionary period" for "consumer spending on durable goods to exceed the growth in total consumer spending." He added: "The severe recession has left the supply of consumer durables in the worst shape in many years. Consumers will try to redress this under-spending on durables in recent years."

The current stock market decline is viewed more somberly by Nicholas Davis, research partner at Boettcher & Co. He asserted that "with interest rates rising, cash alternatives now are more attractive than equities." He looks for a decline of about 100 points in the industrial average and has raised the cash positions of the firm's managed accounts to about 20%. For the longer term, however, he is "still quite bullish."

Weeden's Mr. Simons sees the market in "a resting period" and contends that a possible settlement in the Mideast could send stock prices climbing again.

Big Board volume, heaviest in the first and final hours, expanded to 18,990,000 shares from 15,850,000 Monday. Greater institutional activity was indicated by the gain in trades of 10,000 shares or more to 140 from the prior day's revised 98.

Declines held a slim lead over winners on the American Stock Exchange but its index rose 0.20 to 92.37. Turnover slowed a bit to 2,210,000 shares from 2,290,000. In the over-the-counter market, the National Association of Securities Dealers' NASDAQ composite index eased 0.21 to 85.39.

Stocks touching new 1975 highs on the Big Board fell to 77 from 83 on Monday, and new lows declined to two from three.

One factor that helped buoy yesterday's market was the strength in Polaroid, the Big Board's third most active issue. The stock spurted 2⅝ to 39¼ after the company said it will post second quarter earnings "better than many people anticipated" early this year.

Another encouraging development was General Motors' rise of 1⅛ to a 1975 high of 49⅝ in active trading. Reynolds' Mr. Stovall said some market technicians regard a new high in GM in a recovery phase as indicating "at least another four months of clear sailing."

Among other gainers, Apco Oil, in second place, rose ½ to 17¼; Alaska Interstate plans an offer for about 51% of Apco's common shares. An 111,000-share block, with Goldman, Sachs & Co. on most of the sell side, traded at 16¾.

Taft Broadcasting, which expects to post a 25% to 30% decline in June quarter net, dropped 2⅛ to 26⅜. Upjohn slid 2 to 38⅜; the Food and Drug Administration said it received reports of 13 additional deaths related to two of Upjohn's antibiotics.

Braniff, the Big Board's volume leader, rose ⅛ to 7⅜; a 265,500-share block, handled by Oppenheimer & Co., traded at 6⅞. Spencer Trask & Co. handled a 197,000-share block of Texas Oil & Gas at 18¼; it ended at 18¾, off ¼. A 100,000-share block of Midland-Ross was handled by Roulston Co. at 19; it closed at 19¼, up ¾.

U.S. Steel Climbed

Of the industrial average's 30 issues, 17 fell and nine gained. United Technologies slipped 1¾ to 55¼ and Du Pont, 1½ to 122½. But U.S. Steel climbed 1¼ to 60⅛.

Among American exchange actives, Great Basins Petroleum gained ⅜ to 3¾ on turnover of 71,900 shares, U.S. Filter rose ⅝ to 13⅛ on volume of 48,500 shares and Houston Oil eased ¾ to 24⅞ on volume of 34,200 shares.

In NASDAQ-reported over-the-counter trading, declines outdistanced advances, 481 to 302. Activity quickened to 5,379,300 shares from 4,959,700 Monday. Anheuser-Busch fell 1 to 36, bid.

Source: Reprinted with permission of *the Wall Street Journal*, (July 9, 1975), p. 21.

The *Wall Street Transcript* was started in 1963. This weekly publication presents verbatim and without comment reports issued by many brokerage firms, as well as corporate news items. Another potentially useful feature of this publication is the "Roundtable," in which experts in a given area, such as energy or the mobile home industry, discuss their views on the future.

The *Commercial and Financial Chronicle* is published twice a week. The Monday issue contains a detailed statistical section similar to *Barron's* and a complete set of announcements and corporate news of interest to the investor. Much of this material, although interesting, is more useful to larger investors and financial institutions. The Thursday issue is of more interest to the average investor, since it contains informative articles on the investment world and at least one detailed analysis of an individual common stock.

Forbes, published twice a month, contains industry and company articles on a regular basis. Columnists provide analyses of the market from several different perspectives. The first January issue contains a complete ranking of firms by industry and profitability. The second August issue contains a complete evaluation of the various mutual funds available. Also of some interest to the investor are *Financial World* and The *Magazine of Wall Street* which, like *Forbes*, concentrate on analysis rather than merely factual reporting.

One of the most difficult tasks for the investor is the determination of the quality of a company's management. Chapter 9 discusses the manner in which this difficult assessment may be approached. *Fortune* is a valuable source of information in making this assessment. This magazine often carries detailed articles on a firm's top management people and how they make critical decisions. *Fortune* also has a personal investing section in which specific investment topics are discussed.

Business Week, a weekly general business publication, is a quick way for the average investor to keep abreast of general developments within the economy. In its special issues, *Business Week* discusses topics of great importance to the investor. The topics include such areas as the role of debt usage in all sectors of the economy, the investment outlook for the coming year, and the role of the multinational corporation.

Many other sources of market and financial information are published regularly and most investors are unable to keep up with all of the publications. Consequently, it is often wise to check one or two popular and complete business periodical indexes available in many libraries, such as the *Business Periodicals Index* or the *F&S Index of Corporations and Industries*. Both can be used as basic reference sources to discover the location of articles about a company, an industry, or any general subject of interest to the investor.

Several academic periodicals are also available to help the investor keep abreast of recent investment concepts. The *Financial Analysts Journal* is published bimonthly and contains analytical articles on the economy, investment management, and investment analysis. Its great advantage lies in its policy of presenting complex topics in clear and concise terms. Many sophisticated and complex mathematical techniques and concepts are summarized and evaluated in this publication. Among the many other academic journals concerned with investments are the *Journal of Finance*, the *Journal of Financial and Quantitative Analysis*, and the *Journal of Business*. Each presents articles on recent developments and typically concentrates on theory, using considerable amounts of mathematics and statistics.

Government and Private Economic Publications

Several sources of economic data are available from both private sources and the federal government, and are designed to assist the investor in the analysis of general economic conditions. Two prominent government publications are the *Survey of Current Business* and the *Federal Reserve Bulletin*. Both are published monthly and contain articles about and analyses of the economy as a whole and by sector, as well as considerable quantities of statistical data. The twelve federal reserve banks also publish monthly bulletins that discuss general business and monetary conditions. These bulletins vary widely in the subjects covered and in their usefulness for individual investors. However, the *Monthly Review* published by the New York Federal Reserve Bank and the *Review* published by the St. Louis Federal Reserve Bank may be especially useful. The *Monthly Review* contains a good summary of recent bond market developments, while the *Review* often discusses the importance of monetary considerations to the state of the economy and the markets in which financial securities trade. The St. Louis "Fed" also publishes *U.S. Financial Data*, a weekly issue that gives the latest monetary and interest rate statistics.

As we shall see in Chapter 7, much economic forecasting uses leading indicators of the business cycle. For the novice and experienced investor alike, a good source of information about the course and interpretation of economic indicators is the *Business Conditions Digest*, published monthly by the Department of Commerce. Economic forecasts can also be found in the January issue of the *Journal of Business* and in the *Annual Report* of the President's Council of Economic Advisors.

Several private organizations publish both quantitative and qualitative information concerning the economy. For example, First National City Bank of New York's *Monthly Economic Letter* and Chase Manhattan Bank's *Business in Brief* contain interpretations of the condition of the economy.

OTHER SOURCES OF INFORMATION

Annual Reports to Stockholders

Before investing in a security, it is usually wise to obtain the company's annual report, which is available on request from the company. Modern annual reports are generally quite complete and informative. Of course, one should remember that they are published by the firm and attempt to place the firm in the best possible light given the regulatory and financial reporting limitations on the firm.

Registration Statements and Prospectuses

In addition to annual reports, detailed company information may be obtained from registration statements required when securities are registered for public trading and prospectuses published when a new issue of securities is offered for sale. Although these sources contain a wealth of information, the investor may find the amount of information and the manner in which it is presented somewhat overwhelming. This tends to be especially true for prospectuses issued in conjunction with complex merger arrangements.

Routine SEC Filings

Associated with the required information that companies must supply are several reports that must be routinely filed with the Securities and Exchange Commission (SEC). The 8-K is a monthly report designed to disclose any changes in such things as voting rights, capitalization, legal problems, and management financial interests in the transactions of the firm. The 10-Q report is an unaudited quarterly financial statement. The 10-K is a detailed annual financial report of the firm. This report must be audited and contains virtually all the financial information that even the most sophisticated investor should need. Companies will often send the investor a copy of the 10-K report.

SUMMARY

Information is the key ingredient in an investment decision. Much information or advice is available at no cost, which is what some of it is worth, especially if it comes in the form of a "hot tip" from your barber or beautician or some similar source. However, many free publications are available from brokerage houses, financial institutions, the Federal Reserve System, and similar sources, that can be of value to the investor.

Other information and advice are not free. In these cases, the cost must be related to the benefits to be realized from using the particular source of information. These benefits should appear in the form of better investment decisions than would be the case without the information. The investor should be discriminating in the choice of information and advice purchased; his or her time and money are limited. A final point: The cost of investment information and business related publications is a tax deductible expense for the investor owning securities. Of course, the investor should not purchase more information and advice than needed to make informed investment decisions; each investor must decide how much information is enough.

QUESTIONS

1. The price-to-earnings ratio reported in the *Wall Street Journal* must be used carefully by the investor. Why is this true?
2. The Booklet Corporation's common stock goes ex-dividend $.75 per share today. Yesterday, the closing price was 32½. If today's closing price is 32¼, what will the *Wall Street Journal* price quotations for today show as the net change for the stock?
3. On the same day that Aceto Chemical was quoted at 16½ bid and 18 asked, Presto Products, Inc. was quoted at 16½ bid and 17 asked. What do you think could account for the difference in these quotations and of what significance is this to you as an investor?
4. The Dow-Jones Industrial Index is what is known as a price weighted index since the prices are summed and the total divided by a divisor.
   a) What serious problems might this form of index construction cause for the investor using this index as a measure of the trend of the market?
   b) Will a market value weighted index such as the S&P 500 solve all of these problems?

5. Where might one go to find information regarding:
   a) the state of the general economy?
   b) the movements of business cycle indicators?
   c) industry information?
   d) company information?
   e) interest rates for various types of fixed-income securities?
6. According to comments in the *Wall Street Journal,* the 25 growth companies in the S&P 500 index that had the largest market value went up 23.3 percent during the first seven months of 1972. The 25 cyclical stocks, such as General Motors, with the largest market values went up only 2.1 percent. The remaining 450 stocks went down 5.0 percent during the period. Given the manner in which the S&P 500 is constructed, what do you think happened to the index during the period?

SUGGESTED READINGS

Carter, E. Eugene and Kalman J. Cohen. "Stock Averages, Stock Splits, and Bias." *Financial Analysts Journal,* May–June 1967, pp. 77–84.

Kekish, Bohdan. "Moody's Averages." *Financial Analysts Journal,* May–June 1967, pp. 65–70.

Latané, Henry A., Donald L. Tuttle, and William E. Young. "Market Indexes and the Implications for Portfolio Management." *Financial Analysts Journal,* September–October 1971, pp. 75–85.

Logue, Dennis E. and Donald L. Tuttle. "Brokerage House Investment Advice." *The Financial Review,* 1973, pp. 38–54.

Lorie, James H. and Mary T. Hamilton. "Stock Market Indexes." In *Modern Developments in Investment Management* ed. James H. Lorie and Richard Brealey. New York: Praeger, 1972, pp. 68–83.

Milne, Robert D. "The Dow-Jones Industrial Average Re-examined." *Financial Analysts Journal,* November–December 1966, pp. 83–88.

Molodovsky, Nicholas. "Building a Stock Market Measure." *Financial Analysts Journal,* May–June 1967, pp. 43–48.

Schellback, Lewis L. "When Did the DJIA Top 1200?" *Financial Analysts Journal,* May–June 1967, pp. 71–76.

Schoomer, B. Alva Jr. "American Stock Exchange Index System." *Financial Analysts Journal,* May–June 1967, pp. 57–64.

Stoffels, John D. "Stock Recommendations by Investment Advisory Services: Immediate Effects on Market Price." *Financial Analysts Journal,* March–April 1966, pp. 77–86.

West, Stan, and Norman Miller. "Why the NYSE Common Stock Indexes?" *Financial Analysts Journal,* May–June 1967, pp. 49–56.

*

5

The Tax Environment

The growing affluence of the American population, coupled with a progressive federal income tax, creates a situation in which each investor should be cognizant of tax factors. Death may be inevitable, but the payment of some taxes can either be avoided entirely or postponed until a later date.

Sound tax planning by the investor is the key to a minimization of taxes. Tax planning means that the investor utilizes the *existing tax structure* to minimize the total tax bite. Taxes are avoided using legal methods. Tax evasion, the nonpayment of taxes that are legally payable to various taxing authorities, is not advocated.

Making proper investment decisions from a tax standpoint is a complicated matter. In this chapter, no attempt will be made to cover the many complex accounting and legal problems that an investor may encounter. Investors facing unique and difficult tax problems are well advised to seek expert counseling.

This chapter introduces the reader to the tax environment in which he or she must operate. In addition, the basic tax goals for the investor are discussed. We limit most of the discussion to the federal tax laws although some attention is devoted to state and local taxes. The nature and significance of the federal tax laws is examined following a discussion of the tax goals of the investor. After a brief discussion of the state and local tax environment, ways in which investors can achieve tax goals are examined.

TAX GOALS

A way of approaching the area of taxation as it relates to investors is to establish a ranking of tax goals. Naturally, an investor must always consider whether the achievement of any particular tax goal is worth the cost involved. Three general tax goals are given below:

1. *Tax-Exempt Income.* The first priority is for the investor to attempt to receive income in a form that does not subject it to taxation. This involves many considerations, as we shall see. One of the most important considerations may involve the acceptance by the investor of a lower rate of return than is available on investments yielding taxable income.

2. *Long-term Capital Gains Instead of Ordinary Income.* A capital gain or loss (either long- or short-term) results from the sale or exchange of a capital asset. Capital assets are precisely defined by the Internal Revenue Code, and include virtually all securities normally held by individuals for investment purposes.

Long-term capital gains are subject to lower rates of taxation than ordinary income such as wages. Short-term capital gains are taxed at ordinary income tax rates. If income cannot be received in a tax-exempt form, long-term capital gains are the next most desirable type of income.

3. *Lowest Tax Rate on Ordinary Income.* If an investor must receive investment income in a fully taxable form (ordinary income), it is desirable to have that income taxed at the lowest possible tax rate. Tax planning designed to reduce the total amount of income subject to taxation is obviously required.

FEDERAL INCOME TAX

Since the federal income tax is such a large and fundamental element in the tax area, it is essential for the investor to understand its structure. The basic form for filing (Form 1040) follows the structure shown below:

	Gross income
less	Deductions from gross income
equals	Adjusted gross income
less	Itemized nonbusiness deductions (or the standard deduction)
equals	Net income
less	Personal exemptions
equals	Taxable income

The taxable income times the tax rate equals the income tax payable.

The adjusted gross income figure is important since other items are often based on it. For example, only expenditures for medicine and drugs in excess of 1 percent of adjusted gross income are deductible as itemized deductions. For this reason, deductions from gross income are important. Most investors, however, will have few, if any, deductions from gross income. Two fairly common deductions from gross income that individuals might have are excludable sick pay and moving expenses.

MARGINAL TAX RATE

The taxable income figure determines the *marginal* tax bracket for an investor. For many investment tax considerations, the marginal tax bracket of the individual is of great interest. The marginal tax bracket determines the percentage of tax which will have to be paid by the investor on any income received, regardless of source, *over and above regular sources of income.* Consider the following situation with the income above wages coming in the form of investment income.

The marginal tax rate in the example here is 29 percent. This is a fairly substantial marginal tax rate and may well influence investment decisions. Yet, $15,000 is not an extraordinarily high income. As seen from the example, all the added investment income is taxed at the marginal tax rate and the tax payable increases by $290. Since virtually all investment income is an addition to sources of income such as wages, one can easily see why investors need to know both their own tax situations and the basic tax laws.

Income and Other Information

Wages:	$15,000
Marital status:	Single—filing separate return
Deductions:	Standard deduction
Investment income:	Case A—none
	Case B—$1,000 (ordinary income)

Calculation of Federal Income Tax Payable	*Case A*	*Case B*
Gross income (wages/investment income)	$15,000	$16,000
Deductions from gross income	0	0
Adjusted gross income	$15,000	$16,000
Less standard deduction[1]	2,000	2,000
Net income	$13,000	$14,000
Less personal exemption[2]	750	750
Taxable income	$12,250	$13,250
Tax calculation:		
Tax on $12,000	$2,630.00	$2,630.00
29 percent of excess over $12,000	72.50	362.50
Tax payable	$2,702.50	$2,992.50

PROGRESSIVE NATURE OF TAX

Table 5-1 compares the tax payable for an individual filing a separate return with the tax payable on a joint return for various levels of taxable income. This table shows that the federal tax structure is highly progressive. A progressive tax means that as income increases, the tax payable increases by a larger percentage. In our example of the individual with $15,000 in wages, the added $1,000 of investment income increased total income by 6.7 percent. However, the tax payable went from $2,702.50 to $2,992.50, for an increase of 10.7 percent.

[1]The tax laws effective in early 1975 provided for a standard deduction equal to 15 percent of adjusted gross income up to a maximum of $2,000. Proposals before Congress might change this provision, however.

[2]A $750 per exemption deduction was effective in early 1975. A proposal before Congress would increase this. The example also assumed an individual under sixty-five years of age since an additional exemption is allowed for taxpayers over sixty-five years of age.

TABLE 5-1
Individual Federal Tax Rates—Single and Joint Returns

	Taxable Income	Base Tax	Marginal Rate	Average Rate Paid
Single:	$ 0	$ 0	14%	0%
	500	70	15	14.0
	1,000	145	16	14.5
	1,500	225	17	15.0
	2,000	310	19	15.5
	4,000	690	21	17.3
	6,000	1,110	24	18.5
	8,000	1,590	25	19.9
	10,000	2,090	27	20.9
	12,000	2,630	29	21.9
	14,000	3,210	31	22.9
	16,000	3,830	34	23.9
	18,000	4,510	36	25.1
	20,000	5,230	38	26.2
	22,000	5,990	40	27.2
	26,000	7,590	45	29.2
	32,000	10,290	50	32.2
	38,000	13,290	55	35.0
	44,000	16,590	60	37.7
	50,000	20,190	62	40.4
	60,000	26,390	64	44.0
	70,000	32,790	66	46.8
	80,000	39,390	68	49.2
	90,000	46,190	69	51.3
	100,000	53,090	70	53.1
Joint:	$ 0	$ 0	14%	0%
	1,000	140	15	14.0
	2,000	290	16	14.5
	3,000	450	17	15.0
	4,000	620	19	15.5
	8,000	1,380	22	17.3
	12,000	2,260	25	18.8
	16,000	3,260	28	20.4
	20,000	4,380	32	21.9
	24,000	5,660	36	23.6
	28,000	7,100	39	25.4
	32,000	8,660	42	27.1
	36,000	10,340	45	28.7
	40,000	12,140	48	30.4
	44,000	14,060	50	32.0
	52,000	18,060	53	34.7
	64,000	24,420	55	38.2
	76,000	31,020	58	40.8
	88,000	37,980	60	43.2
	100,000	45,180	62	45.2
	120,000	57,580	64	48.0
	140,000	70,380	66	50.3
	160,000	83,580	68	52.2
	180,000	97,180	69	54.0
	200,000	110,980	70	55.5

Note: As a result of the Tax Reform Act of 1969, the maximum marginal rate on earned income (wages, salary, professional fees, etc.) is 50 percent.

Not only are the federal tax rates progressive in that they become larger with increasing income, but also the highest marginal rate (70 percent) is reached at a taxable income of $100,000 for a separate return and $200,000 for a joint return. These high marginal tax rates have profound implications for the manner in which high-income taxpayers invest.

STATE TAX LAWS

A complete analysis of state income tax laws is beyond the scope of this book. In fact, some states do not even have a state income tax. State income taxes are not as important as federal income taxes since the rate structure at the state level tends to be lower and much less progressive. State income taxes are also an itemized deduction in determining taxable income for federal income tax purposes. This serves to reduce federal income taxes and lessens the impact of state income taxes.

While one cannot argue that an investor should ignore either state or city income taxes, the remainder of this chapter will focus on federal income taxes because of their predominant impact. Any conclusions drawn from examining tax planning under the federal tax laws also apply to state taxes, but to a much lesser degree.

TAX EXEMPT INCOME

Dividend Exclusion

There are several ways an investor can obtain investment income exempt from taxation. The first method involves the way title is held to the assets. The federal tax law allows $100 of dividend income to be excluded from a separate tax return and up to $200 on a joint return provided both parties have $100 of dividend income.

If the single wage earner earning $15,000 also owned stocks paying $200 annually in dividend income, $100 of that income could be excluded from adjusted gross income. Upon getting married, this individual would be allowed to exclude only $100 of dividend income *unless* the manner in which title is held to the stocks is changed. Either all the dividend-producing stocks could be registered under joint ownership or stocks producing $100 of dividend income could be registered in the spouse's name. By taking either of these actions, an additional $100 in dividend income could be excluded. It should be pointed out, however, that if stock producing only $50 in dividend income is registered in the spouse's name, the dividend exclusion is only $150.

Municipal Bonds

As shall be seen in more detail in Chapter 19, the interest income received from bonds issued by state and local governmental bodies is exempt from federal taxation.[3] These bonds are quite popular with taxpayers in high marginal tax brackets. Since the yields on these tax exempt bonds tend to be lower than for taxable bonds of comparable quality, the effective after-tax yield from both types of bonds, given the investor's marginal tax bracket, must be calculated. This calculation is discussed in Chapter 19.

Timing of Income Realization

It is often possible to time the receipt of income so that the income is not taxed. For example, interest income of federal government Series E bonds is not taxed until it is received by the investor when the bond is cashed in, unless the taxpayer elects to be taxed on an accrued interest basis. Under the accrued interest basis, the taxpayer calculates the amount of interest earned during a given tax year and reports it as taxable income that year. Assume that an investor purchased a Series E bond in the name of a minor child twenty years ago. When this bond is cashed in, all the interest earned since its purchase is reported as taxable income in the year of redemption. It would be desirable to time the receipt of this income when other sources of taxable income are low. This situation might occur when the child is in college. In fact, the total income could be low enough to avoid the payment of any income taxes. The net result is that all the Series E bond interest income could escape taxation since the timing of its realization is planned for the maximum tax benefit. In general, investors should plan the receipt of taxable investment income for a time when taxable income in general is low.

Another time of life that often produces significant tax planning benefits is the retirement years. Since Social Security retirement benefits are not taxable, retirees often have either no taxable income or are in rather low marginal tax brackets. An individual approaching retirement and owning securities with unrealized gains might well decide to wait until retirement to realize these gains. In that way, the gains would not be taxed or would be taxed at low rates.

[3]If federal-state revenue sharing continues to increase, it is possible that municipal bonds might eventually be phased out as a means of financing state and local capital expenditure projects.

CAPITAL GAINS VS. ORDINARY INCOME

Timing Considerations

The tax laws regarding gains and losses on the sale of securities place a premium on the timing of transactions. A *short-term capital gain or loss* results when the capital asset has been held six months or less. A *long-term capital gain or loss* results from the sale of a security held more than six months. Whether gains or losses are long term or short term is often not a trivial consideration. The following four statements summarize the tax treatment of short- and long-term capital gains and losses:[4]

1. Short-term capital losses are fully deductible from ordinary income up to a limit of $1,000 per year. Any excess can be carried over to subsequent years to offset any gains or utilized at the rate of $1,000 per year if there are no gains.
2. One-half of long-term capital losses may be deducted from income up to the maximum deduction of $1,000 for any capital loss per year. The carry-forward provisions discussed in 1 apply.
3. Short-term capital gains are fully taxable in the year realized.
4. Only one-half of long-term capital gains are taxed at ordinary tax rates.

Consider the following example as an application of these tax laws:

An investor in the 30 percent marginal tax bracket holds four securities as of early December. While there is no compelling investment reason to sell any security, the investor is willing to sell any or all of the four securities. The securities in the short-term category have been held for three months.

Security	*Short or Long Term*	*Gain or Loss*
A	short term	$1,000 loss
B	short term	1,000 gain
C	long term	1,000 loss
D	long term	1,000 gain

Sale of One Security Only

Sale of A — $1,000 loss is fully deductible and saves $300 in taxes at the 30 percent marginal tax rate. If this loss becomes long term, only $500 is deductible, which reduces taxes by $150.

[4]These summaries and the discussion and examples that follow over-simplify the federal tax laws. While the laws apply reasonably well to taxpayers with moderate incomes and no special transactions (such as the sale of a personal residence), high-income taxpayers and taxpayers with unusual transactions may be subject to special provisions in the federal tax laws.

Sale of B	$1,000 gain is fully taxable resulting in an additional tax of $300. If this is allowed to become long term, only $500 of the gain is taxable, resulting in an additional tax of $150.
Sale of C	$500 of loss is deductible resulting in a tax reduction of $150.
Sale of D	$500 of gain is taxable resulting in an additional tax of $150.

It is clear from the above example that the investor can do nothing regarding the long-term gains or losses. Their holding period cannot be changed. However, given that the investor has decided to dispose of security A for investment reasons, it should be sold immediately to thereby take advantage of the tax benefits associated with realizing the short-term loss. The investor should not allow security A to become a long-term loss. Likewise, the investor should continue to hold security B until the gain falls into the long-term category.

Other factors might influence the investor's decision. If security B happens to be a very speculative security, it might be better to have a short-term gain of $1,000 rather than no gain at all should the security decline in price while the investor is attempting to hold it longer than six months. In other words, the (tax) tail should not wag the (investment) dog.

The tax laws are more complicated when more than one security transaction occurs in a tax year. Before continuing our example by allowing the sale of more than one security, it becomes necessary to discuss the manner in which capital gains and losses are handled on the taxpayer's Schedule D of the federal tax return. The taxpayer is required to net short-term gains against short-term losses and to net long-term gains against long-term losses. The investor is then required to net the short-term transactions against the long-term transactions. The diagram below shows how this works:

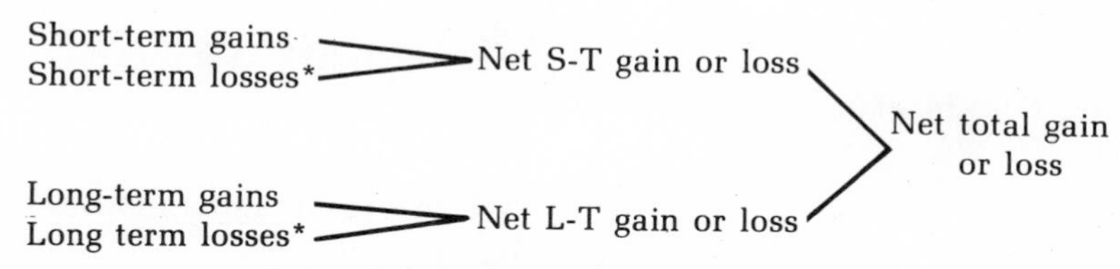

Sale of Two or More Securities

Sale of A,B,C & D	Gains and losses all cancel out resulting in no tax impact.
Sale of A & C	Net total loss of $2,000. The amount deductible is 50 percent of $1,000 (L-T loss) and 100 percent of $1,000 (S-T loss). Federal tax laws require the short-term loss to be used first with the result that the $1,000 long-term loss is carried forward to the next taxable year. In the next year, the long-term loss can be used to offset a gain or to reduce taxable income by $500.

*Includes carryovers of losses from previous years.

Sale of A & D	Short-term loss gets netted against the long-term gain resulting in no tax impact.
Sale of C & D	Long-term gain and loss cancel out resulting in no change in taxes payable.

The above examples of sales of two or more securities do not include all possible combinations of transactions. However, they are illustrative of the type of calculation required when considering the tax consequences of security transactions. The investor considering the sale of securities in early December would not want to sell securities A and D in the same year if these are the only two security transactions. If security A is sold in December, the investor saves $300 in taxes. If security D is sold in January, the investor incurs additional taxes of only $150. It is clearly to the investor's benefit to time sales so that these two transactions fall in different tax years since there is a net tax savings of $150.

Since it is not possible to cover in this book all possible tax situations an investor will encounter, each investor should make a preliminary assessment of the year's income tax situation toward the end of the tax year. In this manner, it is possible to see if security transactions may be made that will be of benefit from a tax standpoint. However, the following three general security transaction rules emerge from our example:

1. Do not let short-term losses become long-term losses.
2. Attempt to hold a security until short-term gains become long-term gains.
3. Do not take long-term gains in the same year you have short-term losses.

Buying Bonds at a Discount

Another method of obtaining long-term capital gains instead of ordinary income is to buy bonds at a discount. In March 1974, one of AT&T's bonds sold for $615. This is a discount of $385 since AT&T is committed to redeem this bond in 1986 for $1,000. The bond pays interest of $27.50 per year. An investor purchasing this bond would receive $27.50 annual interest income in addition to a long-term capital gain of $385 from holding this bond to its maturity date.

As with the purchase of municipal bonds, the investor should determine if a bond selling at a discount is a worthwhile purchase. What one essentially accomplishes by buying the AT&T bond is to trade interest income for long-term capital gains. As might be suspected, the investor can be expected to pay a price in order to receive a different form of income. This price tends to come in the form of a lower yield. In Chapter

17, we examine the nature of this trade-off in detail along with the manner in which the investor would analyze the investment merits of a bond such as the AT&T bond.

Purchase of Stocks of Growth Firms

Investors in high marginal tax brackets are often attracted to growth firms, whose common stocks often pay few, if any, dividends. This is again a situation where the investor makes a decision to give up current income from dividends that would be taxed at ordinary tax rates. In place of this dividend income, the investor seeks growth opportunities in the hope of achieving long-term capital gains. Whether this is to the benefit of the investor is the subject matter of many of the following chapters since the investor needs to be able to identify growth opportunities and invest in them at a reasonable price.

REDUCTION IN ORDINARY TAX RATES

Timing Considerations

The proper timing of both the receipt and expenditure of funds is of concern to the investor in an attempt to stay in the lowest possible marginal tax bracket. We previously noted the importance of timing in the realization of gains and losses on capital assets. In addition, timing with regard to expenditures may make a difference in the total amount of itemized deductions or in their impact on tax savings.

A somewhat obvious example has to do with making sure large charitable contributions are made in years of high adjusted gross income. Another example would be to make sure any loans on which the interest is paid at maturity come due near the end of the taxable year. The investor then has a choice of what year in which to pay the interest. For example, an investor borrowing $5,000 for six months at an annual rate of 9 percent could arrange to have the note mature on December 30. By doing this, the investor may pay the $225 interest on December 30 if the interest expense deduction would be of benefit in that year. However, if taxable income is expected to be much higher the following year, an agreement with the investor's friendly banker should allow the payment of the interest on January 2.[5]

[5]Extraordinary large year-end deductions may come under Internal Revenue Service review. The IRS may determine whether the taxpayer's accounting methods reflect his or her income. The *Wall Street Journal* of February 26, 1975, cited an example of a taxpayer who borrowed $5.4 million in late 1969 and prepaid a year's interest of $377,202. The Tax Court allowed only 3/365ths of the yearly interest as a 1969 interest expense deduction. The court gave consideration to the fact that the taxpayer had a capital gain of $968,000 for 1969.

The tax laws regarding medical and dental expense deductions may have ramifications for the investor in helping to remain in a low marginal tax bracket. Basically, the tax law states that medical and dental expenses may be deducted only to the extent that they exceed 3 percent of adjusted gross income.[6] For a taxpayer with adjusted gross income of $15,000, no medical and dental expense deduction can be taken unless these expenses exceed $450. Assume the taxpayer normally incurs $200 per year in medical and dental expenses, but in September faces an orthodontist's bill of $1,000. The orthodontist has suggested that $50 per month would be an acceptable payment schedule. If the taxpayer pays as the orthodontist has suggested, the following medical and dental expense deductions result:

	Year 1	*Year 2*	*Year 3*
Normal medical and dental expenses	$ 200	$ 200	$ 200
Orthodontist expenses	200	600	200
Total medical and dental expenses	$ 400	$ 800	$ 400
Less 3% of adjusted gross income	450	450	450
Deductible medical and dental expenses	$ 0	$ 350	$ 0

The taxpayer has the option of prepaying the orthodontist's bill at the end of year 1. If this is done, the following medical and dental expense deductions result:

Normal medical and dental expenses	$ 200	$ 200	$ 200
Orthodontist expenses	1,000	0	0
Total medical and dental expenses	$1,200	$ 200	$ 200
Less 3% of adjusted gross income	450	450	450
Deductible medical and dental expenses	$ 750	$ 0	$ 0

In this example, a difference in the timing of the payment of the orthodontist's bill has increased the total medical and dental expense deductible over the three-year period from $350 to $750. Additionally, the taxpayer has managed to obtain this deduction in year 1 instead of year 2. Of course, the investor does need to consider whether the "investment" in prepaying the orthodontist's bill has a better return associated with it than other possible investments. The investor's marginal tax bracket will be a significant factor in this determination.[7]

[6]One-half (but not over $150) of insurance premiums for medical care is deductible without regard to the 3 percent rule. The other 50 percent (or excess over $150) is subject to the 3 percent rule.

[7]For example, assume that the taxpayer is in the 25 percent marginal tax bracket. The taxpayer would then save $100 in taxes over the three years ($750–$350 times .25). What could the investor have earned on the money if the orthodontist's bill had not been prepaid? A simple solution would be that the investor now has an average of $400 (the $800 due in years 2 and 3 divided by 2) to invest for 16 months (year 2 and the first 4 months of year 3). If the investor could earn 8 percent on the $400, investment earnings would be approximately $43 ($400 times .08 times 16/12). Prepayment is desirable in this situation, but might not be at lower marginal tax rates.

Tax-Deferred Pension Contributions

Some employers allow their employees to contribute to pension plans and to avoid paying tax on these contributions until they are received as retirement benefits. The taxable salary of the individual is reduced by the amount of the tax-deferred contributions. The result is a lower taxable income for the employee. To be sure, the tax must be paid when the retirement benefits are received. But this may be many years later and the individual's taxable income may be less than during his or her working years.

Income Averaging

In 1964, a revision in the tax laws allowed taxpayers with substantially increased income in a given year to take advantage of income averaging. The provisions of the law resulted in tax savings under certain conditions.

The income averaging provisions were of little direct use to investors until 1969, however. In that year, a change in the law allowed capital gains to be included in income eligible for income averaging. This had not been the case under the 1964 tax provisions. The 1969 revision also lowered the upward increase in income that was necessary to qualify for income averaging.[8]

ESTATE TAXATION AND PLANNING

Tax planning regarding what happens to your assets upon your demise is just as important as planning for those assets during life. A will is the basic legal document that stipulates how an estate will be divided. Competent legal advice may be sought in drawing up a will.

Federal estate taxes are becoming increasingly important as a result of increasing affluence. This is true since the federal estate tax is a progressive tax similar to the federal income tax. The federal estate tax law provides for a $60,000 exemption for an estate. In addition, a marital deduction for transfer to a surviving spouse is available up to one-half of the gross estate minus expenses and claims. Essentially, these laws mean that an estate over $60,000 is taxable for a single individual and

[8]Federal Income Tax Schedule G, Income Averaging, is difficult to understand. Essentially, however, the taxable income, after deducting $3,000, must be 120 percent of the average taxable income for the last four years before the taxpayer is allowed to income average. For example, if the average taxable income for the past four years was $10,000, unless the taxable income for the current year is over $15,000 ($10,000 times 1.2 + $3,000), a taxpayer may not income average. Prior to 1969, the upward increase needed to be 133⅓ percent rather than 120 percent.

an estate over $120,000 is taxable for a married person. Hence, small estates normally escape taxation, but larger estates can benefit from estate planning.

To illustrate the application of the federal estate tax law, assume a gross estate of $200,000 and funeral and administrative expenses of $10,000. The federal estate tax, ignoring for simplicity any credit allowed for state death taxes, would be calculated as follows:

	Single	*Married*
Gross estate	$200,000	$200,000
Deduct:		
Exemption	60,000	60,000
Funeral and administrative expenses	10,000	10,000
Transfers to surviving spouse (marital deduction)	none	95,000
Taxable Estate	$130,000	$ 35,000
Tax on estate*	$ 29,700	$ 3,900

*Tax rates: $3,000 tax on $30,000 taxable estate plus 18 percent on excess over $30,000 to $40,000. $20,700 tax on $100,000 taxable estate plus 30 percent on excess over $100,000 to $250,000.

A complete discussion of the manner in which estate planning can reduce estate taxes is beyond the scope of this book. However, we will mention two general possibilities. It is possible to establish one or more trusts in such a manner so as to keep some of the estate from being taxed. This is especially important for any surviving spouse not remarrying. The surviving spouse's estate will not have any marital deduction and will be taxed in a manner similar to the single individual example above. Second, it is possible to give a portion of one's estate away prior to death. This will reduce the gross estate. The gift tax laws should be consulted if one plans to do this. It is evident from our brief discussion that competent estate planning advice is needed even if the estate reaches only a moderate size measured by today's standards.

SUMMARY

Taxes have become an increasingly important consideration for all investors as incomes have risen and as tax rates at all levels of government have tended to increase. The federal income tax is of special concern because of its high marginal tax brackets. It is these marginal tax rates which have an impact on the investor since most investment income is an addition to earned income from sources such as wages.

The investor has three basic tax goals. They are: 1) to attempt to have investment income exempt from taxation; 2) to obtain income taxable as a long-term capital gain rather than as ordinary income; and 3) to minimize the income which is taxed at ordinary tax rates. It is possible that the achievement of some of these goals may involve too high a cost in the rate of return sacrificed. The individual investor must make this determination on the basis of his or her own tax situation.

Timing is an important variable. To the extent investors have a choice concerning the timing of realization of gains and losses on their investments, the tax implications should be carefully studied. Both the length of the holding period and the taxable year of income realization may be significant. Timing of expenditures to achieve maximum itemized deductions may also be a goal of the investor.

The tax structure is fixed as far as the investor is concerned. The laws are on the books and the rates are established. The investor should make these laws work to his or her advantage so that the lowest possible legal tax payable is achieved.

QUESTIONS

1. *a)* Define the concept of a marginal tax rate.
   b) How does the marginal tax rate differ from the average tax rate?
   c) Why is the marginal tax rate of importance in the investment decision-making process?
2. What is the difference between tax evasion and tax avoidance?
3. Timing is an important consideration in tax planning. Give examples of situations where timing is either beneficial or detrimental to the investor.
4. What is a progressive tax structure? Are state or federal income tax structures more progressive? What does a progressive tax structure mean to the investor?
5. *a)* Under what circumstances would an investor prefer receiving income in the form of a capital gain instead of as ordinary income?
   b) Under what circumstances would the investor be indifferent about the form in which income is received?
6. If an employee can defer payment of taxes on any contribution to the individual's retirement system, should this be done? Are there any exceptions to your answer?
7. Congress is almost always considering various proposals for changes in the system of taxing capital gains. Some proposals would change the holding period for long-term capital gains and losses to one year. Other proposals would increase the $1,000 maximum deduction per year on capital losses or eliminate the maximum entirely. Another proposal would introduce a "roll-over" provision on long-term capital gains. A "roll-over" provision would postpone payment of a tax at the time of sale as long as the proceeds are reinvested within a specified period of time. "Roll-over" provisions currently apply to the sale of a personal residence. What would be the impact of these various proposals on the investor?

PROBLEMS

1. Using the tax rates in Table 5–1 determine the tax payable, the marginal, and average tax rates based upon taxable income and total income for the following situation:

   Wages = $20,000
   Joint return with two children
   Standard deduction taken ($2,000 maximum)
   Dividend income on jointly held stocks = $2,000
   Long-term capital gains of $3,000

2. What would be the tax consequences for an individual having the following capital gains and losses assuming a marginal tax bracket of 25 percent?
   a) A long-term capital gain of $1,500.
   b) A short-term capital loss of $2,200.
   c) A long-term capital loss of $1,800.
   d) A long-term capital gain of $2,400 and a short-term capital gain of $500.
   e) A long-term capital gain of $2,400 and a short-term capital loss of $500.
   f) A long-term capital gain of $1,600, a short-term capital loss of $800, and a long-term capital loss of $300.
3. An investor in the 40 percent marginal tax bracket can buy a corporate bond at a discount. By doing this, half of the 8 percent return will come in the form of a long-term capital gain and half will come as interest income. Calculate the after-tax rate of return from this bond.
4. What yield would an investor require from a bond bought at par (whose interest income is fully taxable) to prefer the investment over the one suggested in question 3?

SUGGESTED READINGS

Holt, Charles C. and John P. Shelton. "The Financial Implications of the Capital Gains Tax for Investment Decisions." *Journal of Finance,* December 1961, pp. 559–80.

Nichols, Donald R. and Bruce D. Fielitz. "Awareness of Marginal Income Tax Rates Among Taxpayers." *Mississippi Valley Journal of Business and Economics,* Spring 1973, pp. 39–46.

Sommerfeld, Ray M. *The Dow Jones-Irwin Guide to Tax Planning.* Homewood, Illinois: Dow Jones-Irwin, 1973.

U.S. Master Tax Guide. Latest annual edition. Chicago, Illinois: Commerce Clearing House.

"Your Tax Strategy for 1975." *Business Week,* March 10, 1975, pp. 85–90.

6

Introduction to Risk and Return

The investment process involves making a trade-off between expected *returns* and the *risk* of not achieving these returns. In order to make the necessary trade-off, the investor should understand the sources which determine the amount and level of return and risk, and be capable of measuring the magnitude of each in some systematic manner. These problems are the essence of investment decision making.

Our focus in this chapter is on the problem of sources of risk and return. Considerable emphasis is placed on the measurement of the rate of return. Our objective is to evolve certain basic concepts for determining the sources of return from financial investments, and for measuring these returns. While the discussion centers on common stocks, the concepts also apply to other types of investments.

In considering the measurement of the rate of return, it is necessary to begin with a discussion of the time value of money. This central concept in finance simply means that dollars received at the present time have more value than those to be received at some future date.

The discussion of the time value of money leads into the measuring of returns and the present value concept. Since the present value approach requires selection of a discount rate (required rate of return), we will look at historical returns earned by investing in stocks and bonds to obtain a starting point for the discount rate selection. The final section of the chapter considers sources of risk.

TIME VALUE OF MONEY

Suppose an individual was asked to read this book for a fee of $100 to be paid by the authors. In accepting this task, the individual would have the opportunity of receiving the fee immediately upon completion of the reading, or of receiving the fee one year following completion. Most would agree that immediate acceptance of the fee would be the preferred alternative.

If the alternatives were set at $100 taken immediately or $110 if taken in one year, a few would accept the larger sum. Setting the sum at $120 would induce even more individuals to accept the future payment. A $500 future payment would probably find that, given the opportunity, virtually all individuals would prefer to receive $500 in one year to $100 immediately. This phenomenon is known as the *time value of money.*

Utility

The reasons for the general preference for early receipt of money are relatively simple and can be broken down into three categories. The first reason concerns what the money will be used for and is often called its *utility.* Utility refers to the "want-satisfying power" of a given item or sum of money.

It is possible to state that $100 today usually has more want-satisfying power than $100 to be received in one year. For example, plans to spend funds on entertainment would cause most individuals to prefer entertainment today rather than in one year. But there is some quantity of entertainment in one year that would be preferred to a smaller quantity now. If this quantity of future entertainment would cost $150, then $150 received in one year would be preferred to $100 today. The actual trade-off would depend upon the personal values of the individual. Whatever these values, most would require a larger quantity in the future than now to be indifferent between the two alternatives.

Risk

The second reason for the time value of money is *risk.* We distinguish between uncertainty and risk later in this chapter. For now, we define risk as the possibility of an individual's not receiving expected funds at some future time. This book may not sell as well as expected, so the expected return is not received. Whatever the reason, the risk of not receiving expected funds at a later date implies a preference for early receipt of the funds.

As with utility, there is some quantity of future money that will be preferred whatever the risk. If an offer of $100 today or $500 in one year is given and the future payment accepted, the individual is giving up an immediate $100 for the possibility of receiving a future $500. The $500 may never arrive, but the individual prefers that possibility to a certain $100. Any individual's preference may be for more or less than $500. Whatever the preference, risk causes the promise of a dollar to be paid in the future to be worth less than a dollar to be received now.

Opportunity Cost

The third reason for the time value of money centers on the concept of opportunity cost. Most individuals have many "spending" opportunities available to them. Funds can be used in a variety of ways—including various investment opportunities. In our example, one might invest the $100, if received today, in a savings account at a commercial bank. Since such a deposit is insured by an agency of the federal government, the investment can be considered "riskless." At current rates of interest, the $100 deposit would earn approximately $5 in one year, which implies that an individual would require more than $105 one year from now in order to prefer the future payment. The investor is said to be *indifferent* between $100 now and $105 in one year. The $5 is called one's *opportunity cost,* defined as the yield on the best available investment opportunity of equal risk, exclusive of the opportunity under consideration.

In summary, any investment decision requires the decision-maker to consider at least three elements:

1. The investor's time utility preference.
2. The risk involved in the investment.
3. The investor's opportunity cost relative to the potential returns available from comparable risk investments.

MEASURING RETURNS

Let us turn our attention to the manner in which one measures returns. To understand the problems associated with measuring investment returns, it is useful to begin with a savings account example. If we are told that a savings institution is paying 6 percent, most investors would conclude that a $100 deposit would grow to $106 in one year. A rate of return figure is generally expressed in annual terms, as a percentage of the initial investment.

In the case of a one-year investment, the return calculation is straightforward, but suppose the initial $100 savings account is held for two years. How much money would be available at the end of the two-year period? The correct answer is $112.36. During the first year, the 6 percent return generated $6 on the $100 deposit. During the second year, the 6 percent return generated $6.36. Given our definition of return, how can this be? At the beginning of the second year, the deposit is $106 (not $100), and 6 percent of $106 is $6.36. During the second year the depositor earned $6 on the initial deposit and $0.36 on the earnings of the first year. This is the essence of the concept of compound interest.

A mathematical equation exists for determining the value of a deposit at the end of any period of years. It is shown below as equation (1).

$$V_n = V_0(1 + r)^n \tag{1}$$

where: V_n = the value of the investment or deposit at the end of n years
V_0 = the amount of initial investment or deposit
r = the annual rate of return

In our two-year example above, we would solve for V_n as follows:

$$V_n = \$100(1 + .06)^2$$
$$V_n = \$100(1.1236)$$
$$V_n = \$112.36$$

Frequently, a savings institution will advertise a rate of return compounded semiannually. The basic compounding equation still applies except that the annual rate of return is reduced to one-half its value and the number of compounding periods is doubled. A deposit of $100 at 6 percent compounded semiannually would total $106.09 at the end of the first year, as shown by using equation (1).

$$\begin{aligned} V_n &= V_0(1 + r)^n \\ &= \$100(1 + .03)^2 \\ &= \$100(1.0609) \\ &= \$106.09 \end{aligned}$$

Obviously, quarterly, daily, or other time periods may be used for compounding. For example, if the 6 percent rate had been compounded quarterly, the rate of return (r) would be reduced to one-fourth its annual value for four compounding periods. The $100 deposit would equal $106.14 at the end of one year as shown below:

$$V_n = V_0(1 + r)^n$$
$$= \$100(1 + .015)^4$$
$$= \$100(1.0614)$$
$$= \$106.14$$

Nominal versus Effective Rate

When deposits are compounded more frequently than annually, a distinction is made between the *nominal rate* and the *effective rate*. The nominal rate is simply the advertised rate of 6 percent in our example. The effective rate is the rate of return required to produce the result achieved. The effective rate is 6.09 percent for semiannual compounding and 6.14 percent for quarterly compounding.[1]

THE PRESENT VALUE CONCEPT

Many of the calculations involved in determining rates of return are greatly aided by tables, and with a modern calculator, one can do the job in a few short steps. Prior to demonstrating the calculation techniques, let us turn to a financial concept that is an integral part of the rate of return.

Recall that in equation (1) the value of a deposit at the end of n years was:

$$V_n = V_0(1 + r)^n$$

We may face a problem where we know both the nominal rate and the ending value of the deposit or investment. In this case, we would

[1]In general, the *effective rate* is given by the following equation:

$$r^* = \left[\left(1 + \frac{r}{n}\right)^n\right] - 1$$

where: r^* = the effective annual rate
r = the nominal annual rate
n = the number of compounding periods

In certain instances, compounding is done continuously—in which case the equation for the effective rate becomes

$$r^* = e^r - 1$$

where e signifies an exponential function and is equal to approximately 2.71828. An elaboration of the problems of continuous compounding can be found in J. Peter Williamson, *Investments: New Analytical Techniques* (New York: Praeger, 1971), Chapter IX.

want to know what the initial deposit should be. Simple algebra will give us the value immediately. Dividing both sides of equation (1) by $(1 + r)^n$ we obtain equation (2):

$$V_0 = \frac{V_n}{(1 + r)^n} \tag{2}$$

Thus, if we are to receive \$116.64 at the end of two years and desire 8 percent compounded annually, we would need to deposit \$100 initially as determined below:

$$V_0 = \frac{V_n}{(1 + r)^n}$$

$$= \frac{\$116.64}{(1 + .08)^2}$$

$$= \frac{\$116.64}{1.1664}$$

$$= \$100$$

The \$100 is referred to as the *present value* of the future receipts. Present value is defined as the amount of money required initially, in order to produce a given amount at the termination of the investment period, when compounded at a given rate.

An investment producing \$90 at the end of four years would have a present value of \$61.47 if one desires a 10 percent annual return. This figure can be verified by compounding \$61.47 at 10 percent annually for four years. Mathematically, the present value (PV) of one dollar received at the end of n years, assuming a rate of return of r, is given by:

$$PV = \frac{1}{(1 + r)^n} \tag{3}$$

Equation (3) can be used to calculate the present value of the example. The following calculations show the manner in which one would obtain the present value of \$90 rather than just one dollar:

$$PV = \frac{1}{(1.10)^4}(\$90)$$

$$= \frac{1}{(1.464)}(\$90)$$

$$= \$61.47$$

One final example is appropriate and also more representative of a typical investment decision. Suppose we are considering a bond purchase paying $75 at the end of each of the next three years plus the bond's $1,000 face value at the end of the third year. Suppose further that the return on similar bonds is currently 8 percent compounded annually. What price should be paid for this bond? We should be willing to pay the present value of all future bond payments given an 8 percent rate of return.

Exhibit 6-1 illustrates the required present value calculations. Columns one and two show the year and the receipts for that year. Column three is commonly called the *discount factor.* In the example, the discount factor is $1/(1.08)^n$ where n refers to the year in which the payment is to be received. Column four is the product of the payment and the discount factor and represents the present value of each annual cash receipt or payment. The total present value, $987.08, represents the price of the bond required for the investor to earn 8 percent. If the actual price in the market is *more* than $987.08, the investor would earn *less* than 8 percent. A price *lower* than $987.08 would generate a return that is *greater* than 8 percent. The only difference between our hypothetical bond calculation and the price calculation made by bond investors is that actual calculations utilize semiannual payments instead of the annual payments assumed in this example.

EXHIBIT 6-1

Present Value Calculation: Hypothetical Bond

Year (n)	Payment Received at End of Year	Discount Factor ($1/(1 + r)^n$) $r = 8\%$	Present Value
1	2	3	4
1	$ 75	.9259	$ 69.44
2	75	.8573	64.30
3	1,075	.7938	853.34
		TOTAL PRESENT VALUE	$987.08

Using Present Value Tables

The calculations of Exhibit 6-1 are usually facilitated through the use of present value tables as presented in Appendices A-1 and A-2 at the end of this chapter. Appendix A-1 is simply a compilation of various possible values of equation (3): $(1/(1 + r)^n)$. Each column represents a separate value of r and each row a separate value for n. For example, the discount factor of .7938 in Exhibit 6-1 can be found in the column labeled .0800 (8%) and the row labeled 3. This is the present value of $1 received in three years at an 8 percent discount rate, or rate of return.

It may be possible to shorten the present value calculation even further. Whenever periodic payments are constant, we need not make each multiplication but can simply sum the present value factors and multiply this sum by the constant annual payment. An example of this process is given in Exhibit 6-2 where the present value of the hypothetical bond is calculated in the shorter manner. The yearly $75 payment is multiplied by the sum of the three discount factors given earlier in Exhibit 6-1. This product is added to the present value of the $1,000 face value received in the third year.

To facilitate this calculation, Appendix A-2 shows discount factor sums for various returns and various periods. Thus, the first row is a duplicate of the first row of Appendix A-1 and each additional row is generated by adding the next period's discount factor to the previous row(s). In our example, the 2.5771 present value factor may be found in the third row under the column labeled 8%.

EXHIBIT 6-2
Present Value Calculation: Hypothetical Bond

Year 1	Payment Received at End of Year 2	Discount Factor 8% 3	Present Value 4
1-3	$ 75	2.5771	$193.28
3	1,000	.7938	793.80
		TOTAL PRESENT VALUE	$987.08

Present Value of a Stock

As with a bond, the price of a common stock should be the present value of all future receipts. The future receipts will be dividends received *plus* the future selling price of the common stock. We will assume that the investor is certain of these figures for the moment.

Consider an investment in a common stock for a one-year holding period. The investor will receive dividends, if any are paid, and the sale price of the stock, so the initial price should be the present value of these payments as follows:

$$P_0 = \frac{D_1}{1+r} + \frac{P_1}{1+r}$$

where: P_0, P_1 = the beginning and ending price, respectively
D_1 = the dividends received during the year

The price of a common stock for any investment period is given by an extension of the above equation as follows:

$$P_0 = \frac{D_1}{1 + r} + \frac{D_2}{(1 + r)^2} + \frac{D_3}{(1 + r)^3} + \ldots + \frac{P_n}{(1 + r)^n} \tag{4}$$

where: P_n = the ending or sale price
n = the number of periods or years of the investment

This equation assumes that the dividend payment is made at the close of each period. The assumption is strictly for convenience and does not alter the basic nature of equation (4). The equation applies to any common stock investment. If the investor's expected holding period is very short or if the common stock pays no dividend, the dividend portion is very small or zero and the current price is dominated by the selling price at the end of the holding period. If the holding period is very long or dividends very large, the current price (P_0) may be determined primarily by the dividend portion. Accordingly, this theoretical representation (model) is applicable to so-called "growth stocks" paying little or no dividends as well as to high-dividend paying stocks.

The terminal price (P_n) is nothing more than the present value of all future returns expected beyond the close of the nth period. The sale price (P_n) for any investor will always be related to the future returns, in the form of both dividends and sale price, expected by the next investor. As the number of holding periods becomes large and approaches infinity, the present value of the sale price becomes insignificant. Assuming the present value of the final price is approximately zero, the current price of any common stock is given by equation (5), which shows the importance of dividends in the valuation process.

$$\begin{aligned} P_0 &= \frac{D_1}{1 + r} + \frac{D_2}{(1 + r)^2} + \ldots + \frac{D_\infty}{(1 + r)^\infty} \\ &= \sum_{i=1}^{\infty} \frac{D_i}{(1 + r)^i} \end{aligned} \tag{5}$$

where: i = period number

Importance of Dividend Growth

Equation (5) can be simplified even further by noting that in many instances future dividends will be related in some functional manner to the present dividend. Suppose that the present dividend of a firm is $1 and next year's dividend is expected to be $1.05. The implication is that dividends are expected to grow by 5 percent annually. In turn, this suggests that next year's dividend can be represented by this year's dividend plus the growth rate percentage of this year's dividend. Therefore, the first year's dividend (D_1) is given by:

$$D_1 = D_0(1 + g)$$

where: D_0 = the dividend at the time of purchase
g = the growth rate of dividends

The dividend in the second year becomes $D_0(1 + g)^2$ and so on for each year. Given this condition, the current price of the common stock as described in equation (5) becomes:

$$= \sum_{i=1}^{\infty} \frac{D_0(1 + g)^i}{(1 + r)^i} \quad (6)$$

Equation (6) retains some major complexities. However, if the assumptions are made that the growth rate (g) is constant and less than the rate of return (r), the price of the stock reduces to equation (7).

$$P_0 = \frac{D_0}{r - g} \quad (7)$$

To illustrate the use of equation (7), assume three different investors are considering the purchase of a common stock paying a dividend of $1.50 with an expected dividend growth rate of 6 percent. Investor A wants a minimum 10 percent return, investor B wants a minimum 8 percent return, and investor C wants a minimum 12 percent return. As shown below, A should be willing to pay no more than $37.50, while the theoretical maximum prices for B and C are $75 and $25 respectively.

Investor A(r = 10%)	Investor B(r = 8%)	Investor C(r = 12%)
$P_0 = \frac{D_0}{r - g}$	$P_0 = \frac{D_0}{r - g}$	$P_0 = \frac{D_0}{r - g}$
$= \frac{1.50}{.10 - .06}$	$= \frac{1.50}{.08 - .06}$	$= \frac{1.50}{.12 - .06}$
$= \frac{1.50}{.04} = \$37.50$	$= \frac{1.50}{.02} = \$75$	$= \frac{1.50}{.06} = \$25$

Equation (7) is highly abstract and relies on several assumptions about the marketplace that are certainly questionable in practice. These assumptions include:

1. A known and constant growth rate of dividends.
2. A constant rate of return.
3. A rate of return that is greater than the growth rate.
4. An infinite time horizon for the market as a whole.

While these are rather tenuous assumptions, we have a framework for determining the fundamental value of a common stock. Essentially our task becomes one of determining future dividends either in absolute values, equation (5), or by establishing a growth rate for dividends, equation (7). Once either of these has been determined, the present value of the stock to the investor will depend on the *rate of return the investor requires* in order to satisfy unique utility, risk, and opportunity cost characteristics.

If these characteristics desired by the investor can be summarized in a desired return, of say, 10 percent, then the common stock of the firm being considered in the example above would have a value of $37.50. At a market price of $30, the stock would be an appropriate purchase. At $50, it would be a poor purchase for the 10 percent rate of return investor. At the same time, a $50 price would be altogether appropriate for the investor wanting a rate of return of 8 percent. In essence, we have a "model" for price determination on an individual basis.

The dividend valuation model just developed in no way suggests that other factors will not operate in determining the price of a given stock. Such factors as stocks being in "vogue" and rumors about various company policies may have their effect, but in general these aspects of common stock investment are short lived. Typically, prices return to their fundamental values. A *Wall Street Journal* article concluded that the poor experience of common stock investors in the late 1960s and early 1970s could be attributed largely to slow dividend growth expectations and higher returns from other forms of investment.[2]

The emphasis on dividends does not imply that such items as earnings growth, quality of management, financial integrity, and general economic conditions will not influence the price of common stocks. The assertion is that the fundamental value of a given common stock is determined by the dividends of the firm, both now and in the future. All other facets of a company become important as variables influencing the firm's dividend-paying ability.

Problems with Present Value

Although the present value approach is basically sound as a valuation technique, the method of calculation breaks down when it is used to determine a rate of return. The present value approach contains the implied assumption that the rate of return, r, is constant from period to period. In the appendix to this chapter, we discuss the measurement problems caused by this implied assumption. In addition, the appendix introduces the concept of the geometric mean as a preferable way to measure rates of return.

[2]*Wall Street Journal,* June 27, 1973, p. 1.

DETERMINING THE PROPER DISCOUNT RATE

To this point we have discussed the concepts of present value, the source of returns from common stock investment, and the methodology of calculating rates of return. What returns are actually available to the investor? We will not be so bold as to suggest what returns *will* be available, only what returns have been available for investments made in past years. In other words, we shall confine our examination to historical rates of return in an attempt to determine what might be an appropriate rate to use for discounting future values.

Several problems must be considered before actual numbers can be presented. The first question that must be answered is: Rates of return on what? A student's entire college career could be spent answering this question. We could discuss the returns on any and all assets including common stocks, government bonds, the various grades of corporate bonds, real estate, commodities, or even education. Since time and information are limited, only common stocks are considered at this point, with some minor comments on the returns from high-grade bonds.

Which common stocks? This second problem also requires that a limitation be imposed. The discussion is confined to the common stocks listed on the New York Stock Exchange because there is a wealth of high-quality historical data available on these securities. These common stocks also represent a large percentage of the total market value of all publicly owned common stocks. High-grade corporate bonds are examined for the same reasons.

These limitations are still too broad in order to embark on any reasonable discussion. For example, some NYSE common stocks have earned huge rates of return. A common stock purchased for $0.125 and sold one month later for $1 would have a monthly return of 700 percent. Such price movements have happened, but they are quite unrealistic in the sense that they occur infrequently and are not sustainable. Such returns have not been available month after month. Thus, we have two additional questions. What period of time is of interest and what group of stocks (portfolio) shall be considered?

HISTORICAL RETURNS ON NYSE COMMON STOCKS

Individual Securities

For individual securities, annual rates of return for various holding periods are available for periods from 1926 to 1965. Many of these data are too detailed for our purposes, but Table 6-1 presents some highlights. The minimum return in any one year was −100 percent—a complete loss. This has occurred on several occasions although much less than 5 percent of the time. The maximum return for any one-year holding period was 1984.1 percent—an unusual return! The arithmetic mean return for the one-year, nonoverlapping holding periods was 14.8 percent during the 1926 through 1965 period, and 90 percent of all rates of return were between −53.4 percent and 97.5 percent. The other percentage-ranking figures shown in Table 6-1 allow the reader to make similar comparisons for the time periods shown.

TABLE 6-1

Historical Rates of Return, NYSE Listed Stocks (1926-65)

	Holding Periods			
	One Year			Five Years*
	1926-65	1926-45	1946-65	1926-65
Minimum return	−100.0%	−100.0%	−100.0%	−100.0%
Maximum return	1,984.1	1,984.1	444.1	4,785.5
Arithmetic mean return	14.8	15.8	13.8	90.4
PERCENTILE				
5th	−53.4	−64.4	−33.7	−70.9
50th (median)	8.5	7.5	9.1	49.1
95th	97.5	123.0	74.3	387.5

*Eight separate five-year holding periods used; returns are for five years.

Source: Lawrence Fisher and James H. Lorie, "Some Studies of Variability of Returns on Investments in Common Stocks," *Journal of Business*, April 1970, p. 108.

In more recent years, the range of rates of return appears to show less variance. From 1945 to 1965, the average return was 13.8 percent with 90 percent of the returns between −33.7 percent and 74.3 percent. Despite this trend toward greater stability, the data clearly present a picture of both wide variability and high rates of return from common stock investment.

While the variability is fairly represented by Table 6-1, the arithmetic average rate of return misrepresents what was actually available to investors during the period. The 14.8 percent average over the entire forty-year period is a straight arithmetic average, which tends to be misleading (as discussed in the Appendix to the chapter). While the figure is not shown on Table 6-1, the geometric mean of the annual averages of all stocks listed was only 10.25 percent per year. In order to obtain 10.25 percent, an investor would have had to invest equal amounts of money in each security listed on the NYSE at the beginning of each year of the period. An investment strategy of reallocating dollars in the portfolio at the beginning of each year so that each security was represented equally would also need to be followed.

Portfolios

Most investors do not own just one security, but hold portfolios of varying size. In this context, two questions must be considered. First, what has been the performance of the "average" portfolio? Second, to what extent can the typical investor duplicate the performance of the average portfolio?

The data presented in Table 6-2 are geometric returns for various holding periods during 1926-65. The returns are determined under the assumption that an investor purchased all NYSE-listed issues in equal dollar amounts at the beginning of each period. All dividends are reinvested in the security paying the dividend, and the returns are adjusted for commissions to buy but not to sell. The returns of Table 6-2 are equivalent to the returns that would have occurred to the "average" investor.

For the entire period the average geometric return was 9.3 percent, with about one-half of this resulting strictly from price movements (4.6 percent) and the remainder from dividends. This 9.3 percent return assumes a tax-exempt investor (such as a pension fund) still holds the portfolio at the close of each period. Thus, transactions costs of selling the portfolio securities are not included in the calculation of this return. Table 6-2 suggests recent periods have been more lucrative. For example, the period from 1950 to 1965 had a total annual geometric return of 14.5 percent, while 1945 to 1965 period had a return of 12.6 percent.

For periods of about ten years or more, the returns from common stock have been relatively high and accompanied by little long-term variability. Since 1940, the minimum annual return for any period of ten years or more was 10 percent. Thus, while both returns on individual securities and short-run market returns will vary considerably, the long-run portfolio returns from common stock are reasonably stable and high, compared, for example, to returns available from high-quality corporate bonds (Table 6-3).

Of what significance are these returns to the investor? An investment of $5,000 in the market portfolio in December, 1940 would have earned 16 percent per year through 1965. The initial $5,000 would have grown to $204,371 by the end of 1965. It is true that the 1940 to 1965 period has seen considerable inflation and much natural growth, but the same $5,000 investment would have had to increase to only $11,252 to keep up with inflation.

HISTORICAL RETURNS ON HIGH GRADE BONDS

Table 6-3 presents bond rates of return calculated in the same general manner as the common stock rates of return. For any period greater than ten years, the bond returns are far less than the common stock returns. Even if we select the worst times to buy common stocks, the long-term returns from stocks were far better than bond returns. For example, bond investments produced an annual return of 3.7 percent from 1929 to 1965 compared to common stock returns of 9.9 percent. The bond return data do not include bond bankruptcies which, while not great when dealing with high-grade bonds, would lower the return slightly if included. One should note, however, that the 1929 investment in stocks did not begin producing superior average returns until after 1950.

BOND VERSUS STOCK RETURNS

Table 6–4 compares bond and stock returns for varying periods of time. While common stocks have shown long-run superiority, bond returns have been far less variable. For example, the worst five-year investment period for bonds was 1954 to 1959 when the average return was a minus 1 percent. While bond returns were generally low compared to stocks, the return in most periods was positive and fluctuated within a very narrow range around the long-run average of approximately 3.5 percent. There apparently is a positive relationship between risk and return. While average returns for common stocks were greater than for bonds, the risk of substantial loss in any one period was much greater for stocks than for the high-grade corporate bonds.

We can briefly examine more recent experiences with common stocks. Data presently available show an average annual geometric return with dividends reinvested of approximately 9.0 percent for the period, December 1965 to June 1972. On price movements alone, the return was 5.9 percent compared to 4.6 percent for 1926 to 1965. However, dividend yields for that period were lower than for the 1926 to 1965 period. The return of 9.0 percent is quite close to the long-run average of 9.3 percent, but like the earlier period, the market experienced wide fluctuations. For example, during the period November 1968 to June 1970 the stock market declined by approximately 45 percent.

Bond market returns from December 1965 to June 1972 were approximately 1.2 percent annually, considering both interest payments and price movements. It is interesting to note that the actual returns from bond investment were quite different from the returns quoted in the newspapers. The discrepancy lies in the difference between expected returns and actual returns. Expectations do not always materialize, especially over relatively short time periods. Increasing market interest rates caused substantial capital losses for bond investors during this period. This inverse relationship between bond prices and interest rates is discussed extensively in Chapter 17.

TABLE 6–2

NYSE Common Stock Rates of Return, Cash to Portfolio, Tax Exempt, 1926–65

	From																			
To	1/26	12/26	12/27	12/28	12/29	12/30	12/31	12/32	12/33	12/34	12/35	12/36	12/37	12/38	12/39	12/40	12/41	12/42	12/43	12/44
12/26	−2.2																			
12/27	15.1	29.3																		
12/28	23.7	37.4	44.9																	
12/29	7.7	9.4	−0.2	−30.4																
12/30	−2.4	−3.6	−13.2	−31.9	−37.7															
12/31	−11.3	−13.7	−21.9	−36.5	−41.2	−48.7														
12/32	−11.1	−12.9	−19.2	−30.5	−32.4	−31.7	−12.9													
12/33	−2.8	−3.3	−7.8	−15.8	−12.0	−1.7	36.0	105.7												
12/34	−1.3	−1.7	−5.3	−11.4	−7.1	2.2	27.7	54.2	12.5											
12/35	2.1	2.0	−0.9	−5.8	−0.6	9.2	32.6	53.1	30.7	49.0										
12/36	6.5	5.4	3.1	−0.5	5.2	15.2	37.3	54.3	40.6	56.3	62.8									
12/37	0.5	0.1	−2.4	−6.3	−2.9	3.2	16.0	22.8	7.9	6.2	−11.4	−46.6								
12/38	2.7	2.5	0.4	−2.9	0.8	6.9	18.6	25.0	12.7	12.2	0.8	−16.5	29.3							
12/39	2.5	2.3	0.3	−2.7	0.8	5.9	15.6	20.3	10.0	8.8	0.1	−11.5	12.4	−4.4						
12/40	1.9	1.6	−0.3	−3.0	0.1	4.6	12.9	16.8	7.7	6.2	−1.2	−10.0	5.9	−5.5	−10.9					
12/41	1.2	0.8	−0.9	−3.3	−0.6	3.4	10.7	13.7	5.7	4.1	−2.1	−9.4	2.3	−5.9	−9.5	−11.4				
12/42	2.0	1.8	0.3	−2.0	0.8	4.7	11.4	14.1	7.0	5.9	0.7	−5.0	5.9	0.3	0.6	6.8	29.0			
12/43	3.5	3.5	2.2	0.1	3.1	7.1	13.7	16.4	10.1	9.6	5.3	0.8	12.2	9.2	11.8	21.8	46.1	54.7		
12/44	4.5	4.7	3.5	1.6	4.6	8.7	15.1	17.8	12.2	11.9	8.3	4.5	15.5	13.5	16.9	26.5	45.1	48.5	36.8	
12/45	6.2	6.5	5.5	3.8	7.0	11.2	17.5	20.4	15.3	15.4	12.4	9.2	20.2	19.2	23.5	33.4	51.1	55.0	49.5	58.7
12/46	5.5	5.7	4.7	3.2	6.0	9.8	15.5	17.9	13.2	13.0	10.2	7.2	16.2	14.9	17.7	24.0	34.5	34.2	25.6	19.7
12/47	5.3	5.5	4.5	3.1	5.7	9.3	14.6	16.7	12.3	12.0	9.4	6.6	14.5	13.5	15.4	20.1	27.3	26.0	18.6	12.8
12/48	5.0	5.1	4.2	2.7	5.2	8.5	13.4	15.4	11.2	10.9	8.3	5.7	12.6	11.6	13.1	16.9	22.3	20.5	14.0	8.9
12/49	5.7	5.8	4.9	3.5	5.9	9.0	13.8	15.6	11.7	11.4	9.0	6.7	13.2	12.2	13.8	17.1	22.1	20.6	15.0	11.1
12/50	6.5	6.6	5.8	4.5	7.0	10.2	14.9	16.6	12.8	12.8	10.6	8.4	14.7	14.0	15.5	18.9	23.3	22.3	17.8	14.8
12/51	6.9	7.1	6.3	5.1	7.4	10.5	15.1	16.7	13.1	13.1	10.9	8.9	14.7	14.0	15.5	18.5	22.5	21.5	17.6	15.1
12/52	7.0	7.2	6.5	5.3	7.6	10.5	14.8	16.3	13.0	12.9	10.9	9.0	14.4	13.7	15.1	17.8	21.4	20.3	16.7	14.4
12/53	6.6	6.8	6.1	4.9	7.1	9.7	13.8	15.3	12.1	12.1	10.1	8.3	13.2	12.4	13.6	16.0	19.2	18.0	14.6	12.4
12/54	6.1	8.2	7.5	6.4	8.6	11.3	15.5	17.0	14.0	14.0	12.2	10.5	15.4	14.7	16.1	18.6	21.8	20.9	18.1	16.3
12/55	8.4	8.6	8.0	6.9	9.1	11.9	15.9	17.3	14.4	14.5	12.7	11.0	15.8	15.2	16.5	18.8	21.7	21.0	18.5	16.8
12/56	8.5	8.6	8.0	7.0	9.2	11.8	15.7	17.0	14.3	14.4	12.6	11.0	15.6	15.0	16.1	18.1	20.7	20.1	17.9	16.3
12/57	7.7	7.9	7.2	6.3	8.3	10.6	14.3	15.4	12.9	12.9	11.1	9.7	13.8	13.2	14.1	15.9	18.2	17.4	15.0	13.5
12/58	8.8	9.0	8.4	7.5	9.5	11.9	15.5	16.7	14.2	14.3	12.6	11.3	15.5	14.9	15.9	17.7	20.1	19.4	17.2	15.9
12/59	8.9	9.1	8.5	7.6	9.6	12.1	15.5	16.7	14.3	14.4	12.8	11.5	15.5	15.0	15.9	17.6	19.8	19.1	17.0	15.7
12/60	8.7	8.9	8.3	7.4	9.3	11.6	14.9	16.0	13.8	13.9	12.3	11.0	14.7	14.1	15.0	16.5	18.6	17.8	15.8	14.6
12/61	9.3	9.5	8.9	8.0	9.9	12.1	15.4	16.5	14.4	14.5	12.9	11.8	15.4	14.9	15.7	17.3	19.2	18.4	16.5	15.4
12/62	8.6	8.8	8.2	7.3	9.1	11.2	14.2	15.3	13.2	13.3	11.8	10.6	14.0	13.5	14.2	15.5	17.3	16.5	14.6	13.5
12/63	8.9	9.1	8.5	7.6	9.4	11.5	14.5	15.6	13.5	13.6	12.1	11.0	14.2	13.8	14.5	15.7	17.4	16.6	14.8	13.8
12/64	9.1	9.3	8.7	7.9	9.6	11.6	14.5	15.5	13.6	13.6	12.3	11.2	14.4	14.0	14.6	15.8	17.3	16.7	15.0	14.0
12/65	9.3	9.5	9.0	8.2	9.9	12.0	14.9	15.8	13.9	14.0	12.6	11.5	14.6	14.2	14.9	16.0	17.5	16.9	15.3	14.4

TABLE 6–2 (continued)

	From 12/45	12/46	12/47	12/48	12/49	12/50	12/51	12/52	12/53	12/54	12/55	12/56	12/57	12/58	12/59	12/60	12/61	12/62	12/63	12/64
12/46	−10.6																			
12/47	−4.9	−1.5																		
12/48	−3.8	−1.5	−4.0																	
12/49	1.6	5.1	7.6	18.0																
12/50	7.6	12.1	16.2	26.4	34.5															
12/51	9.2	13.1	16.1	22.8	24.6	13.8														
12/52	9.3	12.7	15.0	19.5	19.4	11.9	7.8													
12/53	7.7	10.3	11.9	14.8	13.4	7.1	2.9	−4.3												
12/54	12.4	15.4	17.6	21.1	21.4	17.6	18.1	22.2	53.2											
12/55	13.3	16.1	18.1	21.2	21.6	18.3	18.8	21.8	36.5	17.8										
12/56	13.2	15.5	17.1	19.7	19.8	16.8	16.7	18.3	26.3	12.8	5.4									
12/57	10.5	12.2	13.4	15.2	14.6	11.8	10.9	10.9	14.2	3.0	−4.2	−13.9								
12/58	13.2	15.1	16.6	18.6	18.5	16.4	16.3	17.3	21.6	14.2	12.6	16.8	56.1							
12/59	13.2	15.2	16.6	18.5	18.5	16.4	16.5	17.4	20.9	14.8	13.7	17.2	35.2	13.2						
12/60	12.2	13.9	15.1	16.7	16.4	14.7	14.7	15.2	17.6	12.2	11.0	12.8	21.4	5.8	−3.1					
12/61	13.1	14.8	16.0	17.4	17.2	15.9	15.9	16.5	18.8	14.4	13.7	15.9	23.3	13.2	12.3	26.2				
12/62	11.3	12.7	13.6	14.8	14.4	13.0	12.7	12.9	14.5	10.3	9.2	10.2	14.8	6.0	3.4	5.2	−14.4			
12/63	11.7	13.2	14.0	15.1	14.8	13.4	13.2	13.4	14.9	11.2	10.3	11.3	15.5	8.5	7.1	10.0	1.4	16.3		
12/64	12.0	13.4	14.1	15.2	15.0	13.6	13.4	13.7	15.2	11.8	11.1	12.2	16.0	10.2	9.4	12.5	7.2	17.8	15.0	
12/65	12.6	14.1	14.8	15.9	15.7	14.4	14.3	14.6	16.2	13.0	12.4	13.5	17.5	12.5	12.3	15.7	12.6	22.2	22.7	26.9

Source: Lawrence Fisher and James H. Lorie, "Rates of Return on Investments: The Year-By-Year Record, 1926–65," *Journal of Business*, July 1968, pp. 296–297.

TABLE 6–3

Annual Returns from a High-Quality Bond Portfolio

To	From 12/25	12/26	12/27	12/28	12/29	12/30	12/31	12/32	12/33	12/34	12/35	12/36	12/37	12/38	12/39	12/40	12/41	12/42	12/43	12/44
12/26	7.2																			
12/27	7.0	6.7																		
12/28	5.4	4.5	2.3																	
12/29	4.4	3.5	1.9	1.6																
12/30	5.6	5.2	4.7	5.9	10.4															
12/31	4.7	4.2	3.5	3.9	5.1	0.1														
12/32	4.7	4.3	3.8	4.1	5.0	2.4	4.8													
12/33	5.1	4.9	4.6	5.0	5.9	4.4	6.7	8.6												
12/34	6.2	6.1	6.0	6.7	7.7	7.0	9.5	11.9	15.3											
12/35	6.6	6.5	6.5	7.1	8.1	7.6	9.6	11.3	12.6	9.9										
12/36	6.7	6.7	6.6	7.2	8.0	7.6	9.2	10.4	11.0	8.8	7.7									
12/37	6.3	6.3	6.2	6.7	7.3	6.9	8.1	8.7	8.8	6.6	5.0	2.4								
12/38	6.3	6.2	6.2	6.6	7.1	6.7	7.7	8.2	8.2	6.4	5.3	4.1	5.8							
12/39	6.2	6.1	6.1	6.4	6.9	6.5	7.4	7.7	7.6	6.1	5.2	4.3	5.3	4.8						
12/40	6.1	6.0	6.0	6.3	6.7	6.3	7.1	7.4	7.2	5.9	5.1	4.4	5.1	4.8	4.8					
12/41	5.9	5.8	5.7	6.0	6.4	6.0	6.6	6.8	6.6	5.4	4.7	4.1	4.5	4.1	3.7	2.6				
12/42	5.7	5.6	5.5	5.8	6.1	5.7	6.3	6.4	6.2	5.1	4.4	3.9	4.2	3.8	3.4	2.7	2.9			
12/43	5.6	5.5	5.4	5.6	5.9	5.5	6.0	6.1	5.9	4.9	4.3	3.8	4.0	3.7	3.4	2.9	3.1	3.3		
12/44	5.5	5.4	5.3	5.5	5.8	5.4	5.9	6.0	5.7	4.8	4.3	3.8	4.0	3.8	3.6	3.2	3.5	3.7	4.2	
12/45	5.5	5.4	5.3	5.5	5.7	5.4	5.8	5.9	5.7	4.8	4.3	3.9	4.1	3.9	3.8	3.6	3.8	4.1	4.5	4.8
12/46	5.3	5.2	5.1	5.3	5.5	5.2	5.6	5.6	5.4	4.6	4.2	3.8	4.0	3.7	3.6	3.4	3.6	3.7	3.9	3.7
12/47	5.0	4.9	4.8	5.0	5.2	4.9	5.2	5.2	5.0	4.2	3.7	3.4	3.5	3.2	3.0	2.8	2.8	2.8	2.7	2.1
12/48	5.0	4.9	4.8	4.9	5.1	4.8	5.1	5.1	4.9	4.2	3.7	3.4	3.5	3.3	3.1	2.9	3.0	3.0	2.9	2.6
12/49	5.0	4.9	4.8	5.0	5.1	4.9	5.1	5.2	4.9	4.3	3.9	3.6	3.7	3.5	3.4	3.2	3.3	3.4	3.4	3.2
12/50	4.9	4.8	4.7	4.8	5.0	4.7	4.9	4.9	4.7	4.1	3.7	3.5	3.5	3.3	3.2	3.1	3.1	3.1	3.1	2.9
12/51	4.6	4.4	4.4	4.4	4.6	4.3	4.5	4.5	4.3	3.7	3.3	3.0	3.0	2.8	2.7	2.5	2.5	2.4	2.3	2.1
12/52	4.5	4.4	4.3	4.4	4.5	4.3	4.5	4.5	4.3	3.7	3.3	3.1	3.1	2.9	2.8	2.6	2.6	2.6	2.5	2.3
12/53	4.4	4.3	4.2	4.3	4.4	4.2	4.4	4.4	4.1	3.6	3.2	3.0	3.0	2.8	2.7	2.5	2.5	2.5	2.4	2.2
12/54	4.5	4.4	4.3	4.4	4.5	4.2	4.4	4.4	4.2	3.7	3.4	3.1	3.2	3.0	2.9	2.8	2.8	2.8	2.7	2.6
12/55	4.3	4.2	4.1	4.2	4.3	4.0	4.2	4.2	4.0	3.5	3.2	2.9	3.0	2.8	2.7	2.5	2.5	2.5	2.4	2.3
12/56	4.0	3.9	3.8	3.8	3.9	3.6	3.8	3.8	3.6	3.0	2.7	2.5	2.5	2.3	2.2	2.0	2.0	1.9	1.8	1.6
12/57	4.0	3.9	3.6	3.9	4.0	3.7	3.9	3.9	3.7	3.2	2.9	2.7	2.7	2.5	2.4	2.3	2.2	2.2	2.1	1.9
12/58	3.8	3.7	3.6	3.7	3.8	3.5	3.7	3.6	3.4	3.0	2.7	2.4	2.4	2.3	2.1	2.0	2.0	1.9	1.8	1.6
12/59	3.7	3.6	3.5	3.5	3.6	3.3	3.4	3.4	3.2	2.7	2.5	2.2	2.2	2.1	1.9	1.8	1.7	1.7	1.6	1.4
12/60	3.8	3.7	3.6	3.6	3.7	3.5	3.6	3.6	3.4	2.9	2.7	2.5	2.5	2.3	2.2	2.1	2.0	2.0	1.9	1.8
12/61	3.8	3.7	3.6	3.6	3.7	3.5	3.6	3.6	3.4	3.0	2.7	2.5	2.5	2.4	2.3	2.1	2.1	2.1	2.0	1.9
12/62	3.9	3.8	3.7	3.7	3.8	3.6	3.7	3.7	3.5	3.1	2.9	2.7	2.7	2.6	2.5	2.4	2.4	2.4	2.3	2.2
12/63	3.8	3.7	3.7	3.7	3.8	3.6	3.7	3.6	3.5	3.1	2.9	2.7	2.7	2.6	2.5	2.4	2.4	2.3	2.3	2.2
12/64	3.8	3.8	3.7	3.7	3.8	3.6	3.7	3.7	3.5	3.1	2.9	2.7	2.8	2.6	2.6	2.5	2.5	2.4	2.4	2.3
12/65	3.7	3.7	3.6	3.6	3.7	3.5	3.6	3.5	3.4	3.0	2.8	2.6	2.6	2.5	2.4	2.4	2.3	2.3	2.3	2.2
12/66	3.6	3.5	3.4	3.4	3.5	3.3	3.4	3.3	3.2	2.8	2.6	2.4	2.4	2.3	2.2	2.1	2.1	2.1	2.0	1.9
12/67	3.4	3.3	3.2	3.2	3.3	3.1	3.2	3.1	3.0	2.6	2.4	2.2	2.2	2.1	2.0	1.9	1.9	1.8	1.8	1.7
12/68	3.3	3.3	3.2	3.2	3.2	3.1	3.1	3.1	2.9	2.6	2.4	2.2	2.2	2.1	2.0	1.9	1.9	1.8	1.8	1.7
12/69	3.3	3.2	3.1	3.2	3.2	3.0	3.1	3.1	2.9	2.6	2.4	2.2	2.2	2.1	2.0	1.9	1.9	1.8	1.8	1.7

TABLE 6–3 (continued)

To \ From	12/45	12/46	12/47	12/48	12/49	12/50	12/51	12/52	12/53	12/54	12/55	12/56	12/57	12/58	12/59	12/60	12/61	12/62	12/63	12/64	12/65	12/66	12/67	12/68
12/46	2.6																							
12/47	0.8	-0.9																						
12/48	1.8	1.4	3.9																					
12/49	2.8	2.9	4.9	5.9																				
12/50	2.6	2.5	3.7	3.7	1.5																			
12/51	1.6	1.4	2.0	1.4	-0.8	-3.1																		
12/52	1.9	1.8	2.4	2.0	0.7	0.3	3.9																	
12/53	1.9	1.8	2.3	2.0	1.0	0.8	2.9	1.8																
12/54	2.3	2.3	2.8	2.6	1.9	2.0	3.8	3.8	5.7															
12/55	2.0	2.0	2.3	2.1	1.5	1.5	2.7	2.3	2.5	-0.7														
12/56	1.3	1.2	1.4	1.1	0.4	0.3	0.9	0.2	-0.3	-3.2	-5.7													
12/57	1.7	1.6	1.9	1.7	1.2	1.1	1.8	1.4	1.3	-0.1	0.2	6.4												
12/58	1.4	1.3	1.5	1.3	0.8	0.7	1.2	0.8	0.6	-0.6	-0.6	2.0	-2.2											
12/59	1.1	1.0	1.2	1.0	0.5	0.4	0.8	0.4	0.1	-1.0	-1.0	0.6	-2.2	-2.2										
12/60	1.6	1.5	1.7	1.5	1.1	1.1	1.6	1.3	1.2	0.5	0.7	2.4	1.1	2.7	7.9									
12/61	1.7	1.6	1.8	1.7	1.3	1.3	1.8	1.5	1.5	0.9	1.2	2.6	1.7	3.0	5.7	3.6								
12/62	2.1	2.0	2.2	2.1	1.8	1.8	2.3	2.1	2.2	1.7	2.1	3.4	2.9	4.2	6.4	5.6	7.7							
12/63	2.1	2.0	2.2	2.1	1.8	1.9	2.3	2.1	2.2	1.8	2.1	3.2	2.7	3.7	5.3	4.4	4.9	2.1						
12/64	2.2	2.2	2.3	2.2	2.0	2.0	2.4	2.3	2.4	2.0	2.3	3.4	3.0	3.9	5.1	4.4	4.7	3.3	4.5					
12/65	2.1	2.0	2.2	2.1	1.9	1.9	2.2	2.1	2.1	1.8	2.1	3.0	2.6	3.3	4.2	3.5	3.4	2.1	2.1	-0.3				
12/66	1.8	1.7	1.9	1.8	1.5	1.5	1.9	1.7	1.7	1.4	1.6	2.3	1.9	2.4	3.1	2.3	2.0	0.7	0.2	-1.9	-3.5			
12/67	1.5	1.5	1.6	1.5	1.3	1.2	1.5	1.4	1.3	1.0	1.1	1.8	1.3	1.7	2.2	1.5	1.1	-0.2	-0.7	-2.4	-3.4	-3.4		
12/68	1.5	1.5	1.6	1.5	1.3	1.3	1.5	1.4	1.3	1.0	1.2	1.8	1.4	1.7	2.2	1.5	1.2	0.1	-0.3	-1.4	-1.8	-0.9	1.5	
12/69	1.6	1.5	1.6	1.5	1.3	1.3	1.5	1.4	1.4	1.1	1.2	1.8	1.4	1.7	2.1	1.5	1.2	0.3	0.1	-0.8	-0.9	-0.1	1.6	1.7

Source: Lawrence Fisher and Roman L. Weil, "Coping with the Risk of Interest Rate Fluctuations: Returns to Bond Holders from Naive and Optimal Strategies," *Journal of Business*, October 1971, pp. 425–426.

TABLE 6–4
Bond and Common Stock: Annual Rates of Return, Selected Periods of Time

	Bond	Common Stock
Jan. 1926–Dec. 1965	3.7%	9.3%
Dec. 1929–Dec. 1965	3.7	9.9
Dec. 1940–Dec. 1965	2.4	16.0
Dec. 1950–Dec. 1965	1.9	14.4
Dec. 1960–Dec. 1965	3.5	15.7
ONE-YEAR PERIOD		
Worst: bonds—1966; stocks—1931	−3.9	−48.7
Best: bonds—1930; stocks—1933	10.4	105.7
FIVE-YEAR PERIOD		
Worst: bonds—1954–59	−1.0	
stocks—1927–32		−19.2
Best: bonds—1931–36	9.2	
stocks—1931–36		37.3

Sources: Tables 6–2 and 6–3.

RISK ANALYSIS

Consideration of risk has generally been excluded thus far except to point out the occurrence of negative or very low rates of return. In order to examine risk, three items are required: 1) a reasonably good definition of risk; 2) an analysis of the sources or causes of risk; and 3) a technique with which to measure risk or determine unambiguously which investments have more or less risk. This section discusses the first two items. Measurement is postponed until a later chapter despite the fact that this problem is probably the most important of the three from the decision-maker's viewpoint.

Risk, Uncertainty, and Partial Ignorance

Risk is typically treated as a lack of knowledge regarding future events. This lack of knowledge is often labeled *risk, uncertainty,* or *partial ignorance. Risk* is defined as a state where a decision-maker knows *all* possible future outcomes of a given decision and can assign a probability to each possible outcome. *Uncertainty* exists when the decision-maker knows *all* possible future outcomes of a given act but cannot, for whatever reason, assign probabilities to the possible outcomes. *Partial ignorance* is a condition where some or all of the possible outcomes are unknown.

These definitions are quite arbitrary and the treatment of risk and uncertainty in the investment field usually assumes that they are synonymous. Actually every decision probably represents the partial ignorance condition. If one desires to be less bold, it is certainly clear that *every* decision is a case of uncertainty. In the life insurance industry, mortality tables are well-developed and based upon enormous quantities of actual experience. Yet one insures for the future and the fact that a 20-year-old male had a life expectancy of 49.4 years from his 20th birthday does not necessarily imply that the same condition will exist in the future. In fact, life expectancy has increased markedly during the past century, but this again does not suggest the same increases will occur during the next 100 years.

Classifications of Risk

There are many ways to classify the sources of risk. Two possible methods are outlined in Exhibit 6–3. Even in using these two methods, considerable overlap can be noted.

Systematic versus Unsystematic. The first method of risk classification considers risk either as systematic or unsystematic. Systematic risk results from being involved with the market. If an investor invests in common stocks, that investor accepts the possibility that the market may go down or that the economy may do poorly. There is no way to diversify away this risk by adding more stocks. Adding assets other than common stocks may help reduce this risk somewhat.

At the extreme, imagine a portfolio consisting of all securities on the NYSE. The risk of this portfolio is simply the risk associated with the entire market since all factors unique to the firm and industry have been diversified away. However, no matter what the portfolio composi-

EXHIBIT 6–3
Two Methods of Risk Classification

1.	Systematic (Non-Diversifiable)	Unsystematic (Diversifiable)
	Risks associated with economy and security market	Industry risks Unique risks financial managerial fraud

2. a. Purchasing power (inflation) risk
   b. Interest rate risk
   c. Market risk
   d. Business (industry) risk
   e. Political risk

tion, systematic risk remains. The market portfolio is an extreme and few investors own such a portfolio, but available evidence, discussed in Chapter 13, suggests strongly that most individuals can purchase a portfolio that closely approximates the market portfolio.

Unsystematic or *diversifiable* risk is that risk the typical investor need not accept. In terms of the risk categories to be mentioned below, it is the risk unique to the firm and the industry. These two risk elements are diversifiable since a portfolio of sufficient size will have only market risk. Throughout the booming period of the middle 1960s the steel industry performed poorly because of obsolete equipment, foreign competition, the availability of alternative materials such as copper and aluminum, and perhaps poor management. Whatever the reasons, the investor in steel stocks experienced the consequences of industry risk despite a booming economy. The risk of the individual firm or that risk which is unique to the firm is exemplified by the auto industry since World War II. As a whole, the industry has done well, yet Studebaker, Kaiser, Hudson, and the Edsel are today footnotes to history.

Traditional Classifications

Risk has traditionally been classified into purchasing power risk, interest rate risk, market risk, business risk, and political risk. In many situations, this is a useful way of examining the risk involved.

Purchasing Power Risk. An important source of risk is purchasing power risk, which is the possibility that future earnings will not command the goods and services possible with current dollars. A 10 percent investment return during a period when the inflation rate is 10 percent results in the investor being no better off than before in terms of the use of the earnings. The *real earnings* in this case are zero. If the inflation rate is uncertain, the investment contains risk even if the investment's monetary return is certain. Hence, a bond issued by the federal government is risky even though its monetary return is certain.

We observed common stocks have done quite well even if the returns are adjusted for inflation, but this favorable outcome requires a long-run investment horizon. In this context, common stocks are said to be an inflation hedge since they protect the investor from purchasing power risk. Bonds with fixed returns have far more long-run purchasing power risk. Hence, if inflation is expected, the typical advice is to buy common stocks. If deflation is expected, bonds become more desirable. But this advice applies only on average and for long-run investment horizons.

Interest Rate Risk. A second element of risk is closely related to purchasing power risk and in fact may be partially caused by inflationary problems in the economy. We refer to interest rate risk, which is the potential for loss of principal due to changes in the general level of interest rates.

Suppose an investment promises to pay $105 at the end of a one-year period. If the interest rate is 5 percent, the present value of the investment is $100. All other things being equal, we expect to pay $100 today. If the interest rate changes to 10 percent, the present value and the price of the investment will fall to $95.45. This relationship can be readily observed in the capital markets where an increase in interest rates is generally associated with declining prices of fixed-income securities and decreasing interest rates correlated with rising prices.

Interest rate prediction is far from an exact science, but even if it were, the price effects would be difficult to pinpoint. In the first place, the impact of interest rate movements varies depending upon which security is being considered. In the case of government bonds where the risk of monetary loss is nil, the interest rate changes dominate, so virtually any price change relates to interest rate changes. The lower the quality of securities considered, the less significant interest rate risk becomes. High-grade corporate bonds have a strong interest rate risk element and these instruments undoubtedly experience roughly the same changes as do government bonds with only minor exceptions. The more dominant the risk of monetary loss from bankruptcy, the less pronounced the interest rate risk element.

Interest rate risk is also closely related to an investor's time horizon. For a ten-year investment horizon, it is frequently suggested that interest rate risk can be avoided simply by purchasing a ten-year bond. Aside from the problems of bonds being callable,[3] the appendix to this chapter shows that a given interest rate can be obtained if and only if the periodic cash proceeds are reinvested at the particular interest rate. If a ten-year bond is purchased which pays $50 per year in current income and the purchase price is $1,000, the bond yield or return will be stated as 5 percent. This return is the discounted cash flow return which assumes that the periodic cash flows are reinvested at a return of 5 percent. If the interest rates fall below 5 percent, the actual return will be less than 5 percent for the ten-year investor. If interest rates rise, the ten-year return will be more than 5 percent.

Market Risk. While the impact on an individual security varies, all securities are exposed to market risk. Market risk includes such factors as business recessions or depressions and long-run changes in the tastes and consumption patterns within the economy.

In addition to general economic conditions, all securities are influenced by general stock market movements that occasionally are unrelated to the actual performance of the economy. Figure 6-1 compares

[3]A callable bond is one where the issuer can force redemption of the bond prior to its maturity date. They are discussed in Chapter 17.

the quarterly GNP from 1946 to 1974 with the Standard & Poor 500 Stock Index for the months of February, May, August, and November. Clearly, stock prices have been much more volatile than the basic GNP series although the GNP series, expressed in dollars, does not show the impact of the double-digit inflation of 1974.

Business and Industry Risk. The risks of doing business as a single entity or as part of an industry vary considerably and frequently the analysis can be quite complex. At this point we can itemize these industry risk sources, preserving their analysis until Chapter 8. Business risk is examined in the next section.

FIGURE 6–1
GNP versus S&P 500 Stock Index (1946–74)

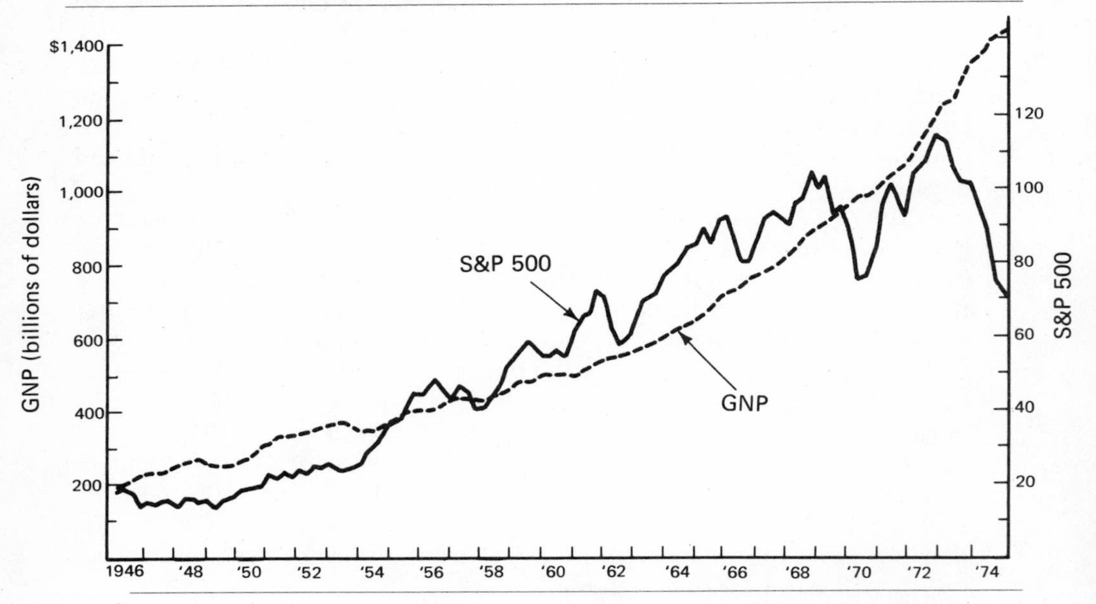

Source: *Survey of Current Business*, various issues, Standard & Poor's *Trade and Securities Statistics, Security Price Index Record*, 1974, p. 4, and *Current Statistics*, January 1975, p. 40.

Tastes and preferences change in a dynamic economy. The status of the auto industry in 1975 is an excellent example. Consumers were expressing a strong preference for smaller cars. Given this change in preferences, the entire auto industry as well as associated industries will need to revise their product mix. No matter what the status of a particular firm within the industry, all are required to change.

New products and technology also produce dynamic changes. Products with origins external to the industry, as was the case with airlines taking passengers from the railroads, will affect the entire industry. But technology also operates at the production and marketing level. Continuous casting in the steel industry has had profound effects on that industry even though the product remained essentially the same. The development of the discount store has had a significant impact on the department store industry.

Political Risk. Foreign competition can have important ramifications. With international trade becoming a larger element in our economy, this source of risk promises to become more important in the future. This risk is discussed more extensively in Chapter 8. It includes such items as tariff and import quota changes, currency fluctuations, business takeovers by foreign governments, and wars.

Unique-to-Firm Risk

We previously observed that risk unique to the firm is a type of unsystematic or diversifiable risk. Unique risk can be classified into financial risk, managerial risk, and risk of fraud. As with other sources of risk, these items are related, but for analytical purposes it is usually preferable to examine them separately.

Financial Risk. Financial risk relates to the ability of the firm to meet its short- and long-run financial obligations and to finance profitable opportunities. A firm may be capable of servicing its debt, but if such action exhausts its financial resources there is considerable financial risk in the sense that innovations such as new products cannot be introduced. Over time, such a firm will perform quite poorly relative to its competitors.

Financial risk may be measured in several ways. The first area to be examined includes the firm's liquidity or the ability to meet short-term obligations from either internal or external sources. The second area is concerned with solvency, or the ability of the firm to meet its long-term obligations through the profitability of its operations. Financial integrity is indicated when a firm can meet short-term debts through the liquidation of short-term assets and long-term debt from the profits of its operations. Financial risk is rarely absolute and, for the most part, the ability to incur financial obligations will depend upon the volatility of sales and earnings. This volatility depends on the industry risk and the firm's position within the particular industry.

Managerial Risk. At the management level we face perhaps the investor's most difficult problem, the need to determine the general skill of management relative to actual and potential competition. The actual performance of management is important since management must transfer the results of their skills to the stockholders. A firm could be quite well managed, but if this does not transfer into dividends and growth for the owners, the firm must be poorly managed for investment purposes. At the performance level, management risk is determined mainly by an examination of operating efficiency. The well-managed firm has a record as good as or better than that of its competitors.

Fraud. "A fool and his money are soon parted," goes the old saying. It does not matter a great deal how much time an investor spends evaluating business risk, interest rate risk, and all other forms of risk if the investment being considered is fraudulent. It is often difficult to know whether a particular investment is an honest venture, but there are certain things investors can keep in mind.

It would be nice to say frauds in the securities business are unknown. Fortunately they are uncommon, but when they occur, huge sums of money are often involved, and they do not help investors' confidence. While space limits our discussion of major frauds that have occurred, one major type of fraud is discussed.

A Ponzi Scheme, named after Charles "Get Rich Quick" Ponzi, involves paying high dividends or interest to early investors with money collected from later investors. During the early 1920s, Ponzi took in $15 million in less than a year with a slogan of "50 percent return in 45 days, double your money in 90." As with many schemes, Ponzi started honestly by discovering that a Spanish postal reply coupon bought in Spain for one cent was redeemable in the United States for five cents. He borrowed $250 from friends and returned $375 to them in a few days. His fame quickly spread—helped along, of course, by some hired agents. The Boston *Post* discovered that only $1 million in Spanish postal coupons had been issued in the previous six years and this could not have supported Ponzi's operation.

Can investors avoid possibly fraudulent ventures such as a Ponzi Scheme? One can probably never be completely sure that any but the most gilt-edged investment is safe. However, any investment which is being promoted heavily and which appears to promise returns substantially above what one would expect to be reasonable should be seriously questioned by the investor.

SUMMARY

Our discussion concentrated on the sources of return and risk with emphasis placed on measuring return. In discussing the problem of return, we noted that any measurement device must consider the time value of money which results from 1) the investor's time utility preference, 2) the investment risk, and 3) the investor's opportunity cost. We then discussed compound interest, noting the basic concept of earnings on the returns of previous periods as well. The concept of compound interest allowed an examination of the investment problem in a present value framework. Present value was defined as the current value of funds received at some point in the future where the adjustment involved discounting future funds at some rate of return.

The price of any investment should be the present value of all future cash flows. For common stocks, this implies that the basic source of returns is from the dividends paid by the firm, although capital gains and losses may be important in examining the investment characteristics of any common stock. One should analyze factors such as earnings, management skill, and product demand to see how they may be expected to influence future dividends.

An historical survey of returns from investments in common stocks and high-grade corporate bonds was undertaken. Over a long period of time, common stocks earned substantially more than bonds (about 9.3 percent per year versus 3.5 percent). At the same time, common stock returns fluctuated much more, so that assurance of the higher returns required a long-run commitment of about ten years or more.

Last, sources of risk were discussed. Risk was classified as either systematic or nonsystematic (diversifiable) risk. Systematic risks cannot be eliminated through diversification. Nonsystematic risks can be diversified away. Another method of classifying risks resulted in the following risks: 1) interest rate risk; 2) purchasing power risk; 3) market risk; 4) business risk; and 5) political risk.

QUESTIONS

1. Why does money have a time value?
2. Many savings institutions advertise that the interest rates they pay on deposits are compounded daily. What is the relationship between the nominal and effective rate of interest in such a situation?
3. Why does an investor need to give so much consideration to the rate of dividend growth in the valuation of common stocks?
4. Is it true that an investor can focus only on dividend growth and ignore other factors such as the financial strength of the company, its market position, and the competence of management?
5. Based upon the historical evidence presented in the chapter regarding the return earned on common stocks, what would you use at the present time as the appropriate discount rate in calculating the present value of a stock? What factors other than the historical evidence might cause you to alter your discount rate?
6. Since bonds have earned a long-term rate of return substantially below the long-term rate of return earned from common stock investments, the logical conclusion is that bonds have no place in the portfolio of an investor. Do you agree? Why or why not?
7. Distinguish among risk, uncertainty, and partial ignorance.

8. Interest rate risk is really only important for the bond investor and can realistically be ignored by the investor in common stock. Do you agree?
9. Are some types of bonds and some types of common stocks more sensitive to interest rate risk than other types of these securities?
10. Risk can normally be classified into risk which can be diversified away and risk which is a part of the system and cannot be diversified away. Give examples of each type of risk.

PROBLEMS

1. Jane Kinney is considering a savings deposit in two different banks. Bank A pays 5¼ percent compounded semiannually, while bank B pays 5 percent compounded quarterly. If Jane plans to keep her money in the bank for a year, which bank should she pick?
2. Harry Smith wants to be able to provide a college education for his five-year-old son. He feels that a four-year college education will cost $25,000 when his son becomes 18. Harry wants to make a common stock investment now and feels an 8 percent annual rate of return is a reasonable expectation. How much will he need to invest now to be able to educate his son?
3. A $1,000 bond pays $80 interest annually at the end of each year and has ten years to go to maturity. What would an investor desiring a 10 percent return be willing to pay for this bond?
4. An investor is considering the purchase of a common stock and estimates dividends per share for the next five years will be as follows: $2.00; $2.10; $2.35; $2.60; and $2.85. The investor also estimates the stock will sell for $60 a share at the end of the fifth year. What will the rate of return be if the stock sells for $45 now? Hint: Guess at a rate and calculate the present value of the returns.
5. A common stock currently pays a $3 dividend per share. The dividend is expected to grow at 4 percent per year in the future. Given the current state of the market and his risk level, Jim Meeks desires a rate of return of 12 percent on this stock. What would he be willing to pay for the stock?
6. His broker calls John Q. Investor and informs him that an offering of bonds is currently being made at par ($1,000 per bond) and will give John $75 yearly in interest income. The bonds have a maturity of twenty years. John knows that interest rates have been volatile in recent years and is concerned about how his investment will fare should he be forced to sell the bonds in two years. He feels that interest rates *two years hence* will not be more than 10 percent nor less than 6 percent. What would be his dollar gain or loss if either extreme occurs?

7. Professor Olson has been a member of the Financial Management Association during its brief one-year life. He has paid dues of $15 to the group. He is considering whether he should accept the FMA's offer of a life membership for $125 less a credit for dues previously paid. This would mean a life membership could be obtained for $110. Olson is thirty-four years old. Government statistics estimate the remaining years of labor force participation for the average thirty-four-year-old male at approximately twenty-nine, while the average life expectancy is estimated at approximately thirty-seven years. If Olson should die before using up the $110 membership at regular annual rates ($15 a year at the time), his estate would be entitled to a refund of the unused life membership.
   a) Olson is wondering what the implied rate of return on the "investment" in a life membership would be using the work-life expectancy figure and assuming dues remain constant at $15 per year (ignore the rebate provision).
   b) If dues should rise because of inflationary factors, what would happen to the rate of return just calculated?
   c) Of what significance is the fact the Olson's estate would receive a rebate in the event of premature death?
   d) What other assumptions has Olson made in arriving at the answer in part *a*?
   e) Would the eight years difference between Olson's life expectancy and his work-life expectancy make a significant difference in the rate of return calculation in part *a*?

SUGGESTED READINGS

Bernstein, Peter L. "What Rate of Return Can You 'Reasonably' Expect?" *Journal of Finance,* May 1973, pp. 273–82.

Brealey, Richard A. *An Introduction to Risk and Return from Common Stocks.* Cambridge, Mass.: MIT Press, 1969.

Fisher, Lawrence and James H. Lorie. "Rates of Return on Investments in Common Stocks." *Journal of Business,* January 1964, pp. 1–21.

——. "Rates of Return on Investments in Common Stock: The Year-By-Year Record, 1926–65," *Journal of Business,* July 1968, pp. 291–316.

Graham, Benjamin. "The Future of Common Stocks." *Financial Analysts Journal,* September–October 1974, pp. 20–30.

Holmes, John Russell. "100 Years of Investment Experience with Common Stocks," *Financial Analysts Journal,* November–December 1974, pp. 38–44ff.

Oudet, Bruno A. "The Variation of the Return on Stocks in Periods of Inflation." *Journal of Financial and Quantitative Analysis,* March 1973, pp. 247–57.

Pinches, George E. and Gary Simon. "An Analysis of Portfolio Accumulation Strategies Employing Low-Priced Common Stocks." *Journal of Financial and Quantitative Analysis,* June 1972, pp. 1773–96.

Reilly, Frank K. *Companies and Common Stocks As Inflation Hedges.* Bulletin 1975-2 of New York University Center for the Study of Financial Institutions, 1975.

Seligman, Daniel. "A Case for Gloom About Stocks." *Fortune,* October 1974, pp. 103-8.

Soldofsky, Robert M. and Dale F. Max. "Securities as a Hedge Against Inflation: 1910-1969." *Journal of Business Research,* April 1975, pp. 165-72.

"The Long-Term Case for Stocks." *Fortune,* December 1974, pp. 97-102.

Appendix A

MEASUREMENT PROBLEMS AND THE GEOMETRIC RETURN

Two common stock investments, A and B, either have or are expected to exhibit with certainty the characteristics shown below during a two-year period. For simplicity, assume that an investment made in either security will be for the entire two-year period with no switching allowed.

	Security A		*Security B*	
Year	*Price*	*Dividend*	*Price*	*Dividend*
0	$10.00	$--	$10.00	$--
1	6.05	1.00	24.20	1.00
2	12.10	1.10	12.10	1.10

Within the context of the present value calculations, the current price of $10 for both A and B would be given by equation (4) in the text in the following manner:

$$P_0 = \frac{D_1}{1 + r} + \frac{D_2}{(1 + r)^2} + \frac{P_2}{(1 + r)^2}$$

$$10 = \frac{1.00}{1 + r} + \frac{1.10}{(1 + r)^2} + \frac{12.10}{(1 + r)^2}$$

Solving for r by using present value tables, we find that the rate of return or discount rate is 20 percent for both securities. Since the investment period is two years, the interim prices of \$6.05 and \$24.20, respectively, do not enter the rate of return calculation.

There is a problem, however. If both investments returned 20 percent, we should find that the investor's wealth at the end of the two-year period should have increased to \$14.40, which is the ending value of a \$10 investment compounded at 20 percent for two years, according to equation (1) in the text. If we sum the final price of \$12.10 and the annual dividends of \$1.00 and \$1.10 for each investment, the final wealth is only \$14.20. What happened?

A straight summation assumes that the cash flows received at the end of the first year earned nothing or were not reinvested. The only way we will obtain a final wealth of \$14.40 is to reinvest the first-year dividend at the calculated rate of return, 20 percent. In other words, the present value calculation assumes that all periodic cash flows are reinvested to earn the return determined from the calculation or assumed in the calculation. In the example, each investment produces a final price of \$12.10, a final cash flow of \$1.10, a first period cash flow of \$1, and earnings of \$.20 on the reinvestment of the first period cash flow. The total is the \$14.40 required.

Such an assumption is typically inconsistent with reality. If we confine ourselves to the securities A and B, which is realistic in the sense that returns do fluctuate from period to period and security to security, it is clear that a 20 percent return in the second year is not possible. The period returns, including both price changes and dividends, are given below, calculated as increases (or decreases) in value as a percent of the beginning of period investment.[1]

Year	*Security A*	*Security B*
1	−29.50%	152.00%
2	118.18	−45.45

No matter which security is purchased, a 20 percent return in the second year on the first-year dividend reinvestment is not possible. The only possibility is reinvesting \$0.40 in A and \$0.60 in B, but this strategy raises portfolio

[1]The reader should be certain that these returns can be reproduced. In period 1 security A lost \$3.95 in price but gained \$1 in dividends for a net loss of \$2.95. Since the initial investment was \$10 the rate of return was −29.5 percent. In period 2 the initial investment is \$6.05 or the price at the beginning of the period. The gain is \$6.05 (12.10 − 6.05) in price and \$1.10 in dividends for a net of \$7.15 or 118.18 percent (7.15/6.05).

problems that we are not prepared to deal with at this time.[2] Furthermore, recall that we are attempting to measure the benefits or return from a particular investment. With this objective, our return should be measured as though the funds were reinvested in the individual security. Thus the $1 dividend of A should be reinvested in A and the $1 dividend of B reinvested in B. In reality, one may not follow such a practice, but in terms of calculating the benefits to be derived from an individual security, such an assumption is justified.

Consequently, the wealth derived from security A is $15.38 while security B produced only $13.75—determined as follows:

Source of Wealth	*Security A*	*Security B*
Final price	$12.10	$12.10
Second dividend	1.10	1.10
First dividend	1.00	1.00
Return from first dividend reinvestment ($1 times year two rate of return)	(1.18	−.45)
	$15.38	$13.75

Geometric Mean

In order to remain consistent with our initial definition of return, any indicated annual rate of return, when compounded annually, should produce a final wealth of $15.38 and $13.75, respectively. Recall equation (1) as follows:

$$V_n = V_0(1 + r)^n$$

For security A, we have $\$15.38 = \$10\,(1 + r)^2$, which produces an annually compounded return of 24.02 percent by solving for r. For security B, we have $\$13.75 = \$10\,(1 + r)^2$, which produces an annually compounded return of 17.26 percent. In essence, security A is equivalent to a savings account which pays 24.02 percent while security B is equivalent to a 17.26 percent savings account. The returns which have just been calculated are referred to as the *geometric mean of the period returns or the time-weighted rate of return.* In our opinion, the term geometric mean is preferable since the time-weighted return is typically not broken down into the equivalent annual rate of return.

The geometric mean is not nearly so difficult to determine as might be implied thus far. All that is required are the annual returns and a table of logarithms, since logarithms convert unequal data to a common or relative base.

[2]Note that the initial investments for the second year return are the security prices of $6.05 and $24.20, respectively. Forty percent in A and 60 percent in B would produce a weighted average return of 20 percent as follows: .4(118.18) + .6(−45.45).

The following steps, with security A as an example, may be used to determine the geometric mean.[3]

1. Convert each annual return into an annual wealth relative. A wealth relative (W_t) is defined as one plus the annual return or the ratio of ending wealth to beginning wealth as shown below (where t can be any period length):

$$W_t = \frac{P_t + D_t}{P_{t-1}} = 1 + r_t$$

For security A, the wealth relatives for periods 1 and 2 are calculated below:

$$W_t = \frac{\$6.05 + \$1.00}{\$10} = 1 + (-.295) = .705 \text{ (period 1)}$$

$$W_t = \frac{\$12.10 + \$1.10}{\$6.05} = 1 + 1.182 = 2.182 \text{ (period 2)}$$

2. Find the product of all period wealth relatives:

$$W_1 \text{ times } W_2 = (.705)(2.182) = 1.538$$

3. Find the nth root of the product of the wealth relatives by finding the logarithm of the product of the wealth relatives and dividing by n.

$$\log_{10} \text{ of } 1.538 = .1871$$

$$.1871/2 = .09355$$

4. Find the antilog of the value found in step 3 and subtract. This is the geometric mean of the period (annual) returns.

$$\text{antilog}(.09355) - 1 = .2402$$

Why not simply average the rates of return? Indeed, in certain instances, such a procedure would be satisfactory. However, such an average would

[3]In more formal terms the geometric mean of the annual rates of return is given by the following equation:

$$r = \left[\prod_{t=1}^{N} W_t \right]^{\frac{1}{N}} - 1$$

$$= \left(\text{Antilog} \sum_{t=1}^{N} \frac{\log W_t}{N} \right) - 1$$

where N is the number of years or periods, Π means to multiply all values of W_t together, and Σ means to add all values.

generally be meaningless. To see why, consider a nondividend paying common stock investment that has an initial price of $10, grows to $20 in the first year, and declines back to $10 in the second year. At the end of the second year, the investor's return was zero. Notice that the return in the first year is 100 percent and the second year return is −50 percent. The average of these returns is 25 percent, but the investor is obviously no better off.[4]

[4]An average annual rate of return will be approximately correct when all annual rates are between approximately plus and minus 15 percent per year. The reason for this is that the natural log of any value $(1 + r)$ is approximately equal to r when r is between plus and minus .15. If, for example, we have period returns of 11 percent and 2 percent, the average return would be 6.5 percent. The geometric mean of the returns would be approximately 6.4 percent. The quality of the estimate deteriorates as the annual returns become large. Straight averages will overstate positive returns and understate negative returns. The geometric of −11 percent and −2 percent is approximately −6.6 percent as compared to an arithmetic average of −6.5 percent.

APPENDIX A–1
Present Value of $1 Received at the End of *n* Years

	Rate of Return (*r*)										
YEARS (*n*)	0.0200	0.0400	0.0600	0.0800	0.1000	0.1200	0.1400	0.1500	0.1600	0.1800	0.2000
1	0.9804	0.9615	0.9434	0.9259	0.9091	0.8929	0.8772	0.8696	0.8621	0.8475	0.8333
2	0.9612	0.9246	0.8900	0.8573	0.8264	0.7972	0.7695	0.7561	0.7432	0.7182	0.6944
3	0.9423	0.8890	0.8396	0.7938	0.7513	0.7118	0.6750	0.6575	0.6407	0.6086	0.5787
4	0.9238	0.8548	0.7921	0.7350	0.6830	0.6355	0.5921	0.5718	0.5523	0.5158	0.4823
5	0.9057	0.8219	0.7473	0.6806	0.6209	0.5674	0.5194	0.4972	0.4761	0.4371	0.4019
6	0.8880	0.7903	0.7050	0.6302	0.5645	0.5066	0.4556	0.4323	0.4104	0.3704	0.3349
7	0.8706	0.7599	0.6651	0.5835	0.5132	0.4523	0.3996	0.3759	0.3538	0.3139	0.2791
8	0.8535	0.7307	0.6274	0.5403	0.4665	0.4039	0.3506	0.3269	0.3050	0.2660	0.2326
9	0.8368	0.7026	0.5919	0.5002	0.4241	0.3606	0.3075	0.2843	0.2630	0.2255	0.1938
10	0.8203	0.6756	0.5584	0.4632	0.3855	0.3220	0.2697	0.2472	0.2267	0.1911	0.1615
11	0.8043	0.6496	0.5268	0.4289	0.3505	0.2875	0.2366	0.2149	0.1954	0.1619	0.1346
12	0.7885	0.6246	0.4970	0.3971	0.3186	0.2567	0.2076	0.1869	0.1685	0.1372	0.1122
13	0.7730	0.6006	0.4688	0.3677	0.2897	0.2292	0.1821	0.1625	0.1452	0.1163	0.0935
14	0.7579	0.5775	0.4423	0.3405	0.2633	0.2046	0.1597	0.1413	0.1252	0.0985	0.0779
15	0.7430	0.5553	0.4173	0.3152	0.2394	0.1827	0.1401	0.1229	0.1079	0.0835	0.0649
16	0.7284	0.5339	0.3936	0.2919	0.2176	0.1631	0.1229	0.1069	0.0930	0.0708	0.0541
17	0.7142	0.5134	0.3714	0.2703	0.1978	0.1456	0.1078	0.0929	0.0802	0.0600	0.0451
18	0.7002	0.4936	0.3503	0.2502	0.1799	0.1300	0.0946	0.0808	0.0691	0.0508	0.0376
19	0.6864	0.4746	0.3305	0.2317	0.1635	0.1161	0.0829	0.0703	0.0596	0.0431	0.0313
20	0.6730	0.4564	0.3118	0.2145	0.1486	0.1037	0.0728	0.0611	0.0514	0.0365	0.0261
21	0.6598	0.4388	0.2942	0.1987	0.1351	0.0926	0.0638	0.0531	0.0443	0.0309	0.0217
22	0.6468	0.4220	0.2775	0.1839	0.1228	0.0826	0.0560	0.0462	0.0382	0.0262	0.0181
23	0.6342	0.4057	0.2618	0.1703	0.1117	0.0738	0.0491	0.0402	0.0329	0.0222	0.0151
24	0.6217	0.3901	0.2470	0.1577	0.1015	0.0659	0.0431	0.0349	0.0284	0.0188	0.0126
25	0.6095	0.3751	0.2330	0.1460	0.0923	0.0588	0.0378	0.0304	0.0245	0.0160	0.0105
26	0.5976	0.3607	0.2198	0.1352	0.0839	0.0525	0.0331	0.0264	0.0211	0.0135	0.0087
27	0.5859	0.3468	0.2074	0.1252	0.0763	0.0469	0.0291	0.0230	0.0182	0.0115	0.0073
28	0.5744	0.3335	0.1956	0.1159	0.0693	0.0419	0.0255	0.0200	0.0157	0.0097	0.0061
29	0.5631	0.3207	0.1846	0.1073	0.0630	0.0374	0.0224	0.0174	0.0135	0.0082	0.0051
30	0.5521	0.3083	0.1741	0.0994	0.0573	0.0334	0.0196	0.0151	0.0116	0.0070	0.0042
31	0.5412	0.2965	0.1643	0.0920	0.0521	0.0298	0.0172	0.0131	0.0100	0.0059	0.0035
32	0.5306	0.2851	0.1550	0.0852	0.0474	0.0266	0.0151	0.0114	0.0087	0.0050	0.0029
33	0.5202	0.2741	0.1462	0.0789	0.0431	0.0238	0.0132	0.0099	0.0075	0.0042	0.0024
34	0.5100	0.2636	0.1379	0.0730	0.0391	0.0212	0.0116	0.0086	0.0064	0.0036	0.0020
35	0.5000	0.2534	0.1301	0.0676	0.0356	0.0189	0.0102	0.0075	0.0055	0.0030	0.0017
36	0.4902	0.2437	0.1227	0.0626	0.0323	0.0169	0.0089	0.0065	0.0048	0.0026	0.0014
37	0.4806	0.2343	0.1158	0.0580	0.0294	0.0151	0.0078	0.0057	0.0041	0.0022	0.0012
38	0.4712	0.2253	0.1092	0.0537	0.0267	0.0135	0.0069	0.0049	0.0036	0.0019	0.0010
39	0.4619	0.2166	0.1031	0.0497	0.0243	0.0120	0.0060	0.0043	0.0031	0.0016	0.0008
40	0.4529	0.2083	0.0972	0.0460	0.0221	0.0107	0.0053	0.0037	0.0026	0.0013	0.0007

APPENDIX A-1 (continued)

Rate of Return (r)

YEARS (n)	0.2200	0.2400	0.2600	0.2800	0.3000	0.3500	0.4000	0.4500	0.5000	0.5500	0.6000
1	0.8197	0.8065	0.7937	0.7813	0.7692	0.7407	0.7143	0.6897	0.6667	0.6452	0.6250
2	0.6719	0.6504	0.6299	0.6104	0.5917	0.5487	0.5102	0.4756	0.4444	0.4162	0.3906
3	0.5507	0.5245	0.4999	0.4768	0.4552	0.4064	0.3644	0.3280	0.2963	0.2685	0.2441
4	0.4514	0.4230	0.3968	0.3725	0.3501	0.3011	0.2603	0.2262	0.1975	0.1733	0.1526
5	0.3700	0.3411	0.3149	0.2910	0.2693	0.2230	0.1859	0.1560	0.1317	0.1118	0.0954
6	0.3033	0.2751	0.2499	0.2274	0.2072	0.1652	0.1328	0.1076	0.0878	0.0721	0.0596
7	0.2486	0.2218	0.1983	0.1776	0.1594	0.1224	0.0949	0.0742	0.0585	0.0465	0.0373
8	0.2038	0.1789	0.1574	0.1388	0.1226	0.0906	0.0678	0.0512	0.0390	0.0300	0.0233
9	0.1670	0.1443	0.1249	0.1084	0.0943	0.0671	0.0484	0.0353	0.0260	0.0194	0.0146
10	0.1369	0.1164	0.0992	0.0847	0.0725	0.0497	0.0346	0.0243	0.0173	0.0125	0.0091
11	0.1122	0.0938	0.0787	0.0662	0.0558	0.0368	0.0247	0.0168	0.0116	0.0081	0.0057
12	0.0920	0.0757	0.0625	0.0517	0.0429	0.0273	0.0176	0.0116	0.0077	0.0052	0.0036
13	0.0754	0.0610	0.0496	0.0404	0.0330	0.0202	0.0126	0.0080	0.0051	0.0034	0.0022
14	0.0618	0.0492	0.0393	0.0316	0.0254	0.0150	0.0090	0.0055	0.0034	0.0022	0.0014
15	0.0507	0.0397	0.0312	0.0247	0.0195	0.0111	0.0064	0.0038	0.0023	0.0014	0.0009
16	0.0415	0.0320	0.0248	0.0193	0.0150	0.0082	0.0046	0.0026	0.0015	0.0009	0.0005
17	0.0340	0.0258	0.0197	0.0150	0.0116	0.0061	0.0033	0.0018	0.0010	0.0006	0.0003
18	0.0279	0.0208	0.0156	0.0118	0.0089	0.0045	0.0023	0.0012	0.0007	0.0004	0.0002
19	0.0229	0.0168	0.0124	0.0092	0.0068	0.0033	0.0017	0.0009	0.0005	0.0002	0.0001
20	0.0187	0.0135	0.0098	0.0072	0.0053	0.0025	0.0012	0.0006	0.0003	0.0002	0.0001
21	0.0154	0.0109	0.0078	0.0056	0.0040	0.0018	0.0009	0.0004	0.0002	0.0001	0.0001
22	0.0126	0.0088	0.0062	0.0044	0.0031	0.0014	0.0006	0.0003	0.0001	0.0001	0.0000
23	0.0103	0.0071	0.0049	0.0034	0.0024	0.0010	0.0004	0.0002	0.0001	0.0000	0.0000
24	0.0085	0.0057	0.0039	0.0027	0.0018	0.0007	0.0003	0.0001	0.0001	0.0000	0.0000
25	0.0069	0.0046	0.0031	0.0021	0.0014	0.0006	0.0002	0.0001	0.0000	0.0000	0.0000
26	0.0057	0.0037	0.0025	0.0016	0.0011	0.0004	0.0002	0.0001	0.0000	0.0000	0.0000
27	0.0047	0.0030	0.0019	0.0013	0.0008	0.0003	0.0001	0.0000	0.0000	0.0000	0.0000
28	0.0038	0.0024	0.0015	0.0010	0.0006	0.0002	0.0001	0.0000	0.0000	0.0000	0.0000
29	0.0031	0.0020	0.0012	0.0008	0.0005	0.0002	0.0001	0.0000	0.0000	0.0000	0.0000
30	0.0026	0.0016	0.0010	0.0006	0.0004	0.0001	0.0000	0.0000	0.0000	0.0000	0.0000
31	0.0021	0.0013	0.0008	0.0005	0.0003	0.0001	0.0000	0.0000	0.0000	0.0000	0.0000
32	0.0017	0.0010	0.0006	0.0004	0.0002	0.0001	0.0000	0.0000	0.0000	0.0000	0.0000
33	0.0014	0.0008	0.0005	0.0003	0.0002	0.0001	0.0000	0.0000	0.0000	0.0000	0.0000
34	0.0012	0.0007	0.0004	0.0002	0.0001	0.0000	0.0000	0.0000	0.0000	0.0000	0.0000
35	0.0009	0.0005	0.0003	0.0002	0.0001	0.0000	0.0000	0.0000	0.0000	0.0000	0.0000
36	0.0008	0.0004	0.0002	0.0001	0.0001	0.0000	0.0000	0.0000	0.0000	0.0000	0.0000
37	0.0006	0.0003	0.0002	0.0001	0.0001	0.0000	0.0000	0.0000	0.0000	0.0000	0.0000
38	0.0005	0.0003	0.0002	0.0001	0.0000	0.0000	0.0000	0.0000	0.0000	0.0000	0.0000
39	0.0004	0.0002	0.0001	0.0001	0.0000	0.0000	0.0000	0.0000	0.0000	0.0000	0.0000
40	0.0004	0.0002	0.0001	0.0001	0.0000	0.0000	0.0000	0.0000	0.0000	0.0000	0.0000

APPENDIX A-2

Present Value of $1 Received at the End of each Year for *n* Years

	Rate of Return (*r*)										
YEARS (*n*)	0.0200	0.0400	0.0600	0.0800	0.1000	0.1200	0.1400	0.1500	0.1600	0.1800	0.2000
1	0.9804	0.9615	0.9434	0.9259	0.9091	0.8929	0.8772	0.8696	0.8621	0.8475	0.8333
2	1.9416	1.8861	1.8334	1.7833	1.7355	1.6901	1.6467	1.6257	1.6052	1.5656	1.5278
3	2.8839	2.7751	2.6730	2.5771	2.4869	2.4018	2.3216	2.2832	2.2459	2.1743	2.1065
4	3.8077	3.6299	3.4651	3.3121	3.1699	3.0373	2.9137	2.8550	2.7982	2.6901	2.5887
5	4.7135	4.4518	4.2124	3.9927	3.7908	3.6048	3.4331	3.3522	3.2743	3.1272	2.9906
6	5.6014	5.2421	4.9173	4.6229	4.3553	4.1114	3.8887	3.7845	3.6847	3.4976	3.3255
7	6.4720	6.0021	5.5824	5.2064	4.8684	4.5638	4.2883	4.1604	4.0386	3.8115	3.6046
8	7.3255	6.7327	6.2098	5.7466	5.3349	4.9676	4.6389	4.4873	4.3436	4.0776	3.8372
9	8.1622	7.4353	6.8017	6.2469	5.7590	5.3282	4.9464	4.7716	4.6065	4.3030	4.0310
10	8.9826	8.1109	7.3601	6.7101	6.1446	5.6502	5.2161	5.0188	4.8332	4.4941	4.1925
11	9.7868	8.7605	7.8869	7.1390	6.4951	5.9377	5.4527	5.2337	5.0286	4.6560	4.3271
12	10.5753	9.3851	8.3838	7.5361	6.8137	6.1944	5.6603	5.4206	5.1971	4.7932	4.4392
13	11.3484	9.9857	8.8527	7.9038	7.1034	6.4235	5.8424	5.5831	5.3423	4.9095	4.5327
14	12.1062	10.5631	9.2950	8.2442	7.3667	6.6282	6.0021	5.7245	5.4675	5.0081	4.6106
15	12.8493	11.1184	9.7123	8.5595	7.6061	6.8109	6.1422	5.8474	5.5755	5.0916	4.6755
16	13.5777	11.6523	10.1059	8.8514	7.8237	6.9740	6.2651	5.9542	5.6685	5.1624	4.7296
17	14.2919	12.1657	10.4773	9.1216	8.0216	7.1196	6.3729	6.0472	5.7487	5.2223	4.7746
18	14.9920	12.6593	10.8276	9.3719	8.2014	7.2497	6.4674	6.1280	5.8178	5.2732	4.8122
19	15.6785	13.1339	11.1581	9.6036	8.3649	7.3658	6.5504	6.1982	5.8775	5.3162	4.8435
20	16.3514	13.5903	11.4699	9.8182	8.5136	7.4694	6.6231	6.2593	5.9288	5.3527	4.8696
21	17.0112	14.0292	11.7641	10.0168	8.6487	7.5620	6.6870	6.3125	5.9731	5.3837	4.8913
22	17.6580	14.4511	12.0416	10.2008	8.7715	7.6446	6.7429	6.3587	6.0113	5.4099	4.9094
23	18.2922	14.8568	12.3034	10.3711	8.8832	7.7184	6.7921	6.3988	6.0442	5.4321	4.9245
24	18.9139	15.2470	12.5504	10.5288	8.9848	7.7843	6.8351	6.4338	6.0726	5.4509	4.9371
25	19.5235	15.6221	12.7834	10.6748	9.0770	7.8431	6.8729	6.4641	6.0971	5.4669	4.9476
26	20.1210	15.9828	13.0032	10.8100	9.1610	7.8957	6.9061	6.4906	6.1182	5.4804	4.9563
27	20.7069	16.3296	13.2105	10.9352	9.2372	7.9425	6.9352	6.5135	6.1364	5.4919	4.9636
28	21.2813	16.6631	13.4062	11.0511	9.3066	7.9844	6.9607	6.5335	6.1520	5.5016	4.9697
29	21.8444	16.9837	13.5907	11.1584	9.3696	8.0218	6.9830	6.5509	6.1656	5.5098	4.9747
30	22.3964	17.2920	13.7648	11.2578	9.4269	8.0552	7.0027	6.5660	6.1772	5.5168	4.9789
31	22.9377	17.5885	13.9291	11.3498	9.4790	8.0850	7.0199	6.5791	6.1872	5.5227	4.9824
32	23.4683	17.8736	14.0841	11.4350	9.5264	8.1116	7.0350	6.5905	6.1959	5.5277	4.9854
33	23.9886	18.1476	14.2302	11.5139	9.5694	8.1353	7.0482	6.6005	6.2034	5.5320	4.9878
34	24.4986	18.4112	14.3682	11.5869	9.6086	8.1566	7.0598	6.6091	6.2098	5.5356	4.9898
35	24.9986	18.6646	14.4983	11.6546	9.6442	8.1755	7.0700	6.6166	6.2153	5.5386	4.9915
36	25.4888	18.9083	14.6210	11.7172	9.6765	8.1924	7.0790	6.6231	6.2201	5.5412	4.9929
37	25.9694	19.1426	14.7368	11.7752	9.7059	8.2075	7.0868	6.6288	6.2242	5.5434	4.9941
38	26.4406	19.3679	14.8460	11.8289	9.7327	8.2210	7.0937	6.6337	6.2278	5.5452	4.9951
39	26.9026	19.5845	14.9491	11.8786	9.7570	8.2330	7.0997	6.6380	6.2309	5.5468	4.9959
40	27.3555	19.7928	15.0463	11.9246	9.7791	8.2438	7.1050	6.6418	6.2335	5.5481	4.9966

APPENDIX A-2 (continued)

Rate of Return (*r*)

YEARS (*n*)	0.2200	0.2400	0.2600	0.2800	0.3000	0.3500	0.4000	0.4500	0.5000	0.5500	0.6000
1	0.8197	0.8065	0.7937	0.7813	0.7692	0.7407	0.7143	0.6897	0.6667	0.6452	0.6250
2	1.4915	1.4568	1.4235	1.3916	1.3609	1.2894	1.2245	1.1653	1.1111	1.0614	1.0156
3	2.0422	1.9813	1.9234	1.8684	1.8161	1.6959	1.5889	1.4933	1.4074	1.3299	1.2598
4	2.4936	2.4043	2.3202	2.2410	2.1662	1.9969	1.8492	1.7195	1.6049	1.5032	1.4124
5	2.8636	2.7454	2.6351	2.5320	2.4356	2.2200	2.0352	1,8755	1.7366	1.6150	1.5077
6	3.1669	3.0205	2.8850	2.7594	2.6427	2.3852	2.1680	1.9831	1.8244	1.6871	1.5673
7	3.4155	3.2423	3.0833	2.9370	2.8021	2.5075	2.2628	2.0573	1.8829	1.7336	1.6046
8	3.6193	3.4212	3.2407	3.0758	2.9247	2.5982	2.3306	2.1085	1.9220	1.7636	1.6279
9	3.7863	3.5655	3.3657	3.1842	3.0190	2.6653	2.3790	2.1438	1.9480	1.7830	1.6424
10	3.9232	3.6819	3.4648	3.2689	3.0915	2.7150	2.4136	2.1681	1.9653	1.7955	1.6515
11	4.0354	3.7757	3.5435	3.3351	3.1473	2.7519	2.4383	2.1849	1.9769	1.8035	1.6572
12	4.1274	3.8514	3.6059	3.3868	3.1903	2.7792	2.4559	2.1965	1.9846	1.8087	1.6607
13	4.2028	3.9124	3.6555	3.4272	3.2233	2.7994	2.4685	2.2045	1.9897	1.8121	1.6630
14	4.2646	3.9616	3.6949	3.4587	3.2487	2.8144	2.4775	2.2100	1.9931	1.8142	1.6644
15	4.3152	4.0013	3.7261	3.4834	3.2682	2.8255	2.4839	2.2138	1.9954	1.8156	1.6652
16	4.3567	4.0333	3.7509	3.5026	3.2832	2.8337	2.4885	2.2164	1.9970	1.8165	1.6658
17	4.3908	4.0591	3.7705	3.5177	3.2948	2.8398	2.4918	2.2182	1.9980	1.8171	1.6661
18	4.4187	4.0799	3.7861	3.5294	3.3037	2.8443	2.4941	2.2195	1.9986	1.8175	1.6663
19	4.4415	4.0967	3.7985	3.5386	3.3105	2.8476	2.4958	2.2203	1.9991	1.8177	1.6664
20	4.4603	4.1103	3.8083	3.5458	3.3158	2.8501	2.4970	2.2209	1.9994	1.8179	1.6665
21	4.4756	4.1212	3.8161	3.5514	3.3198	2.8519	2.4979	2.2213	1.9996	1.8180	1.6666
22	4.4882	4.1300	3.8223	3.5558	3.3230	2.8533	2.4985	2,2216	1.9997	1.8181	1.6666
23	4.4985	4.1371	3.8273	3.5592	3.3254	2.8543	2.4989	2.2218	1.9998	1.8181	1.6666
24	4.5070	4.1428	3.8312	3.5619	3.3272	2.8550	2.4992	2.2219	1.9999	1.8181	1.6666
25	4.5139	4.1474	3.8342	3.5640	3.3286	2.8556	2.4994	2.2220	1.9999	1.8181	1.6667
26	4.5196	4.1511	3.8367	3.5656	3.3297	2.8560	2.4996	2.2221	1.9999	1.8182	1.6667
27	4.5243	4.1542	3.8387	3.5669	3.3305	2.8563	2.4997	2.2221	2.0000	1.8182	1.6667
28	4.5281	4.1566	3.8402	3.5679	3.3312	2.8565	2.4998	2.2222	2.0000	1.8182	1.6667
29	4.5312	4.1585	3.8414	3.5687	3.3317	2.8567	2.4999	2.2222	2.0000	1.8182	1.6667
30	4.5338	4.1601	3.8424	3.5693	3.3321	2.8568	2.4999	2.2222	2.0000	1.8182	1.6667
31	4.5359	4.1614	3.8432	3.5697	3.3324	2.8569	2.4999	2.2222	2.0000	1.8182	1.6667
32	4.5376	4.1624	3.8438	3.5701	3.3326	2.8569	2.4999	2.2222	2.0000	1.8182	1.6667
33	4.5390	4.1632	3.8443	3.5704	3.3328	2.8570	2.5000	2.2222	2.0000	1.8182	1.6667
34	4.5402	4.1639	3.8447	3.5706	3.3329	2.8570	2.5000	2.2222	2.0000	1.8182	1.6667
35	4.5411	4.1644	3.8450	3.5708	3.3330	2.8571	2.5000	2.2222	2.0000	1.8182	1.6667
36	4.5419	4.1649	3.8452	3.5709	3.3331	2.8571	2.5000	2.2222	2.0000	1.8182	1.6667
37	4.5426	4.1652	3.8454	3.5710	3.3331	2.8571	2.5000	2.2222	2.0000	1.8182	1.6667
38	4.5431	4.1655	3.8456	3.5711	3.3332	2.8571	2.5000	2.2222	2.0000	1.8182	1.6667
39	4.5435	4.1657	3.8457	3.5712	3.3332	2.8571	2.5000	2.2222	2.0000	1.8182	1.6667
40	4.5439	4.1659	3.8458	3.5712	3.3332	2.8571	2.5000	2.2222	2.0000	1.8182	1.6667

7

Analysis of Growth Potential: Economy

An analysis of the growth of the economy, both past and projected, is of fundamental importance to the investor. The expected growth of the economy has ramifications for both bond and stock investing. Interest rate movements are closely tied to the growth of the economy. High interest rates normally occur during boom periods, while lower interest rates are more often associated with low or negative rates of growth in the economy. The level of market interest rates is a primary determinant of bond prices for any given quality bond.

Common stock prices are closely associated with the expected rate of growth in the economy. It is, of course, necessary to relate the growth rate of the whole economy to specific industries and then to specific companies within an industry. Chapter 8 will discuss the growth potential for specific industries. Chapter 9 will look at the manner in which an investor analyzes the growth prospects of a specific company. One can see the significance of the growth by recalling the following equation developed in Chapter 6:

$$P_0 = \frac{D_0}{r - g}$$

where: P_0 = the value of the stock
D_0 = the current dividend
r = the rate of return desired
g = the expected rate of growth of dividends

Assume that a stock pays a dividend of $2 per share and that the investor desires a 10 percent rate of return. Given a 5 percent growth of dividends, our hypothetical stock should sell for $40 per share calculated as follows:

$$P_0 = \frac{\$2}{.10 - .05} = \$40.00$$

If no future dividend growth can be expected, the price of the stock would decline to $20 per share as indicated below:

$$P_0 = \frac{\$2}{.10 - 0} = \$20.00$$

This chapter first examines past growth rates for several of the more important economic variables in order to arrive at some reasonable expectation regarding future growth rates. Next, the relationship between business cycles and the stock market is discussed.

Following this historical review of major economic variables and their relationship to stock market movements, some of the more important economic and demographic factors are analyzed for their investment ramifications. These factors include the current population and its age distribution, the role of the government in fostering economic growth, and the behavior of corporations with regard to expenditures on plant, equipment, and inventories.

The last section in this chapter looks at recent long-term projections of the economy. In forecasting the long-term future of the U.S. economy, many noneconomic factors are exceedingly important. The final point examined is the role of these noneconomic considerations.

PAST ECONOMIC GROWTH TRENDS

GNP and Industrial Production

Figure 7-1 shows inflation-adjusted Gross National Product (GNP) from 1889 to 1974. GNP is the dollar value of all final goods and services produced in the economy. While the long-term growth rate of the econ-

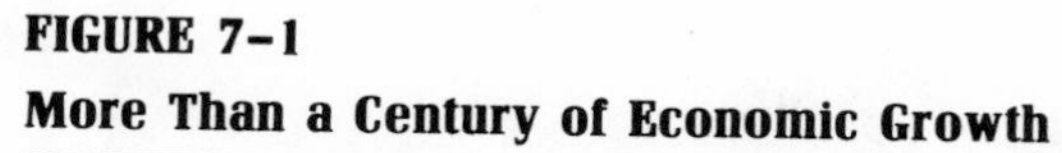

FIGURE 7–1
More Than a Century of Economic Growth

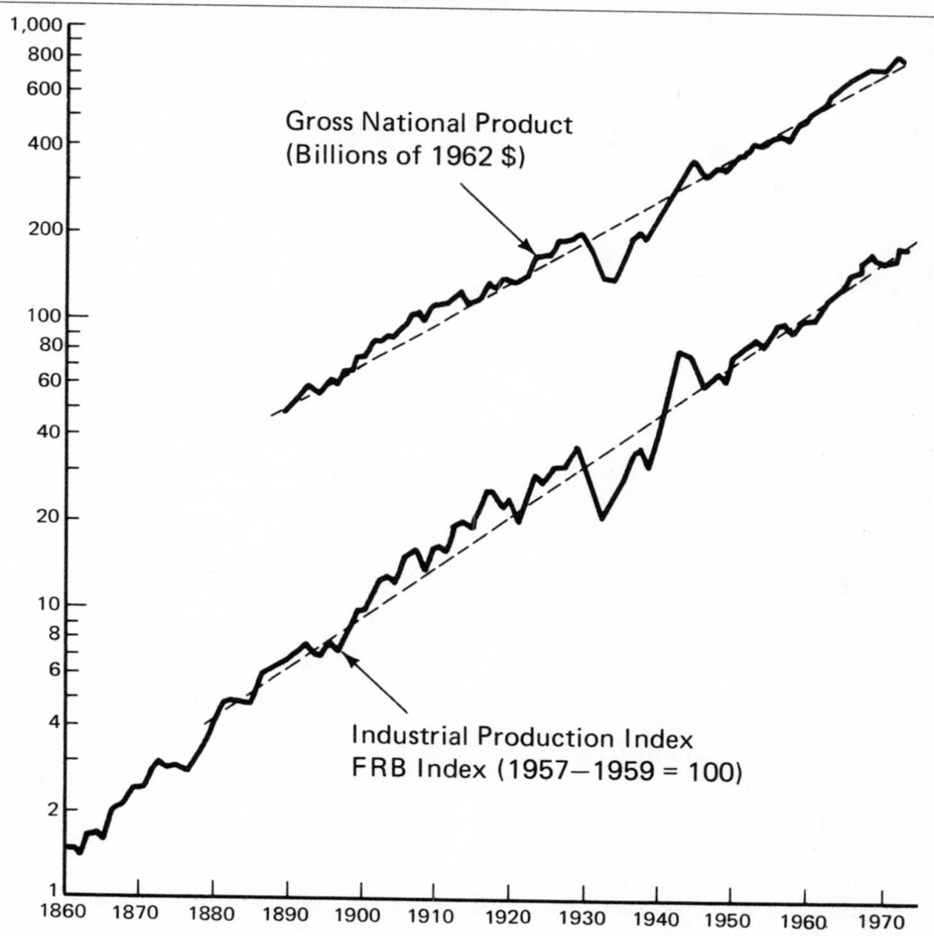

Source: David H. McKinley, et al., *Forecasting Business Conditions*, New York: American Bankers Association, 1965, p. 16. Updated using Department of Commerce data.

omy as measured by the GNP series has been in the neighborhood of 3.5 percent, this growth has been somewhat erratic.

Table 7-1 contains a breakdown of the GNP rates of growth for the economy from 1840 to 1973. With the exception of the decades of 1860–69 and 1930–39, the growth of the economy over ten-year periods has been at a fairly consistent rate, fluctuating in a range of 2.6 percent to 4.95 percent per year.

The Index of Industrial Production is also shown in Figure 7-1. This index covers the period from 1860 to 1974. While this index has

TABLE 7–1
GNP Growth, 1840 to 1973, Percent per Year

1840 to 1960 3.56%	1840 to 1880 4.03%	1840s	4.24%
		1850s	4.95
		1860s	1.99
		1870s	4.95
	1880 to 1920 3.52%	1880s	3.73
		1890s	4.04
		1900s	3.71
		1910s	2.60
	1920 to 1960 3.15%	1920s	3.99
		1930s	1.37
		1940s	4.27
		1950s	3.24
		1959/61 to 1971/73	4.01

Sources: Simon Kuznets, *Economic Growth and Structure* (New York: W. W. Norton & Co., 1965), p. 305, and U. S. Department of Commerce, *Survey of Current Business*, various issues.

the same general growth trends as the GNP series, its fluctuations are more pronounced. This greater volatility of industrial production relative to GNP will probably continue in future years as relatively stable service activities, which are included in GNP but not in industrial production, become more important.

In summary, the past growth of the economy adjusted for changes in the price level has averaged about 3.5 percent per year. Since this historical record covers more than a century, it serves as a benchmark for future growth projections. A long-term growth expectation for the economy of at least 3 percent appears to be indicated by past trends. Nevertheless, future growth projections must consider past trends as only a starting point. The contemporary energy situation demonstrates the problems of blind historical projections.

Unemployment and Inflation

The Employment Act of 1946 established "full" employment as one of the goals of federal government policy. While Congress did not define "full" employment, economists have often thought in terms of 4 percent unemployed. With the federal government committed to keeping the unemployment level "low" by stimulating economic growth when necessary, the post-World War II record of the economy is of special concern to contemporary investors.

FIGURE 7-2
Unemployment Rate, 1948-74

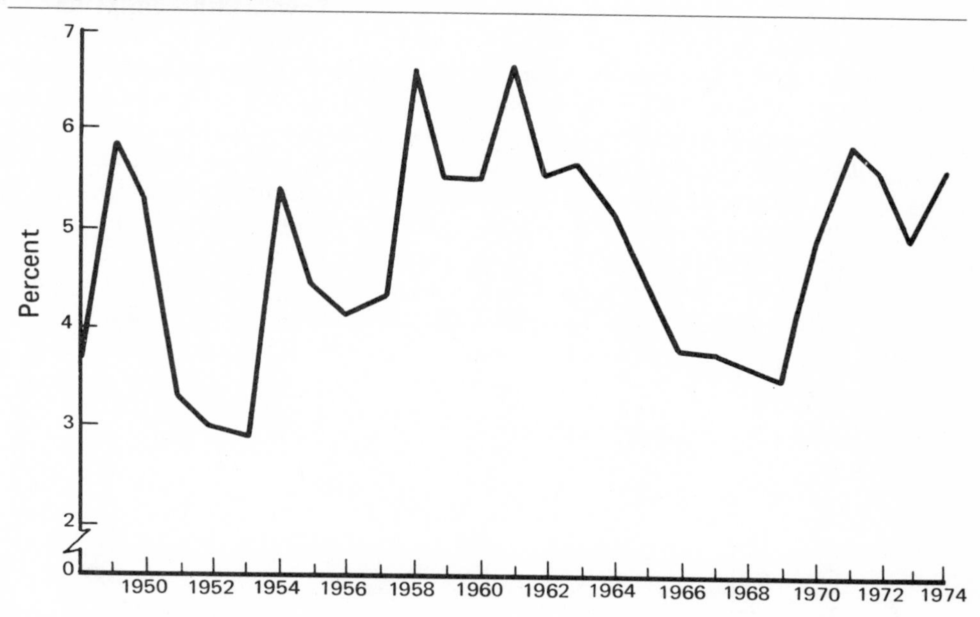

Source: U.S. Department of Commerce, *Survey of Current Business*, various issues.

Figure 7-2 shows the unemployment rate from 1948 to 1974. While 4 percent has represented an unofficial target for the unemployment rate, some economists are now arguing that a figure closer to 5 percent is more reasonable.[1] Their reasoning is that structural changes related to the age, sex, and education of the labor force have taken place within the economy. Later in this chapter we will examine those structural changes. For now, we should recognize that as the economy approaches full employment, the rate of inflation typically increases. The inverse relationship between unemployment and inflation is far from perfect, but nevertheless a pattern exists. Thus, as the economy approaches full employment, however defined, the investor can typically expect more rapid rates of inflation. As we saw in Chapter 6, inflation is the source of purchasing power risk. High rates of inflation may result in high interest rates, causing bond values to decrease. High inflation rates also tend to be associated with short-term difficulties in the stock market.

Inflation is also critical in that uncertainty regarding future rates of inflation may cause people to alter their consumption habits. The public may decide to spend more and save less because of higher rates

[1]"Can the U.S. Bring Unemployment Down to 4 percent?" *Business Week*, November 17, 1973, p. 48.

of inflation. This action may tend to reduce total capital formation and thereby markedly slow economic growth. People may also need to reorder their spending priorities. This may have a differential impact on various industries. During 1973 and 1974, for example, increases in the price of food required American consumers to spend a greater percentage of their income for food. The result of the increased spending for food may be a decline in the purchase of items such as cars, televisions, and stereos. Since consumers may feel that they are not able to maintain their standard of living, indexes of consumer sentiment turn pessimistic and may foreshadow a recession. In early 1974 consumer sentiment was clearly forecasting the 1974–75 recession.[2]

Figure 7-3 shows the history of the U.S. consumer price index (CPI) from 1913 to 1974. The CPI started to increase about 1965 at a faster

FIGURE 7-3
Consumer Price Index, 1913-74

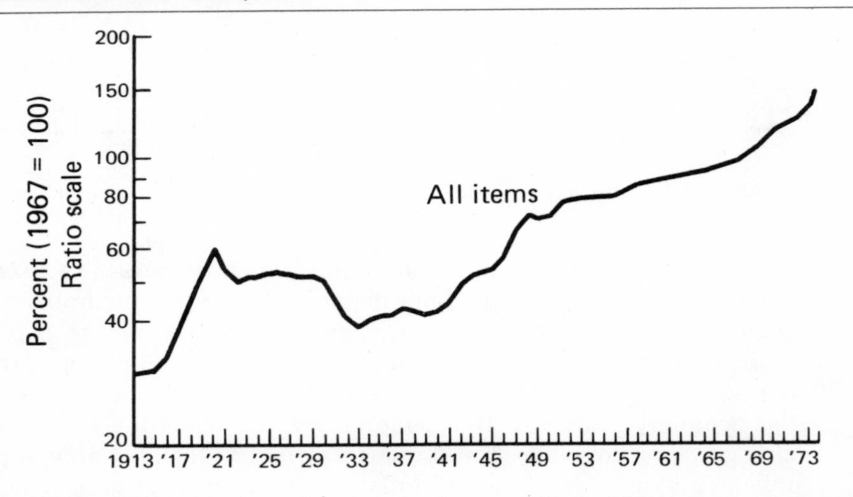

Source: U.S. Department of Commerce, *Survey of Current Business*, various issues.

rate than that observed in the prior fifteen years. The relatively poor performance of stocks and bonds since 1965 can probably be traced to a considerable extent to these more rapid rates of inflation. It should be emphasized that the poor performance is probably not caused by inflation per se. Over long periods of time the growth in stock prices has been more than sufficient to compensate the investor for the rate of inflation. Stock market declines are probably more closely associated

[2]Lawrence G. O'Donnell, "Consumer Poll Shows the Most Pessimism in at Least 22 Years," *Wall Street Journal*, April 5, 1974, p. 14.

with an increasing rate of inflation. In other words, it is the *change* in the rate of inflation that is most directly associated with poor performance in the stock market.

Income—Corporate and Personal

Income at both the corporate and personal level is a significant factor in any investment evaluation of the economy. Corporate income is important since it is the fundamental determinant of the level of stock prices. The growth of personal income is the main determinant of the level of corporate profits. A rising level of personal income tends to produce increased sales and increased profits.

The general rise in the level of corporate profits since World War II is shown in Figure 7–4. Corporate profits after taxes reached a plateau during the late 1960s and early 1970s. In fact, after-tax corporate profits were virtually unchanged from 1968 to 1971. It is not surprising that common stock prices did poorly during this same period. The dividend model suggests a close relationship between market prices and earnings growth. Moreover, Henry Latané and Donald Tuttle have found a high correlation (.829) between growth in market price and the growth in earnings.[3] Therefore, it behooves the investor to consider carefully the future growth of corporate profits.

BUSINESS CYCLES AND STOCK MARKET CYCLES

The relationship between per capita personal income and various business cycle indicators such as GNP, industrial production, and corporate profits, is a general one that exists on the average but may be quite unreliable in specific instances. Stock prices are often more volatile than a general economic series such as GNP. Moreover, stock prices and economic indicators do not always move in the same direction, as Figure 6–1 shows, and often the stock market is a leading indicator of the economy. Some wags have gone so far as to suggest that the stock market has predicted at least *eleven* out of the *five* post-World War II recessions!

We previously observed that industrial production fluctuates more than GNP, since the relatively stable service component of GNP is not included in the industrial production series. Figure 7–5 plots the seasonally adjusted Index of Industrial Production against the Standard & Poor 425 Industrial Stock Average starting with 1947. Notice the way in which these two series parallel each other. Industrial production, quite naturally, is fundamental to the movement of stocks classified as industrials.

[3]Henry A. Latáne and Donald L. Tuttle, "Framework for Forming Probability Beliefs," *Financial Analysts Journal*, July–August 1968, p. 56.

FIGURE 7-4
Corporate Income before and after Taxes, 1945-74

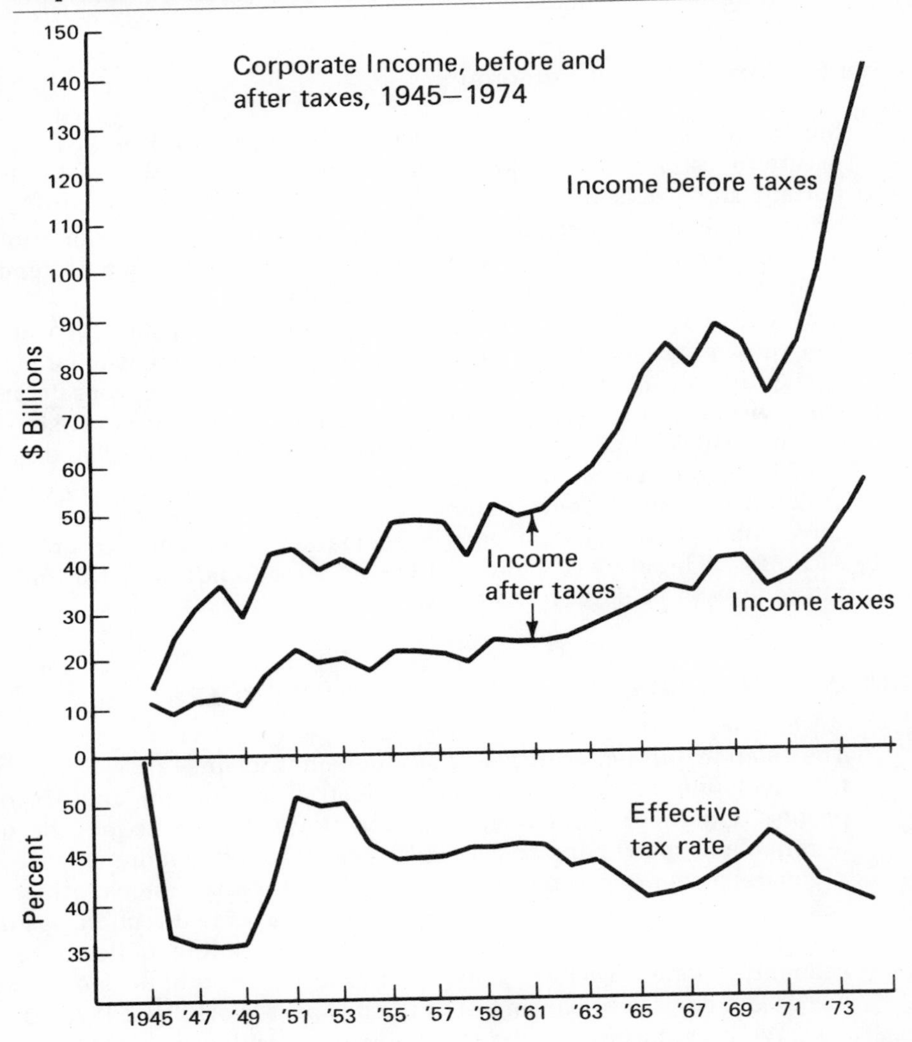

Source: U.S. Department of Commerce, *Survey of Current Business*, various issues.

But Figure 7-5 demonstrates that industrial production is likely to change direction *after* the beginning of a stock market move. The best example of the stock market leading industrial production was in 1970, as Figure 7-5 indicates. The worst example occurred in 1962 when stock prices declined approximately 12 percent without a corresponding decline in industrial production. Stock price movements predicted a recession which did not occur!

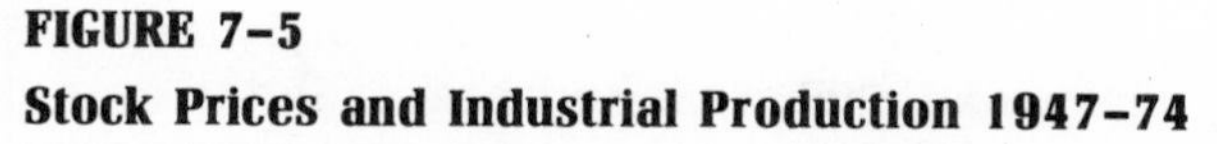

FIGURE 7–5
Stock Prices and Industrial Production 1947–74

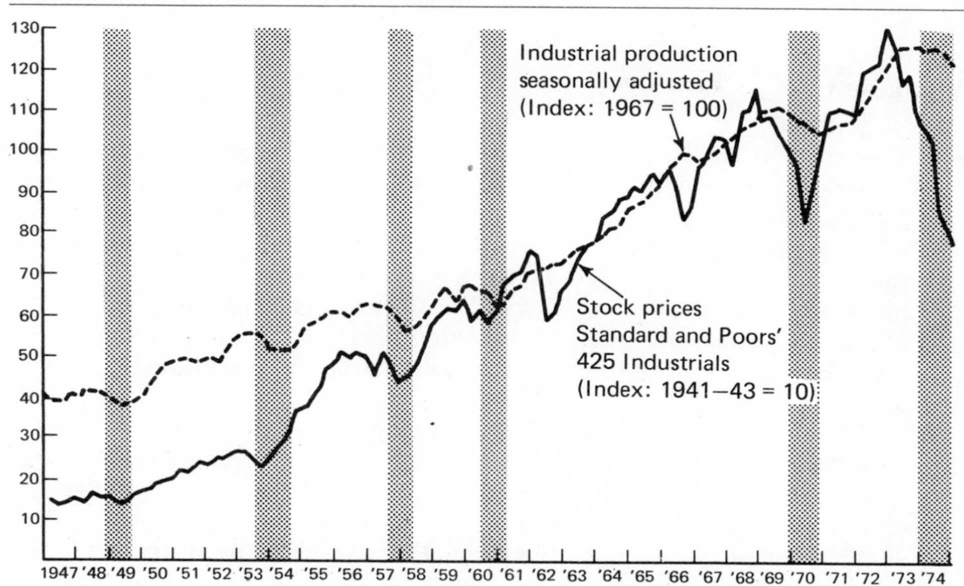

Notes: Shaded areas represent periods of business recession; data are quarterly averages.
Source: *Federal Reserve Bulletin,* various issues.

Much research has taken place in recent years in attempting to forecast stock prices using highly sophisticated analysis of economic and financial forces in the economy. Econometric models have been constructed to analyze such factors as the rate of inflation, the availability of credit, the growth of the money supply, and the overall level of economic activity. At the conclusion of this chapter, we shall see what some of these mathematical forecasting models foretell for the U.S. economy in the next few years.

ANALYSIS OF MAJOR ECONOMIC AND DEMOGRAPHIC FACTORS

Is the population bomb being defused? If so, what ramifications does this have for the investor? Will certain industries benefit from a slower rate of population growth while others are injured? These questions indicate the vital significance population data have for the investor.

This section examines the structure of the U.S. population and its projected growth. Following this, several other economic variables are analyzed for their importance to the investor. These include the importance of changes in the money supply, changes in fiscal policy, capital expenditures, and the significance of changes in inventories in the economy.

Population

The investor should be aware of important developments in the areas of population growth and its distribution. The three panels in Figure 7-6 show selected population statistics. Panel one shows the birth rate per 1,000 population since 1950. The growth in the U.S. population is forecast in panel two, assuming a replacement fertility level of 2.11 births per 1,000 women at completion of child-bearing, and net immigration of 400,000 people per year. Panel three projects the age distribution of the U.S. population in the year 2,000, assuming the replacement fertility level.

The birth rate has declined markedly since the late 1950s. During that decade, the birth rate per 1,000 population averaged 24.9 and was quite stable throughout the decade.[4] Since 1957, the birth rate has declined every year except 1969 and 1970, when the birth rate showed slight increases. Even with the dramatic decline in the birth rate since the "baby boom" of the fifties, panel two shows that the population will continue to grow until about 2040 before zero population growth is reached. This phenomenon is explained by examining the distribution of the population.

Using Census Department Series E population estimates (replacement fertility level assumption), the percentage of the population in the 25 to 44 year age group will grow from 24 percent in 1970 to 31 percent in 1990. A higher percentage of the women in the U.S. will be in the prime child-bearing years so that the actual number of births may show an increase even with a decline in the birth rate.

Panel three in Figure 7-6 illustrates the changing population structure as indicated by the series E forecast for the year 2000. The median age is estimated to increase from 28.1 years to 34.0 years. Since the population will be getting progressively middle-aged, the management of any company will need to adapt to this changing age distribution. Johnson & Johnson, for example, has recently been advertising its baby shampoo as being great for adults.

In addition to a rise in the median age, a large increase in the 30 to 44 year age group can be seen from panel three. The percentage of people in the 45 to 64 year group will also increase somewhat. Stated another way, a larger percentage of our population will be in the labor force. This is especially true when one considers the increasing participation of women in the labor force. The economy will have to grow

[4]"The Stork Takes a Nose Dive," *Business Week*, March 2, 1968, p. 30.

FIGURE 7–6

Selected Population Statistics

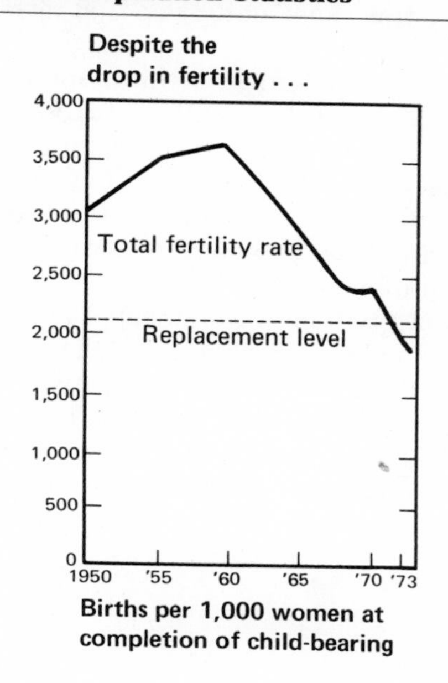

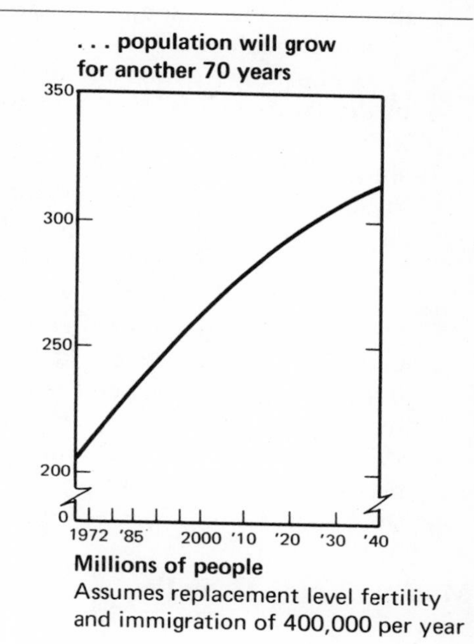

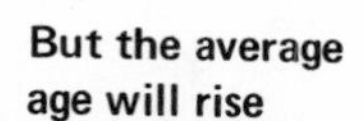

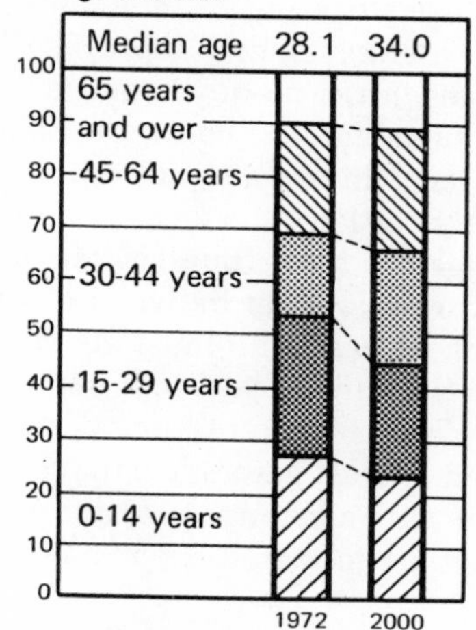

Source: Reprinted from the December 15, 1973 issue of *Business Week* by special permission.

at a fairly rapid rate in future years just to provide employment for new entrants into the labor force. The federal government will more than likely play a major role in stimulating the economy so that needed jobs are created.

The large, expected increase in the percentage of the population in the 30 to 44 year age bracket has profound implications for various industries as well as for the entire economy. This age group is important since it falls shortly after the prime years of family formation. It is during these years that families spend heavily for housing, consumer durables such as furniture and automobiles, and for many expensive luxury items such as vacations and recreational equipment.

Because the 30 to 44 year age group will be well-educated and will probably be having smaller families, per capita income for the family unit should increase markedly. This development should provide the impetus for continued and relatively sustained growth in the years ahead. In short, a much higher standard of living per person should result. While a lower birth rate may be detrimental to specific industries, the economy should prosper.

Money Supply Growth

The relationship between changes in the money supply and stock prices has been the subject of considerable research and debate in recent years.[5] Can one forecast future stock prices by examining current money statistics? How does one define money supply? This section examines the importance of changes in the money supply. However, although considerable research has been conducted on the relationship between money supply and stock prices, the nature and specification of any relationship is still not completely settled.

Several investigators have found what they believe to be the existence of a long-term relationship between changes in the money supply and changes in stock prices. The most generally accepted definition of the money supply is the sum of time and demand deposits at commercial banks, and currency held by the public. Often, the money supply series is seasonally adjusted. Investigators feel that changes in the money supply are an important factor in changes in the general level of prices and corporate income, which in turn exert a major influence on stock prices.

[5]Beryl Sprinkel, *Money and Stock Prices* (Homewood, Illinois: Richard D. Irwin, 1964; Beryl Sprinkel, *Money and Markets,* Homewood, Ill.: Richard D. Irwin, 1971; Richard V.L. Cooper, "Efficient Capital Markets and the Quantity Theory of Money," *Journal of Finance,* June 1974, pp. 887–908; K. E. Homa and D. M. Jaffee, "The Supply of Money and Common Stock Prices," *Journal of Finance,* December 1971, pp. 1045–66; M. Palmer, "Money Supply, Portfolio Adjustments and Stock Prices," *Financial Analysts Journal,* July–August 1970, pp. 19–21; and James E. Pesando, "The Supply of Money and Common Stock Prices: Further Observations on the Econometric Evidence," *Journal of Finance,* June 1974, pp. 909–21.

Beryl Sprinkel has written two books discussing the relationship between changes in the rate of growth of the money supply and stock prices.[6] In *Money and Markets,* he argues that stock prices lead business cycle peaks by an average of five to six months. In addition, growth in the money supply leads business cycle peaks by fifteen to sixteen months, on the average. After conducting a similar study of cyclical downturns, Sprinkel concludes that "changes in monetary growth lead changes in stock prices by an average of about nine months prior to a bear market and by about two or three months prior to bull markets."[7]

Sprinkel also looks at the long-term application of stock market decisions based upon an examination of changing money supply growth. From 1918 to 1970, he maintains, the investor "would have participated in all bull markets" but "would have avoided most bear markets."[8] In recent years, however, it would have been critical for the investor to recognize a reduction of the lead time of monetary changes compared to stock prices for bear market periods. We should note, however, that a recently published study questions the relationship between money and stock prices. The conclusion of this study is that the relationship is weak and if one exists it is more likely that the stock market leads the money supply![9] The money supply is important but the specific relationship remains open to question.

In another study, Michael Keran examines the indirect impact of money supply changes by investigating the theory that stock prices will be determined by the present value of expected future profits as adjusted for inflation.[10] Looking at expected corporate earnings and expected inflation rates, Keran found that expected corporate profits rise with increases in the expected rate of inflation. However, higher inflationary expectations also cause investors to use a higher discount rate for the expected profits. Expected profits and inflation rates were based upon an examination of past and current trends.

Using a computer simulation of historical money supply statistics to verify hypothetical forecasts of stock prices for the 1956 to 1970 period, Keran obtained predicted prices which were closely correlated with actual prices. However, for several reasons care must be observed in the actual application of a study of this type by the investor. First, the investor may still purchase an individual security that does not perform like the market. In Chapter 13, we shall see that this objection becomes less relevant if the investor undertakes a minimum amount of diversification. Second, tax changes may not be correctly accounted for by using

[6]Sprinkel, *Money and Stock Prices* and *Money and Markets.*

[7]Sprinkel, *Money and Markets,* p. 221. A bull market is a rising market and a bear market is a falling market.

[8]*Ibid.,* p. 25.

[9]Michael S. Rozeff, "Money and Stock Prices: Market Efficiency and the Lag in Effect of Monetary Policy," *Journal of Financial Economics,* September 1974, pp. 245–302

[10]Michael Keran, "Expectations, Money and the Stock Market," *Federal Reserve Bank of St. Louis Review,* January 1971, pp. 16–31.

money supply data. Perhaps the most important objection to using money supply data in forecasting stock prices is that other factors may be of great importance. The political risk discussed in Chapter 6, as evidenced by such events as the 1973–74 Arab oil boycott and Watergate, is an important other factor. Money matters, but it may not be the only thing that matters.

Fiscal Policy

Fiscal policy is the way the government handles its finances. The revenue side of fiscal policy has mainly to do with taxation by the federal government. The expenditure aspects of fiscal policy have to do with actions taken by the federal government to increase or reduce expenditures. Both of these aspects are important to the investor, but it is not always possible to separate them. In this section, several instances of fiscal policy important to the investor are discussed, although anything approaching a comprehensive analysis of the implications of federal, state, and local budgets is beyond the scope of this book.

In 1929, state, local, and federal purchases of goods and services amounted to $8.5 billion, or 8.2 percent of GNP. By 1972, these purchases amounted to $254.8 billion, or 22.1 percent of GNP. With government now commanding over 20 percent of GNP, changes in governmental spending can have profound economic consequences. Since spending by state and local government has been rising at a rate which is both quite rapid and quite predictable, it becomes especially important to examine spending at the federal level.

Three instances of tax policy at the federal level will illustrate the importance of this variable for the investor. To help stimulate an economy which had recently gone through two recessions (1958 and 1960–61), President Kennedy urged in 1962 that taxes be cut in order to provide more spending power to American taxpayers. The growing expenditures of the federal government would be financed by deficit financing. The Revenue Act of 1962 substantially lowered taxes for many taxpayers and, as Figure 7–2 reveals, unemployment steadily declined from slightly over 5.5 percent in 1962 to approximately 3.5 percent in 1968. These years were also generally good years for investors in common stocks. In early 1975, a $23 billion tax cut was passed to stimulate the economy and to help to offset the impact of inflation on the average taxpayer. Will history repeat itself in this regard?

Another important piece of tax legislation provided for the establishment of a 7 percent investment tax credit starting in 1962.[11] This law helped to stimulate spending for new machinery since it was equiva-

[11]Only 4% for utilities.

lent to a 7 percent decline in the price of a new machine. For the purchase of a $100,000 machine qualifying for the investment tax credit, the corporation could reduce its tax bill by $7,000.[12]

Not only did the investment tax credit tend to increase the income of corporations, but it also served to stimulate expenditures for more modern equipment. This capital spending, in turn, created new jobs and helped to increase the productivity of workers. While Figure 7-7 shows that the investment credit has been taken off and reinstated twice since its original passage in 1962, the trend of expenditures on producers' durable equipment has been clearly upward.

FIGURE 7-7

Plant and Equipment Expenditures and Investment Tax Credit

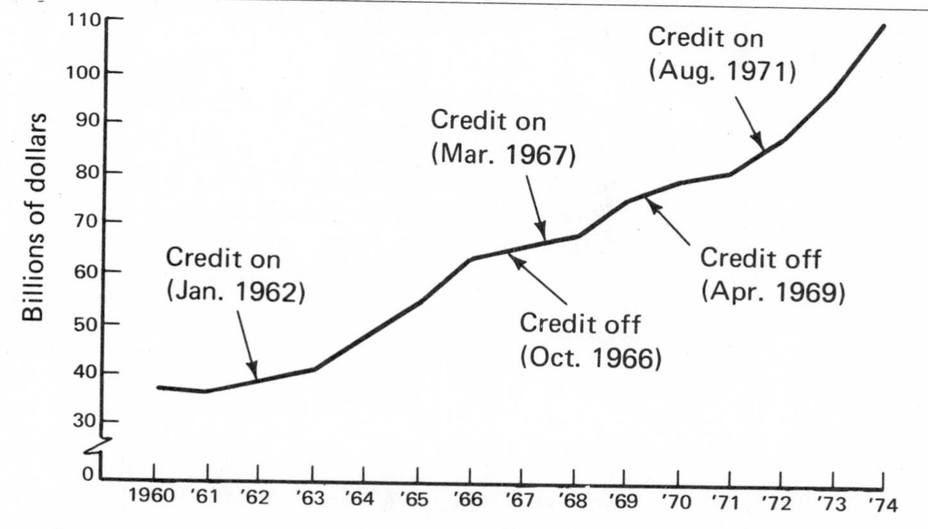

Source: U.S. Commerce Department, *Survey of Current Business*, various issues.

A final illustration of action at the fiscal policy level shows the importance of governmental action to the economy. In April 1970, Social Security pensioners received a 15 percent increase in their benefits. Rather than raise the payroll tax immediately to pay for this increase, the tax increase was postponed until January 1971. This gave a stimulus to a stagnant economy by increasing the spendable income of Social Security recipients, while not immediately decreasing the spendable income of workers contributing to the Social Security System.

[12]Until 1964, depreciation of only $93,000 allowed.

Capital Expenditures

As we observed in the preceding section, government has been concerned with the level of spending for plant and equipment, since this is a powerful economic stimulant. Huge sums of money must be spent just to replace and modernize obsolete equipment. As the economy benefits from ever higher levels of technology, our stock of capital goods becomes both larger and shorter lived.

Our growing population requires substantial increases in productive capacity. To provide jobs for the growing American labor force, U.S. industry will be required to make huge expenditures for research and development and for capital equipment. Any decline in capital expenditures planned by business during any future period could signal a forthcoming recession. The 1974–75 recession was in part the result of a decline in the rate of growth of capital expenditures.

Inventories

The last major economic variable to be considered is the level of inventories in the economy. *Forecasting Business Conditions* describes the role of inventories in the following fashion:

> Inventory investment is one of the bad actors in the business cycle. It has been by far the most unstable of the various categories of spending. Fluctuations in inventory investment were the prime factor in the minor recessions of 1924 and 1927. They played a dominant role in the business pickup of 1936–1937 and the 1937 collapse. The four modest recessions which we have had since World War II have often been referred to as "inventory adjustments."[13]

Businessmen plan their inventories in light of anticipated sales. If these sales do not materialize, it is necessary to reduce inventories to a level consistent with the actual sales volume. In 1974, the automobile industry engaged in such an inventory adjustment as the energy crisis, coupled with a recession, caused a substantial decrease in the sale of cars—especially large ones. The reduction of inventories caused numerous layoffs by the major automobile producers. The inventory adjustments continued into 1975, as evidenced by the rebate plans of that year.

Since inventories for the total economy are large, small changes in the rate of inventory change may cause important adjustments in the economy. At year-end 1974, manufacturing and trade inventories at book

[13]David H. McKinley et al., *Forecasting Business Conditions* (New York; American Bankers Association), p. 73.

value were estimated at $269.2 billion. If, instead of adding to inventories at a 3 percent annual rate, businessmen decide not to increase their inventories, the result is a reduction of spending for inventories of $8.1 billion.

The investor can follow statistics which tend to indicate whether or not the level of inventories is satisfactory. Inventories need to be related to sales, since a given level of inventories may be reasonable at one level of sales and imprudent at a lower level of sales. Figure 7-8 shows the ratio of inventories to sales, a widely followed yardstick,

FIGURE 7-8
Manufacturing and Trade Inventories Sales Ratios, 1955-74

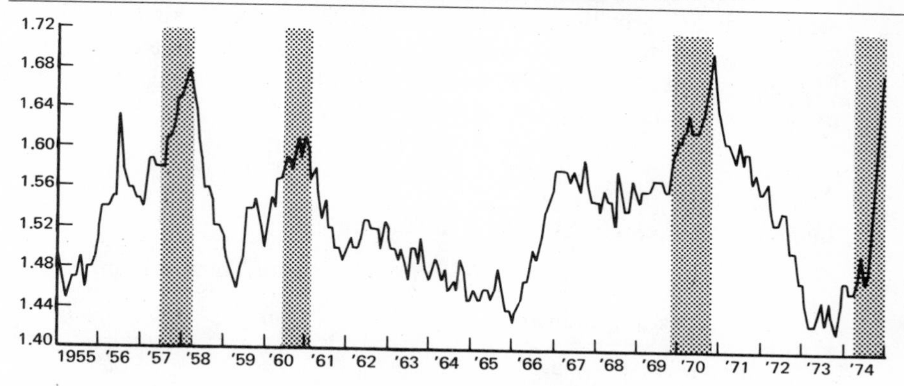

Note: Shaded areas represent periods of business recession.
Source: U.S. Department of Commerce, *Survey of Current Business*, various issues.

for the 1955 to 1974 period. The normal behavior of the inventory series is to decline during the early years of a prosperous period and to start to increase a year or so prior to the start of a recession. It is no wonder that investors monitor closely the rate of change in inventory investment.

LEADING, LAGGING, AND COINCIDENT INDICATORS

The behavior of the inventory series characterizes it as a leading indicator of the business cycle. Other statistical series have shown a tendency either to follow closely the business cycle or to lag behind the pace of business activity. These indicators are known respectively as roughly coincident and lagging indicators.

Over the years, the National Bureau of Economic Research (NBER) has conducted numerous studies on the behavior of various indicators of the business cycle. Many statistical series have been classified by the NBER as either leading, lagging, or roughly coincident and these series are charted monthly in *Business Conditions Digest*, published by the U.S. Department of Commerce.

Unfortunately, these various indicators do not always act in a similar fashion over each business cycle. Not only may the lead and lag times vary but indicators which normally lead the economy may become roughly coincident or lagging indicators during any particular business cycle.

Despite these problems of classification and the additional task of trying to ascertain whether an indicator is really moving up or down at any given moment, the study of business conditions as revealed by business cycle indicators may be a rewarding activity for the investor. Since investors are especially concerned with the trend of future business activity, leading indicators should be followed with special care. Table 7-2 lists some of the more important and widely followed leading indicators along with an approximation of their average lead times for both peaks and troughs in past business activity.

TABLE 7-2

Lead Times—Selected Leading Indicators

	Lead Time in Months	
Leading Indicators	Peaks	Troughs
Industrial stock prices	4	4
New orders, durable manufactured goods	8	2
Housing permits	13	5
Average work week, manufacturing	6	4
Change in consumer installment debt	12	4
Industrial raw material prices	6	0
Change in manufacturing and trade inventories	14	6
Corporate profits after taxes	6	2

Source: Beryl Sprinkel, *Money and Markets* (Homewood, Ill.: Richard D. Irwin, 1971), p. 138.

PROJECTIONS OF FUTURE ECONOMIC GROWTH

Many efforts have been made to predict the growth of the American economy for long periods of time. This section examines some of these efforts as they pertain to the investor. In the next chapter, these studies are examined more closely to determine the impact of expected growth on specific industries.

In 1970, two studies were conducted which produced remarkably similar forecasts.[14] One study forecast the state of the economy in 1980, while the second study forecast the economy until 1985. These two studies are summarized below:

	GE Study	*McGraw-Hill Study*
Growth in GNP adjusted for inflation—per annum	4–4½%	3.9%
Unemployment rate	4% (in 1980)	4½% (annual average)
Rate of Inflation—yearly	3%	3%

Perhaps the most interesting forecast of the American economy occurred in conjunction with the White House Conference on the Industrial World Ahead, held in Washington D.C. during February 7–9, 1972. In the summary of this conference, *A Look at Business in 1990,* the Conference Board presented material dealing with the outlook for the U.S. economy to the year 1990.[15] Figure 7–9 reproduces material presented at the conference dealing with the level of employment, the pace of economic growth, and the utilization of labor. Other general conclusions are summarized below:

GNP expressed in 1971 prices will total more than $2.4 trillion by 1990—a yearly increase of 4.2 percent.

Labor productivity will increase 3.0 percent annually during the 1970s and 3.4 percent annually during the 1980s.

Inflation will probably average 3.75 percent annually until 1990 with a moderate estimate being 3.0 percent per year and a high estimate being 4.5 percent per year.

Social Indicators of Economic Growth

Thus far in this chapter, we have been concerned only with economic considerations. Is not the quality of life of any concern to forecasters? Does the fact that GNP is expected to rise at 4 percent per year mean happiness?

Many individuals feel consideration should be given to statistics in the social area.[16] Without going into great detail, several likely mea-

[14]Earl B. Dunckel, William K. Reed, and Ian H. Wilson, *The Business Environment of the Seventies* (New York: McGraw-Hill, 1970) (GE Study). For a summary of a McGraw-Hill study conducted by the McGraw-Hill Economics Department, see *Business Week*, December 18, 1971, pp. 84–85.

[15]*A Look at Business in 1990* (Washington D.C.: U.S. Government Printing Office, November 1972), pp. 45–73.

[16]For example, see "Adam Smith," *Supermoney* (New York: Random House, 1972), p. 266, and Frederick Andrews, "Government Statistics are Termed Misleading as Gauges of Society," *Wall Street Journal*, December 16, 1971, p. 1.

sures can be suggested. These are data dealing with the level of education, the extent of air pollution, suicide and divorce rates, and statistical measures of congestion per given area of land. Even these statistics are only an indirect proxy for the general well-being of the population.

FIGURE 7-9
Forecasts of Selected Economic Factors

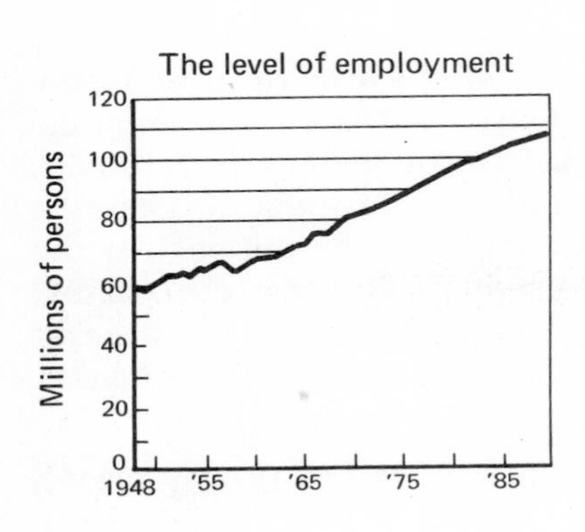

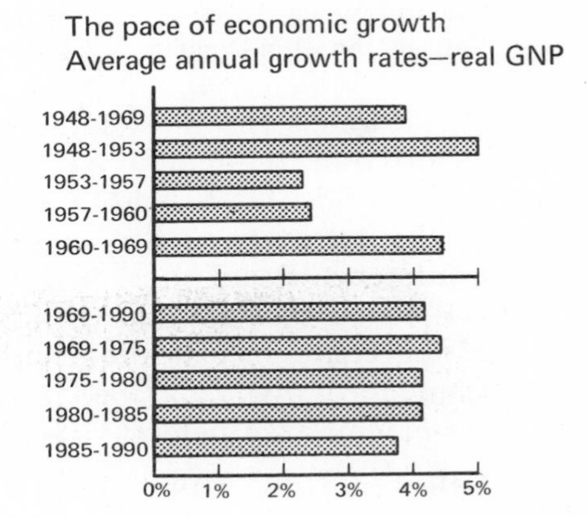

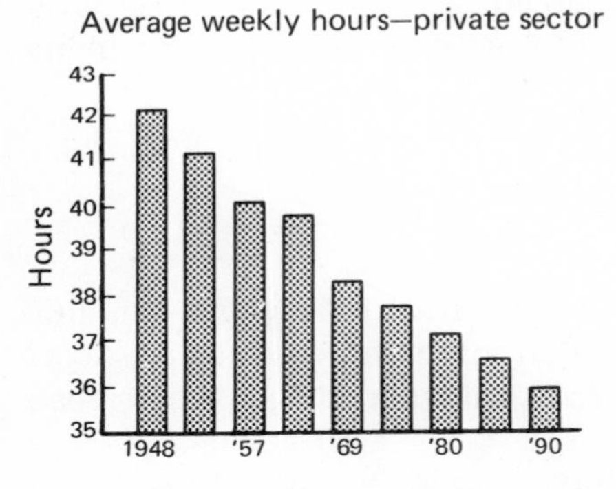

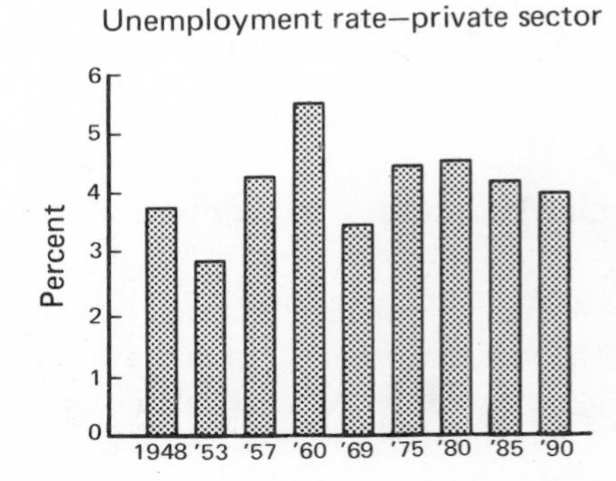

Source: *A Look at Business in 1990,* Washington, D.C.: U.S. Government Printing Office, November 1972, pp. 47 and 49.

The Survey Research Center at the University of Michigan pioneered in the measurement of the mood of the American public. People are asked questions such as whether they feel they will be better off in the coming year than they are at present. Although it is true that there is much economic content in any answer to this question, other things, such as the rate of crime and individual health, will also influence the answer. A pessimistic outlook for the future may tend to have grave consequences for consumer spending. In turn, this will influence the fortunes of the investor.

SUMMARY

From a review of past economic trends in the U.S. economy, it is reasonable to expect long-term sustained future growth. This general conclusion is supported by an examination of the age distribution of the population. The high percentage of the population in the more productive years means a larger labor force and a greater tendency towards consumption since young families have great needs for such fundamental items as housing, transportation, and clothing.

Since 1946, the federal government has been pledged to support the growth of the economy to maintain reasonably low levels of unemployment. The actions of the government, especially in the area of fiscal policy, are important in formulating more accurate predictions of economic activity.

This chapter concluded with an examination of several economic forecasts made for long periods of time. The general conclusions of these studies are quite comparable. Economic growth is expected to be in the 3 to 4 percent range. Inflation is predicted to be a persistent problem with the long-term rate of inflation expected to be in the 3 to 4 percent range. Incomes are expected to grow rapidly and the unemployment rate is expected to range between 4 and 4½ percent.

QUESTIONS

1. Substantial disagreement exists regarding the future potential growth of the U.S. economy. What factors do you think the economic experts use to make their forecasts and what would lead them to arrive at different conclusions with regard to the future of the economy?
2. What has been the significance of the Employment Act of 1946 to our economic growth since World War II? What will be the significance of this legislation in future years?
3. With a declining birth rate in recent years, the expectation is that the American population will become increasingly middle-aged. Of what significance is this to the investor?
4. An extremely important consideration in recent years for the investor forecasting the future of the economy is attempting to determine what will happen to interest rates both in the long run and in the short run. Why is the forecast of interest rates of concern to the investor in stocks and in fixed-income securities such as bonds?
5. President Ford once expressed a desire to reduce federal expenditures and to bring the budget into balance. As an investor, what do you feel

will be the consequences of reducing federal government expenditures by $10 billion?

6. A 10 cent increase in the federal tax on gasoline has been suggested as a means of raising revenue. What would be the impact of this tax increase, if enacted, on the economy? What industries do you feel would be helped or harmed?
7. It is argued that inventory considerations were a fundamental cause of the 1974–75 recession. What is it about inventories that make certain economists relate inventory adjustments to recessions?
8. Concern has been expressed recently that the major industrialized countries in the world have business cycles that are increasingly uniform (*Business Week,* February 16, 1973). The result could be a synchronized slump leading to a world-wide depression. Do you feel this will happen? Why or why not?

SUGGESTED READINGS

A Look at Business in 1990. Washington, D.C.: U.S. Government Printing Office, November 1972.

Heathcotte, Bryan and Vincent P. Apilado. "The Predictive Content of Some Leading Economic Indicators for Future Stock Prices." *Journal of Financial and Quantitative Analysis,* March 1974, pp. 247–58.

Henderson, Hazel. "The Limits of Traditional Economics: New Models for Managing a Steady State Economy." *Financial Analysts Journal,* May–June 1973, pp. 28–32ff.

Homa, Kenneth E. and Dwight M. Jaffee. "The Supply of Money and Common Stock Prices." *Journal of Finance,* December 1971, pp. 1045–66.

Keran, Michael W. "Expectations, Money, and the Stock Market." *Federal Reserve Bank of St. Louis Review,* January 1971, pp. 16–31.

Kreinin, Mordechai E. "Inflation, Recession, and Stagflation." *MSU Business Topics,* Winter 1975, pp. 5–18.

Mayer, Lawrence A. "It's a Bear Market for Babies, Too." *Fortune,* December 1974, pp. 134–37ff.

Meadows, Donella H. et al. *The Limits to Growth.* New York: Universe Books, 1972. This is often referred to as the Club of Rome Study.

Mennis, Edmund A. "The Practical Use of Economic Analysis in Investment Management." In *The Economic Framework for Investors.* Charlottesville, Va.: The Financial Analysts Research Foundation, 1975, pp. 43–56.

Mesarovic, Mihajlo and Eduard Pestel. *Mankind at the Turning Point.* New York: Dutton/Readers' Digest, 1974. This is the second Club of Rome Study.

Moor, Roy E. "The Use of Economics in Investment Analysis." *Financial Analysts Journal,* November–December 1971, pp. 63–69.

Niederhoffer, Victor. "The Analysis of World Events and Stock Prices." *Journal of Business,* April 1971, pp. 193–219.

Palmer, Michael. "Money Supply, Portfolio Adjustments, and Stock Prices." *Financial Analysts Journal,* July–August 1970, pp. 19–22.

Reilly, Frank K. "The Misdirected Emphasis in Security Valuation." *Financial Analysts Journal,* January–February 1973, pp. 54–56ff.

Rose, Sanford. "The Far-reaching Consequences of High-priced Oil." *Fortune,* March 1974, pp. 106–11ff.

Rudolph, J. Allan. "The Money Supply and Common Stock Prices." *Financial Analysts Journal,* March–April 1972, pp. 19–25.

Sprinkel, Beryl W. *Money and Markets: A Monetarist View.* Homewood, Illinois: Richard D. Irwin, 1971.

——. *Money and Stock Prices.* Homewood, Illinois: Richard D. Irwin, 1964.

"The Debt Economy." *Business Week,* October 12, 1974, pp. 44–123.

"The Squeeze on the Middle Class." *Business Week,* March 10, 1975, pp. 52–60.

Tongue, William W. *How Can We Halt Inflation and Still Keep Our Jobs.* Homewood, Illinois: Richard D. Irwin, 1974.

——. "How Money Matters." *Business Economics,* May 1974, pp. 31–38.

U.S. Department of Labor. *The U.S. Economy in 1985: A Summary of BLS Projections.* Washington, D.C.: U.S. Government Printing Office, 1974.

*

8

Analysis of Growth Potential: Industry

The analysis of an industry is a logical follow-up to the analysis of the economy. The investor should attempt to trace economic developments through to specific industries. For example, what will a long and pronounced energy crisis mean to the entire transportation industry? Will the relative competitive positions of railroads, airlines, and automobiles change as a result of this major economic development?

This chapter discusses an approach investors may take to the analysis of an industry. Since the growth potential of different industries varies considerably, it behooves the investor to ascertain the prospects of those industries of investment interest. New industries are born and old industries stagnate and sometimes die. The knowledge of the factors influencing an industry is useful in looking at the risk associated with any given industry. For example, is the industry especially sensitive to interest rate risk? To political risk?

The analysis of industries is not without its problems, however. It is often difficult to define just what constitutes an industry. Even if one is able to accomplish this task, there are very few one-industry companies in the U.S. economy. Most companies are diversified and operate in several different industries. This makes the analysis of a specific industry only partially useful in analyzing a company. The growth of conglomerates is a clear example of this development. As a matter of fact, many firms are currently classified in the conglomerate "industry," which is not really an industry but a group of firms which have no dominant characteristic in common other than a widely diversified product line.

The remainder of this chapter discusses the role of life cycle analysis in the evaluation of an industry along with the factors an investor will want to consider in the examination of a particular industry. A case study analysis of the building supply retailing industry (a segment of the housing industry) is presented. Then, the future growth of various industry groups, as determined by examining the economy as a whole, is discussed.

LIFE CYCLE ANALYSIS

Just as individuals are born, grow to become adults, and eventually die, so do industries. Figure 8–1 shows the life cycle curve, which forms a convenient framework with which to begin the analysis of an industry. The stages of the life cycle curve are commonly known as infancy, growth, maturity, and decline. A brief discussion of each of these stages follows:

Infancy. This refers to the birth of a new industry or a new product. There is no competition of any importance and the public must be educated to the use of the product produced by this industry. There are normally a limited number of product models available and prices

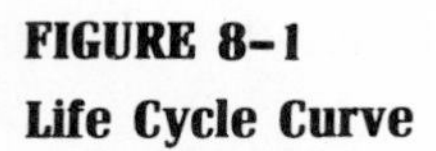

FIGURE 8–1
Life Cycle Curve

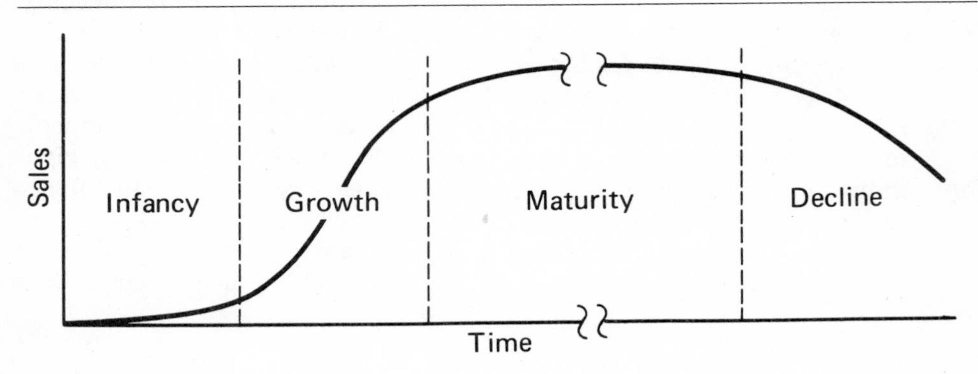

tend to be quite high, although promotional discounts may be used. The birth of the computer industry or the introduction of the Xerox machine are good illustrations. Investors normally incur extremely high risk by making investments in infant industries or in relatively small companies with a major product in its infancy.

Growth. In this stage, aggressive competitors begin to enter the scene. Sales of the industry or product increase rapidly. There may be heavy emphasis on advertising. More models of the product will be available. Prices will be adjusted to create a mass market. The rapid growth of the recreational vehicle industry during the early 1970s is a classic example. Sales increased rapidly, with General Motors finally deciding to become a competitor in this industry. From the investor's viewpoint, there is likely to be substantial reshuffling of the industry participants during this period. It is important to attempt to identify those companies with managerial and financial resources to survive this very competitive period.

Maturity. In this stage of the life cycle, competition is likely to be relatively stable and market shares are unlikely to change much over time from company to company. Advertising is used extensively, as are dealer promotions. Considerable attention is given to cost cutting within the industry. Sales tend to grow slowly compared to the growth of GNP. The automobile and steel industries are probably reasonable examples of mature industries. Investors can make money buying stocks of companies in mature industries, but timing is very important since the industries tend to be cyclical.

Decline. The final stage of the life cycle is the decline stage where sales grow at a rate substantially less than GNP or experience an absolute decline. In this stage, there is normally a decline in the number of competitors in the industry along with a definite attempt to eliminate unprofitable products. Prices are set to maintain profit margins and less concern is given to market shares. It is difficult to identify precisely industries that are in the decline stage, but those industries serving the high school age and younger markets would seem to qualify solely on the basis of the change in the age distribution discussed in the previous chapter. While investors probably should avoid investing in companies serving declining industries, stocks in well-managed companies bought at a reasonable price could prove to be a good investment.

There are definite risks involved in investing in companies in each stage of the life cycle. However, by attempting to classify companies according to their place on the life cycle curve, an investor begins to obtain a feel for whether or not a particular security is reasonably priced. The investor also gets an indication of the risk involved in buying the securities in any given industry.

BASIC INDUSTRY CONSIDERATIONS

In addition to attempting to specify where an industry is on the life cycle curve, the investor needs to take into account many other considerations. To be sure, some of these factors, such as past industry growth trends and the nature of the products, are closely related to the analysis of the life cycle, even though they can be considered separately. In this section, we consider eight relevant industry considerations.

1. *Past Industry Growth Trends.* Just as we examined the past growth trends of the economy, it is possible to examine the past trends for any given industry. Any recent change in growth relative to past growth rates will help the investor to determine where the industry should be located on the life cycle curve.

Figure 8-2 shows the dollar sales of mutual funds each year from 1941 to 1974. Mutual funds, a form of investment company, are discussed fully in Chapters 20 and 21. While not an industry in the normal sense, mutual fund sales clearly demonstrate the life cycle curve. It is still

FIGURE 8-2
Mutual Fund Sales, 1941-74

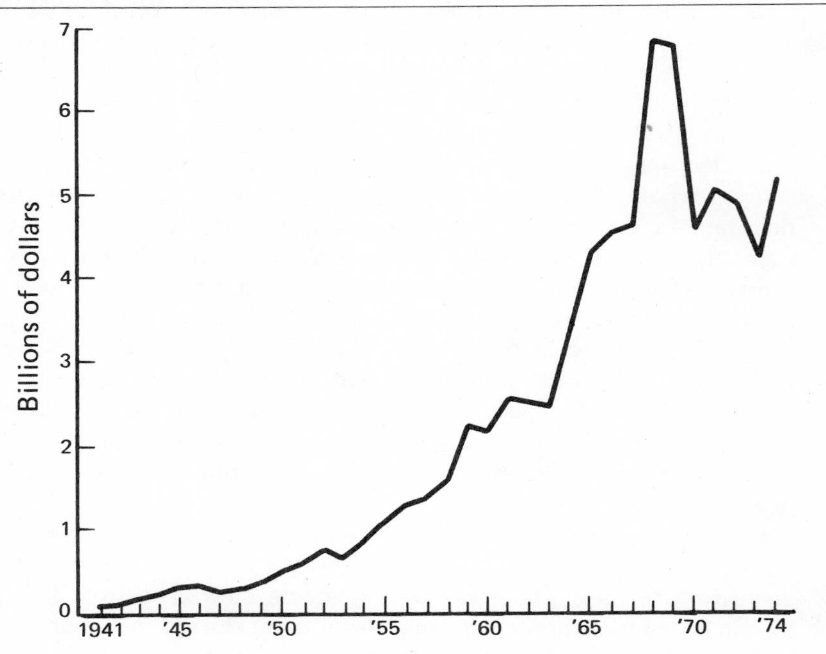

Note: 1974 figure includes $2.3 billion of money market funds (see Chapter 19).
Source: Investment Company Institute, *Mutual Fund Fact Book*, New York, 1975, p. 10.

difficult, however, to determine whether the sales decline is the start of the maturity or decline stages.

2. Supply and Demand. One can attempt to determine the supply and demand situation within any given industry. Has the demand been increasing? Where is the basic source of the demand? Does the industry have enough capacity to accommodate future expected demand? This question may be of critical importance in what has become known as a shortage economy. For example, demand in the electric utility industry has been fairly predictable over the years. One of the continuing problems facing this industry is the need to provide physical capacity to meet expected demand. Money must be raised to construct new generating plants and these plants must be designed many years in advance so that they are available when needed.

The omission of the cash dividend of Consolidated Edison's common stock in April 1974 epitomizes the supply and demand problems of the electric utility industry even though some of Consolidated Edison's problems are unique. This utility is faced with the prospect of increasing demand over the years, but because of severe liquidity problems it may have difficulty financing the needed capacity additions.

3. Nature of Products. One aspect of the demand for the products of an industry concerns the nature of those products. Products of companies in growth industries often exhibit increasing use per capita. Until recent years, more and more high school students have chosen to go to college, making the business of providing college educations a growth industry. Tennis is considered a rapid growth segment within the recreation industry as more and more people take up the game.[1] Computers increasingly occupy a central place in our lives, resulting in increased use per capita. And so the list goes on.

In addition to increased use per capita, an investor needs to determine if a mass market truly exists for the products of any industry or industry segment. The early market research studies of Winnebago Industries apparently identified a mass market for recreational vehicles and the company proceeded to capitalize on that mass market. Xerox found a mass market for its dry process copier and became one of the great growth companies of the past two decades. If a mass market does not exist, the firm or industry may have difficulty in producing a quality product at a competitive price.

The investor should attempt to determine whether the products of any industry are capable of long-run technological improvement. The possibility of the continued technological upgrading of an industry holds promise that the industry will be able to meet competitive challenges from other industries and from foreign competitors. The miniaturization

[1]"The Tennis Industry," *Fortune*, June 1973, pp. 124–32.

of electronic components has allowed continued long-term growth for the computer industry. IBM and Hewlett Packard are examples of companies where technology upgrading has been favorable.

The life expectancy of a product may be of concern and is related to its per capita use. In the hospital supply field, disposable products have created a mass market, resulting in increased use per capita. More profitable investment opportunities may become evident in future years as machine-produced goods continue to be substituted for those made with expensive, on-site labor.

4. Relationship to Income Levels. A reasonably precise method of determining the nature of products is to relate changes in the use of the product to changes in the income level of the consuming group. Economists refer to this relation as the *income elasticity* of the product. A product that is *income elastic* is one where the volume of sales goes up and down at a rate that is faster than the up and down fluctuations of the consumer's income. A product that is *income inelastic* will experience changes in demand that are lower than the consumer's relative changes in income. A more popular way of expressing the same concept is to ascertain whether or not the product or industry is "recession proof." Are the demands of the consumer postponable or do they need to be fulfilled on a fairly regular basis? Is the product a luxury or a necessity?

Items that take a relatively minor part of an individual's total income are considered to have a relatively inelastic income demand function. In other words, changes in income levels leave demand for these products virtually unchanged. Items in this category include chewing gum and newspapers.

Other items accounting for a larger percentage of the consumer's budget may also be relatively recession proof. Items such as beer and cigarettes could fall into this category. In reference to the beer industry, Standard & Poor's states:

> Annual consumption of beer is less affected by the economic well-being of the consumer than is consumption of other food and beverage items. However, brewers, like soft drink producers and, to a lesser extent, the distillers, experience a marked seasonality in demand.[2]

5. Industry Capacity. The physical capacity of an industry may be a vital factor in the investment outlook for an industry. There is often a relationship between the prices charged for a product and the percentage of capacity utilized. The cement industry during the 1960s provides an excellent example of this relationship. Industry capacity was rapidly expanded in the early 1960s, resulting in substantial excess capacity. It sometimes seemed that each company in the industry built enough capacity to accommodate expected increased demand for the

[2]Standard & Poor's Industry Surveys, "Liquor," October 18, 1973 (Section 2), p. L57.

industry for the next several years. The result was that virtually every company in the industry had excess capacity because of overexpansion of plant and equipment.

6. Political Factors. The influence of political factors on an industry involves many different aspects. Political considerations run the continuum from industry regulation by a governmental agency to relatively little governmental influence. Industries such as the public utilities, banking, and transportation have governmental regulation of such matters as the rates charged, the routes served, and the type of service provided.

All industries, to one degree or another, appear to be influenced by a tendency toward intervention by government in their internal operations. Although the authors make no value judgment regarding this trend, it is important for investors to be aware of possible investment implications. The automobile industry has to comply with federal safety and anti-pollution requirements. The cigarette industry has its advertising shaped by governmental regulations. The food industry is subject to nutrition labeling requirements and to regulation regarding food additives. The ban of cyclamates from diet soft drinks in 1970 is an excellent illustration of governmental influence in the food industry.

7. International Considerations. This area could be viewed as part of the political factor just discussed. As modern communication networks effectively shrink the size of the world, investors must give added attention to international considerations. Over the years, American corporations have had property confiscated by foreign governments. At times there has been adequate compensation. At times, there hasn't. Investors purchasing securities in firms operating in politically sensitive areas of the world need to examine the nature of the firms' diversification. During the 1973 Arab oil boycott, investors carefully classified petroleum companies into domestic and foreign producers and then examined the geographic composition of the production of the international producers.

On a more positive side, one can examine the foreign markets for various industry groups. Do certain industries have a good future because of rapidly increasing foreign sales? On the import side, do some industries face increasingly strong competition from foreign producers? How will industries such as steel, automobiles, optical goods, and electronics fare against foreign competitors? How will common markets such as the European Common Market influence the fortunes of domestic industry groups?

Investors have recently had a new concern of an international variety added to their worries. This is the result of fluctuating exchange rates. With rapid currency revaluations, firms not only may make or lose money as a result of currency fluctuations, but also the prices of goods may change in a relative manner. During late 1973 and early 1974, the prices of many foreign automobiles increased faster than those of American-produced automobiles. This relative change in prices was caused, in part, by the currency revaluations that took place. American exports became available for fewer dollars, but more dollars were required to pay for imported goods.

8. Social Changes. While this is the last factor to be explicitly considered in the analysis of an industry, it is not necessarily the least important. In recent years, many changes in consumption patterns of individuals have apparently resulted from social changes. Such changes as the trend toward smaller families noted in the previous chapter, more leisure time, and less emphasis on materialistic goals may have profound investment ramifications. Smaller families may result in increased demand for smaller cars relative to larger automobiles. The toy and baby products industries may suffer unless they diversify. More leisure time may create or wipe out entire industries.

Tastes appear to change slowly, but changing tastes may create excellent investment opportunities. The alcoholic consumption of Americans has shifted somewhat away from heavy spirits such as bourbon to lighter spirits such as vodka and gin. Along with this change in tastes has come an increasing consumption of wine. The consumption figures in Exhibit 8-1 show the changing tastes of the American consumer in this regard:

EXHIBIT 8–1

Consumption per Capita (gallons)

	Distilled Spirits	Beer	Wine	Total
1963	1.37	15.36	.93	17.68
1965	1.52	16.00	.98	18.50
1970	1.84	18.60	1.26	21.68
1972	1.89	19.50	1.57	22.96
1973*	1.92	20.20	1.60	23.72
Change 1963–73	40.1%	31.5%	72.0%	34.2%
Change 1970–73	4.3	8.5	27.0	9.4
Change 1972–73	1.6	3.6	1.9	3.3

*Estimate.

Source: Standard & Poor's Industry Surveys, "Liquor," October 17, 1974 (Section 2), p. L52.

We should note that these data imply that the wine industry has been in the growth stage of its life cycle. The poor performance of the wine consumption figures in 1973 may suggest that the maturity stage is close at hand as per capita consumption levels out. At the same time, one year does not establish a trend.

BUILDING SUPPLY RETAILING—AN INDUSTRY ANALYSIS

Industry Description

This section presents a description and an analysis of the building supply retailing industry, which is a subset of the general retailing industry. As such, the building supply retailing industry is highly fragmented and includes the building supply departments of companies such as Sears and Kresge's as well as those firms that have specialized in the retailing of building supplies, such as Wickes and Lowe's. A brief description of the major competitors in this industry will be given later.

The building supply retailing industry is also an industry which might be considered a part of the housing industry. The level of sales is highly dependent on the trends in such areas as housing starts, remodeling expenditures, and availability of mortgage money. Since the demand for housing and related items is derived from both the expected growth of the population and its age distribution, the general economic factors examined in the previous chapter relative to the importance of population growth are significant. In general, we observed that the contemporary demographic factors are favorable for the housing industry. On the other hand, unfavorable monetary and interest rate factors may serve to curtail demand.

In recent years, many changes have occurred in building supply retailing. There has been considerable growth in large, chain-type operations in contrast to the more traditional lumber yard operation. Product lines have expanded and many companies initially outside the building supply industry have diversified into the field. The growth of the do-it-yourself market has created tremendous marketing opportunities for aggressive firms. The size of stores has increased and additional space is being devoted to attractive merchandising displays.

There are four major types of building supply retailers that may be identified. While the distinctions between each of these four basic types have tended to blur in recent years, it is still useful to examine their characteristics.

1. *The Builder Retailer.* Professional buyers, including builders, developers, and contractors, constitute the major customers for the builder retailer. While the builder retailer may also sell to the general consumer, this business is not actively sought. Because of the volatility in construction, many builder retailers have either gone out of business, diversified into component production or gone into the retailing of specialized types of buildings designed primarily for industrial use.

2. *The General Retailer.* A firm such as Lowe's is classified as a general retailer. Professional buyers accounted for 58 percent of Lowe's $362.5 million sales in fiscal 1974, while retail customers accounted for

the remaining 42 percent. When home building and other types of new construction are strong, the general retailer may tend to concentrate on the professional buyer. When housing starts drop, a firm such as Lowe's will concentrate on obtaining retail business with special advertising promotions and the provision of planning services for the do-it-yourselfer. *Building Supply News,* in a January 1973 issue devoted to an analysis of the 400 largest firms in the building supply industry, estimated that there are approximately 15,800 retailers in the general retailer category, with sales of $6 billion.[3]

3. The Consumer Retailer. While the consumer retailer concentrates primarily on sales to the homeowner, occasional sales may be made to builders. Products offered for sale normally include a full line of electrical and plumbing supplies, appliances, and hardware. In some respects, these retailers can be viewed as the modern version of the general hardware store and are probably best referred to as "home improvement centers."

4. The Mass Retailer. Companies such as Sears and Wards are examples of the mass retailer. These stores often have separate departments appealing to the retail trade. They tend to concentrate on popular items and often offer discount prices along with self-service.

Growth of the Industry

While it is difficult to determine exactly the sales volume of the building supply retailing industry, it is possible to obtain a good approximation. Figure 8-3 shows estimated sales for lumber yards, building material dealers, paint, plumbing, heating and electrical stores on an annual basis from 1965 to 1974. This statistical series corresponds closely to the products offered by the general building supply retailer. As seen in Figure 8-3, sales growth is mildly cyclical, but has shown a generally upward trend. This is the result which would be expected from an analysis of the growth and age distribution of the U.S. population. With the substantial increase expected in the number of people entering the "family formation" years, the building supply retailers should, at the very least, maintain their relative position within the economy and probably do better than the average firm during the next ten to fifteen years.

A Look at Demand

In order to analyze demand, construction expenditures and the housing starts statistical series are examined in this section. Given the great emphasis in this industry on do-it-yourselfers, remodeling expenditures

[3]*Building Supply News,* January 1973, p. 70.

in past years are also analyzed. The three remaining areas to be scrutinized include the cost and price trends in the building industry, the availability of money to finance housing expenditures, and the role of governmental programs in the housing area.

FIGURE 8–3

Estimated Sales for Lumber, Building Material, Paint, Plumbing, Heating, and Electrical Stores, 1965–74

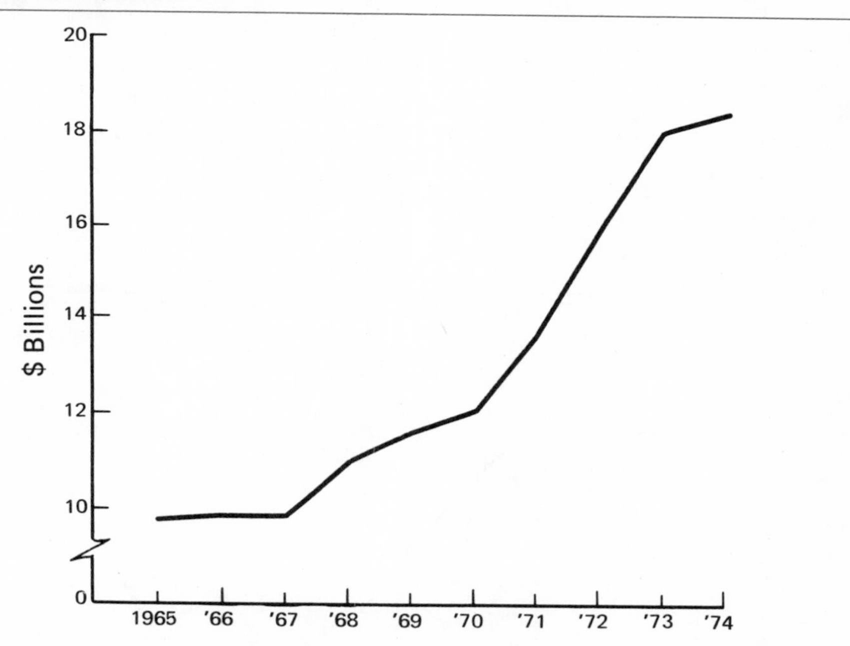

Source: U.S. Department of Commerce, *Survey of Current Business*, various issues.

Figure 8–4 shows the trend in dollar expenditures for residential construction from 1960 to 1974, along with the corresponding percentage of Gross National Product accounted for by residential construction. The impact of credit availability is obvious from Figure 8–4. Credit was difficult to obtain in 1966 and again in 1969–70, and the impact of tight money can be seen in Figure 8–4. Relatively high interest rates in 1973 and 1974 also influenced residential construction spending. One cannot reasonably expect a substantial and sustained growth in residential construction expenditures until credit becomes more available and perhaps less expensive.

While the general trend of residential construction expenditures is useful in analyzing the retail building supply industry, other, more refined measures provide the investor with a better idea of trends directly

FIGURE 8–4
Residential Construction Expenditures, 1960–74

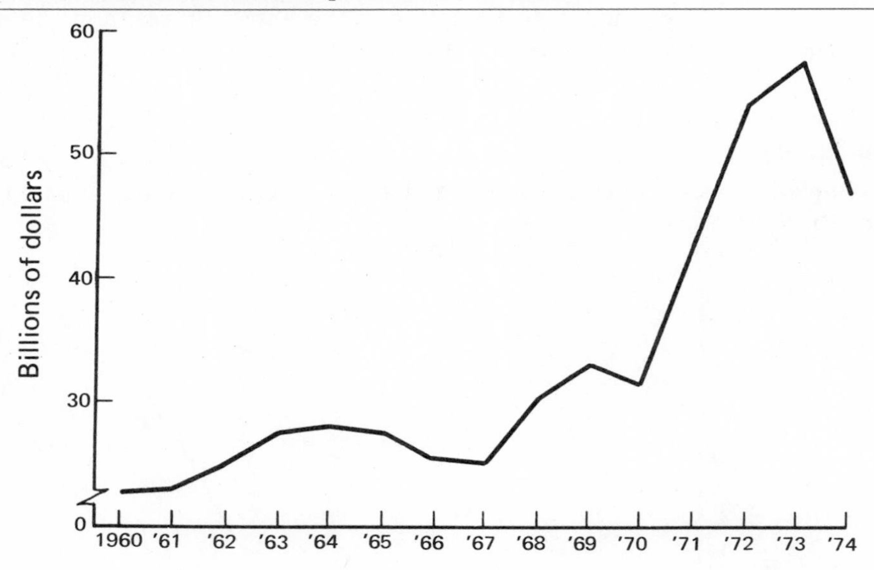

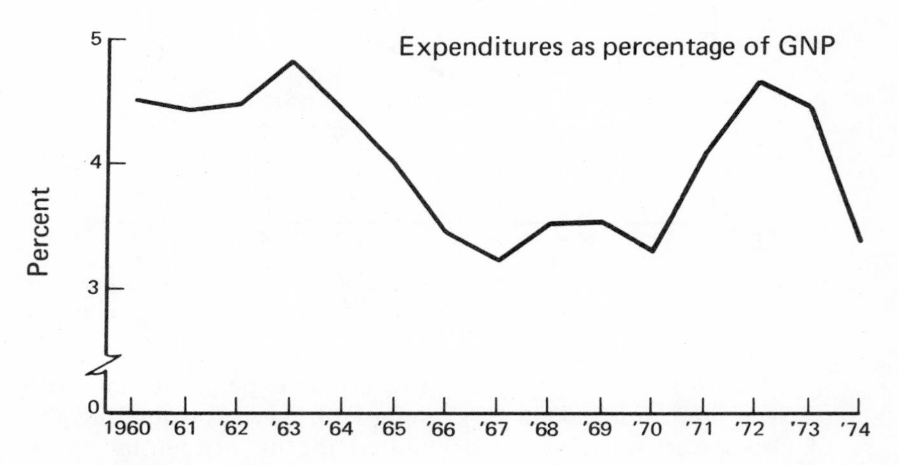

Source: Department of Commerce, *Survey of Current Business*, various issues.

affecting the industry. Figure 8–5 shows the number of housing starts each year from 1960 to 1974. This series measures the demand from the professional segment of the market served by the retail building supply companies.

To obtain an indication of the past growth of the retail customer segment of the market, one can examine the trend of estimated remodeling

FIGURE 8–5
Housing Starts, 1960–74

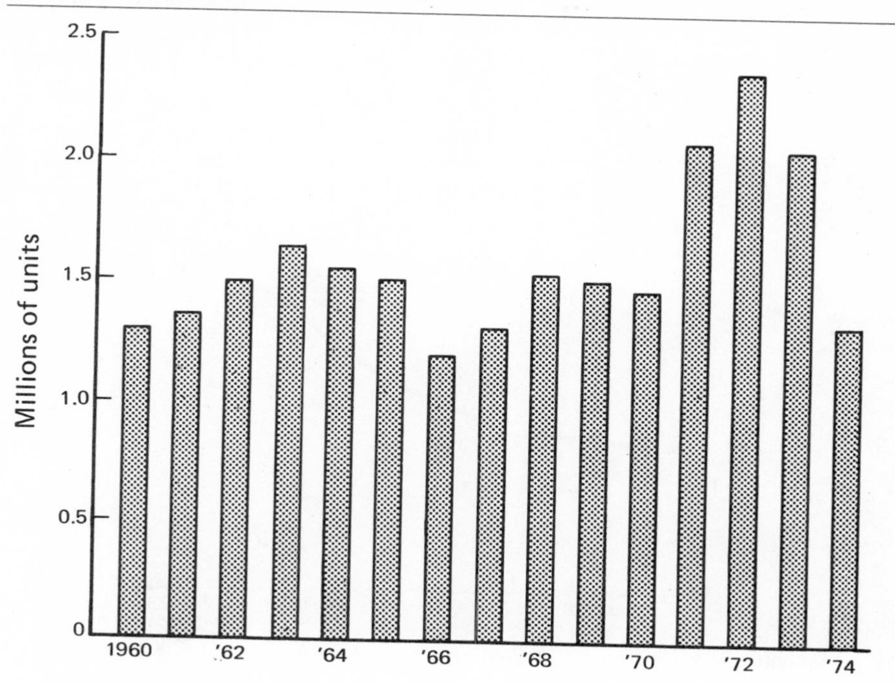

Source: U.S. Department of Commerce, *Survey of Current Business*, various issues.

expenditures for residential alterations and repairs. Figure 8–6 presents these data for the period from 1965 to 1974. As credit becomes less available, customers tend to forego the purchase of new housing units and elect to remodel existing dwellings. From the following tabulation, one can see that this happened in both 1966 and 1970, both of which were years of tight money.

Percentage Change from Previous Year

	1966	1970
Housing starts	−20.8%	−2.1%
Residential construction expenditures	− 7.9	−4.0
Remodeling expenditures	+ 2.6	+9.6

The growth of demand for retail building supplies for remodeling purposes during periods of decline for new housing units helps to cushion the impact of the housing industry's traditionally cyclical nature on the nation's building supply companies.

FIGURE 8-6
Remodeling Expenditures, 1965-74

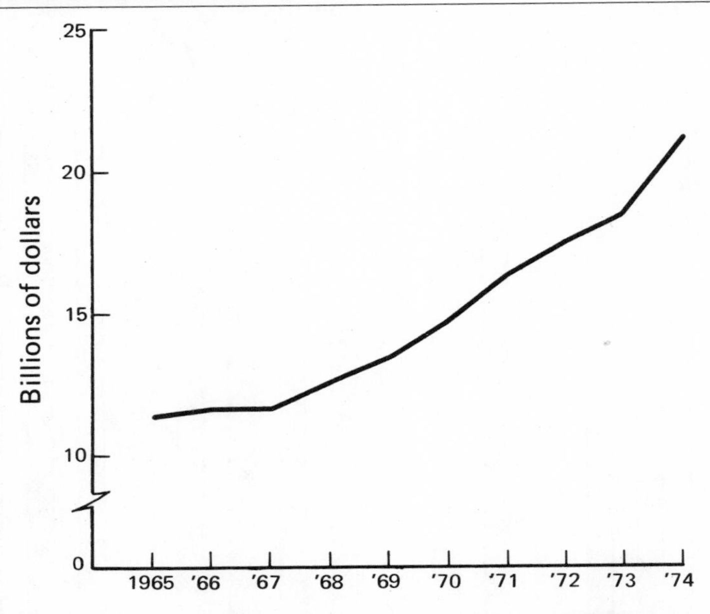

Source: U.S. Department of Commerce, *Residential Alterations & Repairs,* Series C-50.

Cost and price trends in the housing industry have an influence on the demand for housing. If the cost of construction of a new, conventional, one-family house increases at such a pace as to preclude the purchase of this form of housing by some potential purchasers, other segments of the housing market may prosper. Table 8-1 shows the five-year and ten-year compound rate of growth for conventional homes, apartment units started, and for factory shipments of mobile homes. The shift from conventional homes to mobile homes will not be especially favorable to the building supply retailers unless these firms have diversified by adding mobile homes to their product line.

Many of the products carried by the typical building supply retailer vary substantially in demand and price over the housing cycle. Table 8-2 shows the wholesale price index for all construction materials compared to the consumer price index. In addition, the table shows the wholesale price index for lumber and plywood. These price indexes for lumber and plywood illustrate the price volatility of certain types of construction materials. It requires sound inventory management on the part of building supply retailers to maintain respectable profits during periods when the cost of replenishing inventory is changing rapidly.

TABLE 8–1
Annual Growth Rates, Various Types of Housing, Selected Years

	Number of		
	One Family Housing Starts	Apartment Units Started	Mobile Homes Shipped
1964	971,900	450,000	191,320
1969	811,200	571,200	412,690
1974	888,100	381,600	329,300
		Annual Growth Rates	
1964–74	–.9%	–1.6%	5.6%
1969–74	1.8	–7.8	–4.4

Source: U.S. Department of Commerce, *Construction Review,* various issues.

The Availability of Credit

Savings and loan associations (S&L's) provide much of the mortgage money required in our economy. By examining the net savings inflows to the S&L's, it is possible to obtain a crude measure of the availability of credit for the purchase of housing. Figure 8–7 shows the net inflow of savings into S&L's on a quarterly basis from 1968 through 1974.

If one considers the net inflow of savings into the S&L's in conjunction with the rate of interest paid for mortgage money, it is possible to look at both the supply of an essential raw material needed to construct a home (i.e., money) and its cost. We previously saw that the availability of credit is a crucial factor in the actual demand for housing. Clearly, much potential building demand is never realized in the marketplace because of both the unavailability of credit and its cost.

During certain periods such as the third quarter of 1969, more savings flowed out of the S&L's than flowed into them. Savers withdrew their funds in order to purchase securities offering higher rates of return than were available from the S&L's. This phenomenon is known as *disintermediation* since the saver disengages the services of a financial intermediary (S&L) and invests directly in the securities market. The financial institution is not used to channel the saver's funds to the capital market. During early 1974, disintermediation was a major problem for the S&L's because of relatively high rates of return available in the bond market from both federal government and good quality corporate bonds. Disintermediation is important to the retail building supply industry since it indirectly influences the number of dwelling units that are started in any particular period through its impact on the availability of credit.

TABLE 8-2
Consumer Price Index and Construction Material Price Indexes, 1960-74

		Wholesale Price Index*		
	CPI*	All Construction Materials	Plywood	Lumber
1960	88.7	95.5	109.6	92.1
1961	89.6	93.7	107.2	87.4
1962	90.6	93.4	103.5	89.0
1963	91.7	93.6	104.7	91.2
1964	92.9	94.7	103.4	92.9
1965	94.5	95.8	103.5	94.0
1966	97.2	98.8	103.9	100.1
1967	100.0	100.0	100.0	100.0
1968	104.2	105.6	115.7	117.4
1969	109.8	111.9	122.5	131.5
1970	116.3	112.5	108.5	113.7
1971	121.3	119.5	114.7	135.5
1972	125.3	126.6	130.7	159.4
1973	133.1	138.5	155.2	205.2
1974	147.7	160.9	161.1	207.1

*1967 = 100.0.
Source: U.S. Department of Commerce, *Construction Review* and *Survey of Current Business*, various issues.

Governmental Housing Programs

The significance of the federal government in the home construction market should not be underestimated. Although space limitations prevent a complete analysis of all federal programs in the housing area, the three most important activities relate to mortgage insurance, availability of mortgage money, and assistance in the form of subsidies which allow low-income families to obtain adequate housing. Standard & Poor's estimates that well over 50 percent of new housing, in recent years, has been built as the result of either direct or indirect governmental action.[4]

In the mortgage insurance area, various governmental agencies provide loan and insurance guarantees to housing lenders. Both the Federal Housing Administration and the Veterans Administration provide mortgage guarantees for lenders for a flat fee, normally one-half of 1 percent. The availability of mortgage money is at least partially influenced by the Federal National Mortgage Association (Fannie Mae) and the Government National Mortgage Association (Ginnie Mae). Fannie Mae, a private corporation with a public purpose, makes a secondary market for mortgages by buying mortgages from financial institutions. In this manner,

[4]Standard & Poor's Industry Surveys, "Building," August 10, 1972 (Section 2), p. B70.

FIGURE 8–7

Net Quarterly Savings Inflow to Savings and Loan Associations, 1968–74

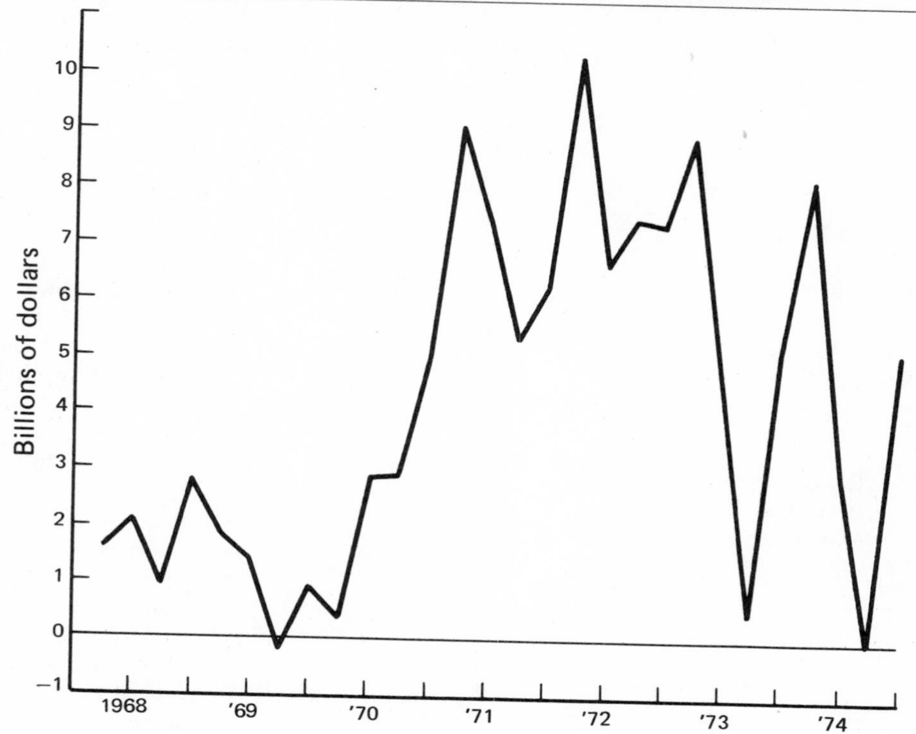

Source: *Federal Home Loan Bank Board Journal,* various issues.

Fannie Mae gives the mortgage portfolios of financial institutions some liquidity. Ginnie Mae's main operation is the sale of mortgage-backed securities. These securities resemble bonds and allow for the "pass through" of interest collected on a portfolio of federally guaranteed mortgages. Ginnie Mae government-backed "pass through" certificates have liquidity and respectable yields as the main attraction for institutional investors. These certificates allow Ginnie Mae to raise money from the sale of existing mortgages. Ginnie Mae also helps in the financing of homes unable to meet the conventional mortgage lending standards of financial institutions in the mortgage market.

Firms within the Industry

The final section of our survey of the building supply retailing industry contains a brief description of the major companies operating in the industry. The survey is outlined in Table 8–3. Clearly, this is a difficult

TABLE 8–3
Selected Building Supply Retailers

Company and Location of Headquarters	Sales Volume ($ mil)	Number of Retail Units	Where Traded	Early Aug. 1974 Price	Comments
Wickes Co. Saginaw, Michigan	1,118.1	258	NYSE	12	Shelter Group (90.1% of fiscal 1973 sales) retails building supplies and furniture. Industrial and Agricultural Group (9.9% of sales). Has outlets in 34 states, the Netherlands, and Great Britain.
Evans Products Braintree, Massachusetts	1,113.6	217	NYSE	6⅛	Retail and Homes Groups (39.9% of 1973 sales) sell building supplies and make pre-cut homes. Building Material Group (44.8% of sales) makes plywood, lumber, etc. Industrial Products Group (15.3% of sales) makes equipment for railroad cars.
Lowe's North Wilkesboro, North Carolina	326.8	100	OTC	34¼–35¼	A general building supply retailer. Also sells mobile homes. Outlets in 14 Southeastern states.
Wolohan Lumber Saginaw, Michigan	66.9	25	OTC	3½–4¼	Located in 5 midwestern states. A general building supply retailer.
Scotty's, Inc. Winter Haven, Florida	66.6	43	NYSE	8	Outlets in Florida. A general building supply retailer.

Payless Cashways Iowa Falls, Iowa	65.9	40	OTC	13¼–14	Caters primarily to do-it-yourself trade with stores in 9 midwestern states.
Pay n' Pak Stores Kent, Washington	51.9	48	OTC	6½–7	A general building supply retailer located in 10 western states and Western Canada.
Channel Companies Whippany, New Jersey	44.2	19	OTC	3½–3⅞	Stores in New Jersey and Pennsylvania. Also operates 6 Play Factory Toy Stores. Lawn and garden suppliers, recreational equipment, and toys accounted for 24% of fiscal 1973 sales.

Sources: Standard & Poor's *Corporation Records*, various issues; *Moody's Industrial Manual*, 1974; "First Annual 400 Report: Profile of Building Supply Giants," *Building Supply News*, January 1973, pp. 69–84; Orville W. Forté III, *The Building Materials Retailing Industry*, San Francisco; Robertson, Colman, Siebel & Weisel [investment bankers], October 23, 1973 and "Update" of May 10, 1974.

industry to define. The survey is limited to those firms that can most accurately be classifed as general building supply retailers. It does not consider firms such as Sears, those building supply companies that are a fairly minor division of a major company, or firms not publicly held.

FUTURE GROWTH, BY INDUSTRY

In the previous chapter, the growth of the economy in future years as projected by various studies was examined. It is possible to relate the impact of economic growth to various industry groups. Both the McGraw-Hill Study and *A Look at Business in 1990*, examined in the previous chapter, did so.

Figure 8–8 shows how selected industry groups are expected to grow between 1970 and 1985, according to the McGraw-Hill Study. This growth is translated into annual rates of increase. Chemicals, electric utilities, and rubber and plastic products are expected to be the prime growth industries during this period. Tobacco, coal, apparel, and certain segments of the metals industry are expected to be the poorest growing industries.

The Report of the White House Conference on the Industrial World Ahead, *A Look at Business in 1990,* projected output growth by industry for the 1970 to 1990 period, using somewhat different industry classifications than those of the McGraw-Hill Study summarized in Figure 8-8.

FIGURE 8-8
Projected Annual Growth Rate, Selected Industries, 1970-85

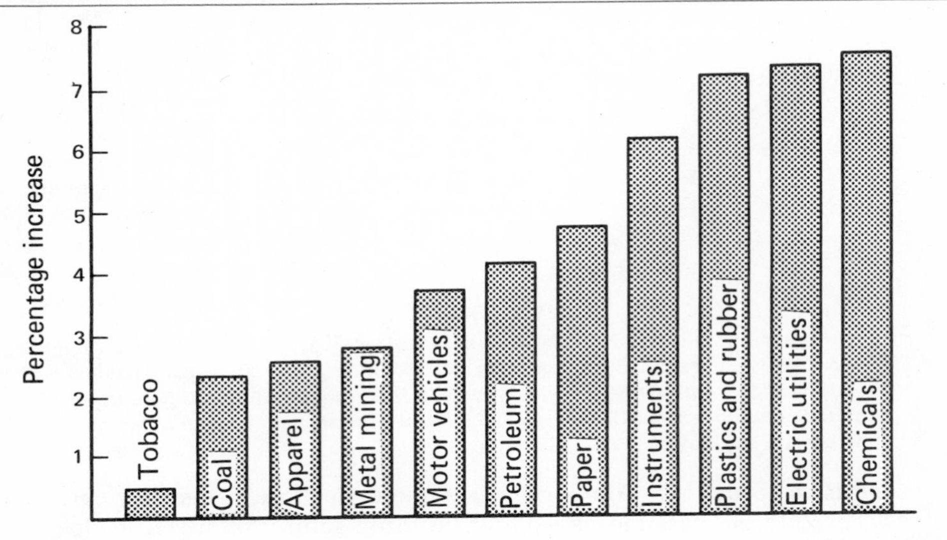

Source: Reprinted from the December 18, 1971, issue of *Business Week* by special permission. © 1971 by McGraw-Hill, Inc.

The communications industry is expected to grow approximately 7.5 percent annually between 1970 and 1990. This would be followed closely by electric, gas and sanitary services at about 7.2 percent per annum. Mining, transportation, and agriculture are expected to be the slowest growing major industries, with growth rates in the 1.5 to 2.2 percent range.

These studies may help the investor to form beliefs regarding both the growth rate of a particular industry and the growth rates for companies wihin an industry. Naturally, one must be careful to note the assumptions under which these estimates were produced. For example, it is doubtful if either study took direct consideration of the energy crisis facing our nation. The explicit recognition of this important factor might allow the investor to substantially increase the growth rates for coal, crude oil, and natural gas industries while decreasing the growth rate for electric utilities. In spite of such difficulties, the investor is provided with a useful starting point in the search for attractive industry groups in which to invest.

SUMMARY

In this chapter, we examined three major topics. First, we examined the major factors accounting for the future growth of an industry. Second, we examined the building supply retailing industry as an example of the application of these factors. Last, drawing upon studies of the future economic growth of the U.S. economy, we examined selected industries to ascertain their expected growth. We saw that future growth expectations for various industries differ widely.

In looking at the future growth potential of an industry, it is often a useful starting point to attempt to locate the industry on its life cycle curve. Four stages of the life cycle were examined. These are: 1) infancy; 2) growth; 3) maturity; and 4) decline. In helping to determine the proper life cycle stage of any given industry, it is important to examine the past growth of the industry. While past growth allows the investor to form preliminary expectations regarding future growth, other factors are also important. These other factors include the nature of the product, the supply, demand, and capacity relationships existing in the industry, political and social considerations, and international developments within the industry.

The analysis of specific industries serves as a starting point for the analysis of companies within the industry. In focusing on the consequences of expected economic growth for any specific industry, we examined studies relating these two factors. These studies pointed out the substantial variations in expected growth for different industry groups. For this reason alone, the investor needs to analyze carefully the growth potential of any industry.

QUESTIONS

1. What are the stages in the life cycle of a firm or an industry?
2. Companies are often concerned with avoiding the final stage of the life cycle. As an investor, how would you identify those firms that are making an attempt to avoid this stage?
3. The utility industry has many problems of both a supply and demand nature. Discuss the nature of these various problems and their significance to the investor.
4. How would you determine if the demand for a given product is income elastic? Give some examples of products that you think would fall into this category.
5. The investor should examine the per capita use of products. However, certain products face natural barriers to sustainable increases in use per capita. What is the nature of these barriers and what products are most vulnerable to the impact of these barriers?

6. Interest rate changes have a varying impact on different industries. What would you expect the impact of rising interest rates to be on the following?
   a) Housing.
   b) Traveler's check industry.
   c) Retailing (i.e., Sears).
   d) Soft drinks.
   e) Savings and loan associations.
7. What is disintermediation? Can you think of any industries that might benefit from disintermediation in the economy?
8. Much attention during the gasoline shortage was focused on the elasticity of demand for gasoline. The price elasticity was estimated as falling between —.1 and —.3 meaning that a 10 percent increase in the price of gasoline would cause a reduction in demand of between 1 and 3 percent. As an investor, what industries would you want to investigate if gasoline prices are rising rapidly? Will some industries benefit while others are injured?
9. The excess demand that was mentioned in the text as existing in the cement industry in the early 1960s has disappeared for all practical purposes. What role would you expect that each of the following factors played in the reduction of excess capacity?
   a) More rigid pollution control requirements.
   b) Increased interest rates.
   c) The nearing of completion of the Interstate Highway System.
   d) An increase in gasoline prices.
10. One of the factors an investor should examine in an industry is the current political environment. What political problems currently exist for both international and domestic petroleum producers?
11. Legislation allowing a 5 percent tax credit (up to a maximum of $2,000) to purchasers of existing, but previously unoccupied homes was passed in early 1975. What impact would you expect this legislation to have on the housing industry?

SUGGESTED READINGS

Cheney, Harlan L. "The Value of Industry Forecasting As an Aid to Portfolio Management." *Appalachian Financial Review*, Spring 1970, pp. 331–39.

Downs, James C. Jr. "Demand and Market for Housing: The Balance of the Decade." *Appraisal Journal*, January 1972, pp. 103-13.

King, Benjamin. "Market and Industry Factors in Stock Price Behavior." *Journal of Business*, January 1966, pp. 139–90.

Latané, Henry A. and Donald L. Tuttle. "Profitability in Industry Analysis." *Financial Analysts Journal*, July–August 1968, pp. 51–61.

Marcin, Thomas C. *The Effect of Declining Population Growth on the Demand for Housing*. Washington, D.C.: U.S. Government Printing Office, 1974.

"Marketing When the Growth Slows." *Business Week*, April 14, 1975, pp. 44–50.

Reilly, Frank K. and Eugene F. Drzycimski. "Alternative Industry Performance and Risk." *Journal of Financial and Quantitative Analysis*, June 1974, pp. 423–46.

Tysseland, Milford S. "Further Tests of the Validity of the Industry Approach to Investment Analysis." *Journal of Financial and Quantitative Analysis*, March 1971, pp. 835–47.

Wenglowski, Gary M. "Industry Profit Analysis—A Progress Report and Some Predictions." *The Economic Framework for Investors*, Charlottesville, Va.: The Financial Analysts Research Foundation, 1975, pp. 19–30.

*

9

Analysis of Growth Potential: Company

Both this chapter and the next are concerned with the analysis of an individual company. This chapter concentrates mainly on the qualitative aspects of the analysis. These qualitative factors include: 1) an assessment of the quality of management; 2) the nature of the products or services provided; and 3) the growth potential as reflected by past performance and current planning efforts. Lowe's, a building supply retailer, serves as the principal example in the analysis of these qualitative factors. Other companies are used as illustrations when appropriate.

Chapter 10 discusses the subject of financial statement analysis. The emphasis in that chapter is upon the use of the financial statement analysis in arriving at conclusions regarding the investment worth of a company and its securities. In Chapter 10, Lowe's also serves as the company for which a financial statement analysis is performed. In practice, it is difficult to segregate the material contained in this chapter from that contained in the next, since both chapters contribute to the formation of beliefs regarding the desirability of any security as an investment.

QUALITY OF MANAGEMENT

Making a determination concerning the quality of management is an arduous task since it requires a judgment which to a considerable extent reflects subjective feelings. In addition, a judgment regarding the quality of management requires more than just a study of the people running a particular company. A careful analysis of the actual performance of the management relative to the opportunities available must be conducted. Despite the existence of these problems, one must still make the effort to ascertain the quality of management. This section conducts the quality assessment from the viewpoint of management's grand design, managerial education and experience, the depth of management, and the track record management has produced as reflected in the historical record.

Management's Grand Design

It is admittedly hard to determine whether any management has a reasonable grand design for the firm. However, careful and thoughtful consideration about the future is one of the major characteristics of a successful management. There are many questions an investor should attempt to answer. Has management established a long-range plan? Are there written policies that employees can rely upon to handle situations that occur in the day-to-day affairs of the business? Is the firm recruiting top-notch young managerial talent and is it willing to pay the price to obtain the services of these people?

In line with the grand design philosophy, Douglas Hayes suggests that managements should have three major goals.[1] These goals are discussed below:

1. The firm should engage in activities of a public relations nature in order to present a good image to the investment community. This would include activities such as presentations to organizations of security analysts and to community groups.
2. The firm should seek to establish appropriate financial policies to enhance the long-run value of the company. In addition, the financial stability of the firm must be considered. Of major importance in this area are the proper use of debt to finance the firm and the establishment of an appropriate dividend policy.
3. A firm should establish and carry out a creative policy in the area of acquisitions. Acquisitions should be consistent with the grand design previously established and should be beneficial to the health of the company being acquired as well as the company doing the acquiring.

[1]Douglas Hayes, "The Evaluation of Management," *Financial Analysts Journal*, July–August 1968, pp. 39–42.

Education and Experience

One of the most useful ways of forming opinions regarding the education and experience of management is actually to have personal contacts with members of the management team or with other parties having contact with management, such as the firm's suppliers or customers. However, limited opportunities exist for the average investor to form opinions regarding top management based upon personal contact. Fortunately, many top management people of major concerns are evaluated in a variety of publications, such as *Fortune, Business Week,* the *Wall Street Journal, Forbes,* and the *New York Times.* The firm's annual report also is a source of information regarding the education and experience of management. The Lowe's 1973 *Annual Report* has a brief description of the five people making up the Office of the President. Their positions within the firm, as well as the societies and other organizations to which they belong, are discussed. The report also states that each of these five people has been with Lowe's fifteen years or more.

Depth of Management

Although important, it is often difficult to determine whether the management of any company is planning for its replacement at some future date. Many companies have been criticized as "one-man shows." These companies may suffer when the one person running the company is no longer energetic and capable enough to keep up with the competition. Occidental Petroleum has been criticized on this point.[2] Dr. Armand Hammer, the founder of the firm, reached his seventy-sixth birthday in 1974. Many industry observers feel he is unwilling to give up any significant control of the operations of the company. Thus, it may be difficult to hire and retain competent senior management people. At the other end of the management depth spectrum, Burnup and Sims, a firm engaged in construction work for public utility firms and for CATV systems, has been mentioned as having one of the few training programs in its industry.[3] The importance of management depth is emphasized in an article in *Business Week* discussing the turnaround at United Airlines. The article concludes:

> The one major point on which Carlson's [sixty-two-year-old chief executive] critics fault him and his management structure is that so far he has not found—nor has the structure produced—a successor to himself. But Carlson is working hard at the problem; he plans to retire in three years.[4]

[2]"Overstaying His Time," *Forbes,* November 15, 1971, pp. 31–32.

[3]Standard and Poor's Corporation, *Over-the-Counter and Regional Exchange Stock Reports,* Vol. 1 (Friday, June 21, 1974, Vol. 40, no. 71, sec. 10), p. 3373.

[4]"How United Airlines Pulled Out of Its Dive," *Business Week,* June 29, 1974, p. 70.

The Track Record

The acid test of the quality of management is in the long-term record that has been produced for the stockholders of the firm. It is possible to infer much about the quality of management by studying the financial statements. To be sure, not everything of significance is revealed in the financial statements but they do represent a good check on evaluations based upon other factors. Many of the inferences made concerning Lowe's management and the firm's position within the building supply retailing industry come from the company's annual report.

PRODUCT ANALYSIS

In the previous chapter, we studied the life cycle framework from the industry vantage point. This approach clearly is relevant for the individual firm within the industry. Where are the firm's products in relation to the life cycle of the product? Are new products continually being introduced to offset the slower sales growth of more mature products? The answers to these and other similar questions should be sought by the investor.

Nature and Diversity of Products

In an old but still relevant article, Jeremy Jenks enumerates the characteristics one might generally find to be true for the products of growth companies.[5] Since these characteristics seem as useful today as they were in 1947, they are listed below:

1. Direct price competition is moderate. This was certainly true for Xerox in its early history. This is a most important generalization since it relates directly to a firm's ability to increase prices to recover higher production costs.
2. The product can be produced at low cost compared to other methods of production.
3. The product can be produced in quantity and with uniform quality. This is similar to the increasing use per capita standard developed in the previous chapter.
4. The market for the products should be broad. A large number of potential customers should exist. This aspect of product demand has an international dimension in our shrinking world.

[5]Jeremy C. Jenks, "Investing in Growth Stocks," *The Analysts Journal*, 2nd quarter, 1947, pp. 38–53.

5. The product has special features or uses to distinguish it from competing products. Polaroid's success with the field of instant photography is a good example of this generalization.
6. The product is frequently protected by patents or by superior managerial "know-how."

The factors listed above refer primarily to the nature of the product. One should also consider whether the firm has the proper mix of products and sources of raw materials to achieve adequate diversification. Investors need to be concerned whether or not a firm has plentiful, low cost, and reliable raw material supplies since shortages of raw materials have occurred on occasion in recent years.

Even a firm such as Lowe's, which has restricted itself essentially to the building supply retailing industry, must remain competitive with regard to the product mix offered to its customers. Lowe's appears to have achieved sufficient variety in its product mix in order to meet competition. In Lowe's 1973 *Annual Report,* four pages are devoted to new directions and programs for the company. In view of the importance of this area, each of the principal items covered in this section of Lowe's 1973 *Annual Report* is discussed below:

1. Lowe's Homestead. In November 1970, Lowe's started to merchandise a low-cost home package of about 1,000 square feet. During 1973, 32 different models were offered to customers, resulting in sales of $23.1 million, up from $3.4 million in 1971. Using computers, Lowe's can give up-to-date, guaranteed price quotations for any of the Homestead houses. In addition, house components have been arranged in such a way so as to give customers sequential delivery.
2. Envi-Ro-Temp. This is a private label home comfort system including such features as central heating and air conditioning, humidity control, and electronic air cleaning.
3. Pre-Assembled Components. Begun in 1971, Lowe's offers custom-built door and window units.
4. Ranchettes. This is Lowe's mobile home sales division. The firm does not build mobile homes, but sells them through nine sales centers located in the Southeastern United States. This geographic area accounts for half the nation's sales of mobile homes.
5. Lowe's Improver Program. This is a three-phase program started in 1973. The program is based upon the realization (phase one) that customers would like to be quoted an installed price for many building supplies requiring installation. Phase two involves having store managers quote installed prices and then arrange and supervise the installation. In the long-run, phase three would involve Lowe's having its own installation crews.

Reputation for Quality Products

In the analysis of the products or services of any firm, an important intangible factor is the firm's reputation for producing a quality product or giving superior service. Maytag washers, for example, have often been cited for their dependable and long-lived service.[6] Naturally, the company has used this reputation to its advantage in its advertising program. Publications such as *Consumer Reports* can be of considerable assistance in helping the investor arrive at an informed decision regarding the quality associated with a firm's products.

Research and Development Program

In order to remain competitive, it is necessary for the firm to invest money continually in research and development (R&D) programs. The investor needs to examine the magnitude of a firm's R&D effort and attempt to determine its financial impact. The investor could calculate expenditures for R&D in relation to sales (or some other suitable measure such as net income). It may also be useful to compare this figure with that of other firms in the same industry. R&D expenditures are clearly a very important consideration in high technology industries such as electronics. In looking at the financial impact of R&D expenditures, the investor should attempt to ascertain the sales and profitability of recent additions to the product line. For example, Polaroid's SX-70 camera represented an enormous investment of approximately $500 million.[7] The company's fortunes are very much tied to the success of this camera.

Two other examples of research and development efforts will be given in light of the importance of this area. Xerox in mid-1974 unveiled its entry into the offset duplicating market with its Xerox 9200 model. The market is expected to be central reproduction departments and large in-plant reproduction facilities. Xerox executives referred to this product as "the most important product we've ever had."[8] *Business Week* stated that Xerox was gambling an estimated $300 million on this market with the Xerox 9200. If this new machine is successful, Xerox may well be able to maintain its past growth rate in spite of a maturing market for its original family of copying machines. Proctor & Gamble's research effort is a second example. In a recent issue of *Fortune,* P&G's research effort was estimated to be over $100 million a year.[9]

[6]"Washing Machines," *Consumer Reports,* October 1973, p. 610.

[7]Dan Cordtz, "How Polaroid Bet Its Future on the SX-70," *Fortune,* January 1974, pp. 82–87.

[8]"Xerox Unveils Its 'Most Important Product'," *Business Week,* June 29, 1974, pp. 92–94.

[9]Peter Vanderwicken, "P&G's Secret Ingredient," *Fortune,* July 1974, pp. 75–79.

ANALYSIS OF PAST GROWTH

We previously mentioned the need to observe management's track record. It is desirable to look at the trend of sales, earnings and dividends and to note growth rates. It is also useful to consider the consistency of the past record. Has management been able to perform well in all kinds of economic environments? Another important measure of growth potential and of management's ability is the rate of return earned on stockholders' equity. This valuable statistic will be discussed in Chapter 10.

Figure 9-1 shows the dollar value of sales, the earnings per share, and dividends per share for Lowe's from 1958 to 1974. The data are plotted on a semilog scale, which shows percentage changes. This makes

FIGURE 9-1

Lowe's Sales, Earnings per Share and Dividends per Share, 1958-74

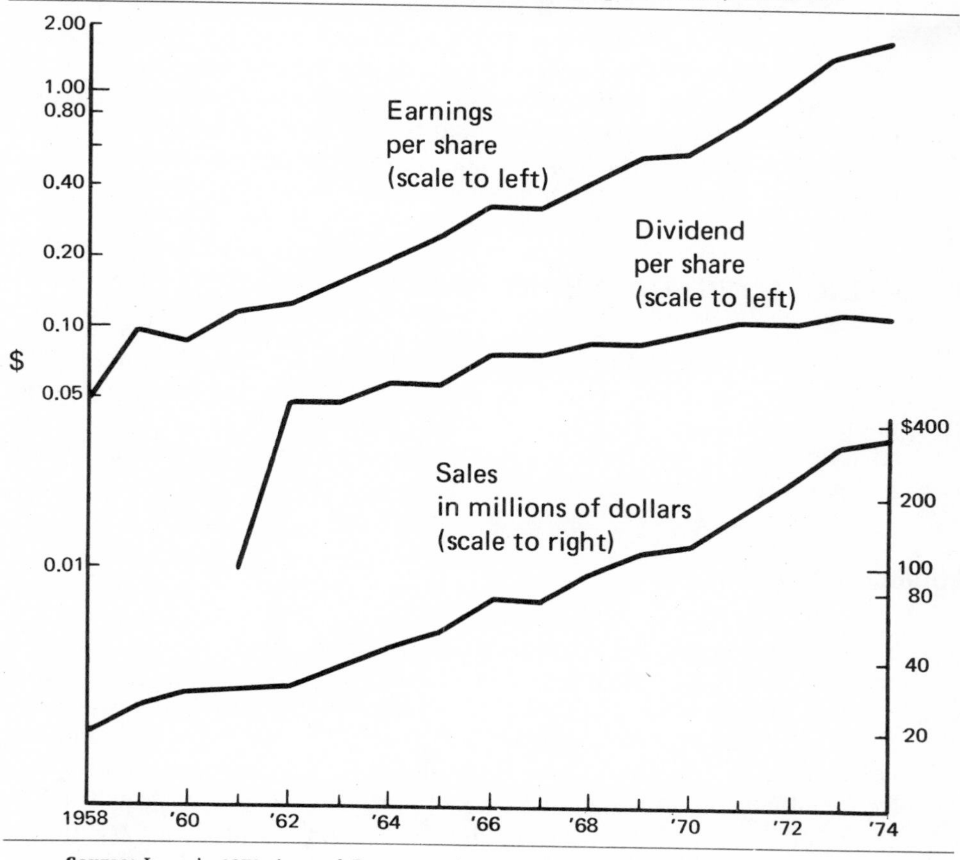

Source: Lowe's 1973 *Annual Report* and 1974 *Fourth Quarter Report.*

it easier to observe consistency of performance from one year to the next. Table 9-1 reinforces the impression of strong and relatively consistent growth given by Figure 9-1.

TABLE 9-1
Lowe's Companies, Inc., Selected Statistics

			Compound Annual Rate of Growth			
	1958	1974	1958-63	1963-68	1968-74	1958-74
Sales	$20,444,000	$362,453,211	13.8%	20.0%	24.6%	19.7%
Earnings per share	$.05	$1.71	26.2	21.9	25.9	24.7
Dividends per share	nil	$ .12	n.a.	12.5	4.9	n.a.

Source: Lowe's 1974 *Fourth Quarter Report.*

Naturally, the investor must use a past growth record such as Lowe's only as a beginning in forecasting what the future will bring. In the last chapter, we saw that the outlook is favorable for the building supply retailing industry. Since Lowe's management has performed well in the past, one would expect that it will continue to perform well in future years given the favorable industry outlook.

PLANNING—LONG AND SHORT RANGE

The final section of this chapter concentrates on the planning efforts of the company that should be examined by the investor. Financial planning, marketing efforts, production planning and control, and diversification efforts are discussed. Illustrations will be drawn from Lowe's and several other companies.

Financial Planning

The investor needs to observe such items as the profit margin achieved on sales, the proper balance in the capital structure of the firm so that prudent debt levels are maintained, and the maintenance of respectable levels of liquidity. Although both the actual ratios for each company will vary over time and the acceptable levels for these ratios will vary from industry to industry, trends can certainly be noted. Much of the work in Chapter 10 will be devoted to an analysis of these trends for Lowe's.

The appropriate dividend policy is a significant part of the financial planning effort. Lowe's has always been rather conservative in its dividend policy. In fiscal 1974, the firm had a dividend payout of only 7 percent of earnings calculated as follows:

$$\text{Dividend payout percentage} = \frac{\text{dividends per share}}{\text{earnings per share}} = \frac{\$\ .12}{\$1.71} = .07$$

The compound rate of growth in dividends per share has been far below the compound rate of growth in earnings per share as seen from Table 9-1. This has resulted in a steadily declining dividend payout percentage for Lowe's for the 1962 to 1974 period shown in Figure 9-2. By lowering the dividend payout, Lowe's has steadily increased the percentage of earnings reinvested in the company to finance future growth. In view of Lowe's rapid sales growth, this dividend policy is probably appropriate. It should be noted that since 1962, the price of Lowe's common stock has risen from approximately $2 per share to approximately $46 per share as of 1975. One should not get the impression, however, that a declining payout percentage implies price advances. If the firm's reinvestment opportunities are improving, as is the case with Lowe's, we can usually expect price advances and a reduced payout

FIGURE 9-2
Lowe's Dividend Payout, 1962-74

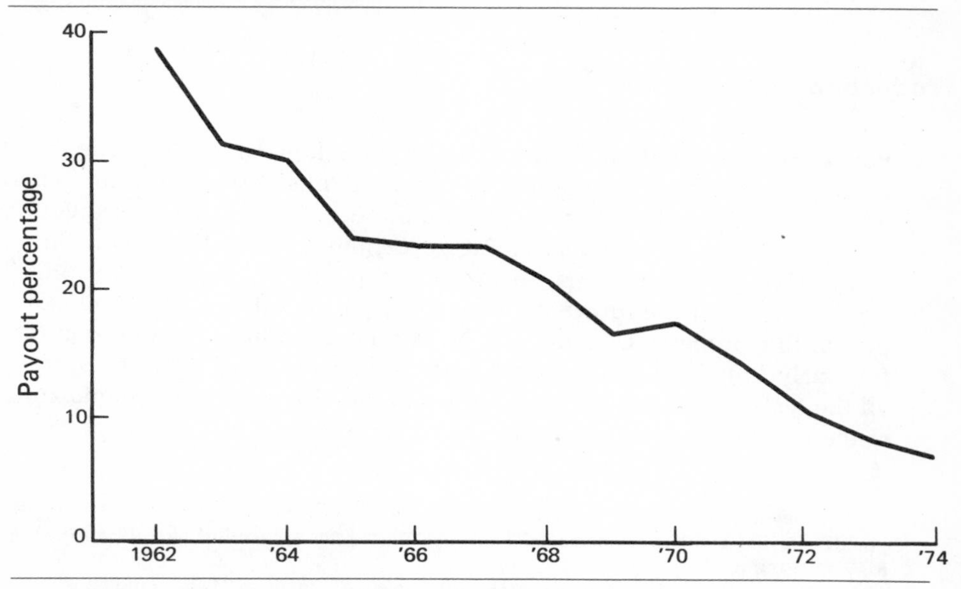

Source: Lowe's 1973 *Annual Report* and 1974 *Fourth Quarter Report.*

percentage. The price increases come from the reinvestment opportunities and the fact that the firm can take advantage of them through a lower payout percentage.

Marketing Efforts

A great deal of the success of any company is attributable to the effectiveness of its marketing activities. The thrust of Lowe's marketing efforts in recent years has already been noted. The investor must determine if these will meet the challenges of the future.

Many of the more successful marketing efforts relative to new products are carefully constructed with regard to the selection of the proper channel of distribution. For example, Avon Products' door-to-door method of selling has had considerable success in the field of cosmetics.[10] Hewlett-Packard, a producer of calculators and other scientific measuring equipment, decided on a direct mail campaign as part of the marketing effort for its high-priced scientific and financial calculators. In addition, Hewlett-Packard decided not to attempt to compete in the market for lower-priced calculators. Hewlett-Packard's marketing effort is generally considered to be successful.[11]

In acquiring companies, it is often an important consideration whether the acquired firm's products can be marketed in the same manner as the products of the acquiring firm. When the Gillette Company acquired the Paper Mate Pen Company, Gillette was able to market the pens through the same distribution system it used for its razors.

Production Planning and Control

For a firm producing a product, the orderly flow of goods through the production process is essential to a sound business operation. There are several dimensions to the proper planning and control of production. First is the careful analysis of future demand. Once this has been accomplished, it is necessary to provide capacity in order to be able to produce to meet the future demand. The public utilities are good examples of this process. Demand can be estimated with reasonable accuracy for fairly long periods of time. Since it takes several years to perform all the tasks necessary to construct many electric generating plants, long-range planning is vital for any electric utility.

[10]Seymour Freedgood, "Avon: The Sweet Smell of Success," *Fortune*, December 1964, pp. 108–13. For another opinion see "Troubled Avon Tries a Face-Lifting," *Business Week*, May 11, 1974, p. 98.

[11]"Packard Returns to a New Hewlett-Packard," *Business Week*, January 29, 1972, pp. 44–45.

Another dimension of production planning and control deals with the physical handling of inventory of both raw materials and finished goods during the production process. Stirling Homex, a producer of modular homes, accumulated sizable inventories of finished modules. It was discovered later that many modules deteriorated during storage, requiring considerable sums of money to refurbish them.[12] The disastrous performance of the Stirling Homex stock testifies to the importance of an evaluation of production planning and control within the firm.

Diversification

As we previously noted, management's grand design should ideally include judicious acquisitions, and these need to be carefully planned. United States Tobacco, the major producer of snuff, has conducted a successful diversification effort in recent years. With the cash generated from profitable snuff operations, the company diversified into snack foods such as nuts and into pet food. As a result, U.S. Tobacco has compiled a respectable earnings growth record in recent years. Many of the major tobacco firms such as American Tobacco and Reynolds, Inc. have also successfully diversified into the food area.

SUMMARY

This chapter develops a framework for determining the growth potential of any company. In this endeavor, the determination of the quality of management is a vital task. While this is to some extent a subjective evaluation, many items can be considered with regard to both the quality of management and the growth potential of the firm and its products. We need to determine the philosophy of management with regard to the future of the business in an attempt to ascertain our interest in investing in the concern. We need to examine the education and experience of management personnel as well as their past record.

In looking at the growth potential of the products of the firm, many factors can be considered. The potential investor should carefully analyze the nature of the products and the environment in which they are marketed. Are the products unique and do they have broad markets? Is competition limited by patents, managerial know-how, or the difficulty of entering the industry because of either capital requirements or other factors? Research and development expenditures are important for the long-run vitality of the firm.

Past growth and plans for the future were the final two major factors examined in our quest to identify the growth potential of a company. An

[12]"Blueprint for Disaster," *Barron's*, July 3, 1972, pp. 11–12.

examination of Lowe's sales, earnings, and dividend growth for the 1958 to 1974 period revealed strong and consistent growth. This past record serves as a starting point for projections into the future. The ability of management to plan for the future should also be evaluated. Are they just keeping up with industry trends or are they pace-setters?

In the next chapter, we look at the results of financial statement analysis in an attempt to approach, in a more quantitative fashion, many of the concerns raised in this chapter. Financial statement analysis does not provide answers to all our questions. However, in conjunction with a serious consideration of many of the qualitative aspects discussed in this chapter, the investor should be well on the road to informed and, we hope, profitable investment decisions.

QUESTIONS

1. In analyzing the quality of management, the goals of the management should be clear and consistent with a "grand design." What would an investor look for to ascertain whether or not this is true in any given company?
2. It is often stated that the size of a company is an important consideration in that some managers seem to be able to effectively manage a relatively small company, but lose control as the firm becomes larger. How would an investor determine whether or not a given management will be able to cope with this "critical size" consideration?
3. Investors disagree on whether or not a company with a large percentage of the stock controlled by one family is a good investment or not. What are the pros and cons on this matter?
4. What are the attributes that are normally associated with products of growth companies? Evaluate the following products in light of these attributes:
   a) Arrow shirts.
   b) A sustained release form of drug delivery for the treatment of glaucoma developed by Alza Corporation.
   c) A Hewlett-Packard pocket calculator.
   d) An automated bank teller produced by Docutel.
   e) Kodak's movie film requiring only regular room light for satisfactory performance.
5. The proper role of diversification in the long-run growth of a firm is important to the investor. From the material contained in the standard financial reference materials, evaluate the two following diversification efforts:
   a) Mobil Oil's takeover of Marcor during August 1974.
   b) The diversification of Household Finance Corporation since 1960 into retailing, manufacturing, and service related activities. HFC owns

National Car Rental System, substantial retailing subsidiaries, and King-Seeley Thermos.

6. Lowe's, a building supply retailer, was used as an illustration in this chapter. What areas of diversification might be reasonable alternatives for Lowe's management to consider?
7. The management of the Great Atlantic & Pacific Tea Company has often been criticized for not being responsive to major industry trends in grocery retailing (*Fortune*, January 1973, pp. 102–106ff). What major industry trends to you feel are important in grocery retailing that A&P may not have responded to? Does it really matter to the investor if a retailer is a little late in following the rest of the industry?

SUGGESTED READINGS

Altman, Edward I. "Bankrupt Firms' Equity Securities As an Investment Alternative." *Financial Analysts Journal*, July–August 1969, pp. 129–33.

Burkhead, J. Gary, William W. Helman, and John B. Walker. *Company Report Guideline*, Smith Barney & Co., Inc., 1974. Reprinted in *Supplementary Readings in Financial Analysis, Volume 3*. Charlottesville, Va.: Institute of Chartered Financial Analysts, 1974, pp. 131–42.

Donaldson, Gordon. *Strategy for Financial Mobility*. Homewood, Illinois: Richard D. Irwin, 1971.

Dutter, Philip H. "Quality of Management." *Financial Analysts Journal*, March–April 1969, pp. 105–8.

Fisch, Gerald G. "Management in Financial Analysis." *Financial Analysts Journal*, July–August 1968, pp. 43–49.

Hayes, Douglas A. "The Evaluation of Management." *Financial Analysts Journal*, July–August 1968, pp. 39–42.

Jenks, Jeremy C. "Investing in Growth Stocks." *The Analysts Journal*, 2d quarter, 1947, pp. 38–53.

Jessup, Paul F. and Roger B. Upson. "Opportunities in Regional Markets." *Financial Analysts Journal*, March–April 1970, pp. 75–79.

Malkiel, Burton G. *A Random Walk Down Wall Street*. New York: W.W. Norton & Co., Inc., 1973, chapters 1–4.

Modak, N. D. "Corporate Planning and the Securities Analyst." *Financial Analysts Journal*, September–October 1974, pp. 51–54ff.

Reilly, Frank K. and Eugene F. Drzycimski. "Aggregate Market Earnings Multipler Over Stock Market Cycles and Business Cycles." *Mississippi Valley Journal of Business and Economics*, Winter 1974–75, pp. 14–36.

Shade, Philip A. *Common Stocks: A Plan for Intelligent Investing*. Homewood, Illinois: Richard D. Irwin, 1971.

Terborgh, George. "Inflation and Profits." *Financial Analysts Journal*, May–June 1974, pp. 19–23.

Wendt, Paul F. "Current Growth Stock Valuation Models." *Financial Analysts Journal*, March–April 1965, pp. 91–103.

*

10

Analysis of Financial Statements

In the stock market environment of the early and mid-1960s it often appeared that about the only item many investors examined was the rate of growth in earnings per share. Frequently, the investment community did not appear concerned with an analysis of the financial statements to ascertain the financial strength that is vital to the investor. We must ask if the firm has sufficient cash and marketable securities in order to run the business. Are the firm's debts being collected promptly? Is the firm using a prudent level of debt given the financial and operating characteristics of the company? The list of potential problems is virtually endless.

In recent years, investors appear to be much more inclined to seek answers to these types of questions. High interest rates and tight money in the 1969–70 period along with the bankruptcy of Penn Central in 1970 caused many investors to be concerned about financial soundness. As Roger Murray put it, "The immediate reaction of financial analysts [to the Penn Central collapse] was to rediscover the significance of the balance sheet, to invoke new emphasis on credit worthiness, and to face the reality of the fading of an inflation-induced euphoria."[1] In addition to this reawakening to the importance of financial statements, several studies relating to the usefulness of financial statement analysis as a risk measure appeared. These studies are discussed later in this chapter.

The first section of this chapter discusses the various types of financial statements available for the investor to analyze, along with the general nature of the information contained in these statements. The next section examines the usefulness of reducing financial statements to a common size by looking at percentage relationships. The third major section deals with ratio analysis. We are concerned with five categories of ratios which will be defined in turn. The categories are liquidity ratios, leverage ratios, activity ratios, profitability-efficiency ratios, and ratios not falling into the other classifications. The trend of these ratios over time will be shown to be of considerable importance. Section four discusses the source and use of funds statement. The next major section discusses the use of financial statement analysis output as a measure of risk. A summary completes the chapter.

TYPES OF FINANCIAL STATEMENTS

There are three major types of financial statements—the balance sheet, the income statement along with the statement of retained earnings, and the statement of changes in financial position. The statement of changes in financial position is sometimes known as the source and use of funds statement.

Balance Sheet

The balance sheet shows the position of the firm at a point in time. Its two major sections show 1) the assets of the firm and 2) the liabilities and shareholders' equity. Exhibit 10-1 shows the consolidated balance sheet from Lowe's 1974 *Fourth Quarter Report.* The balance sheet is called consolidated since it includes the accounts of the company and its subsidiaries. All of Lowe's 118 subsidiary companies are wholly owned.

The balance sheet shown in Exhibit 10-1 indicates that Lowe's total assets as of July 31, 1974, amounted to over $150.6 million. The total assets are classified into current assets, fixed assets (property, improvements, and equipment), and other assets. Current assets include cash and other assets that will become cash within the normal operating cycle

[1]Roger F. Murray, "The Penn Central Debacle: Lessons for Financial Analysis," *Journal of Finance,* May 1971, p. 327.

EXHIBIT 10–1

Consolidated Balance Sheet

LOWE'S COMPANIES, INC. AND SUBSIDIARIES

July 31, 1974 With Comparative Figures for July 31, 1973	1974	1973
ASSETS		
Current Assets:		
Cash	$ 12,986,368	$ 7,858,746
Accounts Receivable Less Allowance for Doubtful Accounts — 1974 — $2,007,200; 1973 — $1,901,168	36,849,859	37,603,195
Inventories at the Lower of Cost (First-In, First-Out) or Market	61,775,133	50,638,619
Prepaid Expenses and Other Current Assets	331,487	290,444
Total Current Assets	$111,942,847	$ 96,391,004
Property, Improvements and Equipment: (Notes 2 and 3)		
At Cost Less Accumulated Depreciation — 1974 — $12,017,619; 1973 — $9,422,442	38,551,555	29,237,863
Other Assets:		
Unamortized Loan Expense	79,300	24,142
Sundry Assets at Cost	60,278	60,808
Total Assets	$150,633,980	$125,713,817
LIABILITIES AND SHAREHOLDERS' EQUITY		
Current Liabilities:		
Accounts Payable — Trade	$ 32,640,087	$ 36,101,215
Notes Payable		4,000,000
Accrued Expenses	6,886,567	6,634,723
Provisions for Employees' Profit-Sharing	2,975,149	2,253,161
Current Maturities of Long-Term Debt	994,546	1,631,757
Provisions for Income Taxes (Note 4)	6,732,005	5,072,915
Total Current Liabilities	$ 50,228,354	$ 55,693,771
Long-Term Debt: (Note 3)		
Notes Payable	33,157,994	18,237,721
Total Liabilities	$ 83,386,348	$ 73,931,492
Shareholders' Equity: (Notes 3 and 5)		
Common Stock — $.50 Par Value, Authorized 20,000,000 Shares; Issued and Outstanding 1974 — 8,591,330 Shares; 1973 — 8,487,313 Shares	$ 4,295,665	$ 4,243,657
Capital in Excess of Par Value	3,756,483	1,915,172
Retained Earnings	59,195,484	45,623,496
Total Shareholders' Equity	$ 67,247,632	$ 51,782,325
Total Liabilities and Shareholders' Equity	$150,633,980	$125,713,817

Source: Lowe's 1974 *Fourth Quarter Report.*

of the firm. For example, accounts receivable should eventually be collected and become cash. Property, improvements, and equipment represent fixed assets such as land, buildings, and machinery. These fixed assets are vital to the operation of the business, but are long term in nature and will not ordinarily be converted directly to cash. The fixed assets are net of an allowance for depreciation to reflect wear and tear and the possible decline in value for these fixed assets.

The total assets have been financed either by incurring a liability (debt) or from capital contributed by the shareholders (equity). Of the total liabilities of over $83.3 million, over $50.2 million are current liabilities. Current liabilities, with a maturity of less than one year, are normally paid off in the normal operating cycle of the business. The long-term debt matures in more than one year. Lowe's stockholders have invested over $67.2 million in the firm. This investment is in the form of both the price originally paid for the shares (common stock plus capital in excess of par value) and earnings retained by the firm for use in the business.

After introducing the other two major types of financial statements, we will analyze the composition of the balance sheet. We will also analyze the composition of the other types of financial statements in the next major section of this chapter.

Income and Retained Earnings Statement

Exhibit 10–2 shows the consolidated statement of both current and retained earnings from Lowe's 1974 *Fourth Quarter Report.* For the fiscal year ending July 31, 1974, Lowe's had sales of over $362 million. Total costs and expenses of doing business amounted to over $333 million, resulting in pretax earnings of over $29 million. Income taxes amounted to about 50 percent of pretax earnings, leaving over $14.6 million in net earnings available for the common stockholders.

Lowe's statement of retained earnings is also shown in Exhibit 10–2. For fiscal 1974, Lowe's had a net addition of over $13.5 million, to increase the total retained earnings at the end of the fiscal year to over $59.1 million. We noted in Chapter 9 that retained earnings have represented an important method of financing for Lowe's, and that the percentage of earnings retained in the business has increased steadily during the last ten years.

Statement of Changes in Financial Position

Lowe's 1974 *Fourth Quarter Report* presents a summary of the statement of changes in financial position for the ten-year period from 1965 to 1974 in addition to data for each of the years in this period. In Exhibit

EXHIBIT 10–2

Consolidated Statement of Current Earnings

LOWE'S COMPANIES, INC. AND SUBSIDIARIES

Year Ended July 31, 1974 With Comparative Figures for 1973	1974	1973
Income:		
Net Sales	$362,453,211	$326,846,108
Costs and Expenses:		
Cost of Sales, Buying, Warehousing and Occupancy	$288,023,372	$266,758,393
Advertising, Selling, Administrative and General Expenses	33,371,208	26,680,888
Depreciation and Amortization (Note 2)	3,458,042	2,790,923
Contribution to Employees' Profit-Sharing Plan (Note 7)	3,649,317	2,695,178
Interest and Loan Expense	2,744,682	1,350,296
Provision for Bad Debts	1,919,598	1,177,354
Total Costs and Expenses	$333,166,219	$301,453,032
Pre-Tax Earnings	$ 29,286,992	$ 25,393,076
Provision for Income Taxes	14,669,889	12,665,144
Net Earnings	$ 14,617,103	$ 12,727,932
Average Shares Outstanding	8,529,499	8,474,124
Earnings per Common Share (Note 1)	$ 1.71	$ 1.50

Consolidated Statement of Retained Earnings

LOWE'S COMPANIES, INC. AND SUBSIDIARIES

Year Ended July 31, 1974 With Comparative Figures for 1973	1974	1973
Balance at Beginning of Year	$ 45,623,496	$ 33,913,091
Additions:		
Net Earnings	$ 14,617,103	$ 12,727,932
Less Cash Dividends	1,045,115	1,017,268
Net Additions	$ 13,571,988	$ 11,710,664
Deductions:		
Stock Dividends (Note 5)		$ 259
Balance at End of Year	$ 59,195,484	$ 45,623,496

Source: Lowe's 1974 Fourth Quarter Report.

10–3, we have reproduced the statement of changes in financial position for the fiscal year 1974 as well as the ten-year totals. We will examine the usefulness of this financial statement later in the chapter.

THE QUALITY OF THE FINANCIAL STATEMENT

These three types of financial statements are the basic raw material of the investor. It is important, however, to recognize that financial statements published by a firm do not always provide an unambiguous source of information. The ambiguity results from the fact that there is considerable leeway in the techniques and accounting principles that can be employed in the preparation of the balance sheet and income statement. Selection of a particular accounting technique is not typically related to corporate dishonesty or an attempt to deceive the investor. In some cases, there is a basic disagreement among the "experts." In other situations, there is a conflict between accounting principles and the economics of the firm. In still other cases, the financial community simply does not know how to reflect certain situations in the financial statements. Finally, we often find that financial information is omitted simply because it is too costly to obtain the omitted data.

Several books have been written on how to solve the problems of financial statements. To examine the problems and proposed solutions is an exhausting task that cannot be given detailed attention here. An example of one problem will suffice as a warning to the unwary investor who is inclined to accept the data given in the financial statements as "correct" and unambiguous.

A contemporary problem of considerable importance lies in the treatment of inventories and their effect on the cost of goods sold. Suppose we have a firm that sells 100 units of its product at a price of $15 per unit. Gross sales are $1,500 as indicated in Exhibit 10–4, which compares two legitimate methods of accounting for the value of inventory. LIFO is the technique that places the cost associated with the last items purchased into the cost of goods sold account and the cost associated with the first items purchased into the inventory account. Under FIFO, the cost associated with the last items purchased is included in the ending inventory account and the cost associated with the first items purchased is included in the cost of goods sold account. Exhibit 10–4 shows income statements using each method. With LIFO the firm has a net profit of $50, but with FIFO the reported profit is $70. The FIFO technique generates an increase in profit of 40 percent but physically there is absolutely no difference. In other words, this firm can increase its reported profits by 40 percent merely by using FIFO instead of LIFO and determination of the correct technique is controversial. The effect on earnings is directly tied to price changes associated with the firm's purchases. As prices increase FIFO will typically generate larger profits.

EXHIBIT 10–3

Consolidated Statement of Changes in Financial Position

LOWE'S COMPANIES, INC. AND SUBSIDIARIES

	Ten Year Totals		7-31-74		7-31-73		7-31-72	
AMOUNTS IN THOUSANDS: ( ) INDICATES A DECREASE	**Amount**	**%**	**Amount**	**%**	**Amount**	**%**	**Amount**	**%**
Source of Funds:								
Net Earnings	$ 63,690	48.0	$14,617	33.2	$12,728	48.2	$ 9,121	50.7
Depreciation and Amortization	14,817	11.2	3,458	7.8	2,791	10.6	2,295	12.7
Total Funds from Operations	$ 78,507	59.2	$18,075	41.0	$15,519	58.8	$11,416	63.4
Sale of Common Stock Under Option Plan	3,281	2.5	1,534	3.4	473	1.8	532	3.0
Disposals of Property and Equipment	1,656	1.3	295	.7	152	.6	302	1.7
Additions to Long-Term Debt	48,258	36.4	23,820	54.0	9,907	37.5	5,714	31.7
Tax Benefit from Optionee Stock Dispositions	703	.5	359	.9	344	1.3		
Other	164	.1					42	.2
Totals	$132,569	100.0	$44,083	100.0	$26,395	100.0	$18,006	100.0
Use of Funds:								
Dividends Paid	$ 8,091	6.1	$ 1,045	2.4	$ 1,017	3.9	$ 946	5.3
Reduction of Long-Term Debt	17,717	13.4	8,900	20.2	1,683	6.4	2,996	16.6
Additions to Property and Equipment	52,642	39.7	13,066	29.6	12,851	48.6	7,840	43.5
Retirement of Preferred Stock	45						45	.2
Other	259	.2	55	.1	40	.2		
Totals	$ 78,754	59.4	$23,066	52.3	$15,591	59.1	$11,827	65.6
Increase in Working Capital	$ 53,815	40.6	$21,017	47.7	$10,804	40.9	$ 6,179	34.4
Changes in Components of Working Capital:								
Current Assets:								
Cash	$ 9,610		$ 5,128		$ 57		$ 1,498	
Receivables	31,264		(753)		10,164		6,495	
Inventories	55,438		11,136		16,163		7,143	
Other Current Assets	277		41		(103)		62	
Totals	$ 96,589		$15,552		$26,281		$15,198	
Current Liabilities:								
Accounts Payable and Other Liabilities	$ 36,460		$(2,487)		$10,530		$ 8,033	
Notes Payable	724		(4,637)		4,959		194	
Provision for Income Taxes	5,590		1,659		(12)		792	
Totals	$ 42,774		$(5,465)		$15,477		$ 9,019	
Increase in Working Capital	$ 53,815		$21,017		$10,804		$ 6,179	

Source: Lowe's 1974 Fourth Quarter Report.

EXHIBIT 10–4
Earnings with LIFO and FIFO

	Income Statement Using			
	LIFO		FIFO	
Sales—100 @ $15		$1,500		$1,500
Cost of goods sold				
Beginning inventory, 10 @ $10	$ 100		$ 100	
Purchases, 50 @ $11	550		550	
50 @ $12	600		600	
	$1,250		$1,250	
Ending inventory	100 (10 @ $10)		120 (10 @ $12)	
		1,150		1,130
Gross profit		$ 350		$ 370
Other expenses		300		300
Net profit		$ 50		$ 70

This inventory example is given to underscore the fact that accounting data do not always provide a clear picture of the financial condition of the firm.

Space does not permit a detailed examination of other accounting problems. Inventory is only one of several areas where potential problems exist. The methods used to depreciate assets are many and varied and may have an impact on the income of the firm. The treatment of stock options is not yet clear and the accounting for employee pension plans can have a marked impact on earnings. There is much controversy concerning whether some expenditures should be treated as a current expense or recorded as a fixed asset and depreciated over time. Mergers represent another special problem.

The list of accounting difficulties could go on and on. Professional security analysts spend considerable time and effort adjusting for these data problems. Most of their adjustments have the two objectives of 1) providing consistency across time within the firm and 2) being certain financial data are comparable to the data of other firms within the industry. They do not attempt to settle the accounting controversy, but instead attempt to generate consistency in their comparisons. In fairness to the accounting profession, in recent years a concerted effort has been made to provide the investor with the necessary information with which to make the adjustments desired.

COMMON SIZE FINANCIAL STATEMENTS

Because of the size differences among firms, it is often convenient to reduce the three major financial statements to a common size by converting the statements to percentage terms. This conversion allows the investor to make a better comparison of one company in an industry with other companies in the same industry. It also allows the investor to observe potentially significant trends which may have developed within the firm over the years. As noted in Exhibit 10-3, Lowe's provided the reader of its financial report with a common size statement of changes in financial position.

Common Size Balance Sheet

Table 10-1 presents balance sheet trends for Lowe's from 1965 to 1974 by major balance sheet categories. In looking at the composition of the various asset categories as a percent of total assets, one notices a substantial long-term decline in *other assets*. *Other assets* consist primarily of cash. The liquidity ratio, to be discussed shortly, also shows a similar decline. Fixed assets have shown a substantial increase as a percent of total assets. During the 1965 to 1974 period, the number of stores operated by Lowe's increased from 35 to 116. This could account for the decline in cash and the increase in fixed assets. The receivable and inventory percentages have remained relatively constant during this period. While the liquidity of the firm has declined, this is not necessarily unfavorable given the growth of the firm in recent years.

Common Size Income Statement

A common size income statement is especially useful to the investor in helping to spot trends in the various expense categories. These trends may be either favorable or unfavorable to the investment value of the

TABLE 10-1

Lowe's Common Size Balance Sheet (1965-74)

	1974	1973	1972	1971	1970	1969	1968	1967	1966	1965
					(In Percent)					
Accounts receivable	24	30	31	30	30	35	34	32	33	31
Inventories	41	40	39	40	39	34	35	32	38	35
Fixed assets	26	23	22	20	21	19	19	19	18	17
Other assets (mainly cash)	9	7	8	10	10	12	12	17	11	17
TOTAL ASSETS	100	100	100	100	100	100	100	100	100	100
Accounts payable	22	29	31	32	31	27	27	28	33	34
Long-term debt	22	15	11	11	7	5	10	12	11	10
All other liabilities	12	15	14	13	12	18	15	13	15	15
Stockholders' equity	44	41	44	44	50	50	48	47	41	41
TOTAL LIABILITIES AND EQUITY	100	100	100	100	100	100	100	100	100	100

Sources: Lowe's 1974 *Fourth Quarter Report.*

firm. Table 10-2 shows a common size income statement for Lowe's for 1965 to 1974. Only major expense categories are shown in this statement. Lowe's cost of goods sold, administrative and other general expenses have declined in recent years as a percentage of sales and have tended to stabilize at approximately 90 percent of sales. This is certainly a favorable situation. In addition, virtually all other expense items shown in Table 10-2 have been quite stable in recent years. One could infer from these data that Lowe's management has been successful in expense control.

TABLE 10-2
Lowe's Common Size Income Statement 1965-74

	1974	1973	1972	1971	1970	1969	1968	1967	1966	1965
					(In Percent)					
Cost of sales, etc.	89.2	90.1	89.9	90.2	90.1	90.2	90.7	91.1	91.5	91.6
Depreciation, etc.	1.0	.9	1.0	1.0	1.0	.8	.9	1.0	.7	.5
Employees' profit-sharing	1.0	.8	1.1	.9	.9	.9	.8	.8	.7	.7
Interest, etc.	.8	.4	.3	.3	.3	.2	.3	.2	.3	.3
Income taxes	4.0	3.9	3.9	3.8	3.9	4.1	3.7	3.1	3.2	3.3
Earnings after taxes	4.0	3.9	3.9	3.9	3.8	3.9	3.7	3.7	3.6	3.6
NET SALES*	100.0	100.0	100.0	100.0	100.0	100.0	100.0	100.0	100.0	100.0

*Columns may not add to 100 due to rounding.
Source: Lowe's 1974 *Fourth Quarter Report.*

P/E RATIO AND CURRENT YIELD

Before examining some of the various ratios in the analysis of financial statements, we need to mention two significant calculations. These are the price-earnings ratio and the current yield on the stock. The price-earnings ratio for Lowe's is calculated below, using a price of $46 for the common stock and 1974's earnings per share of $1.71. Investors are willing to pay almost $27 for each $1 of Lowe's earnings. Whether such a valuation is justified is the investor's major concern.

$$\text{P/E ratio} = \frac{\text{price per share}}{\text{earnings per share}} = \frac{\$46}{\$1.71} = 26.9$$

The price-earnings calculation is not without its problems. First, what price should be used? Although the current market price is probably the most useful price for many calculations, an investor might want to calculate historical price-earnings ratios. For historical calculations, past prices are needed. More difficult problems are evident in deciding what earnings per share figure to use. We will just pose some potential questions, answers to which depend mainly on the individual circumstances of the company under analysis. Should the investor use the most recent twelve-month earnings per share figure? What if the most recent twelve months were abnormal because of such problems as a strike, a recession, an extraordinary income item, or a shortage of raw materials? If earnings per share are in a strong trend, should the investor use the best estimate of earnings per share for the coming twelve-month period? Is the firm under analysis using accounting practices that would cause the investor to adjust the reported earnings per share in some manner?

The current yield is calculated by dividing the dividend per share by the market price per share. The current yield for Lowe's is calculated below using the $46 market price.

$$\text{Current yield} = \frac{\text{dividend per share}}{\text{market price per share}} = \frac{\$.12}{\$46} = .003 \text{ or } .3\%$$

Lowe's current yield is low by any standard. This is not really surprising since the company is retaining approximately 93 percent of its earnings for use in the business. Whether this low current yield is acceptable to an investor given Lowe's growth prospects is a key question. The investor in Lowe's stock is clearly making a trade-off between current income and potential capital gains.

RATIO ANALYSIS

The analysis of financial statements normally entails the calculation of ratios examining various aspects of the business. The potential investor is interested in both the absolute level of the ratio and its trend over time. It is often useful and desirable to compare ratios for different companies in the same industry in order to determine if any particular company differs substantially from industry norms. We will examine various ratio classifications, including liquidity, leverage, activity, profitability-efficiency, and others.

Liquidity Ratios

As indicated by the name, liquidity ratios are concerned with the ability of the firm to meet its obligations out of its cash account or by using assets which will be converted to cash within a relatively short period of time. The three ratios we will examine are the current ratio, the acid-test ratio, and what is called the liquidity ratio. The acid-test ratio is sometimes referred to as the "quick ratio" since the components making up the ratio can be quickly converted into cash. Each of these three ratios will be calculated for Lowe's for 1974 and discussed.

Current Ratio. The current ratio is determined by dividing current assets by current liabilities. Using the data for Lowe's from Exhibit 10–1, the current ratio is calculated below for 1974:

$$\text{Current ratio} = \frac{\text{current assets}}{\text{current liabilities}} = \frac{\$111{,}942{,}847}{\$50{,}228{,}354} = 2.23$$

Since an investor does not know whether a current ratio of 2.23 for 1974 is favorable or unfavorable, the current ratio for Lowe's for the 1958 to 1974 period is shown in Figure 10–1. While the 1973 current ratio is near the low end of the range observed during this fifteen-year period, the current ratio has been quite consistent over time. The 1974 current ratio represents an improvement over 1973. Furthermore, the fact that the firm has operated for sixteen years with a current ratio between 1.6 and 2.2 suggests that a ratio in this range is adequate to meet liquidity needs.

FIGURE 10–1
Lowe's Liquidity Ratios, 1958–74

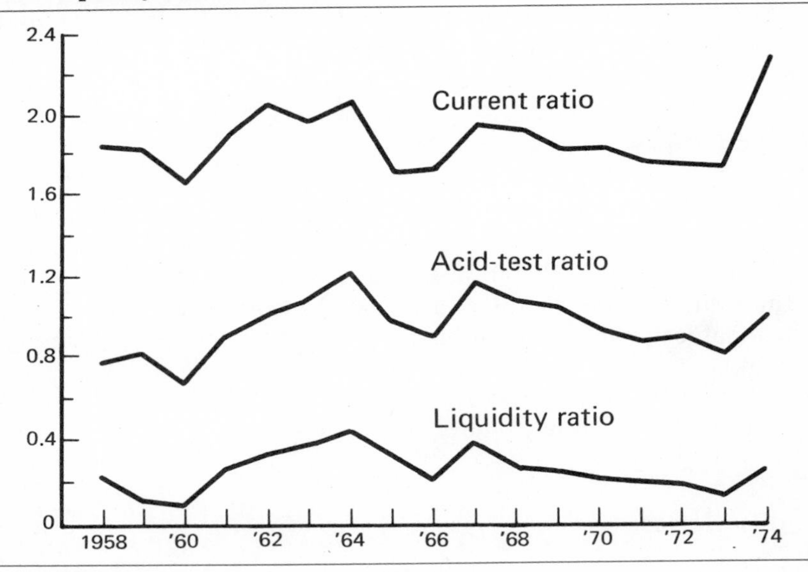

Source: Lowe's 1974 *Fourth Quarter Report.*

Acid-Test Ratio. The acid-test ratio is determined by dividing current assets excluding inventory by the total of current liabilities. By excluding inventory, the least liquid of the current assets, one obtains a more restrictive definition of the ability to meet current liabilities. Using Exhibit 10–1, the acid-test ratio for Lowe's for 1974 is calculated below:

$$\text{Acid-test ratio} = \frac{\text{current assets less inventory}}{\text{current liabilities}} = \frac{\$50{,}167{,}714}{\$50{,}228{,}354} = 1.00$$

A somewhat useful rule-of-thumb is that inventory should normally be equal to about 50 percent of the current assets, although valid exceptions can certainly exist depending on the company and the industry being examined. This would mean that the acid-test ratio should be about half the value of the current ratio. Lowe's is reasonably close to this rule-of-thumb standard for 1974.

Figure 10–1 shows Lowe's acid-test ratio for the 1958 to 1974 period. The same general impression is gained by observing the acid-test ratio that was gained by noting the current ratio. Lowe's liquidity when measured by the acid-test ratio appears acceptable and no unfavorable trends can be noted. It also appears that the acid-test ratio has fairly consistently approximated one-half of the current ratio.

Liquidity Ratio. The most restrictive measure of liquidity is called the liquidity ratio. This ratio is obtained by dividing cash and marketable securities by the total of the current liabilities. Cash and marketable securities are the most liquid of the current assets and the liquidity ratio provides a measure of a firm's immediate debt-paying ability. Lowe's 1974 liquidity ratio is calculated below:

$$\text{Liquidity ratio} = \frac{\text{cash plus marketable securities}}{\text{current liabilities}} = \frac{\$12{,}986{,}368}{\$50{,}228{,}354} = .26$$

Since Lowe's has no marketable securities, only the cash figure from Exhibit 10–1 is used in the calculation. The liquidity ratio for the 1958 to 1974 period is also shown in Figure 10–1. This ratio shows the same general picture for Lowe's as the current and acid-test ratios. We observed in the common size balance sheet for Lowe's, which was presented in Table 10–1, that cash has declined as a percentage of total assets. Clearly, Lowe's is not "cash-rich."

We will want to complete our analysis of Lowe's financial statements before making a final judgment regarding the level of cash. Certainly, the financing flexibility of the firm as indicated by the level of debt in the capital structure will be of considerable interest to the potential investor. Evidence of good financial management in other aspects of the firm will also lessen our concern about the level of cash.

Leverage Ratios

Leverage ratios provide a means of examining the use and impact of debt by a firm. As with the three liquidity ratios, investors have experienced a resurgence of interest in the use of borrowed money by firms.

Capital market conditions in 1974 reinforced investor concern about the need for a firm to have a good credit rating to issue new bonds and the need to have financing flexibility. Many public utilities, for example, have recently had their bond ratings downgraded. Bond ratings, a convenient manner of looking at the quality of a bond, are discussed in detail in Chapter 17. In addition, the investing public has become very aware of quality considerations, and securities of poorer quality have been very difficult, if not impossible, to sell.

In this section, we examine several measures of leverage. These include the composition of the firm's capital structure, the debt-to-asset ratio, the leverage factor (the number of asset dollars per equity dollar), and the times interest earned calculation.

Capital Structure Breakdown. A useful starting point in the analysis of the use of debt by a firm is to calculate the percentage breakdown of the capital structure. In this calculation, we are interested in the breakdown of long-term sources of capital. The calculation below gives Lowe's capital structure as of July 31, 1974:

Long-term debt	$ 33,157,994	33.0%
Total common stockholders' equity	67,247,632	67.0
Total long-term capital	$100,405,626	100.0%

Of Lowe's capital structure, 33 percent is in the form of long-term debt. Whether this is a prudent figure depends upon many different factors. Some of these factors include the amount of short-term debt that the firm is using, the amount of interest relative to net income, the stability of its revenues and earnings, the past and expected growth of income for the firm, and the maturity structure of the long-term debt. While not included in the capital structure breakdown, the amount of short-term debt a firm is using is included in some of the other leverage measures we will now examine.

Debt-to-Asset Ratio. A measure that includes all forms of debt is the debt-to-asset ratio. The total of all the various forms of debt on the firm's balance sheet is divided by the total assets. The resulting ratio tells the investor what percentage of the assets is being financed by various forms of debt. From Exhibit 10–1, the debt-to-asset ratio is calculated as of July 31, 1974. The calculation is shown below and indicates that approximately 55 percent of Lowe's assets are financed by debt of all types.

$$\text{Debt-to-asset ratio} = \frac{\text{total debt}}{\text{total assets}} = \frac{\$83{,}386{,}348}{\$150{,}633{,}980} = .554$$

Leverage Factor. Lowe's 1974 *Fourth Quarter Report* also includes what is called the leverage factor. This statistic is nothing more than the dollar amount of assets financed by one dollar of equity capital. For Lowe's, all the equity is supplied by common stockholders. The leverage factor for Lowe's at the beginning of its 1975 fiscal year is calculated below. It shows that for each dollar of equity capital there is $2.24 of assets.

$$\text{Leverage factor} = \frac{\text{total assets}}{\text{stockholders' equity}} = \frac{\$150{,}633{,}980}{\$67{,}247{,}632} = 2.24$$

Times Interest Earned. One of the fundamental calculations an investor can make is to determine the relationship between the income earned by the firm and the interest charges that must be paid. This relationship is commonly called times interest earned. The ratio is often calculated on a before-tax basis. While it is possible to calculate times interest earned on an after-tax basis, we restrict our discussion to the before-tax method since interest is a before-tax deduction. Based upon data from Exhibit 10–2, the times interest earned for Lowe's for 1974 is calculated below:

$$\begin{array}{c}\text{Times interest earned}\\ \text{(before taxes)}\end{array} = \frac{\begin{array}{c}\text{earnings before}\\ \text{interest and taxes}\end{array}}{\text{interest expense}} = \frac{\$32{,}031{,}674}{\$2{,}744{,}682} = 11.67$$

While Lowe's has 33 percent debt in its capital structure, the interest coverage is substantial. Earnings can decline to roughly 9 percent (1/11.67) of the current level before the firm is technically insolvent. Technical insolvency occurs when earnings are not sufficient to meet the firm's debt obligations. Two points need to be made, however. First, the interest coverage figure does not cover other fixed financial obligations such as lease payments. Lowe's rent expense for real estate leases amounted to $709,138 in 1974. If this amount is added to the interest expense of $2,744, 682 to calculate a times fixed financial charges earned figure, the new figure would be 9.27 ($32,031,674/$3,453,820). Since Lowe's could incur long-term debt to purchase the real estate that it is leasing, the debt component previously calculated tends to be understated by the amount of debt that would need to be incurred to acquire the benefits achieved by use of the lease arrangement. If one assumes an interest rate of 10 percent, over 7 million dollars of equivalent debt would need to be added to the capital structure ($709,138 ÷ .10) to cover the leases outstanding.

The second point deals with the relationship between the ability to carry the burden of debt and the profitability of the firm. As we shall see shortly, Lowe's is a very profitable firm when measured by the rate of return on stockholder's equity. The profitability, combined with the low dividend payout percentage noted in the previous chapter, appears to make the debt burden of Lowe's quite manageable.

In summary, we conclude that the fixed financial obligations of the firm are not excessive. In Table 10–3 the data and various ratios

TABLE 10–3
Capital Structure Analysis

	Without Leases		With Leases*	
	($000)	%	($000)	%
Total debt (all maturities)	83,386	55.4	90,477	57.4
Stockholders equity	67,248	44.6	67,248	42.6
TOTAL	150,634	100.0	157,725	100.0
Debt-to-asset ratio		.54		.57
Leverage factor		2.24		2.34
Times interest earned		11.67		9.27

*$709,138 of annual lease payments discounted at 10 percent for equivalent of $7,091,380 of debt.

used to arrive at this conclusion are summarized. In this particular example, inclusion of leases does not alter the judgment that the capital structure is sound. As we will soon see, the profitability of the firm suggests that Lowe's could easily carry additional debt. Fixed financial obligations can be met and debt capacity exists for future expansion and flexibility.

Activity Ratios

One of the questions an investor needs to consider is how the firm is managing its assets. Are inventories under good control? Is inventory "fresh" or has slow-moving inventory accumulated? Are accounts receivable being collected within a reasonable period of time? These and similar questions can be answered with the assistance of activity ratios. We will examine two activity ratios—the inventory turnover and the accounts receivable turnover.

Inventory Turnover. Inventory turnover measures the speed with which inventory moves from acquisition and manufacture to the ultimate sale. Inventory turnover is calculated by dividing the cost of goods sold by the average inventory during the period for which the ratio is being calculated. It would be desirable to have an average inventory figure based upon weekly or monthly data. These data are not often available to investors, however. The calculation below uses the average of the fiscal year-end figures for 1973 and 1974 to calculate Lowe's inventory turnover figure for 1974:

$$\text{Inventory turnover} = \frac{\text{cost of goods sold}}{\text{average inventory}} = \frac{\$288{,}023{,}372}{\$56{,}206{,}876} = 5.12$$

The inventory turnover of 5.12 times can be transformed into the number of days of sales that is represented by the inventory account by dividing the number of days in a year (365) by the turnover figure. During fiscal 1974 the firm held an average inventory of slightly more than 71 days of sales.

Accounts Receivable Turnover. Just as we calculated an inventory turnover and the average number of days of inventory in stock, it is possible to perform similar calculations for the accounts receivable. By dividing the sales figure by the average of the accounts receivable, we get the accounts receivable turnover figure. Ideally, we should use only credit sales since only credit sales result in accounts receivable. Since this figure is not available in Lowe's annual report, we have to use total sales from Exhibit 10–2. This will not result in any serious distortion of our conclusions as long as the percentage that credit sales comprise of total sales remains relatively constant. We would prefer an average receivable figure based upon weekly or monthly data. As with the inventory calculation, this is not available to the investor from published financial statements. Therefore, we will use the average of the fiscal year-end accounts receivable figures in the calculation below:

$$\text{Receivable turnover} = \frac{\text{sales}}{\text{average accounts receivable}} = \frac{\$362{,}453{,}211}{\$37{,}226{,}527} = 9.74$$

The 1974 figure of 9.74 for accounts receivable turnover for Lowe's represents the second highest value achieved for the 1964 to 1974 period. During this eleven-year period, the lowest value was 8.0 with an average of 9.2. It would appear that accounts receivable are being managed properly and better than has been the case historically.

At the same time one should recognize that increasing receivables turnover may result from an overly strict credit policy which could have a negative impact on sales and earnings. The sales record of Lowe's suggests that credit given by the firm is not overly restrictive or, if it is, there appears to have been little impact on sales.

We can also transform the receivable turnover figure into an average collection figure. To do this, the accounts receivable turnover figure is divided into 365 days to produce the value below:

$$\text{Average collection period} = \frac{\text{365 days}}{\text{annual receivables turnover}} = \frac{365}{9.74} = 37.5 \text{ days}$$

Profitability-Efficiency Ratios

Profitability and efficiency ratios are grouped together for discussion purposes since they are really two different ways of examining the same basic thing. If a firm is efficiently managed, it tends to be profitable.

Likewise, a profitable firm tends to be efficiently managed. Hence, an investor should reach the same general conclusions concerning the quality of management by looking at either type of ratio. We should note, however, that an efficient firm is not necessarily profitable nor is the profitable firm necessarily efficient.

The profitability ratios we will examine are the rate of return on sales, the rate of return on total assets, and the rate of return on stockholders' equity. The rate of return on assets and sales will be examined on a before interest and taxes basis. This will provide a better picture of the efficiency or earning power of the assets and allow the separation of asset efficiency from the firm's use of financial leverage. The rate of return on stockholders' equity will be examined on an after interest and taxes basis in an attempt to measure profitability from the stockholders' point of view.

Several efficiency ratios have already been examined in Lowe's common size income statement for the 1965 to 1974 period (Table 10–2). In this table, we examined the trend of the various expense ratios expressed as a percentage of sales. Our basic finding was that Lowe's expense control appeared reasonable. We concluded that Lowe's is an efficiently managed concern.

Before examining the various profitability ratios, we should mention one special efficiency ratio that is used in many industries—especially regulated industries such as utilities, airlines, and railroads. This is the operating ratio. The operating ratio is the operating expenses divided by the operating income. It is a useful measure of the operating efficiency of management since it excludes the expense items associated with the capital structure, the administrative structure, and other nonoperating financial activity.

Return on Sales. Return on sales is frequently calculated merely as the ratio of net earnings to total sales. Unfortunately, this ratio mixes the earning power of assets with the use of financial leverage. As a consequence, it is less useful for analytical purposes. To eliminate the effect of financial leverage, return on sales is calculated by taking the ratio of earnings before interest and taxes (EBIT) to sales. Table 10–4 presents the return on sales for Lowe's for 1964 to 1974. In 1974 Lowe's achieved a return on sales of 8.84 percent calculated as follows:

$$\text{Return on sales} = \frac{\text{pretax earnings + interest}}{\text{sales}}$$

$$= \frac{\$29{,}286{,}992 + \$2{,}744{,}682}{\$362{,}453{,}211} = 8.84\%$$

Total Asset Turnover. Lowe's 1974 *Fourth Quarter Report* presents the total asset turnover figure for each year during the 1964 to 1974 period. The turnover figures are reproduced in Table 10–4. The total asset turnover data are obtained by dividing sales by total assets. Lowe's 1974 turnover of 2.88 is obtained in the following manner:

$$\text{Total asset turnover} = \frac{\text{sales}}{\text{total assets (start of period)}} = \frac{\$362,453,211}{\$125,713,817} = 2.88$$

TABLE 10-4

Lowe's Return on Sales and Assets plus Total Asset Turnover

Year	Return on Sales %	Total Asset Turnover	Return on Assets %
1964	6.6	3.11	20.5
1965	7.2	3.20	23.0
1966	7.1	3.34	23.7
1967	7.0	2.65	18.6
1968	7.7	3.24	24.9
1969	8.2	3.37	27.6
1970	8.0	3.09	24.7
1971	8.0	3.43	27.4
1972	8.1	3.40	27.5
1973	8.2	3.65	29.9
1974	8.8	2.88	25.4

Source: Lowe's 1974 *Fourth Quarter Report.*

Return on Assets. The return on assets is also expressed on a before interest and taxes basis and is merely the ratio of earnings before interest and taxes (EBIT) to total assets held at the beginning of the year. The earnings figure is the same number used in the return on sales calculation and the asset figure is the same as the one used in the turnover calculation. Lowe's return on assets for the period 1964–74 is presented in Table 10–4. For 1974 the return on assets is calculated as follows:

$$\text{Return on assets} = \frac{\text{EBIT}}{\text{total assets (start of period)}} = \frac{\$29,286,992 + \$2,744,682}{\$125,713,817} = 25.4\%$$

The return on assets can also be expressed as the product of the return on sales and the total asset turnover. This approach is often called the Du Pont System because of its early use by that firm.[2] We have

[2]See T. C. Davis, *How the DuPont Organization Appraises Its Performance,* Financial Management Series Number 94 (New York: American Management Association, 1950), pp. 3–7.

already determined that the return on assets for 1974 was 25.4%. Using the Du Pont method, the 1974 return on assets is determined as follows:

$$\frac{\text{Return on}}{\text{assets}} = \frac{\text{total asset}}{\text{turnover}} \times \frac{\text{return on}}{\text{sales}} = 2.88 \times .0884 = 25.4\%$$

There are several good reasons for separating return on sales from turnover in order to determine the firm's return on assets. In most instances, one observes that a relatively high turnover ratio is associated with a relatively low return on sales. High return on sales is, conversely, usually accompanied by a low turnover ratio. This is best observed in the department store industry where a discount store, such as K-Mart, operates on an extremely low return on sales but a very high turnover. The high-fashion store such as a Neiman-Marcus will show a relatively low turnover but a high return on sales. The profitability of the discount chain and that of the high-fashion department store are approximately equal. The discount chain sells its goods at low prices with a low markup but sells only fast-moving items in order to earn the low margin many times during the year. The prices of the high fashion store are based on a high markup but many of the products stay in inventory for long periods of time. Both types of stores are profitable but they serve separate markets. By observing the turnover and return on sales figures one can determine which marketing strategy has been employed.

Turnover and return on sales figures can also indicate that a trend reversal is imminent. The firm with a steadily increasing return on assets would appear to be an outstanding investment. If, however, the turnover ratio is also increasing with a relatively constant return on sales it may be that the return on asset improvement is about to come to an end. This would be particularly true if the turnover was approaching the turnover of the firm's competitors or the firm's industry. The reverse may hold for an unfavorable trend in the return on asset figures.

An examination of the turnover and return on sales data may also indicate that the firm is going through a basic change in the character of its business. The high turnover, low-markup organization may be changing to a low turnover, high-markup business. If this is the case, our analysis should place less emphasis on the historical record of the firm and more emphasis on an examination of the firm's "new" industry.

One of the most encouraging aspects in the analysis of Lowe's is the rather stable relationship between turnover and return on sales that has existed since the late 1960s, as can be observed in Table 10–4. There is very little in the data to suggest that the return on assets will deteriorate in the near future. The relationship between turnover and return on sales appears to have stabilized. Decreases in profitability because of an inability of the firm to maintain an upward trend in either the return on sales or turnover of its assets, do not seem likely. The data also suggest that downward fluctuations in the firm's profitability are associated with reductions in turnover. In 1967 and again in 1970 and 1974 relatively poor performance was directly associated with reductions in turnover.

Turnover appears to be the item to watch for indications of difficulties in profitability.

Return on Stockholders' Equity. We come to the measure of profitability that is most directly related to the prosperity of the common stockholder. The return on stockholders' equity is the ratio of earnings after taxes to the stockholders equity at the beginning of the period. Since we are attempting to measure the earning power available to the common stockholder, preferred stock and preferred dividends are excluded. For the same reason the calculation is on an after tax and interest basis. The calculation below is for 1974 for Lowe's:

$$\text{Return on stockholders' equity} = \frac{\text{earnings after taxes}}{\text{stockholders' equity at start of period}} = \frac{\$14{,}617{,}103}{\$51{,}782{,}325} = 28.2\%$$

By most standards a 28.2% return is quite satisfactory, but like all the ratios a comparison across time must be made, as should an industry comparison. The return on equity should also be compared to the return on assets figures. If a firm paid no taxes and did not employ financial leverage, the return on assets would be identical to the return on equity. The payment of taxes will, of course, reduce the return on equity relative to the return on assets. If financial leverage is being used wisely, the use of debt will increase the return on equity relative to the return on assets.

To determine the wisdom of financial leverage we merely divide the return on equity by the tax rate. In 1974, Lowe's paid taxes at the rate of 50.1%, obtained by taking the ratio of the provision for income taxes to the pretax earnings. As we saw earlier, the return on assets in 1974 was 25.4% and the return on equity was 28.2%. Dividing the return on equity by the tax rate (.501) gives us a before-tax return on equity of 56.3%. In other words, the return on assets of 25.4% was increased to 56.3% *with the use of financial leverage.* Taxes reduced the return on assets back down to 28.2%, the return available to the common stockholders. There is no escaping the conclusion that the firm has been quite profitable and that financial leverage has been used to the benefit of the common stockholders.

Three Other Ratios and Calculations

Tax Reconciliation. Calculation of the tax rate has other uses in financial statement analysis. If this figure falls substantially below 50 percent, some additional investigation may be needed on the part of the investor. The investigation is usually conducted with a tax reconciliation.

Since the corporate tax rate for larger corporations is approximately 50 percent, an effective tax rate below that figure indicates that some of the income was not fully taxable. This may be important for the investor since nonrecurring capital gains may be included in income. In addition, special tax laws may exist, as in the case of the petroleum industry, which tend to reduce the effective tax rate. If these laws are changed, the investor should have some indication of the impact on the earnings of the firm.

Exhibit 10–5 shows a tax reconciliation presented in the Witco Chemical 1973 *Annual Report.* The investor is presented with information showing the reasons why the effective tax rate for both 1972 and 1973 was less than the 48 percent rate stated in the law.

EXHIBIT 10–5

Witco Chemical Tax Reconciliation

The (income tax) provisions for 1973 and 1972 were 43.9% and 43.2%, respectively, of income before income taxes.

The difference between these rates and the 48% U.S. income tax rate is attributable to the following factors:

	1973	1972
Effective rate per statements of income	43.9%	43.2%
Equity in earnings of associated companies	1.3	1.7
Investment tax credits	1.1	1.4
Percentage depletion allowed for tax purposes in excess of cost depletion booked	.7	.6
All other—net	1.0	1.1
U.S. income tax rate	48.0%	48.0%

The statement of income caption "Equity in earnings of associated companies" is net of income taxes payable directly by such companies. Only the additional income taxes payable by the Company on these earnings are included in the Company's provision for income taxes.

"All other—net" includes such items as tax-exempt interest income and other permanent differences between book and taxable income.

Source: Witco Chemical, Inc. *Annual Report,* 1973.

Depreciation Analysis. It is also useful to determine depreciation as a percentage of sales. We made this determination in Table 10–2 when we constructed Lowe's common size income statement. Since depreciation methods may change over time, this calculation gives the investor an indication whether or not depreciation methods were changed by the firm.

A slight variation relating to depreciation is to calculate a figure known as *cash flow* in the following manner:[3]

Cash flow = earnings + depreciation

All investors recognize that this figure does not really represent the flow of cash. The term *cash flow* is merely a name that has evolved to mean earnings after taxes but before depreciation.

If the method of depreciation is changed so that the depreciation expense is lowered from one year to the next, the net income will tend to be higher by the amount of the change in the depreciation expense. For example, Armco Steel reported depreciation expense for 1968 of approximately $56 million. Depreciation expense for 1967 was over $84 million. In 1967, Armco Steel reported depreciation on an accelerated basis. For 1968, the firm changed its method of reporting depreciation to a straight-line method. Armco Steel reported net income of about $76 million for 1967 and about $95 million for 1968. By adding the depreciation figure to the net income to get the cash flow figure, the following results are achieved:

	1967	*1968*
Net income	$ 76 million	$ 95 million
Depreciation	84	56
Cash flow	$160 million	$151 million

While the reported net income increased as a result of the decline in the depreciation expense from 1967 to 1968, the cash flow figure declined. In view of the change in depreciation methods, the cash flow figures probably give the investor a better measure of the performance of Armco Steel from 1967 to 1968 than do the net income data. The firm actually did worse than would be indicated by the reported net income.

Eugene Comiskey did an empirical study of market valuation changes resulting from the type of accounting change described above for Armco Steel. Eight steel companies made the switch from accelerated depreciation to straight-line in 1968. In comparing the change in the price-earnings ratio for these eight companies with that of a control group of fourteen steel companies making no depreciation method change, Comiskey found that the "P/E ratios of the Changers generally declined while those of the Control group increased."[4] Apparently, investors were

[3]Other expenses such as amortization, which do not require the expenditure of cash, are normally added to the depreciation figure.

[4]Eugene E. Comiskey, "Market Response to Changes in Depreciation Accounting," *Accounting Review*, April 1971, p. 284.

generally aware of the consequences of the change in depreciation method.

Book Value. Book value is the summation of the per share, historic, financial contributions made by the firm's shareholders to the firm. To calculate book value per share, an investor needs to divide the stockholders' equity by the number of shares outstanding. As can be seen from Exhibit 10–1, the stockholders' equity is equal to the assets minus the liabilities. Often, the book value figure is calculated for the investor either in the firm's annual report or in material made available to the investor from the standard reference sources discussed in Chapter 4. For example, Lowe's 1974 *Fourth Quarter Report* states the shareholders' equity (book value) per share at $7.83 at the end of fiscal 1974.

Of what value is the book value per share to the investor? The answer to this question depends primarily upon the industry classification of the company being analyzed. For most industrial companies, the relationship between the market price of the company's stock and the book value per share is not very meaningful. Based upon Lowe's price range for its common stock of 59½ to 31¾ for fiscal 1974, the market price ranged from 4.1 times book value to 7.6 times book value. Clearly, investors are valuing Lowe's common stock primarily on the basis of future earning power rather than on book value.

For firms in the financial service field and for public utilities, book value per share tends to assume a degree of importance. For banks, insurance companies, and investment companies, investors probably should take note of the book value to market value relationship as a part of a complete investment analysis of the firm.[5] This is true since the assets of the financially based firms could be liquidated at a price close to the value carried on the company's books. This does not imply that an investor should necessarily buy the firm in each of these financial areas with the lowest ratio of market price to book value, only that consideration should be given to the historic relationship between book and market value.

Book value becomes important for public utilities because of their frequent need to sell new common stock. The sale of new shares of common stock below book value results in a dilution of the book value of the presently outstanding shares. In addition, the lower the price of the shares, the more shares that will have to be offered. This tends to retard the growth of earnings per share since the prices public utilities can charge are regulated partially on the basis of book value.

[5]For an interesting application of book value in the valuation of savings and loan association stocks, see Howard G. Conklin, "Evaluation of Savings and Loan Stocks," *Financial Analysts Journal,* July–August 1967, pp. 39–42. *Forbes* annually lists what they call the loaded laggards. These are stocks selling for substantial discounts from book value. For an example, see "The Loaded Laggards," *Forbes,* July 15, 1974, pp. 56–57.

THE SOURCE AND USE OF FUNDS STATEMENT

The major use that can be made of the source and use of funds statement is to observe the trends of how the firm is financing itself and the manner in which funds are being spent. We can answer such questions as the following: Are funds from operations providing the greatest percentage of funds or is debt being used extensively? What percentage of funds is being used for additions to property and equipment? Is working capital being increased to finance sales growth?

Table 10–5 summarizes the major sources and uses of funds for Lowe's for 1965 to 1974. The ten-year totals from Exhibit 10–3 are also reproduced to allow the reader to place the trends shown in Table 10–5 into perspective. Funds from operations have historically provided about sixty percent of the total funds, but 1974 is considerably below the historical average. Additional debt was incurred to supplement the funds provided by operations. This does not appear to have harmed the financial condition of Lowe's based upon our previous evaluation of the times interest earned ratio for 1974. It might also be noted that Lowe's has

TABLE 10–5

Lowe's Source and Use of Funds Statement, 1965–74

	1965–74 Summary	1974	1973	1972	1971	1970	1969	1968	1967	1966	1965
					(In Percent)						
Sources of funds											
Operations	59	41	59	63	63	77	97	87	73	69	88
Additions to long-term debt	36	54	38	32	35	21	—	8	20	26	2
Other	5	5	5	2	2	2	3	5	7	5	10
TOTAL*	100	100	100	100	100	100	100	100	100	100	100
Uses of funds											
Dividends	6	2	4	5	7	11	14	15	14	13	19
Repayment of long-term debt	13	20	6	17	4	6	22	10	12	10	11
Property and equipment	40	30	49	44	42	48	43	33	35	39	66
Other	—	—	—	—	—	—	—	2	—	1	1
Increase in net working capital	41	48	41	34	47	35	21	40	39	37	3
TOTAL*	100	100	100	100	100	100	100	100	100	100	100

*Columns may not add to 100 due to rounding.
Source: Lowe's *1974 Fourth Quarter Report.*

been able to finance its growth in sales during the 1965–74 period without the need to have a general sale of common stock.

The uses of funds shown in Table 10–5 have been quite consistent. The increase in net working capital and the additions to property and equipment have been reasonably stable over the period. The increase in net working capital (defined as current assets minus current liabilities) has been favorable and has accounted for a high percentage of the uses of funds. In this sense, Table 10–5 reinforces the conclusions we made by examining the various liquidity ratios. The decline in the use of funds to pay dividends is consistent with our examination of the dividend payout percentage in the previous chapter. The funds have been used for reinvestment in the business and have not been paid to the stockholders to any appreciable extent. Given the superior growth of earnings experienced by Lowe's in recent years, the stockholders should be happy to let Lowe's reinvest a substantial portion of the earnings.

In general, the summary of sources and uses of funds in Table 10–5 shows no unfavorable trends. This is especially true when the data shown in Table 10–5 are considered along with other aspects of financial statement analysis.

FINANCIAL STATEMENT ANALYSIS OUTPUT AS A RISK MEASURE

An examination of financial statement analysis would not be complete without an inquiry into the relationship between the various ratios we have just studied and the contemporary market-determined measures of risk. The measures of risk derived from the stock market will be developed in Chapters 12 and 13. For now, two questions seem especially relevant. First, is there an association between accounting-determined measures of risk and market measures of risk? Does the level of the various financial ratios correspond with the actual risk of the firm's common stock in the market? Second, can the accounting measures of risk, which we have derived in the form of various ratios, be used to estimate the future risk of an investment? We will examine a study by William Beaver, Paul Kettler, and Myron Scholes which addresses itself to these two questions.[6]

We will also examine one other aspect of the results of performing a financial statement analysis. Much empirical work has been undertaken in recent years relating to the ability of financial ratios to predict bankruptcy. We will briefly comment on studies by William Beaver and by Edward Altman. In addition, since the bankruptcy of Penn Central was

[6]William H. Beaver, Paul Kettler, and Myron Scholes, "The Association Between Market Determined and Accounting Determined Risk Measures," *Accounting Review*, October 1970, pp. 654–682.

an event of such financial magnitude, we will examine two studies dealing with whether or not an investor should have been able to predict financial distress for this company.

Beaver, Kettler, and Scholes Study

Beaver, Kettler, and Scholes used several different financial ratios to see if they were associated with the riskiness of a firm's common stock as observed in the market. The following accounting measures were analyzed: 1) dividend payout; 2) a growth measure; 3) a leverage measure; 4) a liquidity measure—the current ratio; 5) asset size; and 6) two different measures of the variability of earnings over a period of time. These are roughly the same types of ratios we have been discussing in this chapter and in the previous one.

The study found earnings variability and dividend payout to be important variables in that they had a close association with the risk as observed in the market. The authors of the study concluded that these accounting measures of risk become impounded as a part of the market assessment of risk. The study also found that dividend payout, growth, and earnings variability were useful in forecasting the riskiness of a security over some future period. It was not clear, however, whether or not the forecasts were an improvement over the forecasts made with market data.

Bankruptcy Studies

In two studies, Beaver examined the ability of financial ratios to predict whether or not a firm will go bankrupt.[7] Essentially these studies pair firms for as many nonfinancial characteristics as possible. The nonfinancial characteristics included such items as industry classification, age, and geographic scope of operations. One of the paired firms actually went bankrupt while the other did not. The investigation then centered upon whether or not financial data could have predicted the outcome for each firm of the paired firms. In his first study, Beaver found that the "ability to predict failure is strongest in the cash-flow to total-debt ratio."[8] Beaver's second study also produced encouraging results in that liquid asset ratios (such as cash flow to total debt) as well as nonliquid asset ratios (such as net income to total assets) showed predictive ability.

[7]William H. Beaver, "Financial Ratios as Predictors of Failure," *Empirical Research in Accounting: Selected Studies, 1966, Supplement to Volume 4 of Journal of Accounting Research*, pp. 71–111 and "Alternative Accounting Measures as Predictors of Failure," *Accounting Review*, January 1968, pp. 113–122.

[8]William H. Beaver, "Financial Ratios as Predictors of Failure," p. 85.

Following the collapse of Penn Central, two studies relating to the analysis of the financial statements of that railroad reached virtually identical conclusions. Paul Dascher's study was based upon the work of Beaver.[9] He found that an investor should have noted a significant deterioration in the financial condition of Penn Central. Murray's study also indicated that an investor might have had some reason for expecting difficult financial times for Penn Central.[10]

One additional study relating to bankruptcy is worth noting. In a paired comparison analysis similar to Beaver's study, Altman used a statistical technique known as multiple discriminant analysis to determine the ability of financial ratios to predict corporate bankrupcy.[11] This statistical technique results in what is known as a discriminant function. The discriminant function allows the investor to classify a firm as either a candidate for bankruptcy or not a candidate for bankruptcy on the basis of a Z value. The Z value that indicates bankruptcy and the predictive equation were determined from an analysis of sixty-six manufacturing firms. The Z score for a particular firm is calculated with the following equation:

$$Z = 1.2X_1 + 1.4X_2 + 3.3X_3 + .6X_4 + .999X_5$$

where: Z = the overall discriminant index number

$$X_1 = \frac{\text{working capital}}{\text{total assets}}$$

$$X_2 = \frac{\text{retained earnings}}{\text{total assets}}$$

$$X_3 = \frac{\text{earnings before interest and taxes}}{\text{total assets}}$$

$$X_4 = \frac{\text{market value of stockholders' equity}}{\text{book value of total debt}}$$

$$X_5 = \frac{\text{sales}}{\text{total assets}}$$

Using Lowe's 1974 financial statements, we find a Z score of 6.992 determined as follows with the dollar figures rounded to the nearest $1,000, except for the $46 price per share:

$$Z = 1.2\left(\frac{\$61,715}{\$150,634}\right) + 1.4\left(\frac{\$59,195}{\$150,634}\right) + 3.3\left(\frac{\$32,032}{\$150,634}\right) + .6\left(\frac{8,591,330 \times \$46}{\$83,386}\right) + .999\left(\frac{\$362,453}{\$150,634}\right)$$

$$Z = .492 + .550 + .702 + 2.844 + 2.404 = 6.992$$

[9]Paul E. Dascher, "The Penn Central Revisited: A Predictable Situation," *Financial Analysts Journal,* March–April 1972, pp. 61–64.

[10]Roger F. Murray, "The Penn Central Debacle."

[11]Edward I. Altman, "Financial Ratios, Discriminant Analysis and the Prediction of Corporate Bankruptcy," *Journal of Finance,* September 1968, pp. 589–610, and "Ratio Analysis and the Prediction of Firm Failure: Reply to Comment," *Journal of Finance,* December 1970, pp. 1169–1172.

A Z score above 2.99 places the firm clearly in the nonbankrupt category, according to Altman's study. A Z score below 1.81 places the firm in the bankruptcy category. Between 1.8 and 3.0, it becomes difficult to predict the future of the firm with regard to bankruptcy. Lowe's is well above the minimum score of 3.0 and certainly qualifies as a firm for which bankruptcy in the next one to three years is quite unlikely. This, of course, is not a surprising result in view of the previous conclusions we have reached regarding Lowe's investment quality.

SUMMARY

This chapter reached the conclusion that investors are experiencing a renewal of interest in financial statement analysis. Not only is this because of the emphasis on quality in the past few years, but several studies have revealed that the output of a financial statement analysis is useful to the investor in analyzing the risk of a security. Hence, financial statement analysis should continue to be an important part of the total valuation process for a security.

Three basic types of financial statements were examined. They are: 1) the balance sheet; 2) the income statement along with the statement of retained earnings; and 3) the statement of changes in financial position, which is often called the source and use of funds statement. Common size financial statements were suggested as a means of adjusting for differing sizes of firms. In addition, common size statements were examined over a period of years to reveal trends of interest to the investor.

Five different types of ratios were examined. The five types and the actual ratios examined under each type are summarized below:

Liquidity Ratios

Current ratio $\dfrac{\text{Current assets}}{\text{Current liabilities}}$

Acid-test ratio $\dfrac{\text{Current assets less inventories}}{\text{Current liabilities}}$

Liquidity ratio $\dfrac{\text{Cash plus marketable securities}}{\text{Current liabilities}}$

Leverage Ratios

Debt-to-asset ratio $\dfrac{\text{Total debt}}{\text{Total assets}}$

Leverage factor $\dfrac{\text{Total assets}}{\text{Stockholders' equity}}$

Times interest earned before taxes $\dfrac{\text{Earnings before interest and taxes}}{\text{Interest expense}}$

Activity Ratios

Inventory turnover	$\frac{\text{Cost of goods sold}}{\text{Average inventory}}$
Accounts receivable turnover	$\frac{\text{Sales (credit)}}{\text{Average accounts receivable}}$

Profitability-Efficiency Ratios

Return on sales	$\frac{\text{Earnings before interest and taxes}}{\text{Sales}}$
Total asset turnover	$\frac{\text{Sales}}{\text{Total assets (beginning of period)}}$
Return on assets	$\frac{\text{Earnings before interest and taxes}}{\text{Assets}}$
Return on stockholders' equity	$\frac{\text{Earnings after taxes}}{\text{Stockholders' equity}}$

Other Calculations

Effective tax rate	$\frac{\text{Income taxes paid}}{\text{Earnings before taxes}}$
Book value per share	$\frac{\text{Stockholders' equity}}{\text{Number of shares outstanding}}$

It is also possible for the investor to calculate a cash flow per share figure by adding depreciation and other noncash expenses to the net income per share. This calculation may be important in adjusting for changes in depreciation methods over time. It is also useful in helping the investor determine if increases or decreases in cash dividends are likely and in estimating the amount of external financing a firm will be required to undertake to finance its growth.

QUESTIONS

1. Would it make any difference to an investor making a financial statement analysis of a firm if the firm's bonds were to be purchased rather than the firm's common stock?
2. If an investor were to purchase a one-year bond as opposed to a twenty-year bond, explain what different items, if any, the investor would want to examine carefully in making a financial statement analysis in each case.
3. Why is it important to examine a firm's capital structure and calculate the debt component and the equity component? Do you feel that this calculation is more important in the mid 1970s than it was ten years ago? Support your position.

4. Some financial analysts feel that it is not sufficient for the investor to examine only the breakdown of the firm's capital structure. What other related items could the investor examine to provide more information regarding the firm's debt paying ability?
5. Describe the three major types of financial statements and the importance of each type for the investor.
6. How does an investor determine a firm's cash flow? Why is its analysis important to the investor?
7. The July 15, 1974 issue of *Forbes* developed a list of "Loaded Laggards" listed on the American Stock Exchange. Satisfying the following criteria was required before a firm was added to the list:
   a) A stock price of one-half or less of book value.
   b) A price-earnings ratio of five or less.
   c) A dividend paying stock.
   d) A current ratio of at least two to one.
   e) A debt-to-total capital ratio of 35 percent or less.
   f) Current earnings regarded as healthy by *Forbes*.
   These are rather stringent standards. Do they mean that the thirty stocks on the list should be profitable investments?
8. What might be the expected impact of an annual rate of inflation in the 10 percent range on the following activity ratios: a) inventory turnover; b) accounts receivable turnover; and c) total asset turnover?
9. Why do you suppose that Armco Steel changed its method of depreciation in 1968 to a straight-line method as described in the chapter?

PROBLEMS

1. In the September 15, 1974, issue of *Forbes* (p. 117), the following statement was made: "with its [du Pont's] high debt-to-equity ratio and excellent record of profitability, du Pont has the financial muscle."
   a) From the du Pont balance sheet and income statement for 1973, calculate du Pont's debt-to-equity ratio. Do you agree with the quotation from *Forbes?*
   b) Calculate the times interest earned before taxes for du Pont for 1973 and see if this calculation supports or refutes your conclusions from part a.
2. Examine du Pont's liquidity by calculating the current ratio, the acid-test ratio, and the liquidity ratio for 1973. Have these ratios deteriorated since the end of 1972?
3. The *Forbes* quotation in question 1 mentions du Pont's profitability. Calculate the return on net sales for both 1972 and 1973. Calculate the return on sales and on assets for 1973. Calculate the rate on the average stockholders' equity (year-end 1972 + 1973 divided by 2) for 1973. Do you agree with *Forbes* regarding du Pont's profitability?

Note: Since stockholders' equity includes preferred stock, the net income figure from du Pont's income statement should be used.

4. What effective tax rate did du Pont pay in 1972 and 1973? If the effective tax rate is less than 48 percent, what might be the cause? How could you find out?

5. du Pont's book value per common share at the end of 1973 was $70.01, while the market price was $159. In addition, the following information is contained in the du Pont 1973 *Annual Report:*

   Dividends per share: 1973 = $5.75; 1964 = $5.19
   Earnings per share: 1964 = $7.72

   Make the following calculations for du Pont:
   a) The market price to book value ratio at year-end 1973.
   b) du Pont's price-earnings ratio for 1973 based on 1973 earnings and the year-end price.
   c) du Pont's dividend yield based upon the year-end 1973 price.
   d) du Pont's dividend payout percentage for 1973 and 1964.
   e) The annual compound rate of growth in dividends and in earnings from 1964 to 1973.

   Can you make any tentative conclusions regarding du Pont as an investment as a result of these calculations? What do you need in the way of additional information to support your conclusions?

6. Below are two statistical series for the Rochester Telephone Company (RTC) for the period from 1958 to 1970. The operating ratio is the amount of operating expenses divided by the operating revenue.

	Operating Ratio	*Times Interest Earned after Taxes*
1958	79.12%	2.73
1959	78.28	2.80
1960	76.96	2.77
1961	74.60	2.87
1962	74.50	2.96
1963	75.33	2.83
1964	75.47	2.81
1965	74.25	2.90
1966	72.23	3.12
1967	68.82	3.26
1968	69.19	3.25
1969	68.14	3.21
1970	68.15	3.21

   a) Why do you think that the operating ratio for RTC dropped almost eleven percentage points from 1958 to 1970? What do you think is likely to happen to this ratio during the twelve years from 1970 to 1982? Why?

b) Do you feel that the interest coverage ratio shown is satisfactory for RTC? Why? What do you think is likely to happen to the interest coverage ratio between 1970 and 1982?

7. Apply Altman's bankruptcy index to du Pont by calculating a Z score for 1973. Additional information needed:
   Retained earnings equals $3,161 million.
   Number of shares outstanding equals 47,801,161.
   Market price per common share equals $159.
   For the book value of the debt, use the total of the current liabilities plus long-term borrowings.

duPont Consolidated Balance Sheet (Dollars in Millions)

	December 31	
	1973	1972
ASSETS		
Current assets		
Cash and marketable securities	$ 343.7	$ 313.9
Accounts and notes receivable	833.9	683.4
Inventories	839.7	793.2
Prepaid expenses	26.8	32.1
Total current assets	2,044.1	1,822.6
Plants and properties	6,268.5	5,689.0
Less: Accumulated depreciation and obsolescence	3,865.7	3,574.7
	2,402.8	2,114.3
Other assets		
Investment in nonconsolidated affiliates—at equity in net assets	277.5	256.1
Goodwill, patents, and trademarks	43.7	43.7
Other assets and investments	64.1	47.0
Total Other Assets	385.3	346.8
TOTAL	$4,832.2	$4,283.7
LIABILITIES		
Current liabilities		
Accounts payable	$ 411.4	$ 291.1
Income taxes	187.4	143.8
Other accrued liabilities	122.7	103.0
Total current liabilities	721.5	537.9
Long-term borrowings	237.8	240.0
Deferred income taxes	49.9	40.0
Deferred investment tax credit	117.9	100.2
Other liabilities and reserves	111.4	97.6
Stockholder's equity	3,593.7	3,268.0
TOTAL	$4,832.2	$4,283.7

duPont Consolidated Income Statement (Dollars in Millions, Except per Share)

	1973	1972
Net sales	$5,275.6	$4,365.9
Other income	92.0	61.2
Total	5,367.6	4,427.1
Cost of goods sold and other operating charges	3,330.5	2,792.0
Selling, general, and administrative expenses	542.5	474.6
Depreciation and obsolescence	423.8	391.9
Interest on borrowings	27.3	20.1
Total	4,324.1	3,678.6
Earnings before income taxes	1,043.5	748.5
Provision for income taxes	457.9	334.0
Net income	585.6	414.5
Dividends on preferred stock	10.0	10.0
Amount earned on common stock	$ 575.6	$ 404.5
Earnings per share of common stock	$ 12.04	$ 8.50

SUGGESTED READINGS

Altman, Edward I. "Financial Ratios, Discriminant Analysis and the Prediction of Corporate Bankruptcy." *Journal of Finance,* September 1968, pp. 589–610.

American Institute of Certified Public Accountants. *Objectives of Financial Statements.* New York: AICPA, October 1973.

Baker, H. Kent and John A. Haslen. "Information Needs of Individual Investors." *Journal of Accountancy,* November 1973, pp. 64–69.

Beaver, William H., Paul Kettler, and Myron Scholes. "The Association Between Market Determined and Accounting Determined Risk Measures." *Accounting Review,* October 1970, pp. 654–82.

Block, Frank E. "The Place of Book Value in Common Stock Evaluation." *Financial Analysts Journal,* March–April 1964, pp. 29–33.

Comiskey, Eugene E. "Market Response to Changes in Depreciation Accounting." *Accounting Review,* April 1971, pp. 279–85.

Dascher, Paul E. "The Penn Central Revisited: A Predictable Situation." *Financial Analysts Journal,* March–April 1972, pp. 61–64.

Edwards, James Don and John B. Barrack. "Last-In, First-Out Inventory Valuation As a Way to Control Illusory Profits." *MSU Business Topics,* Winter 1975, pp. 19–27.

Elam, Rick. "The Effect of Lease Data on the Predictive Ability of Financial Ratios." *Accounting Review,* January 1975, pp. 25–43.

Kaplan, Robert and Richard Roll. "Accounting Changes and Stock Prices." *Financial Analysts Journal*, January–February 1973, pp. 48–53.

Murray, Roger F. "The Penn Central Debacle: Lessons for Financial Analysis." *Journal of Finance*, May 1971, pp. 327–32.

Niederhoffer, Victor and Patrick J. Regan. "Earnings Changes, Analysts' Forecasts and Stock Prices." *Financial Analysts Journal*, May–June 1972, pp. 65–71.

*

11

The Portfolio Decision

Our study of the investment process thus far has concentrated upon the analysis of an individual financial asset with primary emphasis on common stocks. This does not imply that investments other than equities are somehow less important. Indeed, for many of us the most important investment we have is in real estate, namely our home. The purpose of the first ten chapters was to present the concepts of analysis and valuation of financial assets using common stocks. Other securities such as bonds must be carefully examined, but first we will examine the investment decision within the context of an individual's investment opportunities. Few investors make decisions regarding a single common stock or other investments without considering both their existing investments and the other available opportunities. In this chapter we concentrate on the development of a framework that can be used to assess the total set of investment opportunities.

RISK AND RETURN—A SINGLE SECURITY

Assume we must select an investment from the alternatives depicted in Table 11-1 and that one of three possible future conditions or states of nature will occur. For descriptive purposes the states are called 1) prosperity, 2) normality, and 3) recession. The information available indicates that each state of nature is equally likely to occur (i.e., the probability of the occurrence of any one state is one-third). Finally, the information pertinent to each of the individual investment opportunities (Zero Ox, Parent Bell, and Goldfinger), allows an estimate of the rate of return to be obtained given the occurrence of each state of nature. For example, if we invest in Zero Ox and a recession ensues, we will lose 60 percent.

TABLE 11-1
Hypothetical Investment Opportunity Set

Future State of Nature*	Annual Percentage Return on Investment Instrument Given State of Nature		
	Zero Ox	Parent Bell	Goldfinger
1. Prosperity	80%	6%	−60%
2. Normality	10	5	10
3. Recession	−60	4	80

*Each state of nature is equally likely to occur.

Without entering into a detailed discussion of terminology, most of us would agree that Zero Ox and Goldfinger are more risky than Parent Bell. Given an investment in Parent Bell, the worst possible outcome would be a 4 percent return. But an investment in either Zero Ox or Goldfinger could produce a loss of 60 percent. From the viewpoint of risk, Parent Bell would be preferred to either Zero Ox or Goldfinger. However, not all investors would purchase Parent Bell since both Zero Ox and Goldfinger offer rewards that may more than compensate for the exposure to loss. Some investors may be quite willing to accept the possibility of a large loss in order to obtain the opportunity for an 80 percent gain. Thus, on a return basis, Zero Ox and Goldfinger would be preferred to Parent Bell.

In summary, Parent Bell is preferred on a risk dimension while Zero Ox and Goldfinger are preferred on a return dimension. Without knowing anything about a given investor's preference for gain relative to an aversion to loss, we cannot determine which security is the "best investment." Each has its advantages and disadvantages.

RISK AND RETURN—A PORTFOLIO

Investors normally do not confine their analysis to a single security. Instead, they attempt to combine securities to form a portfolio that may be less risky than the individual components. Consider an investment with 50 percent of the investor's resources placed in Zero Ox and 50 percent placed in Goldfinger. If we experience prosperity, the investor's average portfolio return will be 10 percent as calculated in Exhibit 11–1. The occurrence of normal economic conditions also produces an average return of 10 percent and in a recession the investor's average return will be 10 percent. By combining Zero Ox and Goldfinger, the investor faces no risk at all since a 10 percent return results no matter what state of nature occurs.

EXHIBIT 11–1

Portfolio Rate of Return Calculation

	.5 Zero Ox	.5 Goldfinger	Total Portfolio
Prosperity	80% (.5) = 40%	−60% (.5) = −30%	40% − 30% = 10%
Normality	10 (.5) = 5	10 (.5) = 5	5 + 5 = 10
Recession	−60 (.5) = −30	80 (.5) = 40	−30 + 40 = 10

While Parent Bell is preferred on a risk dimension when considered as a single investment, Zero Ox and Goldfinger are preferred on the basis of risk when considered in combination. Combined with the greater average return from Zero Ox and Goldfinger (10 percent certain, as compared to a maximum of 6 percent for Parent Bell), we find that Zero Ox and Goldfinger are the preferred securities when considered in combination. We can conclude that the analysis of a given investment is not complete until we have considered the various combinations of that investment with all other opportunities. In essence, we cannot make a decision regarding a single asset without examining its implications for the portfolio.

Unfortunately, the above example is highly simplified. There are an almost infinite number of states of nature. Even if their number were limited, we would still have the task of determining the probabilities and the returns associated with each state. Furthermore, there are thousands of different securities. In order to determine the best or optimum combination, we would have to examine all possible combinations. Even in our simplified example, the number of combinations is infinite. We could put 1% in Zero Ox and 99% in Parent Bell or 5% in Zero Ox, 50% in Parent Bell and 45% in Goldfinger, and so on. The task is mammoth but necessary since returns do vary and the variations are frequently related in some fashion.

INVESTMENT PORTFOLIO SET

Perhaps the best way to solve the problem is to attack it one step at a time by leaving aside the rather difficult problems associated with determining states of nature and the respective returns. Let us assume investors can measure the risk characteristics of the set of all investment opportunities and the risk associated with their various combinations. In the same context, we assume that returns can be measured and that investors have a preference for returns, but seek to avoid risk. With these measurement and preference assumptions, the set of all investment opportunities and their various combinations can be presented graphically in Figure 11-1.

In any real world situation, an extremely large number of such opportunities and combinations exist. In fact, given more than one individual security, there are an almost infinite number of combinations that could be established, as we previously noted. However, since we assumed we prefer high returns but find risk to be undesirable, we can establish a decision rule that eliminates most of the possible combinations. If we consider all those opportunities that have the same risk, the decision becomes obvious. We would select the combination that provides the maximum expected return. In Figure 11-1, only portfolio Y need be considered for risk level A. Portfolio X, relative to Y, can be immediately rejected since X is equally undesirable based upon its risk, but less

FIGURE 11-1
Hypothetical Opportunity Set Comparing Risk and Return

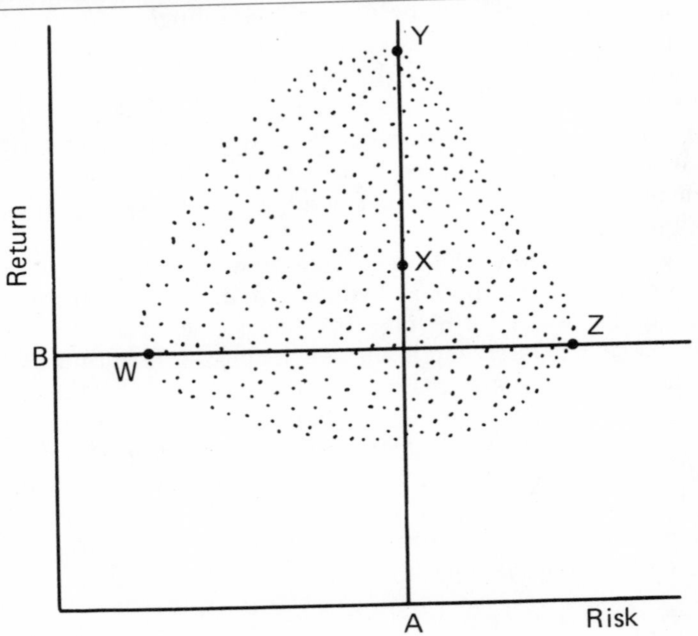

desirable because of its lower rate of return. Conversely, given a set of portfolios with the same expected return, we will select the portfolio which provides the minimum risk. In Figure 11–1, we would not select portfolio Z since portfolio W will provide the same expected return (B), but at a lower level of risk.

THE EFFICIENT FRONTIER

The decision criterion we have established is referred to as the *efficiency criterion.* Portfolios Y and W are efficient as are all portfolios that maximize return for any given level of risk or minimize risk for any given level of return. Use of the efficiency criterion allows the investor to determine all efficient portfolios to form what is known as the efficient frontier. The efficient frontier is the set of all portfolios that meet the efficiency criterion. In Figure 11–2, the efficient frontier is the northwest boundary of the entire set of portfolios.

The most important consequence of establishing the risk-return efficient frontier is that it allows us to eliminate from consideration the great majority of possible investment opportunities. The investor can concentrate on the problem of selecting one portfolio from the efficient frontier instead of examining the entire set of potential portfolios. The establishment of the efficient frontier reduces substantially the number of combinations that must be considered.

FIGURE 11–2
The Efficient Frontier

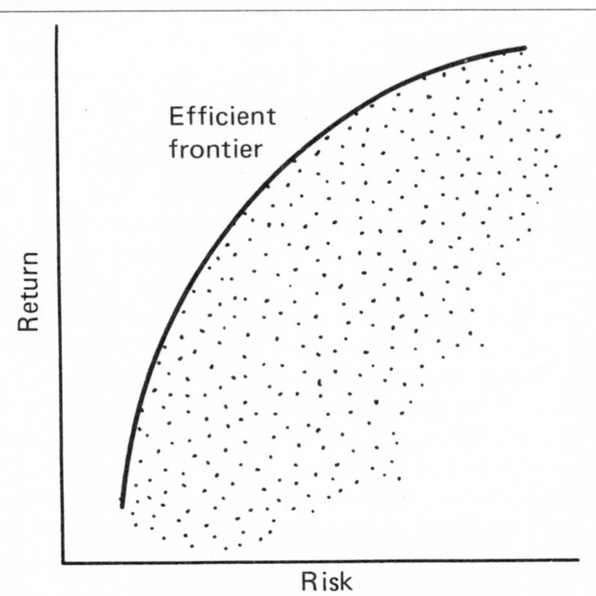

It is appropriate to recognize that the shape of the efficient frontier will always be of the form characterized in Figure 11-2. It will have a positive slope. Higher returns are associated with higher risk, but as risk becomes large the corresponding increases in return become smaller and smaller.

There are two fundamental reasons for the characteristic of a positive but diminishing trade-off between risk and return. The first is economic and the second arises from the techniques of measuring risk and return. The measurement problem will have to wait until we establish the conventional measuring techniques. The economics are most important and, of course, dictate the measurement techniques. The efficient frontier as illustrated in Figure 11-2 implies a positive relationship between risk and return. This is equivalent to the often repeated advice that, in order to obtain high returns, one must accept high risk. High-risk securities produce high returns and low-risk securities produce low returns. In general, such a relationship exists, but there is a paradox. Given a positive relationship, all investors should invest in only those assets with the highest risk. Any other strategy would produce a return less than the maximum available. The paradox is that all investors do not invest in the highest risk securities.

The paradox is generated from a lack of rigor in the original premise. It is only over the long-run that high-risk assets tend to produce high returns. In any given situation the investor cannot use this relationship as a decision criterion. To see why, consider the choice between two investments, A and B. Investment A will produce income of either $1.1 million or $.9 million with each outcome equally likely. Investment B will produce income of either $3.0 million or a loss of $1.0 million, with each possibility equally likely. With no other information, most investors will prefer investment A, but the preference does not necessarily imply that A would be purchased. The actual decision will depend on the respective prices of A and B. No matter how much one prefers A to B, there is some set of prices for A and B that will cause acceptance of B. Suppose that the price of A was $1,000,000 and B was $1,000. Alternative B might then be preferred, but not necessarily.

We cannot determine exactly what the respective prices will be. We can conclude that the market participants through their preference for the more stable income of A will bid up the price of A and bid down the price of B. Thus, the price of B will typically be lower than the price of A. Notice that the income of both A and B will average $1.0 million over the long run. Hence, the average return as a percent of the price of B will be higher than that of A. If it is agreed that B is more risky than A, a positive average risk-return relationship exists, but only over the long run.

The conclusion is that there is no causal relationship between risk and return. Risk does not cause high return. Instead, investor preference for low risk will cause the price of low-risk assets to be relatively higher than the price of high-risk assets. Consequently, high-risk securities will generate the higher average returns observed in the marketplace. We must emphasize, however, that the relationship is an average. One can go bankrupt waiting for the average just as one can drown in a river with an average depth of three inches.

UTILITY THEORY

The relationship between risk and return leads us to believe that the efficient frontier has a positive slope because of investor preference for low risk. The curvature of the efficient frontier is also caused by investor preference. To see this relationship, the general concepts of utility theory need to be introduced. Utility theory also helps to establish the techniques required to select an optimum portfolio from the set of efficient portfolios. The efficient frontier concept reduces the number of portfolio possibilities, but each investor must still select the ideal portfolio from those that are efficient.

An investment with a high expected return is not sought because the return itself is desirable. The objective is to obtain the high return to enjoy the material benefits flowing from the successful investment. We seek the utility of the investment return where utility is generally defined as the *want-satisfying power* of a given quantity of money or rate of return.

The general assumption is that our wants are not satisfied at any point in time. We prefer more to less. There is more utility in $100 than in $10 and, all other things equal, we will prefer to receive $100 if the alternative is the receipt of $10. This conclusion is obvious, but if our preferences were this simple, few investment problems would exist. Suppose, for example, we were offered a bet with a 50–50 chance of winning or losing. Winning would produce a gain of $5,000 and losing would produce a loss of $5,000. A few people might be willing to make such a bet but most would not enter into such a transaction. The reason is that the $5,000 gain does not have the exact opposite utility value as the $5,000 loss. The want-satisfying power of an extra $5,000 is less than the satisfaction that would be given up if we lost $5,000.

The utility of a given quantity of money is, of course, a highly individual matter. Wealth is often of vital importance. A millionaire may attach very little utility to $1,000. But to the student working to finance a college education, $1,000 has a large amount of want-satisfying power. Age and education may be important determinants of the utility of money. Ambition can also enter into the utility valuation of a given return since the drive for success may far outweigh the potential losses one is exposed to in the attempt to be successful. In a similar context, the individual whose job is secure may be quite willing to accept potential loss from investments since the disutility of investment losses is mitigated by the assured employment income.

Diminishing Marginal Utility

While the catalogue of causes of variations in the utility of investment returns is virtually endless, it is possible to characterize the general relationship between returns and the utility of returns. For the most part, investors exhibit a diminishing marginal utility of returns. The investor will prefer the receipt of $100 to the receipt of $10, but not ten times as much. The preference for the $100 will be something less than ten times the preference for the $10. Put another way, the utility of $2 is greater than the utility of $1, but the utility of the first dollar received is greater than the utility of the second dollar.

Diminishing marginal utility can be illustrated by the relationship between return and utility of return shown in Figure 11–3. This figure indicates that as returns increase, the investor receives greater utility. However, increases in utility occur at a diminishing rate. The relationship shown in Figure 11–3 is normally referred to as a utility function.

FIGURE 11–3
Example Utility Function: Diminishing Marginal Utility or Risk-Averter

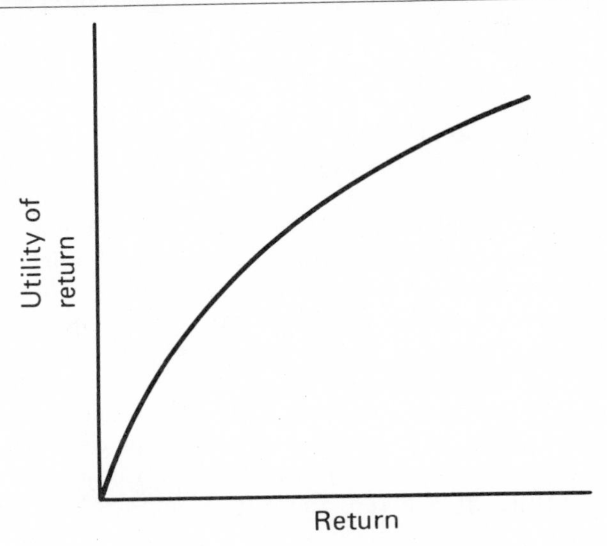

Risk-Averters, Risk-Neutrals, and Risk-Seekers

An investor with a utility function that exhibits diminishing marginal utility is generally defined as a risk-averter. As illustrated in Figure 11–3, a risk-averter will have a utility function that is everywhere increasing but at a decreasing rate. Two other types of utility functions can be described—the risk-neutral and the risk-seeker. The risk-neutral has a utility function with a positive slope or rate of change like the risk-averter, but the slope is constant throughout. The risk-neutral exhibits constant marginal utility of return. The risk-seeker has a utility function that has a positive slope, but the slope increases from point to point. A risk-seeker exhibits increasing marginal utility of return.

Both the risk-neutral and risk-seeker are generally ignored in discussing the investment decision and we shall follow this practice. This does not imply that such people do not exist. However, the vast majority of investment decisions are made on the basis of risk-aversion.

INDIFFERENCE CURVES

Before applying the concept of risk-aversion to the efficient frontier, it is necessary to introduce indifference curve analysis as related to risk and return. Suppose we are considering investment alternatives A and B in Table 11-2 and our utility function is such that we are *indifferent* between selecting A or B. Indifference means the expected utility of A is identical to the expected utility of B. Suppose further that we can agree investment A is more risky than investment B. If this were all the information available, we could construct an indifference curve as has been done in Figure 11-4. The line AB or indifference curve I simply connects points A and B. Any investment with the risk-return characteristics of any point on the line AB has the same utility as A or B or any other point on the line. In short, the investor is indifferent between any investments which have a risk-return relationship that plots on indifference curve I.

TABLE 11-2
Returns from Hypothetical Investment Alternatives

	Investment Alternatives			
State of Nature	A	B	C	D
1	$2,000	$100	$3,000	$200
2	−1,000	50	0	150
Average return	$ 500	$ 75	$1,500	$175

Introducing investments C and D yields a second indifference curve. If the investor's utility function is such that the utility of C is identical to the utility of D, we have a second indifference curve labeled II in Figure 11-4. Indifference curve II is higher than curve I since most of us would prefer investment C to investment A and investment D to

FIGURE 11–4
Indifference Curves

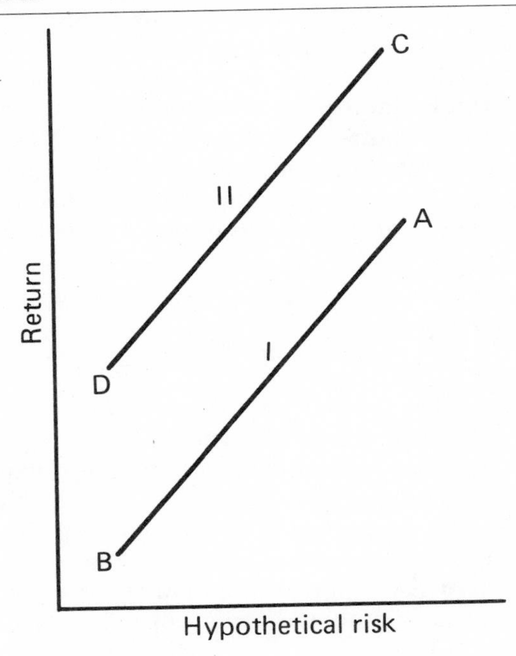

investment B. In other words, A and B are equally desirable as are C and D, but both C and D are preferred to either A or B.

In summary, indifference curves connect all risk-return points having the same utility. Investments with a different expected utility will plot on alternative indifference curves. Greater expected utility implies a higher indifference curve and less expected utility implies a lower indifference curve.

In Figure 11–4, the indifference curves have been drawn as straight lines. This is not the typical shape. If we can imagine that risk is reflective of the potential disutility of an investment, increases in risk should require proportionately greater increases in potential return to compensate the risk-averse investor. Because of diminishing marginal utility, an asset with greater risk must offer even greater returns to maintain indifference. This increasing trade-off between risk and return is depicted in Figure 11–5, which shows several indifference curves for the risk-averse investor. All investments with risk-return characteristics falling on curve I have the same expected utility and are equally desirable. Any investment falling on curve II is preferred to any investment on curve I and any investment with the risk-return characteristics of curve III is preferred to all others. Thus the investor will choose investment X over Y, but will select Z over both X and Y.

FIGURE 11-5
Hypothetical Indifference Curves: Risk-Averse Investor

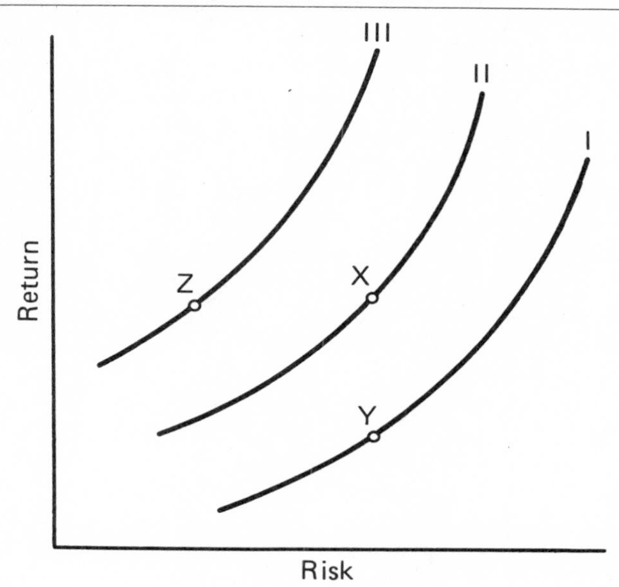

The set of indifference curves for a given investor is called an *indifference map*. The investment strategy is to select the investment or portfolio that falls on the highest indifference curve. This can be clearly seen in Figure 11-5 where investment Z has the same expected return as investment X, but a lower risk level.

SELECTING THE OPTIMUM PORTFOLIO

With the introduction of indifference curves, it is possible to select an optimum portfolio from the set of efficient portfolios. In Figure 11-6, we constructed an efficient frontier from a population of investment opportunities and their various combinations. In addition, we superimposed a risk-averse investor's indifference map. As noted earlier, the decision criterion is to select the portfolio which falls on the highest indifference curve. The optimum portfolio is located where the efficient frontier is tangent to the highest possible indifference curve. In Figure 11-6, the optimum portfolio is portfolio Z. Any other portfolio would lie on a lower indifference curve and provide the investor with less utility than portfolio Z. Higher indifference curves cannot be obtained because of the efficient frontier limitation.

FIGURE 11-6
Hypothetical Optimum Portfolio Selection

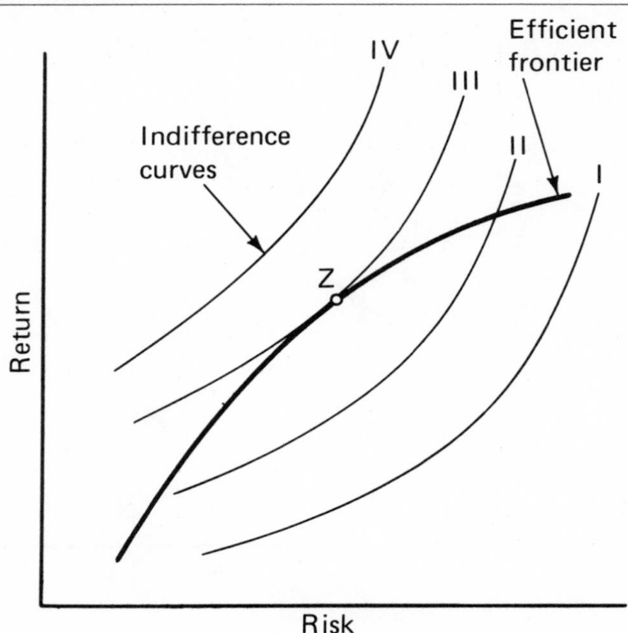

SUMMARY

We began this chapter by recognizing the importance of examining individual securities within the context of their portfolio effects. The concept developed was that a security may be quite risky when analyzed in isolation, but when considered with other securities, the risky security may be capable of reducing the risk of a given portfolio. This important observation implies an enormous problem since the number of potential portfolios is almost limitless even when we consider only a few securities. In recognition of this problem we introduced the *efficiency criterion,* which says the investor must consider only those portfolios that maximize return for a given level of risk or minimize risk for a given level of return. The set of all efficient portfolios is referred to as the *efficient frontier.* In general, the efficient frontier has a positive slope. Higher returns will, on the average, be associated with higher risk. The positive risk-return relationship is due to investor preference for low risk.

Following our brief examination of the efficient frontier, we ventured into the realm of utility theory, where it was noted that a given return provides different benefits to different people. These benefits we described as the *want-satisfying power* of a given quantity of money or return. The typical investor could be classified as risk-averse. The investor's marginal utility declines with higher returns such that $1,000 is preferred to $100. But this preference is not ten times as great. The risk-neutral and risk-seeker were also defined. A risk-neutral has a constant marginal utility, while the risk-seeker exhibits increasing marginal utility. In general, our study of the investment decision assumes risk-aversion.

Given a well-defined utility function we could represent an investor's utility preferences with a set of *indifference curves*. An indifference curve connects all points in the risk-return configuration which have the same utility. The complete set of indifference curves is an *indifference map* where each successively higher curve has greater utility. The investor is indifferent between any two points on a given indifference curve and will always prefer points on higher curves to any point on a lower indifference curve. The indifference map allows us to establish an *optimum portfolio*. The investor should select the efficient portfolio that falls on the highest possible indifference curve since expected utility is maximized at that point. This point is where the efficient frontier and the indifference curve are tangent.

Thus, all the concepts necessary for the investment decision have been established, but in order to apply the theory, we require 1) a measure of risk and return, 2) a technique to find the efficient frontier, and 3) a measure of the investor's indifference map. The great value of the theory we have examined lies in its ability to direct us to the specific problems we need to solve in order to find the optimum portfolio.

QUESTIONS

1. Explain, in your words, why the riskiness of a single security may be completely irrelevant to the investor's decision to buy or sell the particular security.
2. What is meant by the efficiency criterion and the efficient frontier? How do these two concepts relate to each other?
3. Why is it necessary to establish an efficient frontier prior to arriving at an investment decision?
4. Why should we expect the efficient frontier to increase with return but at a decreasing rate? Your explanation should emphasize both the economic principles involved in the investment decision and the investor's particular utility function.
5. Explain why we expect the typical investor to have a utility function that increases at a decreasing rate.
6. Figure 11-5 shows an indifference map for a risk-averter. What would the indifference map of a risk-neutral look like? How would the indifference map of a risk-seeker differ from that of the risk-averter?
7. Discuss the general criterion used to select the optimum or best portfolio

from the set of efficient portfolios. Why might the optimum portfolio of one investor be different from the optimum portfolio of another investor?

8. Itemize the information the investor requires in order to apply the theory of portfolio selection presented in this chapter.

9. Define the following terms:
   a) Utility.
   b) Marginal utility.
   c) Risk-averter.
   d) Risk-seeker.
   e) Indifference curve.
   f) Efficient portfolio.
   g) Optimum portfolio.

SUGGESTED READINGS

Bauman, W. Scott. *Performance Objectives of Investors.* Occasional Paper Number 2. Charlottesville, Va.: Financial Analysts Research Foundation, 1975, pp. 14–29.

Markowitz, Harry H. "Portfolio Selection." *Journal of Finance,* March 1952, pp. 77–91.

——. *Portfolio Selection: Efficient Diversification of Investments.* New York: John Wiley and Sons, Inc., 1959.

Robichek, Alexander A. "Risk and the Value of Securities." *Journal of Financial and Quantitative Analysis.* December 1969, pp. 513–38.

Swalm, Ralph O. "Utility Theory: Insights into Risk Taking." *Harvard Business Review,* November–December 1966, pp. 123–36.

Zinbarg, Edward D. "Modern Approach to Investment Risk." *Financial Executive,* February 1973, pp. 44–61.

12

Measures of Risk and Return

In dealing with the problem of selecting from many investment alternatives, each having many possible outcomes, we established the requirement for a measure of return and a measure of risk. Regarding return, we would like to have a measure that represents our "best" estimate of the actual outcome. The measure of risk should reflect the possibility that the actual outcome will be different than the estimated outcome. The purpose of this chapter is to examine various measures of risk and return. The emphasis is on establishing a technique of measurement in an abstract sense. No effort is made to discuss the problem of assigning numbers to our measurement devices. This application problem is the subject of the next chapter. For now, we concentrate on how risk and return *should* be measured.

If we define our best return estimate as that which minimizes the average error, the obvious choice for a return measure is the average return or expected value, since the average error will be zero over long periods of time. However, such a solution would be unacceptable if we were to use expected value as our only decision variable. We may not want to wait the thirty or more years required to assure that the average error will be close to zero. This is precisely why risk must be considered. As long as risk is a part of the decision, we can employ the expected value as the measure of return. How one obtains a number for the expected value is a major problem, but in order to solve this aspect of the investment decision, one must first establish a measure of risk.

In Chapter 6, we discussed several sources of risk, including market risk, interest rate risk, price level risk, and business risk. The problem is to develop a measure of these risks in the same way as one develops a measure of heat or distance or time. The analogy to a physical phenomenon such as heat is appropriate when we recognize that temperature is not heat, but merely a means of communicating relative differences in heat. The temperature has no necessary relationship to the causes of heat or cold. In a similar fashion, a risk measure should not be thought of as risk or a cause of risk, but merely as a technique to distinguish between assets with different degrees of risk.

DISTRIBUTIONS OF RETURNS

When asked to think of risk, an investor might suggest that risk increases as potential outcomes deviate from the expected value. In the previous chapter, we concluded that investments in Zero Ox and Goldfinger were more risky than an investment in Parent Bell. Zero Ox and Goldfinger each had an expected return of 10 percent (vs. 5 percent for Parent Bell), but were more risky than Parent Bell because of their more widely scattered distribution of returns.

If asked to distinguish, on the basis of risk, among three securities with probability distributions as depicted in Figure 12–1, most would conclude that security X is the most risky and security Z is the least risky. This is simply because X has the greatest dispersion around the expected value and Z has the least dispersion. Each distribution in Figure 12–1 is drawn with the same mean—shown as $E(R)$. The mean, of course, is equal to the expected value. Investors would generally select investment Z due to indifference on a return dimension and a preference on a risk dimension. The preference for Z on a risk dimension is due to the fact that low dispersion is preferred to high dispersion in the same way that low risk is preferred to high risk.

VARIANCE

If dispersion and risk are equivalent, risk can be gauged by measuring dispersion. The most appropriate measure of dispersion is the variance of the probability distribution of returns. The variance is simply the

FIGURE 12–1
Hypothetical Distributions of Returns

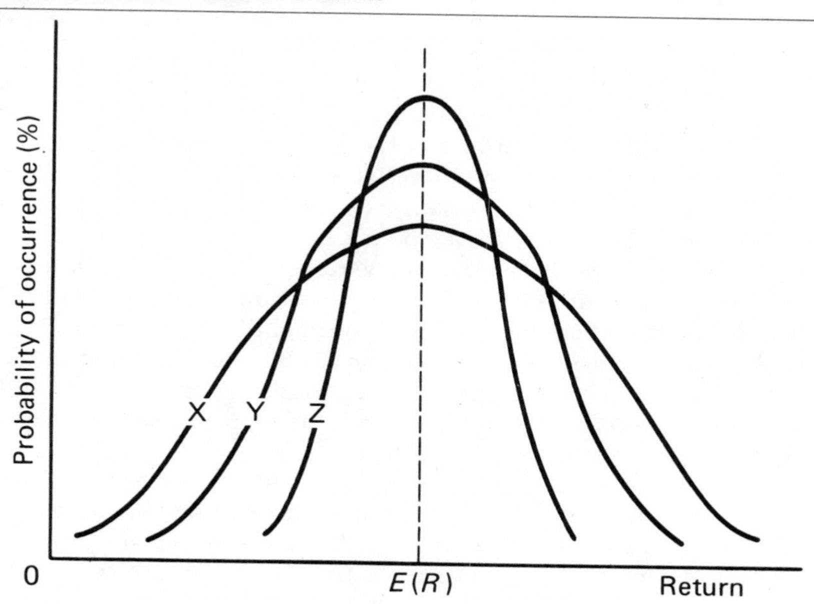

average of the squared deviations from the mean. Variance is easily determined from the potential investment outcomes. We will demonstrate the calculation of the variance later. For now, note that in Figure 12–1 investment X will have the largest variance, while investment Z will have the smallest variance. Investment Y will have a variance between that of investment X and Z. In essence, the greater the dispersion, the greater will be the variance. Consequently, the variance of returns can be used to measure risk if it is dispersion we wish to avoid.

There are other reasons for using variance to measure risk. By recalling our elementary statistics, it becomes clear what the power of the variance can be in an investment decision. Assume that the probability distributions of the returns from security investments are normal. If one were to plot a normal distribution, it would appear as a symmetrical bell-shaped curve similar to those depicted in Figure 12–1. This familiar curve is uniquely described by the expected value (mean) and variance. As a result, knowing the expected value and the variance is all the information we need if the distribution of returns is normal. There is no additional information required.

An individual investing in securities with normally distributed returns will make decisions on the basis of expected value and variance. Since dispersion is undesirable, the investor will attempt to minimize variance for any given level of expected value or to maximize expected value for any given level of variance. If we substitute risk and return for variance and expected value, we have the efficiency criterion developed in Chapter 11. The result is that, given normality, the investor will behave as though variance measures a risk.[1]

Do actual returns in the securities markets have a normal distribution? The available evidence suggests the distributions of the returns from common stocks are not normal. Rather, common stock returns belong to a family of distributions of which the normal is a member but the actual distribution of returns is of a character where variance has no meaning.[2] In other words, actual common stock distributions most closely resemble distributions whose dispersion cannot be measured by variance. Obviously, this evidence is quite damaging to the use of variance as a measure or risk, but variance is still used quite widely. The reason lies in the fact that while deviations from normality clearly exist, the actual difference between a normal distribution and the actual distribution of returns is extremely small. It is so small that investment decisions made using variance are, for practical purposes, no different than the decisions that would be made using a measure of dispersion in keeping with the actual distributions.[3]

Some investment analysts would argue that proximity to normality is an invalid conclusion since even casual observation indicates that stock market returns are highly skewed to the right. As illustrated in Figure 12–2, this means that returns from common stocks are typically quite modest, but on rare occasions very high returns can be observed. However, concluding a lack of normality from such observed behavior results from a failure to specify properly the measure of return.

We saw in the appendix to Chapter 6 that return should be measured using the geometric mean. The geometric mean can be calculated using the logs of the individual returns. Substituting logs in the return calculation has a very important implication. A distribution skewed to the right will become much more symmetrical when the values are converted to logs. Symmetrical means that half of the distribution lies above the mean and half below the mean. Each half is a mirror image of the other half. With common stock returns, the highly skewed distributions become

[1]In addition to dispersion and normality, variance can also be justified as a measure of risk on the basis of the shape of the investor's utility function. This justification involves the mathematics of quadratic functions and will not be developed here. For a complete discussion see William F. Sharpe, *Portfolio Theory and Capital Markets* (New York: McGraw-Hill Book Co., 1970), pp. 196–201; and Harry M. Markowitz, *Portfolio Selection, Efficient Diversification of Investments,* Cowles Foundation Monograph No. 16 (New York: John Wiley & Sons, 1959), pp. 282–89. Variance is also an appropriate measure of risk when the investment objective is to maximize final wealth.

[2]A complete examination of the actual distributions of common stock returns can be found in Eugene F. Fama, "The Behavior of Stock-Market Prices," *Journal of Business,* January 1965, pp. 34–105; and R. R. Officer, "The Distribution of Stock Returns," *Journal of American Statistical Association,* December 1972, pp. 807–12.

[3]See, for example, Marshall E. Blume, "Portfolio Theory: A Step Toward Its Application," *Journal of Business,* April 1970, pp. 152–53; and William F. Sharpe, "Mean-Absolute Deviation Characteristic Lines for Securities and Portfolios," *Management Science,* October 1971, pp. 1–13.

FIGURE 12-2
Distribution Skewed to the Right

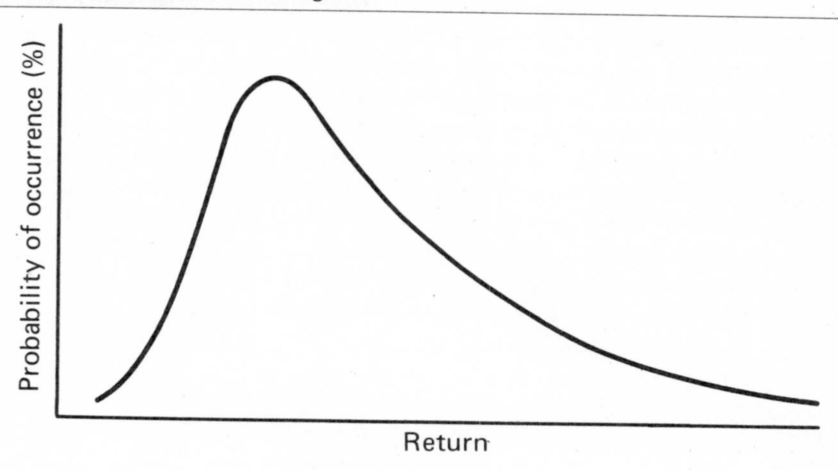

extremely close to normal when the logs of returns are used. Since the logs of returns are the appropriate measure of return over time, the assumption of normality becomes acceptable.[4]

SEMIVARIANCE

There are several situations where the variance may not be appropriate. Dispersion per se is not necessarily undesirable—only dispersion *below* some minimum return. In considering an investment that will earn either \$3 million or lose \$1 million, the use of variance treats both deviations from the expected value equally. But the \$3 million gain is not the positive equivalent of the \$1 million loss as we know from our discussion of utility theory. The typical solution to this conceptual problem introduces semivariance as the measure of risk. The semivariance is identical to the variance except that it considers only those deviations below the mean or some minimum acceptable return such as zero. It is the average of the squared deviations below the mean or minimum return.

Although the problem that semivariance attempts to rectify is an important one, unfortunately the semivariance has very little practical value. Statisticians have not been able as yet to find a convenient method with which to handle semivariance in putting securities together into portfolios. There is no way of determining quickly and cheaply the semivariance of a portfolio of two or more securities, given the individual

[4]Achieving normality by converting returns to logs can best be seen in Lawrence Fisher, "Outcomes for 'Random' Investments in Common Stocks Listed on the New York Stock Exchange," *Journal of Business*, April 1968, pp. 149–61.

semivariances. We also saw that the actual distributions of common stock returns belong to a family of distributions of which the normal is a member. One characteristic of this family of distributions is that they are symmetrical. Given symmetry, the semivariance will equal the variance when the semivariance is calculated using only those deviations below the mean. The result is that variance and semivariance will produce exactly the same decision given symmetry. In other words, use of the semivariance is unnecessary. Furthermore, even if distributions were not symmetrical it would not be appropriate to ignore positive deviations in order to account for the differences in the utility of positive and negative returns. While semivariance is not of much practical use, we have presented the concept to familiarize the reader with the term and the reasons why it is not functionally useful.

SKEWNESS

Several authors have suggested that investors are quite concerned with skewness as well as with dispersion. The suggestion is that given two investment opportunities, such as N and R in Figure 12-3, which have equal variances and equal expected values, the individual will prefer investment R. Investment R will be preferred since its returns are more skewed to the right. The suggestion is intuitively appealing since right skewness provides more opportunities for very large returns. As pre-

FIGURE 12-3
Two Investment Alternatives with Different Skewness

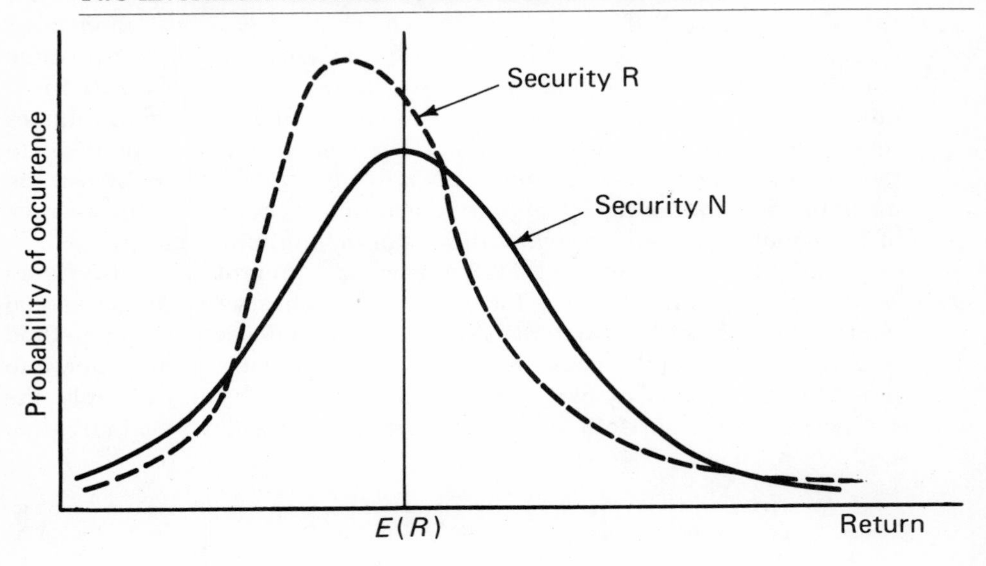

viously noted, however, evidence seems to indicate that common stock returns are distributed in a symmetrical fashion, which implies that right skewness is absent.[5]

STOCHASTIC DOMINANCE

Another problem with using variance as a measure of risk has to do with the size of the variance relative to the expected value. Figure 12–4 illustrates the probability distributions of the returns for securities A and B. The expected values and variances lead us to conclude that neither security will be preferred by all investors, since the highest expected value is associated with the highest variance. The highly risk-averse investor should select security B. A lower aversion to risk may allow the selection of security A.

FIGURE 12–4
Stochastic Dominance

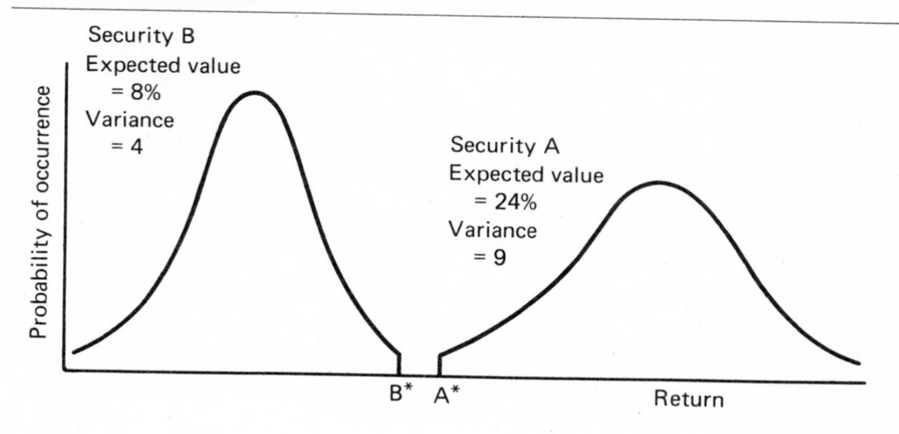

A closer look at the two securities shows a clear preference for security A no matter what our utility function happens to be. Given any reasonable actual future result, the return from security A will be larger than the return from security B. If the return from security A is extremely low (A*), security A will still represent the better decision. Security A is said to *stochastically dominate* security B. All possible outcomes of security A are preferred to all possible outcomes of B despite A's higher variance.

[5]The subject of skewness is handled in greater detail in Clayton P. Alderfer and Harold Bierman, Jr., "Choice with Risk: Beyond the Mean and Variance," *Journal of Business*, July 1970, pp. 341–53; and Fred D. Arditti, "Risk and the Required on Equity," *Journal of Finance*, March 1967, pp. 19–36.

Under a condition of stochastic dominance, variance as a measure of risk is inappropriate. This argument does not imply that we should ignore variance—only that it should not be used when stochastic dominance is present. The real question is whether or not stochastic dominance is a frequent occurrence in the marketplace. The answer is a firm no. Evidence on return distributions suggests that it is unlikely that such a condition will ever exist. If it did, investors would quickly eliminate it by bidding up the price of security A, the dominant security. Bidding up A's price would reduce the rate of return and eliminate the advantage. The existence of stochastic dominance would make the portfolio decision wonderfully easy since we would not have to worry about such items as utility theory and the objectives of the investor.[6]

VARIANCE IN THE DECISION MAKING PROCESS

Calculation of Variance and Standard Deviation

We examined variance and found that there are strong reasons for its use as a measure of risk. Let us examine more carefully the definition of variance in order to see how its use will influence our investment decision. We noted earlier that variance is the average of the squared deviations from the mean. This definition can be expressed in the following manner:

$$V = \frac{1}{n} \sum_{i=1}^{n} [R_i - E(R)]^2$$

where: n = the number of possible outcomes
$E(R)$ = the average rate of return or the expected value of the investment
R_i = the return for the ith outcome.

Fortunately, we can simplify this equation to read as follows:

$$V = E(R^2) - [E(R)]^2$$

This equation states that the variance is the difference between the average of the squared individual return possibilities and the square of the average rate of return.

[6]A complete examination of stochastic dominance in the stock market is in R. B. Porter, "An Empirical Comparison of Stochastic Dominance and Mean-Variance Portfolio Choice Criteria," *Journal of Financial and Quantitative Analysis,* January 1973, pp. 71–81. An application giving consideration to stochastic dominance is in William J. Baumol, "An Expected Gain-Confidence Limit Criterion for Portfolio Selection," *Management Science,* October 1963, pp. 124–82.

An additional term, the *standard deviation,* is frequently used in investments. This is the square root of the variance. If the variance is nine, the standard deviation would be three. Both the standard deviation and the variance can be used to measure risk. Whichever one is used, the same decision will result. The standard deviation is an important concept, since it allows a rigorous interpretation of the variance. Given a normal distribution, approximately 95 percent of the actual returns will fall within a range of plus or minus two standard deviations of the mean. For example, for a security with an expected return of 9 percent and a standard deviation of 5, approximately 95 percent of the actual returns will fall between −1 percent and 19 percent, given normality. The greater the standard deviation or variance, the greater will be the range of possible returns.

The calculation of the variance and standard deviation for a security having four possible outcomes with each outcome equally likely is depicted in Exhibit 12-1. Column 2 lists the returns (R) and column 3 shows the squared values of each return (R^2). Taking averages of each column results in an expected return of 10 percent, a variance of 500, and a standard deviation of 22.36.

It is also necessary to calculate the variance of combinations of securities. Unfortunately, complications arise in determining the variance of portfolios. But it is the variance of combinations that is most important and the power of variance as a decision making tool is most evident when it comes to the risk on combinations of securities.

EXHIBIT 12-1

Calculation of Expected Return, Variance and Standard Deviation

Outcome or State of Nature	Assumed Annual Rate of Return (R)	Squared Annual Rate of Return (R^2)
1	−20	400
2	0	0
3	20	400
4	40	1,600
Sum	40	2,400

$$E(R) = 40/4 = 10$$
$$E(R^2) = 2{,}400/4 = 600$$

$$\begin{aligned} V &= E(R^2) - [E(R)]^2 \\ &= 600 - (10)^2 \\ &= 500 \end{aligned}$$

$$\text{Standard deviation } (\sigma) = \sqrt{500} = 22.36$$

Most investors take the view that portfolios with many securities are in general less risky than portfolios with only a few securities. Diversification is used as a risk-reducing device. In general, the more diversification, the less the risk. The variance behaves in the same fashion in that a portfolio with many securities will typically have a lower variance than a less diversified portfolio. However, there are some very important conditions attached to this conclusion. In Exhibit 12-2 security A is identical to the security described in Exhibit 12-1. Security A has a mean of 10 percent and a variance of 500. Security B has a mean of 30 percent and the same variance as security A. The fourth column of Exhibit 12-2 is the return from a portfolio where equal amounts of money have been invested in securities A and B. The variance of this combination is shown along with the individual variances. Surprisingly, the portfolio variance is identical to the individual variances. The outcome is surprising in that we typically expect risk to be lower when securities are combined, but no risk reduction occurred.

EXHIBIT 12-2

A Hypothetical Two-Security Portfolio Combining Perfectly Positive-Correlated Securities

Outcome or State of Nature	Return from A	Return from B	Return from 50% A & 50% B
1	−20	0	−10
2	0	20	10
3	20	40	30
4	40	60	50
Sum	40	120	80
$E(R)$	10	30	20
$V(R)$	500	500	500

Perfect Positive Correlation

Exhibit 12-2 represents a situation where the returns from each security exhibit perfect positive correlation with each other. This term means the return from security B is directly related to the return from security A. The relationship is perfect in that knowledge of the return of one will tell us, with no error, exactly the return of the other. Security B's return is always 20 percentage points higher than security A's. Given perfect positive correlation, diversification will not reduce risk. Hence, perfect positive correlation implies that we should not diversify. We would select the security with the highest expected return (security B in Exhibit 12-2).

Exhibit 12–2 is highly artificial since securities never exhibit perfect positive correlation. Although perfection does not exist, some positive correlation is quite common. In fact, virtually every security has some positive correlation with every other security. This observation is vital to the portfolio manager since *the greater the positive correlation, the less will be the risk-reducing properties of a given combination of securities.* Perfect positive correlation provides no risk reduction.

Perfect Negative Correlation

Perfect diversification is possible with securities that exhibit perfect negative correlation. Exhibit 12–3 presents returns for two hypothetical securities in the same fashion as presented in Exhibit 12–2. Security C is much different even though the potential return is the same as for security B in Exhibit 12–2. The difference is that security C is at its best when security A is at its worst. For each outcome, security C achieves a return which is equal to minus the return of security A plus forty percentage points as shown by the following equation:

$$\text{security C} = -(\text{security A}) + 40$$

Knowledge of the return from security A tells us all we need to know about the return of security C. Both returns are related in a perfect but negative fashion. When the return of security A is high the return of security C is low and vice versa. When such a situation exists, one can achieve perfect diversification. In Exhibit 12–3, the returns from a combination of securities A and C are recorded in column 4. No matter what the state of nature, the investor will achieve a return of 20 percent. Such perfect diversification is possible because of the perfect negative correlation.

EXHIBIT 12–3

A Hypothetical Two-Security Portfolio Combining Perfectly Negative-Correlated Securities

Outcome or State of Nature	Return from A	Return from C	Return from 50% A & 50% C
1	−20	60	20
2	0	40	20
3	20	20	20
4	40	0	20
Sum	40	120	80
$E(R)$	10	30	20
$V(R)$	500	500	0

Covariance

A measure of the correlation between securities can be developed to evaluate the riskiness of a given portfolio. The measure most frequently used is called covariance. The covariance between two securities may be stated as follows:

$$Cov(R_A,R_B) = E(R_A,R_B) - E(R_A)E(R_B)$$

where: R_A = return from security A
R_B = return from security B

The interpretation of the covariance is that the higher the correlation, the higher will be the covariance. With a positive correlation, the covariance will be positive. When the correlation is negative the covariance will be negative. The covariance will be zero when two securities exhibit no relationship. This special case is referred to as *statistical independence*. Two securities that are said to be independent will have a covariance equal to zero.

To calculate the covariance, it is necessary to sum the products of the returns and take their mean. Exhibit 12–4 illustrates the covariance calculation for the securities shown in Exhibits 12–2 and 12–3. Taking these expected values we find that the covariance between securities A and B is 500. The covariance between securities A and B is large and positive, as we would expect given positive correlation. The covariance between securities A and C is –500, as we would expect since these two securities exhibit negative correlation.

EXHIBIT 12–4

Covariance Calculation

Outcome or State of Nature	Return from A (R_A)	Return from B (R_B)	Return from C (R_C)	A times B $E(R_A, R_B)$	A times C $E(R_A, R_C)$
1	–20	0	60	0	–1,200
2	0	20	40	0	0
3	20	40	20	800	400
4	40	60	0	2,400	0
Sum	40	120	120	3,200	– 800
Expected value	10	30	30	800	– 200

$$\text{Covariance }(R_A, R_B) = E(R_A, R_B) - E(R_A)E(R_B) = 800 - (10)(30) = 500$$

$$\text{Covariance }(R_A, R_C) = E(R_A, R_C) - E(R_A)E(R_C) = -200 - (10)(30) = -500$$

Correlation Coefficient

Interpreting the covariance is difficult since all it really indicates is whether the correlation is positive or negative. By itself covariance does not tell us how close the correlation is to perfection since the magnitude of the variances of the two securities involved will directly influence the magnitude of the covariance. If the variances are large, the covariance can be large even if the relationship between securities is far from perfection. For this reason investors frequently employ the correlation coefficient as the measure of the relationship between security returns. This measure is the ratio of the covariance to the product of the two standard deviations. The correlation coefficient is given by the following equation:

$$r_{AB} = \frac{Cov(R_A, R_B)}{\sigma_A \; \sigma_B}$$

where: r_{AB} = correlation coefficient between A and B
σ_A = the standard deviation of the return from security A
σ_B = the standard deviation of the return from security B

The above equation can be used to calculate the correlation coefficient for security pairs AB and AC as shown in Exhibit 12-4.

$$AB = \frac{500}{(22.36)\;(22.36)} = 1.0$$

$$AC = \frac{-500}{(22.36)\;(22.36)} = -1.0$$

Coefficient of Determination

Squaring the correlation coefficient yields the coefficient of determination (r^2), which has a very rigorous interpretation. The coefficient of determination gives the percent of the fluctuations in the return of one security explained by knowing the return of the other security. In the example, the coefficient of determination in both cases is one. Hence, knowledge of the return of security A explains 100 percent of the potential fluctuations in the return of security B and vice versa. If the correlation coefficient (r) were .80, the knowledge of the return of one security would explain 64 percent (.80 squared) of the fluctuations in the return of the other.

In summary, the covariance can take on any magnitude and tell us only whether the relationship is positive or negative. The coefficient of determination indicates the strength of the relationship. Its maximum value will be one and its minimum value will be zero. A coefficient of determination of zero would indicate statistical independence.

Portfolio Variance

It is possible to calculate the portfolio variance for a portfolio of two securities in a direct fashion by using the following equation instead of considering each state of nature as was done in Exhibit 12-2.

$$V(R_p) = X_A^2\, V(R_A) + X_B^2 V(R_B) + 2X_A X_B Cov(R_A, R_B)$$

where:
X_A = the percent invested in security A
X_B = the percent invested in security B
V = variance of security or portfolio indicated
R_A, R_B = return on securities A, B
R_p = return on portfolio

The portfolio variance is a weighted average of the individual variances plus twice the weighted covariance. The weights are the percent invested in each security. If we invest 60 percent in security B and 40 percent in security A, X_A would equal .4 and X_B would be .6. The doubling of the covariance term comes into play since we are dealing with combinations of securities A and B, and B and A.

In Exhibit 12-2, the variance of a portfolio with half the funds invested in security A and half the funds invested in security B was calculated by taking the sum of the squared deviations. With the covariance term, this value can be calculated directly in the following manner:

$$\begin{aligned} V_{AB} &= X_A^2 V(R_A) + X_B^2 V(R_B) + 2X_A X_B \text{ Cov}(R_A, R_B) \\ &= (.5)^2 500 + (.5)^2 500 + 2(.5)(.5)(500) \\ &= 125 + 125 + 250 \\ &= 500 \end{aligned}$$

As before, the portfolio variance is 500. In the example of perfect negative correlation we found earlier that the portfolio variance was zero. Using the covariance term we arrive at this directly in the same fashion. Exhibit 12-3 summarizes the situation of a two-security portfolio with perfectly negative-correlated securities.

$$\begin{aligned} V_{AC} &= (.5)^2 - 500 + (.5)^2 - 500 + 2(.5)(.5)(-500) \\ &= 125 + 125 - 250 \\ &= 0 \end{aligned}$$

These calculations point out the importance of covariance when measuring the risk-reducing properties of a given combination of securities. In the case of positive correlation, the large covariance term does not reduce the variance at all as should be the case with perfect positive correlation. In the case of negative correlation, the negative covariance reduces the portfolio variance to zero as should be the case with perfect negative correlation.

SUMMARY

The problem of measuring risk is difficult. While variance was chosen as the appropriate risk measure, its use is not free of conceptual problems. The justification of variance is basically twofold. First, most investors agree that risky assets have large dispersion or a large range of possible returns. If dispersion is the basis of our intuitive concept of risk, variance is the appropriate measure of risk since variance measures dispersion. Larger dispersion is always associated with larger variance. The second reason to measure risk with variance concerns the characteristics of the distributions of returns. It was argued that if distributions are normal, all we ever need is the mean and variance. Our decision will be based on the efficiency criterion where we attempt to maximize expected return for a given variance or minimize variance for a given expected return. The evidence presented suggested that for common stocks, the distributions were close enough to normal so that an assumption of normality is reasonable.

The arguments for using the variance to measure risk appear quite strong until some additional considerations are introduced. The first problem mentioned related to the fact that most of us will not consider dispersion above the expected value to represent risk. Potential losses are to be avoided but potential gains are not. Variance treats equivalent gains and losses equally. In light of this observation, the semivariance was introduced as a candidate for measuring risk. The semivariance is calculated using only those deviations below the mean or some minimum loss point. Potentially the suggestion is a good one. Yet, given symmetrical distributions, the semivariance will produce the same decisions as the variance. Since the semivariance is more difficult to work with, variance is preferred, given the symmetry which seems to be the case in the real world.

The existence of stochastic dominance implies that we should not measure risk with variance, but here again the problem appears to be a minor one. If stochastic dominance is present, variance is obviously a poor measure. However, it is highly unlikely that such a condition prevails in the marketplace. If it did the prices of the stochastically dominant securities would be bid up to a point that would eliminate their advantage. In other words, given stochastic dominance investors should, and can be expected to, ignore variance. By their action the dominance should be eliminated.

The calculation of the variance for a specific asset was shown to be the mean of the squared deviations around the average or expected return. If we take the square root of the variance, the result is the standard deviation. With a normal distribution, approximately 95 percent of the possible returns will fall within a range of the expected value plus or minus two standard deviations.

We encounter difficulty with the variance when we seek the variance of a combination of securities. The portfolio variance will be closely related to the extent to which the securities in the portfolio are correlated. In the case of two securities having a perfect relationship, the portfolio variance can be reduced to zero if the relationship is negative. If the relationship is positive, the variance of the combination will at least be as large as the lowest individual security variance in the portfolio. The measure of the relationship between security returns is the covariance. If the correlation is positive, the covariance will be positive, while a negative correlation produces a negative covariance.

In order to interpret the covariance, we introduced the correlation coefficient, the ratio of the covariance to the product of the standard deviations of the two securities. The square of the correlation coefficient is the coefficient of determination. The coefficient of determination achieves a maximum value of one when the correlation is perfect, either positive or negative. When no correlation exists, its minimum value is zero. Between zero and one, the coefficient of determination measures the percentage of the fluctuations in one of the securities explained by the fluctuations in the other security.

The calculation of the portfolio variance demonstrated the importance of the covariance term. If the covariance is large and positive, combining securities into a portfolio does very little to reduce the portfolio risk. When the covariance is large and negative, combining securities will reduce risk dramatically. If the covariance is close to zero, the portfolio risk will be less than that of the individual security risks and diversification will be a valuable risk-reducing strategy. The covariance size will determine the risk-reducing properties of a given combination of securities. The smaller the covariance the greater will be the value of diversification.

The primary emphasis in the chapter has been with the problem of how risk should be measured. Once we have decided upon the form of our measuring rod, we must address the problem of application. In order to actually use variances, covariances, and correlation coefficients, we must find a way to assign numbers to these abstract measuring techniques. This difficult problem is the subject of the next chapter.

QUESTIONS

1. Explain why most investors will typically use expected value to measure the future return of the security.
2. If one recommends that variance be used to measure risk, discuss whether or not it is necessary to relate variance to such important items as interest rate risk, purchasing power risk, and business risk.
3. Critically examine the reasons why variance or standard deviation might be used to measure the risk of financial assets. Can you cite any evidence that suggests the validity of using variance to measure risk?
4. Define semivariance and explain why this statistic might be used to measure risk, including an explanation of the risk measurement problem that semivariance is designed to correct.
5. Give an example of a skewed probability distribution and explain why skewness is typically not considered in the investment decision as made within the context of portfolio theory.

6. Define stochastic dominance. Discuss the reasons why this phenomenon is typically not given consideration in the investment decision.
7. Define and interpret the following terms:
   a) standard deviation,
   b) perfect correlation,
   c) covariance,
   d) correlation coefficient,
   e) coefficient of determination.
8. Why is the covariance such an important concept for the investor when considering the selection of a portfolio of financial assets?
9. Why is it necessary to introduce the coefficient of determination in order to interpret the meaning of the covariance statistic?

PROBLEMS

1. The following rates of return on securities XYZ and ABC are projected for the four states of nature listed below. Each state of nature has an equal probability of occurrence.

	Rate of Return	
State of Nature	*XYZ Company*	*ABC Company*
1	18%	27%
2	11	5
3	− 7	34
4	14	−20

   a) Calculate the following statistics from these data:
      1) Expected value of each security.
      2) Variance of each security.
      3) Covariance.
      4) Coefficient of determination.
   b) Calculate the portfolio expected value and variance under the following conditions:
      1) 40% invested in XYZ and 60% invested in ABC Company.
      2) 25% invested in XYZ and 75% invested in ABC Company.

2. Construct a table of returns for two securities with four states of nature where the two securities exhibit *a*) perfect positive correlation, *b*) perfect negative correlation, and *c*) independence.

SUGGESTED READINGS

Alderfer, Clayton P. and Harold Bierman, Jr. "Choices with Risk: Beyond the Mean and Variance." *Journal of Business*, July 1970, pp. 341–53.

Altman, Edward I. and Robert A. Schwartz. "Common Stock Price Volatility Measures." *Journal of Financial and Quantitative Analysis*, January 1970, pp. 603–25.

Baumol, William J. "Mathematical Analysis of Portfolio Selection." *Financial Analysts Journal*, September–October 1966, pp. 95–99.

Bower, Richard S. and Donald F. Wippern. "Risk-Return Measurement in Portfolio Selection and Performance Appraisal Models: Progress Report." *Journal of Financial and Quantitative Analysis*, December 1969, pp. 417–47.

Pinches, George E. and William R. Kinney, Jr. "The Measurement of the Volatility of Common Stock Prices." *Journal of Finance*, March 1971, pp. 119–25.

Porter, R. Burr. "An Empirical Comparison of Stochastic Dominance and Mean-Variance Portfolio Choice Criteria." *Journal of Financial and Quantitative Analysis*, September 1973, pp. 587–608.

Valentine, Jerome L. *Investment Analysis and Capital Market Theory*. Occasional Paper No. 1. Charlottesville, Va.: The Financial Analysts Research Foundation, 1974.

West, David A. "Risk Analysis in the 1960's." *Financial Analysts Journal*, November–December 1967, pp. 124–26.

13

Capital Asset Pricing

In Chapters 11 and 12, we developed a theoretical structure for making investment decisions. The selection of an optimum portfolio involves 1) determination of the expected return and risk for each investment possibility, 2) determination of the efficient frontier, and 3) selection of the optimum portfolio on the basis of the investor's utility function.

In this chapter, we examine the problem of multiple covariances that exists in attempting to apply the efficient frontier concept. The concept of a risk-free asset is also introduced. The existence of a risk-free asset allows the development of the capital asset pricing (CAP) model. The CAP model provides a convenient way of examining the risk and return characteristics of a portfolio. It may produce a solution to many of the difficult portfolio problems facing the investor. The CAP model essentially provides a simplified approach to the construction of a portfolio that is consistent with the methods introduced thus far. After examining the nature of this model, we examine its practical validity as revealed by several empirical studies. Finally, we examine the use of the CAP model in making the portfolio decision.

THE PROBLEM OF MULTIPLE COVARIANCES

The hypothetical two-security portfolio used in the previous two chapters is an unrealistic situation. Although the principles derived from examining two securities remain unchanged in considering a larger number of securities, a problem does arise. As additional securities are considered, the number of covariance estimates an investor must make increases rapidly. With three securities, there are three covariance terms between securities 1 and 2, 1 and 3, and 2 and 3. For five securities, the number of covariance estimates increases to ten. An investor dealing with 100 securities would need 4,950 covariance estimates.[1]

A RISK-FREE ASSET

The large number of covariance estimates needed is one important reason why the investment community until recently virtually ignored portfolio theory even though Harry Markowitz had introduced the basic concepts in 1952.[2] The introduction of the concept of a risk-free asset did much to stimulate the application of portfolio theory.[3] A risk-free asset provides a return, but has a zero variance (no risk). U.S. Treasury bills are often used as a proxy for the risk-free asset.[4]

The availability of a risk-free asset has some important consequences. When we combine the risk-free asset with any other risky asset or risky portfolio, the result will be a linear (straight-line) relationship between the risk and the expected return of the combination portfolio. In Figure 13–1, we have taken a risk-free asset (R_f) and combined it with portfolio A on the efficient frontier (EF). A straight line from the risk-free return to portfolio A is the risk-return relationship of all combinations of the risk-free asset and portfolio A. Between R_f and A, we are said to be *lending,* since the combination portfolio contains Treasury bills which are loans the investor has made to the federal government.

We have eliminated a portion of the efficient frontier by introducing the risk-free asset. Without a risk-free asset, any portfolio between E and A is efficient and may be purchased by a highly risk-averse investor. With a risk-free asset, no portfolio between E and A will receive consideration. For example, an investor desiring the risk-return combination of portfolio E would be better advised to purchase portfolio D by placing a portion of the funds in portfolio A and the remainder in the risk-free

[1]If we designate the number of securities as N, the addition of one security would require *N* additional covariance terms. In general, an opportunity set with *N* securities will contain $(N^2 - N)/2$ separate covariance terms.

[2]Harry M. Markowitz, "Portfolio Selection," *Journal of Finance,* March 1952, pp. 77–91.

[3]James Tobin, "Liquidity Preference as Behavior Towards Risk," *Review of Economic Studies,* February 1958, pp. 65–86.

[4]Treasury bills are discussed in detail in Chapter 19.

FIGURE 13–1
The Efficient Frontier with a Risk-Free Asset

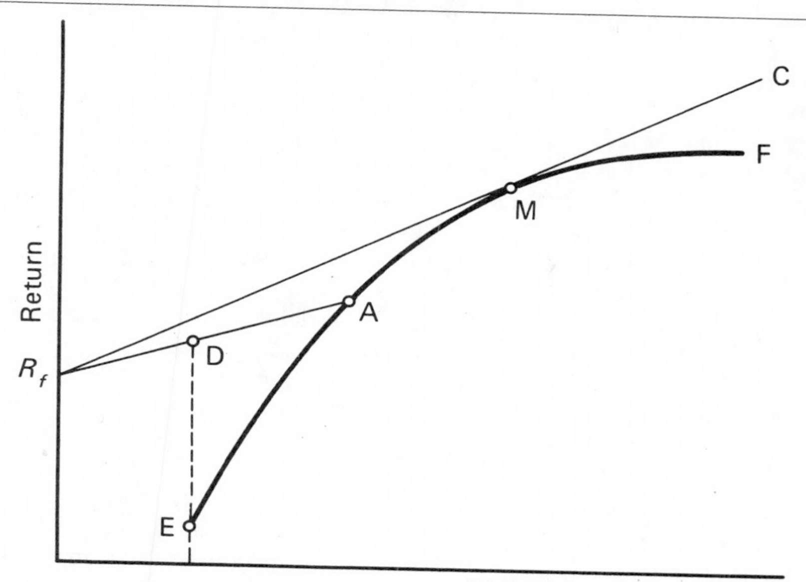

asset. This combination has the same risk as portfolio E but the expected return is higher.

An even greater portion of the efficient frontier can be eliminated by concentrating on portfolio M. We can eliminate the entire efficient frontier except for portfolio M. If we desire the risk associated with any portfolio other than M, we should not purchase that portfolio since we would be better off to purchase M and either borrow or lend to adjust the risk level. Beyond portfolio M through point C, we say we are *borrowing* since all of our own funds have been invested in portfolio M and added funds have been borrowed (perhaps in a margin account) at the risk-free rate. Our total investment in portfolio M amounts to more than 100 percent of our available funds. Combinations of portfolio M and R_f represented by line R_fC produce a higher rate of return for a given level of risk than the return provided by all other portfolios, except M, on the old efficient frontier. In essence, we have developed a new efficient frontier, R_fC.

MARKET PORTFOLIO

If we make the very broad assumption that all investors have *homogeneous expectations* (all investors face identical efficient frontiers and have the same opportunities regarding the risk-free asset), we get some powerful results. All investors will purchase the same optimum risky portfolio (portfolio M in Figure 13-1). The differences in the portfolios of individual investors will lie in the amount they borrow or lend. Given that all investors have the same risky portfolio, the composition of that portfolio is relatively easy to find. If an asset is not in the risky portfolio, nobody will buy that asset. When there are no buyers, the price of the asset must be zero. In other words, the optimum portfolio must contain all securities that have a positive price. The only portfolio of this character is the *market portfolio.* The market portfolio is defined as that portfolio which contains every asset in proportion to its market value.

Use of the market portfolio leads to a relatively simple solution to the portfolio selection problem. The investment decision reduces to one of buying the market portfolio and lending at the risk-free rate if the market portfolio is perceived as too risky or borrowing if one desires a higher risk and return relationship. A highly risk-averse investor might hold a portfolio with only a small proportion of the portfolio invested in the market and the majority of the funds invested in the risk-free asset. The investor with less aversion to risk might buy the market portfolio of common stocks on margin (borrowing) to achieve a higher risk-return relationship than the market. Combinations of the market portfolio and borrowing or lending should satisfy any investor's risk-return preferences.

We have arrived at an astonishing result. Covariances and other complex statistical techniques need not be considered. We need only to buy the market portfolio and borrow or lend. Unfortunately, we have oversimplified. The most obvious difficulty with this result is that nobody actually owns the market portfolio. A small investor with a few thousand dollars cannot buy the market portfolio since brokerage commissions would be prohibitive and fractional shares would be needed. Even a large mutual fund cannot buy the market portfolio. However, all is not lost, as will be seen shortly.

CAPITAL ASSET PRICING MODEL

Capital Market Line

Under the conditions of borrowing and lending, the new efficient frontier, $R_f C$, depicted in Figure 13-1, can be represented with the following formula:

$$R_p = R_f + \left(\frac{R_m - R_f}{\sigma_m}\right)(\sigma_p)$$

where: R_p = the return on the portfolio of the investor
R_f = the return on the risk-free asset
R_m = the return on the market portfolio
σ_m = the standard deviation of the market return
σ_p = the standard deviation of the portfolio return

This formula says that the new efficient frontier will intercept the vertical axis at the risk-free rate. The efficient frontier increases with the portfolio standard deviation at a rate equal to the ratio of the difference between the market and risk-free return to the standard deviation of the market portfolio. With one more step we can transform this formula into the capital asset pricing model, which has important implications for the application of the concepts of contemporary portfolio theory.

The additional step requires the formula above to be rearranged slightly to read as follows:

$$R_p = R_f + (R_m - R_f)\left(\frac{\sigma_p}{\sigma_m}\right)$$

With this formula we can construct the capital market line (CML), which is a pictorial representation of this rearranged equation. Figure 13-2 presents a hypothetical CML. The vertical axis is the expected portfolio return. The horizontal axis is the ratio of the standard deviation of the investor's portfolio to the standard deviation of the market portfolio. This ratio is referred to as *beta*. The CML in Figure 13-2 is equivalent to the new efficient frontier depicted in Figure 13-1 except that the horizontal axis is now beta instead of the standard deviation. In essence, the CML substitutes beta as the measure of risk for the standard deviation.

FIGURE 13-2
Capital Asset Pricing Line

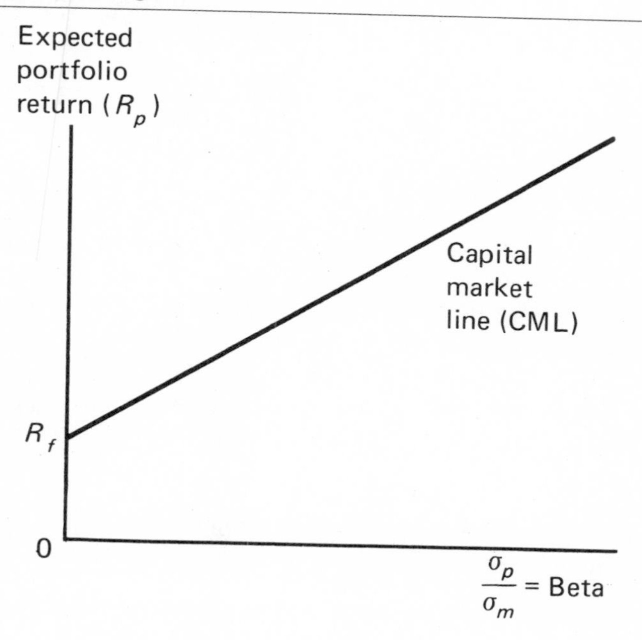

With beta as our measure of risk, we can define the *capital asset pricing* (CAP) model using the formula below:

$$R_p = R_f + \beta(R_m - R_f)$$

where: β = beta or the measure of risk (σ_p/σ_m)

In addition to replacing standard deviation or variance with beta for the measure of risk, the CAP model provides an equation to estimate the future return of a given portfolio. If the model has validity, we can now measure risk and return without encountering the problem of calculating the many covariance terms. Beta measures risk and there is only one beta value for each security.

Interpretation

The CAP model shows that the higher the beta value, the greater the expected return and vice versa. This is exactly what we would expect (i.e., the higher the risk, the higher the expected return). Why not maximize the value of beta in order to maximize the rate of return? Unfortunately, the model requires knowledge of the return on the market portfolio and the risk-free asset. If we knew with certainty that the market return would exceed the risk-free rate, we would want to maximize beta. However, it is the rare investor who knows with certainty what the market return will be in a given future period. One can only estimate the future market return. While the estimates may be quite accurate on the average, the return in any one period may deviate substantially from the average estimate.

To see beta's influence on the portfolio return, suppose an investor purchases the market portfolio on margin (borrowing) so that the beta is 2.0. Borrowing always produces a beta greater than 1 and lending produces a beta less than 1. An investor neither borrowing nor lending has the market portfolio with a beta of 1. The question we need to answer is what will be the return on the portfolio with a beta of 2.0. It depends upon the risk-free rate and the market performance during the investment period. The tabulation below shows the results achieved by this high-risk (high beta) portfolio if the market goes up 20 percent or down 10 percent and the risk-free rate is 8 percent. An up market results in a 32 percent return for the investor, but a down market produces a 28 percent portfolio loss. Similar calculations are shown for a low-risk portfolio (beta = .5).

In general, a "high" beta is greater than one while a "low" beta is less than one. A high-beta portfolio is desirable in a strong up market, but a low-beta portfolio is better in a down market. A portfolio with

Portfolio Return Calculations

	$R_f + \beta(R_m - R_f)$	$= R_p$
Low beta, up market	$= .08 + .5(.20 - .08)$	$= .14$
High beta, up market	$= .08 + 2.0(.20 - .08)$	$= .32$
Low beta, down market	$= .08 + .5(-.10 - .08)$	$= -.01$
High beta, down market	$= .08 + 2.0(-.10 - .08)$	$= -.28$

Summary of Portfolio Returns

		Beta	
		.5	2.0
Market Return (R_m)	.20	.14	.32
	−.10	−.01	−.28

a high-beta will outperform the market when the market return exceeds the risk-free return. A low-beta portfolio will outperform the market when the risk-free return exceeds the market return.

Diversification Aspects

The capital asset pricing model as formulated is not really very practical since it requires the purchase of the market portfolio. However, under certain conditions, we may be able to duplicate the results of the CAP model with a much smaller portfolio than the market portfolio. What we require is a combination of securities having the same risk-return characteristics of the market portfolio, but containing a much smaller number of securities. Whether or not such a portfolio can be found is an empirical question. Fortunately, several studies relating to this question have been conducted with extremely encouraging results.

Our objective is to find a portfolio equivalent to the market portfolio so that we do not actually have to purchase the market portfolio. How many securities are needed in a portfolio in order to approximate closely the movements of the market? The general conclusion of several studies is that a portfolio containing approximately eight to sixteen *randomly selected* common stocks will, for practical purposes, virtually duplicate the market portfolio.

Figure 13–3 shows the results of an investigation by John Evans and Stephen Archer on this question.[5] The horizontal axis is the portfolio size measured by the number of securities contained in the portfolio. The vertical axis is the standard deviation of the portfolio. The portfolio

[5]John L. Evans and Stephen H. Archer, "Diversification and the Reduction of Dispersion: An Empirical Analysis," *Journal of Finance*, December 1968, pp. 761–767.

FIGURE 13–3
Risk and Portfolio Size

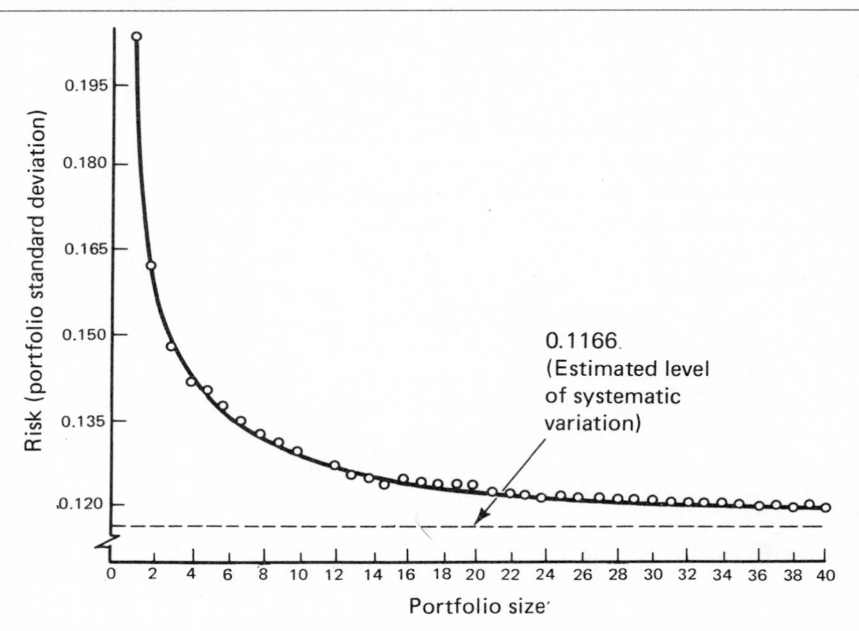

Source: John L. Evans and Stephen H. Archer, "Diversification and the Reduction of Dispersion: An Empirical Analysis," *Journal of Finance,* December, 1968, pp. 761–767.

standard deviations were calculated for a large number of separate portfolios with different numbers of securities in each portfolio. The securities were randomly selected from the Standard & Poor's 500 stock index. The maximum portfolio size was forty securities and the returns used to calculate the standard deviations were taken from the period 1958 to 1967. In addition to the portfolio standard deviations, Figure 13–3 shows the market standard deviation (.1166) for the period studied with the market represented by the S&P 500.

The results of this study indicate that a portfolio of approximately eight to sixteen randomly selected securities will closely resemble the market portfolio in terms of fluctuations in the rate of return. The standard deviation of the randomly selected portfolio is almost identical to the standard deviation of the market portfolio. Other studies have shown similar results and an unusual consistency using different time periods, different groups of common stocks, and different research techniques.[6] Consequently, while theory requires the investor to purchase

[6]For example, see: Lawrence Fisher, and James H. Lorie, "Some Studies of Variability of Returns on Investments in Common Stocks," *Journal of Business,* April 1970, pp. 99–134; and Edward H. Jennings, "An Empirical Examination of Some Aspects of Common Stock Diversification," *Journal of Financial and Quantitative Analysis,* March 1971, pp. 797–813.

the market portfolio, it seems that we can achieve the same result with a much smaller portfolio.

The ease with which the market portfolio can be approximated allows investors to separate total portfolio risk into the two parts mentioned in Chapter 6, diversifiable and undiversifiable risk. Undiversifiable risk is equivalent to the risk associated with the market portfolio and cannot be reduced by simply adding securities to one's portfolio. In the Evans and Archer study, undiversifiable risk was .1166, or the standard deviation of the S&P 500. From the point of view of an individual portfolio or security, undiversifiable risk is represented by the extent to which the portfolio's (or security's) rate of return is correlated with the return on the market portfolio.

Diversifiable risk results from non-market factors and is represented by the difference between total portfolio risk and the undiversifiable or market element. Diversifiable risk is the extent to which individual portfolio (or security) returns are not correlated with the market return. When diversifiable risk is zero or very close to zero we have an approximation of the market portfolio. As indicated, the empirical studies suggest that diversifiable risk is virtually eliminated with a portfolio of approximately eight to sixteen randomly selected common stocks.

In the CAP model, beta represents undiversifiable risk and the model assumes the absence of diversifiable risk. Empirical studies imply that the investor does not need to purchase the market portfolio in order to eliminate diversifiable risk since the same effect can be achieved with a much smaller portfolio. Furthermore, the ease with which the market can be approximated means borrowing or lending is not required. Unless we move to extreme risk situations, the desired risk level (beta) can usually be achieved without borrowing or lending. If we desire a portfolio with a beta of 1.5, we could borrow and buy the market portfolio (or an approximation) but we need not. All we need do is purchase a portfolio (without borrowing) containing enough securities to eliminate diversifiable risk where the average of the betas of the individual securities is 1.5. Hence, any constraints that may prohibit borrowing or lending at the risk-free rate will not necessarily prevent the investor from accomplishing the predictions of the capital asset pricing model.

If the CAP model has validity, it will be unwise for the investor to purchase a portfolio that is not fully diversified. The CAP model states that higher average returns are associated with higher betas (undiversifiable risk) and that there is no association between diversifiable risk and the portfolio rate of return. In other words, investors are *not rewarded* with higher returns for taking on diversifiable risk. This does not mean a portfolio with diversifiable risk will not occasionally achieve a handsome return, but only that on the average, there is no reward for diversifiable risk. This is as it should be, given the ease with which we can eliminate diversifiable risk.

Empirical Validity

Numerous studies dealing with the capital asset pricing model suggest that the model is empirically valid. There seems to be a strong positive relationship between betas and actual rates of return. The evidence also suggests there is no association between return and diversifiable risk. While the relationship between beta and return is linear (straight-line) as the model suggests, the specific relationship seems less clear. Fischer Black, Michael Jensen and Myron Scholes found that the CAP model overstates the high-beta returns and understates the low-beta returns.[7] When the portfolio beta is zero, the investor's portfolio will have a return in excess of the risk-free rate. This relationship is shown in Figure 13-4. For lack of a better name, Black referred to this finding as the zero-beta model.[8] The zero-beta adjustment drops the risk-free assumption and substitutes an asset having a variance, but independent of the market (its beta is zero). Even with the zero-beta substitution for the risk-free

FIGURE 13-4
Comparison Between Theoretical and Empirical Capital Market Line

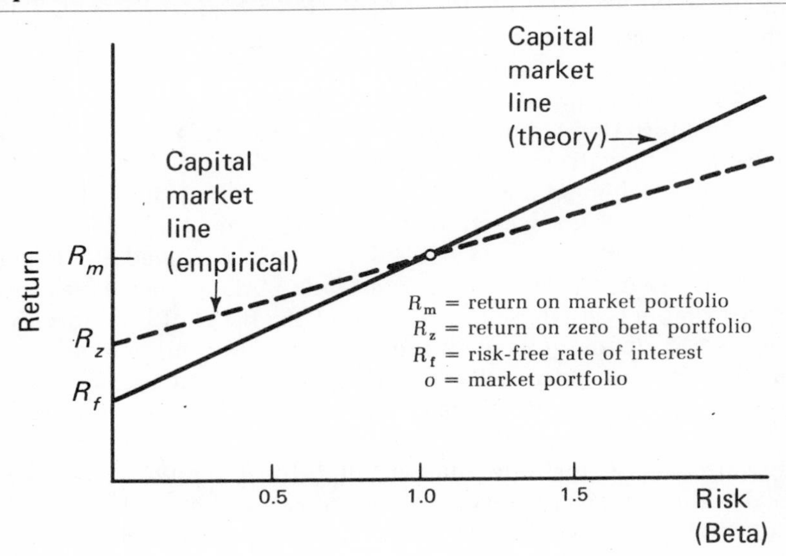

[7]Fischer Black, Michael C. Jensen and Myron S. Scholes, "The Capital Asset Pricing Model: Some Empirical Tests," *Studies in the Theory of Capital Markets,* edited by Michael C. Jensen (New York: Praeger, 1972), pp. 79-121.

[8]The theoretical development of the zero-beta model is in Fischer Black, "Capital Market Equilibrium with Restricted Borrowing," *Journal of Business,* July 1972, pp. 444-54.

asset, the investor seeking high expected returns should seek high betas. Lower returns are associated with lower betas.[9]

APPLICATION OF PORTFOLIO THEORY

Since the capital asset pricing model has reasonable empirical support, we are now prepared to discuss the application of portfolio theory as developed thus far. Application requires the selection of the optimum portfolio from the efficient frontier. To construct an efficient frontier, we require an estimate of the risk and return of each of the securities under consideration.

Estimating Beta

As we have seen, the theoretical and empirical work suggests beta should be used to measure risk. It is relatively easy to discuss beta on an abstract level, but its application requires assigning a number. The number we are looking for must apply to the future, but the only way to obtain such a number is through an evaluation of historical data. The condition under which we could use historical data for our investment decision exists when a stable and predictable relationship exists between historical betas and future betas. If we use past data for decisions regarding the future, we must provide evidence that the past and the future are related in some systematic fashion.

In an important study, Marshall Blume examined this question.[10] Using all common stocks listed on the NYSE from 1926 to 1968, Blume calculated betas for each stock for six separate seven-year periods. The calculations provided betas for the periods 1926–33, 1934–40, and so on to 1968. He then compared the betas in the first period with the betas in the second, the second with the third, and so on to a comparison of the fifth and sixth periods. The comparisons were made along the following lines. If the coefficient of determination between the betas in one period and the following period was zero, he would conclude historical betas were unrelated to future betas. If the coefficient of determination between the betas was close to one, the conclusion would be that historical betas are closely related to future betas.

His results are quite enlightening. In every case, the coefficient of determination was significantly greater than zero. Unfortunately, the

[9]For a review of the empirical work on the CAP model see: Franco Modigliani and Gerald A. Pogue, "An Introduction to Risk and Return (Part II)," *Financial Analysts Journal* May–June 1974, pp. 69–86; and Michael C. Jensen, "Capital Markets: Theory and Evidence," *The Bell Journal of Economics and Management Science*, Autumn 1972, pp. 357–98.

[10]Marshall E. Blume, "On the Assessment of Risk," *Journal of Finance*, March 1971, pp. 1–10.

relationship was a weak one. In general, when the past beta of an individual security was compared to the future beta, the coefficient of determination was approximately .36. In other words, Blume's evidence suggests that knowledge of past betas explains only about 36 percent of the variability in future betas. In relying on this relationship, it seems fair to conclude that past data can be used, but only in a very broad sense. However, this is not the relationship that we are interested in.

In theory, beta should be used as a risk measure only with adequately diversified portfolios. Sufficient diversification can be accomplished with portfolios containing eight to sixteen securities. In other words, we must examine portfolio betas and not betas of individual securities. Blume formed portfolios and determined their betas for each of the six time periods. His portfolios ranged in size from two to fifty securities. The weak relationship found with individual securities became extremely strong with portfolios. With portfolios of only four securities, historical betas explained approximately 65 percent of the variability of future betas, compared with 36 percent with individual securities. With portfolios of ten securities, the past explained approximately 80 percent of the future. By the time we reach portfolios of twenty securities, the future betas exhibited an almost perfect correlation with the historical betas. With a diversified portfolio, we can be quite confident past betas will provide a close approximation of future betas.

A caveat seems appropriate at this point. Since Blume was using seven-year periods, he required at least fourteen years of data on each security. His results are based on only those NYSE common stocks that had been listed for at least fourteen years. Hence, the results may be applicable only to the larger, higher quality common stocks. Perhaps smaller or lower quality firms do not exhibit the stability found by Blume. Secondly, the evidence suggests that while the past and future betas are closely correlated, there is a strong tendency for high betas to decline toward one and low betas to increase toward one. This means an investor having a portfolio with an historical beta of 1.5 may find that the future beta will be somewhat lower, perhaps around 1.4. It will remain high, but not as high. Correspondingly, the low beta will increase slightly. The problem does not appear to be a serious one, since these changes took place over fairly long periods of time.

Estimating Return

The assignment of risk is only half the problem. We require an estimate of the expected return of each security under consideration. Here again, the CAP model can aid us considerably. The conclusion of the model is that the expected return on a portfolio will be the risk-free return plus the product of the portfolio beta and the market risk-premium as shown below. The market risk-premium is the market return less the risk-free rate.

$$\text{Portfolio return} = R_f + \beta(R_m - R_f)$$

Market Return

In order to obtain the return as indicated by the CAP model, we require an estimate of the market return and the risk-free return. The market return is crucial. Chapter 7 examined the techniques required to estimate the market return. It was recognized that the art of investing is not sufficiently developed to allow us to estimate with certainty what the market will do during our investment horizon. Indeed, the forecasting problems of the past few years are ample evidence of the errors even astute investors can make. At the same time, this is precisely why portfolio theory places such a heavy emphasis upon risk. If somehow we *knew* the market would increase by 20 percent over the next year, there would be little need for portfolio theory. We would simply purchase the highest beta portfolio available and sit back and relax. It is because we cannot expect to be right all of the time that we require a risk measure.

Risk-Free Rate

The standard practice employed to determine the risk-free rate is to use the return associated with short-term Treasury bills. They are extremely close to being risk-free. There is no default risk in the sense that we can be assured that the federal government will make good on its short-term obligations. On the other hand, if one must sell a Treasury bill prior to maturity, there is a risk that small losses will be incurred because of changing interest rates. However, the short-term character of Treasury bills implies that liquidation can usually be postponed until maturity in order to receive full value.

Alpha

Let us stop to ask if our conclusions regarding the capital asset pricing model imply that the work on security analysis examined in Chapters 7 through 10 is now to be ignored. If the CAP model can provide us with the value of an asset in the form of a rate of return, why is it necessary to go through the complex task of security analysis?

The capital asset pricing model does not imply that individual securities will not produce returns in excess of the return projected by the CAP equation. It merely says that, on the average, actual returns will correspond to the predictions of the model. For an investor able to interpret the financial statements of a firm better than the market in general, the CAP model does not conclude that these skills should be ignored. If the individual's interpretations are correct, higher rates of return will be produced, since the firm will be more or less prosperous than originally expected by the market in general. Furthermore, as new information regarding the firm becomes available, price changes not associated with the CAP model will occur. These possibilities are reflected in diversifiable risk. If the investor can recognize an incorrect valuation by the market, either through interpretive skills or information that is not generally available, there is no reason why excess profits cannot be obtained.

The primary objective of security analysis is valuation to discover an underpriced security where the calculated value of the security is greater than the current price. The question becomes one of determining how our valuation conclusions fit into portfolio theory. To do this, we employ alphas. Alphas are the measure of the excess return expected from undervaluation or the excess loss expected for overvaluation. Alphas, as we shall see in the next chapter, are a means of measuring the stock selection ability of an investor for any given risk level. Of course, if an investor possesses no special skills or knowledge allowing recognition of deviations between price and value, the estimate of the return will be the capital asset pricing return. Expected alphas will be zero in this situation.

There is no necessary inconsistency between the objectives of security analysis and the implications of the capital asset pricing model. The ability to locate undervalued securities is an empirical question for both the market as a whole and the individual investor. An investor using only the CAP model relies on the elimination of diversifiable risk to balance overvalued securities with undervalued securities.

Forming Efficient Portfolios

With returns and risk determined for each security under consideration by the investor, we are prepared to select a portfolio from the set of efficient portfolios. The formation of efficient portfolios should be examined under two basic situations. The first situation occurs when the investor has decided that rates or return are to be determined solely from the capital asset pricing model. With no security undervalued or overvalued, the return for each security is simply the risk-free rate (or zero-beta return) plus the product of beta and the market risk-premium $(R_m - R_f)$. All alphas are expected to be zero. The second situation occurs when the investor has determined that individual returns will deviate from the return predicted by the CAP model. Securities have been evaluated and found to be either undervalued or overvalued. Alphas are non-zero.

In the first situation, the portfolio problem is relatively straightforward. After the investor has decided upon a suitable level of risk, a portfolio is selected where the average of the individual betas is equal to the beta desired. Any group of securities will do, provided the portfolio beta is the beta desired and the portfolio is sufficiently large to substantially eliminate diversifiable risk.

Table 13–1 presents betas for a population of five securities. An investor wanting a beta of .84 could select portfolio 1 with 40 percent in security B, 25 percent in D, and 35 percent in E. If a 1.11 beta is desired, portfolio 2 would be appropriate.

TABLE 13–1
Individual and Portfolio Betas

		Percent Invested In	
Security	Beta	Portfolio 1	Portfolio 2
A	1.7	— %	15%
B	.8	40	20
C	1.9	—	10
D	1.1	25	30
E	.7	35	25
Portfolio beta		.84	1.11

Neither portfolio is probably adequately diversified, since we normally need more securities to accomplish this objective. However, portfolio 2 is better diversified than portfolio 1. This observation brings up another possibility. If the investor can invest in the risk-free asset, it may be possible to employ portfolio 2 in the same context as the market portfolio is used in the capital asset pricing model. An investor may desire a beta of .84, but prefer not to accept the diversifiable risk of portfolio 1. Investing in a risk-free asset and purchasing portfolio 2 with a portion of the total investable funds will reduce the beta. The proportion invested in portfolio 2 will be the ratio of the beta desired to the beta of portfolio 2. Thus, to achieve a beta of .84, the investor could invest 75.7 percent (.84/1.11) in portfolio 2 and 24.3 percent of the funds in the risk-free asset. Such a strategy would be the equivalent of investing in portfolio 1 but with lower diversifiable risk.

As previously noted, the elimination of diversifiable risk requires approximately eight to sixteen randomly selected securities. Hence, an actual portfolio should contain at least eight to sixteen securities given the zero alpha situation. However, for a group of securities the returns of which are closely correlated to those of the market, fewer securities will need to be included in the portfolio to eliminate diversifiable risk. If a particular security "tracks" the market especially well, it will be wise to place a fairly large percentage of the total funds into that security in order to eliminate diversifiable risk with fewer securities.[11]

If we have determined certain securities are either undervalued or overvalued, it is more difficult to achieve an optimum portfolio without a computer program. At the same time, we can usually come close. If securities A, C, and E in Table 13-1 are currently estimated to be priced about right, while securities B and D are estimated to be undervalued, we will want to include a large proportion of the undervalued securities in our portfolio. The undervalued securities are expected to provide a greater return per unit of risk than the correctly valued securities. Securities should be included in the portfolio in order of the size of their expected return relative to their beta or risk.

The investor with an existing, fully diversified portfolio should examine the problem of adding to the portfolio within the context of the relative return per unit of risk. The decision to purchase a new security should be based on whether or not the particular security has a higher or lower return relative to its risk than the existing portfolio. If it is higher, the security should be purchased. If it is lower, the security should be ignored and the funds used to purchase more of the securities in the existing portfolio.

Risk Level Selection

The solution to the general investment problem is now complete except for the thorny task of selecting the risk-return combination desired. A utility function is needed to determine the proper portfolio for a given investor. We cannot be of much assistance in solving this matter since one's utility function is a very personal thing. At the same time, we should understand that this problem is not unique to portfolio theory. Any investment technique or methodology will require a trade-off between risk and return based on the investor's particular utility function.

While a precise solution to the problem of the utility function is not available, we can offer some insights into how one might make the risk-return trade-off. Initially, one should examine the potential consequences of a given level of risk. For example, in the month of November, 1973, the actual market risk premium ($R_m - R_f$) as measured by the NYSE Composite Index ($R_m = -15\%$) and the three-month Treasury bill rate ($R_f = 8\%$) was a minus 23 percent. The investor holding a diversified portfolio with a beta of 1.5 would have "earned" a risk

[11]An example of the elimination of diversifiable with a well chosen smaller portfolio can be found in Keith V. Smith, and John C. Schreiner, "A Portfolio Analysis of Conglomerate Diversification," *Journal of Finance*, June 1969, pp. 413–27.

premium of minus 34.5 percent. The portfolio with a beta of .5 would have had a risk premium of minus 11.5 percent. The actual returns earned on these portfolios as calculated below would have been minus 26.5 percent for the 1.5 beta portfolio and minus 3.5 percent for the .5 beta portfolio.

$$R_p = R_f + \beta(R_m - R_f)$$

if $\beta = 1.5$	if $\beta = .5$
$R_p = .08 + 1.5(-.15 - .08)$	$R_p = .08 + .5(-.15 - .08)$
$= -.265$	$= -.035$

The future use of investment funds should probably be the first consideration in determining one's risk level. If funds are required for general consumption in the near future, low-risk (low-beta) should be the order of the day. If the use of investment income can be postponed without hardship, the individual may consider a high-risk, high-return portfolio. The selection of high or low risk will be partially related to the investor's need for invested funds and whether or not the expenditures can be postponed during periods like November 1973.

Still, this is only a partial solution. The pension fund manager may feel the fund is in a position where contributions will exceed withdrawals for the foreseeable future, because of the growth of the company responsible for the fund. Under these conditions, short-term market declines will not injure the fund since there will be no need to sell to meet withdrawals. Nevertheless, the fund manager's performance may be measured on a year-to-year basis. A major market decline like that of 1974 may be all that is needed to convince the owners of the fund of the need for a new manager, despite pleading about high betas and good long-run performance. Certainly, any portfolio manager needs to work toward stated objectives by which performance is to be measured.

We must also recognize that even if the consequences of risk can be handled financially, we may prefer a low-beta portfolio. It takes a resolute individual to ride out a major market decline. Quite frequently, major mistakes are made from sheer nerves, since the investor decides to sell at the bottom of a market decline. A high-beta portfolio would magnify this very real problem. The investor should not only examine the consequences of risk, but should also have the ability to watch—without panic—a portfolio decline in value.

The consequences of risk are important but so are the benefits. From year-end 1950 to year-end 1965, the market risk-premium was approximately 12.1 percent per year based upon a market return of 14.4 percent and a Treasury bill yield of about 2.3 percent per year. These results imply a portfolio return of about 17 percent annually for the investor with a beta of 1.2 and about 12 percent for the investor with a beta of .8. In terms of dollar values, these are enormous differences. A $10,000 investment in the 1.2 beta portfolio in 1950 would have been worth approximately $105,000 in 1965 as contrasted to about $55,000 for the .8 beta portfolio.

The more recent performance of the market has been less encouraging for the high-beta investor, yet the facts are clear. During virtually any other ten to fifteen-year period, the market risk-premium has been positive and would have provided substantial rewards for the high-risk investor. At the same time, patience was required. The rewards were available only to the investor who was willing to allow the downward fluctuations to average out.

SUMMARY

We started this chapter with the recognition that as the number of securities being considered increases, the number of covariance terms becomes very large. This makes the covariance approach to portfolio selection impractical. To deal with the covariance problem, we allowed the investor to borrow or lend at a risk-free rate. We found the efficient frontier reduced to a single risky portfolio and the investor could increase or decrease expected risk and return by borrowing or lending. By introducing the assumption of homogenous expectations, this single risky portfolio must be the market portfolio.

Using the market portfolio, we found the risk-return relationship of the efficient frontier reduced to a linear relationship between the portfolio return and the ratio of the portfolio risk to the market risk as measured by standard deviation. This ratio is known as beta. The relationship is the capital asset pricing model where the portfolio return is the risk-free return plus the product of beta and the market risk-premium. Beta becomes our measure of risk. High betas indicate that the investor's return will go up and down faster than the market return. Low-beta portfolios will fluctuate less than the market portfolio.

Using beta to measure risk assumes that the investor's portfolio is fully diversified, which means that it is perfectly correlated with the market portfolio. How many securities does one need to purchase to be adequately diversified? An examination of empirical studies revealed that, for practical purposes, a portfolio of eight to sixteen securities was sufficient to eliminate virtually all diversifiable risk.

Measures of beta can be obtained from historical data provided that we form fully diversified portfolios. Portfolio betas seem to be stable over time in that past betas are closely correlated with future betas. Estimating returns involves a combination of the capital asset pricing model and security analysis. If a given security is priced about right, its future return can be estimated from the CAP model. If a given security is undervalued or overvalued, its estimated return will be the capital asset pricing return plus the undervaluation or minus the overvaluation. Alpha is used to measure the undervaluation or overvaluation.

Selection of the risk level is a personal matter depending directly on the individual's aversion to risk. We suggest the investor examine the financial consequences of portfolio losses, the manner in which performance is to be measured, and the ability to watch a portfolio decline in value. The risk level selection is a trade-off between risk and return. Over long periods of time, small differences in beta may generate large differences in wealth. The rewards from high risk can be great. To achieve these rewards, the investor must be willing to accept the possibility of severe temporary losses.

QUESTIONS

1. Using graphical analysis show how the introduction of a risk-free asset results in a new efficient frontier that is linear and above the efficient frontier (except at one point) without the risk-free asset.
2. Explain why the single point that is common to the efficient frontiers with and without the risk-free asset is the market portfolio. What assumptions must be made to justify your answer?
3. Explain why the introduction of the risk-free asset eliminates the need for covariances and reduces the portfolio decision to one of borrowing or lending on a theoretical basis.
4. Relate the capital market line (CML) to the capital asset pricing (CAP) model including a discussion and interpretation of *beta*.
5. Explain why it is probably not necessary to purchase the market portfolio in order to obtain the same results as suggested by the capital asset pricing model.
6. Distinguish between total risk, diversifiable risk, and undiversifiable risk.
7. Discuss why it is ordinarily unwise to purchase a portfolio which contains diversifiable risk. Under what conditions should the investor accept diversifiable risk?
8. Discuss why it is probably possible to estimate betas, which should be future oriented, from historic data. Include in your discussion the difference between estimating portfolio betas and estimating individual betas.
9. Define the term *alpha* and discuss how alpha relates to security analysis.
10. Discuss several criteria you might use in selecting the risk level of your preference. Which beta should your portfolio have and why do you expect to change your portfolio beta as time passes?

PROBLEMS

1. Assume that the risk-free rate is 6.23 percent. Calculate the portfolio return that is expected for each of the following conditions:
   a) Market return of 15 percent

1) Beta = .75
2) Beta = 1.65
3) Beta = 1.00

b) Market return of 5 percent
1) Beta = .75
2) Beta = 1.65
3) Beta = 1.00

c) Market return of −12 percent
1) Beta = .75
2) Beta = 1.65
3) Beta = 1.00

Are the results what you would expect and why?

2. You are given the following securities from which to select a portfolio.

Security	*Beta*
1	.63
2	1.29
3	1.04
4	.98
5	1.75
6	1.14
7	.82
8	.40
9	1.43
10	.78

a) You are asked to select a portfolio from these ten securities. Why did you pick the securities you did?
b) How would your selection change with different estimates of the market and risk-free return?
c) How would your selection change depending upon your investment objectives?
d) How would your selection change if someone told you that securities 1 and 8 had positive alphas equal to 7 percent?
e) What would your investment strategy be if you were required to invest equal amounts in each security?

SUGGESTED READINGS

Black, Fischer. "Capital Market Equilibrium with Restricted Borrowing." *Journal of Business*, July 1972, pp. 444–54.

Blume, Marshall E. "On the Assessment of Risk." *Journal of Finance*, March 1971, pp. 1–10.

——. "Portfolio Theory: A Step Toward Its Practical Application." *Journal of Business*, April 1970, pp. 152–73.

Crowell, Richard A. "Risk Measurement: Five Applications." *Financial Analysts Journal,* July–August 1973, pp. 81–87.

Evans, John L. and Stephen H. Archer. "Diversification and the Reduction of Dispersion: An Empirical Analysis." *Journal of Finance,* December 1968, pp. 761–67.

Fama, Eugene F. "Risk, Return and Equilibrium: Some Clarifying Comments." *Journal of Finance,* March 1968, pp. 29–40.

Fleming, Robert M. "How Risky Is the Market?" *Journal of Business,* July 1973, pp. 404–24.

Gaumnitz, Jack E. "Maximal Gains from Diversification and Implications for Portfolio Management." *Mississippi Valley Journal of Business and Economics,* Spring 1971, pp. 1–14.

Jennings, Edward H. "An Empirical Analysis of Some Aspects of Common Stock Diversification." *Journal of Financial and Quantitative Analysis,* March 1971, pp. 797–813.

Jensen, Michael C., ed. *Studies in the Theory of Capital Markets.* New York: Praeger Publishers, 1972.

Levy, Robert A. "On the Short-Term Stationarity of Beta Coefficients." *Financial Analysts Journal,* November–December 1971, pp. 55–62.

Lintner, John. "Security Prices, Risk and Maximal Gains from Diversification." *Journal of Finance,* December 1965, pp. 587–615.

Modigliani, Franco and Gerald A. Pogue. "An Introduction to Risk and Return." *Financial Analysts Journal,* March–April 1974, pp. 68–80 (Part I), and May–June 1974, pp. 69–86 (Part II).

Officer, R. R. "The Variability of the Market Factor of the New York Stock Exchange." *Journal of Business,* July 1973, pp. 434–53.

Reilly, Frank K. "Evidence Regarding a Segmented Stock Market." *Journal of Finance,* June 1972, pp. 607–25.

Robichek, Alexander A. and Richard A. Cohn. "The Economic Determinants of Systematic Risk." *Journal of Finance,* May 1974, pp. 439–47.

Sharpe, William F. "A Simplified Model for Portfolio Analysis." *Management Science,* January 1963, pp. 277–93.

——. "Bonds versus Stocks: Some Lessons from Capital Market Theory." *Financial Analysts Journal,* November–December 1973, pp. 74–80.

——. "Capital Asset Prices: A Theory of Market Equilibrium Under Conditions of Risk." *Journal of Finance,* September 1964, pp. 425–42.

——. "Risk, Market Sensitivity and Diversification." *Financial Analysts Journal,* January–February 1972, pp. 74–79.

Smith, Keith V. "Stock Price and Economic Indexes for Generating Efficient Portfolios." *Journal of Business,* July 1969, pp. 326–36.

Upson, Roger B., Paul F. Jessup, and Keishiro Matsumoto. "Portfolio Diversification Strategies." *Financial Analysts Journal,* May–June 1975, pp. 86–88.

Welles, Chris. "The Beta Revolution: Learning to Live with Risk." *Institutional Investor,* September 1971, pp. 21–27ff.

*

14

Measuring Investment Performance

To complete our study of the investment process, we must examine the sometimes unpleasant task of evaluating the results of our investment decisions. If a professional is managing our funds, we want to know the performance of the manager. Can we do better by finding a more skillful manager? Can we do just as well ourselves and avoid the costs of the manager? Performance evaluation is also necessary if we manage our own funds in order to make portfolio adjustments. We should not buy a portfolio and just forget about it. If the portfolio's performance is not up to standard, we want to know why, so the same mistakes will not be made in the future. If the performance is above average, we also want to know why, so the outstanding performance can continue. Whether we are a professional manager or an individual investor, performance is critical and knowledge of our performance aids considerably in future decision making.

This chapter focuses on the evaluation of investment results. We are concerned with the appropriate criteria for judging investment performance, including the establishment of a benchmark portfolio. In establishing the benchmark portfolio, risk adjustments are important and are discussed extensively. In judging investment results, we need to be concerned with the selection of the proper risk level, the degree of diversification achieved by the portfolio, and the security selection and market forecasting ability of the investor.[1]

PERFORMANCE CRITERIA

The Portfolio Perspective

Any performance measurement needs to examine the overall behavior of the portfolio. Stories abound about the investor who purchased a common stock at $5 and sold it a year later at $50. This is certainly an outstanding transaction, but the evaluation of performance must consider all of the investor's securities. Portfolio performance is the critical ingredient when attempting to determine the wisdom of investing. Investing in the stock market can be quite profitable, but it would be foolish to conclude that one can get rich overnight simply because an individual security has doubled overnight. The selection of a security that doubles in value is not very satisfying if the value of the total portfolio declines by 50 percent.

Benchmark Portfolios

While portfolio returns are critical, it is important to evaluate performance within the context of the opportunities available. Most of us would conclude that an average annual return of 12 percent over a twenty-five-year period was adequate performance since an investment of $10,000 twenty-five years ago would now be worth $170,001. Such a return may be adequate but does not necessarily suggest good performance. We must ask what could have been accomplished. For example, had the 12 percent return been achieved during the period 1941 through 1965, we would have to conclude that it was quite mediocre. The New York Stock Exchange averaged a 16 percent return during that period. Had the investor purchased the market portfolio at the beginning of 1941, $10,000 would have grown to $408,742 by the end of 1965. Performance must be judged relative to the opportunities available.

The opportunities used as a benchmark comparison are referred to as *naive opportunities*. Any performance comparison should be made

[1]The performance measurement techniques discussed in this chapter come largely from: Eugene F. Fama, "Components of Investment Performance," *Journal of Finance*, June 1972, pp. 551–67.

to a portfolio that could have been selected by an investor without any special skills, information, or foresight. The most obvious portfolio falling into this category is the market portfolio. Furthermore, since the market return is the average portfolio return for all investors, average investment skills should produce the market return. If you are above average, you should outperform the market.

The Problem of Risk

The use of the market portfolio as a benchmark is not sufficient, however. Any comparisons must be made to a benchmark portfolio of equivalent risk. For example, if the market return for a given year was 10 percent and the risk-free rate was 7 percent, a fully diversified portfolio with a beta of 1.5 would have earned 11.5 percent. If a portfolio had a beta of .5, the return would have been 8.5 percent. The high-risk portfolio outperformed both the market and the low-risk portfolio. It would be incorrect, however, to conclude that the manager of the low-risk portfolio was less skillful than the manager of the high-risk portfolio since the returns have not been adjusted for risk. With hindsight, we know higher risk should have been accepted. But given what was known at the time, the selection of low-risk should not necessarily reflect on the manager's skills. Had the market declined by 10 percent, the high-beta investor would have lost 18.5 percent, while the low-beta investor would have lost only 1.5 percent. Did the high-beta investor suddenly become less skillful? Clearly, the answer is no. In essence, our performance comparison must consider the risk level elected by the investor.

Risk level comparisons may be difficult for two reasons. The first problem concerns whether the investor actually achieved the level of risk sought. In our example, suppose the manager with a beta of .5 was attempting to purchase a portfolio with a beta of 1.5. In this case, we would conclude the performance was quite poor from the standpoint of the risk objective. The actual return achieved may have been consistent with the actual risk, but since the risk objective was much different from the actual risk, the portfolio performance must be considered poor within the context of the risk objective. In essence, we must adjust for the risk objective as well as for the actual risk.

The second problem with risk-level adjustments concerns the diversification achieved by the investor. If the portfolio is not fully diversified, the actual beta does not represent the total risk, only undiversifiable risk, as we saw in Chapter 13. We also saw that, on the average, there seem to be no extra returns associated with taking on risk that can be diversified away. Nevertheless, an investor may be willing to accept diversifiable risk under certain conditions. In finding a security believed to be substantially undervalued, an investor may decide to place a large portion of the investment funds in that security so as not to dilute its return with other securities that promise lower returns. This is perfectly acceptable behavior, but in measuring performance an adjustment must be made for the added risk. The decision not to diversify should result in a return sufficient to compensate for the added diversifiable risk.

Security Selection

Having adjusted for the benchmark portfolio and both diversifiable and undiversifiable risk, we can address the question of the investment manager's ability to select undervalued securities. If the actual return exceeds the risk-adjusted market return, we conclude that the portfolio contained undervalued securities. The investor "picked winners" or perhaps sold overvalued securities short. Either way, the actual return was greater than an investor could have obtained by simply purchasing a fully diversified portfolio with equivalent risk. If the actual return was less, the investor "picked losers." We shall see later that this aspect of performance could also include the ability to make accurate market projections.

The Problem of Chance

One final problem must receive attention and that is the problem of chance or luck. In the real world, one can probably seldom obtain exactly the risk level desired, nor is it possible to buy a portfolio that is perfectly diversified. The selection of undervalued securities could be nothing more than chance. In effect, we must be able to separate the results due to skill from those due to chance. Statistical techniques exist that allow such a separation to be made, but the methods are not perfect and can result in incorrect conclusions. Perhaps the best way to allow for chance is to insist that the performance be measured over fairly long periods of time. The five-year performance of an investor is more likely to be representative of investment ability than performance in any one year. We do not suggest that performance should not be measured from year to year, only that errors due to chance are much more likely to influence the evaluation when it is confined to short periods.

PERFORMANCE MEASUREMENT

Let us now consider the application of the performance adjustments and criteria that we have discussed. The investment results of a hypothetical portfolio are presented in Exhibit 14–1. We will measure portfolio performance given these data. The actual return of the portfolio was a quite respectable 12.6 percent, including dividends and capital gains. In an

EXHIBIT 14–1
Investment Results of Hypothetical Portfolio

	Risk-Free Asset	Market Portfolio	Hypothetical Portfolio
Annual rate of return (R)	6.8%	11.3%	12.6%
Standard deviation (σ_R)	0	.30	.40
Variance (V_R)	0	.09	.16
Coefficient of determination with market	0	1.00	.81
Portfolio beta	0	1.00	1.20

absolute sense the portfolio outperformed the market portfolio by over one percentage point per year. The investor did quite well, but this is merely a surface comparison. We must investigate further.

Market Risk Adjustment

Initially, the investigation should concentrate on the risk accepted by the investor. Exhibit 14–1 shows the portfolio had an actual beta of 1.2, suggesting the need to adjust our benchmark, the market portfolio, to reflect the higher level of risk. Given a beta of 1.2, the portfolio risk-premium should be 20 percent higher than the market risk-premium. In the last chapter, we saw the market risk-premium is the difference between the market return and the return on the risk-free asset. Adjusting the market risk-premium $(R_m - R_f)$ for the actual portfolio beta of 1.2 results in an expected risk-premium of 5.4 percent, as shown in the center column of Exhibit 14–2.

EXHIBIT 14–2
Summary of Risk-Adjusted Performance Measurement

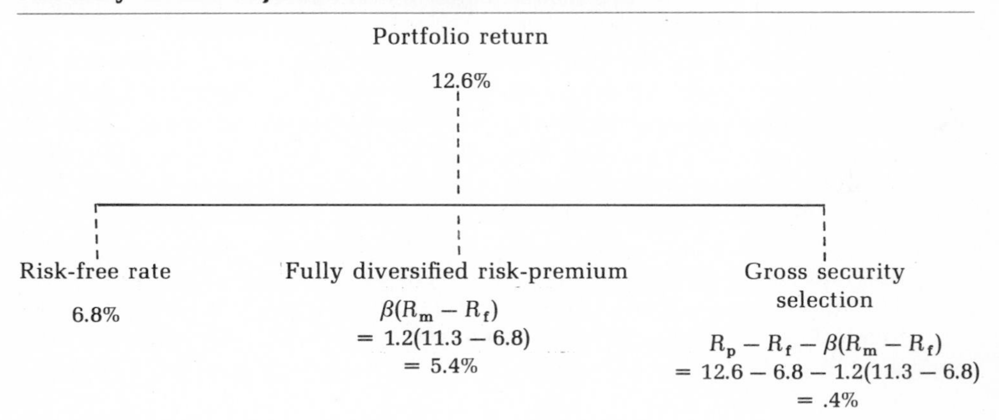

The investor could have achieved a risk-premium of 5.4 percent by simply purchasing a fully diversified portfolio with a beta of 1.2. The actual risk premium ($R_p - R_f$) of 5.8 percent indicates that the investor outperformed the market on a risk-adjusted basis. Not only did the investor beat the market in an absolute sense, but the investor also beat the market after adjusting for risk. The investor beat the risk-adjusted market standard by .4 percent per year, which is labeled gross security selection in Exhibit 14–2.

Exhibit 14–2 summarizes the risk-adjustment process by showing the three return components we have separated at this stage of our analysis. The actual portfolio return of 12.6% includes 6.8% for the risk-free asset, 5.4% to reflect the actual beta, and .4% representing the investor's excess return from security selection. At this stage we conclude the investor earned .4% from the selection of undervalued securities.

Gross Security and Diversifiable Risk

Concluding that the investor picked winners is appropriate even though the difference of .4% is fairly small. However, the analysis of the actual return is not really complete since the utilization of beta assumes a fully diversified portfolio. From Exhibit 14–1, we see the portfolio was reasonably close to being fully diversified, since the coefficient of determination was .81. A fully diversified portfolio would have had a coefficient of determination of one.

A coefficient of determination less than one means the investor has accepted more risk than accounted for in the beta measure. Perhaps this was done deliberately in order to purchase some securities believed to be undervalued. Indeed, it would seem that a failure to diversify completely was wise in view of the fact that the investor actually achieved a return in excess of the risk-adjusted market return.

To determine whether or not the failure to diversify completely was wise, we must determine what sort of return could have been obtained from a benchmark portfolio that was fully diversified and had the equivalent *total risk* of the portfolio under examination. Could the investor have achieved the 12.6 percent return with a fully diversified portfolio without the security analysis required to isolate the undervalued securities? In the previous chapter, we saw the beta of a fully diversified portfolio will be the ratio of the standard deviation of the portfolio to the standard deviation of the market. In our example, this ratio is 1.33. The implication is that our hypothetical portfolio was equivalent in risk to a fully diversified portfolio with a beta of 1.33. The difference between the 1.33 and the actual beta of 1.20 reflects the lack of perfect diversification.

Added risk is perfectly acceptable provided the compensation forthcoming in the form of added return is consistent with the amount of added risk. In our example, the added risk from a lack of diversification is represented by the difference between the actual beta (1.20) and the fully diversified beta (1.33). Since beta is related to the market risk-premium, the added amount of return needed is the product of the market risk-premium and the difference in betas. In our example, the failure to diversify fully should have produced .6 percent per year return calculated as follows:

$$(R_m - R_f)\ (\sigma_p/\sigma_m - \beta) = (11.3 - 6.8)(.40/.30 - 1.20) = .60$$

We previously concluded that .4 percent was earned from the selection of undervalued securities (gross security selection). We see now that these earnings were not sufficient to compensate the investor for the added risk accepted in the form of diversifiable risk. The investor could have purchased a fully diversified portfolio with a beta of 1.33 and earned an additional .6 percent instead of the .4 percent actually earned from security selection.

Exhibit 14–3 summarizes this adjustment for diversifiable risk. Exhibit 14–3 is identical to Exhibit 14–2 except that gross security selection has been separated into two parts. The first part is the return required to compensate for diversifiable risk and the second part is net security selection, or the difference between gross security selection and the return required for diversifiable risk. Net security selection is the added return the investor achieved by selecting undervalued securities. In the example, this activity produced a minus .2 percent, indicating that while added returns were obtained, they were insufficient to compensate for the added risk.

Risk Level Selection

We should also examine the performance of the portfolio manager in the context of whether the actual risk of the portfolio was consistent with the risk expected. Was the portfolio in the right location on the efficient frontier? Suppose an investor actually sought a portfolio with a beta of 1.1. The actual risk achieved, in our example, was 1.2, suggesting that the manager underestimated the actual risk of the portfolio. The consequences of this "mistake" can be evaluated on the basis of the return achieved due to the higher risk. In Exhibit 14–2, we saw that the portion of the investor's return attributable to market risk was 5.4 percent per year. Had the investor achieved the beta desired (1.1), the 5.4 percent would have been 4.95 percent (the desired beta of 1.1 times the market risk-premium of 4.5 percent). The difference of .45 percent represents the return gained as a result of not obtaining the 1.1 beta.

EXHIBIT 14–3
Summary of Risk-Adjusted Performance Measurement

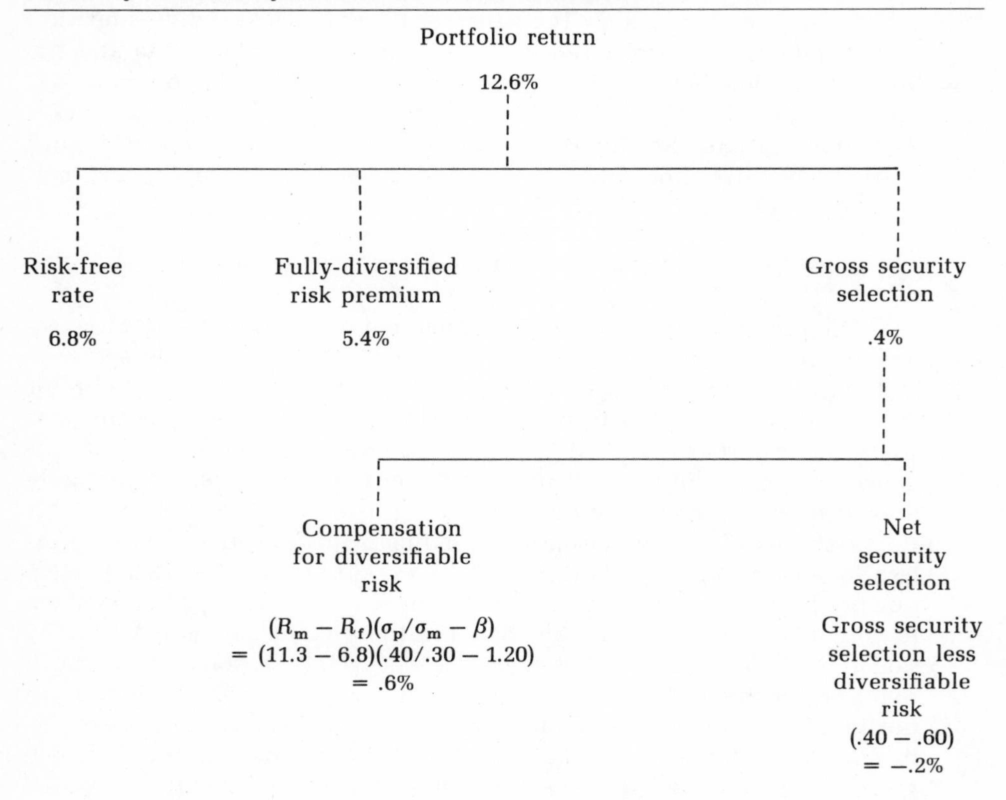

Like gross security selection, the fully diversified risk premium of Exhibits 14–2 and 14–3 has the two components summarized in Exhibit 14–4. The first component is the return associated with the market risk-premium and the desired beta. The second component is the return associated with the market risk-premium and the difference between the desired beta and the actual beta.

Market Projections

The differences between actual market risk and desired market risk may not have been a mistake. Suppose that under normal conditions the investor prefers a portfolio with a beta of 1.1. If the investor predicts the market will perform unusually well over the time period under consideration, the purchase of a portfolio with a higher level of risk may be considered. A more pessimistic prediction might result in a lower level of risk. If the predictions are correct, gains will result from the decision to accept higher or lower risk based on market projections.

EXHIBIT 14-4
Components of the Fully Diversified Risk-Premium

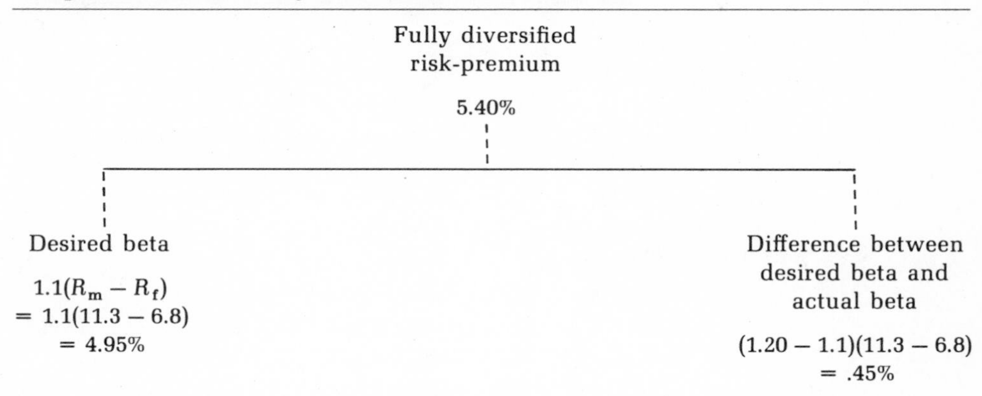

By breaking out the return attributable to differences in the actual risk and the desired risk level, we are isolating the benefits or losses which result from variations in the portfolio risk that may have been made in response to estimates of the market return. However, this breakdown will operate only during the time period of the estimated market movement. Over long periods of time, the changes will average out and we will not be able to detect the benefits of shifting the risk level by examining differences in the return from the actual risk level and the desired risk level. If shifts are made on purpose, the actual and desired risk should be the same over long periods. Nevertheless, the benefits will show up. They will be reflected in the net security selection portion of the return.

The net security selection portion will be positive even if no undervalued securities were selected. In other words, over long periods of time net security selection reflects both the selection of undervalued securities and portfolio shifts in response to market predictions. At this point, there is no way of separating which it is merely by looking at the figures. The only way of making the separation is to examine the period-by-period association between the actual beta and the desired beta. In our example, it appears that the selection of a beta of 1.20 instead of the desired beta of 1.10 was wise. When the market risk-premium is positive, shifts into higher risk are appropriate.

Summary of Measurement Components

Exhibit 14-5 summarizes the performance measurement techniques by depicting the return for each item discussed. The actual total return was 12.6 percent per year. By accepting no risk, the investor could have

EXHIBIT 14-5
Summary of Performance Components for Hypothetical Portfolio

1. Risk-free return		6.80%
2. Fully-diversified risk-premium		
A. Desired beta	4.95	
B. Actual beta	.45	
		5.40
3. Gross security selection		
A. Diversifiable risk	.60	
B. Net security selection	−.20	
		.40
	TOTAL RETURN	12.60%

obtained the risk-free return of 6.8 percent. However, risk was accepted in the form of market and diversifiable risk. Desired market risk should have produced a return of 4.95 percent and the actual market risk another .45 percent. The fully diversified risk-premium should have totaled 5.40 percent. Diversifiable risk should have produced a return of .60 percent. The returns from security selection are found by taking the difference between the sum of the returns assigned to each of the measurement or risk categories. In the example, the investor picked winners but accepted too much diversifiable risk, producing a loss of .20 percent from net security selection.

Overall Performance Measurement

The discussion of performance measurement has centered upon the four basic functions of the portfolio manager, including 1) market risk-level selection, 2) diversifiable risk, 3) security selection, and 4) responses to market projections. All of these items may be summarized by using the ratio of return to risk. We have seen that our basic strategy involves the selection of a portfolio with the maximum return per unit of risk. Whatever risk we prefer, the optimum portfolio will be the portfolio with the highest ratio of return to risk. If we have a fully diversified portfolio, the risk should be measured with beta. If the portfolio is not fully diversified, the risk should be measured with the standard deviation of the return. Given the measure of risk, the "best" portfolio will be the portfolio with the maximum return per unit of risk. If the risk measure is the standard deviation, we call the return per unit of risk the *reward-to-variability ratio.* If beta is used to measure risk, the return ratio is referred to as the *characteristic line.* The appendix to this chapter shows the calculation of these two measures for the example used throughout the chapter.

SUMMARY

The measurement of the performance of an investment manager must consider several aspects of the investment decision. We started by insisting that any measurement techniques concentrate on the performance of the entire portfolio. Single assets that do well contribute to outstanding performance, but the skill of an investor will reside in the outcome of the portfolio. It was also noted that performance must be judged in light of available opportunities. The performance must be compared to a benchmark portfolio. The conventional techniques employ the market portfolio to represent the investor's opportunities. In the same context, the benchmark portfolio must be adjusted for risk. If the portfolio is fully diversified, the risk adjustment can be accomplished with beta, where the portion of the investor's return required to compensate for risk is simply the product of beta and the market risk-premium. When diversifiable risk exists, an additional adjustment must be made. By taking the ratio of the standard deviation of the portfolio to the standard deviation of the market, we get an equivalent beta. We are then able to compare to see if the investor had superior ability in security selection.

We also noted that a comparison must be made between the actual beta of the portfolio and the beta desired by the investor. If the actual beta exceeds the desired beta in an up market, there will be a net benefit from the underestimation of the risk of the portfolio. If the market moves down, the underestimation will produce a net loss. With the actual beta less than the desired risk level, gains will be produced in a down market and losses in an up market. The differences between actual and projected betas could be the result of mistakes or deliberate portfolio shifts in response to market projections. Over long periods of time, the measure of security selection shows both the results of wise security selection and wise portfolio shifts based on market projections.

QUESTIONS

1. *a*) Explain what is meant by benchmark portfolio or naive opportunity.
   b) Why must performance comparisons be made to a benchmark or opportunity set?
2. Evaluate the problems associated with adjusting returns for risk including: *a*) the difference between actual and expected risk, and *b*) the diversification achieved.
3. Discuss how we might decide that a portfolio manager has "picked winners" or "picked losers."
4. In evaluating performance, should the problem of chance be considered and why?

PROBLEMS

1. Over a period of two years investor A and investor B achieved the results listed below. During the same period the market had a return of 4.3 percent with a standard deviation of .30. Treasury bill rates averaged 7.9 percent over the same period. You are asked to evaluate the performance of A and B. Would you hire either to manage your portfolio?

	A	B
Annual return (R)	5.10	4.20
Standard deviation	.28	.40
Actual portfolio beta	.90	1.10
Desired portfolio beta	.75	1.35

2. Using the same data presented in problem 1, calculate the reward-to-variability ratio and the characteristic line for the two portfolios.
3. In the two years following the period described in problem 1, the market had an annual return of 14.7 percent and a standard deviation of .30. The annual treasury bill rate was 5.4 percent during the same period. You are asked to reevaluate investors A and B using the results for the most recent two years noted below. Would these results change your assessment of the competence of Investors A and B?

	A	B
Annual return (R)	11.8%	13.9%
Standard deviation	.25	.43
Actual portfolio beta	.70	1.40
Desired portfolio beta	.75	1.35

4. In comparing the results of the evaluation of managers A and B in questions 1 through 3, why was the compensation for diversifiable risk negative in question 1 and positive in question 3?

SUGGESTED READINGS

Bauman, W. Scott. "Evaluation of Prospective Investment Performance." *Journal of Finance,* May 1968, pp. 276–95.

Cooley, Philip L. and Rodney L. Roenfeldt. "Market Return and Risk of South Carolina Firms and the General Market." *Business and Economic Review,* April 1975, pp. 9–16.

Dietz, Peter O. *Pension Funds: Measuring Investment Performance.* New York: The Free Press, 1966.

Fama, Eugene F. "Components of Investment Performance." *Journal of Finance,* June 1972, pp. 551–67.

Friend, Irwin and Marshall Blume. "Measurement of Portfolio Performance Under Uncertainty." *American Economic Review,* September 1970, pp. 561–75.

Klemkosky, Robert C. "The Bias in Composite Performance Measures." *Journal of Financial and Quantitative Analysis.* June 1973, pp. 505–14.

Melicher, Ronald W. and David F. Rush. "The Performance of Conglomerate Firms: Recent Risk and Return Experience." *Journal of Finance,* May 1973, pp. 381–88.

Robinson, Randall S. "Measuring the Risk Dimension of Investment Performance." *Journal of Finance,* May 1970, pp. 455–68.

Smith, Keith V. "Alternative Procedures for Revising Investment Portfolios." *Journal of Financial and Quantitative Analysis,* December 1968, pp. 371–403.

—— and John C. Schreiner. "A Portfolio Analysis of Conglomerate Diversification." *Journal of Finance,* June 1969, pp. 413–27.

Appendix

In measuring the return on a portfolio relative to the risk assumed, an investor can calculate either a reward-to-variability ratio or a characteristic line. The following discussion presents the method by which each of these two ratios is calculated along with a discussion of each measure. The actual numbers used are found in Exhibit 14–1.

Calculation of Reward-to-Variability Ratio:

$$\text{Portfolio} = (R_p - R_f)/\sigma_p = \frac{.126 - .068}{.4} = .145$$

$$\text{Market} = (R_m - R_f)/\sigma_m = \frac{.113 - .068}{.3} = .150$$

where:
R_p = portfolio return
R_f = return on risk-free asset
R_m = market return
σ_p, σ_m = standard deviation of return on portfolio and market, respectively

Calculation of the Characteristic Line:

$$\text{Portfolio} = (R_p - R_f)/\beta_p = \frac{.126 - .068}{1.2} = .0483$$

$$\text{Market} = (R_m - R_f)/\beta_m = \frac{.113 - .068}{1.0} = .0450$$

where: β_p = portfolio beta
β_m = market beta

Reward-to-Variability Ratio

Using the market portfolio as our benchmark, the reward-to-variability ratio indicates the performance of our portfolio was slightly below standard. The market portfolio had a lower return and lower risk, but the market return as measured relative to risk was higher than for the portfolio.

Since the risk measure is the standard deviation, we need not be concerned with whether or not total risk included diversifiable risk. It is for this reason that the reward-to-variability ratio is used as the most comprehensive measure of overall performance. It includes all elements of performance—the undiversifiable risk, the diversifiable risk, and security selection. Since it is all inclusive, the difference between the reward-to-variability ratio of a portfolio and that of the market will reflect the net benefits of security selection. If security selection results in a positive return, the investor's reward-to-variability ratio will exceed that of the market portfolio. If security selection produces a negative return, the market will have a higher reward-to-variability ratio. In summary, the reward-to-variability ratio is a general measure of performance that combines the various components of performance.

The Characteristic Line

The characteristic line is also designed to reflect overall performance. It measures the return per unit of risk in the same fashion as the reward-to-variability ratio, but uses beta to measure risk. Consequently, the assumption is that the portfolio under consideration was fully diversified. In the example, the portfolio has a characteristic line that exceeds the characteristic line of the market portfolio, indicating superior performance. But the portfolio was not fully diversified. Consequently, we required an additional return of .6 percent to compensate for the risk not considered in the beta measure. The conclusion that followed was that .6 percent of the total actual return of 12.6 percent was not superior performance, but simply compensation for diversifiable risk. The result is that the characteristic line overstates performance by including the diversifiable element in the return, but excluding it from the risk measure.

By removing the diversifiable risk compensation from the actual return we would have a risk-premium of 5.2 percent (12.6 minus .6 minus 6.8). Dividing this adjusted risk-premium by the beta of 1.2 produces a characteristic line ratio of .0433, which is less than the market and indicates inferior performance. With the recognition of the diversifiable risk element, the characteristic line tells the same story as the reward-to-variability ratio. The performance of the portfolio was slightly inferior to the market because of poor security selection. In essence, the characteristic line ignores diversifiable risk and by doing so generates a measure of performance that will overstate the performance of any portfolio that is not perfectly diversified. If the portfolio is reasonably close to full diversification, this does not represent a major problem. Nevertheless, it is probably best to use the reward-to-variability ratio as the measure of overall performance.

15

Technical Analysis and Market Efficiency

An alternative exists to the types of investment analysis examined thus far in the book. Chapters 7 through 10 examined what is called fundamental analysis, where the objective is to determine the value of the firm based upon characteristics, both real and financial, of the firm itself. Chapters 11 through 13 examined the concepts of portfolio analysis, where the broad objective is to determine an optimum combination of individual securities. The primary emphasis was on the trade-off between risk and return.

TECHNICAL ANALYSIS

Supply-Demand Aspects

A third category of investment analysis, usually referred to as technical analysis, represents a methodology of forecasting short-run fluctuations in the price of either individual securities or the market in general.

Technical analysis is not restricted to common stocks, but most applications are directed at common stocks or the market for common stocks. The forecasting technique, by and large, attempts to determine the supply and demand conditions for the shares of a given security or for the market. The emphasis on supply and demand differs from the emphasis on financial and real factors that is the main ingredient of fundamental investment analysis. In its purest sense, technical analysis is not concerned with fundamentals. If excess demand exists for the shares of a particular security, the technician will consider the stock to be an outstanding purchase candidate and not worry about the fundamental characteristics of the stock.

Because of the short-run character of technical analysis, the approach is characterized by an emphasis on the timing of purchases and sales. For example, the technician may advise against the purchase of a security simply because of supply and demand considerations. The technical factors may indicate the security will sell for a lower price in the near future. In other words, technical analysis is designed to forecast temporary changes in either the supply or the demand or both of the security.

The techniques used to make the demand-supply forecasts are based primarily on the isolation of patterns in the fluctuations of stock prices and other market statistics. In the attempt to use pattern recognition, technical analysis relies quite heavily upon empirical observation. If a particular pattern has reappeared several times and consistently forecasts a particular price movement, the technician will use that pattern even if a theoretical justification is absent for the price move that follows. The technician would prefer both theoretical and empirical justification. But if theoretical justification is absent, an historical record of consistent forecasts will admit the particular indicator to the technician's arsenal of forecasting techniques.[1]

Multiple Indicators

By its very nature, technical analysis must rely upon a wide variety of supply and demand indicators. A particular price pattern may have an outstanding forecasting record but may appear rather infrequently. To be useful, a forecasting technique must not only demonstrate reliability, but also appear frequently enough to isolate most demand-supply shifts. Since many technical indicators by themselves do not frequently signal a price movement, the technical analyst may rely on several indicators.

[1]For a good discussion of the general considerations involved in technical analysis, see Robert A. Levy, "Conceptual Foundations of Technical Analysis," *Financial Analysts Journal,* July–August 1966, pp. 83–89.

Several indicators may also be used since many situations require the interpretation of interactions among technical indicators. Most technical analysts do not claim a particular pattern will always forecast a particular price movement. There are usually conditions attached where the conditions refer to patterns in one or more other indicators. Technical analysis is often criticized incorrectly with the observation that a particular technique did not forecast properly. The incorrect forecast may have been the result of a failure to recognize the interaction of the particular technique with other technical indicators. Even if a technical analyst does recognize the interactions of various technical indicators, a particular technique cannot be expected to forecast correctly all the time. Incorrect signals are sometimes given and no technique is infallible. Consequently, as far as possible, the technician makes forecasts on the weight of evidence of several indicators.

Accuracy of Forecasts

With the reliance upon interaction of indicators, it becomes difficult to determine the forecasting accuracy of a particular indicator in a direct manner. In testing the reliability of a particular indicator, one encounters several problems. It may not be possible to obtain enough observations to attach any statistical validity to an empirical test. Two correct forecasts during the past twenty years do not allow any conclusions regarding the reliability of any particular pattern. Likewise, an incorrect forecast does not suggest that a forecasting technique should be discarded. The conditions or interactions may have been absent or the error may not be statistically significant.

The result of these empirical testing difficulties is that the reliability of technical analysis has been and continues to be tested *indirectly*. The indirect tests concentrate upon an examination of whether or not price patterns actually exist, and the extent to which the technician actually earns returns exceeding returns available to the investor not using technical analysis. If patterns exist, technical analysis may have validity. If a particular investor earns excess profits using technical analysis, the methods must be useful. Because the tests are primarily indirect we shall postpone a detailed examination of them until later in the chapter. The tests generally go under the name of the *efficient market hypothesis*, which is designed to examine several characteristics of our capital markets, including technical analysis.

Both the use and empirical validation of technical analysis encounter trouble when it comes to the recognition of patterns in security prices or other market statistics. A particular pattern may be an accurate reflection of the future, but it is often difficult to determine if the pattern is developing or has actually appeared. As with any statistical approach, the technical patterns are never perfect in the sense that it is clear and obvious that the indicator is developing or has appeared. The technician's chart may suggest a particular pattern, but there are always ambiguities and another technical analyst may not "see" the pattern. Moreover, it is often the case that a particular pattern has an excellent forecasting record, but recognition of the pattern comes too late to take advantage of the forecast.

Because of the wide variety of technical indicators, we cannot go into an exhaustive analysis of each one. There are literally hundreds of technical indicators used actively and hundreds of systems of indicators employed by investors. We cannot hope even to discuss all the more popular indicators. We will simply present a sampling of the better known technical indicators with no suggestion that the techniques presented are better than others actively employed.[2]

Technical Indicators Used

Dow Theory. One of the best known and oldest of stock market indicators is the Dow Theory. The primary objective of the Dow Theory is to forecast major changes in the trend of the stock market.[3] Casual observation of the fluctuations in any of the market indexes shows that there are long periods of time when the general trend of the market is upward (a "bull" market) or downward (a "bear" market). Whether we are in a bull or a bear market, there are fluctuations in the opposite direction. The trend may be upward, but every bull market has its reversals, as does every bear market. The Dow Theory is supposed to forecast when the reversals become permanent and the trend changes direction.

Figure 15-1 presents a hypothetical chart of the Dow-Jones Industrial Average (DJIA) during a major bull market. The trend is upward, but on four occasions declines may be observed. The first three declines did not equal the previous advance. The fourth decline is more serious. The decline is greater than the previous advance and the index "breaks through" a previously established *support level*—the bottom of the previous decline. When the DJIA breaks through the support level, the Dow Theory holds that the bull market is finished and a bear market is

[2]A more complete examination can be found in R. D. Edwards and John Magee, Jr., *Technical Analysis of Stock Trends* (Springfield, Mass., Stock Trend Service), latest edition; Joseph E. Granville, *A Strategy of Daily Stock Market Timing for Maximum Profit* (Englewood Cliffs, N.J.: Prentice-Hall), Encyclopedia of Stock Market Techniques (Larchmont, N.Y.: Investors Intelligence, Inc.), latest edition; and Anthony J. Lerro and Charles B. Swayne, Jr., *Selection of Securities: Technical Analysis of Stock Market Prices*, 2nd ed. (Morristown, N.J.: General Learning Press, 1974).

[3]For a more extensive analysis of the Dow Theory, see George W. Bishop, Jr., *Charles H. Dow and the Dow Theory* (New York: Appleton Century Crofts, 1960) or Bishop, "Evolution of the Dow Theory," *Financial Analysts Journal*, September-October 1961, pp. 23-36.

FIGURE 15-1
Hypothetical Dow-Theory Sell Signal

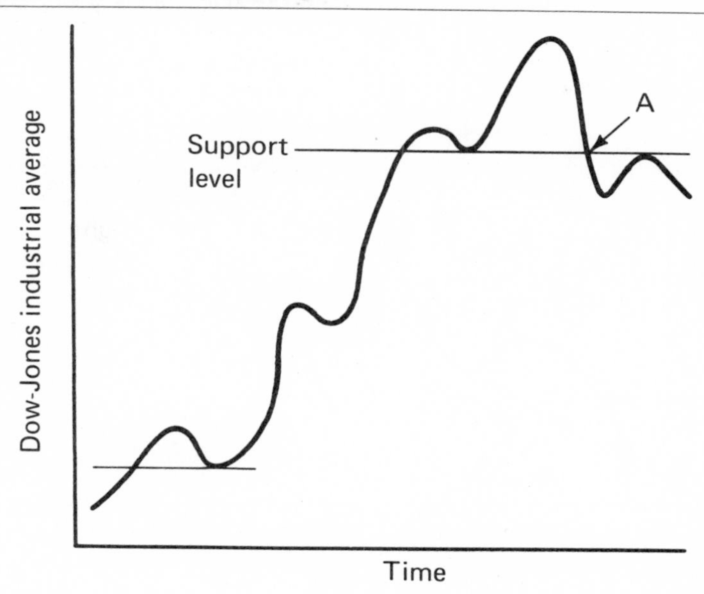

beginning. In Figure 15-1, point A is the sell signal. If the market goes through point A, the Dow theorist sells. If the market does not go through point A the bull market is expected to continue.

The signal given in Figure 15-1 is not complete in that most users of the Dow Theory require confirmation of the signal by the Dow-Jones Transportation Average (DJT). In other words, a sell signal is not complete until a similar breakthrough is observed in the DJT. The beginning of a bull market is predicted in exactly the same fashion when a breakthrough on the *upside* is observed.

The Dow Theory is quite popular mainly because it gave a sell signal a few weeks before the 1929 stock market crash. Its record since that time has been mixed, with the greatest difficulty being the lateness of the predictions. Quite often, by the time the DJT has confirmed the sell signal, we have already passed through 80 or 90 percent of the bear market. Instead of a leading indicator, the Dow Theory turns out frequently to be a lagging indicator of general market trends. The predictions are often accurate but come too late to use as a trading signal. Nevertheless, the Dow Theory forms the basis of the many other widely used technical indicators.

Price Patterns. Virtually all price patterns used in technical analysis are related to breakthroughs around resistance or support levels. A resistance level, such as the highest value of the DJIA in Figure 15-1, is where selling pressures are expected to appear. The technician will

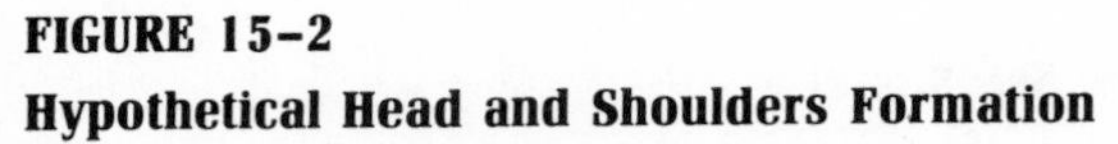

FIGURE 15-2
Hypothetical Head and Shoulders Formation

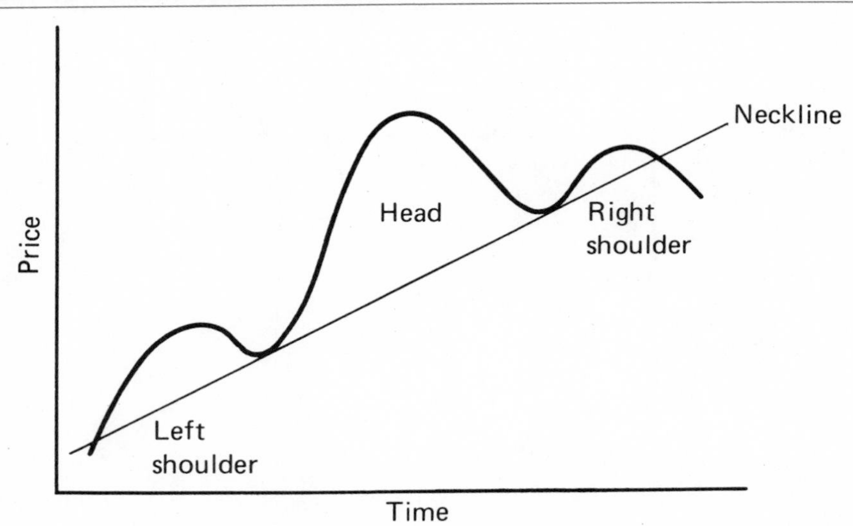

speak of "head and shoulders" formations, pennants, wedges, triangles, gaps, and so on. All these labels refer to some sort of pattern that can be observed in a chart of the price of particular stocks or of the market. Each pattern has a specific interpretation, but all interpretations are based on breakthroughs above and below previous resistance or support levels. For example, Figure 15-2 shows a chart of the price of a hypothetical stock showing a classic pattern known as a head and shoulders formation. The forecasting power of the pattern appears to be strongest when it occurs after a prolonged upward movement in the price of a particular stock. The shoulders of the formation form the base or support levels (typically called the neckline). When the price of the stock breaks through the neckline from the right shoulder, a strong sell signal is given.

In the first quarter of 1975 the Dow-Jones Industrial Average formed a head and shoulders pattern as depicted in Figure 15-3. In this example the movement through the neckline did not materialize, providing a strong buy signal for the market technicians. Had the DJIA broken through the neckline (about 740 on the DJIA) during the week of April 4, 1975, the head and shoulders pattern would have indicated a strong signal for a market decline. Like the Dow Theory, this pattern and many more like it base their forecasts on price movements above and below previous tops and bottoms that the chart of the stock or market traces out.

There are literally scores of price patterns employed as technical indicators. While we cannot begin to discuss them, we should remember that technical indicators are generally based on recurring patterns in the price of a stock or the market. The forecasts generally come from breakthroughs above and below support or resistance levels.

FIGURE 15-3
Head and Shoulders Formation—Dow-Jones Industrial Average, First Quarter, 1975

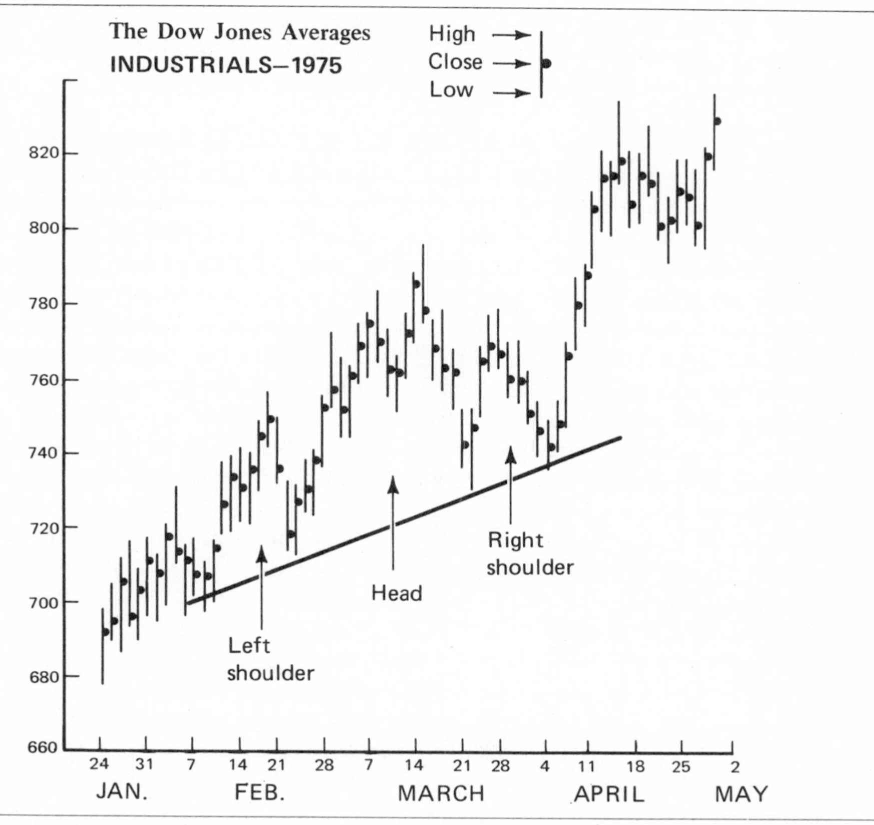

Source: Reprinted with permission of the *Wall Street Journal*, © Dow Jones & Company, Inc. (May 2, 1975), p. 31. All Rights Reserved.

Volume Data. The technical analyst does not stop with merely examining patterns in the price of a stock. Other market statistics are employed as well. One of the most widely used nonprice indicators is the volume of trading in a particular stock or the market. Volume is defined as the number of shares that exchanged hands during a particular time period. The interpretation of volume statistics is often quite complex; however, a general rule is that heavy volume indicates a continuation of recent price trends while light volume implies a reversal. For example, if the market moves up on light volume the technician will forecast a decline. But a movement down on light volume suggests subsequent upward price movements.

The primary exception to the tendencies just noted comes on what are known as key or important reversal days. A major market or stock decline often begins with a very rapid price increase on a given day accompanied by heavy volume. Correspondingly, a major price advance is often preceded by a rapid price decline on a particular day accompanied by heavy volume. These key reversal days are the exception to the general rule that heavy volume signals a continuation of the previous price direction while light volume indicates a reversal.

Advance-Decline Line. The strength or weakness of the market is also judged by changes in the advance-decline line.[4] Each day the financial press reports the number of stocks on the NYSE that had price increases (advances) and the number that experienced price declines. The technician uses these statistics to construct an advance-decline line, which is a daily chart of the cumulative net advances or declines. If we were to begin our chart on a day with 700 advances and 500 declines, our first point would be 200. If on the following day, there were 650 advances and 550 declines the next point would be 300, or the sum of the net advances on the first two days.

The advance-decline line is often referred to as a breadth of the market indicator, since its basic function is to determine whether a particular market movement is sufficiently general and strong to be sustained. For example, if the market has been moving upward as measured by one of the several market averages, but the advance-decline line has been flat or even declining, the indication is that the upward movement will shortly come to an end. The market is moving upward but more stocks are declining than are advancing, suggesting that the general increase is concentrated in relatively few securities. If the advance-decline line was moving up rapidly we would forecast a continuation of the upward movement of the market. In essence, the advance-decline line is an indication of how widespread a particular market fluctuation happens to be. The more widespread a particular movement, the stronger it is likely to be.

In addition to the strength of a market movement, the advance-decline line is also employed as a leading indicator. The termination of a bear market is often preceded by increases in the number of stocks showing gains. Correspondingly, an increase in the number of stocks showing declines frequently signals the end of a bull market. Hence, the advance-decline line should begin to increase prior to the beginning of a bull market and begin to decline prior to the beginning of a bear market.

[4]For an empirical test of the advance-decline technical indicator, which finds that using this indicator is not as profitable as a buy-and-hold trading approach, see: James C. Van Horne, and George G. C. Parker, "The Random-Walk Theory: An Empirical Test," *Financial Analysts Journal*, November–December 1967, pp. 87–92 and Van Horne and Parker, "Technical Trading Rules: A Comment," *Financial Analysts Journal*, July–August 1968, pp. 128–32.

The Confidence Index. Another widely used leading indicator of general market fluctuations is the Confidence Index published weekly by *Barron's*. The Confidence Index is defined as follows:

$$\text{Confidence index} = \frac{\text{high-grade corporate bond yield (10 bonds)}}{\text{lower-grade corporate bond yield (40 Dow-Jones bonds)}}$$

High-grade corporate bonds should always have a yield less than the yield on the lower quality bonds. Thus, the Confidence Index should always be less than one. If bond investors are optimistic about the future, the difference between the yields on high and lower quality bonds will be small. If prosperity is expected, the risk and yield of the lower quality bonds becomes much closer to the risk and yield of high quality bonds. If bond investors are pessimistic, the difference in yields and risk becomes much greater.

The result of this situation is that as bond investors become more confident about the future, the Confidence Index will rise, since the difference between high and low quality bond yields declines. As bond investors become pessimistic about the future, the Confidence Index will decline, since the yield on high-grade bonds decreases relative to the yield on lower quality bonds. The increases or decreases in the Confidence Index are expected to lead the stock market by several months. The lead time varies, but a lead is expected under the hypothesis that bond yields are closely associated with the activities of professional investors managing very large bond portfolios. When the Confidence Index rises, it suggests that these professionals are becoming optimistic. A decline indicates pessimism among the professionals.

Odd-Lot Trading. The confidence index is designed to tell what the professionals are doing under the belief that the "smart money" will make correct forecasts more often than not. Technicians also employ the odd-lot index, which is designed to determine what the less sophisticated investor feels about the future of the market. The general thought here is that the small investor who deals primarily in odd-lot transactions (purchases and sales of less than 100 shares) is less sophisticated in making investment decisions and typically wrong regarding future predictions. Thus, the odd-lot investor will be buying heavily at market tops and selling at market bottoms. If this is true we should expect to see odd-lot purchases increasing relative to odd-lot sales prior to the end of a bull market. The end of a bear market should be preceded by an increase in odd-lot sales relative to odd-lot purchases. We want to discover what the odd-lot investor is doing and do the opposite.

The odd-lot index is the ratio of odd-lot sales to odd-lot purchases. As it begins to decrease, we expect a decline in the market to begin shortly. As it increases, we expect the end of a bear market. It should be emphasized that the odd-lot index is normally interpreted on the basis of changes rather than the absolute level. Long periods of time exist when odd-lot purchases exceed odd-lot sales and vice versa. We should also note that most technicians consider the odd-lot index to be a far better predictor of market tops than market bottoms. The evidence available seems to indicate this to be the case.[5] Many technicians will also use an odd-lot index for individual common stocks as well as for the market in general.

A popular variation of the odd-lot index is the short sales ratio shown below.

$$\text{Odd-lot short sales ratio} = \frac{\text{odd-lot short sales}}{\text{total odd-lot sales}}$$

When this ratio becomes large, the odd-lot theory holds that the market is near its trough and is ready to rally. The rationale for this technical indicator is similar to that for the odd-lot index. Small investors are expected to be "whiplashed" by their emotions and do the wrong thing at the wrong time. Hence, they will sell a stock short just as the stock is near its low point and about to increase in price.

Summary of Technical Indicators. We have examined a few of the many technical indicators used to forecast market and common stock price fluctuations. Our analysis is by no means complete; indeed, we barely scratched the surface.[6] This is unfortunate but necessary since a more detailed study would take us far from the objective of introducing the many and varied factors in the process of investing. At the same time, we said little about whether the technical indicators examined have any validity when making market forecasts. As noted early in the chapter, the interactions of the technical indicators make it difficult to test directly the forecasting power of a particular indicator. Hence, the validity of technical analysis is determined indirectly within the broader context of the general subject of efficient markets.

EFFICIENT MARKETS

Volumes have been written about efficient markets and the subject continues to be controversial. Much of the controversy apparently results from a misinterpretation of the theory and evidence regarding efficient

[5]Thomas J. Kewley, and Richard A. Stevenson, "The Odd-Lot Theory for Individual Stocks: A Reply," *Financial Analysts Journal,* January–February 1969, pp. 99–104; Stanley Kaish, "Odd-Lotter Trading of High and Low Quality Stocks," *Financial Analysts Journal,* March–April 1969, pp. 88–91; and Kaish, "Odd-Lot Profit and Loss Performance," *Financial Analysts Journal,* September–October 1969, pp. 83–89.

[6]For a more complete discussion of studies of technical indicators, see George E. Pinches, "The Random Walk Hypothesis and Technical Analysis," *Financial Analysts Journal,* March–April 1970, pp. 104–10.

markets. For example, an efficient market does not mean that the optimum investment strategy is to select securities randomly—what is popularly known as throwing darts at the *Wall Street Journal*. Nothing could be further from the truth, since an efficient market does not imply that the returns and risk of each security will be the same.

Neither does the existence of an efficient market suggest that security analysis is useless and should be ignored. In fact, if the stock market is efficient, security analysis is being done extremely well. An efficient market is entirely consistent with the proposition that security analysts are generally quite proficient in their analytical abilities. In addition, it has often been noted that analysts can perform an important function for the investor by selecting the "right" security, given the investor's individual characteristics. These individual characteristics include tax brackets, job security, age, family position, and other unique personal circumstances.

Efficient Market Theory

The theory of an efficient market is simple and straightforward. In its most general form, an efficient market fully reflects all relevant information. In such a market, a security or commodity will be priced in accordance with the relevant information. Since the information is complete, the price at any point in time will approximate the true or intrinsic value of the security.

This does not imply that the price of a security will never change. As new information enters the market, the price will adjust to reflect the intrinsic value implied by the new information. In practical terms, this suggests that price changes in an efficient market will be random, since the only cause of a price change is new information. If information is to be new, it must be unpredictable. If a piece of information about a firm is predictable, the information will be incorporated into the price of the security. When the predicted event occurs, nothing will happen since the price already allowed for the event. With new information entering the market in a random fashion, price changes will be random. As "Adam Smith" wrote in *The Money Game*, "Prices have no memory, and yesterday has nothing to do with tomorrow."[7] For this reason, efficient markets are often described as a random walk since price changes are somewhat similar to the steps of a drunk walking down the street.

Price Changes

A *random walk* suggests that successive price changes are independent and knowing yesterday's price change tells us nothing about today's price change. Notice that the emphasis is being placed on price changes and

[7]Adam Smith, *The Money Game* (New York: Random House, 1968), p. 148.

not on prices. Clearly the prices of common stocks and other financial assets are related across time. If a security closes today at a price of 50 most of us would predict a price tomorrow that is close to 50. As long as our prediction was close to 50, the potential error would be extremely small. A prediction of 50 with a result of 55 means a 10 percent error. This error is quite small, particularly when it is recognized that a movement of 5 points on a $50 stock in any one day is quite unusual. *Prices are not random and the efficient market hypothesis does not suggest that they are.*

The efficient market hypothesis suggests that price *changes* are random. If today's price change is plus one-half and we predict the change to be plus one-half tomorrow, an increase of three-fourths would imply a 50 percent error. The error associated with the price would be insignificant (50½ vs. 50¾).

Market Trends

It is also important to recognize that random changes do not prohibit market trends. To see why trends can exist when changes are random, let us construct a market index by tossing a coin. To give the index a sense of time, we will designate the first coin flip as 1944, the second flip as 1945, and so on through 1974. To give the index a sense of proportion, it is set at 7.14 in 1943, which was the value of the NYSE Composite Index at the close of 1943. If a given coin toss comes up heads, we shall increase the index by 20 percent. If a toss comes up tails we shall decrease the index by 5 percent. In Figure 15-4 the index has been plotted from 1943 through 1974 along with the NYSE Composite Index. The first toss was heads and hence the 1944 value of the index is 8.57, or 7.14 plus 20 percent. The second toss turned out to be tails and thus the 1945 value of the index is 8.14, or 8.57 minus 5 percent. This procedure was repeated for each year through 1974.

The coin toss index is amazingly similar to the market index. Both have an obvious trend. A correlation analysis between the two indexes would yield a high correlation. The reason for the trend in the coin toss index is that the average annual change is approximately 7½ percent. Hence, over long periods a trend of 7½ percent per year is evident. If the average change is positive, the trend will be positive. If the average change is zero, no trend will exist. Random changes do not imply that the average change is zero. However, knowing last year's change tells us nothing about what the change will be next year, just as knowing that a tail occurred in 1974 tells us nothing about what the coin flip will produce in 1975.

As investors, our interest lies in the price change and not in the absolute price level. It makes very little difference whether or not a

FIGURE 15-4
The Coin Toss Index and the NYSE Composite Index (1943-74)

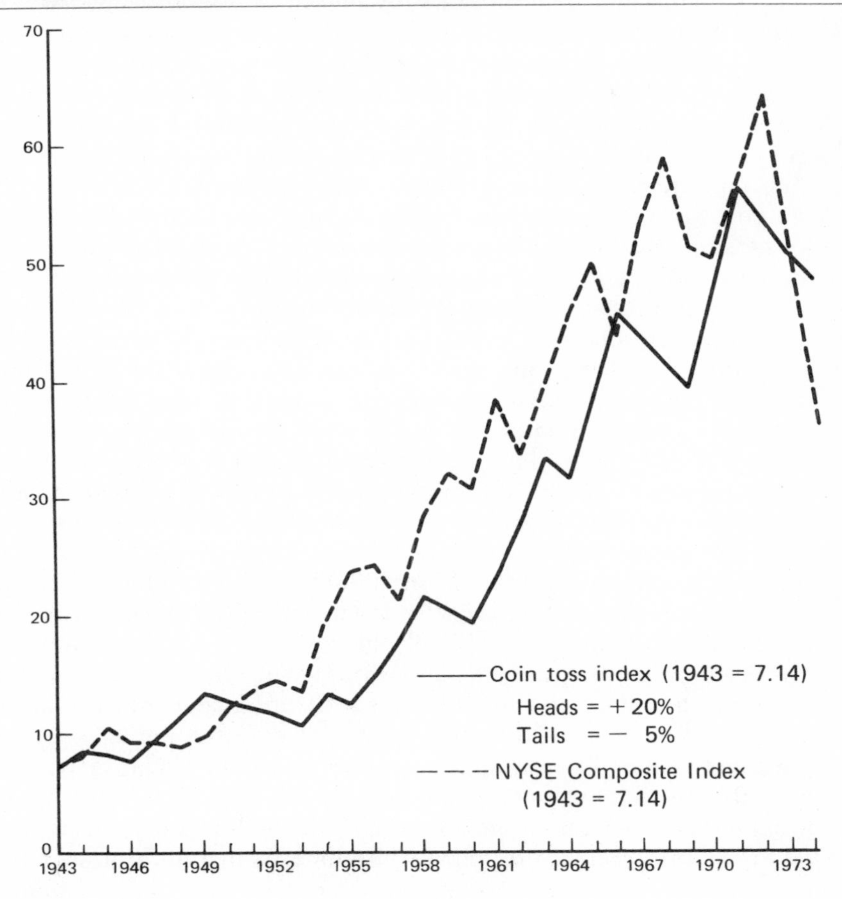

stock is priced at $50 or $5 or $500. The investor's interest is in the rate of return that results from price changes.[8] Moreover, we are not interested in the absolute change. A $5 increase must be related to the current price. Higher priced stocks obviously have higher price changes. As a consequence, changes are always discussed in relative terms. A $5 increase on a $50 stock is a 10 percent change, but only a 5 percent change for a $100 stock. When the efficient market refers to random changes, the change is defined as the relative change.

[8]Dividends, of course, are an important ingredient of rates of return, but for clarity they are omitted from this analysis.

Conditions for an Efficient Market

The coin tossing experiment illustrates the possibility of trends when relative changes are random. The fact that the index is closely associated with the NYSE Composite Index should not be taken as "proof" of the theory of efficient markets. Efficiency is more complicated. We said an efficient market would fully reflect all available information. To do so, capital markets must meet certain rather stringent conditions. The first condition is that information must be available to all investors at no cost. If a cost exists, information may not be incorporated into the price since the cost of the information may exceed the profit that could be earned by acquiring the information. The second condition is that all investors must interpret the information in the same fashion. Price changes could occur in a nonrandom fashion as investors with different interpretations enter and leave the market. The third condition is that an efficient market have no transaction costs. If new information enters the market and indicates that a $50 stock should have a value of $50.25, the price will not adjust to the "proper" value if commissions are equal to or greater than the $.25 differential. Without commissions, buyers would enter at $50 to obtain the $.25 profit. With commissions, the price may remain at $50.

Given these conditions, any market will be efficient. Obviously the conditions do not exist in the real world, but markets could behave in an efficient manner even when the conditions are not strictly adhered to. Price changes could be random allowing for transaction costs, but to obtain a change the market will wait until new information has accumulated sufficiently to generate a change large enough to overcome the commission. Price changes can occur without new information being available to all investors. A few investors may incorporate new information into the price and move the price to its new intrinsic value. Interpretation of information becomes a factor only if one group of investors has a monopoly on interpretative powers. One group should not consistently make better interpretations than the rest of the participants in the market. Following our general policy, we must look to the real world to see if the implications of the theory are observable.

Categories of Efficiency

To test the theory of efficient markets, we need to be much more specific than our statements to this point. Fully reflecting available information is a vague statement that cannot be tested in any meaningful manner. To test the efficient market hypothesis, the theory has been divided into three separate categories. The three categories have been labeled 1) the weak form, 2) the semistrong form, and 3) the strong form.

The *weak form* of the efficient market theory is directed at the information contained in the price behavior of a given common stock.

In the weak form, price predictions cannot be made by using the pattern of historical prices. If the weak form is valid, we should observe a random walk. We should find that the price change in one period is statistically independent of the price change in any other period.

The *semistrong form* states that the price of a stock should reflect all publicly available information. The empirical tests of the semistrong form concentrate on how stock prices adjust to new information when the information becomes public. If the price adjustment is rapid and complete we have confirmation of the efficient market hypothesis.

The *strong form* of the efficient market theory states that stock prices reflect all information, both public and private. The private information is usually referred to as insider information. The tests of the strong form are indirect in the sense that they seek to determine if groups of investors earn "excess" profits. If investors exist who systematically beat the market, we have evidence that the strong form of the efficient market hypothesis is not valid. If one can profit in some regular fashion from the use of insider information, the market is inefficient.

EMPIRICAL EVIDENCE

The efficient market hypothesis in any form can never be proved. We can only offer evidence consistent with the theory. The theory can be disproved with evidence that is inconsistent with the hypothesis, but consistent evidence is not proof. We must rely on the weight of evidence where acceptance of the theory becomes more palatable as consistent evidence accumulates from different sources using different research techniques.

The Weak Form

The empirical tests of the weak form of the efficient market hypothesis are by far the most numerous and the oldest. The possibility of random changes in capital markets was discussed and observed as far back as the early 1900s and the tests continue today. In each test the basic methodology involves correlation analysis where past price changes are correlated with future price changes. If the correlation coefficient is found to be zero, verification of the weak form is indicated. Nonzero correlation coefficients indicate that past price changes could be used to predict future price changes and lead to the conclusion that the current price did not contain all existing information.

The results of dozens of different studies are amazingly consistent.[9]

[9]A compilation of most of the significant weak-form efficient market tests is available in Paul H. Cootner, *The Random Character of Stock Market Prices* (Cambridge, Mass.: MIT Press, 1964); A more recent summary is in Eugene F. Fama, "Efficient Capital Markets: Review of Theory and Empirical Work," *Journal of Finance*, May 1970, pp. 383–417.

In virtually every study the correlation coefficients were significantly different from zero. Most of the tests, however, were massive undertakings using enormous quantities of data. Consequently, the research typically obtained statistical significance with extremely small coefficients. The coefficients that were significantly different from zero were on the order of .03. The figure is extremely small, especially when it is recalled that it is the correlation coefficient. The coefficient of determination is the square of the correlation coefficient and in this case would be .0009. The fluctuations of past price changes seem to explain 9/100's of 1 percent of the fluctuations in future price changes. In essence, correlations of past price changes are extremely small and appear to support the weak form of the efficient market hypothesis.

Nevertheless, correlation analysis can occasionally be overwhelmed by large changes that disguise profitable trends. Consequently, the weak-form research has also examined the problem of "runs." A *run* is simply a series of price changes in the same direction. We could observe runs of two days, three days, or even twenty days. If the weak-form holds, the runs observed will have roughly the same frequency as if we were drawing price changes from a table of random numbers. The research that has examined this problem generally concludes that runs in the stock market occur at random, providing further support for the weak form of the efficient market hypothesis.[10]

It is also possible that small correlations could produce profits for the investor who is willing to devote the time and effort. A set of tests called filter rules has been developed to determine if there is a potential for profit from small correlations. A *filter test* establishes a certain percentage change in the price of a stock as a buy or sell signal. The percentage change is called the filter. Given a filter of 5 percent the investment strategy is to buy on an increase of 5 percent and sell and go short on a decrease of 5 percent. If the filter system works, the strategy will produce profits in excess of the profits available from simply buying and holding. The tests use only the information contained in past price changes and will be profitable if such information is not always incorporated in the current price. If one can profit from the small correlations, the filter rules should produce excess profits.

Many filter tests have been conducted, and like the correlation research, the results are generally consistent from one study to the next.[11] Filter rules do not produce excess profits, and after allowing for brokerage commissions several filters produced substantial losses. The conclusion

[10]The most complete study of stock market runs in Eugene F. Fama, "The Behavior of Stock Market Prices," *Journal of Business*, January 1965, pp. 34–105.

[11]The most outstanding filter rule tests are included in Sidney S. Alexander, "Price Movements in Speculative Markets: Trends or Random Walks, No. 2," *Industrial Management Review*, Spring 1964, pp. 25–46; Fama, "The Behavior of Stock Market Prices," and Eugene F. Fama and Marshall Blume, "Filter Rules and Stock Market Trading Profits," *Journal of Business, Security Prices: A Supplement*, January 1966, pp. 226–41.

holds for filters as small as ½ of 1 percent and as large as 50 percent. The small correlations cannot produce excess profits and the investor would be better advised to buy and hold.

The conclusions regarding the weak form of the efficient market hypothesis seem clear. The market is not perfectly efficient, but it is so close that the practical investor will conclude efficiency. The amount of past price information not contained in the current price is so small that profits cannot be made from this information.

The Semistrong Form

The tests of the semistrong form of the efficient market hypothesis are more difficult, since an inclusive test must specify what public information is and when the information becomes known to the public. The semistrong tests are just coming into their own and more research is required. Each of the tests specifies a certain body of information and attempts to isolate the price changes that result from the release of the information to the public. Ray Ball and Phillip Brown, for example, studied the price effects of the announcement of earnings for a sample of corporations.[12] Their basic findings were that securities which reported earnings increases advanced in price while earnings declines were associated with price declines. Moreover, the price movements occurred well in advance of the actual announcements, suggesting that the market not only responded to the earnings announcements but also anticipated them.

It is often suggested that a stock split will be followed by a market price increase to the benefit of the investor. If a stock is selling for 100 and is split 2 for 1, it is suggested the price will not fall to 50 but to a price somewhat above 50. A study that attempted to isolate the effect of a split found that the returns from such securities were well above what we would expect, given the risk of the security.[13] As a trading device the finding is of very little use since virtually all of the excess returns were incorporated into the price about four months prior to the split. The price splits had been anticipated by the market.

This study was especially interesting from an informational point of view. When a firm splits its stock, it will often change the dividend rate per share. A stock with a one dollar dividend may be split 2 for 1. After the split, the dividend rate is frequently greater than fifty cents per share. The evidence on splits seems to indicate the excess return associated with splits is the result of these dividend increases and not the split itself. The securities with an increased dividend rate remained

[12] Ray Ball and Phillip Brown, "An Empirical Evaluation of Accounting Income Numbers," *Journal of Accounting Research*, Autumn 1968, pp. 157–78.

[13] Eugene F. Fama, Lawrence Fisher, Michael C. Jensen, and Richard Roll, "The Adjustment of Stock Prices to New Information," *International Economic Review*, February 1969, pp. 1–21.

at high prices after the split. Securities with proportionately reduced dividends declined after the split. It seems the excess returns are in anticipation of a dividend increase. The split has informational content and is incorporated into the price. If the information is wrong, the price readjusts to the previous level.

Several other semistrong tests have been conducted with similar results.[14] The current market price seems to incorporate publicly available information. One should note, however, that these tests are by no means exhaustive. Considerable work is still being conducted on the question of the market's response to new information. At this point, the evidence seems to favor the semistrong form of the efficient market theory, but the conclusion is not nearly as definitive as is the case for the weak form. The quest for public information that is not included in the current market price continues and is by no means complete.

The Strong Form

The strong form of the efficient market hypothesis suggests that the market price of a security reflects all information, both public and private. The empirical tests must be indirect since the specification of private information is impossible. We should note also that even if private or insider information does not exist, public information could produce superior returns for individuals who can interpret the information in a superior fashion. In other words, the strong form asks whether or not investors can earn excess returns from private information or better interpretation or both. The tests are indirect and take the form of measuring the actual returns of professional investors. The basic hypothesis is that in a strongly efficient market no one will be able to profit consistently from insider information or superior interpretation. In dealing with professional investors the proposition is that these individuals or institutions are the most likely candidates for superior returns. Since they are being paid for their services they should perform better than the average investor. Most of the research is centered on the investment company manager for whom considerable performance data are available.

The strong-form studies are quite numerous and generally reach similar and rather uniform conclusions.[15] While Chapters 20 and 21

[14]See, for example, Myron S. Scholes, "The Market for Securities: Substitution versus Price Pressure and the Effects of Information on Share Prices," *Journal of Business,* April 1972, pp. 179–221.

[15]Some of the more prominent studies include Irwin Friend, Marshall Blume, and Jean Crockett, *Mutual Funds and Other Institutional Investors, A New Perspective* (New York: McGraw-Hill, 1970); William F. Sharpe, "Mutual Fund Performance," *Journal of Business, Security Prices: A Supplement,* January 1966, pp. 119–38, and J. Peter Williamson, "Measuring Mutual Fund Performance," *Financial Analysts Journal,* November–December 1972, pp. 78–84.

discuss investment companies in detail, we will briefly discuss here the major conclusions of the studies of investment company performance. Generally, investment company (mutual fund) returns are about what could be expected, given their risk. Probably the most comprehensive study of mutual fund returns examined 115 funds during the period 1945 to 1964.[16] The study examined average returns, the average risk-adjusted returns, and the risk-adjusted returns for each of the 115 funds. Both the average returns, before management compensation, and the risk-adjusted returns were not significantly different from the market returns. When the risk-adjusted returns of individual funds were examined, differences were substantial. However, none of the differences was outside what could reasonably be expected from chance.

The investment company studies all lend support to the strong form of the efficient market hypothesis. They do not prove the theory, since proof would require evidence that there are no individual investors who consistently beat the market.

INVESTMENT IMPLICATIONS AND SUMMARY

It is appropriate to conclude that strong empirical support exists for all forms of the theory of efficient markets. Price changes are uncorrelated through time, current market prices seem to incorporate all public information, and there is no evidence to suggest that any group of investors can systematically outperform the market after adjusting for risk. These results have frequently been interpreted to mean that the investor should be passive in making investment decisions and simply select a random portfolio without security analysis, portfolio analysis, or market projections: The investor should throw darts at the *Wall Street Journal*. Some have even gone so far as to conclude that the evidence on the efficient market implies that our stock market is little more than a casino where profits depend on the roll of the dice. These interpretations are gross misrepresentations of the efficient market hypothesis.

If these are misrepresentations, what are the implications? Validation of the efficient market hypothesis provides strong support to those who conclude that the investment community is performing its tasks of security analysis and portfolio management quite well. There are so many highly skilled investment analysts with virtually complete information that it becomes extremely difficult for any individual investor to obtain a competitive advantage allowing the earning of excess profits. Stock splits cannot be used as a trading device to earn excess profits, not because they have no informational content, but because the investment community at large quickly and accurately incorporates the economic implications of a split into the market price. If the investment community began ignoring the economic behavior of the firm, we would

[16] Michael C. Jensen, "The Performance of Mutual Funds in the Period 1945–64," *Journal of Finance*, May 1968, pp. 389–416.

revert to an inefficient market since the investor could once again earn excess profits from an economic analysis of the firm. If we throw out security analysis and portfolio analysis, we also throw out the efficient market.

Empirical evidence suggesting that capital markets are inefficient would suggest that legislation be designed to make them efficient. In a competitive economy, we expect the profits of a given firm or industry to be just sufficient to compensate for risk. Any excess profits suggest that there are noncompetitive elements at work and that the particular market is not operating to maximize the social welfare. The finding that differences in rates of return can be explained on the basis of risk suggests that the stock market is a competitive market where no single element has any particular advantage. The existence of mutual funds that earn excess profits would suggest legislation to "break up" the monopoly, just as excess profits in any other industry would suggest the need for antitrust legislation.

None of this of course implies that the average individual investor cannot earn a return that exceeds the average return, only that if one is not willing to accept higher risk, one cannot normally expect higher returns. This is precisely why so much of security analysis and portfolio management is concerned with risk. From the individual investor's viewpoint, securities can be undervalued and overvalued even if undervaluation and overvaluation do not exist in the market on any systematic basis. An investor may be quite unwilling to purchase a security with a given risk and expected return since the return is not considered sufficient to compensate for the risk. Another investor may consider the return quite adequate and conclude that the security is undervalued.

As a final note, it seems fair to conclude that technical analysis that attempts to predict future price changes strictly on the basis of past price changes is bound to fail. Price patterns are probably random occurrences as determined from the studies on the weak form of the efficient market hypothesis. Technical analysis will not produce excess profits. Of course it will not produce excess losses either. In this context, charting and other forms of technical analysis are harmless unless the costs are significant. The weak-form empirical results suggest that technical analysis is nothing more than a disguised form of random selection. Random selection will produce average returns but no more and no less. Naturally, chartists do not accept these conclusions.

QUESTIONS

1. What is the fundamental purpose of technical analysis?
2. Why would technical analysts be tempted to use more than one technical indicator?
3. Technical analysis relies heavily upon the concepts of support and resistance levels.

   a) Why does the technical analyst consider these levels to be so important?
   b) Can you offer a rationale for using support or resistance levels on the basis of investor psychology?
4. What is the fundamental difficulty in using the Dow Theory as a technical indicator?
5. What is the rationale for using price patterns as a technical indicator?
6. *Barron's* Confidence Index ranged from about .91 to about .96 during 1974. If the Confidence Index should decline to .87, what would this signal to the investor? Why?
7. In his studies dealing with odd-lot trading behavior, Stanley Kaish found that moderate fluctuations in the market cause no problem for odd-lot investors, but large and consistent moves in either direction usually result in unprofitable trading. Why do you believe that this is the case?
8. In Chapter 1, we examined the increasing affluence of the U.S. economy. As investors' income increases over the years, what impact might one expect this to have on the forecasting ability of the odd-lot index?
9. What is an efficient market? What conditions need to be present for an efficient market to exist?
10. What are the three categories of efficiency?
11. Is the efficient market theory inconsistent with either the use of the techniques of security analysis or the use of portfolio theory?
12. What sort of challenge does the concept of an efficient market (especially the random walk hypothesis) raise for technical analysts?
13. What is the function of a filter test in the empirical testing of the weak-form efficient market theory?
14. Why would one expect prices of securities to adjust rapidly to the information content of new information entering the market?

SUGGESTED READINGS

Bishop, George W. Jr. *Charles H. Dow and the Dow Theory.* New York: Appleton Century Crofts, 1960.

Black, Fischer. "Implications of the Random Walk Hypothesis for Portfolio Management." *Financial Analysts Journal,* March–April 1971, pp. 16–22.

Brealey, Richard A. *Security Prices in a Competitive Market.* Cambridge, Mass.: MIT Press, 1971, chapters 7–13.

Drzycimski, Eugene F. and Dennis R. Fredrickson. "A Relative-to-Market Test of the Random-Walk Theory." *Mississippi Valley Journal of Business and Economics,* Fall 1970, pp. 33–47.

Fama, Eugene F. "Efficient Capital Markets: A Review of Theory and Empirical Work." *Journal of Finance,* May 1970, pp. 383–17.

——. "Random Walks in Stock Market Prices." *Financial Analysts Journal*, September-October 1965, pp. 55–59.

—— and Arthur B. Laffer. "Information and Capital Markets." *Journal of Business*, July 1971, pp. 289–98.

Fanning, James E. "A Four-Indicator System for Forecasting the Market." *Financial Analysts Journal*, September-October 1971, pp. 49–56.

Gup, Benton E. "A Note on Stock Market Indicators and Stock Prices." *Journal of Financial and Quantitative Analysis*, September 1973, pp. 673–82.

Kaish, Stanley. "Odd Lot Profit and Loss Performance." *Financial Analysts Journal*, September-October 1969, pp. 83–89.

——. "Odd Lotter Trading of High and Low Quality Stocks." *Financial Analysts Journal*, March-April 1969, pp. 88–91.

Kewley, Thomas J. and Richard A. Stevenson. "The Odd-Lot Theory for Individual Stocks: A Reply." *Financial Analysts Journal*, January-February 1969, pp. 99–104.

Lerro, Anthony J. and Charles B. Swayne, Jr. *Selection of Securities: Technical Analysis of Stock Market Prices*, 2nd ed. Morristown, N.J.: General Learning Press, 1974.

Levy, Robert A. "Conceptual Foundations of Technical Analysis." *Financial Analysts Journal*, July-August 1966, pp. 83–89.

——. "Relative Strength as a Criterion for Investment Selection." *Journal of Finance*, December 1967, pp. 595–610.

Malkiel, Burton G. *A Random Walk Down Wall Street*. New York: W. W. Norton & Co., Inc., 1973, chapters 5–6.

Pinches, George E. "The Random Walk Hypothesis and Technical Analysis." *Financial Analysts Journal*, March-April 1970, pp. 104–10.

Seligman, Daniel. "Playing the Market with Charts." *Fortune*, February 1962, pp. 118–19ff.

——. "The Mystique of Point-and-Figure." *Fortune*, March 1962, pp. 113–15ff.

Smidt, Seymour. "A New Look at the Random Walk Hypothesis." *Journal of Financial and Quantitative Analysis*, September 1968, pp. 235–61.

Van Horne, James C. and George G. C. Parker. "Technical Trading Rules: A Comment." *Financial Analysts Journal*, July-August 1968, pp. 128–32.

Vasicek, Oldrich and John A. McQuown. "The Efficient Market Model." *Financial Analysts Journal*, September-October 1972, pp. 71–84.

16

Preferred Stock

"The preferred-stock *form* is fundamentally unsatisfactory."[1] Why did the fourth edition of *Security Analysis* by Graham, Dodd, and Cottle make such a bold and uncompromising statement? It is primarily because preferred stock is a hybrid security with certain undesirable features. However, this does not imply that investment in preferred stocks should be avoided at all times by the average investor.

HYBRID NATURE OF PREFERRED STOCK

Preferred stock is a hybrid security since it combines elements of both the common stock (equity) and bond forms of investment. This form of security gets its name because of its preference both with regard to

[1]Benjamin Graham, David Dodd, and Sidney Cottle, *Security Analysis*, 4th ed. (New York: McGraw-Hill, 1962), p. 375.

dividends and to the distribution of assets upon liquidation of the corporation. The preferred shareholder receives dividends prior to any payment to the common shareholders. The preferred shareholder also receives payments upon liquidation of the firm before payments are made to common shareowners.

Legally, preferred stockholders are considered owners of the firm since no debtor-creditor relationship exists as occurs between the firm and the bondholders. Preferred dividends are declared by the Board of Directors in the same fashion as cash dividends on common stock. While legally an owner, the preferred stockholder does not share the "normal" benefits of the common stockholder. The preferred stockholder does not share directly in the growth and prosperity of the firm, as the common shareholder can. There is no opportunity to receive a growing stream of dividend income, which may occur with common stock ownership.

Since the preferred stockholder receives a fixed dividend payment, the holder's position is much like that of the bondholder. The bondholder receives a fixed contractual amount of interest, while the preferred stockholder looks forward to a noncontractual fixed amount of preferred dividends. The preferred dividend is stated either as a percentage of the par value or as a dollar amount. If stated as a percentage of par, the dollar figure is arrived at by multiplying the par value by the stated percentage.

PREFERRED STOCK ISSUES

Just as preferred stock has its disadvantages for the investor, it has disadvantages for the firm. Since preferred dividends are legally payments to owners of the firm, these dividends come from earnings after taxes.[2] Bond interest, on the other hand, is a tax deductible expense. Therefore, bond interest is paid with before-tax dollars, while preferred dividends are paid with after-tax dollars. With a corporate income tax rate of about 50 percent, preferred stock financing becomes approximately twice as expensive as bond financing.

As might be expected, preferred stock issues have accounted for a relatively minor part of money raised as a result of new security issues in recent years. Figure 16–1 shows the cash raised by preferred stock issues as a percentage of total security issues since 1920. In recent years, preferred stock has accounted for only about 3 percent of cash raised with the exception of the last three years shown, 1971 to 1973. During

[2]A proposal has been put forth that would allow the dividends on preferred stock issued for cash after a certain date to be considered a tax deductible expense for the firm. See: "A Presidential Sweetner for Preferred Stock," *Business Week*, November 2, 1974, p. 73.

FIGURE 16-1
Preferred Stock Issued (Percentage of total securities issued)

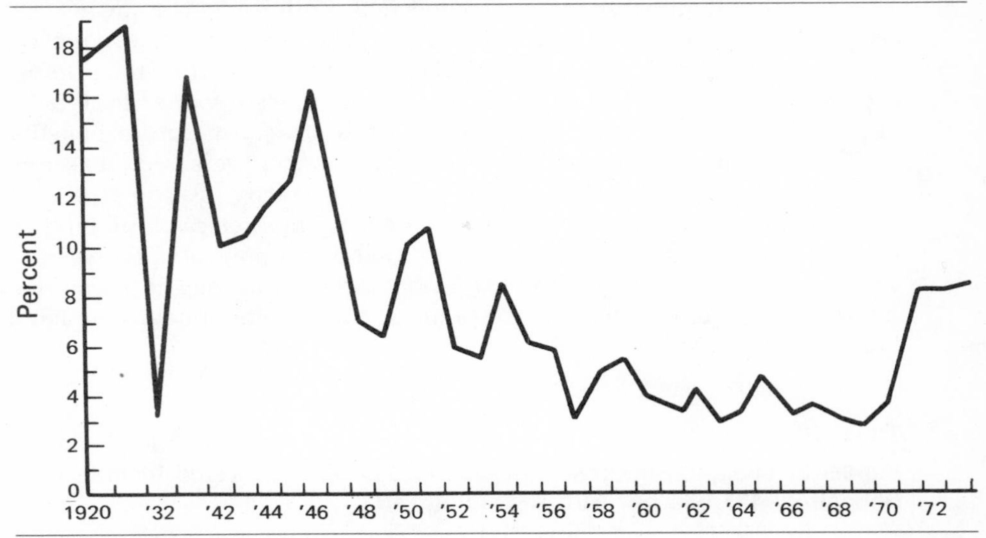

Sources: Gordon Donaldson, "In Defense of Preferred Stock," *Harvard Business Review*, July-August 1962, pp. 123-36, and U.S. Securities and Exchange Commission, *Statistical Bulletin*, several issues, 1962-74.

these three years, preferred stock accounted for approximately 8 percent of new corporate cash offerings.

During the decade from 1964 to 1973, utilities accounted for approximately 87 percent of all preferred stock issued by corporations for cash.[3] Despite the cost of preferred stock financing, utility firms have required such enormous quantities of capital that preferred stock has been issued in order to maintain a prudent balance between debt and equity in the capital structure.[4]

Not only have industrial firms refrained from issuing new shares of preferred stock, but there has also been a pronounced trend for these firms to retire outstanding issues of preferred stock.[5] The incentive for redemption emanates from the tax laws, which make preferred stock a relatively expensive component of the capital structure of the firm.

[3]Calculated from data contained in *SEC Statistical Bulletin*.

[4]The logic of this position is argued in Gordon Donaldson, "In Defense of Preferred Stock," *Harvard Business Review*, July-August 1962, pp. 126-36 and Ward S. Curran, "Preferred Stock in Public Utility Finance—a Reconsideration," *Financial Analysts Journal*, March-April 1972, pp. 71-76.

[5]For an example of this trend see Richard Stevenson, "Retirement of Non-Callable Preferred Stock," *Journal of Finance*, December 1970, pp. 1143-52.

INTEREST RATE RISK: BONDS VERSUS PREFERRED STOCK

The fixed dividend payment associated with preferred stock means preferreds are subject to interest rate risk. The present value concepts discussed in Chapter 6 suggest that the longer the period of time before receipt of the principal repayment, the less its present value. Preferreds are similar to bonds since they have a fixed stream of future benefits. Unlike most bonds, they have no maturity. Hence, preferred stocks are similar to *consols,* which are bonds with no maturity.

Table 16-1 shows the impact of varying market rates of interest on a fixed income obligation having a stated or coupon rate of 8 percent. The maturity of the obligation is of no consequence as long as the market interest rate is at 8 percent—corresponding to the stated rate on the fixed income obligation.

Table 16-1

Impact of Changing Interest Rate on Various Maturity Fixed Income Obligations ($1,000 par with 8% stated rate)

Maturity	Present Value (Price with Market Level of Interest Rates		
	8%	10%	6%
1 year	$1,000	$981.40	$1,019.10
5 years	1,000	922.80	1,085.30
10 years	1,000	875.40	1,148.80
20 years	1,000	828.40	1,231.10
30 years	1,000	810,70	1,276.80
40 years	1,000	804.00	1,302.00
50 years	1,000	801.50	1,316.00
No maturity (preferred stock or consol)	1,000	800.00	1,333.33

Source: Reproduced from Expanded Bond Values Tables, Publication No. 83, p. 355, copyright © 1970, Financial Publishing Company, Boston, 1970.

If the market interest rate moves upward to 10 percent, the stream of expected future benefits must be discounted at the 10 percent rate. The future benefits in this example are the $80 yearly income plus the principal repayment. As the maturity lengthens, the present value (price) of the security declines. For a security with no maturity, the price would be only the present value of the dividend income or $800 as shown in Table 16-1.

It is possible to compute the $800 preferred stock price in the above illustration by using the following equation:

$$\text{Preferred stock price} = \frac{\text{annual preferred dividend in dollars}}{\text{market rate of interest}}$$

$$= \frac{\$80}{.10} = \$800$$

A decline in the market interest rate to 6 percent produces an increase in the present value of the security. The longer the maturity, the greater the increase in the present value of the obligation. For a preferred stock, the price would increase to $1,333.33. This would be the result of dividing $80 by .06 in the equation above.

Of what practical value is all this to the investor? If an investor has strong expectations regarding a pronounced decline in interest rates, Table 16-1 shows that the investor should seek a fixed income obligation *with the longest possible maturity.* In this manner, interest rate risk will work to the maximum benefit of the investor. Since preferred stocks do not have a maturity date, they become a suitable investment for realizing capital gains during interest rate declines.[6]

CALL PROVISIONS

Table 16-1 shows a fixed income security with no maturity increasing to $1,333.33 (or 133.33 percent of whatever the par value is for the security), when the market interest rate falls to 6 percent. This price increase may not occur because of the existence of a call feature associated with most fixed income obligations. For example, if a preferred stock is callable for redemption by the issuing firm at 108 percent of par, this effectively limits the upward price appreciation potential of the preferred stock to approximately $1,080 for the Table 16-1 illustration.

A call provision works only to the advantage of the firm and not the investor. The firm will tend to call the preferred for redemption when it can refinance the preferred at a lower interest rate. This means that the investor must take the money received as a result of the call and reinvest at the lower rate of return prevailing in the market. Clearly, the terms of a call provision are of concern to the investor. The standard references sources such as the *Moody's Manuals* may be consulted to ascertain the call feature attached to any preferred stock.

An investor anticipating a decline in interest rates would not be likely to purchase the preferred stock used as the example in Table 16-1. A preferred stock with a coupon rate of 8 percent would likely be called long before it reached its maximum theoretical possible price (133.33 percent of par in Table 16-1). However, an investor could buy a preferred

[6]As can be noted in Table 16-1, bonds with thirty or more years to maturity are also good securities with which to speculate on interest rate movements.

with a 5 percent coupon rate instead of the 8 percent coupon rate with the following result:

Market interest rate = 8 percent:

$$\text{Purchase price (\$100 par 5\% preferred)} = \frac{\$5}{.08} = \$62.50$$

Market interest rate falls to 5 percent:

$$\text{Price of preferred stock} = \frac{\$5}{.05} = \$100$$

In this example, the investor buys a preferred stock which is selling at a discount. Any call price, such as 105 percent of par ($105), would be of little practical concern. The investor gets the full benefit of the decline in interest rates without bumping into the call price and running the risk of having the preferred stock called by the firm.

In summary, preferred stocks selling at less than par may be excellent investments during a period of interest rate decline. The capital appreciation of a discounted preferred stock may be greater than for preferreds selling near their call price. Naturally, one needs to determine the commission costs of purchasing preferred stock rather than bonds. Preferreds are subject to the same commissions as common stocks. In Chapter 3, we noted that commissions on bond transactions are often less than on stock transactions. Despite the greater interest rate risk and return potential of preferred stocks, the investor might purchase bonds because of commission considerations.

ANALYSIS OF PREFERRED STOCK

The preferred stock investor should become familiar with certain features associated with preferred stocks. These features concern the manner in which dividends are paid and a special tax provision which influences greatly the market for preferred stock. This section also briefly discusses the manner in which preferred stock may be evaluated. Last, preferred stock yields are compared with yields on bonds of comparable quality. This is an especially important consideration for the individual investor because of certain tax laws.

Dividend Payment Methods

Preferred stocks have dividend provisions which are either cumulative or noncumulative. Most preferred stocks have the *cumulative provision,* which means that any dividend not paid by the company accumulates. Normally, the firm must pay these unpaid dividends prior to the payment of dividends on the common stock. These unpaid dividends are known as *dividends in arrears* or *arrearages.*

Noncumulative dividends do not accumulate if they are not paid when due. Under the noncumulative provision, unpaid dividends are lost forever. Hence, an investor contemplating the purchase of a preferred stock with a noncumulative dividend provision needs to be especially diligent in the investigation of the firm because of the investor's potentially weak position with regard to dividends. Actually, the holder of a preferred stock with a cumulative dividend provision is not in a much stronger position, as we shall see shortly.

Tax Considerations

A provision exists in the tax laws allowing a corporation to exempt from taxation 85 percent of all dividends received as a result of holding the stock of another corporation. The intent of this law is to reduce the burden of triple taxation. If Company A earns a profit, that firm pays a tax. If Company B owns some of Company A's stock and receives a dividend, Company B would have to pay a tax on the entire amount of the dividend in the absence of special tax legislation. Triple taxation would occur when Company B's stockholders received dividends on their stock and were required to include the dividends in their taxable income.

Although this provision applies to dividends paid on both common and preferred stock held by a corporation, it is especially important for preferred stocks. Since preferred stocks have a fixed dividend payment, they tend to compete with bonds for the fixed income investment dollars of a portfolio. This tax provision has produced a market for preferred stocks which favors the institution as opposed to the individual. This can be seen from the following example of an 8 percent preferred and an 8 percent bond held by a corporation and by an individual. We are interested in the after-tax yield from either security.

	Corporation Holding		*Individual Holding*
	Bond	*Preferred*	*Bond or Preferred*
A. Pre-tax yield	8.0%	8.0%	8.0%
B. Non-taxable portion of yield	.0	6.8	.0*
C. Taxable portion of yield (A–B)	8.0	1.2	8.0
D. Tax—50% corporate** Tax—25% individual**	4.0	.6	2.0
E. After-tax yield (A–D)	4.0%	7.4%	6.0%

*Ignores any possible benefit from the $100 dividend exclusion discussed in Chapter 5.
**Assumed marginal tax rates.

Three conclusions may be drawn from this example. First, the tax benefits for a corporation from owning a preferred stock rather than a bond can be substantial, as indicated by the difference of 3.4 percentage points in after-tax yield. At any positive marginal corporate tax rate, benefits would still exist. To be sure, the higher the marginal rate the larger the benefits. Second, because of the high after-tax yield, insurance companies and other financial institutions tend to be large purchasers of preferred stock. These institutions may be willing to accept a lower before-tax yield than they would accept for a bond of comparable quality. This results in a situation in which the yields on the preferred stock of a company may be either equal to or less than the yield on a bond *of the same company*. For example, in early March 1974, Philadelphia Electric had the following securities outstanding.

Issue	*Price*	*Current Yield**
8.25% bond, due 1996	99⅞	8.26%
8.75% preferred	105	8.33
4.68% preferred	58½	8.00
4.40% preferred	54¾	8.04
4.30% preferred	52	8.27

*Dollar interest or preferred dividend divided by the price.

When risk premiums were discussed in Chapter 6, we indicated that securities with more financial risk should sell at higher yields. On this basis, one would not anticipate having a preferred stock of a company selling for a lower yield than the firm's bonds.

A third conclusion to be drawn from the example is that with the possible exception of a minor benefit from the $100 dividend exclusion, an individual investor would be indifferent between the 8 percent bond and preferred because of the identical after-tax yields. However, if financial institutions seek preferred stock and drive the before-tax yields down, the individual would choose the bond since it would have a greater rate of return. If the bond and preferred were issued by the same company, the bond would normally represent a more secure investment. Hence, preferred stocks are not normally an attractive investment for individuals because of yield considerations.

Quality Assessment

In many respects, the analysis of the quality of a preferred stock is very similar to the analysis of a bond. A potential investor in preferred stock needs to examine the terms of the preferred stock for the same general features to be discussed in detail in the next chapter. These include such features as the call price, the size of the issue, the nature of any sinking funds designed to retire the issue, and quality ratings.

Just as coverage ratios are of great importance in the determination of bond quality, as we shall see in the next chapter, the same is also true for preferred stocks. Bond quality gets expressed in a bond quality rating issued by either Moody's or Standard & Poor's. Likewise, preferred stock gets quality ratings upon which investors rely. Table 16–2 shows selected statistics for different quality preferred stocks, including Standard & Poor's preferred stock quality ratings.

TABLE 16–2
Selected Preferred Stocks

S&P Rating	Issue	Call Price	Par Value	No. of Shares Outstanding (000)	4/9/75 Price	Yield
AAA	duPont pfd B $4.50 cum	120	None	1,689	59½	7.56%
AAA	General Motors pfd A $3.75 cum	100	None	1,000	49⅛	7.63
AA	ATT pfd A $3.64 cum	53.54*	$1	10,000	42¼	8.62
A	Commonwealth Edison pfd C $1.90 cum	27½*	None	4,250	20	9.50
A	Southern Railway 5% non cum	10	10	5,856	5⅞	8.51
BBB	Duke Power pfd G $8.20 cum	110*	100	600	78½	10.45
BBB	Philadelphia Elec. pfd K 9.50% cum	109½*	100	750	81	11.73
BB	Burlington Northern 5½% cum	10½*	10	3,082	7	7.86
BB	Consolidated Edison pfd A $5 cum	105	None	1,915	40	12.50

*Call price changes over time.
Source: Standard and Poor's Corporation, *Security Owner's Stock Guide*, March 1975.

PREFERRED WITH ARREARAGES

Should an investor buy a preferred stock with dividends in arrears? What has been investor experience with stock of this nature? On an intuitive basis, it is not clear that investors should seek out preferred stocks with dividends in arrears. The inability to pay preferred dividends is a sign of financial distress. Additionally, preferred shareholders have a weak bargaining position compared to bondholders, since they cannot force the company into bankruptcy. Considering these factors, it would appear that preferreds with arrearages represent an attractive investment only under special circumstances. If the firm's financial condition is improving rapidly, the firm may want to eliminate preferred arrearages so it may make dividend payments on the common stock and improve its credit standing.

Even in an improving financial situation for the firm, the investor may not receive a payment equivalent to the full amount of the arrearage. In 1964, Michigan Sugar Company decided to recapitalize in order to eliminate arrearages of $7.25 a share on its 6 percent, $10 par value preferred stock. The arrearages dated back to 1926. Each share of preferred stock in arrears was exchanged for the following package of cash and securities:

	Estimated Value
$5 in cash	$ 5.00
$5 principal amount of a new $6 bond	4.37
1 share of new $4 par value 6% preferred stock	3.00
½ share common stock	2.38
	$14.75

The estimated value was determined by observing the price at which the various new securities traded shortly after they were issued. The preferred stockholder apparently did reasonably well in this situation. The new $4 par value preferred would yield 8 percent as the result of the 24¢ annual dividend and the $3 price. On the basis of an 8 percent yield, the old $10 par value stock was worth $7.50 ($.60 divided by .08). Adding the $7.25 in arrearages to the $7.50 imputed value results in exactly the estimated value received by the holders of the old preferred stock as a result of the recapitalization.

Table 16–3 shows selected statistics for Michigan Sugar from 1956 to 1963. The earnings per share on the common stock were positive with the exception of 1960. Regular dividends were paid on the preferred stock, although little progress was made on reducing the amount of the arrearage. While the timing of the offer to eliminate the arrearage was somewhat uncertain, the preferred stockholders apparently expected

TABLE 16–3

Michigan Sugar Company, Selected Statistics

Year	Earnings per Share—Common*	Dividend Paid per Share—Preferred	Price Range per Preferred Share
1956	$.34	$.60	8 –10½
1957	.30	.60	8¼–10⅝
1958	.15	.60	8½–15
1959	.70	.60	12⅜–15
1960	(.07)	.90	10⅞–13⅛
1961	.29	.60	10⅞–13
1962	.30	.60	9⅞–12
1963	.70	.60	11⅜–16⅞

*Disregarding preferred arrearages.
Source: *1964 Moody's Industrial Manual.*

recent profitable operations to result in clearing of the arrearages, although the price of the preferred appeared to be undervalued in 1961 and 1962.

Investor experience during the 1961 to 1974 period with preferred stocks having arrearages was more favorable than one might expect. An investor purchasing all ASE- or NYSE-listed preferred stocks with arrearages at the beginning of 1961 and holding them to the end of the year (or the resolution of the arrearage if it occurred first), and repeating the process each year, would have achieved the results shown in Table 16–4. This table also shows the returns from the S&P 500 Stock Index and Moody's Aaa Bond Index calculated on the same basis as the preferred returns. All returns include dividends or interest as well as capital gains or losses.

The mean annual arithmetic return of 8.1 percent compares favorably with the 5.9 percent from common stocks and the 3.1 percent from bonds. This is especially true considering the standard deviation of returns from preferreds in arrears is only slightly higher than that of the S&P 500. Preferreds in arrears not only produced higher returns than common stocks, but also did not appear to be significantly more risky. This conclusion takes on added significance since the correlation coefficient between the annual returns from common stocks and from preferreds in arrears for the 1961 to 1974 period was .41. We noted in Chapter 12 that a low correlation coefficient is desirable for risk reduction in a portfolio context. Not only did preferred stocks with arrearages produce a higher return than common stocks, but they also would have reduced the risk of a portfolio of common stocks if included in that portfolio. The most pronounced example of this occurred in 1974, when the S&P 500 declined 24.8 percent, but a portfolio of preferreds with arrearages produced a positive return of 29.8 percent.

TABLE 16–4

Returns from Preferreds with Arrearages, S & P 500, and Moody's Aaa Bonds, 1961 to 1974

	S&P 500	Aaa Bonds	Preferreds in Arrears
Mean arithmetic annual return	5.9%	3.1%	8.1%
Standard deviation	16.8	4.7	22.5
Maximum annual return	29.3	12.2	41.1
Minimum annual return	–24.8	–3.5	–21.3

Correlation coefficients
S&P 500 to preferreds = .41
Aaa bonds to preferreds = –.27

Source: Richard A. Stevenson, "Returns from Preferreds with Arrearages," unpublished manuscript.

SUMMARY

It is no secret that most investors generally are not "turned on" by preferred stock. But we observed that preferred stocks are attractive investments for corporate holders because of the tax provision which makes 85 percent of dividends tax exempt for the corporate holder. In some instances, this has the effect of reducing before-tax yields on preferreds below the level existing for bonds of comparable quality.

For the individual investor, preferred stocks have several disadvantages, which tend to reinforce the investor's dislike of preferred stock. The yield is normally equal to or less than what can be obtained on comparable quality bonds. The purchaser of a preferred also owns a hybrid security that is part common stock and part bond, but which lacks the principal advantages of each form.

Despite the generally undesirable nature of preferred stocks for investment by individuals, one should not conclude that the individual investor should own no preferred stock. Preferred stocks are sensitive to interest rate fluctuations since they lack a maturity date. Therefore, an investor expecting a pronounced decline in interest rates might seek a high-quality preferred stock to attempt to maximize interest rate risk and achieve capital gains. We also saw that the rate of return during the 1961 to 1974 period from a portfolio of preferred stocks having arrearages was superior to that available from common stocks. The investor could even reduce the risk of a common stock portfolio, since the correlation coefficient between the returns from these two portfolios was low.

QUESTIONS

1. Why is preferred stock referred to as a hybrid security? Of what significance is this to the investor?
2. Some preferred stocks have par values and some do not. Does this matter to the investor?
3. Many writers have pointed out the declining importance of preferred stock in the financing of corporations. Why has preferred stock declined in importance in the financing plans of most corporations? Why do you suppose public utilities only recently started issuing substantial quantities of preferred stock in marked contrast to general trends relative to preferred stock?
4. It might be said that there is a time and purpose for virtually every form of investment security in an investor's portfolio. Under what circumstances would an investor desire to hold preferred stock? What qualities would the investor desire to have associated with the preferred stock in the portfolio?

5. In early 1974, Virginia Electric had the three preferreds shown below traded on the NYSE.

Coupon	*Price*	*Current Yield*
8.84%	100¾	8.77%
7.72	89	8.67
5.00	60	8.33

What factors can you think of that might explain the differences noted in the current yields?

6. Distinguish among the different types of dividend provisions associated with preferred stock and their importance to the investor.
7. Discuss the general significance of tax considerations that are important in the analysis of preferred stocks.

PROBLEMS

1. A $50 par value preferred stock is paying an annual dividend of $2.75 and is selling in the market at $35 per share. If the market rate of return desired on this quality preferred stock falls to 6.5 percent, what will happen to the price of the preferred stock? What will happen if the market demands an interest rate of 9 percent?
2. In mid-August 1974, AT&T's $4 preferred stock was selling for $49.50 per share. Calculate the after-tax yield for an individual in the 30 percent marginal tax bracket and for a corporation in the 48 percent corporate marginal tax bracket.

SUGGESTED READINGS

Bildersee, John S. "Some Aspects of the Performance of Non-Convertible Preferred Stocks." *Journal of Finance,* December 1973, pp. 1187–1201.

Donaldson, Gordon. "In Defense of Preferred Stock." *Harvard Business Review,* July–August 1962, pp. 123–36.

Fischer, Donald E. and Glenn A. Wilt, Jr. "Non-Convertible Preferred as a Financing Instrument, 1950–1965." *Journal of Finance,* September 1968, pp. 611–24.

Kreidle, John R. and Walter W. Perlick. "The Current Status of Participating Stocks." *Mississippi Valley Journal of Business and Economics,* Fall 1968, pp. 83–89.

Pinches, George E. "Financing with Convertible Preferred Stock, 1960–1967." *Journal of Finance,* March 1970, pp. 53–63.

Stevenson, Richard A. "Retirement of Non-Callable Preferred Stock." *Journal of Finance,* December 1970, pp. 1143–52.

*

17

Corporate Bonds

In 1970, Sidney Homer wrote: "[The] choice between buying or avoiding long-term bonds is, no doubt, the single most important investment decision facing the portfolio manager today."[1] This decision is still important in the present environment with its relatively high interest rates on good quality bonds. Bonds may very well have a place in an investor's portfolio.

This chapter concentrates on the principles of investing in corporate bonds. The next chapter discusses fixed income securities convertible into common stock. Chapter 19 examines investments in bonds of governmental issuers. The basic principles of bond investing are applicable to all these types of securities.

What is a bond? The term *bond* is normally used to refer to a long-term promissory note given under seal by a debtor. The holder

[1]Sidney Homer, *Bond Investment in the 1970's* (New York: Salomon Brothers, November 1970), pp. 8–9.

of that note becomes a lender or creditor of the issuer. There are normally many lenders in a given bond issue. A bond issued by a private firm is called a corporate bond. The firm promises to repay the principal at some specified future date and to pay interest to compensate the lender for the use of the funds during the life of the bond. For example, in 1957 AT&T created a debt obligation of $250 million. The issue itself contained 250,000 separate $1,000 bonds that were sold to many different investors. Often, all the separate bonds are sold to a single investor in what is known as a *private placement*. We will concentrate on the public offering, where the mass borrowing is divided into units which are sold to many investors.

BOND TERMINOLOGY

Indenture

The AT&T issue is a typical corporate bond in that the entire obligation is created under what is known as an indenture, the legal document spelling out the obligations and terms of the borrowing. It is the contract between the corporation and its creditors. The indenture stipulates the total amount of the borrowing, the number of bonds to be issued, the date of interest payments, and other crucial features of the contract.

Denomination

Corporate bonds are normally issued in units of $1,000. The $1,000 is the face value or par value of the bond and is the amount to be received when the principal is repaid. However, we should note that bond quotations in the financial press are listed in $100 units. The *Wall Street Journal* of October 14, 1974, shows the last sale of the AT&T bond at 69½. This means that an investor wishing to purchase one of these bonds might pay $695. The quoted price should be multiplied by ten to arrive at the actual price.

Interest Payments

The indenture stipulates the interest payments to be made at the *coupon rate*. The coupon rate states the amount of money the bondholder will receive each year. The AT&T issue has a coupon rate of 4⅜ percent, meaning that the bondholder will receive $4.375 per year per $100 of face value or $43.75 per year for a $1,000 bond. The typical corporate bond pays interest semiannually, with the timing of the semiannual payment stated in the indenture. The usual arrangement is for the first payment to be made six months after the date of original issue and every six months thereafter. Thus, for a bond issued in February, the coupon payments will be made in August and February.

The method of interest payment depends upon how the indenture stipulates legal ownership. There are two basic forms evidencing ownership—*bearer bonds* and *registered bonds.* In a bearer bond, no record of ownership exists. The bond certificate, as shown in Exhibit 17-1, does not show an owner's name and possession of the bond amounts to proof of ownership. The investor collects interest by simply removing the appropriate coupon from the bond certificate and redeeming it. In practice, interest coupons are redeemed through a bank in much the same way checks are cashed. The principal is collected in the same fashion.

Registered bonds are similar to stock certificates. The owner's name is recorded and a check for each interest payment is sent directly to the owner. Occasionally bonds are registered as to principal and the investor clips interest coupons as with bearer bonds. Principal repayment is by check. With revised government regulations and theft problems, most bonds issued today are registered, but many bearer bonds exist in the market and will be around for years to come.

Maturity

The principal repayment date, stated in the indenture, refers to the date when all of the bonds are to be retired and is usually called the maturity date. However, a maturity date of April 1, 1985, such as for the AT&T bond we have been examining, does not necessarily mean the corporation will retire all the bonds on April 1, 1985. It simply means all the bonds must be paid off by then using one of several principal repayment techniques to be discussed shortly.

Trustee

In practice, interest and principal payments are not made directly by the issuing corporation but by an intermediary called a trustee. The trustee is usually a commercial bank and is responsible for enforcement of the bond indenture. In addition, the trustee acts as an intermediary for purposes of payment of principal and interest. If the corporation fails to live up to any part of the indenture, it is the responsibility of the trustee to take whatever action is necessary on behalf of the bondholders. With bond ownership so widespread, any violation of the indenture would be difficult to enforce without a trustee.

EXHIBIT 17-1
Bearer Bond Certificate

BOND PRICES AND YIELDS

We now have enough information to identify a particular bond as reported in the financial press. Exhibit 17-2 shows selected bond quotations from the NYSE as reported in the financial press for October 11, 1974. The first item is the name of the issuing corporation followed immediately by the coupon rate and bond maturity. The AT&T bonds show a coupon rate of 4⅜ percent and a maturity of 1985, shown as 85. The Atlantic Richfield Company has an issue with a coupon of 7 percent that matures in 1976. That issue is listed as follows: AtlRich 7s76.

EXHIBIT 17-2

Selected Bond Trading as Reported in the Financial Press for October 11, 1974

Bonds		Cur Yld	Vol	High	Low	Close	Net Chg
ATT	4⅜s 85	6.2	29	69½	69	69½	+ 2⅜
ATT	2⅝s 86	4.6	18	56½	56	56⅜	+ ⅜
Atchsn	4s 95	8.1	9	49⅛	49⅛	49⅛	+ 1
AtlRich	7s 76	7.2	24	96¾	95⅝	96¾	+ 1⅝
BalGE	10s 82	9.8	47	102	102	102	. . .
ElPaso	6s 93	cv	12	63	62½	63	+ ½
vjEriR	5s 20f	. . .	1	4	4	4	+ ½
vjEri	3⅛s 90f	. . .	5	8⅛	8⅛	8⅛	− ½

Current Yield

Following the identification of the bond in Exhibit 17-2 is the current yield, which is defined as follows:

$$\text{Current yield} = \frac{\text{annual coupon rate}}{\text{closing price of bond}}$$

For the AT&T 4⅜ percent issue of 1985, the current yield is shown in Exhibit 17-2 as 6.2 percent (4.375 divided by 69.5). The current yield would be the investor's return if the bond were purchased for $695 and later resold for $695 and if all coupon payments were made on time during the investment's holding period. For the AT&T bond, the current yield may represent a poor measure of the rate of return expected from holding this bond since the current yield ignores any potential capital gain or loss. An investor holding this bond to maturity would receive a capital gain of $305. While the financial press routinely reports current yields, the investor should exercise caution in using these yield figures because of the potential for capital gains or losses.

Following the current yield is the number of bonds traded that day. Twenty-nine of the AT&T 4⅜ percent bonds traded on October 11, 1974. The next set of figures indicate the highest price, the lowest price, and the closing or last transacted price of the trading day, respectively. The final figure is the difference between the current closing price and the closing price of the previous day on which a trade occurred. Thus, the net change for the AT&T bond was +2⅜ or an increase of $23.75 per bond.

Price plus Accrued Interest

The typical corporate bond trades on the basis of *price plus accrued interest*. The AT&T 4⅜ percent bond makes interest payments on April 1 and October 1. Since interest payments are made only every six months, purchase of the AT&T bond for $695 on October 15 would deprive the seller of one-half month's interest to which the seller is entitled. A coupon of 4⅜ means an annual payment of $43.75 and an equivalent monthly payment of approximately $3.65. Thus, buying the bond at $695 on October 15 requires paying an additional $1.83 for accrued interest. The total cost would be $696.83 plus commission. The investor will recover the $1.83 on April 1 when he or she receives interest for the entire six-month period.

Accrued interest calculations can become rather complex. The basic rule is that any full month is counted as thirty days and any partial month is calculated as the exact number of days. There are occasions when bonds are traded "flat," which means that trading is conducted without regard to accrued interest. Corporate bonds are traded "flat" when the receipt of the scheduled interest payment is in doubt because of such events as bankruptcy. Bonds traded "flat" are noted with an "f" as can be seen for the Erie Railroad bonds in Exhibit 17–2.

Yield-to-Maturity and Bond Tables

An important concept for bond rates of return is the yield-to-maturity. Here we encounter "our old friend," present value. The yield-to-maturity for a given bond is the discount rate that equates the present value of the future cash flows (interest payments and principal repayment) with the current price of the bond. We frequently speak of a bond that is "selling to yield" a figure such as 9.2 percent. This means that if 9.2 percent is used as the discount rate, the present value of the cash flows will equal the current price.

The calculation of the yield-to-maturity is as difficult as any other present value problem. In practice, most bond investors use a book

EXHIBIT 17–3

A Portion of a Bond Table

YEARS and MONTHS — 4⅜%

Yield	8-3	8-6	8-9	9-0	9-3	9-6	9-9	10-0
2.00	117.98	118.48	118.98	119.47	119.96	120.46	120.94	121.43
2.20	116.32	116.78	117.22	117.67	118.11	118.55	118.99	119.43
2.40	114.70	115.10	115.50	115.90	116.29	116.69	117.08	117.47
2.60	113.10	113.46	113.81	114.16	114.51	114.86	115.20	115.54
2.80	111.53	111.84	112.14	112.45	112.75	113.06	113.35	113.65
3.00	109.98	110.25	110.51	110.77	111.03	111.29	111.55	111.80
3.20	108.46	108.68	108.90	109.13	109.34	109.56	109.77	109.99
3.40	106.96	107.15	107.32	107.51	107.68	107.86	108.03	108.21
3.60	105.48	105.63	105.77	105.91	106.05	106.19	106.32	106.46
3.80	104.03	104.14	104.24	104.35	104.44	104.55	104.64	104.75
4.00	102.61	102.68	102.74	102.81	102.87	102.94	103.00	103.07
4.20	101.20	101.24	101.26	101.30	101.32	101.36	101.38	101.42
4.40	99.82	99.82	99.81	99.82	99.81	99.81	99.80	99.80
4.60	98.46	98.43	98.39	98.36	98.31	98.28	98.24	98.21
4.80	97.13	97.06	96.99	96.92	96.85	96.79	96.72	96.66
5.00	95.81	95.71	95.61	95.51	95.41	95.32	95.22	95.13
5.10	95.16	95.05	94.93	94.82	94.70	94.59	94.48	94.38
5.20	94.52	94.39	94.25	94.13	94.00	93.88	93.75	93.63
5.30	93.88	93.74	93.58	93.45	93.30	93.17	93.02	92.89
5.40	93.24	93.09	92.92	92.77	92.61	92.46	92.30	92.16
5.50	92.61	92.44	92.26	92.10	91.92	91.76	91.59	91.43
5.60	91.99	91.80	91.61	91.43	91.24	91.07	90.88	90.72
5.70	91.37	91.17	90.96	90.77	90.57	90.38	90.19	90.01
5.80	90.75	90.54	90.32	90.12	89.90	89.70	89.49	89.30
5.90	90.14	89.92	89.68	89.47	89.24	89.03	88.81	88.60
6.00	89.54	89.30	89.05	88.83	88.58	88.36	88.13	87.91
6.10	88.94	88.69	88.43	88.19	87.93	87.70	87.45	87.23
6.20	88.34	88.08	87.81	87.56	87.29	87.04	86.79	86.55
6.30	87.75	87.48	87.19	86.93	86.65	86.39	86.13	85.88
6.40	87.17	86.88	86.58	86.31	86.02	85.75	85.47	85.21
6.50	86.59	86.29	85.98	85.69	85.39	85.11	84.82	84.55
6.60	86.01	85.70	85.38	85.08	84.77	84.48	84.18	83.90
6.70	85.44	85.12	84.78	84.47	84.15	83.85	83.54	83.25
6.80	84.87	84.54	84.19	83.87	83.54	83.23	82.91	82.61
6.90	84.31	83.96	83.61	83.28	82.94	82.62	82.28	81.98
7.00	83.75	83.40	83.03	82.69	82.33	82.01	81.66	81.35
7.10	83.19	82.83	82.45	82.10	81.74	81.40	81.05	80.72
7.20	82.64	82.27	81.88	81.52	81.15	80.80	80.44	80.11
7.30	82.10	81.71	81.32	80.95	80.56	80.21	79.84	79.49
7.40	81.56	81.16	80.76	80.38	79.98	79.62	79.24	78.89
7.50	81.02	80.62	80.20	79.81	79.41	79.04	78.65	78.29
7.60	80.49	80.08	79.65	79.25	78.84	78.46	78.06	77.69
7.70	79.96	79.54	79.10	78.69	78.28	77.88	77.48	77.10
7.80	79.44	79.00	78.56	78.14	77.72	77.32	76.90	76.52
7.90	78.92	78.47	78.02	77.60	77.16	76.75	76.33	75.94
8.00	78.40	77.95	77.49	77.06	76.61	76.19	75.77	75.37
8.10	77.89	77.43	76.96	76.52	76.06	75.64	75.21	74.80
8.20	77.38	76.91	76.43	75.98	75.52	75.09	74.65	74.24
8.30	76.88	76.40	75.91	75.46	74.99	74.55	74.10	73.68
8.40	76.38	75.89	75.40	74.93	74.46	74.01	73.55	73.13
8.50	75.88	75.39	74.88	74.41	73.93	73.48	73.01	72.58
8.60	75.39	74.89	74.38	73.90	73.41	72.95	72.48	72.04
8.70	74.90	74.39	73.87	73.39	72.89	72.42	71.95	71.50
8.80	74.41	73.90	73.37	72.88	72.38	71.90	71.42	70.97
8.90	73.93	73.41	72.88	72.38	71.87	71.39	70.90	70.44
9.00	73.46	72.93	72.39	71.88	71.36	70.88	70.38	69.92
9.20	72.51	71.97	71.41	70.90	70.37	69.87	69.36	68.89
9.40	71.58	71.03	70.46	69.93	69.39	68.88	68.36	67.88
9.60	70.67	70.10	69.52	68.98	68.42	67.91	67.38	66.88
9.80	69.77	69.19	68.60	68.04	67.48	66.95	66.41	65.91
10.00	68.88	68.29	67.69	67.12	66.55	66.01	65.46	64.95

Source: Reproduced from Expanded Bond Values Tables, Publication No. 83, p. 355, copyright © 1970, Financial Publishing Company, Boston, 1970, p. 355.

containing tables like the one presented in Exhibit 17–3. A book of bond tables contains prices for a large number of maturities, coupon interest rates, and yields-to-maturity. Exhibit 17–3 is a portion of a bond table for bonds having maturities ranging from 8 years, 3 months to 10 years, a coupon rate of 4⅜ percent, and yields-to-maturity from 2.00 to 10.00 percent. The AT&T bond has a coupon of 4⅜ percent, a maturity of approximately 9 years and 6 months as of October 11, 1974, and is selling for 69½. Using the bond table, we would read across the top row to the column labeled 9 years, 6 months and down to 69.5. The AT&T bond has a yield-to-maturity of 9.27 percent given the price of 69.5. If the bond price should fall the next day to 66, the bond table tells us that the new yield-to-maturity would be approximately 10 percent.

Basis Points

Within the context of the yield-to-maturity, the term *basis point* is often used. A basis point is one-hundredth of one percentage point. Thus, a bond selling to yield 8 percent would have a yield of 800 basis points. The term is used most often when considering changes in the yield-to-maturity. If yields increase from 8 to 8.25 percent, we note the change with the statement that the yield has increased 25 basis points.

Estimating the Bond Price

If we are interested in the price of a bond given a particular yield-to-maturity, the value can be obtained by using a bond table. If an investor expects market interest rates to fall immediately so that the 4⅜ percent AT&T bond maturing in 1985 should yield an investor 8 percent, the bond would sell for $761.90, according to the bond table in Exhibit 17–3. In this way, the investor can ascertain the price of a bond for any given maturity and coupon rate.

CORPORATE BOND RISK

The yield-to-maturity calculations assume that the investor will hold the bond to maturity and that all interest payments and principal will be paid by the issuing firm when due. The assumption is also made that *all interest received will be reinvested at the yield-to-maturity.* The assumptions may not hold and, if not, one's return will be different than expected. The possibility of return variability is, of course, the risk of corporate bond investment. Typically, bond investment is subject to three sources of risk: 1) purchasing power risk; 2) interest rate risk; and 3) credit risk. We have examined these risks within the context of common stocks. Although the basic concepts are applicable to corporate bonds, certain differences emerge that are vital to the bond investor.

Purchasing Power Risk

Purchasing power risk, as we have seen, involves the possibility that the proceeds of an investment will not purchase the goods and services expected because of a change in the general price level. We speak of a real rate of return, which is the rate of return after consideration of changes in the price level. The usual method of estimating the real rate of return is to take the difference between the actual monetary rate of return and the inflation rate. If a bond has a yield-to-maturity of 8 percent and we expect inflation to be 4 percent per year, the real rate of return would be 4 percent.

Unfortunately, an adjustment for the inflation rate is not the only problem associated with purchasing power risk. If you are not planning to hold a particular bond to maturity, changing rates of inflation can affect the market price of your bond quite drastically. Suppose you have purchased a twenty-year, 8 percent bond for $1,000 and at the time of your purchase, you and the market were expecting an inflation rate of 4 percent. You have purchased a bond with a monetary rate of 8 percent and a real rate of 4 percent provided inflation expectations are realized. If, a year later, you and the market conclude that the future inflation rate will no longer be 4 percent, but 6 percent, you will not be able to obtain $1,000 for the bond. For investors to obtain the same real rate of 4 percent, the monetary yield must be 10 percent. The bond now (one year later) has a nineteen-year maturity and must sell for a price of $831.30 in order for the yield-to-maturity to be 10 percent. This value was obtained from a bond table and is the present value of all the future returns from the bond discounted at 10 percent.

The price change potential resulting from interest rate changes is precisely why it is often said that a constant rate of inflation does not trouble the bond investor. As long as the rate of inflation is constant in the future, there is no inflation risk provided the monetary rate is high enough to compensate for the rate of inflation. What the bond investor is worried about is a *changing rate of inflation*. If a bond investor can predict a change in the inflation rate accurately and ahead of the market, the profit potential is quite large.

Interest Rate Risk

The price changes associated with inflation rate changes are closely related to interest rate risk and are frequently discussed within the same context. Interest rate risk is twofold. It includes the effect on price due to an interest rate change and the lost opportunity associated with purchasing a bond selling to yield 8 percent where market interest rates subsequently rise to 10 percent.

Maturity Effects. The general rule is that an increase in interest rates is associated with bond price declines and an interest rate decrease is associated with bond price increases. Bond prices and interest rates move in opposite directions. This general rule is important but we must be more specific. First, a given interest rate change will produce the greatest price change for bonds with long maturities. The longer the maturity, the greater will be the price change associated with a given interest rate change.

If we wished to maximize price changes, we would purchase long maturity bonds. We might well want to follow this investment strategy if we expect interest rates to fall. However, the price change due to a change in interest rates increases at a decreasing rate as the maturity increases. Figure 17-1 shows the prices of the bond originally examined in Table 16-1 for various maturities. An investor wishing to maximize price changes resulting from interest rate changes would select a bond with a long maturity. However, the investor need not go much beyond thirty years to obtain a reasonable approximation of the maximum price change, since the present value of cash flows to be received many years in the future is quite small.

FIGURE 17-1
Bond Prices for 8% Bond for Market Rates of 6%, 8% and 10% by Maturity

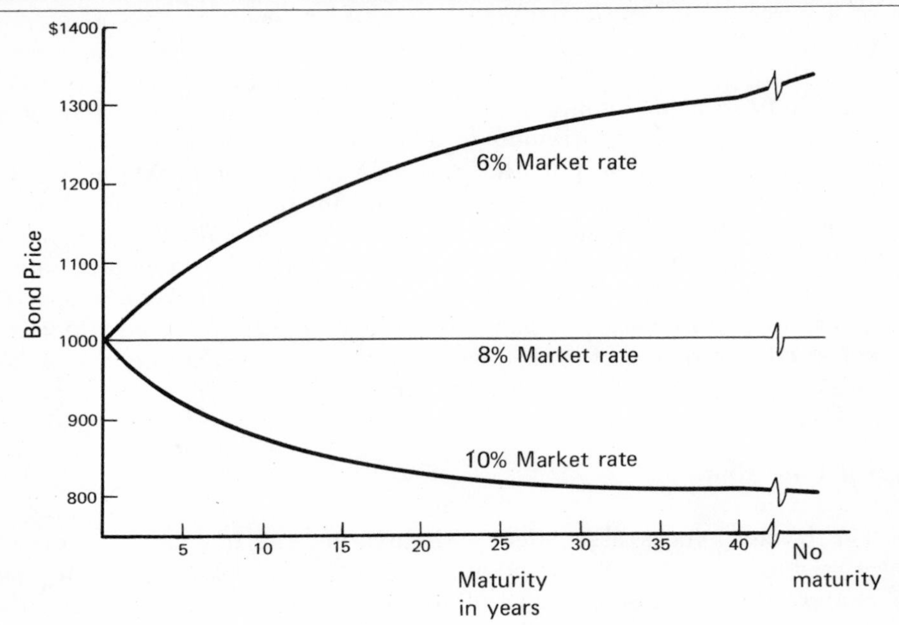

Symmetry of Interest Rate Risk. It is also a characteristic of bond prices that changes are nonsymmetrical. An increase in interest rates does not have the opposite impact on the bond price as the same decrease in interest rates. Bond prices will decline at a slower rate than they will increase for a given absolute interest rate change. Consider the 8 percent, twenty-year bond in Figure 17–1. If the market interest rate changes to 6 percent, the bond price will increase from $1,000 to $1,231.10 (a 23.11 percent increase). If the market interest rate changes to 10 percent, the bond will sell for $828.40 (a decline of 17.11 percent). While the exact percentage change cannot be generalized, for any given absolute interest rate change, the percentage bond price increase will be greater than the percentage price decline.

Coupon Effect. The coupon rate of any bond will also influence the price change that results from an interest rate change. The higher the coupon rate, the smaller will be the price change for a given change in the market interest rate. If both bond A and bond B have a twenty-year maturity, but A's coupon is 8 percent while B's is 4 percent, a decrease in the market rate of interest from 10 to 8 percent will produce the following results:

	Bond Price with Market Interest Rate of		
	10%	*8%*	*Capital Gain*
Bond A (8%)	$828.40	$1,000.00	20.71%
Bond B (4%)	485.20	604.10	24.51

The above result occurs because the 4 percent bond sells for a low price relative to the 8 percent bond. When the market interest rate declines, the lower priced bond increases by a greater percentage because of the smaller size of the initial base price. If one's objective is to maximize the percentage capital gain, bond B with its lower coupon rate should be purchased. Deep discount bonds will always perform this way if they are of good quality.

Credit Risk

Credit risk, the third element of corporate bond risk, is the chance that the corporation will default on the bond. Default is the failure to make one or more interest payments or to repay the principal when due. The least troublesome default occurs when the firm experiences temporary insolvency and one or more interest payments must be delayed. The worst situation is bankruptcy, since virtually all future interest payments and the principal repayment are in jeopardy.

Bond indentures typically contain an *acceleration clause* stipulating that if an interest payment is missed, the entire debt becomes due immediately. In practice, repayment of the principal is not possible. Hence, a defaulted bond normally continues to be traded while the firm, the courts, and the bondholders seek a settlement. Settlement of defaulted bonds frequently requires years and the final outcome is often quite unsatisfactory for the bondholder.

We should also recognize that the difference between the credit risk of a corporate bond and the risk of the common stock of the same company is often far less than assumed. A corporation issues long-term bonds with the intention of repaying the principal and making the interest payments from the earnings of the assets purchased with the proceeds of the bond issue. If the earnings of the firm materialize, the bondholder receives the principal and interest with no problem and the common stockholder should also do well and probably better than the bondholders. When firms do well, the owners should earn more than the creditors. When firms do poorly, both bondholders and stockholders tend to suffer. The great advantage of bonds relative to common stocks is that when a firm experiences *temporary difficulties,* its bonds may decline in price less than its common stock.

Bond Ratings

Determination of the credit risk of the bonds of any corporation is a complex task involving many of the analytical techniques used in the evaluation of common stocks. Because of the complexities, many bond investors rely on the credit evaluations of two prominent bond rating agencies, Moody's and Standard & Poor's. These rating agencies do not place an absolute value on the credit risk of corporate bonds but rank bonds from the highest credit risk to the lowest credit risk. The ranking takes the form of placing each bond evaluated into a risk category. The highest quality bonds are designated Aaa by Moody's and AAA by Standard and Poor's. These bonds are often referred to as triple A bonds. As the credit risk increases, both rating agencies assign lower ratings.

Moody's rates bonds as Aaa, Aa, A, Baa, Ba, and so on, down to C. Standard & Poor's rates bonds as AAA, AA, A, BBB, BB, and so on, down to C. Standard & Poor's rates defaulted bonds as low as D. The rating of defaulted bonds indicates the relative salvage value. Moody's does not rate defaulted bonds.

The bond ratings say nothing regarding purchasing power or interest rate risk. In general, bond investors will consider the first three categories (triple, double, and single A) to be the highest quality where the risk of default is low.[2] The medium quality bonds are those with the next two ratings, triple and double B. These bonds are for more aggressively managed bond portfolios, but are still normally less risky than many

[2]Bonds rated triple B or higher are often considered to be investment quality bonds since they are generally eligible as commercial bank investments.

common stocks. The third general category is the speculative grade of bonds and includes bonds rated B or lower. These bonds have high risk and are somewhat similar in their risk characteristics to common stocks. In fact, they may frequently be much more risky than the common stocks of firms having bonds rated triple A.

The two rating agencies do not always agree on the rating of a given bond. When this occurs, it is known as a *split rating*. Split ratings are not uncommon, but it would be rare to find the rating agencies disagreeing by more than one rating category. In addition, all bonds are not rated by the agencies. This is especially true of the debt issues of financial concerns such as bank-holding companies and consumer finance companies.

Ratings are not carved in stone. Although the ratings are assigned with a long-term perspective, bond ratings are changed as the fortunes of the firm change. Moreover, the changes are more frequently in a downward direction.[3] Boston Edison's bonds are an example of extremely swift downward ratings revisions, as can be seen from the following Standard & Poor's ratings from various monthly issues of the *Standard & Poor's Bond Guide:*

January 1970 Guide	*AAA rating*
July 1970	Changed from AAA to AA
May 1973	Changed from AA to A
June 1974	Changed from A to BBB

Why were the bonds of Boston Edison downgraded so swiftly? Part of the answer to this question concerns the problems the utility industry faces, such as rapidly increasing costs of fuel and the difficulty of obtaining rate relief (often called "regulatory lag"). Moody's also downgraded Boston Edison's bonds in June 1974 from A to Baa. In announcing this decision, Moody's referred to a deterioration of the firm's financial condition in the past few years.[4] For example, from 1968 to 1973, interest coverage fell from 4.88 to 1.94 times. Moody's opinion was that this deterioration resulted from an increase in the percentage debt in the capital structure without adequate rate relief to support the level of the debt.

Returns by Rating

Investors typically require higher rates of return as bond quality decreases. Thus, triple A bonds will typically have the lowest yield-to-maturity and the yield will increase as one moves down the rating scale.

[3]For example, according to the monthly issues of Standard & Poor's *Bond Guide* for 1974, 39 companies had bond issues upgraded while 75 had issues downgraded. Forty-one utilities were downgraded while only 10 utilities were among those upgraded.

[4]Moody's *Bond Survey*, June 3, 1974, p. 856.

TABLE 17–1
Yields by Moody's Bond Rating, October 10, 1974

Moody's Rating	Bond Yields (%)			
	Corporate	Industrial	Railroads	Public Utilities
Aaa	9.37	9.12	*	9.61
Aa	9.45	9.42	8.96	9.96
A	10.10	9.81	9.69	10.80
Baa	10.39	9.92	10.30	10.96

*Series discontinued December 18,1967.
Source: *Moody's Bond Survey,* October 14, 1974, p. 374.

Table 17–1 lists yields-to-maturity for several of Moody's rating classifications as of October 10, 1974. The data in Table 17–1 contain the assumption that interest will be paid when due and the principal repaid at maturity. For triple A bonds, the probability of default is so small that the assumption is valid. For the lower quality bonds, there is a higher probability of default. If default occurs, the actual yield will be lower than the yields presented in Table 17–1.

The relevant question when considering yields for the various bond ratings is whether or not the yields actually earned by investors are higher or lower than the stated yield-to-maturity for various risk classes. Braddock Hickman calculated the actual rates of return for various bond ratings for the 1900 to 1944 period.[5] The returns were for portfolios of bonds. Some of his results are presented in Table 17–2. This table shows that, in terms of actual (realized) returns, higher rated bonds produced the lowest rates of return.[6] Hickman concluded that low rated bonds during the 1900 to 1944 period produced higher returns, even with consideration given to defaults. As with all investments decisions, the relationship Hickman found is an average and does not imply that the investor should automatically purchase low rated bonds. The higher yields may be possible only with a diversified low-quality bond portfolio and a long-term investment horizon.[7]

The risk of a particular bond, summarized in its agency rating, is important to the investment decision, but risk in the portfolio context is also important and probably more so to most investors. The beta of corporate bonds must be evaluated in the same light as we have suggested

[5]W. Braddock Hickman, *Corporate Bond Quality and Investor Experience* (Princeton, N.J.: Princeton University Press, 1958).

[6]For a different approach, see Harold G. Fraine and Robert H. Mills, "Effects of Defaults and Credit Deterioration on Yields of Corporate Bonds," *Journal of Finance,* September 1961, pp. 423–34; they found realized yields to be almost identical over quality ratings (p. 433).

[7]Even this might not be possible since Hickman's results depend on the Great Depression for their validity.

TABLE 17-2

Default Rates and Yields for Bonds Classified by Industry and Quality at Offering, 1900-44

	Default Rate	Promised Yield	Realized Yield
All industries	17.3%	5.3%	5.4%
Railroads	28.1	5.5	5.2
Public utilities	10.6	5.0	5.4
Industrials	14.8	5.4	5.8
Agency rating			
I (AAA)	5.9	4.5	5.1
II (AA)	6.0	4.6	5.0
III (A)	13.4	4.9	5.0
IV (BBB)	19.1	5.4	5.7
V-IX (BB and less)	42.4	9.5	8.6
No rating	28.6	4.8	4.6

Notes: The default rate is a life-span default rate. In other words, a bond is considered to have defaulted if it failed to make an interest or principal payment during its existence. The realized yield may be greater than the yield promised to the investor at the offering because of such items as bonds called prior to maturity at a premium. The ratings from I to IX are those of Hickman and roughly correspond to the ratings of AAA, and so on. Bonds not rated include mainly those of financial institutions.

Source: Walter Braddock Hickman, *Corporate Bond Quality and Investor Experience*, New York: National Bureau of Economic Research, 1958, p. 10. Used with permission.

for common stocks. Sharpe has provided us with some evidence regarding the beta of "high-grade" corporate bonds.[8] As can be expected, these financial instruments have a beta that is substantially below one. Using the Dow-Jones Industrial Average as the "market" portfolio, Sharpe found betas on the order of 0.25 during the period 1946-71. In other words, high-grade corporate bonds are not only less risky than common stocks on an individual basis but less risky than common stocks when considered within the context on one's portfolio. In the same study the returns on stocks and corporate bonds were examined and as expected, bonds experienced lower returns. What is surprising is that adjusted for risk (beta), the bond returns remained below the stock returns.

Quality of Bond Ratings

The methods used by Moody's and Standard & Poor's to rate bonds include an economic analysis of the firm, examination of financial information, liquidity tests, and an examination of the bond's collateral and

[8] W. F. Sharpe, "Bonds versus Stocks: Some Lessons from Capital Market Theory," *Financial Analysts Journal*, November-December 1973, pp. 74-80.

sinking fund provisions. It is fair to conclude that the analysis is complete and reasonably accurate.[9] It is also fair to conclude that a credit risk analysis by virtually any bond investor should come to approximately the same conclusion as the rating service. One might rate a Baa bond as Ba or A, but one would generally not want to change the rating more than one grade.

We do not suggest that an investor wishing to purchase an A-rated bond will find any A-rated bond acceptable. Analysis is still required since each bond is different and a given bond may not fit particular needs. Moreover, there are differences within a rating category that should not be ignored. On May 30, 1974, $125 million of F. W. Woolworth 9 percent debentures were offered by underwriters at 99.25 to yield 9.08 percent in 25 years. These debentures were rated A, but sold poorly. Part of the explanation for the poor response from bond purchasers related to investor concern with Woolworth's substantial business in Great Britain and the problems being encountered there.[10] In effect, some bond investors were apparently skeptical of the firmness of Woolworth's bond rating of single A and felt the rating might soon be downgraded, perhaps to triple B.

Call Provision

A bond with a call provision enables the corporation to repay the debt at its discretion. Such bonds are said to be *callable*. If the bond is called, the investor is obligated to return the bond to the corporation and, upon doing so, the corporation will repay the principal. The investor has no choice in the matter since the call provision is written into the indenture. If the investor retains the bond, no additional interest payments are received.

The call provision normally requires the corporation to pay a premium to call the issue. The bond indenture will stipulate this *call premium* in the form of a price the firm must pay when the bond is called. If bonds are callable at 105, the investor will receive $1,050 for each bond, if called. In this case, the call premium is 5 or $50 per $1,000 bond. The call premium is usually not constant over the life of the bond, but typically declines as the bond gets closer to maturity. The investor should determine whether a given bond is callable and the terms of the call price by consulting Moody's *Manuals* and other sources.

[9]See Thomas F. Pogue and Robert M. Soldofsky, "What's in a Bond Rating," *Journal of Financial and Quantitative Analysis*, June 1969, pp. 201–28 and A. F. Hussey, "Double-or-triple A: Bond Rating Services Get High Marks for Accuracy, Fairness," *Barron's*, July 30, 1973, p. 5ff.

[10]"Issues to Woolworth, Central P&L Shunned Due to Financial Woes," *Wall Street Journal*, June 21, 1974, p. 14.

A corporation is unlikely to call outstanding bonds unless new bonds can be sold at a lower interest rate to replace the called bonds. With call provisions existing in most bond issues, most corporations will not hesitate to call the bonds when interest rates decline substantially. The result is that the bond investor loses some of the benefits of a decline in interest rates because of the operation of the call provision.

Even if the corporation does not call the bonds, the investor will not reap the entire benefit of a price increase resulting from a decline in interest rates. Given a call feature and an interest rate decline, the bond market is unlikely to value a bond at a price much above the call price. We saw from Table 16–1 that a twenty-year 8 percent bond should sell for $1,231.10 if the market interest rate is 6 percent. However, given a call price of $1,050, the price of the bond will tend not to exceed $1,050. The risk of a call prevents the bond price from moving higher as would be the case without the call provision.

In essence, a call provision is of great benefit to the corporation and a major disadvantage to the investor. If interest rates increase, the investor has either a capital loss or an opportunity loss if the bonds are held to maturity. If interest rates decline, the capital gain or opportunity gain that would accrue to the investor is reduced by the call provision.

In times of high interest rates the investment community frequently insists on what is called a *deferred call provision*. The deferred call is identical to the ordinary call provision except that the firm is unable to call the bonds for several years after the date of issue. For example, a bond issue may be callable after being issued five or ten years. The deferred call is actually a compromise between the corporation and the investor. It provides some of the advantages of a callable bond to the corporation without the call provision being such a one-sided affair. In a similar way, high call premiums also contribute to the terms being less one sided.

The investment community has adapted to the deferred call with the concept of the *yield-to-call date* as compared to the yield-to-maturity. Suppose a twenty-year, 8 percent bond is callable in ten years and market interest rates have dropped to 6 percent. Without the call provision, the bond would sell for $1,231.10. If the bond were callable immediately, the bond would sell for the call price, which was assumed to be $1,050. However, given that the call provision does not become effective for ten years, we can determine a bond price that will provide us with a 6 percent return under the assumption that the bond will be called in ten years. The price of a ten-year bond with an 8 percent interest coupon given a 6 percent rate of discount is calculated below.[11] In this case, the principal repayment is $1,050 instead of the usual par value of $1,000, since it is the call price we shall receive ten years hence.

[11]These calculations assume that payments are received at the end of each year. Hence, the calculated figures would be slightly lower than if a bond table could be used.

Present value of bond = present value at 6 percent of principal repayment in year 10 + present value at 6 percent of interest payments in years 1 to 10
= $1,050 (.558) + $80 (7.360)
= $585.90 + $588.80
= $1,174.70

A corporation is willing to accept a deferred call, since without it the firm will be required to pay a higher rate of interest. It is difficult to generalize about how much more interest the firm will be required to pay, since it depends on what the investment community thinks will happen to interest rates after the bond has been issued. If there is a good chance that interest rates will increase, the call provision will not be very expensive. If, on the other hand, the investment community believes that interest rates may fall sharply, it will demand considerable payment for a call provision and typically insist on either a deferred call or a very high call price. In recent years, the deferred call of five to ten years has become popular.

Sinking Fund

Closely associated with the call provision is the sinking fund provision of the bond indenture. Contrary to its name, a bond with a sinking fund does not require the corporation to establish a fund of money with which to repay the principal at maturity. Rather, the sinking fund is a method of repaying a portion of the bond issue prior to the maturity date. The sinking fund works on the same principle as any sort of installment loan. With corporate bonds, the sinking fund is established in the indenture as a payment schedule. The typical payment arrangement calls for partial payment each year so a portion of the principal has been retired by the maturity date. At maturity, the corporation is required by the bond indenture to make a final *balloon payment.* For example, a firm may sell a $50 million bond issue with a twenty-year maturity. The indenture may establish an annual sinking fund payment of $2 million at the start of the sixth year with a balloon payment of $20 million at maturity. Like any installment plan, the credit risk is reduced as time goes by since the payments gradually reduce the principal and interest obligation.

A bond with a sinking fund presents a problem to the investor. The problem lies in the method of satisfying the sinking fund. A $50 million bond issue will contain 50,000 separate $1,000 bonds and each bond will have the same maturity in the typical corporate bond issue. In our example, the sinking fund provision would require 2,000 bonds be retired at the beginning of each year starting with the sixth year, but would not stipulate which of the 50,000 bonds were to be retired in any given year. In practice, the sinking fund can be satisfied in one of two ways. The bonds may be purchased in the market at the current market price. Alternatively, the trustee can select 2,000 bonds at random and notify the owners that these bonds have been selected. A holder of a registered bond would be notified by mail. The notice of a call for redemption of bearer bonds would appear in the financial press (i.e., the *Wall Street Journal*). The owners of these 2,000 bonds must return them and receive the call price as stipulated in the indenture.

Which call alternative will the firm select? If it selects bonds at random, the amount paid will be the call price stipulated in the indenture. If the firm purchases the bonds in the market, the price will be the market price. Obviously, the market purchase alternative will be selected when the market price is below the call price. The market price will be below par if interest rates have increased since the issue date. In effect, an increase in interest rates allows the firm to retire $2 million face value of bonds per year for less than $2 million. The bond's market price is determined independently of the sinking fund requirement. Hence, the sinking fund provision is of no harm to the bond investor if interest rates increase.

If interest rates decline, the firm will satisfy the sinking fund requirement with a call for the appropriate number of bonds when the market price exceeds the sinking fund call price. We again face the problem encountered with a general call provision. The difference is that only a portion of the issue will be retired as a result of the call. Nevertheless, the bond price is unlikely to increase to its theoretical market price. The sinking fund requirement will prevent the price from increasing much above par (if that is the sinking fund call price) with an interest rate decline since an investor may face a call.

Collateral

An important feature of all corporate bonds is the collateral behind the bond. If a bond has collateral, the bond investors as a group have a claim to the assets described in the indenture if and when the bonds are in default. The collateral can be sold and the proceeds of the sale used to satisfy the debt obligation. However, a firm that has defaulted on its bonds is having serious financial problems and these problems usually result from an inability of the assets of the firm to produce sufficient earnings to satisfy the financial obligations.[12] When bonds are in default, the assets of the firm have lost their earning power for that use. If the problems are permanent, the market value of the assets will be low for that use and possibly even lower for alternative uses. In this context, the "best collateral" is an asset capable of producing a wide variety of products. Specialized assets are much less valuable as collateral since their value depends entirely on one product or process.

[12]Protective covenants such as restrictions on either dividend payments to common stockholders or the ability to obtain additional funds using the same collateral help to protect the bondholder.

While collateral is to be preferred in any debtor-creditor situation, it may do little to reduce the risk of loss of principal in a given default.

The types of collateral are many and varied. Often the characteristics of the collateral dictate the label attached to a particular bond. A *debenture* is a bond issue with no collateral. A *subordinated debenture* is a corporate bond the holder of which, in the event of liquidation, has a claim that is subordinated (inferior) to the claims of some or all other creditors. The subordinated debenture holder is usually inferior in rank to other bondholders. In addition, the claim may also rank behind that of the firm's general creditors. The nature of the subordination is stated in the bond indenture. A *mortgage bond* is a bond that is secured by a lien on the property of the corporation. The lien is usually confined to specified real property of the firm. The typical mortgage arrangement is a lien on all real property. The mortgage bond may also contain an *after-acquired clause* stipulating that any real property acquired after the bonds have been issued will come under the mortgage agreement. The intent of the after-acquired clause is to maintain the bondholder's relative position as the firm grows.

Mortgage bonds may be *senior* or *junior;* the distinction is made on the basis of the bond having first claim. The senior mortgage bonds must be completely paid off from the sale of the assets prior to any payment to the junior mortgage bondholders. The value of the junior claim will be related to the market value of the assets in the event of bankruptcy. If the senior claim is $50 million and the market value of the collateral is $200 million, there is $150 million available for the junior claim. The market value to be used is the collateral's market value given bankruptcy.

Collateral trust bonds are corporate bonds backed by stocks and bonds of another corporation. The stocks and bonds are frequently the financial securities of one or several of the firm's subsidiaries or simply the financial investments of the firm. The quality of the collateral is directly related to the fortunes of the firm(s) whose securities are being used as collateral.

The Carolina, Clinchfield and Ohio Railway has a bond outstanding that is a *guaranteed bond.* The payment of the principal, interest, and sinking fund is unconditionally guaranteed, jointly and severally, by the Seaboard Coast Line Railroad Company and the Louisville & Nashville Railroad Company. If the issuing firm cannot pay the interest, principal, or sinking fund payments, the two railroads guaranteeing the bond will do so.

The bond rating of any guaranteed bond is influenced by the financial strength of the firm or firms making the guarantee. On October 18, 1974, the Exxon Pipeline Company sold, through underwriters, $250 million of 9 percent Guaranteed Debentures due in 2004. This issue was given a triple A rating since all payments on the debenture are guaranteed by Exxon Corporation.

Another form of mortgage bond is the *equipment trust certificate,* where the bonds are backed by specific equipment or machinery. These generally high-quality securities are frequently used by railroads and airlines where the equipment is the rolling stock of the railroad or the airplanes of the airline. The unique feature of equipment trust certificates is that the trustee of the bond retains legal title to the equipment until the bonds have been paid in full. For example, a plaque on many railroad freight cars shows a bank as trustee owner. Consequently, there is a compelling reason to meet the financial obligations of the bonds since the trustee can prevent use of the equipment at any time without the necessity of obtaining a court order. For a firm in the transportation business, its equipment is essential to continued operation.

Coverage Ratios

The potential bond buyer should examine the extent to which the firm is capable of satisfying the obligations of the bond. A measure of repayment ability is the coverage ratio. This ratio is designed to indicate the extent to which earnings of the firm can deteriorate before the firm is

EXHIBIT 17–4

Income Statement—Hypothetical Company

Sales	$200,000,000
Expenses	185,000,000
Earnings before interest and taxes (EBIT)	$ 15,000,000
Interest*	4,500,000*
Net income before taxes	$ 10,500,000
Taxes at 50 percent	5,250,000
Net income	$ 5,250,000

$$\text{Times interest earned (before taxes)} = \frac{\text{EBIT}}{\text{interest}} = \frac{\$15 \text{ million}}{\$4.5 \text{ million}} = 3.33$$

*Composed of the following:
$40 million, 8% senior mortgage bonds (interest = $3.2 mil).
$13 million, 10% junior mortgage bonds (interest = $1.3 mil).

Annual sinking fund payment of $1 million for each bond ($2 million total). Paid with after-tax income.

$$\text{Charges coverage ratio} = \frac{\text{EBIT}}{\text{interest + before-tax sinking fund payment}}$$

$$= \frac{\$15}{\$4.5 + \$2.0/.5}$$

$$= 1.76$$

unable to meet its creditor obligations. Times interest earned, introduced in Chapter 10, is the ratio of earnings before interest and taxes (EBIT) to the interest obligation. In Exhibit 17-4, the interest obligation is $4.5 million and EBIT is $15.0 million. The exhibit shows a times interest earned ratio of 3.33. The interpretation is that the firm's earning power is presently 3.33 times the interest obligation.

In Exhibit 17-4, we have two bond obligations, one of which is junior to the other. The senior bond must be paid prior to the junior bond. Coverage ratios could be calculated for each bond obligation. Since the senior bond is first in line, the firm needs only to earn the interest necessary to pay the senior obligation. Hence, the coverage ratio for the senior bond is the ratio of EBIT to the interest payment for the senior bond. The senior obligation has a times interest earned of 4.69 (15.0/3.2).

In order to pay the junior bondholders, the firm must earn both the junior and senior interest payment. Thus, we use the *cumulative method* of calculating the coverage ratio for junior bonds where the EBIT remains the same, but we add the junior interest payment to the denominator of the ratio. The coverage ratio for the junior bond is 3.33. In this example, the coverage ratio for the junior bond is identical to the ratio for the entire firm. The reason is that the junior bond is last in line for interest payments and generally the ratio for the most junior bond will be the lowest ratio and equal to the overall interest coverage ratio.

We use the cumulative technique since junior bonds may appear less risky than the senior bonds if we didn't. In our example, if we simply used the junior bond interest of $1.3 million and the EBIT after the senior interest payment ($15.0 less $3.2 million), we would obtain a coverage ratio of 9.08 (11.8/1.3). This coverage ratio is greater than the coverage ratio for the senior bonds. This calculation is obviously incorrect and should not be used.

Many bond investors employ a *charges coverage ratio* as well.[13] This ratio is identical to the times interest earned except that it is designed to reflect both interest and principal payments that must be made by the firm. It is the ratio of EBIT to the interest and sinking fund payments. Suppose that both of our bonds in Exhibit 17-4 had a $1.0 million annual sinking fund requirement designed to retire the bonds by the final maturity date. In order to meet the sinking fund obligation from earnings, the firm must earn $4.0 million before taxes since the illustrative tax rate is 50 percent. In our example, the charges coverage is 1.76, which is the ratio of EBIT to the sum of the interest payments and the before tax sinking fund payment.

Can a generalization be made regarding the minimum acceptable times interest earned for a given bond or firm? An absolute standard such as three or four is often inappropriate since the adequacy of a

[13]This is sometimes referred to as the burden coverage ratio.

given coverage ratio will depend on such factors as the industry, the stage of the business cycle, and the efficiency of management. While the coverage ratio must be judged in light of the business risk faced by the firm, the rating agencies often tend to require a given interest coverage to maintain a specific rating (i.e., 3.0 for a utility to maintain a triple A rating).

YIELD CURVES

A yield curve is a useful graphic representation of the relationship between the yield-to-maturity and the maturity date for fixed income securities of a given risk class. Figure 17-2 shows the yield curve which existed at various dates for securities issued by the U.S. government. As we shall examine more fully in Chapter 19, a U.S. government security has no credit risk. Thus, the yield curves of Figure 17-2 represent the term (maturity) structure of riskless interest rates as of each date. However, yield curves can also be drawn for corporate bonds of various risk classes or ratings. At any given time, these corporate yield curves

FIGURE 17-2
Yields on U.S. Government Securities

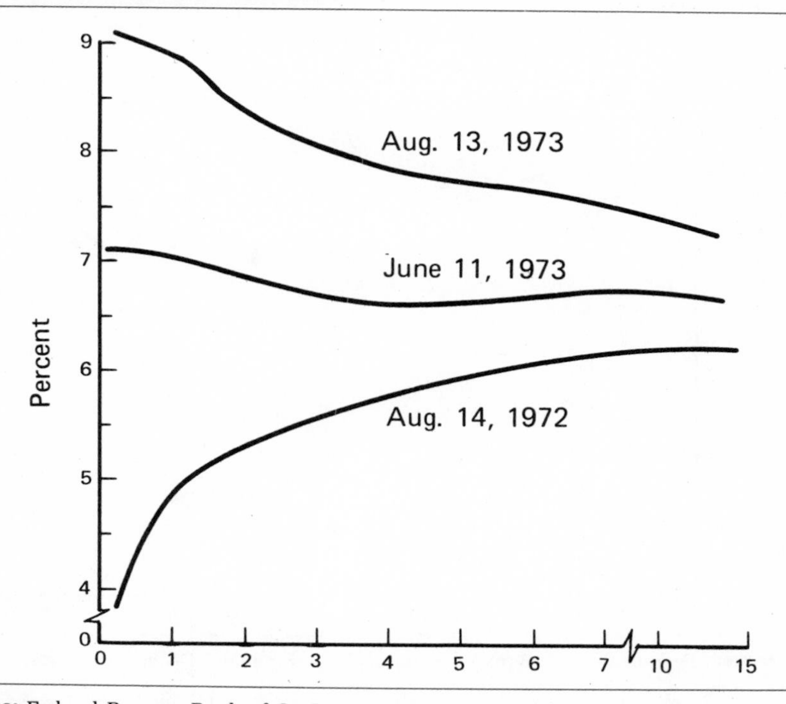

Source: Federal Reserve Bank of St. Louis, *U.S. Financial Data*, several issues.

would tend to have the same general shape as a yield curve using U.S. government securities, but would show higher yields for comparable maturities.

Figure 17-2 demonstrates that many different shapes for the yield curve can exist depending upon the time chosen to draw the yield curve. The yield curve is useful to the potential bond investor in helping to decide whether short-term bonds should be purchased rather than long-term bonds. The investor has a picture of the differences in yields for the various maturities under consideration. Explanations for the various shapes have been proposed and are known as the expectations hypothesis, the liquidity preference hypothesis, and the market segmentation hypothesis. These three explanations for the shape of the yield curve are discussed in the appendix of this chapter.

Expected Inflation

The shape of the yield curve allows an investor to obtain a glimpse of the judgment of the bond market regarding the future rate of inflation for various periods of time. For example, for a bond free of credit risk

FIGURE 17-3
Real Interest Rate

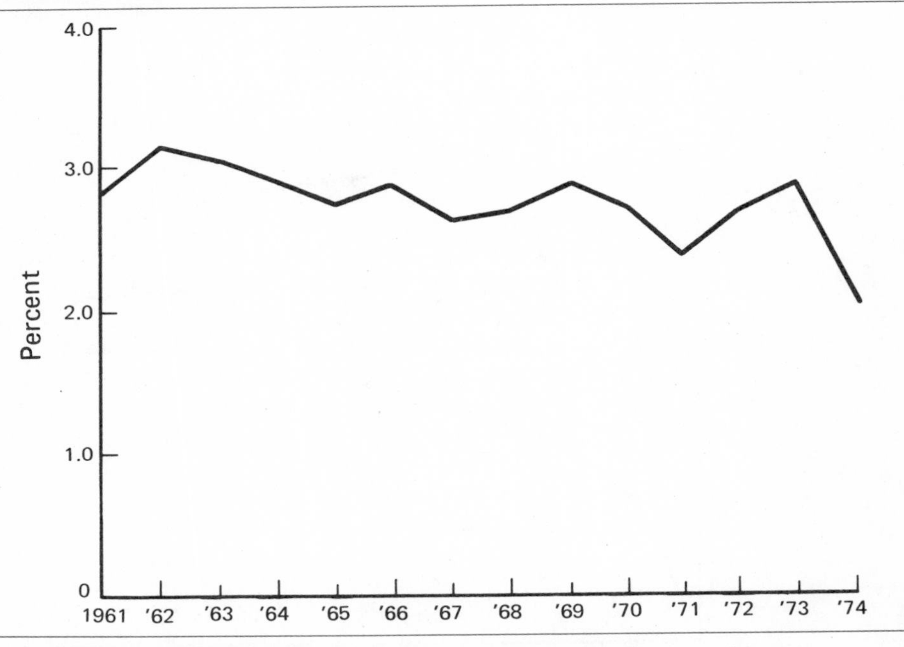

Source: Federal Reserve Bank of St. Louis, *U.S. Financial Data*, several issues.

and selling to yield 9.5 percent, we might conclude that the *real interest rate* is approximately 3.5 percent and the expected inflation rate will be 6 percent. Figure 17-3 shows that real rates of interest have been amazingly consistent since 1961 at around 2½ to 3½ percent.

If it is reasonable to conclude that real rates will continue to fluctuate in a narrow range, an estimate of expected inflation rates can be obtained by examining market rates on bonds free of credit risk such as those issued by the U.S. government. If five-year U.S. bonds are selling to yield 7.8 percent, this yield implies that the market expects inflation during the next five years to be between 4.3 and 5.3 percent per year. The expectation is merely the market rate less the historical real rate of 2.5 to 3.5 percent.

CONTEMPORARY DEVELOPMENTS IN THE BOND MARKET

This section summarizes various bond market developments mentioned previously in various parts of the chapter. In addition, the introduction of floating rate notes in June 1974 is examined from the viewpoint of the bond investor. These notes represent an unusual type of security for the bond investor to consider.

The developments are as follows: 1) The trend toward issuing bonds with deferred call provisions. Many of these bonds are not callable for five years, although many utilities have placed a ten-year, noncallable provision on their new issues to increase their marketability. With interest rates at relatively high levels in the mid 1970s, deferred call provisions are likely to be demanded by the bond buyer. 2) The marketing of substantial quantities of intermediate-term bonds having maturities of five to eight years. These bonds are generally noncallable for their entire life. These bonds appeal to investors as a means of participating in the bond market with relatively little interest rate risk because of their fairly short maturity. 3) Related to the preceding development has been the marketing of split maturity offerings to appeal to all types of bond buyers. For example, on November 7, 1974, du Pont issued $350 million of thirty-year debentures and $150 million of seven-year notes. Both of these issues were rated triple A. 4) A sustained and high level of bond offerings as firms refinance their short-term debt obligations with longer-term debt issues. 5) A trend toward negotiated bond underwritings rather than competitively bid offerings. This trend has occurred because of extremely difficult capital market conditions in the summer of 1974. Some public utility bond issues put up for competitive bidding received little attention by Wall Street underwriters. Many underwriters feel that a negotiated issue is easier to market in difficult times, since the underwriters have more time to develop buyer interest in a given bond offering than is true in the case of a competitively bid offering. In the case of a competitive offering, the underwriting syndicate will often wait until bids are opened before starting a concentrated marketing effort so that its marketing efforts are not wasted.

Floating Rate Notes

In June 1974, Citicorp, the one-bank holding company controlling the First National City Bank (New York), proposed selling a floating rate note.[14] Floating rate notes are unsecured debt obligations issued by corporations. The interest rate paid on these notes varies from time to time. In addition, the holders of these notes may redeem them at their face value at preset dates.

Citicorp's issue provides a good example of the operation of floating rate notes. The issue matures on June 1, 1989. It carried an interest rate of 9.7 percent from issuance to November 30, 1974, and a minimum rate of 9.7 percent from December 1, 1974, to May 31, 1975. Starting December 1, 1974, the interest rate is determined for six months and is set at one percent above the three-month U.S. Treasury bill rate (minimum rate of 9.7 percent). The rate is then determined every six months thereafter until the note reaches maturity. On June 1, 1975, the interest rate was set at one percent above the three-month Treasury bill rate existing during the first three weeks of May 1975. No minimum interest rate provision would apply to rates starting with the June 1, 1975 period. Beginning on June 1, 1976, and every six months thereafter, the holders of the Citicorp notes may redeem them on any semiannual interest date, at the holder's option, by giving thirty days notice to Citicorp. This is sometimes referred to as the put provision. While the initial minimum purchase applicable to this $650 million issue was $5,000, the bonds are traded on the NYSE in units of $1,000.

What are the advantages of floating rate notes for the investor? First, if inflation rates increase, causing interest rates to go higher, the investor will probably receive a higher interest yield on the note, since the rate is reset every six months. Second, the notes are actually renewable short-term obligations once the first redemption (put) date is reached. Every six months the investor can decide whether the money should be left in the Citicorp issue or placed in more attractive investments. Third, because of the short-term character of the notes, interest rate risk is minimal. The price of the notes is unlikely to vary much from the $1,000 par value since that value can be obtained by redemption every six months once the first redemption date is reached.

On the other hand, floating rate notes may not be a desirable security for an investor. An investor expecting a decline in interest rates would

[14] "Citicorp to Offer $250 Million of Notes: Yield to be Keyed to Treasury-Bill Rate," *Wall Street Journal*, June 20, 1974, p. 23. Because of investor interest, the amount eventually issued was $650 million.

not be attracted to floating rate notes. As we previously noted, long-term, high-quality bonds would be a better holding because of the potential for capital gains. The holder of a floating rate note might also be adversely influenced by changes in the shape of the yield curve. If the yield curve changes from upward sloping (Figure 17–2, Aug. 14, 1972, curve) to downward-sloping, short-term interest rates will drop faster than long-term rates. In fact, long-term rates might even remain unchanged or increase slightly. In this situation, the investor would do much better with a long-term bond rather than a floating rate note.

As of October 1974, approximately $1.3 billion of floating rate notes were outstanding.[15] The question of whether this form of security is an effective means of combating inflation risk has not been completely settled. However, the various underwritings generally receive good support from the investing public. While many of the floating rate notes have been issued by firms with excellent credit ratings, the investor must still examine any potential floating rate note investment from the viewpoint of credit risk.

SUMMARY

Bond investing is, in some ways, easier than investing in common stocks. Once the potential bond investor has studied the terms of the issue and its quality, the investor need only determine if the promised yield-to-maturity is satisfactory for the particular issue. The quality of a bond issue gets expressed in a rating given to the bond issue by a bond rating agency. While these bond ratings are extremely useful guides to bond quality, the investor should also do some credit risk assessment, since even bonds having the same rating often have different characteristics.

Credit risk is only one of three risks facing the bond investor. The other two risks, purchasing power risk and interest rate risk, are not only somewhat related, but also have been extremely important factors in bond investing since 1965. We noted in Chapter 7 that the annual rate of inflation has generally increased since 1965. As inflation rates increase, interest rates tend to increase. When interest rates increase, bond prices decline with the longer maturity bonds declining most.

Purchasing power risk relates to the buying power of the principal when it is returned to the investor either at the maturity of the bond or as a result of resale of the bond prior to maturity. With high rates of inflation, the purchasing power of the bond's principal gets eroded quickly either through a decline in the price of the bond, if sold before maturity, or through a decline in the real income when the principal is returned at maturity.

The terms of the issue of concern to the investor include the maturity date, the coupon rate, the interest payment dates, the call price and call provisions, the sinking fund provisions, and the collateral behind the bond.

[15]Margaret D. Pacey, "Floating Rate Notes," *Barron's*, October 14, 1974, p. 5.

Using the current price of a bond, its maturity date, and the coupon rate, it is possible for the bond investor to calculate a current yield and a yield-to-maturity for the bond. Investors generally compare bonds of comparable quality using yield-to-maturity. In addition, bond investors should not ignore the potential tax benefits of buying bonds at a discount. These benefits were discussed in Chapter 5.

The choice of whether to buy a short-term bond or a long-term bond is perhaps the most important decision facing a bond investor. By buying a short-term bond, the investor reduces interest rate risk and the price of the bond will be relatively stable in the face of interest rate changes. When the bond matures, however, the proceeds may have to be reinvested at a substantially lower interest rate. By buying a long-term bond, the investor may "lock-in" a favorable interest rate for a long period of time. However, a long-term bond will fluctuate more than a short-term bond for any given interest rate change. If the investor believes interest rates are near their peak, a long-term bond would be desirable. However, the investor does need to realize that the purchase of a long-term bond contains a fair amount of interest rate risk because of the volatility of interest rates in recent years.

QUESTIONS

1. What is the relationship between the coupon rate of interest on a bond, its current yield, and its yield-to-maturity?
2. Bonds may be fully registered (principal and interest), partially registered (principal only), or coupon bonds. What difference does this make to the investor?
3. If a bond investor expects interest rates to increase, what are the characteristics of the bond that should be purchased?
4. Graham, Dodd, and Cottle, authors of *Security Analysis* (1962 ed.), maintain that the absence of a lien (a secured position) in any bond is of minor consequence. Would you agree with them?
5. What is the significance of a deferred call provision as far as the investor is concerned?
6. Hickman concluded in his study, *Corporate Bond Quality and Investor Experience*, that some of the best buys in the bond market appear to be low grade issues near the date of default. Do you think that this conclusion would be a good operating guideline for bond investors at the present time?
7. The text refers to the split-maturity issue of du Pont that was issued November 7, 1974. Do you think that different types of investors would be attracted to the thirty-year debenture as opposed to the seven-year note?

8. Under what conditions would the interest rate on a floating rate note decline?
9. The original proposal put forth by Citicorp for its floating rate note was to have the note redeemable on *any* semiannual interest date rather than the delayed put provision its issue actually contained. *Business Week* of July 13, 1974, had an article titled, "Citicorp's Offering Kicks Up a Storm." Obviously, this was a controversial issue and caused the original proposal to be modified. What groups were the most concerned? Why?
10. Table 17–1 shows that the yields for public utility bonds tend to be higher than for those of industrial firms. Why do you think that this is the case?
11. If inflation stabilizes at an annual rate of 5 percent, good quality corporate bonds should yield about 9 percent. Since the long-term rate of return on common stocks has been about 9 percent, it does not matter whether the investor buys bonds or common stocks. Do you agree?
12. A recent *Wall Street Journal* article was titled, "Gimmicks for Raising Long-Term Funds May Live on After Interest Rates Subside." What gimmicks do you suppose the author of the article had in mind?

PROBLEMS

1. An 8½ percent bond pays interest on June 1 and on December 1. If an investor purchases this bond on August 15, how much accrued interest will the buyer need to pay?
2. A bond carrying a coupon interest rate of 4⅜ percent has a maturity of 8½ years.
   a) If the bond sells for $766.30, what will be its yield-to-maturity according to Exhibit 17–3?
   b) If three months later, the market demands a yield-to-maturity of 7.75 percent on this quality bond, what will be the price of the bond?
3. A twenty-year 9 percent bond is noncallable for ten years and is currently selling for $1,000. When the issue can be called, the call price on that date will be $1,060. What is the yield-to-first call date for this bond?
4. AT&T's outstanding bonds include the two shown below.

Coupon Rate	*Maturity*	*Call Price*	*Oct. 1974 Market Price*	*Yield-to-Maturity*
8.70%	12/1/2002	107.09*	$930	9.41%
7.125	12/1/2003	105.55**	770	9.45

* Not callable until 1975.
**Not callable until 1977.

If a bond investor expects the yield-to-maturity on AT&T bonds of this maturity to drop to 7 percent by the end of 1977, which bond would the investor purchase?

5. The following tabulation shows statistics from Standard & Poor's *Bond Guide* of October 1974 for nine petroleum firms.

Name	*Times Fixed Charges Earned after Taxes**		
	1971	1972	1973
Amerada Hess	5.23	2.31	7.52
Ashland Oil	3.82	4.36	4.37
Continental Oil	3.67	4.28	5.02
Exxon	7.03	6.95	9.66
Gulf Oil	5.23	4.19	7.19
Phillips Petroleum	3.11	3.52	4.70
Skelly Oil	8.93	9.08	7.22
Texaco	11.92	9.38	10.16
Union Oil of California	3.84	4.04	5.40

*All are December year-end except Ashland Oil (September year-end).

Using these data alone, assign a bond rating to the various companies noting the reasons for your rating.

6. Calculate the times interest earned before interest and taxes for the senior and junior bonds shown below.

Earnings before interest and taxes	$45
Less interest (senior = $15, junior = $5)	20
Earnings before taxes	$25

SUGGESTED READINGS

Ang, James S. and Kiritkumar A. Patel. "Bond Rating Methods: Comparison and Validation." *Journal of Finance,* May 1975, pp. 631–40.

Atkinson, Thomas R. and Elizabeth T. Simpson. *Trends in Corporate Bond Quality.* New York: National Bureau of Economic Research, 1967.

Baskin, Elba F. and Gary M. Crooch. "Historical Rates of Return on Investments in Flat Bonds." *Financial Analysts Journal,* November–December 1968, pp. 95–97.

De Pamphilis, Donald M. "Long Term Interest Rates and the Anticipated Rate of Inflation." *Business Economics,* May 1975, pp. 11–18.

Ederington, Louis H. "The Yield Spread on New Issues of Corporate Bonds." *Journal of Finance,* December 1974, pp. 1531–43.

Fisher, Lawrence and Roman L. Weil. "Coping with the Risk of Interest-Rate Fluctuations: Returns to Bondholders from Naive and Optimal Strategies." *Journal of Business,* October 1971, pp. 408–31.

Hickman, W. Braddock. *Corporate Bond Quality and Investor Experience.* Princeton, N.J.: Princeton University Press, 1958.

Homer, Sidney. *Bond Investment in the 1970s.* New York: Salomon Brothers, November 1970.

Joehnk, Michael D. and James E. Wert. "The Call-Risk Performance of Discounted Seasoned Issues." *Mississippi Valley Journal of Business and Economics,* Winter 1973–74, pp. 1–15.

Katz, Steven. "The Price Adjustment Process of Bonds to Rating Reclassifications: A Test of Bond Market Efficiency." *Journal of Finance,* May 1974, pp. 551–58.

Miles, Joseph E. "Formulas for Pricing Bonds and Their Impact on Prices." *Financial Analysts Journal,* July–August 1969, pp. 156–61.

Pinches, George E. and Kent A. Mingo. "A Multivariate Analysis of Industrial Bond Ratings." *Journal of Finance,* March 1973, pp. 1–18.

——. "The Role of Subordination and Industrial Bond Ratings." *Journal of Finance,* March 1975, pp. 201–6.

Pogue, Thomas F. and Robert M. Soldofsky. "What's in a Bond Rating?" *Journal of Financial and Quantitative Analysis,* June 1969, pp. 201–8.

Soldofsky, Robert M. "A Note on the History of Bond Tables and Stock Valuation Models." *Journal of Finance,* March 1966, pp. 103–11.

——. "*Ex Ante* and *Ex Post* Yields on Bonds: Concepts and Measurements." *Mississippi Valley Journal of Business and Economics,* Spring 1970, pp. 1–10.

Thackray, John. "The Launching of Floating Rates." *Institutional Investor,* September 1974, pp. 43–47ff.

Zaentz, Neil. "Relative Price Performance Among Coupon Areas in Corporate Bonds." *Financial Analysts Journal,* July–August 1969, pp. 146–55.

Appendix

Yield Curve Explanations

The yield curve concept is of assistance in helping the investor select the maturity of any fixed income investment. Before using the yield curve, it is useful to ask why the yield curve has its particular shape at any given time. There are several explanations which have some validity, but none can completely explain the shape of the yield curve. The yield curve is often referred to as the term structure of interest rates.

Expectations Hypothesis

The first explanation is called the expectations hypothesis. If one-year bonds are selling to yield 8 percent and two-year bonds are selling to yield 9 percent and the investor is planning to invest for two years, one of two basic strategies could be followed. The investor could buy the two-year bonds and simply hold them to maturity. Excluding credit risk, the investor would be assured of a 9 percent return.

An alternative strategy is to invest in the one-year bond and, at the end of the first year, purchase another one-year bond. Whether the investor picks this alternative will depend upon the investor's expectations regarding interest rates at the end of the first year. Suppose that the investor expects one-year interest rates to be 12 percent in one year instead of the current 8 percent. If this expectation materializes, an investment of $1,000 would grow to $1,209.60, which is the compound value of 8 percent for one year and 12 percent for the second year. With $1,000 invested at 9 percent for two years, the compound value at the end of the second year would be only $1,188.10.

In this example, the investor's expectations differ from those of the market. Recall that the market rate for one-year bonds was 8 percent and that the two-year rate was 9 percent. The implication is that the market expects one-year rates to be approximately 10 percent one year from now. A two-year investment will produce a compound value of $1,188.10 if the 9 percent two-year bonds are purchased. In order for an equivalent return to be made from the strategy of purchasing consecutive one-year bonds, the rate of interest in the second year must be 10.01 percent.[1]

The expectations hypothesis concludes that the yield curve's shape exists because of different expectations regarding the course of future interest rates. If short-term rates are expected to increase, the yield curve will be upward sloping. If interest rates are expected to decline, the yield curve will be downward sloping.

Liquidity Preference

Expectations enter into the interest rate picture and investors can get a good idea of the market's expectations by examining the yield curve. However, two problems exist. The most obvious problem is that the market could be wrong and often is, although studies suggest that, on the average, market expectations are reasonably close. The fact that expectations are not always correct leads us to the second problem with the expectations hypothesis. The hypothesis is based on equating the yields of two separate investment alternatives in our example. If we are to equate yields, we must equate risk. The recognition that risk may vary with the maturity goes under the general name of the liquidity preference hypothesis.

It is fair to conclude that a long-term bond is more risky than a short-term

[1]The rate of 10.01 percent is calculated as follows:

$$(1.09)^2 = (1.08)(1 + r)$$

$$(1 + r) = \frac{(1.09)^2}{(1.08)}$$

$$r = 10.01\%$$

bond from the investor's viewpoint and less risky from the corporation's viewpoint. Consequently, the investor demands a higher yield on the long-term bond and the corporation will be willing to accept the higher rate in order to obtain the less risky funds.

We have seen several examples of risk increasing with a longer maturity. The mathematics of bond returns implies greater price fluctuations for a given interest rate change with long-term bonds. The uncertain course of future interest rates and purchasing power risk will make a long-term bond less desirable than the short-term bond. With the long-term bond, we have seen that the investor can "lock-in" the current interest rate. If interest rates rise, the investor must wait to reinvest at the higher rate. In addition, the uncertainties regarding the fortunes of the issuing corporation are considerably greater in the long run than in the short run. A one-year bond may be paid with the liquidation of short-term assets, while a long-term bond must be paid from the earning power of the firm. These risks to the investor imply that long-term interest rates will be greater than short-term rates.

From the viewpoint of the corporation, an upward sloping yield curve is also to be expected. Given the existence of call provisions, the firm will prefer long-term bonds since it can "lock-in" a given rate. If rates increase, it has a long-term bond at a lower rate than the market rate. If rates decrease, the bond will be called and refinanced at the lower rate. From the repayment of principal standpoint, the firm also prefers a long maturity. We could continue to examine these risks, but the point is that the investor will demand higher rates on long-maturity bonds while the firm will be willing to accept high rates in exchange for a longer maturity. The result will be an upward sloping yield curve, which is the general situation in our modern capital markets.

Segmentation Hypothesis

Some bond market analysts suggest a third explanation of the yield curve, which has been labeled the *market segmentation theory.* It is suggested that our capital markets are segmented in that investors tend to purchase certain types of securities and ignore others. The segmentation theory implies that some investors will buy and sell only short maturities while others will trade only long maturities. The segmentation hypothesis is typically not confined to maturities, but also will claim segmentation among various types of financial securities. In support of this, it is noted that several bond investors, such as life insurance companies, must purchase long maturities since their assets require such a strategy. They must match maturities of their assets and liabilities. In addition, many investors must confine their investments to certain types of instruments by law or tradition or both. Trust departments usually confine their investments to legal list securities, savings and loan associations to home mortgages, commercial banks to short- and intermediate-term loans, and so on. Finally, it must be recognized that many large investors may find that specialization in a particular type of corporate bond is beneficial because of the high cost of information and analysis of the data.

There is little doubt that segmentation exists along the lines suggested. However, to conclude that interest rates are influenced by such segmentation is an extremely large step that is probably not supportable. Basically, segmentation assumes that although investors specialize, there are no investors who specialize in arbitrage between markets. Many investors buy nothing but short-term securities and others buy nothing but long-term securities. However, many investors exist who specialize in taking advantage of differences between rates. To support the segmentation theory, one would have to show that arbitrage either does not exist or is done poorly. There is no such evidence and it is fair to conclude that the market segmentation supporters cite facts that could imply segmentation, but do not show an actual influence on interest rates.

SUMMARY

A general explanation for the shape of a given yield curve seems to be a combination of the expectations and liquidity preference hypotheses. In essence, it seems appropriate to conclude that yield curves express investor expectations and the preference by investors to own short-term bonds coupled with the preference by borrowers to issue long-term bonds. Because of this dual causation, determination of market expectations is more difficult than would be the case if the expectations hypothesis were the only explanation. We cannot determine precisely the market consensus regarding future rates. If the yield curve is downward sloping or flat, we can conclude that the market expects declining rates. A rising yield curve is much less informative since, given the liquidity preference hypothesis, we could have a rising yield curve with an expectation of no change in interest rates. The expectations are reflected in how rapidly the yield curve rises. If the rate of increase is greater than the historic norm, an increase in yields can be expected. If the yield curve rises slightly, it may be reflecting an expectation of a slight interest rate decline.

*

18

Convertible Securities

"Convertible Securities: The Parachute That Failed to Open" is the title of a 1969 article in *Forbes*.[1] What are convertible securities? What is the parachute and why did it fail to open? This chapter examines these questions by discussing the desirability of having convertible securities in the investor's portfolio.

A convertible security can be exchanged, at the holder's option, for a fixed or determinable number of shares of a security junior to it in rank. This normally means that the convertible bondholder or convertible preferred stockholder receives common stock in the same firm upon exercise of the conversion privilege. Since the convertible security may eventually become common stock, the convertible has features of both a debt and an equity security. In essence, the convertible is a hybrid security and must be analyzed accordingly. The basic form of the analysis does not differ markedly whether the convertible is a preferred stock or a bond. Consequently, both are discussed together.

[1]*Forbes*, September 15, 1969, pp. 30–31.

Convertible securities are attractive to the investor because they are hybrid securities. This is in contrast to the undesirable hybrid nature of nonconvertible preferreds discussed in Chapter 16. The investor hopes to combine the stability of a fixed income security with the growth potential of a common stock investment. The convertible security, if analyzed properly, can provide a limit on the amount of loss, while giving the investor an opportunity for a capital gain. A nonconvertible preferred stock, however, does not give the holder a direct method of participating in the growth of the common stock.

ANALYSIS OF A CONVERTIBLE

Conversion Price

The conversion price is usually stated as a formal part of the terms of the indenture. Xerox issued a convertible bond in 1970. The conversion price during the life of the bond until its maturity on November 1, 1995, is $92 per share of Xerox common stock. When the investor finds the conversion price, the next step is to divide the conversion price into the par value of the security to determine the *conversion ratio.*

The conversion ratio and the conversion price are actually two different ways of measuring the same thing. Dividing $92 into the $1,000 par value of the Xerox bond results in a conversion ratio of 10.87 shares of common stock for each bond. Should the holder of a $1,000 par value, 6 percent Xerox convertible bond maturing in 1995 elect to convert this bond to common stock, he or she would receive 10.87 shares of Xerox common stock. Some investment advisory services give the investor the conversion ratio, while others do not.

The Xerox bond has a constant conversion price until its maturity date. However, this price will change if Xerox splits its common stock, issues a stock dividend, or takes other action, such as the acquisition of another company by merger, that results in an increase in the number of shares outstanding. In other words, the Xerox bondholder is fully protected by an *antidilution clause.*

Although most convertible securities are fully protected against dilution, the investor should check the antidilution feature, since some securities do not change the conversion price for stock dividends below a certain percentage. For example, Litton Industries 3½ percent convertible subordinated debenture, due 1987, contains a provision stating that the conversion price will not be adjusted for stock dividends not exceeding 3 percent in any one year. From 1959 to 1974 inclusive, Litton paid a 2½ percent stock dividend on its common stock and no adjustment had to be made for the debenture's conversion price.[2] This is an undesirable feature for the holder of the convertible bond.

[2]*Moody's Industrial Manual,* 1975, pp. 3196–97.

It is not unusual for a convertible security to have a conversion price that changes over time. For example, the Litton Industries convertible debenture, maturing in 1987, provides that the conversion price increases from $42.50 a share to $45.00 a share after April 1, 1982. This would decrease the number of shares received upon conversion from 23.53 shares to 22.22 shares. The potential purchaser should carefully examine a convertible security having a changing conversion price, since this feature can influence the value of the security over its life.

Bond Value

The analysis of convertible securities also uses what is known as the bond (or preferred stock) value. The bond value is an estimate of the market value of the convertible if it were not convertible. The bond value is often referred to as either the straight value or the investment value. The term *straight value* is used because the investor is looking at the convertible bond as a nonconvertible or straight bond.

Like any corporate bond, a convertible bond has a credit rating. The investor needs to be aware of the credit rating of a given convertible bond before attempting to calculate the bond value. In essence, the bond value reflects what the bond would reasonably be expected to sell for in the market with the conversion feature stripped from it. The investor can attempt to calculate a bond value, or else use the investment advisory services that often make bond value estimates. The determination of the bond value of most convertible securities is far from an exact science, however, primarily because of the low bond ratings carried by most convertible bonds. The following tabulation summarizes the bond ratings given all the convertible bonds listed in Standard & Poor's *Bond Guide* for October 1974:

S&P Rating	*Number*	*Percentage*
AAA	0	.0
AA	2	.3
A	14	2.4
BBB	60	10.3
BB	150	25.7
B	153	26.2
CCC or lower	75	12.8
Not Rated*	129	22.1
Called	1	.2
TOTAL	584	100.0

*Includes many financial companies.

The low bond ratings reflect two major factors. First, a company needing to sell a bond issue will often attach a convertible feature to the bond to enhance its marketability. Companies with low bond ratings are the firms most likely to do this. Second, convertible bonds are usually subordinated debentures having a rank in the liquidation of the company equal to that of other unsecured creditors and superior only to the common and preferred stock. Whatever the cause, the low bond ratings make an estimate of a given convertible's bond value a difficult task because of the existence of considerable business and financial risk.

If an investor must calculate a bond value, he or she needs to know such items as the convertible bond's rating, its maturity, and what comparable bonds yield in the market. Xerox's 6 percent convertible bond is A-rated and matures in 1995. Once the investor finds the yield-to-maturity on comparable bonds, a bond table can be used to estimate the selling price. Naturally, a change in market yields or the business or financial risk of the firm results in a different bond value.

It is possible that the various investment advisory services have already made an estimate of the bond's value as a nonconvertible bond. An examination of several bond advisory services resulted in the following prices for the Xerox bond's value as a bond only:

Moody's Bond Survey (Oct. 21, 1974)	67⅜ (to yield 9.65%)
Standard & Poor's Opportunities in Convertibles (Sept. 21, 1974)	66⅞
Value Line Convertible Survey (Oct. 21, 1974)	69

What bond value should the investor use in the analysis which follows of the investment merits of the Xerox 6 percent bond, based upon its closing price of $1,012.50 on November 12, 1974? Since interest rates declined between mid-October and November 12, the investment values from the investment advisory services are probably somewhat low. An estimated bond value of $700 on November 12 will be used.

Conversion Value

The conversion value of a convertible security is obtained by multiplying the conversion ratio by the current market value of the common stock. The resulting figure is the market value of the convertible if it were immediately exchanged for the common stock. On November 12, 1974, Xerox common stock closed at 66⅛. Multiplying $66.125 by the conversion ratio of 10.87 gives a conversion value of $718.78 for the Xerox bond.

The Minimum Market Value

To judge the value of a convertible, we must establish the minimum market value. By definition, the price of a convertible should never fall below the greater of its bond value or its conversion value. For the

Xerox bond, the bond value was estimated to be $700, and the conversion value was $718.78. Hence, the minimum price of the Xerox convertible bond must be $718.78 on November 12.

We can illustrate this concept graphically, if we assume that the bond value is $1,000 for any given bond and that it will remain unchanged. Figure 18-1 shows the bond value constant at $1,000. The

FIGURE 18-1
Stock and Bond Values for a Convertible Bond

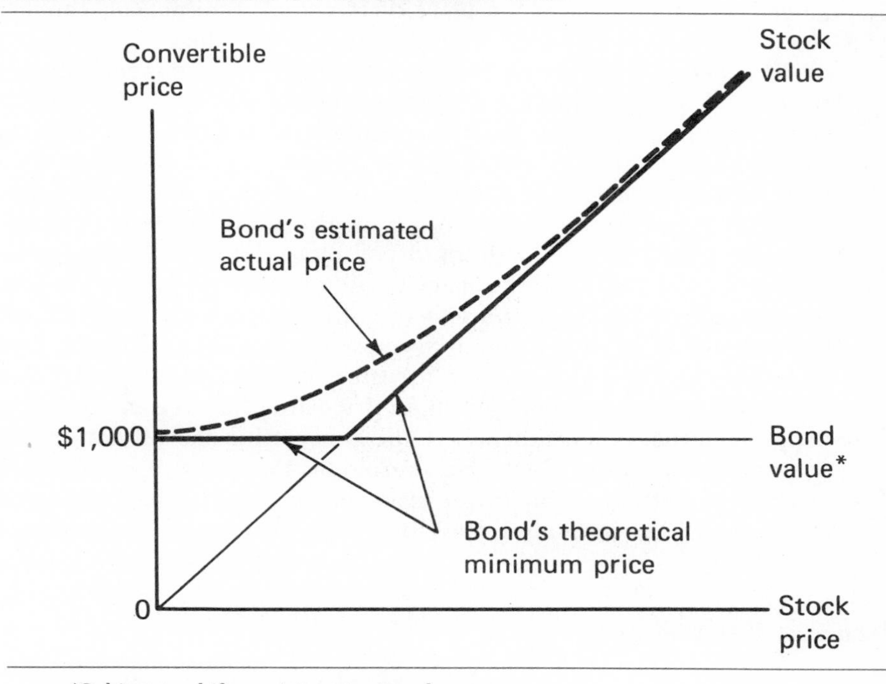

*Subject to shifts as interest rates change.

straight upward sloping line in Figure 18-1 is the conversion value determined by multiplying the various stock prices by the conversion ratio. The heavy portion of these two lines represents the convertible's minimum market price given a particular stock price. The price of the convertible should never drop below these theoretical values, since the convertible can always trade as a pure bond or as a pure stock. Of course, the bond value line may shift up or down as interest rates change.

It is unusual for a convertible to sell for exactly its theoretical minimum value. Convertibles normally sell at a price higher than the minimum value as represented by the dashed line on Figure 18-1. Why would anyone pay more than the bond or stock value? Probably the most important reason has to do with the reduced risk resulting from the bond value of the convertible bond. Suppose we are examining a convertible bond with a conversion ratio of 50 shares, a stock price of $22, and a bond value of $1,000. The minimum market price of the convertible would be $1,100, its conversion value. Its actual market price is likely to be somewhat higher than $1,100 as explained below.

The alternatives facing the investor can be viewed as purchasing the convertible bond or fifty shares of the common stock. In either situation, the investor will profit from an increase in the price of the stock. What happens if the price of the stock declines? If the common stock is purchased and its price declines to $15, the loss is $7 per share, or 31.8 percent of the initial investment. If the convertible bond is purchased and the price of the stock declines to $15, the loss will be considerably less, since the convertible should sell for no less than its $1,000 bond value. In summary, an investment of $1,100 in the stock would produce a loss of $350 given a stock price of $15, but the same investment in the convertible bond would produce a loss of only $100.

Most investors are willing to pay more than the $1,100 stock value for the convertible bond in order to obtain the loss protection provided by the convertible. The purchase of fifty shares of the stock exposes the investor to all of the potential losses of the stock, while the purchase of the convertible exposes the investor to losses which cannot exceed the difference between the purchase price and the bond value. Whatever happens to the price of the stock, the convertible should not drop below its bond value. This "floor price" provides the investor with an element of risk protection. With lower risk, the price must be higher. Hence, the convertible bond should sell for a price that exceeds the stock value.

Premium Calculations

The investor can calculate two values to assist in the investment decision regarding convertibles, the *loss premium* and the *conversion premium.* Xerox's 6 percent convertible bond serves as an example for the calculation of these premiums and their interpretation.

Loss Premium. The loss premium measures the amount of loss an investor would suffer if a convertible security were purchased at its current price and the price fell to the security's bond value. This might happen if the underlying common stock fell in price. Xerox's bond sells for $1,012.50 and has an estimated bond value of $700. Hence, the bond investor could lose $312.50 (30.9 percent of the purchase price) by buying this bond provided that interest rates remain unchanged. The loss premium of 30.9 percent for the Xerox bond is calculated as shown below:

$$\text{Loss premium} = \frac{\text{market value} - \text{bond value}}{\text{market value}}$$

$$= \frac{\$1{,}012.50 - \$700}{\$1{,}012.50}$$

$$= 30.9\%$$

As the loss premium becomes larger, the less "bondlike" the convertible becomes. If the common stock into which the convertible security is converted rises in price, the price movements of the convertible security will become more like those of the common stock. In this situation, the convertible feature dominates the bond feature of the convertible security. The loss premium will also become larger if everything remains the same except for an increase in interest rates. We noted previously that bond values drop if interest rates increase. If the bond value for the Xerox bond were to decline to $600, the loss premium would increase to 40.7 percent ($412.50/$1,012.50). This is the parachute that failed to open referred to in the 1969 *Forbes* article. The bond value was expected to cushion the fall of the price of the convertible bond even if the common stock fell, but rising interest rates kept reducing the altitude at which the parachute (bond value) would open.

Conversion Premium. To calculate the conversion premium, the convertible security is viewed solely as the purchase of the common stock. The Xerox bond is viewed as the purchase of 10.87 shares of Xerox common stock having a conversion value of $718.78 for a cost of $1,012.50. This is a conversion premium of $293.72. The conversion premium of 40.9 percent can be calculated as follows.

$$\text{Conversion premium} = \frac{\text{market value} - \text{conversion value}}{\text{conversion value}}$$

$$= \frac{\$1{,}012.50 - \$718.78}{\$718.78}$$

$$= \frac{\$293.72}{\$718.78}$$

$$= 40.9\%$$

Combined Premium

The conversion premium for the Xerox bond tends to be high, especially given the loss premium of 30.9 percent. The investor can lose almost one-third of the investment in the Xerox bond, yet pays a high conversion premium to be able to participate, at least partially, in any capital gain achieved by the common stock. It may be useful for the investor to add the loss premium to the conversion premium to obtain the combined premium.

The combined premium becomes a useful starting point for an analysis of the attractiveness of any convertible security. Table 18-1 shows selected statistics, including the combined premium for eight different convertible bonds. An investor would desire a loss premium of zero and a conversion premium of zero, resulting in a combined premium of zero. With all these premiums at zero, the investor would purchase a bond at bond value that was also worth the bond value in common stock. Naturally, this situation is quite unlikely to exist, since both the risk protection of the bond value and the possibility of participating in the growth of the common stock are valuable to the investor. Consequently, these valuable features are unlikely to be available at a zero cost.

The combined premium should be low to obtain both benefits of a convertible security, the risk limitation feature and the capital gains potential. We recommend the combined premium be no more than approximately 40 percent. This is based upon a 20 percent loss premium and a 20 percent conversion premium. The investor stands to lose only 20 percent of the investment if interest rates remain unchanged. In addition, the investor pays only a 20 percent premium to obtain the conversion feature. By staying within the suggested guideline of 40 percent, the investor purchases convertible bonds having relatively limited risk as well as capital gains potential obtained at a modest conversion premium.

The investor may want to trade some risk for some growth potential and purchase a convertible with a loss premium of 30 percent and a conversion premium of 10 percent. The suggested 40 percent guideline gives investors the flexibility to satisfy different risk preferences while remaining true to the desirable hybrid nature of a convertible security—a reasonable risk limitation and a capital gain possibility.

For the Xerox bond, the combined premium is 71.8 percent, higher than the 40 percent we recommend. Should this bond automatically be ignored by the investor? Whether the purchase of a Xerox bond with a combined premium of 71.8 percent is a reasonable purchase depends upon many factors associated with the company and the convertible issue itself.

Determinants of Convertible Premiums

Yield Differences. A consideration in the premium determination is the income of the convertible relative to the income of the common stock. The Xerox 6 percent convertible bond has an annual income of $60 per bond. The common stock of Xerox, as of November 1974, pays common cash dividends at an annual rate of $1. The current yield for

TABLE 18–1

Convertible Bond Statistics—Selected Bonds

Description Name, Rate, Maturity	S&P Rating	Amount Outstanding	Price (11/12/74)	Conversion Value	Bond Value	Premiums Loss	Premiums Conversion	Premiums Combined
American Airlines, 4¼, 1992	BB	$167 mil	$ 440.00	$ 172.33	$350	20.5%	155.3%	175.8%
Beaunit, 4¼, 1990	B	25	505.00	448.73*	420	16.8	12.5	29.3
Brunswick, 4½, 1981	BB	17	680.00	199.86	690	(1.5)	240.3	238.8
Ford Motor Credit, 4⅞, 1998	BBB	174	610.00	481.60**	490	19.7	26.7	46.4
Houston Lighting, 5½, 1985	AA	40	821.25	630.76	750	8.7	30.2	38.9
Penn Dixie Ind., 5, 1982	B	23	650.00	239.91	660	(1.5)	170.9	169.4
Union Pacific, 4¾, 1999	A	63	1,250.00	1,273.13	560	55.2	(1.9)	53.3
Xerox, 6, 1995	A	155	1,012.50	718.78	690	30.9	40.9	71.8

*Convertible into common stock of El Paso Gas

**Convertible into Ford Motor Company common stock

Sources: *Standard & Poor's Bond Guide*, October 1974; *The Wall Street Journal*, November 13, 1974; and *Value Line Convertible Survey*, November 4, 1974, for the estimated bond value figure.

the bond is 5.88 percent, while the stock yields 1.50 percent. This means the convertible bond should sell for a price greater than its stock value. A portion of the premium on the conversion value of the Xerox bond can be attributed to this difference in income.

Brokerage Commissions. Convertible bonds may carry a positive combined premium, resulting from differences in the brokerage commissions for stocks as opposed to bonds. The commission for the purchase of a bond is around $5 to $10 per bond, while the commission to purchase approximately $1,000 worth of common stock is in the neighborhood of $25 to $30. Thus, the purchase and sale of a convertible requires around $10 to $20 in commissions, while the purchase and sale of the equivalent stock requires approximately $50 to $60. The actual stock commission depends upon the conversion value of the bond, but a difference of about $30 to $40 is representative.

This savings from purchasing the convertible should be reflected in the combined premium, with the size of the premium a function of the difference between the two commission rates. Both yield and commission differences may appear to be much ado about very small values. However, relative to the loss premium or the conversion premium, they can assume considerable significance.

Growth Prospects. A crucial element in determining the reasonableness of the loss and conversion premiums is the growth prospects for the common stock to be obtained upon conversion. Because of Xerox's good past record of growth and favorable prospects for future growth, the investor may accept a combined premium greater than the suggested 40 percent standard. This decision will, of course, require a complete analysis of Xerox's desirability as a common stock investment. It will also depend upon a person's utility function, discussed in Chapter 11.

Other Terms of the Convertible. There are several other factors that may influence the premium, but their impact is usually small. The duration of the conversion option, and the period of time over which the option can be exercised, can influence the size of the premium. The longer the duration of the conversion feature, the greater the period over which the expected growth of the firm can be realized in the marketplace.

The extent to which the conversion ratio declines over time may influence the size of the premium investors are willing to pay. Empirical studies have shown that the effect of both duration and a changing conversion ratio appears small.[3] Nevertheless, if we are close chrono-

[3]For a recent study, see Edward H. Jennings, "An Estimate of Convertible Bond Premiums," *Journal of Financial and Quantitative Analysis,* January 1974, pp. 33–56. In Roman I. Weil, Jr., Joel E. Segall, and David Green, Jr., "Premiums on Convertible Bonds," *Journal of Finance,* June 1968, pp. 445–63, the authors omit duration as a variable because of the lack of an operational measure of the duration of the conversion premium.

logically to either a change in the conversion terms or to the expiration of the conversion feature, these factors may assume considerable importance.

The convertible bond buyer should also study the antidilution clause previously mentioned. We noted that antidilution clauses have not been standardized, and that an unusual clause may have a profound impact on the price of a given convertible security.

Convertible bonds, like common stocks, are controlled by the Federal Reserve with regard to initial margin requirements. As of November 1974, an initial margin requirement of 50 percent applied to both common stocks and convertible bonds. In the past, typically, the initial margin on common stocks has been slightly higher than that for convertible bonds. A higher initial margin for common stocks relative to convertible bonds could make bonds a more attractive investment, because of the greater financial leverage potential of convertible bonds purchased on margin. Hence, the convertible bond would tend to sell at a premium compared to its conversion value.

What is the reason for a margin requirement on convertible bonds? If the conversion value dominates in the determination of the market price of the convertible, an investor could violate the spirit of the margin controls if allowed to purchase convertible bonds on very low margins. Formal initial margin requirements set by the Federal Reserve on convertible bonds have existed only since 1968, however.

Call Provision

Convertible bonds are almost always callable in some form and the typical corporation will insist upon a call provision. The call feature is necessary, given the motivation behind the use of a convertible. Suppose a corporation has decided it requires capital in the form of a public offering. It has decided to issue common stock, which is selling for $20 a share, in order to raise the needed capital. The firm believes that $20 per share is a depressed price and the stock is actually worth $30 per share. The firm could wait until the market recognizes the "true value," but this is frequently impractical, since the capital needs are pressing. One solution is to issue a convertible bond with a conversion price slightly below $30 per share. When the common stock reaches $30, the firm will "force conversion" and thus convert the debt into common stock. The firm has its equity capital, but at slightly below $30 per share instead of at $20 per share.

A firm is able to force conversion with the use of the call provision. The Xerox 6 percent bond has a call price of $1,045. We previously calculated that this bond is convertible into 10.87 shares of Xerox common stock. If the price of Xerox common stock increases to $110, the conversion value becomes $1,195.70. If Xerox calls this bond when the common stock is selling for $110, the investor has the choice of either accepting the call or of converting the bond into common stock. The choice is obvious, since accepting the call would mean receiving $1,045, whereas conversion would mean receiving common stock with a market value of $1,195.70.

By forcing conversion, the firm has converted the bond into common stock. The possibility of a forced conversion is an important consideration to the convertible bondholder. The investor considering the purchase of the Xerox convertible bond, with the common stock selling for $110, would need to consider carefully what price should be paid for the bond. If the investor pays more than $1,195.70 for the bond, he or she runs the risk that Xerox will soon force conversion of the bond. Then, the difference between the price paid and the conversion value will be a loss for the investor. For example, if the investor were to pay $1,300 for the Xerox bond and the bond were called, the investor would convert the bond into common stock worth only $1,195.70, incurring a loss of about $104. As a result, the convertible is not likely to sell much above $1,195.70.

If a convertible security is selling at a substantial premium over its conversion value and the conversion value is greater than the call price, the investor will need to determine the probability of a call actually occurring. Many questions need to be answered. Has the firm called convertible bonds in the past? Does the firm have a need to sell more debt? If so, does the firm need to call the convertible to alter its debt-to-equity ratio to facilitate the sale of a new debt issue? What is the coupon rate on the convertible bond compared to the rate the firm will have to pay on a new debt issue? The firm might not be willing to give up a low interest rate debt security unless compelled to do so by pressing needs to raise new capital by selling a new debt issue.

A PORTFOLIO APPROACH

We previously saw that risk is easier for the investor to evaluate if considered in a portfolio framework. If returns from the securities in the portfolio are uncorrelated, the fact that a given security is risky is of little importance, since that risk can be diversified away. If the risk of a common stock can be diversified away at a nominal cost, there is no need to purchase a convertible bond in order to reduce the risk of a decline in the price of a given common stock. There is no need to pay a cost to obtain the risk reduction ability of a convertible if the same degree of risk reduction can be obtained with a diversified portfolio of common stocks.

Figure 18–2 shows a hypothetical probability distribution of the price of a given common stock for an assumed one-year holding period. The mean of the distribution, $1,210, is the expected price one year from now. The current common stock price will be the expected price discounted at an appropriate rate or return. Let us also assume that the

FIGURE 18–2
Hypothetical Distribution of Common Stock and Convertible Bond Prices

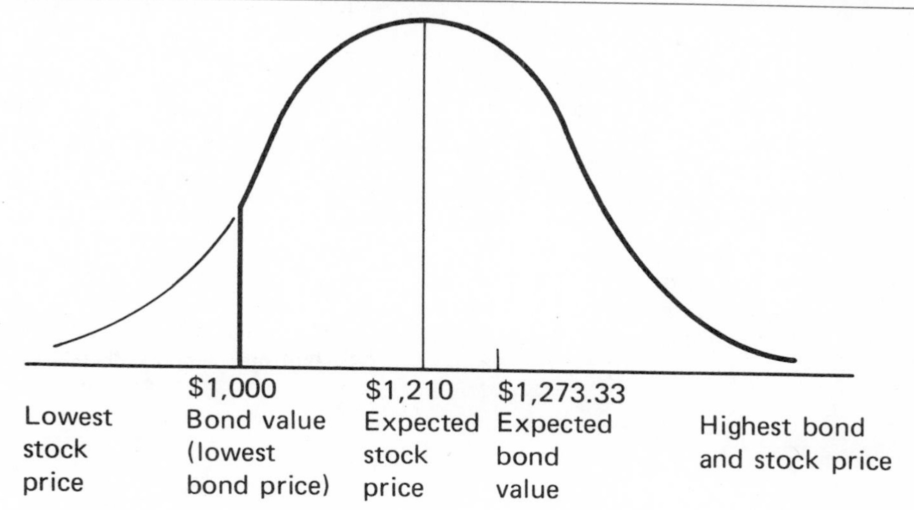

same firm has issued a bond convertible into one share of common stock. Thus, if the current price of the common stock is $1,100 per share, the convertible bond has a conversion value of $1,100.

We also assume that the convertible has a bond value of $1,000 and the discount rate is 10 percent. Figure 18–2 shows both the bond value of $1,000 and the expected stock price of $1,210. The probability distribution associated with the convertible's price can be represented by the portion of the distribution shown by a heavy line in Figure 18–2. Any possible prices below the bond value are eliminated, since the bond value will prevent the convertible from falling below that value, no matter how low the stock price falls. The expected price of the convertible bond will be the mean or average of the truncated probability distribution shown in Figure 18–2. This expected bond value will be greater than the $1,210 expected value for the common stock.

Exhibit 18–1 gives a numerical example of the calculation of both an expected stock price and an expected convertible bond price under assumed economic conditions of prosperity, normality, and recession. Each outcome has an equal chance of occurring. For each economic condition, an expected stock and an expected convertible bond price are given. The expected convertible bond price is simply assumed to be the expected stock price except for the recession outcome, where the bond value would dominate the conversion value of the bond.

The expected price of the convertible one year from now is calculated to be $1,273.33. When this expected price is discounted at the 10 percent rate, the present value of the convertible bond is $1,157.58, or $57.57 more than the present value of the common stock. We might want to discount the convertible's expected price at a lower rate if it

EXHIBIT 18–1
Calculation of Expected Stock and Convertible Bond Prices

Economic Event	Probability	Expected Convertible Price	Expected Stock Price
Prosperity	⅓	$1,610	$1,610
Normal	⅓	1,210	1,210
Recession	⅓	1,000 (bond value)	810

Average expected price: Convertible = $3,820/3 = $1,273.33
Stock = 3,630/3 = 1,210.00

Present value (10% discount rate and one-year holding period): Convertible = $1.273.33 times .9091 = $1,157.58
Stock = 1,210.00 times .9091 = 1,100.01

Conversion premium = $1,157.58 – $1,100.01 = $57.57

is less risky than the common stock. For example, if an 8 percent discount rate is used for the bond in Exhibit 18–1, its present value would be $1,178.98 rather than $1,157.58.

In practice it is difficult to arrive at meaningful values to use in the analysis performed in Exhibit 18–1. One approach that has experienced some success is to employ the capital asset pricing model with betas and the expected returns from the market portfolio.[4] The expected stock price is determined by estimating the expected return from the market portfolio and applying the beta of the stock to this return. The beta is used under the proposition that the bond value protection is valuable only to the extent that the risk of a stock price decline cannot be diversified away. Even with this approach, convertible premiums are difficult to determine. Nevertheless, if premiums exist because of the risk protection element of convertible bonds, they must be related to the theory presented in Exhibit 18–1, and the size of the premium should be closely related to the underlying beta of the common stock.

CONVERTIBLES AS FIXED INCOME INVESTMENTS

An investor may view the purchase of a convertible only as the purchase of a fixed income security. The conversion feature is effectively ignored in this situation, and the bond or preferred stock is analyzed only on its merits as a fixed income security. This situation occurs when the

[4]Edward H. Jennings, "An Estimate of Convertible Bond Premiums," pp. 33–56.

loss premium is at a relatively low level, indicating that the convertible security is essentially a bond.

In Table 18–1, both the Brunswick and Penn Dixie convertible bonds have small negative loss premiums. These negative loss premiums result from the inability to specify precisely the bond value for a low quality bond. In essence, an extremely small loss premium or a negative loss premium means the bond is selling for its bond value and little consideration is being given by the market to the convertible feature. Both the Brunswick and Dixie bonds can be viewed as the purchase of a pure bond.

An investor could follow the strategy of buying bonds such as the Brunswick or Penn Dixie bonds. This means the investor looks for convertible bonds with very low loss premiums (probably less than 5 percent) and gets the conversion feature thrown in at very little additional cost. The investor actually buys a straight bond and a conversion feature of dubious value. However, the conversion feature might be of value at some future date.

CONVERTIBLES AS COMMON STOCK SUBSTITUTES

The strategy of buying convertible securities as a substitute for the common stock may be a better strategy than buying convertibles for their bond value, especially since convertible bonds are generally of rather low quality. The Union Pacific 4¾% bond of 1999 listed on Table 18–1 is a good example of the possibility of buying a convertible security as a common stock substitute. The bond sells for $1,250, but the conversion value of the bond is $1,273.13. Reasons for this slight discount are mentioned below. It is probably not feasible for the investor to arbitrage this situation by buying the bond and selling short the stock, with the short sale to be covered by the stock received upon conversion. Commissions would normally prevent this.

If the investor is willing to accept the risk inherent in the purchase of Union Pacific common stock, the bond is an attractive purchase as a common stock substitute. Not only is the Union Pacific bond selling at a slight discount from its conversion value, but also the bond is rated A by Standard & Poor's. We previously observed that the commission for purchasing one Union Pacific bond would be substantially less than for purchasing an equivalent dollar amount of common stock ($1,273.13 in this case). The current yields from both securities are approximately equal, as shown below:

Current Yield From

Bond	*Common Stock*
$\frac{\$\ 47.50}{\$1{,}250} = 3.80\%$	$\frac{\$\ 2.80}{\$72.75} = 3.85\%$

The $2.80 dividend from each share of common stock results in a slight yield advantage for the common stock. In addition, the dividend on the common stock may increase over time, while the coupon interest rate on the convertible bond is fixed. This may be one reason why the bond is selling at a slight discount from its conversion value. Another reason might be that the investor would need $1,250 to purchase the bond, but a lesser amount could be invested in the common stock. It should also be recognized that the markets for the common stock and the convertible bond are separate and subject to their own short-term supply and demand considerations. This might temporarily cause a slight discount from conversion value. Finally, a time difference between the last trade of each security might account for some of the discount.

One thing has become evident as a result of examining the Union Pacific convertible bond. If an investor discovers a common stock that appears to be an attractive investment, he or she should examine the capital structure of the firm to determine if a convertible security exists that provides an even better investment alternative.

SUMMARY

In recent years, the number of convertible securities available for the investor to consider has increased substantially. Convertible bonds have been sold as a means of raising new capital, and convertible preferred stocks have been used as the currency to facilitate many mergers. As a result, convertible securities have become an important area for the investor, with a large number of different securities available.

The basic attraction of a convertible security is the possibility of having your cake and eating it too. As a hybrid security, a convertible is part bond and part equity. The bond element of a convertible is important because of the fixed income it provides. In addition, the bond element is supposed to act as a means of reducing the risk of investing in a convertible compared to a direct investment in the common stock. The convertible should not decline in price below its value at that specific time as a fixed income security. Since the convertible has a common stock aspect, its price may increase as the price of the stock into which it is convertible increases.

In analyzing a convertible, the investor should determine its bond value, the price the security would sell for if it were nonconvertible. Of course, the bond value will change as interest rates change: Increasing interest rates will cause the bond value to decline and vice versa. In addition, the generally low quality of convertible securities means that considerable business and financial risk may be present in any given situation as well as interest rate risk. Only 13 percent of all the convertible bonds listed in the October 1974 issue of Standard & Poor's *Bond Guide* were rated triple B or better. Even if we include those nonrated convertible bonds of large commercial banks as being of investment grade, only about 17 percent of the convertible bonds would be investment grade.

The loss premium is a measure of the possible loss from buying a convertible if both interest rates and the quality of the convertible remain unchanged. The loss premium is the difference between the convertible's current price and its bond value expressed as a percentage of the current price. The higher the loss premium, the greater the potential loss if the underlying common stock declines in price.

The conversion value of a convertible is determined by multiplying the number of shares to be received upon conversion by the market price of each share. Once the conversion value has been determined, the investor can calculate the conversion premium. The conversion premium relates the conversion value to the price of the convertible to determine the price paid for the convertible feature as opposed to buying the common stock directly. A conversion premium of 20 percent would mean that the investor is paying 20 percent more for the shares into which the convertible can be converted than what these shares could be purchased for directly. The investor is willing to pay a premium mainly because of the risk reduction feature of the convertible.

By adding the loss premium to the convertible premium, the investor obtains a combined premium. A very high combined premium means the convertible is effectively either mostly fixed income security or mostly a common stock substitute. As a result, the convertible may not provide both a risk reduction function and an opportunity to participate in the growth of the common stock. We suggested a 40 percent combined premium as a guideline, which should not be exceeded unless the investor views the growth prospects of the common stock very favorably. The investor might also buy a convertible with a high combined premium in that situation where the high combined premium results from a high loss premium and a low conversion premium. In this case, the investor is essentially purchasing the convertible as a substitute for the common stock.

QUESTIONS

1. What are the main reasons why an investor would purchase a convertible security?
2. Most convertible bonds are subordinated debentures. As a result, the bond rating of convertible bonds is usually one quality rating below the nonconvertible bonds of the same company. Why do you feel this is the case?
3. Is it possible to lose a greater percentage of your investment in a convertible bond than you could lose by investing directly in the common stock into which the bond is convertible?
4. In comparing two convertible securities, the investor finds that one of the securities has a high loss premium while the other security has a low loss premium. What does this tell the investor?

5. Why would an investor purchase a convertible security rather than the related common stock if the convertible's bond value is far below the current market price of the convertible security?
6. An investor can voluntarily convert a convertible security into the common stock at anytime during the life of the convertible provision. Under what circumstances would the convertible security holder want to do this?
7. The text mentions that convertible preferred stocks are often used as the medium of exchange in a merger offer. If you own the common stock of a firm that is going to be acquired, what would convince you to accept a convertible preferred stock in exchange for your common stock?
8. It is possible to calculate both a current yield and a yield-to-maturity for a convertible bond. It is sometimes suggested that the yield-to-maturity calculation is not an apporpriate yield concept to apply to a convertible bond. Do you agree?
9. An article in *Business Week* of September 28, 1974, stated: "Some portfolio managers are loading up on convertible debentures in hopes of double-barrelled action." What do you think the article had in mind by "double-barrelled action"?
10. A special type of convertible security, referred to as an exchangeable security, will sometimes be encountered by the potential investor in convertible securities. For example, Dart Industries has a convertible security outstanding that is convertible into 10.75 shares of Minnesota Mining and Manufacturing Company common stock per $1,000 par value bond. Would the investor need to modify the standard form of analysis for convertible securities in considering this security for purchase?

PROBLEMS

1. Standard Oil of Indiana had outstanding $200 million of a 5 percent convertible bond maturing August 1, 1996. This bond was convertible at a price of $70.50 for the common stock. On October 18, 1974, the convertible bond's closing price was $1,270 and the common stock closed at $90.75 per share.
   a) What is the conversion ratio for this bond?
   b) What is the bond's conversion value and the conversion premium?
   c) *Value Line*, as of October 21, 1974, estimated that the bond value of this bond was $590. Using this bond value, calculate the loss premium and the combined premium.
   d) What is your interpretation of the calculations you have just made?
2. If Sue King views the prospects for the common stock of Standard of Oil of Indiana favorably, what are the merits of purchasing the common stock as opposed to purchasing the convertible bond? The bond is rated double A. The dividend per share on the common stock is $3.60.

3. In late October 1974, Standard of Indiana called its 5 percent convertible bond for redemption on November 29, 1974, at a price of $1,042.50. On November 22, 1974, Sue King knew she would soon have to make a decision regarding the bond she purchased on October 18, 1974. On November 21, the bond closed at $1,160 and the common stock closed at $83.50.
   a) What alternatives are available for Sue King?
   b) What would you recommend that she do?
4. Occidental Petroleum has the following securities outstanding:

Issue	*Nov. 1974 Market Price*	*Convertible Into*	*Call Price*	*Estimated Straight Value—11/18/74*
Common	$13.50	–	–	–
$4 preferred	44.875	3.107 sh.	$115*	$27
$3.60 preferred	44.50	3.191	100	24
$2.16 preferred	24.75	1.581	47.50	15

*$105 after March 31, 1975

Calculate:
a) The loss premium for each preferred issue.
b) The conversion value and conversion premium for each preferred issue.
c) The combined premium for each preferred issue.
d) The yield on each preferred stock.

The company resumed dividends on the common stock by declaring a 25¢ dividend per share payable in January 1975. Using the implied $1 annual rate on the common stock, compare the investment merits of the various preferred stocks compared to the common. What other information might you as an investor want to have?

SUGGESTED READINGS

Brigham, Eugene F. "An Analysis of Convertible Debentures." *Journal of Finance,* March 1966, pp. 35–54.

Jennings, Edward H. "An Estimate of Convertible Bond Premiums." *Journal of Financial and Quantitative Analysis,* January 1974, pp. 33–56.

Noddings, Thomas C. *The Dow Jones-Irwin Guide to Convertible Securities.* Homewood, Illinois: Dow Jones-Irwin, 1973.

Soldofsky, Robert M. "Yield-Risk Performance of Convertible Securities." *Financial Analysts Journal,* March-April 1971, pp. 61–65ff.

Vinson, Charles E. "Rates of Return on Convertibles: Recent Investor Experience." *Financial Analysts Journal,* July-August 1970, pp. 110–14.

Weil, Roman L., Jr., Joel E. Segall, and David Green, Jr. "Premiums on Convertible Bonds." *Journal of Finance,* June 1968, pp. 445–63.

*

19

Government Bonds and Money Market Securities

To complete our analysis of fixed income securities, we must examine the characteristics of debt instruments issued by the many governmental units within the United States. These include federal, state, and local bond issues. There are distinct differences among these various bond issues, and consequently, each type is considered separately. Since many of the characteristics of government bonds are shared by short-term, fixed income securities issued by private corporations, these securities are also examined. The chapter concludes with an analysis of the manner in which the average investor can participate in these markets indirectly.

FEDERAL GOVERNMENT SECURITIES

Ownership

At the end of 1974, the federal government had outstanding over $492 billion (face value) of fixed income securities.[1] As Table 19-1 indicates, the ownership of these securities is widespread, with the largest single owner the federal government itself, holding approximately 29 percent of the total. If we include the Federal Reserve System, the government ownership is approximately 45 percent of the total outstanding federal issues. The large portion of the federal debt owned directly by the federal government is held in a variety of investment accounts. These accounts include reserves for the Social Security System, the insurance reserves of the Federal Deposit Insurance Corporation, and the retirement plan for federal government employees.

TABLE 19-1

Ownership of the Federal Debt December 31, 1974

Held By	Amount in Billions			
U.S. gov't agencies and trust funds			$141.2	(28.7)*
Federal Reserve Banks			80.5	(16.3)
Private Investors				
Commercial banks	$56.5	(11.5)		
Mutual savings banks	2.5	(.5)		
Insurance companies	6.1	(1.3)		
Other corporations	11.0	(2.2)		
State and local governments	29.2	(5.9)		
Individuals**	84.5	(17.2)		
Foreign and other	80.8	(16.4)		
Total private investors			271.0	(55.0)
Total federal debt			$492.7	(100.0)

*Figures in parenthesis indicate percentages of total.
**Includes $63.4 billion of savings bonds.
Source: *Federal Reserve Bulletin*, February 1975.

Although the various accounts are extremely large, they are much less significant as a market force than might be indicated by their size, since the securities in the accounts are typically not traded. They are purchased at the time of issue and redeemed at maturity. The redemption process often does not involve cash, but merely the exchange of the maturing issue for a new issue.

The private ownership of U.S. government securities is strongly influenced by the stage of the business cycle. In expansionary times,

[1]*Federal Reserve Bulletin*, February 1975, p. A36.

commercial banks, insurance companies, and other financial institutions tend to be heavy sellers of federal government issues in order to invest in the private sector of the economy. During a contraction in the economy, the reverse occurs; financial institutions tend to accumulate government securities. The individual investor tends to accumulate government securities when the rates are better than the rates of return available on the time deposits of commercial banks and other financial institutions. This accumulation by individuals is known as financial disintermediation.

Risk of Government Bonds

The changes in the ownership of U.S. government securities during various stages of the business cycle are directly related to the characteristics of these securities. In our examination of corporate bonds, we noted three elements of risk: 1) interest rate risk, 2) purchasing power risk, and 3) credit risk. In the case of U.S. government securities, the element of credit risk is absent, since there is no credit risk associated with fixed income securities of the federal government. The owner can be completely certain the principal and interest will be paid in full and on time. The reason for the absence of credit risk lies neither in the financial condition of the federal government nor in its taxing power. An understanding of both the financial condition of the government and its taxing power is vital to an understanding of the economy, but it is not important to the safety of the principal and interest of U.S. government bonds. The federal government has the constitutional power to issue and create money. In the final analysis, new money can simply be issued in order to meet the obligations of the federal debt. With this power, defaults on U.S. government issues will not occur unless the government is overthrown and previous debt issues are not honored.

It is true that the act of creating money may help to create inflationary economic conditions so that the face value of the bonds will purchase less than originally expected. But this situation has to do with purchasing power risk and perhaps interest rate risk; it is not credit risk. The return of principal and interest may represent a real income loss, but in monetary terms, the investor can be assured of the absence of defaults.

Liquidity

The absence of credit risk makes U.S. government bonds unique in U.S. financial markets. The bonds that are marketable (some are not, as we shall see) also hold a special place in our economy, since they are the most liquid of all financial securities. Virtually all trading in U.S. government bonds is conducted in the over-the-counter market. The Association of Primary Dealers in Government Securities has a membership of about twenty-three brokerage firms, representing important dealers in these financial securities. These dealers make the market in government securities and are regularly in contact with buyers and sellers. Large institutions and corporations may deal directly with one of these firms, while the smaller investor may make transactions through a local bank or brokerage firm. The large volume of activity assures the investor that a holding can be liquidated in minutes at a price very close to that of the previous trade. The spread, the difference between the bid and asked price, is often less than 10 cents per $1,000 of par value. Most transactions are made on a net basis, which means that no commission is involved. Occasionally, a service charge will be made for small transactions and the price execution for the small investor is usually not as good as for the larger investor.

Types of Government Securities

Treasury Bills. Over 32 percent of the federal, publicly issued, interest-bearing debt is represented by Treasury bills.[2] These instruments have a maturity of up to one year, although they are more typically issued for periods of three to six months. Bills carry no coupon or interest payment and are issued at a discount. Because of this, Treasury bills are quoted on a bank discount basis. For a ninety-day Treasury bill quoted at 8 percent, the price would be determined with the following equation:

$$\begin{aligned} P &= 100 - Y\left(\frac{M}{360}\right) \\ &= 100 - 8\left(\frac{90}{360}\right) \\ &= 98 \end{aligned}$$

where: Y = quoted yield
M = days of maturity

Of course, the quoted yield is not the actual investment yield. The investment yield is approximately the ratio of the quoted yield to the price. Thus, the 8 percent Treasury bill is a security with an investment yield of 8.16 percent—the ratio of 8 to 98. This calculation is an approximation, since the quoted yield is based on a 360 day year. To adjust for this, one would multiply the restated yield of 8.16 percent by the ratio of 365 to 360. Using this exact technique the investment yield becomes 8.27 percent on the 90 day bill. In practice, the quoted bank discount rate is used and is usually very close to the actual yield. The

[2]As of December 31, 1974, Treasury bills outstanding amounted to $119.7 billion compared to $373.4 billion publicly issued, interest bearing federal debt.

actual yield (8.27 percent) will always be slightly higher than the quoted rate. The difference, however, may become important for an investor with millions of dollars to invest.

The typical procedure for issuing three- and six-month Treasury bills is a weekly auction usually held on Monday. Delivery of the bills and payment for them is normally made the following Thursday. It is possible for an individual investor to enter a noncompetitive bid. Noncompetitive bids (usually up to $200,000), entered without a stated price, may be made in person or by mail at the Bureau of the Public Debt or at any of the 36 banks and branches of the Federal Reserve System. A noncompetitive bidder pays the average price of all competitive bids that are accepted and is assured of getting the Treasury bills. Some brokerage firms will enter a noncompetitive bid for their customers for a modest fee. The brokerage firm will then keep the securities in the customer's account and collect the principal at maturity.

Bills are issued on a bearer basis, with a minimum denomination of $10,000. Although the income on an investment in Treasury bills comes entirely in the form of a capital gain, the tax authorities treat the income as ordinary income and not as a capital gain. However, like all income from U.S. government securities, it is exempt from state and local taxes.

It is difficult to generalize about the return available from an investment in Treasury bills. Since 1970, Treasury bill yields have been as low as 3 percent and as high as 9½ percent. The only generalization that can be made is that of the many short-term financial instruments available to the investor that are also marketable, the Treasury bill will have the lowest return. This is because of the absence of credit risk.

Tax Anticipation Securities. Tax anticipation securities, as their name implies, are short-term securities that can be used to pay one's income taxes. If an investor owes $10,000 in federal income tax that is due in four weeks, the investor could purchase a tax anticipation bill at a discount and use the face amount of the bill to pay the tax liability when due. The motivation for wealthy investors and for corporations to use tax anticipation bills is that the maturity of these bills is set several days after the tax due date, but the Internal Revenue Service allows the bills to be redeemed at par on the tax date. Thus, the earnings on a tax anticipation bill will be earned over a somewhat shorter period of time than the stated maturity period.

Treasury Notes and Bonds. The federal government also issues longer-term marketable securities at a stated or coupon rate. The two categories of long-term federal debt instruments are called Treasury notes and bonds. Notes represent approximately 35 percent of the federal, publicly issued, interest-bearing debt and have an initial maturity of one to seven years. Notes are typically sold in registered form and carry a minimum denomination of $1,000. Bonds represent approximately 9 percent of the federal, publicly issued, interest-bearing debt, and carry initial maturities of five years or more, with the typical issue having a maturity longer than five years. The minimum denomination is $500, but since mid-1971, all new issues of marketable U.S. government bonds carry a minimum denomination of $1,000. With the many issues of both notes and bonds outstanding, an investor can usually arrange virtually any maturity schedule desired, up to about twenty-five years.

When purchasing either bonds or notes, an investor must be aware of the method of quoting U.S. government bonds in the financial press. These securities are quoted exactly like corporate bonds *except* that prices are reported and traded in 32nds instead of 8ths. The usual method of reporting prices is in decimal form where a price reported as 91.17 would be read as 91 and 17/32nds. Occasionally, a quotation may be made in 64ths and the price might be reported as 91.17+, which would be interpreted as 91 and 35/64ths.

Treasury bonds are often callable at par during the last five years of their maturity. For example, the 4¼ percent bond maturing in 1992 is callable at par beginning in 1987. In order for the investor to be aware of this feature, the bond is described as 4¼, 1987–92, where the first date refers to the initial call date and the later date the maturity. In reporting prices for this bond, the financial press retains this label.

Savings Bonds. With some very minor exceptions, bills, notes, and bonds represent the total marketable debt issued directly by the federal government. As of December 31, 1974, these three categories represented about 57 percent of the federal debt, or more than $282 billion of par value. Another 18 percent ($88.2 billion) is represented by nonmarketable securities available to the public. The remaining 25 percent consists of issues sold directly to government agencies and trust funds. Of the nonmarketable issues, the most important for the average investor is the United States Savings Bond. This security is designed mainly for the small investor, and has the attractions of small denominations and safety. There are two categories of savings bonds, the Series E and the Series H.

There are important differences between these two types of savings bonds, as noted in Exhibit 19–1. The minimum denomination for the Series E is $25 of par value, while the Series H can be purchased in multiples of $500. The income from Series E bonds comes in the form of appreciation in the value of the bond, as opposed to the current income received every six months from Series H bonds. Series E bonds carry an initial maturity of five years, while Series H bonds have an initial maturity of ten years.

Since the income from a Series E bond comes in the form of price appreciation, the bonds are purchased from the Treasury at a discount of 25 percent of the face value of the bond. If you were to purchase a $25 Series E bond, the purchase price would be $18.75. At this price, the bond has a yield-to-maturity of 6 percent. However, the holder should be aware of the fact that a penalty is attached to early redemption.

EXHIBIT 19–1
Comparison of Series E and Series H Bonds

Characteristic	Series E	Series H
Denominations	$25, 50, 75, 100 200, 500, 1,000	$500, 1,000, 1,500
Purchase price	75% of denomination	Denomination value
Interest rate	6% to maturity 4½% the first year with gradually increasing rate to maturity	6% to maturity 5% the first year 5.8% for years 2 to 5 6.5% for years 6 to 10
Maturity	5 years	10 years
Payment of interest	Increase in the redemption value	by semiannual check to the bondholder
Tax status of interest	Taxed as current income or may be deferred until redemption	Taxed as current income
Redemption	Any time after two months from issue date	Any time after six months from issue date
Exchange provision	May be exchanged for Series H bond; $500 minimum	None

As shown in Exhibit 19–1, the yield on a Series E bond held for only one year is 4½ percent. The terms of the bond are such that the annual return required to produce a rate of return of 6 percent over the original maturity increases with time.

Series H bonds have a similar arrangement except that instead of the price appreciation of a Series E bond, the income payments increase with time. The first payment is $21 per $1,000 of face value. The second payment is $29 and this rate continues for the next eight semiannual interest payments. Beginning in the sixth year, the interest payment increases to $32.56 every six months and remains at that level until maturity.

Because of the interest penalties, it is often wise to hold a savings bond to maturity even when one has opportunities for seemingly greater returns from investment of comparable adjusted risk. The actual yield on savings bonds is low relative to some other investment opportunities, but once the bond is purchased, the redemption decision should be made on the basis of the marginal yield, the bond's yield for the rest of its life, and not the total yield from the bond.

Like all U.S. government issues, the income from savings bonds is exempt from state and local taxes, but not from federal income taxes. However, in the case of Series E bonds, the tax payment need not be made until the bond is redeemed. This may be an advantage to the saver if redemption occurs after retirement or in a low income year. In addition, a Series E bond may be exchanged, at its current redemption price, for a Series H bond without having to pay taxes on the accrued income of the Series E bond. With such a conversion, the tax payable is postponed until either the redemption or final maturity of the newly acquired Series H bond.

The maturity of both a Series E and H bond will be automatically extended if the investor chooses not to redeem the bond at its original maturity. No special action is required to take advantage of the extension feature. As a result of this feature, all Series E and H bonds outstanding are still earning interest regardless of their issue date.

"Flower" Bonds. The individual investor also has available for purchase a number of somewhat unusual securities. For example, several U.S. government bonds are known as "flower" bonds. The advantage of these bonds is that when the bond is redeemed for the purpose of paying federal estate taxes, payment of the tax on any capital gain on the bond itself is not required. In addition, a "flower" bond purchased at a discount can be used at par in the payment of the estate taxes. If death were to occur shortly after a person purchased a "flower" bond at 80, the person's estate would benefit, since this bond is accepted at 100 for the payment of estate taxes. Since no new bonds with this special provision have been issued since March 1971, the supply of these bonds gets smaller each year as outstanding bonds are used to pay estate taxes.

Federal Agency Bonds. We emphasized the fact that bonds issued by the federal government are free of credit risk. For this reason, U.S. government bonds have a promised yield below all other investment opportunities of comparable maturity. However, a set of issues with over $85 billion in face value exists that provides the investor with a yield higher than that on U.S. government securities without much increase in risk. These securities are fixed income securities issued by agencies of the federal government. Some of the larger issuing agencies include Banks for Cooperatives, Federal Land Banks, Federal Home Loan Banks, Federal Intermediate Credit Banks, and the Government National Mortgage Association (Ginnie Mae). Some of the smaller agencies include the U.S. Postal Service, the Small Business Administration, and the Tennessee Valley Authority (TVA).

In terms of return, federal agency bonds frequently sell to yield as much as one hundred basis points more than equivalent maturity securities issued directly by the U.S. Treasury. A few of the agency bonds are backed by the federal government, but most rely on the earning power of the particular agency. In other words, if you owned bonds issued by the TVA, the principal and interest payments would be paid from the earnings of TVA. If these earnings were insufficient, the bondholder could not look to the taxing power or money-creating power of the federal government as a source of funds to meet the obligation of the TVA bonds. As with a corporate bond, the credit risk lies in the earning power of the particular agency issuing the bond.

The lack of a direct government guarantee is a problem in theory only. It is probably fair to conclude that although there is no explicit guarantee by the U.S. Treasury, there exists a strong implied government guarantee. It is difficult to imagine the federal government allowing TVA to enter the bankruptcy courts because of the inability to meet principal and interest obligations on outstanding debt. It would seem that the only real credit risk lies in potential delayed payments. Financial problems might cause a delay in payments, but it seems doubtful that the U.S. Congress would allow the liquidation of the assets of one of the agencies. In essence, it would appear that purchase of a federal agency bond requires sacrificing a very slight amount of protection in return for an added yield.

Like direct debt issues of the U.S. Government, federal agency bonds are subject to federal income tax, but are exempt from state and local income taxes. The state and local exemption is not applicable, however, to agency bonds issued by Fannie Mae, Ginnie Mae, and the Export-Import Bank.

MUNICIPAL BONDS

Tax Status

Other government units besides the federal government issue marketable fixed income securities. State and local governmental units also issue debt securities that are generally referred to as municipals or tax-exempts. Municipals basically include all fixed income financial instruments issued by a governmental unit other than the federal government. These securities have a variety of characteristics that separate them from United States government bonds, but the most outstanding feature is their tax status. The income received by the owner of a municipal bond is exempt from the federal income tax. In addition, most states will allow a tax exemption on the interest received from its own state and local issues. However, the federal exemption is by far the most important of the tax exemption features.

To see the significance of the tax exemption feature, let us suppose that an investor filing a joint return has taxable income of $22,000. This places the investor in the 32 percent marginal tax bracket. If the investor is trying to decide between the purchase of a municipal bond yielding 6 percent and a corporate bond, the corporate bond of equal risk would need to yield 8.82 percent for the investor to be indifferent between the two alternatives. Since the corporate bond is taxable, the after-tax return from the corporate bond will be only 68 percent (one minus the marginal tax rate) of the 8.82 percent. Sixty-eight percent of 8.82 percent is a return of 6 percent. The after-tax yield on the municipal bond is 6 percent since its income is tax exempt. A resident of the issuing state would find the municipal even more attractive because of the state and local tax exemption feature.

Tables known as taxable equivalent tables have been prepared to show the taxable yield equivalent to a given tax-exempt yield for a given tax filing status. Exhibit 19-2 is a taxable equivalent table for a joint return tax filing status. The 8.82 percent taxable return can be determined by reading down the 6.00 percent column and across the $20,000 to $24,000 line. From Exhibit 19-2, it is readily apparent that municipal bonds become more attractive the larger the taxable income level.

Unless the investor is the original buyer of the municipal bond, the tax exemption applies only to the coupon payments. If an investor purchases a ten-year municipal selling to yield 6 percent with a coupon of 5 percent, its price will be $925.60 per $1,000 of face value. When the bond is redeemed at its face value in ten years, a capital gain of $74.40 per $1,000 face value results. This capital gain is taxable like any other capital gain. The $50 annual interest is tax exempt, but a tax at capital gains rates must be paid on the discount. Even if the bond is sold prior to maturity, any capital gain is taxable.

Categories of Municipals

The risk associated with the purchase of municipals is typically much different from the risk associated with U.S. government bonds. In order to examine the risk associated with a municipal, we must understand three categories of municipals: general obligation, revenue, and assessment bonds.

General obligation bonds, or full faith and credit bonds as they are often called, are backed by the overall financial and taxing power of the issuing political entity. The risk of default is tied to the resources of the entire state, county, city, or other political entity issuing the bonds. These bonds typically carry the highest credit ratings with corresponding low risk and low returns. We need to recognize, however, that even general obligation bonds carry credit risk since taxing power is limited and state and local governments do not hold the power to create money. For example, some of the financial problems of New York City forced investors to consider very carefully the quality of New York City's full faith and credit bonds.[3]

Revenue bonds form the second large category of municipal bonds. The principal and interest payments on these bonds can be made only

[3]For example, see Phil Hawkings and Lindley B. Richert, "New York City, Fighting off Insolvency, Is Bolstered by $396 Million State Loan," *Wall Street Journal,* April 4, 1975, p. 34.

EXHIBIT 19-2
Taxable Equivalent Table—Joint Return

TAXABLE INCOME JOINT RETURN	Tax-Free Yield 2.00	2.50	3.00	3.50	4.00	4.50	5.00	5.50	6.00	6.50	7.00
$16,000 20,000	2.77	3.47	4.17	4.86	5.56	6.25	6.94	7.64	8.33	9.03	9.72
20,000 24,000	2.92	3.68	4.41	5.07	5.88	6.62	7.35	8.09	8.82	9.56	10.29
24,000 28,000	3.12	3.91	4.69	5.47	6.25	7.03	7.81	8.59	9.37	10.16	10.94
28,000 32,000	3.27	4.10	4.92	5.74	6.56	7.38	8.20	9.02	9.84	10.66	11.48
32,000 36,000	3.44	4.31	5.17	6.03	6.90	7.76	8.62	9.48	10.34	11.21	12.07
36,000 40,000	3.63	4.55	5.45	6.36	7.27	8.18	9.09	10.00	10.91	11.82	12.73
40,000 44,000	3.84	4.81	5.77	6.73	7.69	8.65	9.62	10.58	11.54	12.50	13.46
44,000 52,000	4.00	5.00	6.00	7.00	8.00	9.00	10.00	11.00	12.00	13.00	14.00
52,000 64,000	4.25	5.32	6.38	7.45	8.51	9.57	10.64	11.70	12.77	13.83	14.89
64,000 76,000	4.44	5.56	6.67	7.78	8.89	10.00	11.11	12.22	13.33	14.44	15.56
76,000 88,000	4.76	5.95	7.14	8.33	9.52	10.71	11.90	13.10	14.29	15.48	16.67
88,000 100,000	5.00	6.25	7.50	8.75	10.00	11.25	12.50	13.75	15.00	16.25	17.50
100,000 120,000	5.26	6.58	7.89	9.21	10.53	11.84	13.16	14.47	15.79	17.11	18.42
120,000 140,000	5.55	6.94	8.33	9.72	11.11	12.50	13.89	15.28	16.67	18.06	19.44
140,000 160,000	5.88	7.35	8.82	10.29	11.76	13.24	14.71	16.18	17.65	19.12	20.59
160,000 180,000	6.24	7.81	9.38	10.94	12.50	14.06	15.63	17.19	18.75	20.31	21.88
180,000 200,000	6.45	8.06	9.68	11.29	12.90	14.52	16.13	17.74	19.35	20.97	22.58
over 200,000	6.66	8.33	10.00	11.67	13.33	15.00	16.67	18.33	20.00	21.67	23.33

Source: *Investing for Tax-Free Income,* New York: Merrill Lynch, March 1972, pp. 22-23. Printed courtesy of Merrill Lynch, Pierce, Fenner & Smith, Inc., New York, New York.

from the revenues generated by the assets financed from the proceeds of the issue. The building of a bridge, for example, may be financed with revenue bonds. The revenue bonds issued will be serviced from bridge tolls for the life of the bond. If the income from the bridge is not sufficient to meet the debt obligation, the bondholder has no recourse to state or local authorities. However, since the assets built with revenue bonds may become indispensable to the particular state or other political entity, it is not unusual for the political entity to intervene in the case of a revenue bond in default. Generally speaking, however, revenue bonds are more risky than general obligation bonds, although some revenue bonds are of very high quality.

Bonds in the much smaller third category are usually issued for the purpose of improving existing governmental facilities. These *assessment bonds* take their name from the fact that principal and interest will be paid from the proceeds of specific assessments on the property in the political entity. The property tax is set up so that a certain portion will go to meet the debt obligation. If the value of the assessed property declines, the bonds may be in risk of default.

The Market and Risk of Municipals

The market in municipal bonds is enormous, with over $180 billion outstanding. The market deals in $1,000 units, but in recent years most municipal bonds have been issued in $5,000 units, and in bearer form. Like corporate bonds, the large municipal issues are given a credit rating by Moody's or Standard & Poor's; essentially the same letter grade notation is used for municipals as for corporate bonds. The credit rating techniques are complex, with consideration given to the aggregate tax burden of the community, the per capita income, the trend of expenditures, the stability of employment in the community, and the growth of the community. The quality of credit ratings for municipal bonds is quite good and an independent credit analysis of the credit standing of a given municipal bond would usually produce a rating close to the rating given by Moody's or Standard & Poor's.

Although the ratings are generally reliable, many municipal issues are too small to merit attention by the rating agencies. Consequently, the smaller investor will often choose from only the larger issues available. There are thousands of small issues available, but these are usually for the local investor only. It is usually unwise to purchase or attempt to gain information on the small issues unless one has a special interest in the community issuing the bond. Even with large issues that have received a rating, it is probably wise to remain with large issues of high-quality municipals where the rating is at least single A. Like corporate bonds, municipals with the lower ratings are more appropriate for the investor with either special expertise in the analysis of fixed income municipal securities or sufficient capital to diversify widely.

There is another important reason for staying with the large, high-quality municipals. The secondary market is almost entirely over-the-counter and unless the issue is large and well known, the investor may face a liquidity problem when attempting to sell. The sale of a holding of a small municipal bond may require several days and a considerable sacrifice in price. Even with larger issues, one should probably not consider the purchase of less than a round-lot, which is $25,000 of face value. Anything less than a round-lot will normally produce liquidity problems that will be manifested in a price sacrifice. The round-lot advice has nothing to do with commissions, since in the municipal bond market there are no commissions. Rather, the dealer earns a fee through a price difference between the buyer's price and the dealer's cost.

Maturity Structure

Many municipal bonds are issued in the form of serial bonds. A serial bond issue exists when the individual bonds under the indenture have their own special maturity. A municipality may issue $10 million in debt with a twenty-year maturity. The indenture will stipulate that $500,000 matures in the first year, $500,000 in the second year, and so on. It should be noted that most toll road bonds are term bonds in which each bond issue matures at one time instead of serially on an annual basis. The difference between a serial bond arrangement and the typical sinking fund in a corporate bond issue is that the indenture for a municipal bond issue will stipulate particular bonds for the annual maturities. The advantage for the investor is that the purchase of a municipal can be made without the risk that the investment will be called prior to the expected maturity.

The typical serial issue does not maintain a constant coupon interest rate for all maturities. This is no problem for the investor since the secondary market will adjust the prices of the various maturities to reflect the difference in coupon rates. At the same time, one should note that the low coupon may cause the bond to sell at a discount depending on the general level of interest rates. Since the interest is tax exempt, but capital gains are subject to capital gains tax rates, the investor will normally prefer a high coupon municipal bond. This situation is just the reverse of the tax preference in the corporate bond market.

OTHER MONEY MARKET SECURITIES

Our survey of the financial securities issued by the various governmental units in the country is now complete. As we saw, a large portion of the federal debt is represented by Treasury bills. Bills are a part of what is commonly referred to as the money market. In general, the money market includes short-term debt securities with a maturity of less than one year where the credit risk is zero or quite low. We observed that the credit risk of Treasury bills is zero, but several other types of securities issued by private corporations exist where the credit risk is close to zero. These instruments include commercial paper, certificates of deposit, bankers' acceptances, a few short-term municipals, and some European securities. All are considered money market securities and are viewed as slightly more risky substitutes for Treasury bills.

Commercial Paper

Short-term promissory notes issued by a private corporation are called commercial paper. The issuing corporation generally belongs to the "honor roll" of financially sound organizations. The commercial paper issue is often backed by unused lines of bank credit. This means that a firm with a $100 million in commercial paper outstanding will have borrowing capability of at least $100 million at a commercial bank. The maturities for commercial paper range from a few days up to one year. Commercial paper is usually issued in bearer form and sold on a discount basis in the same manner as Treasury bills. However, some commercial paper has been issued recently on an interest bearing basis. In general, investors in commercial paper are other large corporations, since the minimum round-lot transaction is $250,000 and the typical minimum denomination is $100,000 of face value. The yields available on commercial paper are typically 50 to 100 basis points above the yields on Treasury bills with equivalent maturities. However, the difference in yields expanded to as much as 300 basis points during the summer of 1974. Concern on the part of investors about the quality of commercial paper outstanding and a strong demand for short-term funds by corporations were responsible for the widening yield differential.

Although the risk associated with commercial paper is greater than that associated with Treasury bills, in most cases the risk is insignificant and need not be given a great deal of consideration. Risk is not absent, however; witness the 1970 default on the commercial paper issued by the Penn Central Corporation.

Certificates of Deposit

Another important money market instrument of recent vintage is the certificate of deposit, which is popularly known as a CD. Money market CD's are *negotiable* time deposits issued by a large commercial bank. Since 1970, Federal Reserve controls have been gradually suspended on CD's of $100,000 or more, so that the rates today generally follow the rates on all other uncontrolled money market securities. CD's generally come in denominations of $100,000 to $1,000,000, and are usually traded in lots of $1,000,000. They can be issued with virtually any maturity, but most frequent maturities are in units of 30 days up to 90 days with some 180-day maturities. When issued by a commercial bank, they cannot be redeemed until maturity. However, since they are negotiable, the investor can sell the CD as any other market instrument could be sold. The market for CD's is quite liquid, with several large banks actively making a market in CD's. As with commercial paper, the risk is only slightly higher than that of Treasury bills and yields in late 1974 were approximately 100 basis points above short-term U.S. government securities. Risk is not absent, however, as the failure of the Franklin National Bank (New York) illustrates.

Bankers' Acceptances

Money market investors also have available to them bankers' acceptances, which can be used for short-term, low-risk investments. Bankers' acceptances are usually created as the result of a foreign trade transaction. If a large retailer in the United States wishes to purchase a shipment of toys on credit from an English firm and the English firm would like payment immediately, the usual arrangement is for the U.S. firm to arrange a letter of credit with a local bank made out in favor of the exporting firm. The letter of credit is then sent to the English firm, which negotiates it at a local bank receiving payment in British pounds. The letter of credit is then sent to the U.S. bank along with the shipping documents where the letter is stamped "accepted" by the U.S. bank. This means the U.S. bank has accepted responsibility for payment. The letter of credit is now a bankers' acceptance and is usually sold to an acceptance dealer with the proceeds of the sale returned to the foreign bank. The toys are turned over to the retailer and the transaction is complete. The credit has been provided by the acceptance dealer, or more properly by the money market investor purchasing the acceptance from the acceptance dealer.

In late 1974, over $8 billion in bankers' acceptances were outstanding with maturities usually set at 180 days. The denominations vary but are usually over $100,000. The purchase and sale of acceptances is done on a discount basis in the same manner as Treasury bills and commercial paper. At maturity, the acceptance is presented to the accepting bank for payment. The bank collects from the original importing firm in the form of payments to the bank as the toys are sold. The risk associated with bankers' acceptances is directly related to the risk of the accepting bank's becoming insolvent. It is interesting that there has never been a principal loss to investors from an investment in bankers' acceptances and these instruments have been available in the secondary money market since the early 1920s. Because of the very low risk, the returns on banker's acceptances have been quite close to those available from Treasury bills.

GOVERNMENT BOND AND MONEY MARKET FUNDS

Whether one is interested in federal government bonds, municipal bonds, or other money market investments, direct participation in the market usually requires substantial amounts of money. In the municipal market, a minimum of $25,000 face value is recommended, and Treasury bills require a minimum purchase of $10,000 face value. Smaller investments are usually excluded either because of liquidity considerations or because smaller denominations are simply not available. With interest rates at high levels in recent years, the investment company concept has been used with increasing frequency for the purpose of providing the small investor with the opportunity to invest in a portfolio of government bonds, municipal bonds, or money market securities. We discuss the general subject of investment companies in the next two chapters. For now, we will simply state that an investment company is a managed portfolio of financial securities; the investor purchases units or shares of the portfolio at current market prices.

Federal Government Securities Fund

A few investment companies have specialized in recent years in U.S. government securities. Table 19-2 shows three such investment companies. Fund For U.S. Government Securities, Inc., established in 1969, is the largest of these three investment companies. This fund has a minimum initial investment of $250 with a minimum subsequent investment of $25. The maximum commission for buying (called a load or sales charge) is 1.5 percent and may be lower for transactions of $10,000 and over. There is no redemption fee. The investor does pay an average annual management advisory fee of .25 percent (or less if the net assets are over a certain size) of daily net assets.

Tax-Exempt Bond Funds

Several municipal bond investment companies have also come into existence since 1961. An estimate by Standard & Poor's is that 244 separate funds have been sold and assets total approximately $3.8 billion. From a legal standpoint, these tax-exempt bond funds are actually trusts, but for our purposes may be considered identical to investment companies. Although these trusts offer units in "nonmanaged" portfolios rather than shares in managed portfolios and cannot make continuous offerings, they do provide the investor with the opportunity of purchasing a diversified portfolio of municipal bonds with a small investment outlay. However, in the case of a tax-exempt bond fund, a small outlay is less important since investors interested in municipals usually are not classified as small investors.

TABLE 19–2

Selected Investment Companies for Government Bonds and Money Market Securities

	Asset Size	Sales Charge*
Federal Government securities‡		
Franklin U.S. Gov't Sec.	$15 mil	8¾%
Fund for Federal Sec., Inc.	6	1¾
Fund for U.S. Gov't Sec., Inc.	88	1½
Tax-exempt bonds:§		
E. F. Hutton (31 Series)	209	4
Municipal Inv. Trust Fund† (95 Series)	2,114	3½
Nuveen (62 Series)	1,030	4½
Money Market Funds: ‖		
Dreyfus Liquid Assets	513	None
Fidelity Daily Income Trust	299	None
Money Market Management	208	None
Reserve Fund	402	None

*The maximum sales charge; may be lower for large investments.

†Sponsored by Merrill Lynch and partners.

‡Asset size as of September 30, 1974, except for Fund for Federal Securities (11/30/74).

§Asset size and number of series data from *S&P Outlook*, December 23, 1974.

‖Asset size as of October 24, 1974.

Sources: "Money Market Funds' Appeal Waning," *Standard & Poor's Outlook*, November 4, 1974, p. 475; "Municipal Bond Funds Offer Tax-Free Income," *Standard & Poor's Outlook*, December 23, 1974, pp. 392–93; and Wisenberger Services, *Investment Companies, 1974*. (New York: Wiesenberger Services, 1974), pp. 487–93.

To see how tax-exempt bond funds operate, we will examine Series 63 of the Nuveen Tax-Exempt Bond Fund. The prospectus for Series 63, dated November 26, 1974, contains the basic information an investor would need regarding this investment opportunity. The potential investor in Series 63 is offered 250,000 units of a $25 million diversified municipal bond portfolio. The units are valued at $100 each with a minimum purchase of 50 units. The investment carries an estimated current rate of return of 7.47 percent based upon the public offering price. All but two of the twenty-four bonds in the trust were rated A or better by Standard & Poor's. Although not required to do so, John Nuveen & Co. plans to maintain a market based upon the bid prices of the bonds in the trust. Unit holders may redeem without a redemption fee.

Money Market Investment Companies

Money market investment companies (or funds as they are called) allow the smaller investor to participate indirectly in investments in commercial paper, bankers' acceptances, certificates of deposit, and other money market securities. Normally, no sales charge is made for either purchasing or redeeming shares of a money market fund, although the investor does pay a management fee and other expenses equal to approximately 1 percent annually of the net assets. When money market rates reached 12 percent in 1974, money market funds were very popular. However, as money market rates declined to the 6 to 7 percent range by the spring of 1975, investor interest in the money market funds started to wane.[4] If money market rates should increase substantially, money market funds should again become popular with investors, especially since they are very liquid investments.

Table 19-2 shows data for four large money market funds. These money market funds pay interest on a daily basis and some even allow the investor to withdraw money by using special checks provided by the money market fund. These favorable withdrawal arrangements, plus the liquidity inherent in a portfolio of money market securities, attracted investors during the poor stock market conditions of 1974.

SUMMARY

Government securities include securities issued by the federal government, a federal agency, or a state or local political entity. Huge quantities of government securities are outstanding, representing the issues of thousands of political entities. The quality ranges from securities issued by the U.S. government that are free of credit risk to municipal bonds of a very speculative nature. Some highway toll bonds, such as the Chicago-Calumet Skyway 3⅜% bonds of 1995 and the Chesapeake Bay Bridge & Tunnel 5¾% bonds of 2000, are in default.

U.S. government marketable securities include Treasury bills, notes, and bonds. Bills have a maturity of one year or less. Notes have a maturity of one year to seven years, while bonds mature in five or more years. Federal securities are free of credit risk since the government can always create money to make principal and interest payments. The interest income on federal securities is exempt from state and local income taxes. Another special tax feature is attached to certain issues of U.S. bonds allowing these bonds to be used at par in the payment of estate taxes. This may make these so-called "flower" bonds attractive if they sell at a discount from par and if the demise of the holder is imminent. Securities issued by federal agencies are also available and usually carry slightly higher yields than do the direct issues of the federal government.

Savings bonds are nonmarketable U.S. government securities; an investor desiring to liquidate a holding of savings bonds must present them to an

[4] "Money Market Funds' Appeal Waning," *Standard & Poor's Outlook,* November 4, 1974, p. 475, and Byron Klapper, "Money Market Funds, Highfliers in '74 Amid Wall Street Ills, May Face Drought," *Wall Street Journal,* April 21, 1975, p. 20.

authorized agency such as a commercial bank for redemption by the federal government. Series E bonds are sold at a discount and income is earned in the form of capital appreciation. Series H bonds are sold at par and pay interest by semiannual check. Both Series E and H bonds pay interest at an annual rate of 6 percent, if held to maturity. While this is not a high rate in comparison to other possible marketable securities, Series E bonds have a tax advantage: Taxes on the interest earned need not be paid until the bond is redeemed. In addition, the bonds are safe and can be purchased through the employee's payroll savings plan.

State and local issues are called municipals or tax-exempt securities, since their interest is exempt from federal income taxes. The three main categories of municipal bonds are general obligation bonds, revenue bonds, and assessment bonds. General obligation bonds are backed by the taxing power of the issuing political entity. Revenue bonds must rely on the revenue produced by the projects financed by the proceeds of the bond issue unless the revenue issue is also backed by the full faith and credit of a political entity. Assessment bonds are serviced by property taxes collected to finance a specific improvement to governmental services, such as a sewage system.

Treasury bills belong to a group of securities known as money market instruments. These high-quality, short-term, marketable securities also include commercial paper, bankers' acceptances, short-term municipals, and negotiable certificates of deposit. The yields available from the various money market instruments depend to a considerable extent on the quality of the issuing organization.

When investing in governmental securities and money market instruments, the investor must examine the yields available on the various alternative investments, the amount of money needed to purchase the particular security, the risks of the various alternative investments, and his or her tax and liquidity positions. The tax situation becomes especially critical in municipal bond investing, since the interest from municipal bonds is exempt from federal income taxes.

QUESTIONS

1. Why would an investor consider the purchase of securities issued by the federal government?
2. What are the advantages and disadvantages of Treasury bills as an investment for the individual investor?
3. What is the meaning of the following U.S. government bond quotation taken from the *Wall Street Journal*?

   7½s, 1988–93 Aug. 97.28 Bid 98.28 Asked – .8 Change

4. *a)* What general sort of investor should purchase U.S. Savings Bonds?
   b) Is there any difference in the kind of investor who should purchase a Series E bond as opposed to a Series H bond?

5. What is a "flower" bond? What type of investor should purchase such a bond?
6. Briefly discuss the major types of municipal bonds available to the investor.
7. In purchasing corporate bonds, it may be desirable for the investor to purchase a bond at a discount if the investor is in a high marginal tax bracket. Is this also true for the purchase of a municipal bond?
8. What factors are important in the determination of the quality of a municipal bond?
9. An alternative to government securities exists and is called by the general name of money market securities.
   a) What major types of securities are considered as money market securities?
   b) What are the disadvantages of these securities for the average investor?
10. An investor filing a joint return has a taxable income of $22,000. The investor can purchase a triple A corporate bond at par to yield 8.5 percent. Using Exhibit 19-3, what yield would this investor require from a municipal bond of comparable quality before it would be purchased?
11. "Toll Roads' Income Down, Finance Costs Up as the Gasoline Shortage Cuts into Traffic" was a *Wall Street Journal* headline on March 4, 1974. As an investor owning a portfolio containing several tollway bonds, what would you examine to determine the soundness of each of your holdings?

SUGGESTED READINGS

Farmer, Richard N. "The Death of Cities—And What to Do About It." *MSU Business Topics,* Autumn 1971, pp. 11–18.

Ganis, David R. "All About the GNMA Mortgage-Backed Securities Market." *Real Estate Review,* Summer 1974, pp. 55–65.

Handbook of Securities of the United States Government and Federal Agencies and Related Money Market Instruments. 26th ed. New York: The First Boston Corporation, 1974.

Hastie, K. Larry. "Determinants of Municipal Bond Yields." *Journal of Financial and Quantitative Analysis,* June 1972, pp. 1729–48.

Hemple, George H. "An Evaluation of Municipal Bankruptcy Laws and Procedures." *Journal of Finance,* December 1973, pp. 1339–51.

——. *Postwar Quality of State and Local Debt.* NBER General Series No. 94. New York: Columbia University Press, 1971.

Hoffland, David L. "The Price-Rating Structure of the Municipal Bond Market." *Financial Analysts Journal,* March–April 1972, pp. 65–70.

Packer, Stephen B. "Municipal Bond Ratings." *Financial Analysts Journal,* July-August 1968, pp. 93–97.

20

Investment Companies: Introduction

An investment company may be generally defined as any company whose assets consist mainly of securities of other companies. The Investment Company Act of 1940 defines an investment company as a company with over 40 percent of its assets in securities other than United States government obligations or majority-owned subsidiaries. Investment companies have grown rapidly during the post-World War II period; the growth of investment company assets and the number of shareholders owning investment company shares is shown in Figure 20–1 for the period from 1950 to 1974.

The number and variety of investment companies has proliferated to such an extent that any investor should be able to find the appropriate investment company to satisfy virtually any investment objective. As of June 30, 1974, the Securities and Exchange Commission reported that 1,377 investment companies were registered under the 1940 act.[1]

[1]U.S. Securities and Exchange Commission, *40th Annual Report* (Washington, D.C.: Government Printing Office, 1974), p. 153.

FIGURE 20-1
Mutual Fund Shareholders and Assets—1950-74

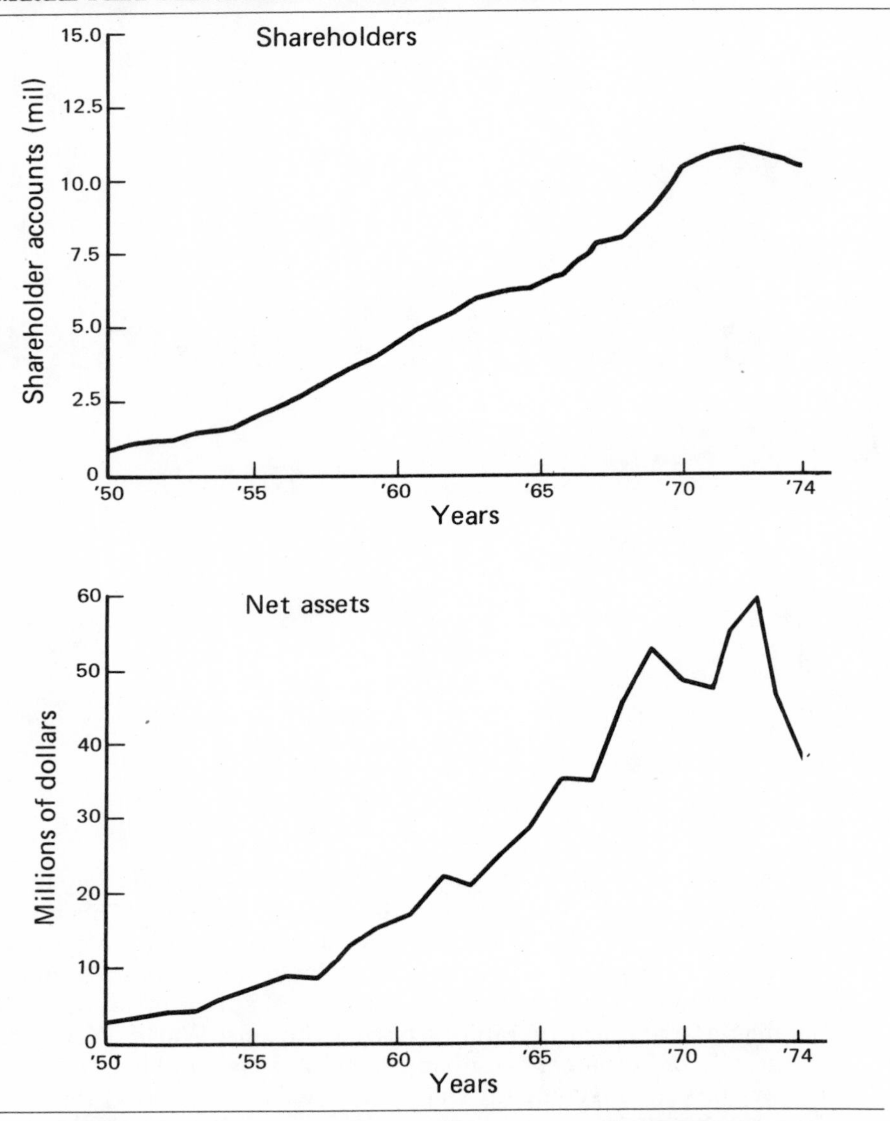

Source: Investment Company Institute, *Mutual Fund Fact Book*, 1975, p. 7.

This chapter discusses the nature, history, and functions of investment companies. Special features available to investors using the investment company format for investing are also discussed. The next chapter discusses the regulatory aspects of investment companies and the evaluation of their performance. With so many investment companies available to the investor, it is crucial to be able to make an appraisal of their past performance.

FUNCTIONS OF INVESTMENT COMPANIES

Investment companies have at least four primary functions: 1) diversification, 2) professional management, 3) liquidity, and 4) allocation of equity funds within the economy. The first three are directly beneficial to the investor. The fourth concerns the functioning of the economy as a whole.

Since the investment company allows an individual to purchase a fractional interest in a well-diversified portfolio, the small investor can achieve the risk-reducing properties that diversification provides. As noted in Chapter 13, owning about ten to fifteen properly selected stocks is sufficient to substantially eliminate diversifiable risk. This implies that an investor without sufficient funds to purchase ten to fifteen separate securities may find investment companies a useful investment vehicle. But there is more to the story than just the number of securities. An investor might purchase ten securities with $2,000, but this would entail a substantial commission. The exact commission would involve considerations such as minimum charges per order, but between $200 and $300 could be spent for commissions for both buying and selling. In addition, the investor would be limited to selecting low-priced stocks. While the purchase of an investment company involves a cost, the sale normally does not. This cost can range from approximately 9 percent for certain investment companies down to a very small management fee for others. The value of the diversification service then becomes a trade-off between commission rates and the investment company charges. In the authors' opinion, a person with less than about $20,000 to invest may find the diversification service of an investment company valuable.

The second function of an investment company is to provide the investor with professional management. The investment decisions of a professional investor may well be "better" than the decisions of most of the investing public. The professional may have greater interpretative skill, more and better information, economies in processing the information, and private or "insider" information. Hence, an investment company will be beneficial to an investor insofar as the decisions of the individual investor can be expected to produce lower returns or higher risk or both compared to the decisions of the investment company management.

Even if investment companies in general earn a rate of return greater than could be earned by a given investor, the individual is not relieved of the task of evaluating alternative investment companies. It is not clear that the skills required to evaluate an investment company are any different than those required to evaluate an individual security. The appraisal of the actual performance of investment companies will be examined in the next chapter.

Some investment companies stand ready to redeem shares upon written notice by the investor, while the shares of other investment companies must be sold in the open market. Rarely will an extended delay be encountered in attempting to liquidate all or a portion of an investor's holdings. In fact, the investor faces a similar situation with actively traded securities. This does not imply that the investor will be able to liquidate at a particular value, only that the current value can be turned into cash almost immediately.

To the extent that these three services are desired by the community at large, the existence of investment companies within the economy probably has generated a larger portion of equity funds than would otherwise be the case. As such it is probable that the allocation of real resources is more efficient than would be the case without an investment company industry. At the same time, this conclusion is extremely difficult to prove in any absolute sense.

TYPES AND HISTORY OF INVESTMENT COMPANIES

There are only two major types of investment companies of significance at the present time—open-end investment companies and closed-end investment companies.[2] Open-end investment companies are commonly called mutual funds. The nature of both types of investment companies will be discussed shortly. Exhibit 20-1 presents a detailed classification of investment companies.

Investment companies trace their origins to the early nineteenth century in Europe. Investment trusts were quite popular in England and Scotland in the period from 1870 to 1890, until a financial crisis slowed their rate of growth.[3]

Early American investment companies were either fixed trusts or closed-end investment companies. The first open-end investment company, as we know it today, was the Massachusetts Investors Trust formed in March 1924. However, these open-end investment companies ran a very poor second to the closed-end funds. The SEC estimated that only

[2]The 1940 Investment Company Act divides registered investment companies into three classes: (1) face-amount certificate companies; (2) unit investment trusts; and (3) management companies. Face-amount certificates are contracts under which the investment company agrees to pay a fixed amount at maturity. Unit investment trusts sell redeemable interests as units of specific securities such as municipal bonds. Management companies, which include both open-end and closed-end types, are by far the dominant form of investment company.

[3]See Hugh Bullock, *The Story of Investment Companies* (New York: Columbia University Press, 1959), for an excellent history of investment companies.

EXHIBIT 20–1
Classification of Investment Companies

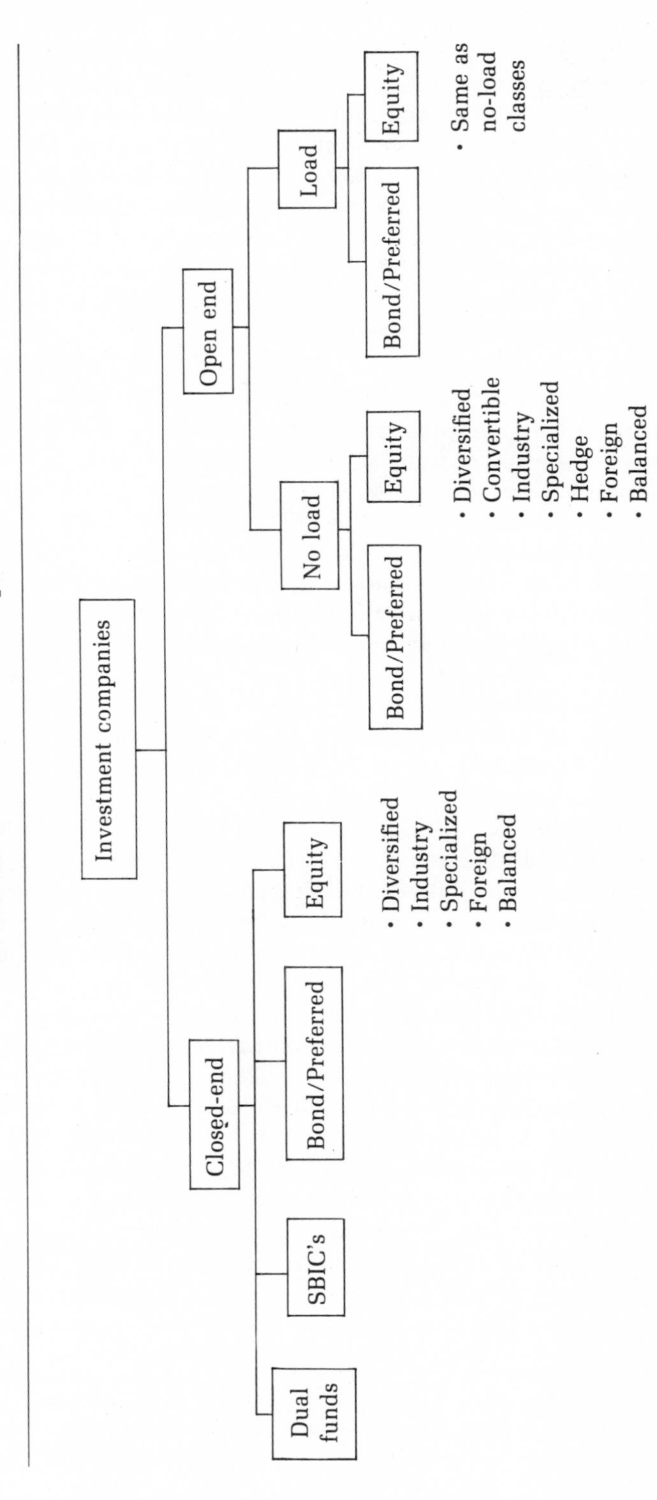

19 open-end investment companies having assets of $140 million or more were in existence as of December 31, 1929.[4]

Many of the closed-end investment companies of the 1920s were heavily margined and very speculative. As a result, their investment performance during the 1930s was a disaster. This poor performance of closed-end funds seriously damaged the reputation of the whole investment company concept.

Open-End Investment Companies

Open-end investment companies derive their name from their capital structure. New shares are continually sold by the investment company to any interested purchaser. Outstanding shares are redeemed by the investment company for cash at the option of the shareholder. Sales and redemptions take place at net asset value plus any sales commission or less any redemption fee that may be imposed.

Net asset value is determined by valuing the assets in the mutual fund's portfolio and subtracting any liabilities. The net asset value is divided by the number of shares outstanding at the time to determine the current net asset value per share. For many funds, the net asset value is determined daily and published in the financial section of many newspapers. Exhibit 20-2 shows part of the mutual fund section from the *Wall Street Journal* of February 7, 1975.

Load Funds. Mutual funds may be classified into load and no-load funds. Load funds, such as American Express Funds in Exhibit 20-2, have a sales commission called a loading charge, which the purchaser must pay when buying shares. There is normally no sales or redemption fee, although occasionally an investor may encounter a modest redemption fee.

Load funds generally have a sliding load charge based upon the amount of the purchase. The loading fee schedules for three different funds are shown in Table 20-1. Clearly, not all load funds have the same loading fee schedule. The dollar amount at which the load fee declines also may be different from fund to fund. In addition, not all funds start their loading fee schedule at the same level. Dreyfus starts at 8¾ percent, Chemical Fund at 8½ percent, and the Istel Fund has a maximum loading charge of 3 percent. Funds such as Istel are sometimes referred to as *low-load funds.* The load charges quoted above are stated as a percentage of the offering price. A $1,000 investment incurring a 8½ percent load charge would have a load fee of $85. Expressed as

[4]U.S. Securities and Exchange Commission, *Investment Trusts and Investment Companies* (Washington, D.C.: Government Printing Office, 1939-42), Part Two, chapter II, p. 27.

EXHIBIT 20–2

Selected Mutual Fund Prices as Reported in the Financial Press for February 6, 1975

	NAV*	Offer Price	NAV Chg.
American Express Funds			
Capital	4.94	5.40	+.01
Income	7.23	7.90	. . .
Invest	6.41	7.01	−.01
Spec Fund	4.77	5.21	+.02
Stock Fund	5.62	6.14	−.01
Am Invest	3.83	N.L.	−.02
Anchor Group			
Daily Inc	1.00	N.L.	. . .
Growth	5.53	6.06	−.02
Income	6.25	6.85	+.05
Reserv	10.09	11.06	+.01
Spectm	3.35	3.67	−.03
Fund Inv	5.63	6.17	. . .
Wa Natl	8.27	9.06	+.01

* net asset value

a percentage of the *amount actually invested* in the fund's shares, the load fee would be 9.3 percent ($85/$915).

No-Load Funds. A growing number of mutual funds, known as *no-load funds,* do not charge a load fee. American Investors Fund in Exhibit 20–2 is a no-load fund as shown by the "N.L." in the offering price column. Both the net asset value and offering price for American Investors are $3.83 per share. No-load funds have no sales charge since

TABLE 20–1

Load Charges, Selected Investment Companies

Istel		Dreyfus Fund		Chemical Fund, Inc.	
Amount	Sales Charge	Amount	Sales Charge	Amount	Sales Charge
$1–$ 9,999	3.0%	$1–$24,999	8.75%	$1–$ 9,999	8.5%
10,000– 24,999	2.5	25,000– 49,999	6.0	10,000– 24,999	7.5
25,000–999,999	2.0	50,000– 99,999	4.0	25,000– 49,999	6.0
1,000,000–or more	None	100,000–249,999	3.0	50,000– 99,999	4.5
		250,000–499,999	2.0	100,000–199,999	3.0
		500,000–or more	1.0	200,000–499,999	2.5
				500,000–999,999	2.0
				1,000,000–or more	1.0

Sources: Prospectuses of the investment companies.

they sell directly to the investor and compensate no salesman or broker for a sales effort. Most no-load funds have no redemption fee. Investors must normally initiate contact with the fund to obtain a prospectus and transact business.

Given the wide variation in sales and redemption charges, it behooves the investor to analyze a potential mutual fund investment carefully. There may even be small service fees such as an account servicing charge that one might consider. In deciding whether to purchase a load or a no-load fund, the relative performance records of each type are important. These performance records will be examined in the next chapter.

Closed-End Investment Companies

There are many different varieties of closed-end investment companies, but they all have one common element. All closed-end funds have a fixed number of shares outstanding and trading takes place in these

TABLE 20–2

Statistics of Selected Closed-End Funds

Type and Fund Name	Net Assets 9/30/74	Net Asset Value per Share 2/7/75	Price 2/7/75	Premium (+) Discount (–)
Diversified common stock				
Lehman	$315.8 mil.	$12.15	$10.50	– 13.6%
Madison Fund	212.7	11.15	8.75	– 24.2
Tri-Continental	407.7	20.38	18.00	– 11.7
Nondiversified common stock				
Standard Shares	49.1	19.64	13.00	– 33.8
Specialized equity				
Diebold Venture Capital	10.5	6.47	2.375	– 63.2
Value Line Development	11.4	4.53	1.625	– 64.1
Foreign security				
Japan Fund	100.4*	10.23	8.625	– 15.7
Convertible funds				
American General Convertible	43.3	16.29	17.375	+ 6.7
Chase Convertible Fund	43.5	9.10	8.25	– 9.3
Bond funds				
American General Bond	191.0	21.29	24.25	+ 13.9
Drexel Bond Debenture Trading Fund	39.0	17.92	16.75	– 6.5

*As of 6/28/74.

Sources: *Wall Street Journal,* February 10, 1975, p. 31, and *Supplement to Investment Companies,* September 30, 1974, New York: Wiesenberger Services, Inc.

shares. There is no continuous offering and redemption of shares as occurs in mutual funds. Table 20-2 shows selected closed-end investment company statistics.

The price of a closed-end investment company share is determined by the forces of supply and demand in the marketplace. The market price per share will only by coincidence equal the net asset value per share. In fact, many closed-end investment companies sell at discounts from net asset value. The "quality" of the net asset value figure appears to be an important factor in the size of the discount. "Quality" relates to the ability to obtain a given value upon liquidation of the holdings of the closed-end investment company. Large blocks of stock and securities with no active markets or relatively inactive (thin) markets may cause large discounts from net asset value.

Closed-end investment companies are allowed by the Investment Company Act of 1940 to issue bonds and preferred stock up to the legal limits. Asset coverage following the sale of the senior security (bond or preferred stock) must be at least 300 percent if a bond is issued and 200 percent if a preferred stock is issued. There is also a provision for restriction of dividend declarations if asset coverages fall below the minimums described above. An open-end investment company generally does not have senior securities in its capital structure.

Closed-end investment companies for equity investment may hold a diversified portfolio. Tri-Continental had investment assets of $650 million as of December 31, 1973, representing an investment in 108 common stocks.[5] Other closed-end funds such as National Aviation tend to specialize in particular industries. Japan Fund, on the other hand, allows an investor to buy a diversified portfolio of Japanese securities. The Japan Fund will be analyzed in Chapter 23, which deals with the methods of foreign investing. Dual funds, discussed in Chapter 24, hold a diversified portfolio, but issue both income and capital shares.

Bond Funds. In 1970, American General Life Insurance Company launched the first closed-end public bond fund. It is estimated that about $3 billion was publicly raised in 1972 and early 1973 by about 30 closed-end bond funds.[6] During this period, the yield on double A utility bonds was in the 7¼ to 7½ percent range.

Bond funds invest in fixed income debt securities. Many of these bond funds have relatively conservative investment policies. They invested in high quality bonds in an attempt to achieve an annual yield in the 7 to 7½ percent range existing at the time most of them were sold. Investors have been attracted to these funds because of the favorable yields relative to savings accounts, the inability of small investors to enter the bond market directly, and the poor performance experienced by many investors in the 1969-70 stock market decline.

[5]*Investment Companies* (New York: Wiesenberger Services, Inc., 1974), p. 528.
[6]Armon Glenn, "Premium to Discount," *Barron's*, September 9, 1974, p. 3.

Some of the bond funds are more speculative; their managements are counting on profits from bond trading to augment interest income. For example, the prospectus of Standard & Poor's Inter-Capital Income Securities, Inc. states that capital appreciation is a secondary objective of the fund. This bond fund plans to have portfolio turnover of up to 200 percent in pursuit of capital appreciation in the bond market and may also borrow an amount up to 50 percent of its assets.

It is yet unclear whether bond funds will be able to perform as investors expect. If interest rates decline from the level existing when the fund was underwritten, some of the bonds in the portfolio may be called for redemption. In this case, the proceeds would have to be reinvested at lower yields. If interest rates increase as they did during the two-year period following the sale of these bond funds, the investor suffers from interest rate risk in about the same manner as an investor purchasing bonds directly.

Another problem facing bond funds is illustrated with the figures below. If a bond fund is to return investors 7½ percent on their original capital contribution, the fund will have to earn enough to compensate for the underwriting fee and to pay the expenses of running the fund. Using an assumed ½ percent management fee and assumed other expenses equal to ⅜ percent, a bond fund would need to earn 8.94 percent on its net assets as shown below:

$25 assumed offering price less assumed 7% load ($1.75) = $23.25 initial net asset value

Income needed for 7½% return on original investment = .075 × $25.00 = $1.875

Income needed to cover fees:
½% annual management fee = .005 × $23.25 = $.116
⅜% other expenses = .00375 × $23.25 = $.087

Total income required = $1.875 + .116 + .087 = $2.078

Yield needed on net asset value $= \frac{\$2.078}{\$23.25} = 8.94\%$

Given the interest rates existing at the time most bond funds were underwritten, approximately 1½ to 2 percentage points of the 8.94 percent required return needed will have to come from bond trading profits. Whether this magnitude of return can consistently be earned by active trading of a bond portfolio remains to be determined.

SBICs. Small business investment companies (SBICs) are a unique form of investment company. Closed-end in form, SBICs were authorized by the Small Business Investment Company Act of 1958 as a means of alleviating the alleged equity financing gap for small, growing businesses. It was thought that companies which had outgrown the capital resources of their founders, but which were still not large enough for a public sale of stock, could obtain needed debt and equity capital from an SBIC.

The SBIC concept allowed private capital to combine with government loan funds and several SBICs went public in the early 1960s. Investors quickly came to the conclusion that investment in an SBIC gave them the main advantages of the investment company—liquidity, professional management, and diversification. Moreover, SBICs yielded some important special features. The diversification was over a portfolio of small businesses that on an individual basis either could not be brought into the public market or might be extremely risky for the average individual investor if direct investment were possible. By obtaining a portfolio of thirty to forty small companies via an SBIC investment, the total portfolio risk might be reduced to an acceptable level, especially if the SBIC was only one of the securities in the investor's portfolio.

The professional management of SBICs was also an attractive feature. The SBIC managers choose what they feel are sound, small growth companies, and venture capital management of this type often takes special talent. Additionally, the assistance to the portfolio companies is not limited to capital, but often encompasses managerial assistance.

In order to make the SBIC concept attractive to investors, several tax incentives were written into the original legislation. The most important provision for the individual investor is one that allows deduction, *as an ordinary loss,* for any loss resulting from the sale, exchange, or worthlessness of SBIC shares. Losses on ordinary corporate stock are subject to normal capital gains tax provisions. The maximum SBIC loss which can be deducted in any given year is $25,000 on an individual return or $50,000 on a joint return. This special tax treatment made SBIC shares an especially attractive investment for taxpayers in high marginal tax brackets.

Despite all the promise of the SBIC concept, both as an investment medium and as a means of financing small businesses, SBICs generally have not prospered. Many SBICs were under-capitalized and many managerial problems quickly surfaced. Even SBICs with adequate capital and competent management have generally proved to be disappointing investments. For example, Midland Capital shares were first offered to the public on February 3, 1961 at a price of $12.50. After deducting underwriting commissions, the initial net asset value was $11.375. During early February 1975, Midland Capital was bid at $1.875 or 16½ percent of its original net asset value despite a general market rise during the intervening period and no stock splits for Midland Capital during the period.

Midland Capital's rate of growth in assets and in the number of portfolio companies has declined or become negative in recent years, and its shares have also sold at huge discounts from net asset value. The main problem for an investor in an SBIC is the manner in which the net asset value is determined. Most SBIC portfolio companies are either not traded or are traded in thin markets. Hence, their valuation is difficult, if not impossible.

The competence of the SBIC management is the principal factor to analyze. Managerial competence is much more difficult to evaluate for an SBIC than for the average industrial company since SBIC assets are purchased with a fairly long time horizon in mind and some total investment failures can normally be expected. The best approach is probably to follow management's portfolio choices from year to year with two objectives in mind. First, are the investments being made in areas one would normally associate with exceptional future growth prospects? Second, have past portfolio investments been successful? Success could be indicated by a public offering of the stock followed by favorable market action.

SPECIAL INVESTMENT COMPANY FEATURES

Over the years, investment companies have developed many ways to accommodate the desires of the investing public. This section discusses the more important features that have been developed, since their presence or absence may be significant to an investor.

Accumulation Plans

An accumulation plan allows the investor to make periodic, noncontractual purchases of investment company shares. After a stipulated initial investment, payments may be sent to the fund at any time to purchase additional shares at the existing net asset value plus any applicable sales charges. These periodic payments may need to be of a certain dollar size.

Along with the accumulation plan, some load funds have two other features known as the letter of intent and the right of accumulation discounts. With a *letter of intent,* an investor planning to purchase more than a specified dollar amount of fund shares within a thirteen-month period may receive reduced sales commissions that apply to all purchases within the letter of intent period. Letters of intent usually include provisions for retroactive sale charge adjustments if the investor actually ends up qualifying for lower sales charges. A letter of intent may normally be terminated by the shareholder at any time. The *right of accumulation discount* allows an investor to combine the value of existing holdings with the amount of the current purchase in order to determine the loading fee applicable to the purchase.

Withdrawal Plans

Withdrawal plans allow an investor whose account has a minimum specified dollar value to request stated monthly or quarterly payments be sent from the fund. These plans are often used as a means of supplementing other sources of retirement income, although withdrawal plans do not provide a guaranteed annuity. If payments cannot be made from the fund's dividends, shares in the account are redeemed to make up the difference. In declining markets, these redemptions could deplete an investment account.

Dividend and Capital Gains Reinvestment

A fund shareholder may elect to have dividends and capital gains paid in cash or reinvested at existing net asset values. Many shareholders not needing current income elect to have the fund reinvest for them at net asset value. Loading fees are normally not charged on these reinvestments.

Keogh Plans and Group Investment Plans

In conjunction with the Self-Employed Individuals Tax Retirement Act of 1962 (Keogh Act), individuals may use investment company shares as one of the qualifying investment alternatives. Individuals are allowed to contribute a portion of their income from self-employed activities to an investment company under the Custodial Agreement required by the act. Income taxes on these contributions are deferred until the individual receives payments from the fund or other qualifying alternative at retirement.

Keogh plans are designed to assist self-employed persons in providing for their retirement years with the tax deferral privilege as the main incentive. Investment companies typically charge either a small fee upon opening the account or an annual maintenance fee or both. Some mutual funds charge a small fee for each distribution under the plan.

Many mutual funds have corporate pension sharing and profit plans, which have been approved by the Internal Revenue Service. Corporate contributions to these plans on behalf of the participants qualify as a tax-deductible expense for the corporation. Some mutual funds allow the individual participant to make voluntary contributions under the plan. All contributions accumulate dividend income and capital gains, taxes on which are deferred until retirement.

Exchange Provisions

If two or more funds are managed by the same management group, such as the American Express Funds in Exhibit 20-2, investors will normally be allowed to exchange shares of one fund in the group for shares of another fund in the group. This exchange takes place at net asset value, although a small service fee is often charged. Other restrictions sometimes placed require that the shares to be exchanged have been held a specified length of time or have a value of a specified dollar amount.

The main advantage of an exchange privilege is that a fund with a different investment objective may be acquired without paying another load fee. For example, an investor feeling that the stock market will decline in the next year or two could exchange a growth stock fund for an income fund managed by the same management group. For federal tax purposes, an exchanging shareholder will realize a gain or loss on the transaction depending on the relationship between the cost of the exchanged shares and their net asset value.

SUMMARY

Investment companies possess many advantages for the average investor. For those investors whose resources are too small to allow adequate diversification or to make stock purchases large enough to avoid paying disproportionately high brokerage commissions, investment companies may be the solution. Investment companies may also be attractive to an investor unable to analyze individual stocks or to assume the risks of direct stock ownership.

Investment companies exist in so many different forms and have such differing investment objectives that an investor should be able to find an appropriate fund after a reasonable amount of searching. The investor cannot escape making certain decisions, however. Market timing decisions still have to be made unless the investor adopts an investment strategy designed to mitigate timing problems. For example, the investor could make regular monthly or quarterly payments to the investment company under the voluntary accumulation plan with no consideration given to the level of the market.

Moreover, the investor must decide between closed-end and open-end funds; the latter are popularly known as mutual funds. Open-end funds allow the investor to purchase shares directly from the investment company. The investment company redeems the shares offered by the investor. As a result, the number of shares outstanding is continually changing, which accounts for the open-end label. Closed-end funds have a fixed number of shares outstanding and trading takes place in those shares.

The investor must also choose between no-load and load mutual funds. With a no-load, the investor pays no loading (sales) charge on the purchase of the shares as he does with the load fund. An investor desiring to purchase a no-load fund must determine which mutual funds are no-load and then proceed to obtain information regarding them. The standard reference sources may be consulted, but the investor must normally write the investment company to obtain a prospectus and a new account form.

Special features have been developed by investment companies over the years to accommodate the desires of the investing public. Most mutual funds have a voluntary accumulation plan, which allows the investor to make periodic payments to the fund. Many mutual funds have withdrawal plans allowing the investor to obtain periodic payments from the fund to supplement other sources of income. In addition, most mutual funds have qualified as a Keogh plan investment alternative. Keogh plans allow self-employed persons to gain tax deferral benefits while saving for retirement. All these special features make many investment companies especially attractive to some investors.

QUESTIONS/PROBLEMS/and SUGGESTED READINGS

(See Chapter 21.)

*

21

Investment Companies: Regulation and Evaluation

The regulatory environment and its impact on the investment company shareholder are examined in the first major section of this chapter. The second major section focuses on the way an investor can evaluate the desirability of a given investment company. The investor can examine the size of the investment company, its efficiency as measured by its operating expense ratio, and the investment company's portfolio turnover. The performance measurement techniques discussed in Chapter 13 are applied to the investment results of an actual investment company. Empirical studies are also examined that relate to the evaluation of investment company performance.

REGULATION OF INVESTMENT COMPANIES

The modern era of investment companies started with the Investment Company Act of 1940. Many investors fared poorly during the 1930s in speculative closed-end investment companies. Mutual funds also suffered in the 1930s as a result of unfavorable publicity associated with an SEC investigation into the speculative abuses of the closed-end funds. The SEC investigation ultimately resulted in the passage of the 1940 Act, which has done much to restore the respectability of the investment company concept.

This section discusses regulations dealing with adequate disclosure, the protection of the rights of shareowners, sales charges, and taxation. A discussion of the state "blue sky" laws precedes the section dealing with the implications of federal regulation.

State Laws

From the viewpoint of investment companies, the important fact is that "blue sky" laws vary from state to state. They may deal with such matters as sales procedures, sales charges, operating costs, and diversification policies. Some mutual funds have decided not to register their shares for sale in all states because of the legal and administrative work involved.

Investment Company Act of 1940 and Amendments of 1970

Congress felt that investment companies were important from a public policy standpoint. Hence, the objectives of the 1940 Act were formulated within this public policy framework. The Act mentions the possibility of domination and control of other companies by an investment company, the vital impact investment companies have on savings flows into the capital markets, and the difficulties of state regulation given the wide geographic distribution of investment company shareowners.

Given these public policy considerations, the Investment Company Act of 1940 stated that investors were adversely affected when:

1. Adequate information is unavailable so that informed decisions can be made.
2. Certain shareholders are discriminated against as a result of special classes of securities, inequitable provisions in securities, or inequitable concentration of control.
3. Unsound or misleading accounting methods are employed.
4. Major changes in the character of an investment company are made without shareholder consent.
5. Investment companies do not have adequate assets or reserves to transact business.

In conjunction with the 1940 Act, the Securities Act of 1933 requires that investment companies desiring to sell shares to the public file certain information with the SEC via a registration statement. Following an examination by the SEC of the information submitted, a prospectus is printed. The prospectus gives potential investors needed information under the basic federal regulatory concept of full and adequate disclosure. The following items represent the more common items that are disclosed:

1. The objectives of the fund and its general investment policies.
2. Restrictions regarding investments of the investment company. These vary and should be studied by a potential investor. Typical restrictions relate to the use of borrowed money, short sales, participation in underwritings of securities, purchase of real estate or commodities, and the size of individual portfolio holdings.
3. The management of the fund.
4. Management fees and the method by which they are determined.
5. Past performance of the investment company including portfolio turnover rates.
6. Methods by which the shares of the investment company may be purchased and the loading fee schedule, if applicable.
7. Special services offered by the investment company.
8. How net asset value is determined.
9. How shares may be redeemed.
10. Taxation of the fund's income.
11. Audited financial statements including the composition of the portfolio.

In 1966, the SEC submitted to Congress a study dealing with the problems faced by the investment company industry.[1] As a result of this study and recommendations proposed by the SEC, several important changes in the areas of management fees and sales charges were legislated by the Investment Company Amendments Act of 1970. This act, signed into law in December 1970, represents the first major revision of the 1940 Act.

Protection of Shareholders' Rights

The 1940 Act and the 1970 Amendments contain several provisions designed to protect the rights of shareholders. The board of directors of any investment company must consist of no more than 60 percent interested parties, defined as persons connected with fund's management. This means at least 40 percent of the directors must be completely unaffiliated with the investment advisor of the fund.

[1]U.S. Securities and Exchange Commission, *Public Policy Implications of Investment Company Growth,* 89th Congress, Second Session, House Report #2337 (Washington, D.C.: Government Printing Office, 1966).

The permissible activities of the fund's management are carefully spelled out in the 1940 Act. A stockholder vote is necessary before the basic investment objectives and policies, as stated in the comprehensive SEC registration statement, may be altered. SEC approval is required before any business transactions between the investment company and its advisors may take place. This requirement is intended to prevent insiders from selling assets to the investment company at inflated prices. Likewise, a fund is not allowed to sell its shares to anyone at a price less than that stated in the prospectus. Insiders may not buy fund shares under net asset value.

The management contract between the investment company and its advisor is also regulated. After initial shareowner approval of a two-year contract, future contracts must be approved yearly either by a majority of both the entire board of directors and a majority of the independent directors or by the shareholders themselves. Management contracts are not transferable from one investment advisor to another. This lack of transferability prevents sudden changes in management, which might not be in the best interests of the investment company shareholders.

Sales Charges

Over the years, the SEC has been interested in the level of loading fees and the manner in which they are charged. As a result of the 1970 legislation, the National Association of Securities Dealers is responsible for promulgating rules regarding the sales charges of an investment company. Legally, these sales charges shall not be excessive. The 1966 SEC study advocated a maximum load charge of 5 percent of net asset value, but this recommendation did not become law.

Sales charges by *contractual front-end load* funds have also been studied carefully by the SEC and new requirements incorporated in the 1970 Amendments. Contractual front-end load funds require an investor to make periodic payments over the life of the plan. An investor, for example, may agree to pay $50 per month for ten years for a total investment of $6,000. It is important to emphasize that a contractual plan does not represent a legal contract since the investor is not compelled to maintain scheduled payments and may drop from the plan at any time.

If an investor pays $50 a month for ten years, the sales commission for the whole transaction might be in the neighborhood of 8½ percent of the investment ($510). Prior to the 1970 legislation, 50 percent of the payments during the first year ($300) could be taken as a commission, with the remaining sales commission ($210) spread over the remaining nine years. Investors dropping out of the contractual plan within the first year or two would incur high sales commissions since there was no provision for a sales commission refund.

Front-end load funds may now select either of the following methods for calculating sales charges. No matter which method is used, the investor has the right to a complete refund of sales fees during a forty-five-day period following the mailing of the investor's certificate.

Method One: Continue the present 50 percent sales charge in the first year, but the investor has a right of refund upon withdrawal for a period of 18 months. The refund would be equal to the net asset value of the shares in the account plus an amount equal to sales charges in excess of 15 percent of gross payments. No refunds are made for custodial charges or insurance premiums.

If an investor had paid $600 during the first year and then dropped the plan, the refund would be calculated as follows under method one:

Investment: $600 at an average net asset value of $10 per share

The number of shares purchased would be calculated as follows:

$$\$600 - \$300 \text{ commission} = \frac{\$300}{\$10} = 30 \text{ shares}$$

Refund calculation when investor drops plan when net asset value per share equals $9·

Value of shares = 30 shares at $9 per share	=	$270
Sales charge refund = $300 less 15%	=	255
Total refund	=	$525

Method Two: Sales charges are limited to 20 percent of any payment and an annual average of not more than 16 percent for the first forty-eight monthly payments.

The voluntary accumulation plan discussed in the previous chapter actually allows the investor to accomplish the same objective as that of a contractual front-end load fund. Since the contractual plan is not binding in a legal sense, the investor can drop out of the plan just as a voluntary accumulation plan can be discontinued. The investor may perceive the contractual plan as having a "forced" savings element, but the 1966 SEC study revealed substantial "dropouts" from contractual plans in the early years.[2] Even with the new methods of determining sales charges for contractual front-end loads, the sales charges may exceed those of a voluntary accumulation plan, especially if the contractual plan is terminated early in its life.

Taxation

Virtually all investment companies elect to be taxed as regulated investment companies. On the theory that investment companies are only a conduit between the investor and the securities in the investment com-

[2] *Public Policy Implications of Investment Company Growth,* pp. 223–50.

pany portfolio, the regulated investment company can distribute its income to its shareholders without itself paying taxes.[3] Within forty-five days after the close of its taxable year, the investment company informs the shareholder of his or her proportionate share of the income and its breakdown into ordinary income, capital gains, and other income. These figures are entered in the appropriate place on the individual's tax return.

Investment companies must meet the following requirements to qualify as a regulated investment company:

1. As a domestic corporation, obtain at least 90 percent of corporate gross income from dividends, interest, and capital gains from securities transactions. Personal holding companies do not qualify as regulated investment companies.
2. Invest at least 50 percent of assets in a diversified group of securities (including cash) and have no more than 25 percent of its assets invested in one company.
3. Have no more than 30 percent of corporate gross income derived from securities held for less than 3 months.
4. Distribute at least 90 percent of investment income, excluding capital gains, to stockholders.
5. Make a binding election to be taxed as a regulated investment company and be registered under the Investment Company Act of 1940.

PERFORMANCE EVALUATION

The evaluation of the typical open-end investment company is similar in concept to the evaluation of any investment portfolio, with some minor exceptions. Prior to the general use of the geometric mean technique of determining rate of return, any evaluation had to consider the timing of contributions and withdrawals of funds from the investment company.[4] Without the use of geometric means, a mutual fund that had large contributions just before a market expansion would look better than a fund which followed an identical investment policy, but had low contributions. If it is presumed that a fund manager has little or no control over contributions and withdrawals, the manager should not be penalized accordingly. The geometric mean alleviates these problems

[3]A provision exists for regulated investment companies to retain capital gains rather than pay them out to shareholders. Shareholders are required to report retained capital gains on their individual tax returns, but the investment company pays the maximum capital gains tax. The shareholder enters the proportional share of any capital gains tax paid by the investment company as a credit on his or her tax return. In addition, the investor must adjust the cost basis of the shares to recognize the undistributed capital gain and its tax impact.

[4]See the appendix to Chapter 6 for a discussion of the geometric mean rate of return.

so that the size and fluctuations in the size of the fund do not influence the return calculation.

Mutual fund evaluation is a market value evaluation as well. However, the rate of return determination requires not only beginning and ending market values, but also income and capital gain distributions made during the period. For example, The Anchor Growth Fund had the following results from 1970 to 1972:[5]

	Year-End	*Dividends*		
	Net Asset Value	*Capital Gains*	*Income*	*Rate of Return*
1970	$10.37	—	$.20	—
1971	11.56	$.69	.16	19.7%
1972	10.71	.84	.08	.6

The returns indicated are calculated as follows:

$$1972 \text{ return} = \frac{10.71 + .84 + .08}{11.56} - 1$$

$$= \frac{11.63}{11.56} - 1 = .6\%$$

This is the conventional return calculation with the inclusion of the capital gain distribution. This return calculation does not subtract any loading charges. The typical performance evaluation treats this item as a cost.

In Chapter 14, we established four performance criteria, including: 1) diversification; 2) maintenance of the risk level desired; 3) selection of undervalued securities or "picking winners"; and 4) market projections. Without exception, every study that has considered diversification has found that funds do an excellent job of eliminating diversifiable risk. They have performed well on the basis of the diversification criterion. It seems clear that an investor unable to purchase the ten to fifteen securities required to substantially eliminate diversifiable risk will be able to achieve the required diversification through the purchase of a mutual fund.

The majority of the evidence regarding the risk level tends to suggest that the actual risk level achieved is generally consistent with the fund's stated policy toward risk.[6] A fund that claims to invest in growth stocks

[5]Data taken from *Investment Companies, 1973,* New York: Wiesenberger Services, Inc., p. 182.

[6]Michael Jensen, "Risk, the Pricing of Capital Assets, and the Evaluation of Investment Portfolios," *Journal of Business,* April 1969, pp. 167–247; William Sharpe, *Portfolio Theory and Capital Markets* (New York: McGraw-Hill, 1970); and John C. Bogie, "Mutual Fund Performance Evaluation," *Financial Analysts Journal,* November–December 1970, pp. 25–33.

will generally have a beta greater than one. The fund that maintains it is an income fund will generally have a low beta. However, this observation cannot be taken as law since there is a good deal of variation, as Table 21-1 indicates. Growth funds have high risk, but there are some exceptions, as is the case with income funds. One should also note from the table that high beta funds do not really have much more risk than the market. The high risk category has an upper limit on beta of 1.1.[7] Investors seeking a very high risk investment will generally find it difficult for a mutual fund to satisfy their needs.

With regard to picking winners, we can be virtually certain that funds do not consistently outperform randomly selected portfolios of equivalent risk. There is no empirical evidence that efforts to select securities to generate an above average risk-adjusted return have been successful. In general, investment company managers have not picked winners. Furthermore, this conclusion appears to apply to all funds and not just to the average fund.

While there are individual funds with outstanding performance, their alpha is not statistically greater than zero. There is some slight evidence that low beta funds have a positive alpha and high beta funds have a negative alpha, but the evidence is weak. In essence, outperforming the market by purchasing mutual funds does not appear to be a reasonable investment alternative.

A similar conclusion is apparent when considering a fund's ability to predict the market and adjust the risk level accordingly. Jack Treynor and Kay Mazuy note that superior market timing should result in a characteristic line that is curved instead of linear.[8] Figure 21-1 shows a hypothetical curved characteristic line. Treynor and Mazuy found no curvature in their study. Their results suggest that fund managements did not make superior market predictions. However, the data do not tell us whether the average performance observed was due to average market predictions or an inability or failure to act on any superior predictions actually made.

Size

What is the ideal size of an investment company? Can funds be too large or too small? What has been the performance of small funds as opposed to large funds? These are important questions for the potential investment company investor.

[7]Irwin Friend, Marshall Blume and Jean Crockett examined 119 mutual funds and found that 12 of them had a beta below .5 and 4 of them had a beta above 1.1. These funds with a beta below .5 and above 1.1 are not presented in the results of Table 21-1. They also omitted very small funds and those formed between April 1964 and June 1968 (the termination of their study).

[8]Jack L. Treynor and Kay K. Mazuy, "Can Mutual Funds Outguess the Market?" *Harvard Business Review*, July-August 1966, pp. 131-36.

TABLE 21-1

Comparison of Investment Performance of Mutual Funds with Different Investment Objectives (January, 1960—June, 1968)

Risk Class (Beta Coefficient)	Number in Sample				Mean return			
	Growth Funds*	Growth-Income Funds	Income-Growth Funds	Income-Growth-Stability Funds	Growth Funds*	Growth-Income Funds	Income-Growth Funds	Income-Growth-Stability Funds
Low risk (β = .5–.7)	3	5	4	16	6.9%	10.1%	9.7%	9.1%
Medium risk (β = .7–.9)	15	24	7	7	11.2	10.0	10.0	12.2
High risk (β = .9–1.1)	20	1	0	1	13.8	9.5	—	13.5

*Investment objectives for 1967 as classified by Arthur Wiesenberger Services.

Source: Friend, Blume, and Crockett, *Mutual Funds and Other Institutional Investors* (New York: McGraw-Hill, 1970), p. 160.

FIGURE 21-1
Hypothetical Characteristic Line Showing Good Market Timing Decisions

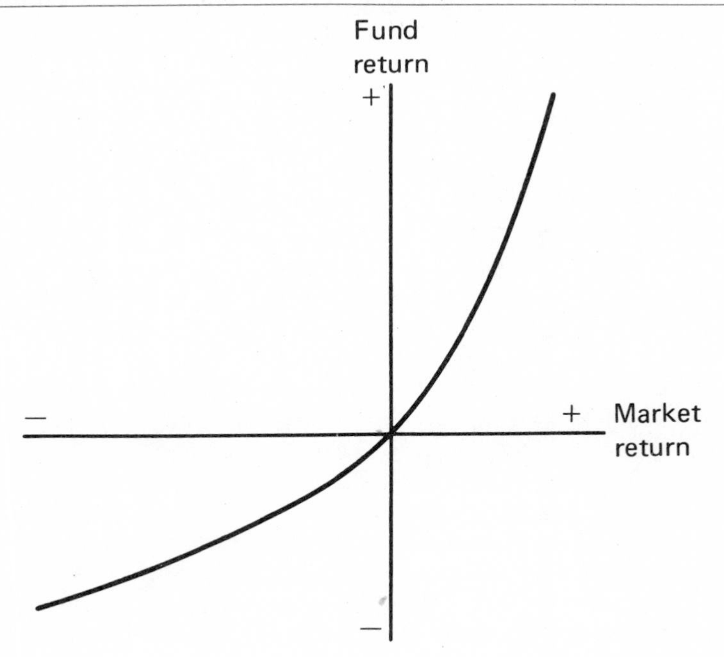

Small funds may have problems recruiting and retaining a competent managerial staff. A fund with $5 million in assets at an annual investment advisory fee of ½ percent will have only $25,000 to support its activities. This will not hire many competent financial specialists. Other expenses for small funds tend to be proportionately high. While small funds may have considerable market trading flexibility, their transactions may not be large enough to qualify for substantial discounts on brokerage commissions. Small funds also have had high portfolio turnover rates. The brokerage fees resulting from trading activity directly affect investment performance.

Large funds also have their managerial problems. The main problems result from the need to invest large sums of money in individual stocks. Large blocks of stock may be both difficult to acquire and dispose of at a price reasonably close to the current market price. Large funds, when they do take a position in a smaller company, may be able to invest such a relatively small percentage of the total assets of the fund that performance is not really affected very much even if the small company's stock does well in the market. On the positive side, large funds have the advantage of large research staffs, lower brokerage costs, and economies of scale in operating costs and management advisory fees.

The Wharton Report found no relationship between the size of a fund and its performance.[9] Smaller funds had a slightly different portfolio composition than large funds, which largely accounted for some slight differences in performance by size that were observed in the study. The SEC staff examined performance during the 1956 to 1965 period and found that growth patterns were positively related to performance, but that there was "no consistent pattern of change in the relative performance of these funds as their assets have grown."[10] The more recent Friend, Blume, and Crockett study also found no difference in fund performance when funds were classified by asset size.[11]

Operating Expenses and Portfolio Turnover

Potential fund shareholders should determine whether the fund is managed so the operating expense ratio is consistent with funds of comparable size. Portfolio turnover is another factor that may influence an investor's decision regarding a fund.

Friend, Blume, and Crockett found that there were no consistent statistical relationships between mutual fund performance and either the fund's operating expense ratio or its portfolio turnover.[12] However, it still appears prudent for the potential investor to be satisfied that the operating expense ratio and the portfolio turnover are reasonable for the size of fund being considered. There is no valid reason for deliberately subjecting oneself to higher expenses and portfolio turnover with the higher brokerage commissions that result if these higher expenses may not make any difference in the performance achieved.

A Performance Appraisal

A brief example of measuring mutual fund performance will demonstrate the general nature of our conclusions. During the period from 1962 to 1972, Massachusetts Investors Trust (MIT) had a geometric mean annual return of 6.3 percent per year while the market as measured by the S&P 500 returned 7.9 percent per year. Both returns assume the reinvestment of income and capital gains distributions. Did MIT perform poorly? Perhaps it did. To tell for sure, we must make a risk-adjusted performance evaluation.

[9]Committee on Interstate and Foreign Commerce, *A Study of Mutual Funds* (Washington, D.C.: Government Printing Office, 1962).

[10]*Public Policy Implications of Investment Company Growth*, p. 24.

[11]Irwin Friend, Marshall Blume, and Jean Crockett, *Mutual Funds and Other Institutional Investors* (New York: McGraw-Hill, 1970), p. 21.

[12]Ibid., p. 21.

Using regression analysis, MIT's beta was .83 during the period examined. This is about what one would expect from a fund classified as a growth-income fund. In terms of Table 21-1, MIT should be a medium risk fund and the beta shows that to be the case. They accepted the risk advertised and hence performed well on the risk selection criterion. The standard error of the beta coefficient was found to be .058, suggesting that our conclusion is reasonable in that the "real" beta probably falls within a range of .94 and .72 (plus or minus two standard deviations of the beta estimate).

In terms of our performance criteria, MIT did an excellent job in eliminating diversifiable risk as measured by the very high coefficient of determination (r^2 of .96) between MIT's annual return and that of the market. Only 4 percent of the fluctuation in MIT's return was diversifiable.

Regarding the possibility of superior security selection or market prediction, the regression analysis indicates an alpha of −.012. Recall that average performance will be indicated by an alpha of zero. In absolute terms, the negative alpha of −.012 suggests poor selection or poor market prediction. However, a conclusion of poor performance is unwarranted since the actual value is not significantly different from zero.[13] On the basis of picking winners, MIT did no better and no worse than the average.

The results for MIT during those eleven years are consistent with our conclusions regarding mutual funds in general. They diversify well. They appear to select the risk level that buyers expect on the basis of the fund description, and their security selection is average. They do not consistently select undervalued stocks.

Performance of Load versus No-Load Funds

The performance of no-load funds compared to load funds has been much debated and researched. In 1963, one source recommended no-load funds only for short-term temporary investments.[14] With no sales commissions when purchased and normally no redemption fees, no-load funds are a good vehicle for speculative short-term commitments. But no-loads were not otherwise recommended for two reasons. First, those no-loads with favorable performance records were organized after World War II and had not been tested by sustained bear markets. Second, no-loads with favorable short-term performance records had not achieved

[13]The t statistic on alpha is −1.55, which implies insignificant deviation from zero.

[14]C. Russell Doane, and Edward J. Hills, *Investment Trusts and Funds from the Investor's Point of View,* Economic Bulletin of the American Institute for Economic Research, Vol. III, No. 2, March 1963.

results similar to leading closed-end investment companies. However, this short-term performance comparison was never made directly. The number of no-load funds examined was small and multiple time periods were not carefully examined.

More convincing research by Robert Carlson concluded that, from 1958 to 1967, no-load funds tended toward above-average performance compared with all funds, although performance figures were examined for only eight no-load funds.[15] Friend, Blume, and Crockett, based upon results which are summarized in Table 21-2, made the following conclusion about the relationship between performance and sales charges:

To the extent that a relationship exists between performance and sales charges, the funds with the lowest charges, including the "no-load" funds, appear to perform slightly better than the others.[16]

TABLE 21-2

Mutual Fund Performance, 1960-68, by Risk Class and Sales Charge

Risk Class (Beta Coefficient)	Average Annual Rate of Return January 1960 to June 1968 — Sales Charges: Below 8.25%	8.25% to 8.5%	Above 8.5%
Low risk (β = .5 to .7)	9.0%	9.1%	9.9%
Medium risk (β = .7 to .9)	11.2	10.4	9.4
High risk (β = .9 to 1.1)	15.1	12.9	13.5

Source: Friend, Blume, and Crockett, *Mutual Funds and Other Institutional Investors* (New York: McGraw-Hill, 1970), p. 157.

While these studies and others are not clearly in favor of either type of fund, no-load funds have been growing more rapidly in the recent years than load funds. Apparently, investors have become increasingly aware of the existence of no-load funds and have decided to avoid transaction costs. Perhaps investors are becoming more sophisticated

[15]Robert S. Carlson, "Aggregate Performance of Mutual Funds, 1948-67," *Journal of Financial and Quantitative Analysis,* March 1970, pp. 1-32. Some of the analysis, however, concentrated on the decade 1958-67.

[16]Friend, Blume, and Crockett, p. 21.

in their personal financial management and view the sales load in the same way the SEC did in its 1966 report—"purely a payment for selling effort."[17]

SUMMARY

The Investment Company Act of 1940 is the cornerstone of the federal regulation of the investment company industry. Since investment companies have public policy aspects, they are subject to disclosure requirements regarding investment objectives, the management of the fund, and management advisory fees. The SEC is concerned with the level of the load charge. For investment companies having a front-end contractual load charge, the method of determining load charge refunds changed in 1970 as a result of the 1970 Amendments to the 1940 Act. However, the investor must decide whether a front-end load is desirable, since a voluntary accumulation plan can accomplish virtually the same investment objective.

A portfolio approach should be taken to evaluate the performance of an investment company. An annual rate of return can be calculated by considering changes in the net asset value of the investment company and any dividends (either income or capital gains) declared by the investment company. To compare the performance of one investment company against other investment companies, the investor needs to develop a risk-adjusted rate of return. This involves the calculation of an alpha and a beta for the investment company using past returns. Alpha is a measure of the ability of the investment company to select stocks. Beta is a measure of the risk level of the investment company. The relationship of the fund's past returns to those of the market is given in the r^2 statistic. This becomes a measure of the degree to which the investment company has diversified. A high r^2 indicates that the investment company has sufficiently diversified to eliminate most of the diversifiable risk. A low r^2 would indicate inadequate diversification.

Investors must make practical decisions regarding the size of the investment company, the reasonableness of both the expense ratio and the portfolio turnover, the proper investment objective, and the desirability of a load fund as opposed to a no-load fund. Many of these practical decisions relate directly to the risk preference of the investor. If investment companies are properly analyzed and the prudent decisions made, investment companies may be an attractive investment for many investors.

QUESTIONS

1. Why have investment companies, especially mutual funds, had such good asset growth in the past twenty-five years?
2. *Forbes,* in its issue of August 15, 1972, applied a marketing product life

[17]*Public Policy Implications of Investment Company Growth,* p. 215.

cycle model (see Chapter 8) to mutual funds. The four phases in this model are infancy, growth, maturity, and decline. What phase of the product life cycle do you feel mutual funds are in? Why?

3. Marketing theory states that the product decline phase (see question 2) can be delayed by product innovation, new ideas, and variations of the old product. What evidence do you see of investment companies attempting to delay the product decline phase? What might investment companies do in the future to avoid the product decline phase?

4. The First Multifund of America was first offered to the public in September 1967, with the objective of investing in securities of fifteen or more selected American mutual funds. The loading fee established at the time of organization was 1½ percent of the first $50,000, 1¼ percent from $50,000 to $199,999, and 1 percent on purchases above $200,000. What would an individual investor gain by owning a mutual fund that invests in other load funds? What disadvantages might exist for an investor in First Multifund?

5. "Do-good" mutual funds have a policy of investing exclusively in companies that the fund management regards as socially responsible. For example, The Third Century Fund, a member of the Dreyfus mutual fund group, has a policy of investing in companies "with evidence of positive performance in the areas of protection of the environment, occupational health and safety, consumer protection and equal employment opportunity."

   The *Wall Street Journal* of August 9, 1972, wrote of the poor performance of "do-good" funds. In addition, sales of these funds have generally been far below original expectations. What, in your opinion, could account for the poor sales and investment results?

6. Wells Fargo Bank in San Francisco established a $100 million closed-end fund marketed by direct placement in an attempt to attract pension fund money. This fund will invest all its assets in all of the stocks in the Standard & Poor's 500 Stock Average. What would be the general name for such a fund? Why would a pension fund be willing to purchase it?

7. Certain mutual funds belong to a category of funds known as "closed-up" funds. These funds originally had a continuous sale and redemption of shares to anyone interested in purchasing them. However, when they reached a predetermined asset size, sales were suspended except for sales to current shareholders. What would be the motivating factor(s) behind "closing-up" a fund?

8. The Keystone management group has thirteen different investment companies under its management. A brief summary of the investment objectives of several of these funds along with selected statistics is given below. The value column represents the value of the particular fund as of December 31, 1973, if $10,000 had been invested on January 1, 1964, and

all dividends and other distributions of the particular fund had been taken in stock.

Fund	Objective	Income dividend Yield—1973	Value
S-1	Long-term growth in high quality equities	1.0%	$15,626
S-2	Growth and income from investment grade issues	1.1	15,999
S-3	Growth from volatile stocks	none	18,332
S-4	Growth from speculative stocks	none	14,178
K-1	Income from any class of security	6.4	13,542
K-2	Maximum growth with prudent, flexible investment policy	.5	17,457

a) Does it appear that the performance of each individual fund is in line with its investment objectives?

b) What might explain the lower value for the S-4 fund when compared to the S-3 fund?

PROBLEMS

1. Selected performance statistics for American Investors Fund, Enterprise Fund, and Johnston Mutual fund are given on the next page.
   a) Compare and contrast the performance of these funds over the time period shown.
   b) Ignoring the fact that Enterprise is a load fund, while the other two funds are no-loads, which fund would you buy at the present time as a result of the data you have just analyzed?
   c) What information other than what you were given might you desire to obtain before determining which of these three funds to purchase?
2. The Foursquare Fund has an investment restriction that prohibits the fund from investing in companies that derive a substantial proportion of their revenues from the sale of alcoholic beverages, tobacco, or drugs. The following data show the quarterly performance of Foursquare Fund for the years of 1967 to 1972. In addition, the quarterly performance data for the Standard & Poor market indexes for liquor stocks, tobacco (cigarette) stocks, and drug stocks are given as well as the performance of the S&P 500 stock index.

   a) Evaluate the performance of the Foursquare Fund. What conclusions can you draw regarding the performance of this fund during the 1967 to 1972 period?
   b) Evaluate the performance of the liquor, tobacco, and drug stocks. What are your conclusions regarding their past performance?

Year	Year-End Asset Size ($ mil)	Dividend Income	Percentage Change* Net Asset Value-Fund	S&P 500	Portfolio Turnover	Oper. Expenses (% net assets)
American Investors:						
1973	$156	1.0%	− 16	− 15	n.a.	1.02%
1972	207	.3	+11	+19	66%	.92
1971	220	.7	+ 4	+14	73	.98
1970	227	—	− 29	+ 4	93	1.02
1969	295	.5	− 29	− 8	71	.86
1968	342	.1	+11	+14		.86
1967	242	.2	+46	+24		.88
1966	87	.5	+ 3	− 9		1.09
1965	58	.2	+49	+12		1.29
1964	25	.2	+15	+16		1.42
1963	11	—	+37	+23		1.42
Enterprise Fund:						
1973	269	1.1	− 22	− 15	106	1.00
1972	414	1.3	+ 6	+19	56	1.00
1971	485	2.2	+23	+14	60	1.00
1970	449	4.0	− 26	+ 4	98	.90
1969	770	.6	− 25	− 8	56	1.13
1968	953	.1	+42	+14		1.07
1967	247	.2	+115	+24		.82
1966	29	.5	+ 4	− 9		.99
1965	17	.5	+40	+12		.97
1964	6	.5	+24	+16		1.04
1963	3	1.0	+28	+23		1.04
Johnston Mutual Fund:						
1973	297	1.6	− 21	− 15	9	.63
1972	333	.7	+25	+19	18	.62
1971	221	.8	+26	+14	29	.58
1970	155	1.7	− 6	+ 4	54	.61
1969	143	1.4	0	− 8	39	.72
1968	124	1.4	+ 8	+14		.63
1967	101	1.3	+30	+24		.67
1966	65	1.7	+ 6	− 9		.68
1965	54	1.7	+23	+12		.66
1964	41	2.0	+12	+16		.70
1963	37	2.1	+18	+23		.71

*includes all dividends.

c) Do you feel that the investment performance of the Foursquare Fund has been hindered because of its restrictive policy regarding investments in liquor, tobacco, and drug companies? How can you support your conclusions?

Quarter	Foursquare Fund—Net Asset Value	Liquor	Tobacco	Drugs	S&P 500
1972—IV	5.2%	8.2%	2.3%	7.3%	5.8%
III	.1	(.2)	(13.3)	3.7	4.1
II	(1.9)	11.5	9.3	8.6	(.1)
I	4.2	(.6)	16.4	7.6	5.0
1971—IV	2.8	18.0	1.3	4.8	3.8
III	(3.9)	1.5	(.4)	1.7	(1.4)
II	(.8)	(5.7)	(7.0)	1.4	(.6)
I	12.0	7.1	19.3	8.6	8.9
1970—IV	2.3	.9	26.3	9.0	9.4
III	14.4	9.4	3.7	8.4	15.8
II	(16.1)	(14.7)	5.9	(13.3)	(18.9)
I	(2.3)	1.1	(7.8)	(6.8)	(2.6)
1969—IV	(4.8)	2.8	10.8	12.0	(1.1)
III	(3.0)	(1.0)	2.9	8.7	(4.7)
II	(9.1)	2.1	(7.5)	5.2	(3.7)
I	(4.9)	(3.9)	(7.3)	(5.2)	(3.0)
1968—IV	4.9	5.8	15.5	5.3	1.2
III	(.1)	9.0	(2.3)	(2.7)	3.1
II	9.2	13.7	11.4	17.9	10.4
I	(10.4)	1.5	(2.5)	(11.4)	(6.5)
1967—IV	2.2	(6.4)	2.5	(4.1)	(.2)
III	3.9	.2	(2.1)	3.5	6.7
II	7.9	1.7	(.3)	5.7	.5
I	14.6	23.1	17.2	15.2	12.3

3. Sara Gray has heard that common stocks have had a rate of return close to 10 percent over long periods of time. She has been investing in the American Investors Fund for several years in anticipation of retirement.

At the close of 1968, Sara decided to stop making payments to the fund and establish an annual withdrawal plan with the fund. American Investors makes this plan available without charge to accounts valued at $10,000 or more. Sara's account is valued at $60,000 at American Investor's 1968 year-end net asset value of $10.68 per share.

Sara instructs the fund to send her $6,000 annually beginning with December 31, 1968. She feels that her principal should remain reasonably intact if the fund can earn close to 10 percent annually in the future.

The following figures show the record of American Investors since Sara established her withdrawal plan.

	Income Dividends per Share	*Year-End NAV per Share*
1969	$.04	$7.51
1970	none	5.31
1971	.04	5.50
1972	.02	6.07

No capital gains distributions were made during the years from 1969 to 1972. Income dividends are paid in January and you may assume that they are reinvested at the previous year-end net asset value.

a) Calculate the value of Sara's account at the end of each year under the withdrawal plan she set up after she has withdrawn her $6,000.
b) Why do you think that Sara's account has fared the way it has?
c) Has Sara gained any benefits from the establishment of the withdrawal plan?
d) Obtain American Investors 1973 Year-end NAV per share from standard reference sources. What does this mean for Sara?

4. The Keystone Group has the following exchange policy: Shares of one fund may be exchanged for those of any other Keystone Custodial Fund at one-half the normal sales charge with the exception of K–1 and K–2. Conversions into these funds may be made at asset value, once each twelve months, for a $5 service charge. A record of the year-end net asset value of funds K–1 and K–2 is shown below.

	NAV	
Year-end	*K–1 (Income)*	*K–2 (Growth)*
1967	$9.34	$7.35
1968	9.73	6.69
1969	7.69	5.23
1970	7.48	4.67
1971	8.16	6.20
1972	8.29	7.59
1973	6.88	5.59

If an investor owned the growth fund at the end of 1967, would an exchange between K–1 and K–2 have been advantageous during the 1967 to 1973 period? Under an optimal exchange arrangement with exchanges made at year-end (no exchanges may be optimal), how would an investor with $10,000 in K–2 at year-end 1967 fare relative to another investor making no exchanges but retaining a position in fund K–2? You may ignore the $5 exchange fee for ease of calculation.

5. On May 1, 1973, the *Wall Street Journal* carried an announcement of the proposed merger of Eberstadt Fund, an open-end mutual fund, with Surveyor Fund, a closed-end investment trust. The proposed merger had been approved by the directors of Surveyor Fund and was to be considered by the directors of the Eberstadt Fund around mid-May.

Following approval of the merger by both Boards of Directors, the shareholders of each investment company must vote on the proposal. Under the proposed merger terms, the surviving company would be known as Surveyor Fund and would be an open-end fund with its assets redeemable at net asset value. The merger would be accomplished by an exchange of shares at the net asset values existing on the effective date of the merger.

Under the provisions of the Investment Company Act of 1940, an open-end investment company is not permitted to have a debt issue outstanding, although bank borrowings are allowed up to stipulated limits. Hence, regulatory clearance was being sought from the Securities and Exchange Commission to allow Surveyor's $20 million issue of 5 percent convertible debentures to remain outstanding.

The debentures that are outstanding are callable at a price equal to 105½ percent of the principal amount, plus accrued interest. If SEC approval to retain the debenture issue is not obtained, the debenture issue would have to be called. The right to convert the issue would terminate on the redemption date.

At the time of the merger announcement, Eberstadt Fund had about 8,000 shareholders and assets of approximately $30 million. Surveyor Fund had assets of approximately $130 million. Just prior to the merger announcement, Surveyor Fund's market price was $19.50 per share and its net asset value per share was $25.63.

a) In a merger transaction, the shareholders of both firms should achieve net positive benefits. What advantages and disadvantages exist for the shareholders of both funds if this merger is consummated?

b) What effect will the redemption of the 5 percent convertible debentures have on the net asset value of the Surveyor Fund?

c) In your opinion, should a shareholder of the Surveyor Fund vote for the proposed merger if the convertible debenture issue has to be called because SEC approval to retain it cannot be obtained?

d) The conversion rate on the debentures is 32.97 shares per $1,000 principal amount. As the holder of a debenture, what would be your action upon receiving notice of their call?

e) Do you think that there will be more mergers in the future between open-end and closed-end investment companies? What might prevent these mergers from taking place in future years?

SUGGESTED READINGS

Boudreaux, Kenneth J. "Discounts and Premiums on Closed-End Mutual Funds: A Study in Valuation." *Journal of Finance,* May 1973, pp. 515–22.

Carlson, Robert S. "Aggregate Performance of Mutual Funds, 1948–1967." *Journal of Financial and Quantitative Analysis,* March 1970, pp. 1–32.

Fishbein, Richard. "Closed-End Investment Companies." *Financial Analysts Journal*, March–April 1970, pp. 67–73.

Friend, Irwin, Marshall Blume, and Jean Crockett. *Mutual Funds and Other Institutional Investors*. New York: McGraw-Hill, 1970.

Investment Companies. Latest annual edition. New York: Wiesenberger Services, Inc.

Jensen, Michael C. "The Performance of Mutual Funds in the Period 1945–1964." *Journal of Finance*, May 1968, pp. 389–416.

Malkiel, Burton G. *A Random Walk Down Wall Street*. New York: W.W. Norton & Co., Inc., 1973, chapter 9.

McDonald, John G. "Objectives and Performance of Mutual Funds, 1960–1969." *Journal of Financial and Quantitative Analysis*, June 1974, pp. 311–33.

Murray, Roger F. "Indirect Investment in the Securities Market and the Individual Investor." *Journal of Contemporary Business*, Winter 1974, pp. 63–71.

Roenfeldt, Rodney L. and Donald L. Tuttle. "An Examination of the Discounts and Premiums of Closed-End Investment Companies." *Journal of Business Research*, Fall 1973, pp. 129–40.

Smith, Keith V. and John C. Schreiner. "Direct vs. Indirect Diversification." *Financial Analysts Journal*, September–October 1970, pp. 33–38.

Treynor, Jack L. "How to Rate Management of Investment Funds." *Harvard Business Review*, January–February 1965, pp. 63–75.

—— and Kay K. Mazuy. "Can Mutual Funds Outguess the Market?" *Harvard Business Review*, July–August 1966, pp. 131–36.

Williamson, J. Peter. "Measurement and Forecasting of Mutual Fund Performance: Choosing an Investment Strategy." *Financial Analysts Journal*, November–December 1972, pp. 78–84.

*

22

From Picasso to Pork Bellies

Oriental carpets, race horses, Tiffany lamps, gold coins, paintings, vintage cars, postage stamps, and porcelain figurines are some of the exotic investments people have been attracted to in recent years. In fact, anything that people collect and will pay a price for is a legitimate alternative to security investments. This chapter considers the investment merits of many of these non-security investments, including real estate and commodities.

The first section discusses the risk and return problems involved in nonsecurity investments. Real estate investment, both on a direct and an indirect basis, is the subject of section two. Investing in precious metals and in stamps is discussed in the next section. Section four deals with investments in art masterpieces and antiques. Commodity trading is discussed in section five. The role of these investments in portfolio theory and a summary complete the chapter. To be sure, entire books have been written on each of the investment alternatives considered in this chapter. Our purpose is only to introduce the reader to these areas, not to provide a comprehensive treatment of each investment alternative.

RISK AND RETURN PROBLEMS

With the possible exception of commodity trading, an investor considering the purchase of the nonsecurity assets discussed in this chapter faces a number of problems. To a large degree, each asset is unique and must be valued in this context. Every share of AT&T common stock is identical to every other share of AT&T, but not every piece of real estate, every original painting, or many of the other nonsecurity assets are identical to each other. Because of this heterogeneity, the secondary markets for these assets are relatively inefficient. Trades in roughly comparable assets occur infrequently, making it difficult to value one's holdings. In addition, transaction costs are often a substantial percentage of the value of the asset, especially if the asset must be sold at auction, which is the case with many art masterpieces. These relatively high transaction costs mean that the asset must normally be held for a longer period of time than is true for securities.

The heterogeneous character of many exotic investments has added implications. Because the quality of the asset is the predominant consideration in valuation, expert knowledge is often required. An investor must be well informed in such areas as art, real estate, and antiques to make investments that will earn respectable rates of return. The need to possess expert knowledge regarding a particular investment tends to increase the probabilities that a fraudulent transaction will occur, since counterfeiting becomes both relatively easy and quite profitable.

Not only is the return on these nonsecurity assets difficult to calculate, since the market is relatively inefficient and the asset must usually be sold to produce a final accounting, but nonmonetary returns are often very important. One article dealing with investment in art stated this concept in the following manner:

> Although art objects do not provide an annual cash flow, the psychic income derived from possessing them can be enormous. The day-to-day experience of living with fine objects is extremely rewarding. [The] psychic rewards . . . [may] become more important than [the] original objective of capital appreciation.[1]

REAL ESTATE

Forms of Ownership

Real estate ownership can be considered as either direct or indirect. Direct ownership refers to having title to the real estate registered in the name of the investor. This would include a homeowner's personal

[1]James O. and Joanne T. Winjum, "The Art Investment Market," *University of Michigan Business Review*, November 1974, p. 5.

residence even though subject to a mortgage. As we observed in Chapter 11, a person's equity in a personal residence may be large compared to other assets owned and have a profound influence on the type of other investments made by that person.

Indirect ownership of real estate can take many forms, but a financial instrument is normally involved. An investor may hold directly a mortgage or a portfolio of mortgages on real estate properties, although this is somewhat unusual for the average investor. The investor may also participate as a partner in a real estate syndicate formed to buy and manage real estate, or may own a Ginnie Mae mortgage-backed security. Since the Ginnie Mae alternative is essentially the purchase of a form of bond, we will not discuss it in this chapter.

Another form of indirect ownership of real estate is the real estate investment trust (REIT, pronounced "reet"). Following a brief discussion of the risk and return considerations involved in both direct and indirect real estate ownership, the investment characteristics of REITs are examined.

Risk and Return Characteristics

The basic investment characteristic of real estate is the fact that new land is not being produced. At the same time, real estate investment has many of the risk and return problems discussed in the previous section. Real estate is a heterogeneous product to a considerable extent and requires expert knowledge. Real estate is relatively illiquid, as people trying to sell a personal residence during periods of tight money discover. Additionally, transaction costs may be significant.

Two additional considerations are important in real estate investing. First, most real estate purchases require an outside source of financing. Hence, the potential real estate investor must give serious consideration to the availability of financing, its cost, and any restrictive covenants that may be imposed by the lender. During tight money periods, these three factors may be dominant in a consideration of any real estate transaction, although they are always important. Tight money conditions may result in distress sales of real estate and provide opportunities for the well-financed investor to profit at the expense of other real estate holders.

Taxes are the second important consideration. Not only are there substantial tax incentives for home ownership, but many real estate transactions depend on the impact of the income tax laws. The manner in which depreciation may be taken on a real estate project and its impact on the profitability of a project will generally require the assistance of competent tax advisors.

REITs

The vast majority of REITs are organized as closed-end investment companies designed to invest in a diversified portfolio of real estate and mortgage investments. REITs provide a means for both large and small investors to obtain a share of a professionally managed real estate portfolio. In this regard, REITs provide diversification similar to that of other investment companies.

The REIT industry came into existence as the result of an act of Congress in 1960.[2] From 1961 to 1968, about $350 million of REIT shares were sold to the public by slightly over fifty REITs.[3] When money became tight in 1969 and 1970 and the traditional real estate lenders such as savings and loan associations curtailed their lending activities, lending by REITs grew rapidly. As a result, REIT assets amounted to about $5 billion at the end of 1970. REITs continued to grow to the end of 1973 when their assets exceeded $20 billion. Innovative financing techniques and a strong construction market during this period contributed to their growth. Then came 1974 and a host of problems, as we shall soon see.

Types of REITs. As with any industry, more than one way exists to classify the firms within the industry. For example, some REITs are regional in the scope of their operations, while others are national. Probably the most useful method of classification for investment purposes is to classify REITs into short-term trusts, long-term trusts, and equity trusts.[4] Short-term trusts are often called construction and development trusts since they provide the funds needed during the construction phase of a project. The long-term trusts provide the regular long-term mortgage loans needed after the project is completed. Equity trusts all own property, but come in several different forms that may be described as regular equity trusts, land trusts, and development trusts. The regular equity trusts own developed property and generate cash flow from rents and depreciation. Land trusts purchase the land under the income producing properties and lease it back to the original owner. The development trusts, as the name implies, own and develop property themselves.

[2]The Real Estate Investment Trust Act, which became law as of January 1, 1961. See E. Norman Bailey, "Real Estate Investment Trusts: An Apprisal," *Financial Analysts Journal,* May–June 1966, pp. 107–14, for a discussion of REITs and their historical development. Bailey recognized that a potential cash flow problem existed as a result of the tax laws under which REITs operate.

[3]The statistics in this paragraph were obtained from *REIT Fact Book 1974* (Washington, D.C.: National Association of Real Estate Investment Trusts). This is the first edition of this publication.

[4]These classifications are not mutually exclusive since REITs will often make the type of loan dictated by the situation, although there is a tendency to specialize. For a more extensive discussion of the various types of REITS, see "The REIT Way," *Forbes,* May 1, 1972, pp. 47–48.

It is important for the potential REIT investor to distinguish among the various types of REITs. REITs make money from the spread between their cost of funds and the interest rate they charge. Short-term trusts are especially sensitive to changes in this spread during periods of tight money. The long-term trusts and the equity trusts tend to be less sensitive to changes in the cost of funds, although they are by no means immune.

Problems of REITs. A host of problems intensified during 1974 to make that year a horrendous one for REITs. The S&P REIT stock price index declined 79.1 percent during 1974 against 29.8 percent for the S&P 500 stock index.[5] What happened? Money became very expensive in 1974, with the result that the spread on which REITs operate narrowed or even became negative in certain instances. Some sources of funds for the REIT virtually disappeared. As the market value of REIT shares declined, it became impossible to sell new shares to the public. Commercial paper, representing about 20 percent of the sources of REIT funds at the end of 1973, became difficult to renew as commercial paper purchasers became very quality conscious.[6] Retained earnings have never been an important source of funds because of the closed-end investment company form of operation and the requirements for qualifying as a regulated investment company.[7] Finally, the commercial banks began to examine their REIT lines of credit very carefully. The banks started to demand lower REIT debt-to-equity ratios as a condition for the continuation of the lines of credit.

The rapid growth of nonearning portfolio assets in certain REITs has resulted in either greatly reduced or omitted dividends. As the percentage of nonearning assets increased, investors became concerned with the level of loan loss reserves. Since there had been few defaults in the mortgage portfolio in previous years, the reserves for portfolio losses were based upon experience and were a small percentage of the value of the portfolio. Many of these reserves appeared too low to investors given the problems facing the industry. Investors expected additional earnings to be set aside in the loss reserve account. This action would reduce earnings and dividends.

Industry Outlook. This industry is going through an adjustment period. Given the performance of REIT shares during 1974, the sale of new REIT shares will probably not be possible for some time. REITs

[5]The S&P REIT price index is constructed using the prices of six REITS. With 1970 equal to 10, this index went from 6.13 on January 2, 1974, to 1.28 on December 31, 1974. This decline followed a decline of approximately 47 percent in 1973.

[6]*REIT Fact Book 1974,* p. 66.

[7]Some REITs have given up their regulated investment company status recently, since under the tax laws, the REIT is required to pay out at least 90 percent of net income in the form of dividends.

still need to reach the lower debt-to-equity ratios demanded by the commercial banks. Lower interest rates should be of considerable help to the REITs, but any real recovery in the industry will depend primarily on the level of construction expenditures and the competition REITs face in providing real estate financing. Several REITs have already gone into bankruptcy and mergers between existing REITs are likely in the future. As the number of industry participants is reduced and the economy recovers, the stronger REITs should eventually prosper.[8]

Direct Real Estate Ownership

The decision to purchase a home for use as a personal residence is a "mixed" decision for a person, because elements of both consumption and investment are present. Investment elements include the build-up of equity over the years as the mortgage is repaid and the possibility that the residence will increase in value. There are also significant tax advantages for the home owner. Property taxes and interest on the mortgage are allowable itemized deductions from the taxpayer's income. For a person with a moderately high income, the after-tax cost of owning a home may be less than that of renting comparable housing even without considering any potential equity accumulation. At the same time, liquidity is a major problem for the homeowner, since a quick sale is often extremely difficult.

As with many nonsecurity investments, it is difficult to calculate a rate of return from home ownership. The reason is that many nonquantifiable benefits may result from owning a home. These qualitative benefits may be psychological, personal, and social. They include social prestige, pride of ownership, a sense of security, the ability to achieve greater personal expression, a potentially better credit rating, and freedom from the authority of a landlord. These qualitative benefits make precise rate of return calculations impossible and indicate that many decisions to purchase a personal residence or rent housing will be made on the basis of personal considerations.

The direct purchase of other real estate should be analyzed on the same basis as other competing investment alternatives. However, the investor does need to realize the lack of diversification that results from direct real estate investment in either a personal residence or other real estate ventures unless substantial sums of capital are available to the investor. In addition, the real estate investor should be aware that this country has experienced land booms and busts in the past, in Florida during the 1920s, for example.[9]

[8]See "Hard-Pressed REITs Are Risky Holdings," *The Standard & Poor Outlook*, December 2, 1974, pp. 429–30, for an analysis of the problems of the industry and its future.

[9]"What Walt Hath Wrought," *Forbes*, June 1, 1972, pp. 21–22, discusses the land boom created by the development of Disney World and also discusses the boom and bust in the Florida land market in the Twenties.

PRECIOUS METALS AND POSTAGE STAMPS

While the great gold rush of 1975 proved to be a bust, investments in precious metals such as gold and silver and investments in other collectible items such as coins and stamps may prove to be profitable. For the first time since 1933, it is now legal for U.S. citizens to buy and hold gold bullion. Many U.S. and foreign coins made of all kinds of metal are also available for investment purposes. In this section, we discuss the ways in which an investor can hold gold and the advantages and disadvantages of each method. Numismatic activities are also discussed. Philately, the collection and study of postage stamps, is also introduced as an investment alternative.

Gold

The four basic ways of directly investing in gold are: 1) gold bullion; 2) gold coins; 3) gold futures; and 4) investment companies specializing in gold investment, if they are eventually sold to the public.[10] An indirect method of investing in gold is to buy the common stock of gold mining companies. Why buy gold? Gold is considered by some authorities to be a method of hedging against poor economic conditions.[11] The price of gold may move in contrast to general economic conditions since people seek the security of gold during troubled times. Certainly, the mystique of gold has existed for many centuries.

Gold Bullion. Private holdings of gold bullion became legal for U.S. citizens at the start of 1975. Some banks and dealers started to handle transactions in gold bars. The investor has a wide range of gold bar sizes from which to choose, but there are important disadvantages in holding gold in this form. As with all direct methods of owning gold, there is no current income. Also, small gold bars are often purchased at a premium price and sold at a discount price. Hence, the investor should purchase the biggest gold bar possible. Once you have your gold bar, you have to do something with it. You can store it yourself or you can arrange to have a financial institution store it for a fee; you should also provide the proper insurance for your holding.[12] Estimates of these costs run in the range of 2 to 3 percent annually of the gold's value.[13]

The opportunity cost of giving up current income, the commissions and sales taxes on gold transactions, and the costs incurred while owning

[10]Bars of Gold, Inc. was planning to sell shares to investors (see *Wall Street Journal*, November 1, 1974, p. 16) but later cancelled the offering.

[11]For an example, see "Will Americans Buy the Catastrophe Hedge?" *Business Week*, December 21, 1974, pp. 134–36.

[12]"Personal Business" section, *Business Week*, July 27, 1974, pp. 69–70.

[13]"The $1 Billion Hobby," *Forbes*, December 15, 1974, p. 35.

gold mean that the price of gold must increase substantially for the investor to break even. An article in *Forbes* stated that "the metal must nearly double every *three* years to outperform a frumpy-looking 6% municipal bond."[14] Assay fees may also be required upon sale if the investor decides to accept physical delivery of gold bullion. In addition, unless the investor deals with bullion dealers of the highest reputation, fraudulent gold bars are a possibility.

Gold Coins. Gold coins may have relatively little or considerable numismatic value. Certain gold coins have been traded for a long time, so the market is well established. Coins are considered more difficult to counterfeit than bullion, although the counterfeiting of gold coins is by no means unknown. The U.S. Treasury's Secret Service has no jurisdiction over the counterfeiting of coins that do not qualify as legal tender.[15] Many counterfeit coins are made in foreign countries where it is not illegal to produce copies of U.S. coins. Just as with bullion, an investor must take steps to insure and protect a collection of gold coins.

Gold Futures. Trading in gold futures began at the start of 1975. Futures trading is discussed extensively later in this chapter and the basic concepts do not differ when applied to gold futures. Exhibit 22-1 shows

EXHIBIT 22-1
Gold Futures Trading Report

Gold Futures

Tuesday, January 14, 1975

	Open	High	Low	Close	Change	High	Low
CHICAGO MERC. EXCH.–x100 TROY OUNCES							
Jan	178.00	178.20	177.50	178.20	– 2.30	190.50	164.50
Mar	177.00	180.90	177.00	180.70-.80	+ .80to.90	195.00	165.00
June	182.10	184.90	182.00	184.70	+ .70	205.00	170.00
Sept	187.00	189.70	186.20	189.30-.70	+1.5to1.9	209.00	178.00
Dec	190.50	194.20	190.40	193.8-194.2	+2.0to2.4	215.00	182.00
Sales estimated at: 1,546 contracts.							
COMMODITY EXCH. (N.Y.)–x100 TROY OUNCES							
Jan	177.00	179.00	176.50	178.60	+ .20	190.50	164.00
Feb	177.00	178.60	176.50	178.60	. . . .	191.50	165.00
Mar	177.70	180.00	177.50	179.90	– .10	192.50	167.00
Apr	179.50	181.50	178.70	181.20	– .20	195.40	168.00
June	182.80	184.50	182.80	184.20	– .20	198.00	174.50
Aug	185.60	187.20	185.50	187.20	– .20	200.00	177.00
Oct	189.00	190.20	189.00	190.20	– .20	202.00	180.00
Dec	192.00	193.20	192.00	193.20	– .20	205.00	183.50
Feb76	195.00	196.20	195.00	196.20	– .20	208.00	190.00
Apr	198.20	199.20	198.20	199.20	– .20	210.50	194.80
Sales estimated at: 1,061 contracts.							

Source: Reprinted with permission of *the Wall Street Journal,* © Dow Jones & Company, Inc. (January 15, 1975), p. 24.

[14]Ibid. (italics in original).
[15]Ibid., p. 29.

the gold future prices for January 14, 1975, as reported in the *Wall Street Journal* for major contracts traded on U.S. commodity exchanges.[16]

Using futures as a method of speculating in the price of gold has some significant advantages over methods requiring physical ownership of gold in bullion or coin form. There are no storage, security, or assay problems for the investor to worry about. The futures market offers a good secondary market with reasonable transaction costs. The purchase of a gold future requires the deposit of margin in the neighborhood of 10 to 15 percent of the value of the contract. The nature of this margin deposit is discussed in the commodities section. However, these advantages do not mean that the gold futures market is a less risky method of speculating in the price of gold than the other methods described. The price of gold has been volatile in recent years, as shown in Figure 22-1, and the value of a gold future tends to mirror the movements of gold prices.

Gold Mining Company Shares. The shares of gold mining firms are an indirect method of investing in the gold market. The shares of gold mining firms have low betas, indicating that their price movements

FIGURE 22-1
Gold Mining Stocks and the Gold Price—1971-74

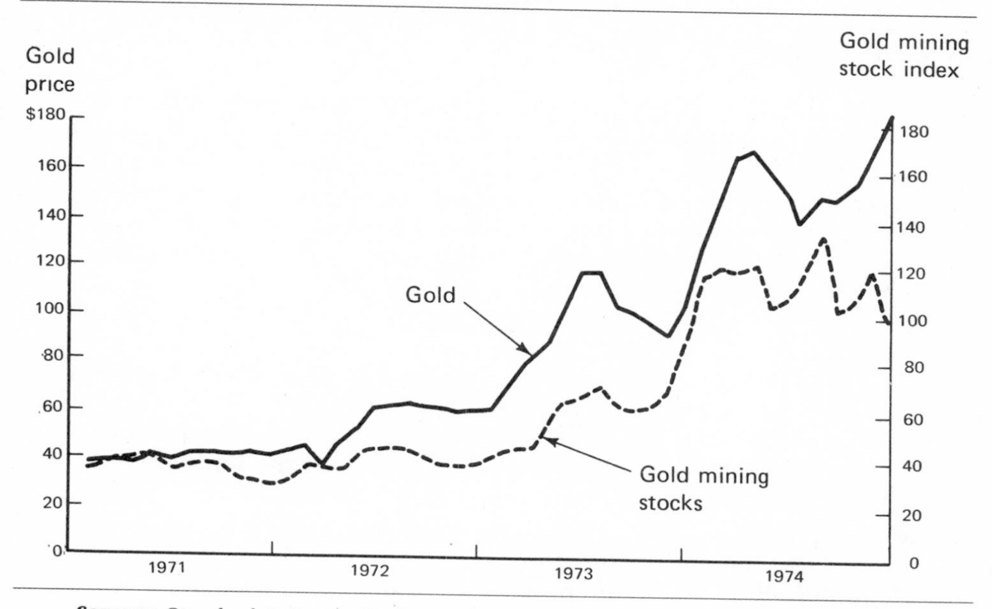

Sources: Standard & Poor's *Trade and Securities Statistics, Security Price Index Record,* 1974, p. 55; S&P's *Current Statistics,* June 1975, p. 33.

[16]A troy ounce is equal to 1.097 avoirdupois ounces.

do not correspond closely to those of the general market.[17] If an investor expects the market to decline, gold mining shares may be a good investment. For example, during 1974, the S&P price index of gold mining stocks declined 8.6 percent compared to 29.8 percent for the S&P 500. Figure 22-2 shows the quarterly movement of the S&P 500 and the S&P gold mining stock price index from 1963 to 1974.

FIGURE 22-2
Gold Mining Stocks and the S&P 500—1963-74

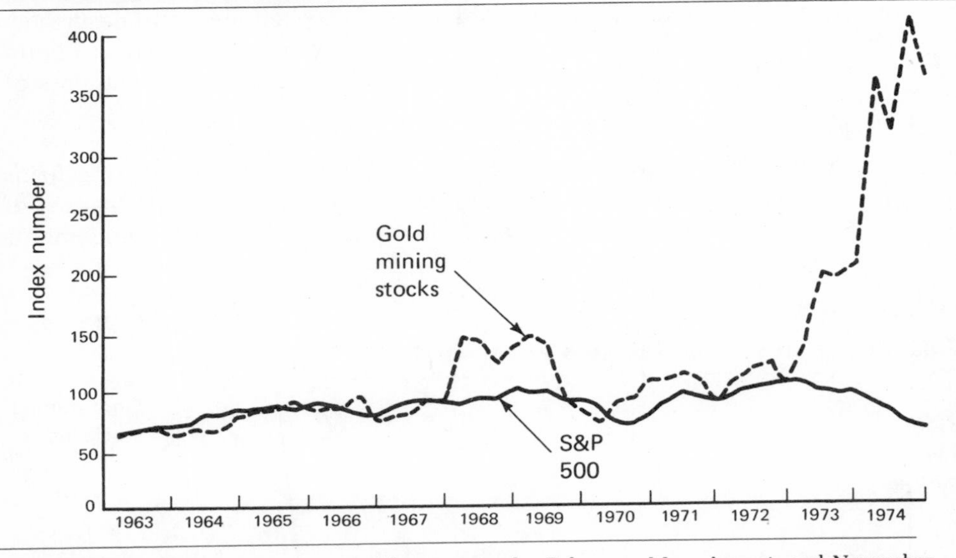

Note: Data plotted are the monthly averages for February, May, August, and November.
Sources: Standard & Poor's *Trade and Securities Statistics, Security Price Index Record,* 1974, p. 55; S&P's *Current Statistics,* June 1975, p. 33. The S&P gold mining stock index is multiplied by a factor of three.

In investing in gold mining companies, the investor does not get a "pure" play on price movements in the gold market. First, other metals may be produced at the same time the gold is mined. The price of these metals will influence the profitability of a gold mining company. As with an investment in any company, the investor must give consideration to the quality of management and how this might change over time. Gold is also mined in foreign countries where political considerations are important. Last, as the price of gold increases, it becomes economi-

[17] *Value Line* beta estimates in early 1974 for the gold mining stocks were as follows: ASA Limited (an investment company with 89 percent of its assets in gold shares), .16; Campbell Red Lake, .15; Dome Mines, .12; and Homestake Mining, .11.

cally feasible for the firm to mine marginal facilities. While the firm will make money doing this, the costs of doing business may increase as a percentage of the revenues of the firm. In other words, the profits of the firm may not increase as rapidly as the price of gold.

Coin Collecting

According to estimates from several sources, approximately eight million Americans are coin collectors.[18] Coins come essentially in two varieties, the numismatic or rare coin and the "common date" coin purchased for its metallic content. Gold and silver coins fit into both of these categories, depending on the particular coin. Since we previously discussed investing in gold coins for their gold value, this section will concentrate on numismatic coins and on investing in silver coins for their silver value.

In 1965, the United States started minting dimes, quarters, and half dollars with a core of copper instead of silver. This action gave the trading in silver coins its start as pre-1965 silver coins started disappearing into coin collections or were melted down for their silver content when the federal government lifted its ban against this practice in 1969. Estimates are that approximately $1.8 billion of silver coins were originally minted and that only about $500 million of these coins exist today.[19]

A recent article estimated that coin prices increased approximately 14 percent annually from 1969 to 1974.[20] However, the investor faces great risks in this type of investment as we have already noted. Collecting coins for their numismatic value is much like investing in many of the other assets discussed in this chapter: Expert knowledge is needed.

Investing in silver coins for their silver value is more risky than investing in numismatic coins, since silver prices are quite volatile. One source states that silver "is notorious for its sharp reactions, and even sophisticated investors frequently get burned on the downside."[21] Various articles have discussed some of the advertising and trading practices that have occurred in the merchandising of bags of silver coins.[22] Investors are able to buy bags of silver coins on margin with the typical payment equal to 25 percent or less. The financing, storage,

[18]Dana L. Thomas, "Double Eagles Soar," *Barron's*. January 14, 1974, p. 5ff; "When a Nickel Is Worth a Small Fortune," *Business Week*, December 14, 1963, p. 132ff; and "Personal Business" section, *Business Week*, May 8, 1971, p. 83. Actually, the estimates range from 700,000 to 15 million depending upon the definition of coin collector. The low estimate is for serious collectors willing to pay more than face value for a coin.

[19]Dana L. Thomas, "Three Bags Full," *Barron's*, January 21, 1974, p. 11ff.

[20]"The $1 Billion Hobby," p. 24.

[21]Thomas, "Three Bags Full," p. 13.

[22]For example, see "Small Investors Flock to Bags of Silver Coins, But Pricing Is Tricky," *Wall Street Journal*, February 4, 1974, p. 1ff; "Who's Holding the Bag?" *Forbes*, September 1, 1974, pp. 32–34; and Thomas, "Three Bags Full."

and commission costs involved in these transactions may make it difficult for the investor to realize a respectable rate of return on the investment. An article in *Barron's* stated:

> As for the coin side of the business, elements within the industry have been charged with misleading promotional and pricing practices. On this score, the recently-initiated actions by government regulatory agencies should tighten standards and weed out poorly-financed operators.[23]

Philately

Postage stamps have a reputation for being a good hedge against inflation. According to one study, U.S. stamps increased in value about 5 percent annually from 1949 to 1969, with the annual rate of gain from 1964 to 1969 at 10.5 percent.[24] Another study indicates that during the decade ending with 1970, American stamps increased an average of 10 percent annually.[25] Rare stamps are estimated to have increased about 30 percent in 1972, 150 percent in 1973, and about 55 percent in 1974.[26] Although recent rates of return have been very high, the long-term historical rates of return are not especially high relative to the return earned on common stocks during the same period. However, the positive rates of return do indicate potential profit in stamp collecting.

The condition of a stamp is the all-important factor in the determination of its value.[27] Poor quality stamps sell at large discounts from the prices received for stamps in good condition. The philatelist needs to know many things about a stamp, including the type of paper on which it is printed, watermarks present, the type of separation used, and the method of printing. It might even be interesting and useful to know the historical background behind many of the more famous stamps.[28]

Perhaps the most famous American stamp is the 1918 24¢ Air Mail Invert on which the picture of the airplane is upside down. The original block of 100 stamps was purchased in 1918 for $24 and resold to another party a week later for $15,000.[29] Using the first resale price of $150 per stamp as a starting point, Exhibit 22-2 shows annual rate of return calculations for selected holding periods for this stamp.

[23]Thomas, "Three Bags Full," p. 13.

[24]Cited in "Taking Stamp Deals Public," *Business Week*, March 11, 1972, p. 106.

[25]"Personal Business" section, *Business Week*, November 20, 1971, p. 83.

[26]Franz Pick, "Hedges Against Inflation," *Barron's*, January 1, 1973, p. 11ff and "Better Than Gold," *Barron's*, January 6, 1975, p. 11ff.

[27]For a good discussion of condition, see Richard Cabeen, *Standard Handbook of Stamp Collecting* (New York: Thomas Y. Crowell Company, 1957), pp. 48–57.

[28]L. N. and M. Williams, *Famous Stamps* (London: W. & R. Chambers Ltd., 1946), is excellent for this purpose.

[29]Williams, *Famous Stamps*, pp. 228–32, gives the early history of this stamp.

EXHIBIT 22-2

Prices and Rates of Return for 1918 24¢ U.S. Air Mail Invert—Selected Data

Year	Price per Stamp	Annual Rate of Return from Previous Period
1918	$ 150	–
1939	4,100	17.1% over 21 years
1946	4,250	.5 over 7 years
1971	31,750	8.4 over 25 years
1974	47,000	14.0 over 3 years

OTHER RATE OF RETURN CALCULATIONS

1918 to 1974	(56 years) =	10.8%
1946 to 1974	(28 years) =	9.0
1964 to 1969*	(5 years) =	15.4

*Estimate from *Business Week*, March 11, 1972, p. 106.

Sources: L.N. and M. Williams, *Famous Stamps* (London: W & R Chambers, Ltd., 1946), p. 230 (1918 and 1939 prices); Henry R. Ellis, *How to Gain Pleasure and Profit from Stamp Collecting* (New York: Funk & Wagnalls Co., 1947, p. 42 (1946 price); "Taking Stamp Deals Public," *Business Week*, March 11, 1972, p. 106 (1971 price); and Franz Pick, "Better Than Gold," *Barron's*, January 6, 1975, p. 11 (1974 price).

ART AND ANTIQUES

"They [paintings] are a good investment compared with other investments, including real estate and the stock market."[30] Along with antiques of all kinds, much attention has been given in recent years to investing in art masterpieces. The rates of return on these investments have generally been good, although risk and return problems are clearly present in this investment as well.

As previously noted, the return from art and antiques comes in both a monetary and a psychic form. The monetary return is in the form of capital appreciation or losses. It is, of course, not possible to calculate the psychic return.

Richard Rush calculated monetary rates of return over a long period of time for both art masterpieces and antiques by using auction prices.[31] Rush encountered many problems in his rate of return studies. For example, for his art index rate of return calculations, he restricted the analysis to what might be described as average size paintings of excellent quality. Even so, no two paintings are the same even if they are of the same size, the same quality, and were painted by the same artist. The large number of artists whose paintings are sold at auction also caused problems for Rush.

[30]Richard H. Rush, *Art as an Investment* (Englewood Cliffs, N.J.: Prentice-Hall, 1961), p. 403.

[31]Richard H. Rush, *Art as an Investment*, and *Antiques as an Investment* (New York: Bonanza Books, 1968).

The use of auction prices itself results in some unique problems. The retail price of a given painting is often higher than the auction price. Also, the quality of paintings varies considerably in the auction market. Since Rush used American, English, and French auction prices, some problems in exchange conversion existed. The biases of the buyers in each of these three countries for or against certain artists or schools of art also may have influenced the auction prices. In addition, buying "rings" of dealers may artificially depress prices. On the other hand, sentimental bidding, such as might occur in conjunction with estate sales, is often responsible for high prices. Notwithstanding all the construction problems, the art price index compiled by Rush, which is based upon five-year intervals, compares favorably with the trend of stock prices for the 1925 to 1960 period.

The Times-Sotheby Index for the 1950 to 1970 period showed that most categories of art were able to show a performance superior to that of the average mutual fund.[32] Both this index and the work of Rush do not present data for the 1970s, however. According to *Business Week,* the art and antique markets "came to a speculative boil" in 1972 and 1973.[33] Subsequently, the economic downturn that occurred in 1974 and 1975 took its toll on art and antique prices. Rush put it quite well in his 1961 book when he wrote:

> In a recession, paintings tend to hold up better than either the stock market or prices of commodities, although in a real depression there is no justification for assuming that art prices will not decline significantly.[34]

In his book on antiques, Rush constructed an index for antiques similar to the one he constructed for art. The antique index covered the period from 1925 to 1968 and showed the results given below:[35]

	Percentage Change in	
	Antique Index	*S&P 500*
1925 to 1968	785%	801%
1950 to 1968	562	225
1960 to 1968	486	160

It is evident that only in recent years has the antique market "taken off." Evidence contained in various articles in the financial and business press indicates that the boom in antiques and other collectible items, especially where nostalgia is an important element, continues despite some softening because of economic conditions.

[32]Winjum and Winjum, "The Art Investment Market," p. 2. The index is prepared by the London *Times* in conjunction with one of England's leading auction houses.

[33]"Exotica: The Bargain Hunter May Find Some Super Buys," *Business Week,* December 21, 1974, p. 158.

[34]Rush, *Art as an Investment,* p. 403.

[35]Rush, *Antiques as an Investment,* pp. 438–39.

Problems for the Investor

The need to be an expert is crucial in the fields of art and antiques. The investor needs to know how to evaluate the condition of a painting or an antique, its rarity, and its historical significance. Moreover, one expert recommends ten years as the minimum safe holding period.[36] This means that the investor has a ten-year, relatively illiquid, nonincome-producing investment.

Rush stresses the foolishness of investing in just one painting. Rather, he urges the investor to purchase a "portfolio" of paintings, "a dozen rather than one, and these purchases should be divided among several artists."[37] The advice is remarkably similar to the conclusion we observed regarding the number of stocks one needs to hold to achieve adequate diversification. But the purchaser of paintings may well pay $5,000 and up for a good-quality holding. The investor also needs to keep in mind maintenance costs such as insurance.

The successful collector of art or antiques must be a knowledgeable person. Rush summarizes the basic traits needed:

> A successful collector of art must be a person who appreciates quality in art. He buys because the quality is there, and he arrives at his conclusion as to the quality through his native taste, through study of art and schools of art, and through an intense enthusiasm for art and for collecting.[38]

Supply and Demand Factors

Except for living artists, the supply of paintings is fixed. The same is true for genuine antiques. At the same time, the demand for art has increased over the years because of a number of factors. The growth of museums has resulted in a decreased supply of art available for public trading, since a museum will ordinarily purchase a painting for its permanent collection. Then too, the income tax laws encourage wealthy collectors to donate paintings to museums rather than sell them at auction. In addition, corporate purchasers of art and antiques have recently become important. Add the increasing interest by individuals to these other demand elements and one has what appears to be an almost perfect investment situation—limited and declining supply and increasing demand. Rush recognizes this situation, but warns that "paintings, although a good investment, do not provide any such thing as absolute security against a price drop, particularly against the effect of a major business

[36]"Ars Gratia Pecuniae," *Forbes*, August 1, 1973, p. 48, contains this recommendation of Hugh Hildesley, the chief appraiser for Sotheby Parke Bernet, the major U.S. auction house.

[37]Rush, *Art as an Investment*, p. 227.

[38]Ibid., p. 264.

recession."[39] For example, high-priced paintings declined from 10 to 20 percent during the recession of 1969–70 and also appear to have declined during the recession of 1974–75.[40]

Future Outlook

While the economic slowdown of 1974–75 cooled the speculative boom in exotic investments such as art and antiques, the long-term future looks favorable. A recent article argues that the prospect for continued, relatively high rates of inflation, plus a corresponding desire for capital appreciation rather than current income, effectively reduces the importance of the fact that art investment lacks a current income.[41] One might quarrel with the assumption that cash yields have become less important in the past couple of years, especially in view of the growth of such institutions as the money market investment companies, but it is probably true that exotic investments will continue to become increasingly important as an investment alternative. The evidence indicates that the monetary rate of return can compete reasonably well with common stocks over long periods of time. Finally, the illiquid nature of these investments is offset to a considerable extent by their psychic income.

COMMODITIES

Commodity trading has increased substantially in recent years, and new commodities have been traded: Witness the start of trading in gold futures on major U.S. commodity exchanges in early 1975. Figure 22–3 shows the estimated dollar volume of trading in commodities compared to the trading volume of the NYSE for the 1962 to 1974 period. Commodity trading volume was substantially greater than NYSE volume during 1973 and 1974.

A person desiring to trade in a given commodity buys or sells a future. A *future* is a bona fide contract providing for future delivery of the actual commodity. Although the contract calls for future delivery, the speculator can avoid accepting physical delivery by closing out the position prior to the time of delivery. There is no reason for the speculator to wake up one morning and find 5,000 bushels of soybeans in the front yard. Actually, the speculator in this situation would own soybeans stored in a grain elevator somewhere.

A future is standardized in many important ways. The size of the contract is standardized. Most grain future contracts are denominated in 5,000 bushel units. The live cattle future calls for delivery of 40,000 pounds of cattle, while the pork belly (unsliced bacon) future calls for the delivery of 36,000 pounds of pork bellies. Other standard features

[39] Ibid., p. 222.
[40] "Exotica: The Bargain Hunter May Find Some Super Buys," p. 158.
[41] Winjum and Winjum, "The Art Investment Market," pp. 2–3.

FIGURE 22-3
NYSE and Commodity Trading Volume, 1962-74

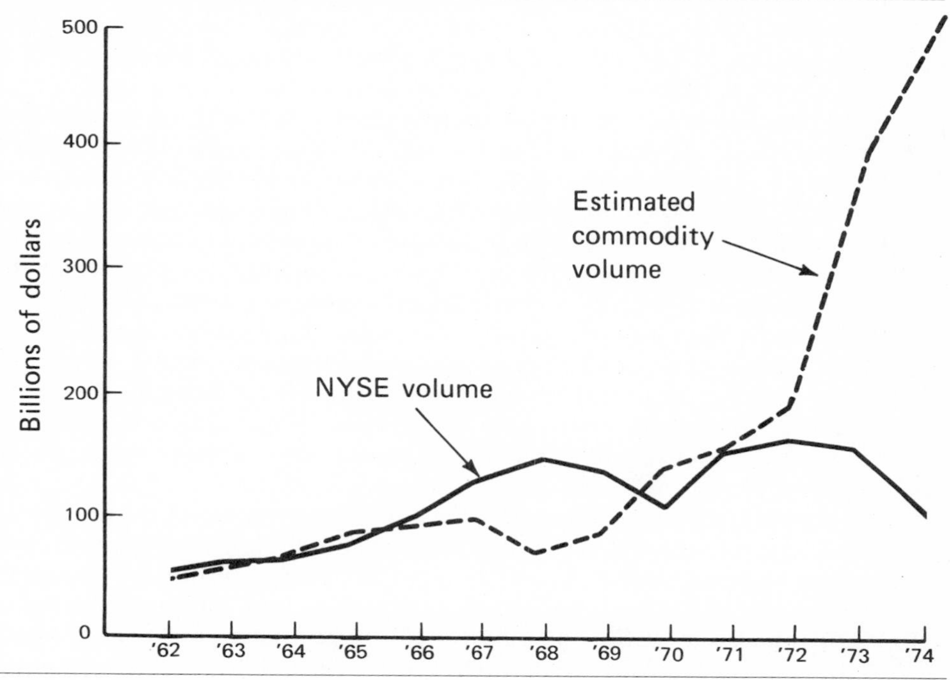

Note: NYSE data are calendar year; commodity data are fiscal year.
Sources: *New York Stock Exchange 1974 Fact Book* (New York: NYSE, June 1974), p. 73; *SEC Statistical Bulletin* (Washington, D.C., U.S. Government Printing Office, February 1975), p. 137; and Association of Commodity Exchange Firms.

of a future concern the grade of the commodity deliverable to satisfy the contract, the delivery period, and approved delivery points. These standardized features make commodity trading viable.

Growth of Commodity Trading

In the past, trading in futures grew to accommodate certain needs or problems that arose as the U.S. economy grew, and many of the needs still exist in a modern agribusiness environment. These problems include the need for capital, inventory management problems, pricing decisions, and the ownership risk involved in the movement of goods from the point of production to the point of consumption.

As the nineteenth-century U.S. economy grew, marketing areas ceased to be local and became regional or national. "To-arrive contracts" developed as a means of adjusting to the growth of these marketing areas. Grain might be sold now with arrival in Chicago to occur at a later date, perhaps two or three weeks. The "to-arrive contract" had a number of defects, including unreliable delivery, nonstandardized quality, and the lack of a good secondary market for the contract. As a result of the experience with "to-arrive contracts," the Chicago Board of Trade, in October 1865, established general rules to govern trading in specified commodities.[42] This date is considered the start of modern futures trading in the United States.

The major U.S. commodity exchanges are the Chicago Board of Trade (CBOT), the Chicago Mercantile Exchange (CME), the New York Mercantile Exchange, the New York Cotton Exchange, the New York Coffee & Sugar Exchange, and the Commodity Exchange, Inc. Corn, soybeans, oats, and other grains along with plywood and silver are the main commodities traded on the CBOT. Grains are also traded on the Midamerica Commodity Exchange, the Kansas City Board of Trade, and the Minneapolis Grain Exchange. The main commodities traded on the CME are eggs, live cattle, live hogs, pork bellies, and lumber. Through its subsidiary, the International Monetary Market, foreign currencies, gold, and silver coins are traded. The other exchanges trade in commodities such as potatoes, platinum, cotton, orange juice, cocoa, sugar, silver, and gold.

Some major requirements exist for a futures market to develop in any given commodity. The commodity should be homogeneous and capable of being graded. There should also be an uncertain and competitive supply-demand relationship for the commodity, and numerous producers and users of the commodity. If one producer controls too much of the supply of a given commodity, the futures market could be manipulated and speculators would be reluctant to deal in that commodity. Further, the commodity traded is often in a raw or semiprocessed state.[43] It is also helpful if the major merchandising firms associated with the commodity participate in the futures market or at least not oppose its establishment. This is quite an extensive list, but trading has been started in a number of new commodities in recent years.[44]

Stocks versus Commodities

A convenient method of discussing commodity trading is to compare it with investing in stocks.[45] One must understand a number of differences before speculating in commodities. These differences involve

[42]The Chicago Board of Trade was organized in 1848 and futures trading actually started in 1859.

[43]Exceptions include currencies, gold bars, silver coins, sugar, lumber, plywood, and interest rates.

[44]For example, pork bellies (1961), live cattle (1964), live hogs (1966), gold (1975), and natural rubber (1975).

[45]For an extended discussion of these differences, see Mark J. Powers, *Getting Started in Commodity Futures Trading* (Columbia, Md.: Investor Publications, Inc., 1973).

the manner in which trading occurs, the risks involved, and the sources of information.

Market Participants. Two major groups participate in the futures market, the hedgers and the speculators. Hedgers already hold a position in the commodity and use the futures market to establish a position opposite to that already held in the cash (spot) market. For example, a country grain elevator operator may agree in June to purchase at the time of harvest 5,000 bushels of corn at $3.30 a bushel from a local farmer. Essentially, the price is determined in June with delivery to take place in November. The elevator operator now has a position in 5,000 bushels of corn. If corn sells for $2.70 a bushel in November, the elevator operator will lose $.60 a bushel, since the farmer receives $3.30 a bushel.

To reduce this risk, the elevator operator will hedge by selling short one corn future contract at the time the price of $3.30 is agreed upon. If the price drops to $2.70 at harvest, the elevator operator makes money on the short position in the futures market. This should offset to a large extent the money lost by having to pay the farmer $3.30 a bushel in November. However, since the emphasis of this book is on investments, we will not devote additional time to the interesting topic of hedging.

Speculators compose the second major group participating in the futures market. They accept the risk the hedgers want to avoid by taking positions in the market. In this sense, they perform an economic function. When the country elevator operator wants to sell a corn future, a speculator may be the party purchasing it. The speculator helps to give the market liquidity, and will accept the risks of commodity trading in an attempt to make large profits.

Margin. A margin transaction in the securities market involves the use of credit. The investor purchases a security by putting up equity and borrowing the rest of the purchase price through the use of a margin account. Margin accounts are regulated by the Federal Reserve Board.

In the futures market, the speculator is not buying or selling the actual commodity, but only agreeing to buy or sell at some future date. Because of this, the nature of margin in the futures market is quite different from that in the securities market. In essence, the margin in a commodity transaction is nothing more than a security deposit to provide the brokerage firm with some protection from default on the contract by the speculator and to absorb trading losses.

Margins are also much lower for commodities than for securities. This makes commodity trading quite speculative, since modest sums of money can control large commodity positions. For example, a live cattle contract selling for 40 cents per pound means that one contract of 40,000 pounds is worth $16,000. The initial margin on this contract will be approximately $1,000. For every dollar put into margin, the speculator controls $16 worth of commodity. It is difficult to find this kind of leverage in the stock market.

Margins in commodities do somewhat resemble those for securities in that there are initial margin and maintenance margin requirements. The initial margin requirement is set by the commodity exchange, although brokerage firms may require that their customers put up more margin than the exchange minimum. Margin calls typically come when the equity in the commodity trading account declines to 75 percent of the initial margin requirement. If the purchase of a live cattle contract were the only transaction, a margin call would come if the speculator loses $250 on the contract.

Daily Price Limits. The relatively low margins for commodities make commodity trading quite risky. The live cattle contract needs to decline only 6.25 percent for the speculator's entire $1,000 margin to be wiped out. The protection of speculators and member firms of the exchange is the main reason why daily price limits exist in the commodities market. Live cattle futures can move up or down only one and one-half cents per pound from the previous close (i.e., a three-cent trading range) on any given trading day. Since this is a maximum of $600 per contract, it would take 1⅔ days for the speculator to be wiped out if unfavorable market limit moves occurred. Of course, the speculator should be sold out before all the risk capital is gone.[46] Margin requirements and daily price limits are changed frequently so that the potential commodity trader will need to check with the brokerage firm handling the trading account.

Time Horizon. Even if an investor purchases a security after a careful security valuation and attention to portfolio ramifications, an unfavorable market move may result in a loss. However, if the analysis was done properly, the investor should eventually get "bailed out" as the market improves. Such is not the case in the futures market.

Commodity futures have a maximum life of two years or less. If still in existence, the contract must be fulfilled by the end of the month in which it expires (delivery month). Since the holder knows when the contract expires, there is no reason to be put into a position to accept delivery. In general, only the more experienced commodity traders should trade a future during the delivery month.[47]

Selling Short. In the commodity market, it is as easy to sell short as to buy long. Since the short sale does not require physical delivery, the commodity does not have to be borrowed from someone, as is the case with the short sale of a common stock. Nor are there special uptick

[46]If a series of limit moves occurs accompanied by no trading, the speculator could lose the entire margin amount and wind up owing the brokerage firm money before the position could be eliminated.

[47]See Gerald Gold, *Modern Commodity Futures Trading*, 6th ed. (New York: Commodity Research Bureau, Inc., 1971), pp. 39–40.

rules for going short, as exist in the stock market. If a short position is closed out before the contract expires, no physical delivery of the commodity is required. Inexperienced commodity speculators may have a bias toward long positions rather than short positions. This appears to be the result of a long-term upward trend in the stock market. However, it is just as easy in the commodities market to make (or lose) money by going short as it is by going long.

Zero-Sum Game. The futures market is what is known as a zero-sum game. For every long position, there is a short position. Thus, an upward price movement will cause one side of the market (the long position) to make exactly what the other side (the short position) will lose. A downward market move will produce the opposite result. Since commissions must be paid, the market is often referred to as a zero-sum game less commissions.

The stock market is not a zero-sum game. There is not a short position for every long position. It is conceivable for virtually every participant in the stock market to make money if the market moves up or to lose money if the market moves down. This difference between stocks and commodities, coupled with the leverage available in commodity trading, means that a commodity trader needs superior skills to make money consistently.

Specialist versus Auction Market. We saw in Chapter 2 that each stock traded on the major exchanges is the responsibility of a specialist. The specialist is responsible for seeing that the trading in the security is conducted in a fair and orderly manner. There are no specialists in the commodities market; trading is conducted only by open outcry in conformity with the auction method used. However, scalpers exist on the floor of the exchange. They operate by buying and selling futures for very small price differences. In essence, they operate and function much like the specialist on the stock exchanges.

Fundamental and Technical Analysis. The manner in which one performs a fundamental or a technical analysis of a commodity differs little from the way one would do it for a stock. Fundamental analysis may be easier for commodities than for stocks because there are fewer commodities than stocks and because the data needed are provided at little or no cost by the U.S. Department of Agriculture. The commodity speculator does need to follow closely new information regarding a commodity, since new information indicating a relatively small change in supply may result in large changes in price. The drought and early frost that occurred during the growing season of 1974 are good examples of how changes in supply projections can result in large changes in price.

For example, the January 1975 soybean future went from $5.43½ per bushel on May 30, 1974, to $9.60 on October 4, 1974—a gain of $20,825 per contract!

Spread Transactions

A spread is a simultaneous purchase of a future for delivery in one month and sale of a future in the same commodity for delivery in another month. A straddle is a simultaneous trade across two different but related markets, such as corn and oats. Actually the terms *spread* and *straddle* tend to be used interchangeably. Hence, we will refer to all related transactions involving the purchase of one future and the sale of another future at approximately the same time as a spread.

Why would a commodity speculator enter into a spread transaction? The object is to profit from a change in the *price difference* between the two futures. This price difference is commonly referred to as the basis. We can distinguish three fundamental types of spread transactions: 1) the intermarket spread; 2) the intracommodity spread; and 3) the intercommodity spread.

Intermarket Spread. The intermarket spread attempts to take advantage of a price difference that exists for the same future trading on two different commodity exchanges. For example, if the July wheat future trading on the Chicago Board of Trade differs from the July wheat future trading on the Kansas City Board of Trade by a price difference that cannot be justified by location differences or quality differences, the speculator could sell short the overvalued contract and buy the undervalued contract. The spreader would wait for the market to correct itself before closing out the spread. This type of transaction clearly requires expert knowledge regarding all the possible variables that will influence the price of wheat on each exchange. Because of commission costs and timing consideration, intermarket spreads are normally profitable only for commodity firms with memberships in each of the exchanges and with a representative on each trading floor.

Intracommodity Spread. The intracommodity spread involves the purchase of one future and the sale of a different future for the same commodity. Suppose that a speculator sees that the May and August 1975 soybean futures are both selling for $7.04 a bushel in mid-January 1975. The speculator feels that the August future should be higher than the May future because it costs money to store soybeans from May to August. The speculator feels that the August future should be 10 cents higher than the May future and decides to take the following action:

January 1975	Sell May soybean future @ $7.04
	Buy August soybean future @ $7.04

If the speculator is correct and August soybeans do sell for 10 cents more than May soybeans as of April 1975, the speculator can close out the spread in the following manner:

April 1975 Buy May soybean future @ $6.70
Sell August soybean future @ $6.80

Notice that the price of both contracts declined during the holding period. This is of little concern to the trader since it is the price difference that the trader is trying to predict. The trader achieved a net profit of 10 cents a bushel as shown below:

May soybeans = profit of $.34 a bushel
August soybeans = loss of $.24 a bushel

Of course, it is possible the price difference between these two contracts will not perform as the trader expects. The prices of both futures could be $6.70 in April 1975 and the trader would have neither gained nor lost except for commission costs. Since the August future is subject to different supply and demand factors from the May future, the August future might actually sell for less than the May future in April 1975, resulting in a net loss for the spread position. Although spread transactions do tend to reduce the risk involved in commodity trading, they are far from a sure thing.

Intercommodity Spread. An intercommodity spread involves the price relationship between two different but related contracts such as corn and oats, or pork bellies and live hogs. We will consider the corn-oat spread. The rationale for the spread is that a bushel of oats weighs a little more than one-half a bushel of corn, but on a pound-for-pound basis, the feeding value of oats is a little better than that of corn.[48] Since the two grains are substitutes for each other in feeding, a bushel of oats should sell for a little more than one-half the price of a bushel of corn. Oats are harvested in July and August, while corn is harvested in October and November. Harvest selling pressure should produce a relatively low price for oats about August and a relatively low price for corn about November. The spreader could buy oats and sell corn in August and reverse the spread at a later date, perhaps November.[49] Consider the following actual situation that existed on September 20, 1974:

	May Corn	*May Oats*	*Oats (% of corn)*
Sept. 20, 1974 prices	$3.58	$1.68½	47.06%

[48]Ibid., p. 234.

[49]This analysis ignores the fact that corn may have more uses than oats and that the number of uses for corn is increasing. It is even possible that the historical price relationship between these two commodities has changed over time.

If a commodity speculator feels that the price of oats is too low relative to the price of corn, an intercommodity spread is indicated. The speculator could buy two May 1975 oats futures and sell one May 1975 corn future. The spreader will be long 10,000 bushels of oats and short 5,000 bushels of corn. The spreader will buy two oats futures since it is normally desirable in a spread transaction to have the dollar amount long and short approximately equal.

As of October 3, 1974, May corn was selling for $4.06¾ while May oats were selling for $2.04, or 50.15 percent of the price of corn. If the speculator decided to liquidate the spread at this time, the following would be the result:

Sept. 20	Buy 10,000 bu. oats	$(16,850)	Sell 5,000 bu. corn	$17,900
Oct. 3	Sell 10,000 bu. oats	20,400	Buy 5,000 bu. corn	(20,338)
	Gain on oats	3,550	Loss on corn	(2,438)
	Net profit = $1,112 excluding commissions			

Requirements of Successful Speculation

Commodity trading is not for everyone. Should you trade? This question is important and must be answered fairly and honestly. The answer involves a consideration of whether you have genuine risk capital, can manage your capital prudently, and have the temperament for commodity trading. All three are essential elements for successful speculating in commodities.

Genuine Risk Capital. "One must approach commodity trading as a business venture and apply good business techniques and judgment."[50] One important element in this business venture is whether or not you have sufficient capital to withstand a series of initial losses before a profit occurs. This capital should be available exclusively for trading in commodities and not be needed for normal living expenses. Because of the leverage in commodity trading, the speculator should be willing to lose all risk capital committed and still be able to live in a reasonable fashion. Hence, many speculators (especially inexperienced ones) commit only a portion of their risk capital to commodity trading.

Some brokerage firms are quite strict regarding the accounts they will accept, while others are less stringent. Merrill Lynch, for example, will not normally accept a commodity trading account unless the would-be speculator has a personal net worth of $50,000 *excluding* equity in a personal residence. But if a person wants to trade in commodities, a brokerage firm can probably be found to accept the account. Thus, it is up to the individual to assess the risk capital requirement.

[50]Leo Melamed, "A Professional's View of Commodity Trading," in *Before You Speculate* (Chicago: Chicago Mercantile Exchange, August 1973), p. 16.

Temperament. If you do not know who you are, the commodities market is a poor place to find out. These markets are very competitive and a highly disciplined personality is required to trade in them. The trader has to have the ability to take loss after loss and not admit defeat. The trader must also have the ability to take a gain if circumstances warrant. We have seen that the time horizon for commodity trading tends to be much shorter than for stocks and the leverage much larger. Quick, decisive action becomes very important in this environment or total ruin may result. The trader should not be vain or greedy. Indeed, every farmer knows that the greediest hogs get slaughtered first.

Capital Management. It is essential that the commodity trader establish trading objectives so risk capital committed can be prudently managed. Many rules of thumb have been suggested to assist the trader in using proper capital management techniques. The number of commodities traded should be severely limited to about three or four.[51] Stop orders should be placed at the same time that the initial position is established. The trader should add to an existing position only if a profit exists in the original position. An inexperienced trader should never carry more than three open contracts in any one commodity. If a margin call occurs, consider liquidating the position instead of meeting the call. Don't overtrade, since this action will tend to warp your judgment. All these rules of thumb and more that could be mentioned suggest that the potential commodity trader maintain a realistic and cautious attitude when trading. The rewards can be substantial, but for every dollar someone gains, someone else loses a dollar.

PORTFOLIO IMPLICATIONS

Because of the problems involved in calculating precise rates of return, relatively little quantitative work has been done on the portfolio impact of the investments discussed in this chapter. Robichek, Cohn, and Pringle discuss the portfolio implications of investing in selected assets including farm real estate, cotton, wheat, and copper futures, and Japanese and Australian stocks in addition to U.S. stocks and bonds.[52] They attempted to determine the extent to which investments other than U.S. stocks and bonds influence the construction of the efficient frontier.

In examining farm real estate using the U.S. Department of Agriculture index of average value per acre of farm real estate from 1950 to 1970, they found an annual rate of return of approximately 9.5 percent. The

[51]For the beginner, we would suggest only one or two commodities be traded.

[52]Alexander A. Robichek, Richard A. Cohn, and John J. Pringle, "Returns on Alternative Investment Media and Implications for Portfolio Construction," *Journal of Business*, July 1972, pp. 427–43.

variability of this rate of return was quite low.[53] The authors attributed this to increasing farm productivity and to inflation. Farm real estate returns were also negatively correlated with returns from stocks and bonds. We know that a negative correlation is useful in reducing the risk of a portfolio. Not only is farm real estate (and presumably other real estate, too) an investment with a reasonable rate of return, but it possesses portfolio risk-reducing properties.[54]

Returns from the three futures examined were highly variable from year to year. Their mean rate of return and the standard deviation around the mean are shown below along with the statistics for farm real estate:

	Mean Annual Rate of Return*	*Standard Deviation*	*Correlation with S&P 425*
Cotton futures	3.80%	66.77%	.29
Wheat futures	−22.88	64.07	.29
Copper futures	26.60	244.02	.32
Farm real estate	9.47	4.50	−.13

*Period from 1949 to 1969 except for farm real estate, which is from 1951 to 1969.

The correlation coefficient between the three commodities and the Standard & Poor 425 Industrial stock price index is quite low. This raises the possibility that commodity futures contracts have low betas and hence are low risk assets when placed in a portfolio context. In a study of wheat, corn, and soybean futures over the period 1952 to 1967, Katherine Dusak found these contracts to have betas that were zero for practical purposes.[55] Moreover, the returns over this period averaged out at approximately the risk-free rate. In other words, the evidence leads to the conclusion that commodity futures contracts are free of risk and the average returns are about equal to what one would expect from a risk-free asset. As we have seen so often, commodities seem to be another example of an asset that is quite risky when considered by itself, but the risk and return are substantially reduced when the asset is placed in a portfolio.[56]

[53]The coefficient of variation was .84, lower than observed for any other long-term investment medium examined (p. 435).

[54]In his study, "Returns from Real Estate and Common Stocks: A Regional Portfolio Analysis," presented at the Eastern Finance Association Meetings, April 19, 1975, Roger B. Upson found a total return on Minnesota rural real estate for the period from 1947 to 1969 of better than 10 percent annually. Using regions of Minnesota, Upson found that the return from some regions had a low correlation with the return from other regions.

[55]Katherine Dusak, "Futures Trading and Investor Returns: An Investigation of Commodity Market Risk Premiums," *Journal of Political Economy*, November–December 1973, pp. 1387–1406.

[56]Dusak, however, does not consider the role of margin in commodity trading since she uses only price differences.

SUMMARY

We have examined a wide range of investment alternatives available to the investor in addition to common stocks and bonds. These alternatives included real estate, precious metals, coins with numismatic value, stamps with philatelic value, art masterpieces, antiques, and commodity futures. Although not all these alternatives are equally suitable for every investor, they should not be ignored in a consideration of investment alternatives.

Good reasons may exist why the investor would choose not to invest in any of the alternatives discussed in this chapter. These reasons fall into two main categories, those inherent in the markets for these investments and personal considerations unique to each investor. The markets for these investments may require an investment time horizon that is unacceptable to the investor. This is clearly a consideration in such areas as real estate, art, and antiques. The liquidity of the markets in which these assets trade and the transaction costs involved are relevant to the time horizon problem. The risk level implied by investing in certain assets may be unacceptable to the investor. For example, an investor may have this attitude toward any form of commodity trading and exclude that alternative from consideration.

On a personal level, expert knowledge is required to be a successful investor in many of the areas discussed in this chapter. If the investor does not possess this expert knowledge or is unwilling to employ the services of experts, the proper decision is to avoid that form of investment. Since psychic income is an important element in areas such as art and antiques, those not appreciative of these investments should stay out. If you can't tell the difference between a Rembrandt and a Utrillo, investing in art is probably not for you. We saw that the decision to purchase a personal residence or to rent living quarters is very much a personal decision in addition to having strong investment elements.

While the majority of the investments discussed in this chapter involve the investor taking possession of a physical object such as a gold bar, an antique, a painting, or a stamp, there are some alternatives available that might accomplish the same investment objectives without the problems associated with physical ownership of an object. The whole concept of futures trading is based upon the ability of the trader to trade in a commodity without having to take physical possession of the commodity unless he or she wants to. Thus, indirect investments in gold, silver, copper, silver coins, and platinum are possible in addition to the numerous agricultural commodities important in the futures market. The futures market may be the best way to speculate in the price changes of such commodities as gold and silver.

Securities may exist that allow the investor to purchase a financial asset with a good secondary market and still come close to achieving the benefits of direct ownership of such investment as real estate and gold. Real estate investment trusts allow the investor to obtain a share of a portfolio of diversified real estate investments. REITs differ widely in risk and investment objective, so the investor must examine each REIT. REITs have faced a number of problems including unfavorable interest spreads, a poor construction market, loss of financing sources, and an increase in nonearning portfolio assets. Hence, the future for REITs is clouded with uncertainty.

Gold may be purchased indirectly by purchasing the shares of gold mining firms. We noted that the movements of the price of gold and the price of shares of gold mining companies have been roughly comparable. As a result, the investor gets many of the potential benefits of gold ownership plus the additional benefit of owning a security with a good secondary market. The shares may have a current income not achieved by physical possession of gold in bullion, coin, or futures form. Transaction costs may also be less with gold mining shares, and the possibility of a fraudulent transaction is less.

Commodity trading attracts investors because of the possibility of turning a small sum of money into an important sum of money. Commodities may be purchased with relatively low margins compared to stocks; hence, the leverage in trading commodities is substantial, and the resulting risk is clearly not acceptable to all investors. Commodity trading differs from stock investing in a number of other important ways. The main differences are that a commodity trading position is limited to the life of the future, which is between one and two years, depending on the commodity. Moreover, daily price limits exist in the commodity markets. It is as easy to sell a future short as to purchase a future and no special rules apply to the short position. Finally, commodity trading is a zero-sum game less commissions; any gain on a futures contract means a corresponding loss for the other trader(s).

QUESTIONS

1. What problems does the investor face in calculating rates of return on investments in such items as art masterpieces and antiques?
2. What are the basic considerations in real estate investments?
3. Why is it important for the investor to distinguish among the various types of REITs available for investment?
4. As a shareholder in a REIT that proposes to give up its regulated investment company status and become a regular operating company, what would be your considerations in deciding how to vote on the proposal?
5. In what ways may an investor speculate on the price movements of gold? What are the disadvantages of each method?
6. In a business recession, why might one expect the price of art masterpieces to decline by a smaller percentage than the price of common stocks?
7. What economic role does the commodity futures market play in the U.S. economy?
8. Compare the concept of margin as it applies to common stocks and to commodities. Are there any important differences as far as the investor is concerned?

9. What is the relationship between margins in commodity futures transactions and the existence of daily price limits?
10. a) What is a spread transaction in commodity trading?
    b) What is the rationale one would use in establishing an intercommodity spread?
11. a) What personal characteristics are necessary for an individual to be a successful commodity trader?
    b) Are there any reasons why a successful investor in common stocks might not be successful as a commodity trader?

PROBLEMS

1. Herman Pickett sold a December 1975 gold future in mid-January 1975 at $194, making the contract worth $19,400. Herman's broker required a $2,000 margin deposit. By July, this contract was selling for $172.
   a) What is his dollar profit on the contract should he sell in July?
   b) He has held the contract six months. What would be his annualized rate of return should he sell?
   c) If he had originally purchased this contract rather than sold, what would have happened?
2. Bob Bear faced the following soybean futures prices in January 1975:

March	594
May	604
July	610
August	611
Sept.	603

   Carrying charges for a bushel of soybeans are 3.5 cents per month including interest.
   a) If Bob expected the price difference to widen between the May and August soybeans, what spread would be established?
   b) What is a reasonable expectation for the maximum profit that may be made in this spread?
   c) What would be Bob's gain (loss) if the spread were closed out when May soybeans were 601 and August soybeans were 605?
3. Looking at the same prices given in question 2, Jackie Downing expects the price difference to narrow between the March and August soybeans.
   a) What action will she take?
   b) The spread is eventually closed out when March soybeans are 597 and August soybeans are 607. How did Jackie come out on this spread?
4. The prices of the futures shown in question 2 reveal that the September soybean contract is priced 8 cents below that of the August contract. It would seem that a spread should be established in the expectation that the September contract would rise relative to the August contract. Can you detect any potential problems with the spreading opportunity?

5. Sidney Phelps is considering the establishment of a spread between gold and silver. As of July 1975, the December 1975 gold future sells for $172 (100 ounce contract) while December silver sells for $4.80 (10,000 ounce contract). Sidney is thinking of selling one silver contract and buying three gold contracts.
   a) What does Sidney expect to happen to the prices of the two metals?
   b) Why might Sidney expect the metal prices to move in this manner?
   c) Do you feel that this is a bona fide spread?

SUGGESTED READINGS

Bailey, E. Norman. "The Future of REITs." *REIT Review*, Spring 1975, pp. 33–8.

Bear, Robert M. "Margin Levels and the Behavior of Futures Prices." *Journal of Financial and Quantitative Analysis*, September 1972, pp. 1907–30.

Bleck, Erich K. "Real Estate Investments and Rates of Return." *Appraisal Journal*, October 1973, pp. 535–47.

Brewer, Robert E. "REITs in Transition." *Appraisal Journal*, July 1974, pp. 429–40.

Commodity Trading Manual. Chicago: Chicago Board of Trade, 1973.

Cooper, James R. and Stephen A. Pyhrr. "Forecasting the Rates of Return on an Apartment Investment: A Case Study." *Appraisal Journal*, July 1973, pp. 312–37.

Dusak, Katherine. "Futures Trading and Investor Returns: An Investigation of Commodity Market Risk Premiums." *Journal of Political Economy*, November–December 1973, pp. 1387–406.

Gold, Gerald. *Modern Commodity Futures Trading*. 6th ed. New York: Commodity Research Bureau, 1971.

Harlow, Charles V. and Richard J. Teweles. "Commodities and Securities Compared." *Financial Analysts Journal*, September–October 1972, pp. 64–70.

Hieronymus, Thomas A. *Economics of Futures Trading*. New York: Commodity Research Bureau, Inc., 1971.

Hines, Mary Alice. "What Has Happened to the REITs?" *Appraisal Journal*, April 1975, pp. 252–60.

Hoppe, Donald J. *How to Invest in Gold Coins & Avoid the Pitfalls*. New Rochelle, N.Y.: Arlington House, 1972.

"Investing in Art and Antiques." *Business Week*, October 27, 1973, pp. 105–10.

Lewis, James E. "An Examination of Real Estate Investment Trusts." *Appraisal Journal*, July 1973, pp. 350–60.

Mark, Morris et. al. "Pitfalls in Real Estate Accounting." *Financial Analysts Journal*, January–February 1972, pp. 29–36.

McQuade, Walter. "Invest in the Art Market? Soybeans Might Be Safer." *Fortune*, May 1974, pp. 201–6.

Powers, Mark J. *Getting Started in Commodity Futures Trading*. Columbia, Md.: Investor Publications, Inc., 1973.

Real Estate Investment Trusts, an Industry Profile. Washington, D.C.: National Association of Real Estate Investment Trusts, 1973.

Ricks, R. Bruce. "Imputed Equity Returns on Real Estate Financed with Life Insurance Company Loans." *Journal of Finance,* December 1969, pp. 921–37.

Robertson, Wyndham. "Gold Bugs Are on the March." *Fortune,* June 1974, pp. 150–53ff.

Robichek, Alexander A., Richard A. Cohn, and John J. Pringle. "Returns on Alternative Investment Media and Implications for Portfolio Construction." *Journal of Business,* July 1972, pp. 427–43.

Roulac, Stephen E. "Economics of the Housing Investment Decision." *Appraisal Journal,* July 1974, pp. 358–71.

Rush, Richard H. *Antiques as an Investment.* New York: Bonanza Books, 1968.

——. *Art as an Investment.* Englewood Cliffs, N.J.: Prentice-Hall, Inc., 1961.

——. "The New Investment Boom." *Wall Street Transcript,* April 15, 1974, pp. 36577ff.

Schulkin, Peter A. "Real Estate Investment Trusts." *Financial Analysts Journal,* May–June 1971, pp. 33–40ff.

Smyth, David and Laurence Stuntz. *The Speculator's Handbook.* Chicago: Henry Regnery Co., 1974.

Stevenson, Richard A. and Robert M. Bear. "Commodity Futures: Trends or Random Walks." *Journal of Finance,* March 1970, pp. 65–82.

Teweles, Richard J., Charles V. Harlow, and Herbert L. Stone. *The Commodity Futures Game: Who Wins? Who Loses? Why?* New York: McGraw-Hill, 1974.

Wendt, Paul F. and Sui N. Wong. "Investment Performance: Common Stocks vs. Apartment Houses." *Journal of Finance,* December 1965, pp. 633–46.

Winjum, James O. and Joanne T. Winjum. "The Art Investment Market." *University of Michigan Business Review,* November 1974, pp. 1–5.

*

23

Foreign Investing

Investor interest in a global approach to investments has increased in recent years. This attention to foreign investing arises from several causes. The economy of a foreign country may be growing more rapidly than that of the United States. Moreover, foreign countries may have advantages in certain natural resources or in unit labor costs. Whatever the reasons, investors appear to be more concerned of late with the international aspects of a portfolio.

The first section of this chapter examines the manner in which foreign investments may be made. In the indirect approach, the investor purchases shares of U.S.-based multinational firms to achieve adequate international diversification. The various ways a direct foreign investment may be made are also discussed. After presenting this descriptive material, we discuss the risk and return considerations of foreign investing to see the portfolio benefits achieved by international diversification. Special problems that may confront the investor in achieving this diversification are also noted.

INDIRECT FOREIGN INVESTMENT

Wealthy investors might be able to invest directly in real assets such as land and buildings located in foreign countries. For many investors, though, an indirect approach is more practical. A domestic corporation is normally used as the means through which the investor achieves the benefits of foreign investments in real assets. In this way the investor need not purchase either real assets located in a foreign country, or securities issued by foreign firms, or any portfolio consisting mainly of foreign securities. This indirect approach requires the purchase of the securities of U.S.-based multinational firms.

The purchase of these multinational stocks reduces the need for the investor to obtain expertise regarding the investment environment in foreign countries. In the years since World War II, American firms have made substantial foreign capital expenditures. This is especially true in certain industries such as petroleum, retailing, and drugs. The investor must identify those firms having a significant international business, and then examine the nature of the foreign sales of the firm to determine the risks involved. Is the capital investment in danger of being nationalized? Will adequate compensation be made if nationalization does occur? Is the foreign country experiencing unique problems with its economy? While questions of this type should be considered, one can also reduce the business risk by deliberately diversifying across U.S.-based multinational firms. Combining firms having few foreign sales with those firms having strong international business might also be desirable.

How is the investor to identify those firms having large foreign sales and profits? Some of the reference sources mentioned in Chapter 4 carry feature articles relating to foreign investments. For example, *The Outlook*, published by Standard & Poor's Corporation, carried a table of U.S.-based firms having a large percentage of their 1973 sales from foreign sources.[1] Caterpillar Tractor had 50 percent of its 1973 sales from foreign sources, Eastman Kodak had 39 percent, and Pfizer had 52 percent. Of course, just because a firm has foreign sales does not necessarily mean that these sales are profitable. Deere and Co., for example, had many years of unprofitable foreign business before finally achieving a profit on this business in fiscal 1972.[2] In addition, the profitability of foreign business may change dramatically within a relatively short period of time; such a change happened to Occidental Petroleum in Libya in the early 1970s.[3]

[1]"Overseas Investment by U.S. Companies Accelerating," *The Outlook*, September 6, 1974, pp. 564–68.

[2]Deere and Co., *Annual Report*, 1972.

[3]Occidental's earnings as stated in its *Annual Report* for 1973, went from $2.92 per share in 1970 to a deficit of $1.61 per share in 1971.

Despite potential risks related to the unique problems of foreign investment, the indirect method of using U.S.-based multinational firms has several advantages for the investor. Most of these firms are listed on a major American stock exchange. This carries the benefits of marketability and liquidity. In addition, the foreign investments are handled by the management of the U.S.-based firm. One should be able to achieve reasonable international diversification if one gives some attention to the geographic and product mix of U.S.-based firms.

DIRECT FOREIGN INVESTMENT

Direct foreign investment has two basic forms: The investor can purchase real assets located in foreign countries or he or she can purchase, either individually or in a portfolio, financial securities issued by foreign firms. Our discussion considers only the direct purchase of financial securities of firms located in another country. There are three basic methods for purchasing these securities. First, the investor may purchase American Depositary Receipts (ADRs) or American shares.[4] Second, the investor may purchase an investment company specializing in foreign securities. Third, the investor can purchase shares listed on a foreign stock exchange.

American Depositary Receipts

Many of the larger foreign companies have their shares traded either on a major U.S. securities exchange or in the U.S. over-the-counter market. British Petroleum and Sony Corporation trade on the New York Stock Exchange, for example, while Honda Motors trades over the counter. An investor purchasing these shares will normally purchase an American Depositary Receipt (ADR). Guaranty Trust Company, the predecessor to the Morgan Guaranty Trust Company, first issued ADRs in 1927.[5] ADRs look much like a standard stock certificate, but actually represent shares of the foreign company being held by the bank issuing the ADRs.[6] In essence, the foreign shares have been Americanized by the use of the ADR. ADRs will be issued by a bank when it perceives

[4]American shares are issued in the United States by a transfer agent acting on behalf of the foreign company.

[5]"Importing the Action in Foreign Securities," *Business Week*, February 8, 1969, p. 90.

[6]A distinction is sometimes made between sponsored and unsponsored ADRs. Sponsored ADRs exist for foreign firms that are fully registered with the Securities and Exchange Commission and are often traded on either the New York or American Stock Exchange. Unsponsored ADRs trade over-the-counter and are not fully registered with the SEC. See "So You Want to Buy a Foreign Stock," *Forbes*, October 15, 1972, p. 86ff.

that there is sufficient investor interest in the stock to warrant the effort. One source recently estimated that 375 foreign companies have securities that trade in the U.S.[7]

The use of ADRs gives foreign shares good marketability, especially if they are actively traded on a major U.S. securities exchange. However, the list of firms with ADRs outstanding is relatively small and consists primarily of large foreign firms. The investor still must perform an analysis of the investment merits of the firm whose ADRs are being considered. Investments in foreign companies involve some expertise even if one purchases an ADR.[8] There may be accounting variations from country to country, especially in the area of accounting reserves. The role of the foreign government in its economy may be quite different from the role of the U.S. government in the U.S. economy. Many commonly accepted financial ratios may have little use when applied to a foreign company. The capital structure of a foreign company may be quite different from that of a U.S. firm in the same industry. Inflation may be a more important consideration in foreign investing, especially for a foreign firm with heavy export sales.

Investment Company Approach

Several open-end and closed-end investment companies exist that invest primarily in foreign securities.[9] Exhibit 23-1 lists four mutual funds and four closed-end investment companies one might want to consider for direct foreign investing. All four closed-end investment companies are listed on the New York Stock Exchange. Of the four mutual funds, Scudder International Investments is the only no-load fund.

The purchaser of shares in an investment company shown in Exhibit 23-1 obtains the general benefits associated with investment companies. Special consideration needs to be given, however, to the portfolio composition of an investment company with a portfolio of foreign securities, since the portfolio may not be well diversified from the standpoint of geography or industry participation. For example, ASA Limited invests almost exclusively in South African gold mining securities, while

[7]Neil A. Martin, "Sophisticates Abroad, Savvy Investors Are Eyeing Foreign Securities," *Barron's*, April 1, 1974, p. 11.

[8]For a comprehensive discussion of the considerations involved in buying Japanese securities see Edgar M. Barrett, Lee N. Price, and Judith Ann Gehrke, "Japan, Some Background for Security Analysts," *Financial Analysts Journal*, January-February 1974 (Part one), pp. 33-44, and March-April 1974 (Part two), pp. 60-67.

[9]This discussion does not consider the offshore funds that do not register with the SEC. It is illegal for U.S. citizens to invest in offshore funds.

EXHIBIT 23-1
Investment Companies for Foreign Investing

	Net Asset Value March 31, 1975 $ millions	Percentage Change in Net Asset Value 1974	1970–1974	1965–1974
Mutual Funds:				
Canadian Fund	$ 28.1	−21.4	12.2	47.9
International Investors	132.0	10.9	240.2	301.2
Scudder International Investments	18.3	−23.1	− 9.3	24.7
Templeton Growth	17.5	−11.8	51.5	215.4
Closed-End Investment Co.				
ASA Limited*	329.9	36.7	367.4	505.5
International Holdings	67.9	−34.3	−24.3	16.9
Japan Fund	102.9	− 5.1	29.4	580.9
U.S. & Foreign Securities	95.8	−28.9	−12.9	3.0
Standard & Poor 500 Stock Index		−26.0	− 7.8	17.5

*Formerly American-South African Investment Company, Ltd.

Source: *Supplement to Investment Companies, 1974* and *Supplement to Investment Companies, 1975* (New York: Wiesenberger Services, Inc., 1975).

Japan Fund invests in Japanese securities. These specialized investment companies may not provide the degree of risk-reducing diversification provided by the typical investment company. In this context, it might be appropriate to view these specialized investment companies as essentially a one-security input to the investor's portfolio.

Exhibit 23-1 also demonstrates the need to analyze the investment company being considered. Both International Investors and ASA Limited are heavily invested in gold mining securities. This portfolio composition accounts for their positive rate of return during 1974. Even eliminating these two investment companies, the performance of the investment companies in Exhibit 23-1 varies considerably. The ten-year performance of the Japan Fund was the best of any investment company listed in Exhibit 23-1. While its performance in recent years has been better than the S&P 500 Stock Index, the potential investor in this investment company needs to consider carefully the growth prospects of the Japanese economy. Japan's real economic growth declined 2 percent in 1974 compared to annual increases of approximately 10 percent for the 1960s and early 1970s.[10] Economic growth in the future may be considerably slower than in the past.

[10] "Japan's Economy in Transition," *Business Week*, July 7, 1975, pp. 44–50.

Foreign Listed Securities

While an investor can purchase securities listed on a foreign stock exchange, it may not be prudent because of a number of potential problems. For example, there may be limits on the amount that may be invested in a foreign security. The most important problems, however, arise from the transaction's being conducted in a foreign currency. This involves the acquisition or sale of a foreign currency and the need to take physical delivery of the securities. These transactions require specialized knowledge, and even those investors with such specialized knowledge are exposed to risks resulting from fluctuations in relative currency values. A hedging transaction in the foreign currency can reduce foreign exchange fluctuation risks, but again this requires specialized skills and may be expensive. Finally, tax problems may result. Taxes in the foreign country may be collected in addition to the capital gains tax in the U.S. For all these reasons, either the ADR or the investment company approach is more suitable for the average investor than the purchase of a security listed on a foreign stock exchange.

RISKS AND RETURNS FROM FOREIGN INVESTING

Portfolio Approach

The risk of any security should ideally be evaluated in the context of a portfolio. The question facing the potential investor in foreign securities is whether the purchase of these securities reduces the risk of the portfolio compared to a portfolio that is not diversified internationally. If the return from the portfolio remains unchanged or increases, while the risk decreases, the purchase of foreign securities is a sound portfolio strategy.

From our previous discussion of the portfolio approach, we learned that an important consideration is how the returns from different investments vary with each other. Hence, in considering the addition of foreign securities to a portfolio of domestic securities, we are interested in the covariance of the foreign security returns with those from the domestic securities. We might intuitively expect that the covariance of returns between foreign and domestic securities would be low. Different countries face different natural resource constraints and varying growth possibilities. The market for particular products may be mature in the United States, but still in the growth stage in a foreign country. Foreign exchange fluctuations may be harmful to one country, yet beneficial to a second foreign country. An increase in the price of petroleum may cause economic difficulties for highly industrialized countries, yet create marketing opportunities in oil-producing countries. The list of situations where the risk may be reduced by international diversification is large.

Problems in Foreign Investing

A number of risks are involved in foreign investing that arise from the pursuit of nationalistic interests by foreign countries. The foreign assets of a U.S.-based multinational company may be expropriated without adequate compensation. In addition, an investor may overestimate the potential market growth of a given foreign market. Foreign exchange fluctuations and controls may prevent the realization of expected returns from an investment. Political risks are important: Tariffs may be raised or lowered to accommodate national interests, and high rates of inflation may be tolerated to accommodate the growth of a country's economy. Finally, the securities markets in many countries are not as well developed as those in the United States, leading to problems in marketability and liquidity for the investor. For example, an estimated $721 billion in market value of NYSE-listed securities as of December 31, 1973, compares to only $439.4 billion for securities listed on the principal foreign stock exchanges.[11]

Empirical Evidence

A number of articles in recent years have been concerned with the benefits achieved from international diversification. The general conclusion from all these studies is that the benefits from international diversification are important. Bruno Solnik writes:

> The gains from international diversification are substantial. In terms of variability of return an internationally well-diversified portfolio would be one-tenth as risky as a typical security and half as risky as a well-diversified portfolio of U.S. stocks (with the same number of holdings).[12]

Figure 23–1 shows the risk reduction achieved by Solnik by combining stocks from eight different countries compared to a portfolio consisting only of U.S. stocks. The internationally diversified portfolio is constructed by assuming an equal chance of holding a security from the eight different countries. The systematic risk from the internationally diversified portfolio is 11.7 percent compared to 27.0 percent for the portfolio consisting of U.S. stocks. While the investor still needs to give consideration to the rate of return that may be achieved, the risk reduction possibilities are evident.

[11] Ruben Shohet, "Investing in Foreign Securities," *Financial Analysts Journal*, September–October 1974, pp. 64–65.

[12] Bruno H. Solnik, "Why Not Diversify Internationally Rather Than Domestically?" *Financial Analysts Journal*, July–August 1974, p. 51.

FIGURE 23-1
Risk Reduction from International Diversification

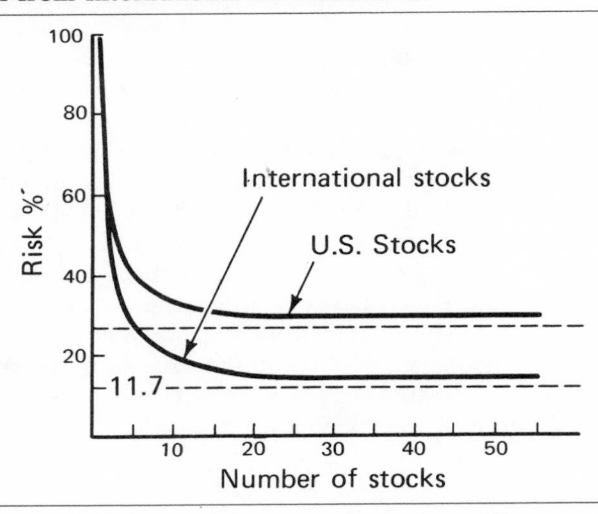

Source: Bruno H. Solnik, "Why Not Diversify Internationally Rather Than Domestically?" *Financial Analysts Journal*, July-August, 1974, p. 51.

SUMMARY

As the world becomes more and more economically interdependent, foreign investments become a more viable investment alternative. Developments favorable to one country or a group of countries may be detrimental to other countries. This provides risk-reducing possibilities from a strategy of international diversification. In addition, since the growth of countries has varied in the past and future variations in growth rates by country are likely, potentially profitable investment opportunities are created.

There are several ways of making foreign investments. By deliberately seeking those U.S. firms having strong positions in foreign countries, the investor should be able to obtain many of the risk-reducing benefits of international diversification. The investor may also purchase shares of foreign firms that are traded in the United States. Most of these shares come in the form of American Depositary Receipts (ADRs). ADRs are issued by banks and are backed by foreign shares held in the bank's custody. The investor is essentially buying an Americanized foreign security. The investor may also purchase shares of an investment company whose objective is to invest in foreign securities. One should analyze the past performance of these investment companies in the same manner as one would analyze any investment company. Direct purchase of shares on a foreign stock exchange is a difficult venture for the typical investor lacking specialized knowledge and is generally not recommended.

Although a number of risks exist for the investor in foreign securities, especially the risk of expropriation without adequate compensation, numerous studies have observed that foreign securities can potentially reduce the risk of a portfolio of domestic securities. The systematic risk of the portfolio is reduced considerably as a result of international diversification. One or two investment companies specializing in foreign investments would appear to be a worthwhile holding for the average investor seeking to achieve risk reduction in a portfolio.

QUESTIONS

1. Special knowledge is often needed in foreign investing to judge the risks involved. What are the risks that require this expertise?
2. Despite the risks involved in foreign investments, securities of foreign firms may be a desirable holding for the investor. Why?
3. Foreign investments may be made indirectly using U.S.-based multinational firms. What are the advantages of this approach?
4. What is an ADR? What are the advantages of purchasing ADRs rather than shares listed on a foreign securities exchange?
5. Investment companies may be a convenient method of achieving international diversification.
   a) What are the advantages of using the investment company concept for foreign investments?
   b) What special factors does the investor need to consider?
6. Exhibit 23–1 gives the percentage change in net asset value for four closed-end investment companies having foreign securities in their portfolios. For these investment companies, what other important factor(s) does the investor need to consider before making an investment decision?
7. Why has the growth of the Japanese economy slowed since 1973? What principal factors do you feel would be useful in making a projection of future growth rates?
8. An internationally diversified portfolio would be especially desirable compared to a domestic portfolio if lower risk could be achieved at the same time that higher rates of return are realized. Do you think the investor is likely to achieve these desirable results? Why?
9. How will fluctuations in foreign exchange rates influence the foreign investments of an individual?
10. Solnik suggests the development of a multinational mutual fund where investments are proportional to the source of the investment capital. For example, if German residents bought 15 percent of the fund's shares,

the portfolio would contain 15 percent German securities. (*Financial Analysts Journal,* July–August 1974, p. 52).
a) What do you see as advantages of this arrangement?
b) Do you foresee any difficulties with the arrangement?

SUGGESTED READINGS

Agmon, Tamir. "The Relations Among Equity Markets: A Study of Share Price Co-Movements in the United States, United Kingdom and Japan." *Journal of Finance,* September 1972, pp. 839–56.

Altman, Edward I., Bertrand Jacquillat, and Michael Levasseur. "Comparative Analysis of Risk Measures: France and the United States." *Journal of Finance,* December 1974, pp. 1495–512.

Barrett, M. Edgar, Lee N. Price, and Judith Ann Gehrke. "Japan, Some Background for Security Analysts." *Financial Analysts Journal,* January–February 1974, pp. 33–44 (Part One), and March–April 1974, pp. 60–67 (Part Two).

Cohn, Richard A. and John J. Pringle. "Imperfections in International Financial Markets: Implications for Risk Premia and the Cost of Capital to Firms." *Journal of Finance,* March 1973, pp. 59–66.

Esslen, Rainer. *How to Buy Foreign Securities.* Arlington, Va.: Columbia Publishing Co., 1974.

Gaskins, J. Peter. "Taxation of Foreign Source Income." *Financial Analysts Journal,* September–October 1973, pp. 55–64.

Grubel, Herbert G. "Internationally Diversified Portfolios: Welfare Gains and Capital Flows." *American Economic Review,* December 1968, pp. 1299–314.

—— and Kenneth Fadner. "The Interdependence of International Equity Markets." *Journal of Finance,* March 1971, pp. 89–94.

Lees, Francis A. and Maximo Eng. *International Financial Markets.* New York: Praeger Publishers, 1975.

Lessard, Donald R. "World, National, and Industry Factors in Equity Returns." *Journal of Finance,* May 1974, pp. 379–91.

Levy, Haim and Marshall Sarnat. "International Diversification of Investment Portfolios." *American Economic Review,* September 1970, pp. 668–75.

Martin, Neil A. "Sophisticates Abroad, Savvy Investors Are Eyeing Foreign Securities," *Barron's,* April 1, 1974, p. 11ff.

McDonald, John G. "French Mutual Fund Performance: Evaluation of Internationally-Diversified Portfolios." *Journal of Finance,* December 1973, pp. 1181–86.

Oltramare, Yves. "How Currency Changes Can Affect International Investments." *Institutional Investor,* June 1974, pp. 69–72.

Shohet, Ruben. "A New Investment Environment for the U.S." *Financial Analysts Journal,* September–October 1973, pp. 26–32.

——. "Investing in Foreign Securities." *Financial Analysts Journal,* September–October 1974, pp. 55–72.

Solnik, Bruno H. "Why Not Diversify Internationally Rather Than Domestically?" *Financial Analysts Journal,* July–August 1974, pp. 48–54.

24

Leverage-Inherent Securities

Certain securities exist which can be called leverage-inherent. While these securities differ somewhat in the various forms in which they exist and the markets in which they trade, they have the common characteristic of leverage associated with them. This chapter discusses the concept of leverage and analyzes the various leverage-inherent securities. Warrants, call options, rights, and dual funds are securities classified as leverage-inherent.

NATURE OF LEVERAGE

In an elementary physics class, a student may learn that a large rock can be moved by inserting the end of a lever under the rock and using a fulcrum to multiply the student's power. The student can move the rock because of the fixed point, the fulcrum, and its ability to increase the force exerted by the student.

In finance, the important concept of leverage is quite similar to the physics example. A small change in one variable, such as the revenue of a firm, produces a larger change in a second variable, such as the firm's profits. Any leverage situation has a fixed element present corresponding to the fulcrum in the physics illustration. In the case of *operating leverage,* the fixed operating costs of the firm become important in relation to the total costs of the firm. An airline typically has a cost structure in which fixed costs are a substantial proportion of total costs. This occurs because of the heavy investment in fixed assets such as airplanes and support facilities. Since the revenues of the airline tend to change by a greater percentage than fixed costs, the profits of the airline are quite sensitive to small changes in revenue. In this instance, we would state that the airline has a high degree of operating leverage.

Another leverage concept is that of financial leverage. *Financial leverage* occurs when the firm incurs fixed financial expenses in a form such as interest. Firms with large amounts of debt in their capital structure typically must make large interest payments. These interest payments are a fixed financial expense and operate (as the fulcrum as in the physics example) to magnify small changes in the earnings before interest and taxes into larger changes in the earnings after taxes. Firms such as some of the major airlines in the United States have both a high degree of financial leverage and a high degree of operating leverage and are likely to have earnings after taxes that are quite volatile over the business cycle.

In summary, leverage results from the existence of a fixed element in the company, the security, or the portfolio being examined. Since our concern in this chapter is with the investment aspect of leverage, we focus on the possibility of leverage in a portfolio or in an individual security. To do this, we must distinguish between external leverage and inherent ("built-in") leverage. This, of course, does not imply that the investor should ignore the operating and financial leverage existing in any given company, since these are clearly important elements in the risk assessment of any given security.

EXTERNAL VERSUS INHERENT LEVERAGE

It is possible for an investor to add leverage to a security or a portfolio simply by buying the security or portfolio on margin. If this is done, the investor has added leverage of the external variety. The capital asset pricing model discussed in Chapter 13 referred to borrowing as a way of increasing the risk of the market portfolio if the investor is not satisfied with the risk level implied by the market. The investor would buy using a margin account in an attempt to increase the rate of return of the portfolio.

An alternative to buying securities in a margin account is to purchase a security that, because of its terms, already has "built-in" leverage. Warrants, call options, rights, and dual funds are leverage-inherent securities. Since the existence of leverage requires that a fixed element be present, we expect to find a fixed element associated with the terms of the security. The fixed element occurs in the form of either a fixed exercise price for the security or a fixed redemption value. We should add that leverage-inherent securities have been receiving increasing attention from the investment community.

WARRANTS

The number of warrants available for purchase by investors has increased dramatically since the early 1960s. As of early December 1974, there were twelve warrants listed on the NYSE, and over sixty warrants listed on the ASE, in addition to warrants listed on regional exchanges and those traded over the counter. A warrant is a security giving the holder the option, exercisable at the pleasure of the holder, of purchasing from a company a given number of shares of a specific security at a stated or determinable price for a specified period of time. The Greyhound Corporation has a warrant outstanding that allows the holder to purchase one share of common stock for $23.50 per share until May 14, 1980. As of early December 1974, the warrant sold for $1.50 and the common stock for $10.

Warrants are a leverage-inherent security since the stock can be purchased at a fixed exercise price. For the Greyhound warrant, the fixed exercise price is $23.50 per share. As a result of this fixed exercise price, a warrant is generally more speculative than the related common stock. The percentage increase or decrease in the market price of the warrant will tend to be greater than the percentage increase or decrease in the market price of the common stock.

Figure 24–1 shows the price movements of both the Greyhound common stock and the warrant, from May 1971 to November 1974. A ratio scale is used for Figure 24–1 so that the percentage price changes may be read directly from the graph. One can note the wider price movements for the warrant. For example, Greyhound common stock declined from 19⅛ at the end of May 1971 to 10¾ at the end of November 1974, a decline of 43.8 percent. During the same period, the warrant fell from 7⅛ to 1¾, a decline of 75.4 percent. However, should the price of the common stock subsequently increase to 19⅛, the warrant probably would not sell for 7⅛, as it did in May 1971. A price of less than 7⅛ is to be expected since the time left before the warrant expires has decreased.

FIGURE 24-1
Prices of Greyhound Common Stock and Warrants—May 1971 to November 1974

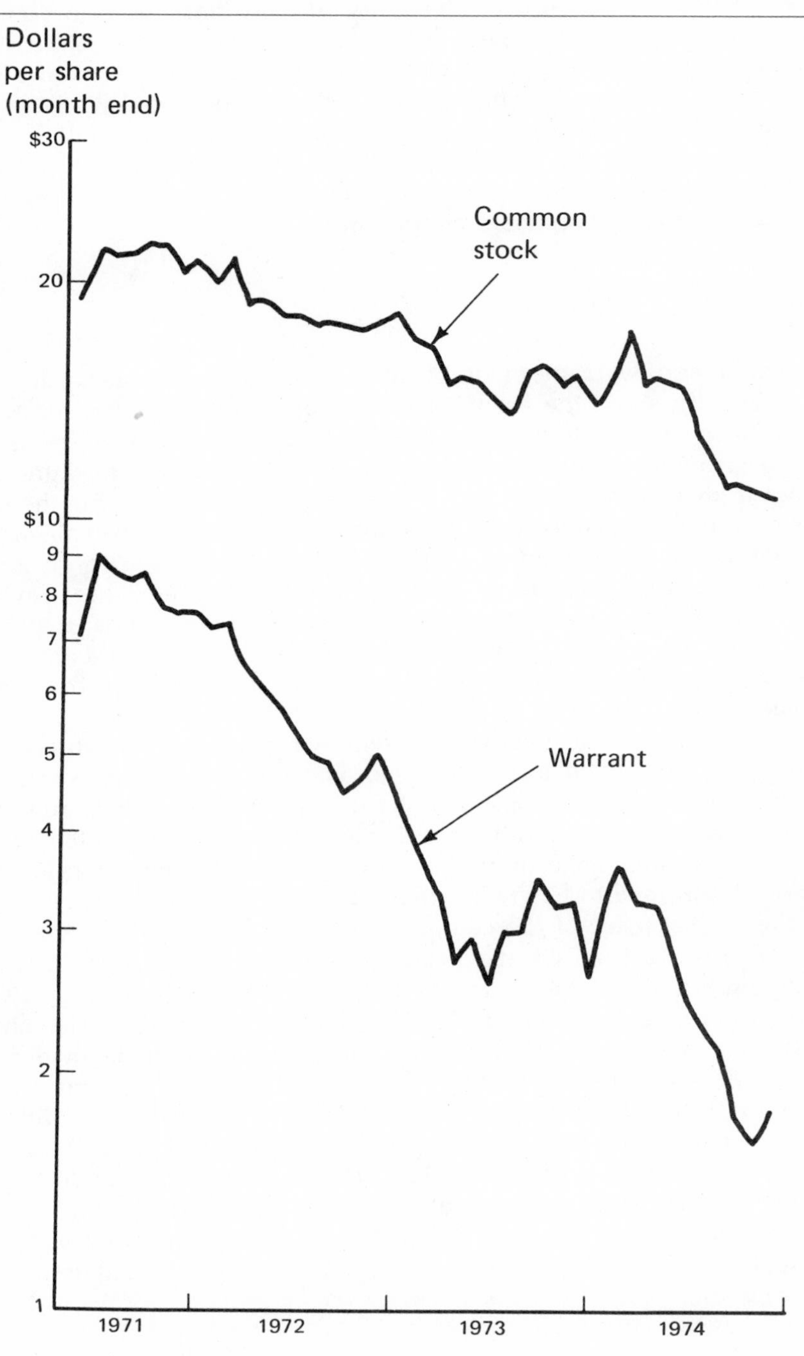

Warrant Valuation

The price of a warrant is the sum of two factors, the price difference and the speculative premium. The price difference, often called the warrant's theoretical value, is obtained by subtracting the warrant exercise price from the market price of the common stock. The price difference is zero unless the common stock is selling above the warrant exercise price. The Greyhound warrant has a price difference of zero with the common stock selling at $10 and the warrant exercise price at $23.50. Hence, the entire $1.50 market value for the Greyhound warrant represents the speculative premium investors are willing to pay for the opportunity of purchasing Greyhound common stock at $23.50 during the remaining life of the warrant.

The amount of the speculative premium depends upon such variables as the time remaining before the warrant expires, the relationship between the common stock price and the warrant exercise price, the dividend yield on the common stock, whether or not the warrant is listed, and investor expectations regarding the future price movements of the common stock. Exhibit 24–1, which shows selected data as of early December 1974 for warrants listed on the NYSE, reveals a wide diversity in both the warrant terms and in the type of company with warrants outstanding.

The time remaining before expiration and the relationship between the common stock price and the warrant exercise price are certainly two significant variables. In the Shelton valuation method to be discussed

EXHIBIT 24–1

NYSE Listed Warrants, Selected Data

	Shares per Warrant	Total Exercise Price	Expiration Date	Price 12/11/74	
				Warrant	Stock
AT&T	1	$52.00	5/15/75	5/8	43 5/8
Avco	1	56.00SS‡	11/30/78	5/16	2 3/8
Chrysler	1	34.00	5/15/76	1 1/4	8 1/8
City Investing	1.02	28.25	7/15/78	1/2	2 3/4*
Commonwealth Edison	1	30.00†	4/30/81	7 5/8	23 1/4
Greyhound	1	23.50	5/14/80	1 1/2	10
Gulf & Western Ind.	1.027	55.00	1/31/78	3 5/8	22 1/8
North Central Airlines	1	5.50	10/31/79	15/16	2 1/2
Northwest Industries	1	25.00SS	3/31/79	8 7/8	18 3/8
Tenneco A	1	24.25	11/01/75	1 1/2	22 1/2
United Telecommunications	1	17.50	10/14/75	1/2	12 3/8
Williams Companies	1	20.00	1/01/76	48 5/8	69 1/4

*Warrant gives holder right to obtain General Development stock.
†Warrant also convertible into one-third share of common, at any time.
‡.SS means that a senior security provision exists; see text.

FIGURE 24–2
Impact of Shelton's Warrant Longevity Adjustment

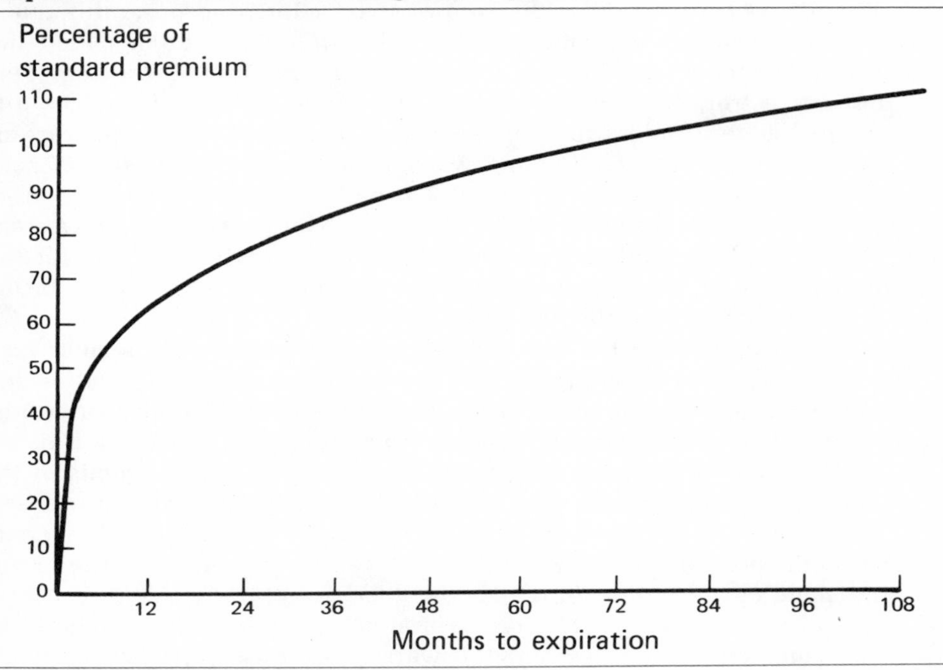

Source: Calculated from formula given in John P. Shelton, "The Relation of the Price of a Warrant to the Price of Its Associated Stock," *Financial Analysts Journal,* July–August 1967 (part II), p. 90.

in detail shortly, a longevity adjustment factor, $\sqrt[4]{\frac{M}{72}}$, is used.[1] Figure 24–2 shows the impact of this adjustment on the standard premium of a warrant. The major impact of the expiration date comes in the two years prior to expiration with the rate of decline becoming especially steep in the six months prior to expiration. Hence, an investor needs to exercise special caution in buying warrants that expire in less than two years.

In another study dealing with the impact of longevity on warrant values, Jerry Miller argues that the time before expiration should become increasingly relevant as the price of the common stock relative to the warrant exercise price decreases.[2] He developed a model in which the

[1]John P. Shelton, "The Relation of the Price of a Warrant to the Price of Its Associated Stock," *Financial Analysts Journal,* May–June 1967 (Part I), pp. 143–51, and July–August 1967 (Part II), pp. 88–99.

[2]Jerry D. Miller, "Effects of Longevity on Values of Stock Purchase Warrants," *Financial Analysts Journal,* November–December 1971, pp. 78–85.

warrant price and the common stock price are standardized by dividing each value by the warrant exercise price. Using these standardized values, Miller found that the longer the life of the warrant, the greater its value. In essence, he has combined the life of the warrant with the relationship between the common stock price and the warrant exercise price.

As a result of empirical testing of several possible explanatory variables, Shelton developed a six step approach to the valuation of warrants. His approach is applied in Exhibit 24–2 to both the Greyhound and Williams Company warrants. Shelton's method produces a valuation for the Greyhound warrant of $1.50, which is exactly equal to its market price in December 1974. For the Williams Company warrant, Shelton's method produces a value of $50.33 compared to a market value of $48.63, indicating a slightly undervalued warrant in December 1974.

It is useful to examine the Williams Company warrant in somewhat greater detail. The theoretical value of the warrant is $49.25 as calculated in step 2 of Exhibit 24–2. The warrant is selling for $48.63, a price that is approximately the theoretical value less the 60 cent annual dividend on the common stock. This relationship is not just a coincidence. Two reasons help to explain the result. First, the warrant expires in about a year, leaving relatively little time before expiration. Second, the warrant is high priced and sells for a high percentage of the price of the common stock. With the warrant selling for a high percentage of the price of the common stock, the warrant has a somewhat limited leverage potential and would tend to sell for close to its theoretical value. In addition, the warrant holder must forego any dividend income from the common stock. The limited leverage potential can be seen by assuming a 20 percent increase in the price of the common stock, to $83.10. The warrant's theoretical value would increase to $63.10 ($83.10 less the $20 exercise price) for a 29.8 percent increase. The leverage factor in this case is slightly less than 1.5 (29.8%/20%). Since the common stock in early December 1974 is only about 10 percent below its 1974 high despite a depressed stock market, market participants may feel that the Williams Company common stock is not undervalued.

Shelton's valuation method has no adjustment for the price volatility of the underlying common stock. In his study, he examined the past price volatility of the common stock as measured by the average of the ratio of the annual high to low stock price for the three preceding years. He found that this variable would not help explain differences in the prices of warrants.[3]

[3]James C. VanHorne, "Warrant Valuation in Relation to Volatility and Opportunity Costs," *Industrial Management Review*, Spring 1969, pp. 19–32, obtains a positive relationship between common stock volatility and warrant prices. See David F. Rush and Ronald W. Melicher, "An Empirical Examination of Factors Which Influence Warrant Prices," *Journal of Finance*, December 1974, pp. 1449–66, for a summary of previous empirical studies. Rush and Melicher find stock price variability to be a significant variable.

EXHIBIT 24–2

Application of Shelton's Warrant Valuation Method as of Early December 1974

Basic Data:

Greyhound warrant allows holder to obtain one share at $23.50 until May 14, 1980

Greyhound common selling for $10 with a dividend of $1.04

Williams Company warrant allows holder to obtain one share at $20 until January 1, 1976

Williams Company common selling for $69.25 with a dividend of $.60

Shelton's Six Steps:	Greyhound	Williams Co.
1. Multiply the common stock by 75%.	$10(.75) = $7.50	$69.25(.75) = $51.94
2. Subtract the warrant exercise price from stock price (but not less than zero).	$10 – $23.50 = zero	$69.25 – $20 = $49.25
3. Use steps 1 and 2 to determine the zone of plausible warrant prices.	zero to $7.50	$49.25 to $51.94
4. Use the following formula to determine where in the zone the warrant will be priced*: $\sqrt[4]{\frac{M}{72}}\,(.47 - 4.25Y + .17L)$ where: M = months to expiration (maximum of 120); Y = dividend yield on common; L = listing variable, 1 if listed, 0 if not listed	$\sqrt[4]{\frac{65}{72}}\,[.47 - 4.25(.104) + .17]$ $(.98)(.20) = .20$	$\sqrt[4]{\frac{13}{72}}\,[.47 - 4.25(.008) + .17]$ $(.65)(.61) = .40$
5. Multiply the answer in step 4 by the width of the zone.	.20 × $7.50 = $1.50	.40 × $2.69 = $1.08
6. Add the answer in step 5 to the answer in step 2 to obtain the value for the warrant.	zero + $1.50 = *$1.50*	$49.25 + $1.08 = *$50.33*

*The fourth root is obtained by taking the square root of the square root.

Since warrants appear to have been issued by a greater variety of companies since the time of the Shelton study, the potential warrant purchaser should probably give consideration to the volatility or beta of the underlying common stock even if the Shelton model is used. A case in point is the AT&T warrant with an expiration date of May 15, 1975. The Shelton valuation approach has consistently produced a value much higher than the actual price of the AT&T warrant. For example, two years prior to the expiration date, AT&T common sold for $53.13 and the warrant sold for $6.63. With a dividend of $2.80 per common share, Shelton's valuation approach produces a value of $13.12 for the warrant. A similar valuation one year before expiration produced a value of $8.10 compared to an actual warrant price of $2.75. One reason for these differences could be that the beta of AT&T's common stock is less than the average beta of the stocks originally studied by Shelton.

Unique Warrant Features

In valuing a warrant, an investor must be aware of some unique features that may be associated with the warrant. As indicated in Exhibit 24–1, warrants are sometimes exercisable into more or less than one share per warrant. The Gulf & Western warrant allows its holder to obtain 1.027 shares for a total cost of $55. The effective exercise price per share becomes $53.55 for this warrant.

The Commonwealth Edison warrant shown in Exhibit 24–1 also has a unique feature. In addition to allowing the warrant holder to purchase one share of Commonwealth Edison common stock for $30 until May 1, 1981, the warrant can be converted into one-third of a share of common stock at any time. The conversion feature remains after the warrant exercise feature expires in 1981. Applying the Shelton valuation model as of early December 1974 to this warrant results in a value of $4.01 in contrast to a market price of $7.63 as shown in Exhibit 24–1. In this instance, the price of the warrant is dominated by the warrant's convertible feature. The price of the warrant is approximately one-third the price of the common stock.

Warrants also exist where the warrant exercise price changes over time. For example, Cott Corporation's warrant is exercisable at $15 until January 31, 1977, and at $20 after that date until its expiration date of January 31, 1982. Another form of warrant exercise provision *effectively* alters the warrant exercise price over time. These are the so-called CD warrants where the holder of the warrant can use either cash (the C) or the par value of specified debt (the D) in exercising the warrant.[4]

[4]Kenneth L. Yeasting, "CD Warrants," *Financial Analysts Journal*, March–April 1970, pp. 44–47.

CD warrants are often referred to as senior security warrants since a senior security, the bond issue, can be used in the exercise of the warrants.

In Exhibit 24-1, the Avco and the Northwest Industries warrants are shown with an SS behind the total exercise price, indicating a senior security provision. An Avco warrant holder can use Avco's 7½% debenture of 1993 *at its par value of $1,000* in the exercise of the warrant. Likewise, Northwest Industries 7½% debenture of 1994 can be used at its par value to exercise the Northwest Industries warrant. If these debentures sell at a discount, the warrant terms are effectively changed. The adjusted exercise price for the warrant can be calculated in the following manner:

$$\text{Adjusted exercise price} = \begin{matrix}\text{exercise} \\ \text{price}\end{matrix} \times \frac{\text{bond price}}{\text{par value of bond}}$$

Both the Avco 7½% debenture of 1993 and the Northwest Industries 7½% debenture of 1994 sold at a discount in early December 1974. Using the Avco debenture price of $411.25 and the Northwest Industries debenture price of $700, the adjusted exercise price for the two warrants would be calculated as follows:

$$\text{Adjusted exercise price (Avco)} = \$56.00 \times \frac{\$411.25}{\$1{,}000} = \$23.03$$

$$\text{Adjusted exercise price (Northwest Ind.)} = \$25.00 \times \frac{\$700}{\$1{,}000} = \$17.50$$

As these bonds increase or decrease in price, the adjusted exercise price will change. Thus, the warrant exercise price becomes interest rate sensitive. An increase in interest rates will tend to reduce the price of the bond, which in turn reduces the adjusted exercise price of the warrant. The opposite will tend to occur if interest rates decrease. However, if the bond price is above $1,000, the adjusted exercise price would be above the cash exercise price and the investor would use cash to exercise the warrant.

It appears that warrants with a senior security provision attached to them represent good investments if interest rates are expected to increase. As interest rates rise, the adjusted exercise price declines and, other things being equal, the warrants would become more valuable. Care should be used, however, since other things may not be equal. If the higher interest rates are associated with lower stock prices and vice versa, as generally occurred during 1974 and early 1975, the impact of interest rate risk (either favorable or unfavorable) is diluted by stock price changes in the opposite direction. Hence, a potential investor needs to develop expectations with regard to both interest rate and stock price movements.

Uses of Warrants

One of the principal motivations behind purchasing a warrant is the desire to take a speculative position in a leverage-inherent security. The warrant holder hopes the price of the underlying security will increase with the result that the warrant increases by a much greater percentage. Naturally, this form of speculation is profitable only in an up market, since the leverage feature of warrants is a two-edged sword. In a bear market, the investor's capital can be reduced quite quickly. Additionally, a warrant has no voting rights, no dividend income, and no claim on the assets of the company.

Warrants may also be used to hedge a position in the common stock. The hedge can take two forms, the *warrant hedge* and the *reverse warrant hedge*. A hedging transaction involves two opposing but related transactions that occur at roughly the same time. The transactions in both these hedges are summarized below:

Warrant Hedge	*Reverse Warrant Hedge*
Buy the warrant	Sell the warrant short
Sell common short	Buy the common

Warrant Hedge

With the warrant hedge, the objective of the hedger is to reduce some of the risk of taking a short position in the common stock. To reduce the risk, the warrant is purchased. If the common stock goes up, the loss on the short position is at least partially offset by an increase in the warrant price. Consider a warrant hedge entered into on June 11, 1974, and liquidated at the prices shown in Exhibit 24-1 for both the Greyhound and Williams Company securities. The following results would occur:

June 11, 1974	*Greyhound*	*Williams Co.*
Short common stock at	14⅞	56⅛
Buy the warrant at	3	38
December 11, 1974		
Buy the common stock at	10	69¼
Sell the warrant at	1½	48⅝
Gain (loss) per Share Excluding Commissions		
Common stock	4⅞	(13⅛)
Warrant	(1½)	10⅝
Hedged position	3⅜	(2½)

In the Greyhound example, the common stock declined as expected. In retrospect, the Greyhound hedger would have done better with just a short position in the common stock. By hedging to reduce the risk, the hedger also reduced the return. The Williams Company common stock increased in price and the hedger suffered a slight loss on the total transaction.

Reverse Warrant Hedge

The object in a reverse warrant hedge is to "capture" the speculative premium that exists in warrants approaching their expiration date.[5] The hedger sells the warrant short and buys the common stock. For example, if a stock trades at $30 and has a warrant outstanding to purchase one share of the common stock at $35 during the next eighteen months, the warrant might sell for $7.[6] If a reverse warrant hedge is executed and the price of the common remains unchanged for the next eighteen months, the price of the warrant will gradually approach zero. The hedger makes a profit on the short position of the warrant. The common stock would have to sell above $42 before the hedger would lose money, if commission costs are ignored.

In order for the warrant hedger to undertake a reverse warrant hedge, he must first make sure that the warrants are available for shorting. Reverse warrant hedges have been popular in recent years, and it may not be possible for the warrants to be sold short since no warrants are available for shorting. If a large number of warrants have been sold short in a particular issue, one may encounter problems if many of the hedgers that are short all try to cover their short positions at approximately the same time. This buying action could drive the price of the warrant up, producing a higher speculative premium and a loss on the hedge. In addition, some special risks have appeared in recent years of which the warrant trader must be aware.[7]

Special Risks of Warrant Trading

The expiration date of a warrant has been extended in some recent instances. This may be detrimental if the warrant was sold short in a reverse warrant hedge, the object of which is to profit from the decline

[5]Edward O. Thorpe and Sheen T. Kassouf, *Beat the Market* (New York: Random House, 1967), and "A Game of Hedging," *Business Week*, April 27, 1974, p. 104.

[6]The Shelton valuation method in this case results in a value of $10.13 if the common stock has no dividend and $4.73 if the dividend is 8 percent. The average of these two values is $7.43.

[7]Daniel Turov, "Trampled Rights," *Barron's*, March 19, 1973, p. 11; "A Game of Hedging," p. 104; and "The New Risk in Warrants," *Business Week*, August 3, 1974, p. 42.

in the premium on the warrant as expiration approaches. If the expiration date is extended, which happened with the warrants of Continental Telephone on March 4, 1974, the price of the warrant could increase in price because of the extended life.[8] In fact, the price of the Continental Telephone warrants went from ⅞ to 1¾ overnight—much to the anguish of the short seller![9]

Another problem is the treatment of the warrant holder in the event the firm merges with another firm. In July 1974, Indian Head's warrants were selling for approximately $5 even though they had no theoretical value since the exercise price was $25 and the common was at $22. Another firm made a tender offer for Indian Head's common stock at $27 per share and also offered to purchase the warrants at their theoretical value of $2.[10] This warrant price in the tender offer was later increased to $2.25, the price at which the warrants sold, since effectively their expiration had been shortened from 1990 to 1974 as a result of the tender offer. The warrant holder suffered a severe loss as a result of this tender offer.

Last, it must be emphasized that the price of a warrant is greatly dependent on the appeal of the underlying stock. Hence, the potential warrant buyer should be especially alert to trends and fads in the stock market. Despite all the sophisticated mathematical formulae that have been developed, good common sense is still an especially valuable asset in warrant trading.

OPTIONS

"To my mind, this Exchange is unquestionably the most exciting and potentially important experiment now occurring in the securities industry."[11] These remarks by U.S. Senator Harrison A. Williams, Chairman of the Securities Subcommittee of the Senate Banking Committee, were made on the occasion of the first anniversary of the opening of the Chicago Board Options Exchange (CBOE). Opened in April 1973 as a project of the Chicago Board of Trade, the CBOE provides an exchange for the trading of call options in certain securities.[12]

A *call* is a financial instrument that gives the holder the right to purchase a specified number of shares of a given stock from another investor at a specified price for a specified period of time. The similarity

[8] *Standard & Poor's Corporation Descriptions*, 1974, p. 3250. The directors of Continental Telephone announced a two-year extension of the warrant terms.

[9] March 4, 1974, to March 5, 1974.

[10] See "The New Risk in Warrants," *Business Week*, August 3, 1974, p. 42.

[11] Chicago Board Options Exchange, Reprint of Senator Williams' speech—copies available from the CBOE.

[12] The American Stock Exchange started trading in options as of January 13, 1975; see "Stock Options Trading Begins on Amex as Board Bids to Boost Sagging Volume," *Wall Street Journal*, January 14, 1975, p. 25. Options also trade on the PBW Exchange.

of this definition to that of a warrant is immediately apparent with the exception that the holder of the call option purchases the shares from another investor and not from the company itself. In addition, a call is normally written for a much shorter period of time than the original life expectancy of a warrant. Calls traded on the CBOE have a maximum longevity of nine months. Because of their similarity to warrants, we would expect the prices of calls to be quite consistent with the pricing patterns of short-term warrants. Naturally, call options are a leverage-inherent security because of their fixed exercise price (often called a striking price).

Development of the CBOE

Prior to the opening of the CBOE, an investor desiring to purchase either a put or a call option would have a brokerage firm contact a special put and call broker to obtain a price for the desired option.[13] Because of tax considerations, the six month and ten day option was popular. The put and call broker would arrange to have the option written by an investor with a portfolio containing the desired stock. If a holder of an option decides to exercise the option, another investor must be willing to deliver the shares of stock to the holder of the option. The investor agreeing to make this delivery, if desired, is known as the *writer of the option*. The striking price of the option would usually be the market price at the time the option was written. The secondary market for options was poor and the holder of the option usually had to either exercise it or attempt to sell the option back to the put and call broker.

Burton Malkiel and Richard Quandt describe the state of the options market prior to the opening of the CBOE:

> The process of getting an option buyer and seller together is currently inefficient and cumbersome. There is no central marketplace . . . . If an option on an inactively traded stock is demanded, the middleman may at times be unable to find an option writer who is willing to sell options on that particular security. Even if the option firm is successful in arranging the trade, the procedure may have involved as many as fifteen telephone calls to potential writers. In addition, there is no systematic reporting of either actual option trades or of offers to buy and sell, except on a limited number of actively traded issues.[14]

The CBOE has dramatically changed the market for call options. Among the major developments are the following: 1) standardization of the option contract with respect to the number of shares under option,

[13]A put option is similar to a call option except that it gives the holder the right to sell shares.

[14]Burton G. Malkiel and Richard E. Quandt, *Strategies and Rational Decisions in the Securities Options Markets* (Cambridge, Mass.: the MIT Press, 1969), p. 165.

the expiration date, and the striking price; 2) standardization of trading practices; and 3) the existence of a good secondary market for options, including continuous public reporting of prices and volume similar to that which exists for common stocks.

Description of CBOE Options

The standardization of both the maturity date and the option exercise price were critical to the development of a good secondary market for options. Call options on the CBOE expire on the last Monday of the months of January, April, July, and October (or February, May, August or November). Trading in any given option starts approximately nine months prior to the expiration date. As a result, trading in three different expiration months usually occurs at any given time. For example, in December 1975, trading would occur in the following options: January 1976, April 1976, and July 1976. About the time that the January 1976 option expires, trading would be open in the October 1976 option. Exhibit 24-3 shows the report of option trading for December 11, 1974, as carried in the *Wall Street Journal.*

EXHIBIT 24-3
Portion of Option Trading Report

Chicago Board Options Exchange

Wednesday, December 11, 1974

Closing prices of all options. Sales unit is 100 shares. Security description includes exercise price.

	– Jan –		– Apr –		– Jul –		Stock
Option & price	Vol.	Last	Vol.	Last	Vol.	Last	Close
Am Tel 50	19	1/8	b	b	b	b	43 5/8
Am Tel 45	191	15-16	140	2	41	2 3/4	43 5/8
Am Tel 40	18	4	31	4 5/8	b	b	43 5/8
Atl R 90	227	4	62	7 1/8	7	10	87 3/4
Atl R 80	211	9	70	12 3/8	2	15	87 3/4
Avon 45	30	1/8	b	b	b	b	30 1/2
Avon 40	87	7-16	b	b	b	b	30 1/2
Avon 35	417	1 3/8	235	3 3/8	b	b	30 1/2
Avon 30	579	3 1/4	188	5 3/4	21	7	30 1/2
Avon 25	238	6 1/2	91	8 1/4	16	9 1/2	30 1/2
Avon 20	42	11	60	12	21	13 1/2	30 1/2
Beth S 30	91	1/4	49	1 1-16	32	1 3/4	24 3/4
Beth S 25	71	1 1/4	38	2 1/4	16	3	24 3/4
Beth S 35	19	1/8	b	b	b	b	24 3/4
Bruns 15	31	3-16	68	1/2	b	b	8 3/4
Bruns 10	171	1 1-16	222	1 7-16	118	1 7/8	8 3/4
Citicp 35	219	5/8	b	b	b	b	29 1/4
Citicp 30	270	1 3/4	119	3 3/4	13	5 1/2	29 1/4
Citicp 25	44	5	14	6 1/2	b	b	29 1/4
Eas Kd .. 100	60	1-16	42	7/8	b	b	61 3/8
Eas Kd .. 90	4	1/8	56	1 1/2	b	b	61 3/8
Eas Kd .. 80	252	7-16	117	2 5/8	4	5 1/4	61 3/8
Eas Kd .. 70	313	1 5/8	93	5 1/8	12	8	61 3/8
Eas Kd .. 60	176	5	28	8 3/4	6	10 1/2	61 3/8

b denotes no option offered.

Source: Reprinted with permission of *the Wall Street Journal,*

When trading is opened in a new expiration month, the exercise price is set at a dollar figure that approximates the market price of the common stock. If the market price changes during the period of the option, the CBOE may open trading in a new option having the same expiration date but a different striking price. Exhibit 24-3 shows that this has occurred in the case of many options. For example, call options expiring in April 1975 are traded for Eastman Kodak with the following exercise prices: 100, 90, 80, 70, and 60. Each of these call options allows the holder to purchase 100 shares of Kodak common stock until the last Monday of April 1975 at the exercise price stipulated in the option. Exhibit 24-3 shows that 93 Kodak April 70 option contracts were traded with a closing price of 5⅛ per share or $512.50 per option contract.

Option Writers

The principal reason an investor will write call options is to realize a return if the stock declines or remains unchanged in price. An option buyer and an option writer will agree, through their respective brokers, to the price of the option (often called the premium). Let us assume that an investor writes an option for Kodak common stock with a striking price of $70 and an April expiration date. The premium agreed to is 5⅛, the closing price shown in Exhibit 24-3. When the transaction is completed, the writer gets the premium less transactions costs. If Kodak does not go above $70 per share by the end of April, the writer will not have to fulfill the option agreement. The writer has earned $512.50 in the form of the premium paid for writing the option less a commission.

The main risk assumed by the writer of call options is that of an increase in the price of the common stock on which the option is written. In Figure 24-3, the profit and loss position of the option writer is displayed. With a market price on the stock above $70, the striking price, the writer begins to lose a portion of the premium. As the market price of the stock passes the sum of the striking price and the premium, absolute losses are incurred.

When writing options, the most typical situation occurs when the writer is "covered." The writer owns the stock required to satisfy the option agreement. When the option is covered, the risk is reduced since losses on the option will be offset by gains on the stock. It is also possible for an individual to write "naked" options, in which case the writer does not own the stock and must purchase it if delivery is required. This situation is much more risky than the covered option. The investor is exposed to all of the losses depicted in Figure 24-3.

For accepting this risk, it has been estimated that the average annual rate of return to the option writer will be in the 20 to 30 percent range.[15]

[15] *Options Trading on the Chicago Option Exchange* (Chicago: CBOE, 1973), p. 12.

FIGURE 24–3
Profit and Loss Position of Option Writer (Excluding Commissions)

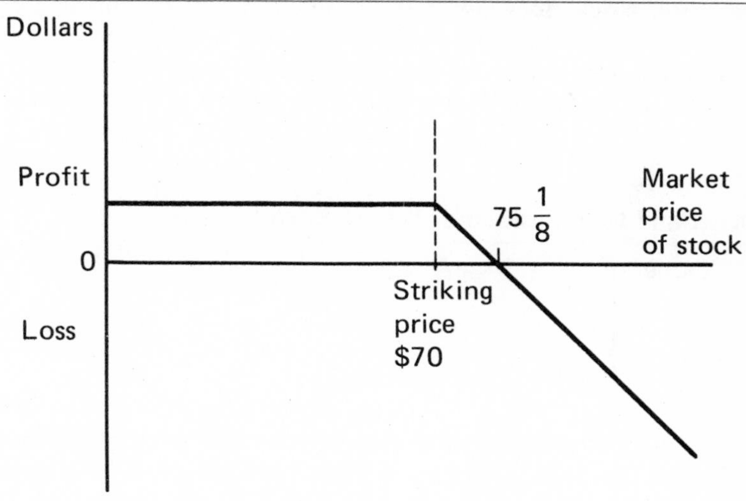

The actual rate of return realized on any option-writing venture depends upon the amount of premium received and what the common stock does during the life of the option. During the bear market of 1974, option writing of call options would generally have been a profitable activity since the option writer would seldom have been called upon to make delivery of the stock.

Option Buying

The purchase and valuation of an option is quite similar to that of a short-term warrant. The price of any option is composed of two elements, as is the case with warrants. The Kodak April 60 option in Exhibit 24–3 is "in the money" 1⅜, since that is its theoretical value. The theoretical value is the difference between the stock price and striking price. A call that has a positive theoretical value is said to be "in the money." The speculative premium is the difference between the price of the call and its theoretical value or zero if the theoretical value is negative. The Kodak option has a speculative premium of 7⅜ (price less theoretical value).

As with warrants, the principal attraction of purchasing a call option is the leverage potential from the fixed striking price of the option. As an example of the leverage potential, consider the Atlantic Richfield April 90 option shown in Exhibit 24–3. If the price of the common stock increases 15 percent by April from 87¾ to $100.91, the option would sell for at least its theoretical value of $10.91. This minimum price would mean an increase of 53.1 percent over the current option price of 7⅛.

Actually, the option might sell for somewhat more than its theoretical value if time remains before it expires. Of course, if Atlantic Richfield's common stock does not sell for at least $90 by the expiration of the option, the investor will suffer a total loss. The speculator might reduce the loss somewhat by selling the call before its expiration date. For the buyer, the profit and loss potential is shown in Figure 24-4.

FIGURE 24-4
Profit and Loss Position of Option Buyer

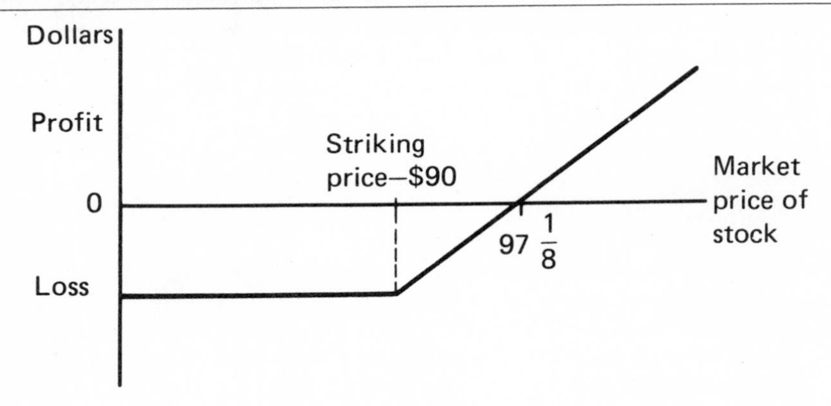

Uses of Options

It is obvious from the previous discussion that one important use of CBOE options is to speculate on price changes with a relatively small amount of capital. In comparison to using warrants for speculative purposes, options have some advantages. First, some of the special risks that exist in the warrant market do not exist in the option market. The life of a call will not be extended nor will the option holder incur problems of the type that have occurred recently for warrant holders in some mergers. The CBOE will alter the terms of an option in the event of such events as recapitalizations and reorganizations. Also, CBOE options are actively traded and have a better secondary market than exists for many warrants.

In summary, because of the powerful leverage potential in the option form, the option market is not for the conservative investor. The time horizon is short and the speculator has little time for the market to "bail out" a poor investment decision. We have not discussed all the possible strategies available for speculating in the options market, but the CBOE is clearly not a place for the average investor looking for good quality investments with a reasonable return. However, for those investors willing to accept substantial risk, the establishment of the CBOE provides a good market in which to speculate with a portion of investable funds.

RIGHTS

If a common stock carries a pre-emptive right feature, the present shareholders have the opportunity of purchasing new shares of common stock before that stock is offered to the general public.[16] This procedure allows the stockholder to retain the same ownership percentage after the new stock offering as existed before the offering. For each share of stock held, the shareholder receives one right. With a specified number of rights and a cash payment, the shareholder can subscribe to a new share of common stock. Since the subscription price is normally set below the current market price, the rights have a value and are actively traded. In this section, we examine both the manner in which rights should be valued and the advisability of speculative trading in rights.

Value of a Right

If a firm's common stock is selling for $40 per share and the firm makes a rights offering giving each shareholder the privilege of buying one share of common stock at $30 for each ten shares presently held, the rights are clearly valuable. The investor owning 10 shares of stock worth $400 can buy one new share for $30. The investor now has a total of 11 shares at a combined valuation for the old shares and payment for the new share of $430. Dividing the $430 total by 11 gives a figure of $39.09 per share, which is what the new market price of the shares should be. The value of the right is $.91, which is the difference between the old market price and the market valuation of each share after giving consideration to the impact of the rights offering.

It is possible to construct a formula to calculate the value of a right before the common stock goes ex-rights. Since a right is similar to a dividend, after a specified date set by the company, the purchase of the common stock will no longer carry the privilege of receiving the rights. The formula for the value of a right before the stock goes ex-rights is as follows:

$$\text{Value of a right} = \frac{\begin{matrix}\text{market value of a} \\ \text{share of old stock}\end{matrix} - \begin{matrix}\text{subscription price} \\ \text{of a new share}\end{matrix}}{\begin{matrix}\text{number of rights needed to} \\ \text{purchase one new share}\end{matrix} + 1}$$

$$= \frac{\$40 - \$30}{10 + 1}$$

$$= \$.91$$

[16]Even without a pre-emptive feature, a firm might use a rights offering.

Handling of Rights

If an investor owns common stock and receives a certificate evidencing the ownership of rights in the mail, the investor can do one of three things with the rights: 1) exercise the rights and buy an additional share(s) at the subscription price; 2) sell the rights in the market; and 3) let the rights expire. Rights usually have an expiration date of about three weeks after the stock goes ex-rights. The decision whether to exercise the rights or to sell them in the market is essentially a portfolio management question. Does the investor want to purchase more shares of the common stock given its risk-return characteristics, or should a small percentage of the holding be sold via the sale of the rights? Of course, the rights should be allowed to expire if the market price (including brokerage commissions) falls below the subscription price, which would make the rights worthless.

Speculation in Rights

Rights are a leverage-inherent security since they allow the holder to purchase shares of stock at a fixed subscription price. They are much like very short-term warrants. If a speculator expects the price of the common stock to rise during the rights offering period, the rights could be purchased for speculative purposes.

Whether or not a speculator ought to deal in rights is an open question. Because of the small number of days in which rights are traded, the speculator's time horizon is necessarily short. Not much time exists for errors in judgment to be corrected. Robert Soldofsky and Craig Johnson studied the advisability of the Wall Street adage, "Stockholders should sell rights early."[17] This adage, if actually sound advice, means that it would generally be unprofitable for speculators to trade rights since the highest prices would come early in the rights subscription period. The study found that, when the trading period for rights is broken into thirds, there is a slight tendency for rights to sell at their highest price in the first period. This would indicate that rights should not be bought for speculative purposes.

There are two other reasons to avoid speculating in rights. First, when a firm issues new shares of common stock, there may be a tendency for downward price pressure to develop during the rights subscription period, since additional shares of common stock will soon be outstanding. Second, the commission costs involved in trading rights, given the typi-

[17]Robert M. Soldofsky and Craig R. Johnson, "Rights Timing," *Financial Analysts Journal*, July–August 1967, pp. 101–04. Also see George L. Leffler, "Stock Rights," *Barron's*, September 16, 1957, p. 15.

cally low dollar value per right, tends to restrict the profit after transactions costs are considered. In summary, it appears that warrants and CBOE options represent a much better speculative vehicle than do rights.

DUAL FUNDS

Dual purpose funds, or dual funds as they are commonly called, are a unique form of closed-end investment company. The first dual fund sold to the public, Dualvest, was marketed by Samuel Montague & Company of London in May 1965. American investors were first offered dual fund shares in 1967. The British form of dual funds is somewhat different from the American form and our discussion will be restricted to U.S. dual funds.

Dual funds have two types of shares outstanding, income and capital shares. In the initial offering of dual fund shares, equal dollar amounts of both types are sold and the money invested in a single portfolio. The income shares receive all the dividend and interest income from the total portfolio while all capital gains accrue to the capital shareholders. The income shareholders are "guaranteed" that they will receive a certain dollar amount per share each year. Any unpaid dividends are cumulative and, if unpaid, result in arrearages.

This specialized form of closed-end investment company has a limited life of about twelve to eighteen years, depending on the provisions stated at the time of the underwriting. At the termination date, the income shares are redeemed. The redemption price is stated in the prospectus of the initial offering and is typically equal to the offering price plus any accrued and unpaid dividends existing at the time of redemption. Any remaining asset value in the portfolio is distributed to the capital shareholders unless the required annual dividends have not been paid to the income shareholders. If dividends are in arrears, they will be paid from the value of the capital shares prior to either the final distribution of assets or the fund's continuation as an open-end investment company, if that is the desire of the capital shareholders. Notice that income shares possess many of the characteristics of preferred stock.

In this section, our principal focus is on the capital shares as a form of leverage-inherent security. Wide differences exist in the past performance of the capital shares of the various dual funds. These differences in performance are especially important to the potential investor in a dual fund's capital shares.

Leverage Aspects

Dual fund capital shares are a leverage-inherent security because of the fixed redemption price of the income shares at the end of the fund's life. We can demonstrate the leverage potential this situation creates with the following example of a dual fund having just sold 1 million income shares and 1 million capital shares at $10 each. A total of $20 million is available for investment in securities. The example assumes that the total value of the portfolio goes up or down by 25 percent, which causes the net asset value of each capital share to change by 50 percent.

	Percentage Change in Total Portfolio		
	None	*25% increase*	*25% decrease*
Value of total portfolio	$20 mil	$25 mil	$15 mil
Less redemption price of income shares	10	10	10
Equals value of capital shares	$10 mil	$15 mil	$ 5 mil
Percentage change in the value of capital shares	–	+50%	–50%

The closer the total portfolio value gets to the fixed redemption value of the income shares, the greater the leverage potential. For example, assume that the value of the total portfolio in the previous example has fallen to $12 million. If the portfolio then increases in value to $15 million (+25%), the net asset value of the capital shares will increase from $2 million to $5 million (+150%). In the same fashion, the higher the total portfolio value relative to the fixed redemption value of the income shares, the less the leverage potential. In essence, the theoretical beta of the capital shares will tend to change over time as the relationship between the total portfolio value and the redemption price of the income shares changes.

Importance of Past Performance

With the leverage inherent in the dual fund capital shares, the past performance of the total portfolio is important, since both good and poor performance is magnified by the leverage inherent in the capital shares.[18] Figure 24–5 summarizes the performance of the seven major dual funds from the end of 1967 to September 30, 1974. The Gemini and Scudder Duo Vest Funds have performed the best and the Hemisphere the poorest. It is evident that the generally down market (–34.1%) from year-end 1967 to September 30, 1974 has not treated the capital shares of any of the dual funds favorably. The capital shares performed poorly even for those funds such as the Gemini Fund, where the total portfolio performed better than the S&P 500.

In picking a dual fund capital share to invest in, one might be tempted to pick the capital share with the greatest apparent leverage.

[18]Performance is also important to the income shareholder, especially since poor performance reduces the value of the assets on which income may be generated.

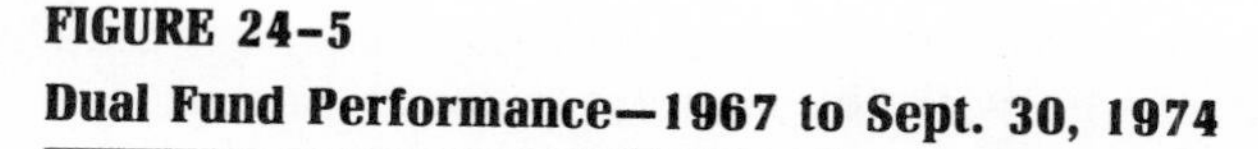

FIGURE 24–5
Dual Fund Performance—1967 to Sept. 30, 1974

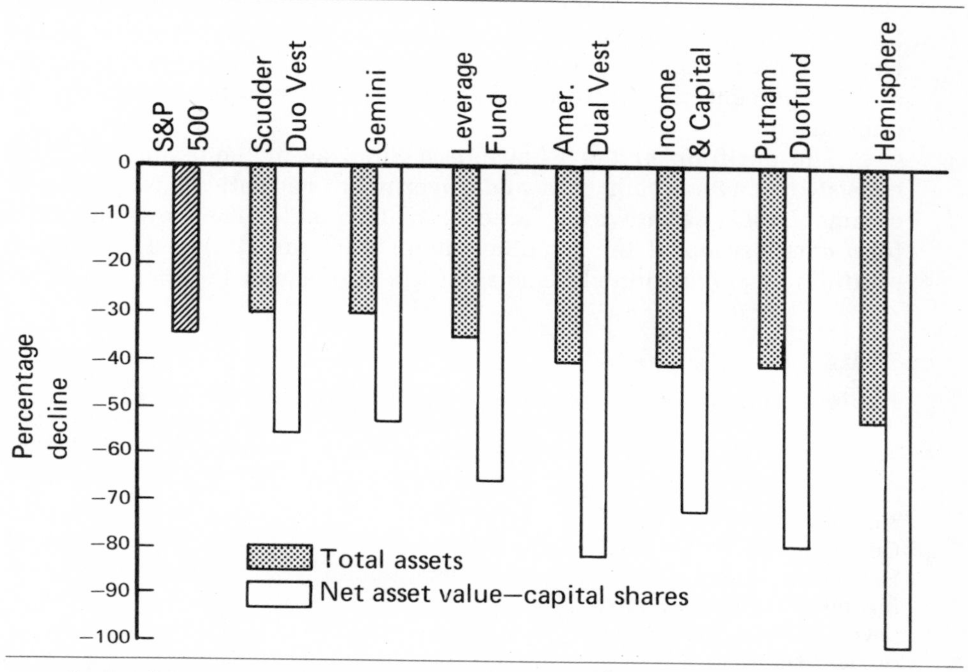

Source: "Management Results," in *Supplement to Investment Companies*, 1974 (New York: Wiesenberger Services, 1974).

The asset value leverage for the capital share at any time may be calculated in the manner shown below: The Gemini Fund and the Hemisphere Fund are used as illustrations.

$$\text{Asset value leverage (AVL)} = \frac{\text{redemption value per income share} + \text{net asset value per capital share}}{\text{net asset value per capital share}}$$

Gemini Fund

$$\text{AVL} = \frac{\$11.00 + \$6.62}{\$6.62} = 2.66$$

Hemisphere Fund

$$\text{AVL} = \frac{\$11.44 + \$.03}{\$.03} = 328.33$$

Picking the Hemisphere Fund for its greater leverage could be a poor investment decision. Because of the high asset value leverage, the Hemisphere capital shares sold for $1.25 a share on December 20, 1974. This price amounts to a premium of 4,067 percent over the net asset value of $.03 on the same day. Hence, if the total portfolio shows only a fairly modest increase, the net asset value of the capital shares would increase dramatically. But even with the leverage potential, the Hemisphere capital shares might not be a good investment because of the fund's portfolio composition. In addition, as the net asset value of the Hemisphere Fund's capital shares increases, say to $.20, the premium of 4,067 percent may narrow and the market price of the shares remain unchanged.

The portfolio of the Hemisphere Fund as of September 30, 1974 consisted of 98 percent cash and government securities and 2 percent common stock, as shown in Table 24-1. This table also shows the portfolio composition of the six other major dual funds. The Hemisphere portfolio is so constituted because of the interests of the income shareholders. Since a slight decline in the value of the portfolio could cause the value of the portfolio to fall below the redemption value of the income shares, the income producing objective dominates the capital gain objective of the fund. In other words, the portfolio becomes structured to preserve the fund's principal and not necessarily to make it grow. In addition, the management of the Hemisphere Fund has taken a conservative attitude toward common stock investment in light of the fund's poor past performance and expectations of the management regarding the future performance of the stock market. As a result of the heavy fixed income emphasis in the fund, it would probably not participate to a significant extent should the market stage a significant upturn.

TABLE 24-1

Portfolio Composition of Dual Funds as of September 30, 1974

	Cash and Gov't Securities	Bonds and Preferred	Common Stock
American Dual Vest Fund	38%	38%	24%
Gemini Fund	2	3	95
Hemisphere Fund	98	—	2
Income and Capital Shares	14	16*	70
Leverage Fund of Boston	14	15*	71
Putnam Duofund	8	47*	45
Scudder Duo Vest	20	13*	67

*Entirely or substantially in convertible securities.

Source: "Management Results," in *Supplement to Investment Companies, 1974* (New York: Wiesenberger Services, 1974).

If an investor expects the market to rise significantly, a dual fund's capital shares may be a suitable leverage-inherent security, provided the portfolio is composed almost exclusively of common stocks or convertible securities. It might even be important to identify which common stocks the investor expects to lead the market recovery and choose the dual fund with the portfolio closest to that description. For instance, if high-quality common stocks are expected to perform well in the near future, the investor would pick a dual fund with a high-quality portfolio.

Investing in the Income Shares

The income shares might be an attractive investment from a yield standpoint. Since the income shareholders get all the income from the portfolio, good economic conditions could result in higher dividend income from the portfolio. This development would tend to increase the rate of return over time to the income shareholders. In addition, since the income shares have a fixed life and a fixed redemption value, they are somewhat like a bond. As a result, a potential investor could calculate what amounts to a yield to redemption date for the income shares. If the income shares sell for less than their redemption value, a capital gain may result when the shares are redeemed. The investor in the income shares will have to give consideration to the possibility that the portfolio will do poorly and the value of the portfolio at the redemption date for the income shares will be insufficient to pay the entire redemption price.

The "margin of safety" calculation is a way for the investor to determine the percentage that the total portfolio can decline in value and still allow the income shares to be redeemed at their full redemption value. Exhibit 24-4 demonstrates the "margin of safety" calculation and the yield to redemption date calculation for the American Dual Vest income shares as of December 1974.

EXHIBIT 24-4

American Dual Vest, Inc.—Yield and "Margin of Safety" Calculations

$$\text{Current yield} = \frac{\text{annual dividend}}{\text{market price}} = \frac{\$\ .87}{\$10.625} = 8.19\%$$

Yield to redemption date = rate of return which discounts the following returns back to the value of the investment ($10.625)

Returns:

estimated annual dividend for 5 years = $.87

redemption value in 5th year = $15.00

Rate of return is equal to 14.4%

$$\text{"Margin of Safety"} = \frac{\text{income share redemption value} + \text{capital share's net asset value}}{\text{capital share's net asset value}} - 1$$

$$= \frac{\$15.00 + \$3.69}{\$15.00} - 1 = 1.25 - 1 = .25 \text{ (25\% decline in value)}$$

SUMMARY

Leverage-inherent securities provide an interesting alternative for the investor. Instead of purchasing securities on margin, the investor can increase the risk of a portfolio by purchasing warrants, options, rights, or dual fund capital shares. The prices of these securities tend to be more volatile than that of the average security since they have a fixed redemption price or a fixed exercise price as part of their terms.

Warrants, call options, and rights are similar in nature since they give the holder the privilege of obtaining shares of another security at a fixed price per share. The main differences in these securities are the party from whom the shares are obtained and the length of time during which the shares may be obtained. Warrants and rights allow the holder to obtain shares from the company itself, while a call option holder obtains shares from another investor. At time of issue, warrants allow the holder to obtain shares for a longer period of time than call options. Rights are actually short-term warrants with a life of about three weeks.

Warrants pose an interesting valuation problem for the investor. What is the privilege of purchasing a security at some future date at a fixed price worth at the present time? The speculative premium is the value the market places on this privilege. The speculative premium combined with any theoretical value for the warrant equals the warrant's market price. The theoretical value is obtained by subtracting the warrant exercise price from the stock price. The theoretical value is never less than zero.

The principal use of warrants is to speculate on the price movement of the underlying stock because of the leverage feature inherent in the warrant. Additionally, warrants can be used to hedge a position in the market. In a warrant hedge, the speculator buys the warrant to hedge a short position in the common stock. In a reverse warrant hedge, the speculator sells short the warrant and buys the common stock. Hedging transactions are entered into to reduce the risk of a position taken in the market. Since they tend to reduce the risk, they also tend to reduce the rate of return which may be expected. In both hedged and unhedged warrant speculation, the speculator should be aware that some special risks exist with warrants. The two main special risks are that the life of the warrant may be extended by the company and that the warrant may be retired prematurely as a result of a merger transaction.

The call option market has undergone a dramatic change as a result of the establishment of the Chicago Board Options Exchange in April 1973. In addition to providing a good secondary market for call options, the CBOE standardized option terms. The expiration date is now standardized along with the number of shares per option and the striking price of the option. Since call options are similar to short-term warrants, the same general principles of valuation apply to call options as apply to warrants.

Dual funds were first sold in the U.S. in 1967 and are an attractive investment under some circumstances. Equal dollar amounts of income and capital shares were sold. The income shares receive all the income during the life of the closed-end investment company while all the capital gains accrue to the capital shares. In essence, the dual fund concept allows each investor to choose an appropriate dividend policy. An investor in a high marginal tax bracket might desire the capital shares because of the capital gains aspect and the lack of current income. An investor needing income might be attracted to the income shares.

We observed that the expected performance of a dual fund is especially important because of the inherent leverage, which magnifies the results of both good and poor performance. In addition, the past performance, along with the need to pursue the two portfolio objectives of income and growth at the same time, may influence the composition of the dual fund's portfolio. Hence, a potential dual fund capital share investor will need to give consideration to the portfolio composition. For example, we noted that the Hemisphere Fund's portfolio is composed almost exclusively of fixed income securities and might not participate to any significant extent in a bull market.

While not for the average investor, leverage-inherent securities provide the investor willing to take above average risks with a means of participating in a bull market. Since a leverage-inherent security, if properly analyzed, will tend to increase in price by a greater percentage than the underlying stock or the market in general, good rates of return relative to the market are possible. Of course, if the investor is incorrect in making an investment decision, the inherent leverage tends to produce poor relative rates of return.

QUESTIONS

1. *a*) Distinguish between financial and operating leverage.
   b) Identify industries having a low degree of either operating or financial leverage.
2. Since an investor can add leverage to a portfolio by buying securities on margin, why might the investor choose to purchase leverage-inherent securities?
3. Distinguish among warrants, rights, and call options.
4. What factors should the investor consider in determining whether the speculative premium for any given warrant is reasonable?
5. What is a CD warrant? Why is this type of warrant an interest rate sensitive security?
6. What does the investor expect to accomplish with a warrant hedge and with a reverse warrant hedge?
7. What risks does the investor face in the establishment of a reverse warrant hedge?
8. Compare the put and call market as it existed prior to the establishment of the Chicago Board Options Exchange with the trading that occurs on the CBOE.

9. When the sale of the first U.S. dual fund was proposed, the Securities and Exchange Commission expressed concern regarding the pursuit of the two objectives of capital growth and income with only one portfolio. What problems might be encountered in pursuing two objectives at the same time? Why might this not be a problem?
10. Why does the leverage inherent in dual fund capital shares change over time? Why is this important to the investor?
11. An investment in the income shares of a dual fund is somewhat like buying a corporate bond. What are the similarities and differences?

PROBLEMS

1. Greyhound's warrants went from $1.50 in December 1974 to $2.875 in July 1975. During the same period, the common stock went from $10 to $14.375.
   a) Calculate the respective percentage changes in these prices and the *ex post* leverage factor (percentage change in warrant divided by percentage change in the common).
   b) Why did the warrant go up so fast relative to the common?
   c) The warrant allows the holder to purchase one share of Greyhound common stock at $23.50 until May 14, 1980. With the common at only $14.375, why would an investor pay $2.875 for the warrant?
2. Commonwealth Edison's warrant (see Exhibit 24–1 for terms) went from $7.625 in December 1974 to $9.25 in July 1975. During the same period, the common went from $23.25 to $28.
   a) Calculate the relative percentage changes and the *ex post* leverage factor.
   b) Why are the results you obtained so different from those of Greyhound in question 1?
3. Apply Shelton's warrant valuation approach to the two warrants listed below to determine their overvaluation or undervaluation using this method. Greyhound's warrant trades at $2.875 (July 1975) while the North Central Airlines warrant trades for $.81.

	Common Price	*Dividend*	*Months Left (M)*
Greyhound	$14.375	$1.04	58
North Central Airlines	2.625	.10	51

4. Both the warrants of Avco and Northwest Industries have a senior security provision as described in the text. Using the terms from Exhibit 24–1:
   a) Calculate the adjusted exercise price as of July 1975. The Avco 7½%, 1993 bond sold for $565 and the Northwest Industries 7½%, 1994 bonds sold for $780.
   b) The following prices existed for the common stocks and warrants as of July 1975:

	Common	*Warrant*
Avco	7	1⅛
Northwest Industries	32½	15

Calculate the percentage changes in prices from those in Exhibit 24–1. Can you explain the results you obtain?

5. A warrant hedge in Greyhound was established in December 1974 when the common was at $10 and the warrant was at $1.50. By July 1975, the common had risen to $14.375 and the warrant was at $2.875.
   a) Calculate the profitability of this warrant hedge (ignoring commissions and dividends) if a 100 share transaction had been executed in each security.
   b) Calculate the profitability of this hedge (ignoring commissions and dividends) if equal dollar amounts had been executed (use 300 shares of common and 2,000 warrants).
   c) Which hedging strategy do you favor? Would your answer change under different circumstances?
6. In December 1974, a reverse warrant hedge was established in Tenneco at the following prices (100 shares each): common, $22.50; warrant, $1.50. By July 1975, the common was at $26.125 and the warrant was at $2.875.
   a) Ignoring commissions and dividends, determine the profitability of this hedge.
   b) Why was this hedge successful (or unsuccessful)?
7. The following CBOE October 1975 options were traded in July 1975.

   Eastman Kodak 100 at 9¼ with the common at 103⅛
   IBM 220 at 11 with the common at 206⅞
   Xerox 70 at 7 with the common at 69⅛

   a) Norman Betz is considering using his stock portfolio for the writing of options. What is his breakeven point for each option? What percentage change is this from the July 1975 price of each common stock?
   b) Sheila Stone is considering the purchase of one of these options. If she expects a 10 percent increase in the price of each common stock by late October 1975, which option should she purchase?
8. American Dualvest's income shares sold for $12.25 in July 1975. The net asset value of the capital shares was $6.44. Using the dividend data and redemption terms shown in Exhibit 24–4, calculate:
   a) The current yield.
   b) The yield to maturity assuming four years to redemption.
   c) The margin of safety.

   Why have these values changed from those shown in Exhibit 24–4?
9. The following data for July 1975 relate to the Gemini and Hemisphere capital shares:

	Market Price	*Net Asset Value*	*Discount/Premium*
Gemini	$10.50	$15.52	−32.3%
Hemisphere	1.50	.81	+ 85.2

a) Calculate the asset value leverage (AVL) for each dual fund. Use the redemption value for the income shares contained in the text.

b) The following values existed as of December 20, 1974 for the capital shares:

	AVL	*Net Asset Value*	*Market Price*
Gemini	2.66	$6.62	$5.125
Hemisphere	328.33	.03	1.25

Calculate the percentage change since December 20, 1974 for the net asset value and the market price of the capital shares. Why are the results for these two variables so different?

SUGGESTED READINGS

Clasing, Henry. *The Dow Jones-Irwin Guide to Put and Call Options.* Homewood, Illinois: Dow Jones-Irwin, 1975.

Fischer, Donald E. "Shorting Expiring Warrants." *Mississippi Valley Journal of Business and Economics,* Winter 1974–75, pp. 73–83.

Gentry, James A. and John R. Pike. "Dual Funds Revisited." *Financial Analysts Journal,* March–April 1968, pp. 149–57.

Johnston, George S., M. Louise Curley, and Robert A. McIndoe. "Are Shares of Dual-Purpose Funds Undervalued?" *Financial Analysts Journal,* November–December 1968, pp. 157–63.

Kassouf, Sheen T. "Warrant Price Behavior—1945 to 1964." *Financial Analysts Journal,* January–February 1968, pp. 123–26.

Malkiel, Burton G. and Richard E. Quandt. *Strategies and Rational Decisions in the Securities Option Market.* Cambridge, Mass.: MIT Press, 1969.

Miller, Jerry D. "Effects of Longevity on Values of Stock Purchase Warrants." *Financial Analysts Journal,* November–December 1971, pp. 78–85.

Rush, David F. and Ronald W. Melicher. "An Empirical Examination of Factors Which Influence Warrant Prices." *Journal of Finance,* December 1974, pp. 1449–66.

Schwartz, William. "Warrants: A Form of Equity Capital." *Financial Analysts Journal,* September–October 1970, pp. 87–101.

Shelton, John P. "The Relation of the Price of a Warrant to the Price of Its Associated Stock." *Financial Analysts Journal,* May–June 1967, pp. 143–51 (Part One) and July–August 1967, pp. 143–51 (Part Two).

——, Eugene F. Brigham and Alfred E. Hofflander, Jr. "An Evaluation and Appraisal of Dual Funds." *Financial Analysts Journal,* May–June 1967, pp. 131–39.

Thorpe, Edward O. and Sheen T. Kassouf. *Beat the Market.* New York: Random House, 1967.

Van Horne, James C. "Warrant Valuation in Relation to Volatility and Opportunity Costs." *Industrial Management Review,* Spring 1969, pp. 19–32.

Yeasting, Kenneth L. "CD Warrants." *Financial Analysts Journal,* March–April 1970, pp. 44–47.

25

Integrated Financial Planning

We suggested in Chapter 1 that an integrated approach to asset management was necessary. Financial planning should start with a financial inventory. In addition, all the elements of an investor's financial management program should be as coordinated as possible, since the relationship between the risk and return associated with individual assets becomes especially important in a total asset context.

Our final chapter attempts to put into proper perspective the various elements of asset management. The first section discusses the concept of a lifetime portfolio. The objective in this section is to ascertain how persons in different stages of life should plan their investments and manage their other assets. The second section discusses the nature of pension plans, their benefits, and how these benefits relate to other elements in the investor's financial planning. The purpose and types of insurance are introduced in the third section, which includes a discussion of life, health, and property and casualty insurance. Section four consists of three case studies of people in various personal and financial circumstances. A summary completes the chapter.

LIFETIME PORTFOLIO APPROACH

As people age and experience different demands upon their incomes, the mix of investment objectives tends to change. The relative importance of the investment objectives of liquidity, income, capital appreciation, and safety of principal depends upon such variables as the investor's age, income level, wealth, marital status, number of dependents, and debt level.[1] Even though an investor's utility function is a personal thing, as we noted in Chapter 11, it is still possible to make some generalizations about what might be the typical mix of investment objectives over an investor's lifetime.

Figure 25-1 shows hypothetical investment preferences of an investor from age twenty-five to seventy-five. At age twenty-five one might weigh investment objectives in the following manner:

Liquidity	30%
Income	10
Appreciation	30
Safety	30

The typical investor in this age group is just getting started on a career and normally has few accumulated assets to fall back on in difficult times. Hence, liquidity and safety might rank relatively high, since investments are often needed to make a down payment on a home, to pay for moving expenses, or to finance additional education. Capital appreciation also ranks as moderately important, but income generation is relatively unimportant.

As the person enters the peak earning years from age thirty-five to fifty-five, the objective of capital appreciation becomes quite important, because assets need to grow to pay for such things as sending children to college and to supplement other sources of retirement income. Since a person should have adequate salary income for normal living expenses, investment income should be of relatively low priority. At age forty-five, the relative weights of investment objectives might look like this:

Liquidity	10%
Income	10
Appreciation	70
Safety	10

The typical investor in this age group should have accumulated enough assets so that the objectives of safety of principal and liquidity are of

[1]For a discussion of these considerations, see Keith V. Smith, "The Major Asset Mix Problem of the Individual Investor," *Journal of Contemporary Business,* Winter 1974, pp. 49-62.

FIGURE 25-1

Hypothetical Relative Investment Objectives, by Age

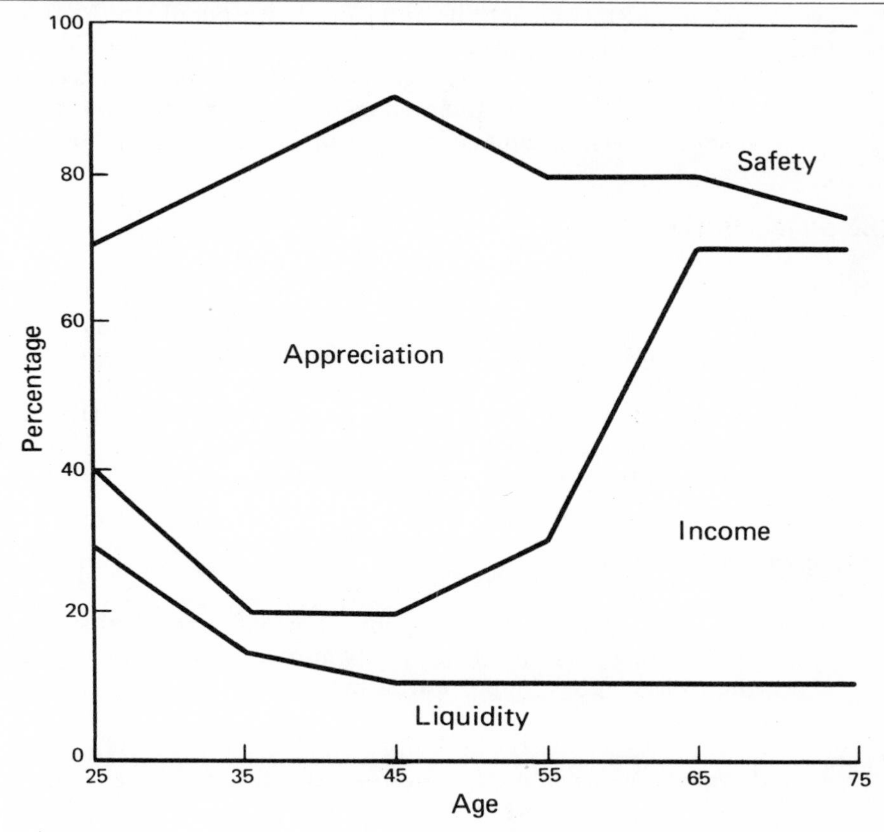

relatively minor importance. Above average risks could be taken in the pursuit of above average returns.

By the time a person reaches retirement at age sixty-five, the mix of investment objectives should shift again and the following relative weights might be appropriate:

Liquidity	10%
Income	60
Appreciation	10
Safety	20

Adequate income for the retirement years from relatively safe investments becomes the most important consideration. Liquidity is still needed to allow the person to handle unexpected expenses. Capital appreciation is a relatively unimportant objective, but still of some concern, especially in view of recent annual increases in the cost of living.

Using these general lifetime portfolio guidelines, the portfolio of assets held by a person should undergo rather radical long-term changes as age, wealth, and income change. A portfolio consisting mainly of growth common stocks might be appropriate for people in the thirty-five to fifty-five age group. However, growth common stocks should probably account for only a small percentage of the portfolio of a retired person. Institutionally provided financial benefits such as pension plans and group insurance also influence the mix of investment objectives.

PENSION PLANS

Many workers and retirees are covered by one or more pension plans.[2] These plans, which may be either private or public (e.g., the Social Security System), are important elements in asset management, as the three case studies presented shortly will indicate. Pension plans typically call for an accumulation period and a payout period. Contributions are made to the pension fund during the accumulation period. Upon retirement, benefits are paid to those entitled to them.

Private Pension Plans

In order to understand how a pension plan works, one must know the jargon of pension plans. While probably more relevant to private pension plans, the following are important terms also applicable to some public retirement plans:

Vesting. A pension plan vests when the employee receives an irrevocable right to a future pension benefit from the pension plan. Actually, the employee owns the pension benefits when they vest and cannot lose vested pension benefits if he or she either quits or is fired. Vesting provisions range from those that provide for immediate vesting of all contributions to those that provide for vesting after a longer period of employment.[3]

Portability. A pension is portable when the employee can transfer accumulated pension rights from one employer to another through a clearinghouse or through some type of government sponsored centralized fund. It is possible for an employee to have vested benefit rights, but not be allowed to transfer them to the next employer. Portable plans are sometimes found within certain industries.

[2]An excellent general discussion of pension plans is contained in "The Push for Pension Reform," *Business Week*, March 17, 1973, pp. 46–58.

[3]For a discussion of vesting provisions under the Employee Retirement Income Security Act (ERISA) of 1974, see Michael S. Gordon, "Q's and A's of Vesting," *Financial Executive*, June 1975, pp. 44–49.

Funded. A pension plan is funded if there are enough assets in the plan to cover present and estimated future benefits. Contributions are made by either employers or employees or both to provide money to fund the pension plan.

Retirement Benefit Determination. This refers to how retirement benefits are calculated under the pension plan. Many plans base their benefit formula on both the number of years of service and earnings over the life of the plan (or a specified number of years such as the highest three of the last five worked). Other arrangements are possible, such as a set amount for each year of service. Some plans integrate their benefits with those from Social Security.

Death Benefit Provision. Some pension plans will pay the amount of the vested benefit to a named beneficiary if death occurs prior to retirement. A vested pension need not contain a death benefit provision.

Disability Waiver of Premium. Some pension plans and many life insurance policies provide for continued contributions to the pension plan (or continued in force life insurance) if the individual should become disabled. This provision helps provide retirement income even though the employee is disabled.

Settlement Options. A pension plan typically allows an individual about to retire to choose from a number of options for the provision of a lifetime retirement income. For example, the retiree might choose to receive an income for as long as he or she lives or an income for as long as either the retiree or spouse is alive.

Private pension plans differ substantially from one employer to another. Employees should know and understand provisions of the employer's pension plan. The presence or lack of certain features in a pension plan may have profound implications for the manner in which the person manages other financial assets. As we shall observe from our case studies, pension plans are especially important in determining the type and amount of life insurance needed. Ramifications also exist for the risks that may be prudently taken in direct investments in stocks and bonds.

Public Pension Plans

Many public employees at the local, state, and national level are covered by government pension plans, most of which have provisions somewhat similar to private pension plans. The most important relate to retirement benefit determination, vesting provisions, death benefit provisions, and settlement options. As with private pension plans, the employee needs to determine the nature of provisions in the pension plan in order to manage other assets effectively.

The Social Security System is an important element in asset planning for many people. For our purposes, the following four main aspects of Social Security are of interest:

Retirement benefits. Monthly retirement benefits payable in full at age sixty-five with reduced benefits available if retirement occurs at age sixty-two.

Survivors benefits. Monthly payments to the survivor of a participant in the Social Security System. This includes widows, dependent children, and dependent parents. In addition, a lump-sum payment is made to the surviving spouse of a deceased worker or to the person paying burial expenses.

Disability benefits. Monthly payments to participants who become totally and permanently disabled. At age sixty-five, the disability payments change to retirement payments without any change in the amount of the payment.

Medicare. This is a two-part health insurance program for older people. One part covers hospital expenses and the other part covers doctor bills.

The determinations of both the amount of benefits and eligibility for benefits are complex under Social Security. While it is beyond the scope of this book to give a detailed treatment of the complex and technical aspects of the Social Security System, the appendix to this chapter presents an outline of the manner in which benefits are determined and the eligibility requirements for various classes of benefits.

INSURANCE

The provision of proper insurance coverage must be considered by the investor in making a financial inventory prior to the purchase of securities. This section considers various types of insurance along with the major considerations for the purchase of any specific kind of insurance. Although a comprehensive treatment of the technical aspects of insurance is impossible here, we will examine the ramifications of purchasing various types of insurance.

We will consider three basic types of insurance: life, health, and property and casualty. Our discussion will focus on the various types of policies available, the rationale for the purchase of each type, and the benefits and drawbacks of each type. The main purpose of life insurance is to provide an immediate estate in the event of the untimely death of the insured. How much of an estate is needed is a highly personal question, as we shall observe in the three case studies to be presented. Health insurance reduces the possibility of financial ruin resulting from an illness. Property and casualty insurance reduces the risk of financial loss resulting from the accidental destruction of life or property.

Life Insurance

Group and Individual Policies. Life insurance comes in a variety of forms and may be purchased in a number of ways. It is useful to distinguish between group and individual policies. Group life insurance policies are often provided to the employee by the employer with the employer paying part or all of the policy's costs. Individual policies are purchased directly from the company by the person to be covered. Group policies often require no medical examination, and they may be an important part of a person's asset management considerations. However, they frequently expire when the employee takes another job unless they are converted to an individual policy within thirty days.

Participating and Nonparticipating Policies. The premium paid for life insurance may be either participating or nonparticipating. With a participating policy, the purchaser of the policy pays an amount in excess of the probable cost of the insurance. After the insurance company determines its expenses and the benefits paid out, the premium overpayment is returned to the policyholder in the form of a dividend. This dividend reduces the actual cost of the insurance. A nonparticipating policy does not pay a dividend. The insurance premium covers the estimated benefits payable and the expenses of the insurance company. Normally, the premium for identical coverage is lower for a nonparticipating policy, but the net cost of each policy is the important comparison.[4] How does the participating policy considering the estimated dividend compare in cost to the nonparticipating policy?

Term and Cash Value Policies. There is also a fundamental difference in insurance policies between term and cash value policies. Cash value policies are also known as straight or whole life policies, and they combine an insurance feature with a savings feature. As a policy ages, the amount of the insurance benefit decreases while the cash value increases. These two elements are arranged so their total value remains level and equal to the face value of the insurance policy over its life. Should the policyholder cancel the policy, the amount of the cash value is payable to the policyholder. In addition, the policyholder may normally borrow the cash value at an interest rate that is typically below market rates; the amount borrowed against a cash value policy reduces the

[4]The cost of life insurance varies from one insurance company to another. Hence, one cannot state that the participating policy premium will always exceed the non-participating premium for identical coverage.

amount of insurance protection. Term insurance contains no savings feature. The policyholder buys only insurance. Hence, term insurance has no borrowing feature like that of cash value life insurance.

The basic decision, from an investment viewpoint, in deciding to buy term insurance is whether or not the insurance element should be separated from the savings element. The rate of return earned on the savings portion of the whole life insurance policy is difficult to calculate. Complex questions regarding estate planning and personal taxation enter into the decision, along with unique personal circumstances. If a person is unable to save without a "forced" savings plan, whole life insurance may be desirable. In spite of all the complexities involved in the calculations, the return on the savings portion of a whole life policy is not likely to exceed that available from a passbook savings account and may well be lower. Many reasonably sophisticated investors can probably earn rates of return exceeding those of the savings element of a whole life policy.

Since term insurance does not carry a savings feature it is generally cheaper than whole life coverage. Hence, the insurance buyer can obtain a greater amount of coverage for the same expenditure. This may be especially important for the young family in need of a large immediate estate, but with relatively little money for an insurance program. Table 25-1 shows representative nonparticipating insurance premiums for various policies of a large insurance firm.

The potential insurance purchaser needs sound, unbiased advice regarding a proper life insurance program, and insurance salesmen may not always provide such advice. As with stockbrokers, the quality of insurance salesmen varies widely. The potential purchaser should perform some analysis of needs before contacting an insurance salesman so that an informed decision may be made.

Whole life policies have a variety of methods of premium payment. Ordinary whole life requires a premium payment for as long as the insured lives and is the least expensive form of whole life insurance. Other premium payment plans call for the policy to be completely paid for in a limited number of years such as ten or twenty. These limited pay policies require larger annual premiums than the ordinary whole life policies.

Term insurance also has a variety of payment plans. Table 25-1 shows annual premiums for a ten-year renewable term policy. Other policy forms might be five-year renewable term, ten-year term, twenty-year term, or term to age sixty-five. *Renewable* term may be continued for successive periods without a medical reexamination. The premiums are based upon the age of the insured at the time of each renewal. *Nonrenewable* term requires a medical examination before a new policy is issued.

A somewhat specialized type of term insurance is known as *decreasing term* or *home protection* insurance. While the standard term insurance policy has a level face value throughout its life, the face value

TABLE 25–1

Representative Non-participating Insurance Premiums, per $1000 for Selected Policies, Male Rates

	Whole Life					Term		
							Decreasing‡	
Age	Ordinary	Paid Up at 65	20 Pay Life	Endowment at 65	Retirement Income at 65*	10 Year Renewable†	15 Year	25 Year
20	10.06	12.00	17.94	14.17	19.89	4.57	4.11	4.46
25	11.43	14.17	20.23	17.26	24.34	4.80	4.11	4.46
30	14.06	17.26	22.86	21.26	30.06	5.26	4.57	5.14
35	16.57	21.14	26.40	26.40	37.37	6.17	5.26	6.17
40	20.80	26.74	30.63	34.29	48.69	8.11	6.86	8.34
45	24.80	35.43	35.43	45.94	66.51	11.20	9.26	11.54
50	31.31	49.83	40.46	65.37	95.54	16.46	12.80	16.91

*Death benefit $1000 or cash value if higher; at age 65, $10 monthly income per $1000 face amount with 120 months of income certain, cash value equals $1,587.

†Cannot be renewed to extend coverage beyond age 65.

‡Premiums for 12 and 20 years respectively.

Note: Premiums are for $10,000 policies. Lower rates apply to larger policies.

Source: *Best's Flitcraft Compend 1975,* 88th Annual Edition (Oldwick, N.Y.: A.M. Best, 1975).

of a decreasing term policy declines over its life. The name, home protection insurance, comes from the fact that the face value of the insurance policy declines over time in much the same manner that the principal amount of a home mortgage declines as it is repaid. Purchasers of homes often purchase a decreasing term policy so the home mortgage will be repaid in the event of the insured's death. It is also possible to use decreasing term policies as an integrated part of total asset planning by carefully estimating insurance needs in conjunction with the growth of other financial assets, including employer-provided fringe benefits. One of the case studies to be discussed shortly illustrates this point. Decreasing term policies tend to be the least expensive form of term insurance since the face amount declines as the insured ages (and the probability of death increases).

Endowment policies are a form of cash value life insurance that emphasizes the savings aspect of the policy. If the insured dies before the policy matures, the face amount is paid to the beneficiary. If the policyholder lives to the maturity date of the policy, the face amount of the policy is paid to the policyholder. Endowment policies might be useful in saving to meet some specified goal, such as a child's education or an early retirement. If the policyholder should die before completing the goal, the savings program is completed by the insurance feature of the endowment policy.

One final type of insurance policy is the *family income* plan. Family income policies provide three basic types of benefits: 1) a lump-sum cash payment at time of death; 2) monthly income from the date of death until the maturity date of the policy; and 3) the face value of the policy at the end of the period. For example, a person purchasing a family income to age fifty-five policy might receive the following benefits per $1,000 of face value if death occurs prior to age fifty-five: 1) $150 in cash at death; 2) $20 monthly to maturity of policy; and 3) $1,000 at the maturity date of the policy. If the insured lives to the maturity date of the family income policy, some plans reduce the premium to the ordinary whole life rate and continue the face amount of the policy for the rest of the insured's life. In essence, this type of insurance contract provides for a stated face amount of permanent ordinary whole life coverage (such as $1,000) combined with the amount of decreasing term insurance needed to provide the family income benefits. The relevant question in purchasing this type of policy involves the wisdom of purchasing both whole life and decreasing term insurance. In reality, it is the whole life vs. term insurance debate again.

Health Insurance

There are three basic types of health insurance for our purposes. First is the *Blue Cross/Blue Shield* type of coverage that pays for many hospital and doctor expenses. Whether or not one elects to purchase this form of coverage depends upon one's ability to handle normal medical expenses. If a person would face severe financial problems from any illness, of even short duration, this type of insurance is desirable. Even if one elects not to carry the Blue Cross/Blue Shield form of coverage, one should be covered by a *major medical* insurance plan. Typically, these plans require the insured to pay 100 percent of medical expenses up to a certain level, such as $500, with the major medical insurer paying 80 percent of medical expenses in excess of this level. For example, if the insured incurred medical expenses of $20,000, the major medical policy would pay $15,600 (.8 times $19,500) and the insured would pay the remaining $4,400.[5]

The third type of health insurance is *disability* insurance. We noted previously that the Social Security System has a disability benefit section as part of its program. However, the Social Security disability benefits are payable only for total and permanent disability. It is equally important to have protection for a temporary disability, such as the recovery period following a heart attack.

Many employers provide some form of temporary or permanent disability protection. Paid sick leave is a form of disability protection; often the sick leave is tied to some form of insurance, which provides benefits after the sick leave is exhausted. If this form of protection is not provided as part of the fringe benefit package, the employee should seriously consider purchasing private coverage. The purchaser needs to choose among policies having various waiting periods before a disability benefit is paid. The longer the waiting period, the less the cost of the disability income protection. This is an example of the need to establish an emergency fund. It should be of sufficient size to handle any disability income waiting period.

Are there other benefits to the investor from having a good disability income policy? One very important benefit is that it allows the investor to continue a systematic investment program despite being disabled. If the investor were using a *dollar cost averaging* approach to investments, this technique could be continued. In dollar cost averaging, the investor purchases equal dollar amounts of a security (or portfolio in the case of an investment company) at regular time intervals without regard to the level of the stock market. When prices are high, few shares are purchased. When prices are low, more shares are purchased. Hence, this approach relieves the investor of timing decisions and results in a cost per share purchased that is lower than the average of the prices at which these shares were purchased. This is true since more shares are purchased at lower prices than at higher prices. Dollar cost averaging does not relieve the investor of the security selection problem, however. A poor security selection is not "bailed out" by using dollar cost averaging.

[5]The policy might contain a provision requiring the insured to pay no more than a given dollar amount (such as $3,000) for any illness.

A second benefit of a disability feature is that it allows the investor to maintain an adequate life insurance program. Many policies provide a disability premium waiver, which pays the premium in the event of disability. A cash value life insurance policy will continue to accumulate cash value. In addition, the investor should be able to seek the same risk level as before the disability.

Property and Casualty Insurance

Most people own some type of property and casualty insurance. Automobile insurance, for example, is purchased to protect against financial loss from an automobile accident. In view of increasingly larger damage settlements arising from automobile accidents, a person should purchase a policy with relatively large liability limits if possible. It would seem that a $100,000/$300,000 policy would be appropriate for many drivers. This means that the policy will pay benefits up to $100,000 for one person injured as the result of an accident and up to $300,000 for all injuries as the result of an accident. Whether collision coverage should also be carried depends primarily on the value of the automobile being insured, the cost of the coverage, and the ability of the owner of the automobile to bear the financial loss should the automobile become damaged as the result of an accident.

Another common form of property and casualty insurance is *homeowner's* insurance. This insurance protects the insured from severe financial loss as the result of damage to or destruction of the insured's residence. Financial institutions normally require that coverage be provided in an amount equal to the amount of the mortgage. However, with increases in property values and construction costs, the homeowner will typically want to carry coverage in excess of the value of any amount owed on the property. Coverage should be sufficient to replace the home without suffering substantial financial loss. This means the homeowner will want to insure the home for an amount close to its replacement cost.[6]

Many homeowner policies now incorporate some form of inflation adjustment feature, allowing the amount of the insurance to be adjusted automatically based upon annual changes in a cost of construction index. For example, a house originally insured for $40,000 would be insured for $44,000 if the construction index increased 10 percent during the year; the new premium would be based upon the $44,000 coverage. This desirable feature allows the investor to protect the investment made in

[6]In order to recover full payment for the amount of a loss, coverage equal to 80 percent of the replacement cost must be carried. For example, if a $60,000 home is insured for $30,000 and suffers $4,800 in damage, the insurance company will pay only $3,000 ($30,000/$48,000 times $4,800). If the residence were insured for $48,000, the company would pay $4,800 for the loss.

a residence without having to make a conscious effort to update coverage limits.

Homeowner policies normally provide two other major forms of protection. First, the contents of the residence are normally insured to an amount equal to a given percentage of the insurance on the building itself. However, a homeowner with substantial sums of capital invested in art masterpieces, antiques, precious stones, and similar assets will often need to provide additional coverage for these assets, since they may not be adequately covered by the homeowner's policy. Second, the homeowner's policy typically provides a coverage amount to cover situations where the homeowner is personally liable. This covers such situations as having the mailman fall from slipping on an icy sidewalk or hitting someone with a golf ball.

CASE STUDIES

A summary of the relevant personal and financial data for the three cases is presented in Exhibit 25-1. Although our analysis of these three situations may not be completely comprehensive, it is adequate to observe the integrated financial planning approach. Since financial planning is an individual process, other recommendations than those given in our analysis may be perfectly proper.

The approach taken for the three cases is a four-stage one. First, we make general comments on each situation, and discuss the investment objectives considered the most important. Second, we make specific comments to supplement the information presented in Exhibit 25-1. The third stage presents an analysis of each case. Finally, a summary of the recommendations for each case is presented.

Case One

General comments: Henry Hunter is a young college professor, age 29 in 1974, starting on what he hopes will be a rewarding career. His annual income of $15,000 comes entirely from his salary. With a wife and two small children to support, Henry must provide for an immediate estate, should he die, sufficient to allow the family to maintain a comparable standard of living and also allow the children to receive a suitable education. Hence, adequate life insurance is of primary importance. An emergency fund should also be established. Any investments made by Henry should stress good quality and growth. While adequate retirement income might be an objective, Henry still has a number of years to meet this objective.

Specific comments: Henry participates in a pension plan called the Teachers Insurance and Annuity Association (TIAA) and the College

EXHIBIT 25–1
Case Study—Financial and Personal Statistics

	Case One	Case Two	Case Three
Age	29	45	55
Sex	M	F	M
Marital status	Married	Widow	Married
Annual salary income	$15,000	N.A.	$35,000
Dependents	wife and 2 children (3 and 1)	2 children (20 and 16)	Wife
Replacement value of home	$40,000	$40,000	$70,000
Mortgage on home	$33,000 8½% for 29 years	$15,000 6½% for 15 years	$ 8,000 5½% for 5 years
Pension plan	TIAA-CREF	None	Co. plan fully vested
Social Security	Yes—participant	Survivor's benefits	Yes—participant
Life insurance	$30,000 group	None	$35,000 group $30,000 whole life
Blue Cross/Blue Shield or Comparable Plan	Yes	No	Yes
Major Medical	$100,000	No	$50,000
Value of automobile	$2,500	$1,200	$5,000
Automobile insurance	25,000/50,000 and $50 deductible	100,000/300,000	100,000/300,000 and $100 deductible
Homeowner's insurance	$35,000	$30,000	$50,000
Other assets:			
Savings account	$700	$1,000	$12,500
Common stocks	None	None	100,000
Corporate bonds	None	None	50,000
Series E Bonds			
Redemption value	None	5,500	12,500
Cost	None	3,750	7,500
Insurance proceeds	None	60,000	None

Retirement Equities Fund (CREF). Funds paid into the TIAA portion of his retirement plan are invested in fixed-income investments, while CREF contributions purchase part of a diversified portfolio of stocks, consisting mostly of growth common stocks.[7] The college for which he works contributes an amount equal to 5 percent of Henry's salary and Henry matches this for a total of 10 percent contributed to the pension

[7]CREF, started in 1952, is considered to be the first significant variable annuity plan allowing participants to invest in common stocks. See William C. Greenough, *A New Approach to Retirement Income* (New York: Teachers Insurance and Annuity Association of America, 1964).

plan. Allocations to CREF may range from 0 to 100 percent of the contributions made to the retirement plan. Henry is presently at an allocation of 50 percent to CREF. TIAA-CREF has an *immediate vesting* provision for all contributions made to the plan. In addition, vested benefits are paid as a death benefit should death occur prior to retirement.

Henry also contributes to the Social Security System, and his payments into the system were based on the following earnings: 1969, $6,000; 1973, $10,800; and 1974, $13,200. Payments will be made on earnings of $14,100 for 1975.

Analysis: Based upon the current contribution rate, the vested death benefit in TIAA-CREF increases at $1,500 per year, ignoring any growth from the investment income of the pension plan.[8] Figure 25-2 shows the vested benefits of TIAA-CREF for the next twenty years assuming salary growth of 5 percent per year and investment earnings averaging 7 percent annually. The vested benefit starts out small but grows rapidly during the twenty-year period. Under the assumptions made, if Henry should die at age forty-nine, a death benefit of over $90,000 would be paid to named beneficiaries. Even if Henry should leave the teaching profession, he still retains his vested benefits and they continue to earn income.

FIGURE 25-2
Hypothetical TIAA-CREF Death Benefit

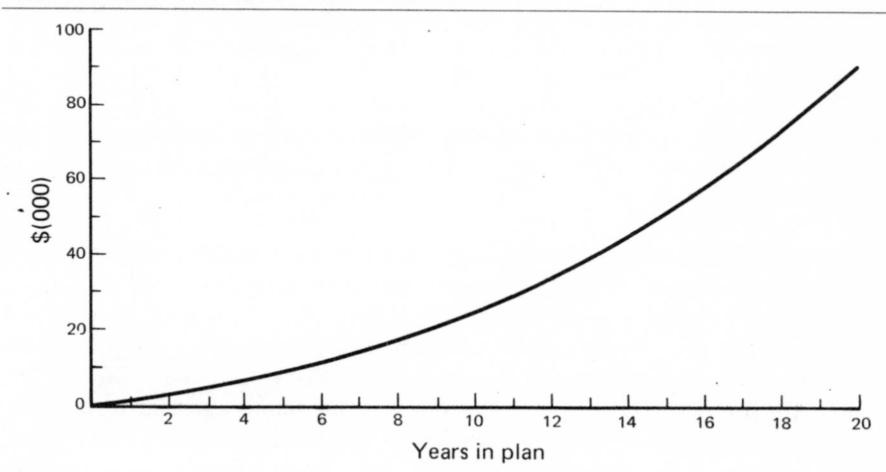

Social Security survivor's benefits are also an important consideration in this case. If one follows the procedure for the determination of the average monthly wage outlined in the appendix, wages starting with 1967 must be listed, but the five years of zero earnings (1967, 1968, 1970, 1971, and 1972) may be dropped. This leaves three years (1969, 1973, and 1974) with earnings to count for the determination of the average

[8]We also ignore minor load charges for TIAA-CREF in our analysis.

monthly wage. The average monthly wage for these years is $833.33 ($30,000 ÷ 36). If 1975 earnings are included at $14,100, the average monthly wage increases to $918.75 ($44,100 ÷ 48). If Henry died at the end of 1974, the family benefit payable would be $778.80 per month in nontaxable income. If he died in 1975 after paying into the Social Security System based on $14,100, the family benefit would be $814.66 per month. Survivor's benefits under Social Security are definitely an important consideration in this situation.

How much life insurance is needed given the benefits payable under TIAA-CREF and Social Security? What type of insurance should be purchased? One method of determining the amount of life insurance needed is to estimate how much is needed to produce an income of $15,000, Henry's present salary. For ease of calculation, we assume that Social Security would provide $800 a month in survivor's benefits. The calculations showing the life insurance needed are given below:

Salary to be replaced	$15,000
less Social Security benefits ($800 times 12)	9,600
Life insurance proceeds need to produce an income of	$ 5,400

If the proceeds earn 8 percent, the following calculation yields the amount of insurance needed:

$$\frac{\$5{,}400}{.08} = \$67{,}500$$

Group life of $30,000 is provided leaving private insurance of $37,500 required.

The amount of insurance needed of $37,500 is only an approximation. Social Security benefits are nontaxable, while Henry's entire $15,000 in salary is subject to taxation. An allowance should probably be made for Henry's personal consumption that no longer needs to be provided. No allowance has been made for changes in the cost of living or in interest rate levels. As the children reach age eighteen (or twenty-two if they are still in school) the family benefit decreases and stops after the last child reaches these age limits. Under the Social Security System, the widow gets no additional benefits until age sixty. Even though it is difficult to quantify all these factors, privately purchased life insurance of between $50,000 and $70,000 should be adequate. This amount of insurance would leave some margin of safety in the calculations to cover unconsidered needs and factors.

As the death benefit from his TIAA-CREF plan increases over time in a manner similar to the example in Figure 25–2, the need for insurance should gradually decrease. This is also true since fewer years of support for the children would be required. Given the immediate vesting provision coupled with the death benefit provision, a decreasing term policy is a logical choice. The amount of the insurance coverage decreases as the vested death benefit increases. Since Henry works for a college, he can purchase an insurance policy from TIAA, which is also a nonprofit, legal reserve life insurance company in addition to managing both the TIAA and CREF pension plans. Figure 25-3 shows the amount of insurance provided yearly for the first twenty years from a $70,000 twenty-five-year decreasing term policy. The estimated amount of the vested death benefit from Figure 25-2 has been added to the benefit amount of the decreasing term policy to show the death benefits payable from both sources. In this example, the total increases gradually over time. A $70,000 decreasing term TIAA policy for Henry requires an annual participating premium of $236.60 for twenty years. Dividends would be approximately $80 per year for a net annual cost of about $156. Adequate insurance coverage is provided at a modest cost, although the TIAA-CREF death benefit provision is very important in making this insurance purchase decision.

Henry's health insurance coverage is adequate, given the Blue Cross/Blue Shield and the major medical policy provided as a fringe benefit. The automobile liability limits are probably too low and he should consider increasing them. The $50 deductible on the collision coverage is satisfactory, but might be raised to $100 without much additional risk. The amount of the homeowner's insurance coverage is cur-

FIGURE 25-3

Death Benefits from $70,000 TIAA 25-Year Decreasing Term Policy and Hypothetical TIAA-CREF Pension Plan

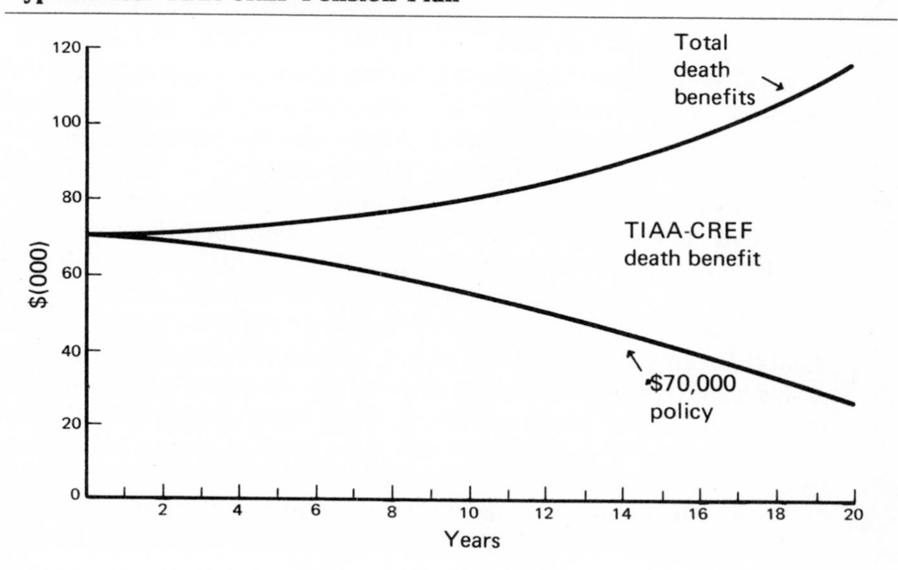

rently satisfactory, but should be tied to some cost of living provision so that it remains adequate. Finally, Henry's emergency fund is low—only $700 in a savings account. Prior to a direct investment program, he should increase the emergency fund to at least two or three months' salary ($2,500 to $3,750).

Summary of recommendations:

1. Purchase $50,000 to $70,000 decreasing term policy.
2. Increase the automobile insurance liability limits. Consider raising the deductible on the collision coverage to $100.
3. Make sure an inflation provision exists in the homeowner's policy. Add one if it does not presently exist.
4. Determine the personal liability coverage contained as part of the homeowner's policy. An adequate level should be approximately $250,000. Increase this coverage if necessary.
5. Give priority to increasing the emergency fund with the first resources available for investment purposes.
6. While TIAA-CREF provides for systematic investment in the pension plan, consider also a systematic program for other investments. An investment company might be an appropriate vehicle.
7. In view of the risk and rate of return evidence presented in Chapter 6, consider increasing the percentage of pension contributions going to CREF. The family is in fair shape financially given the fringe benefits provided and more risk could prudently be accepted in the form of a larger CREF allocation. However, this is a personal consideration.

Case Two

General comments: Jane Edwards' husband died in late 1974. Jane is forty-five and has two children, a twenty-year-old son and a sixteen-year-old daughter. Jane's assets consist primarily of $60,000 in life insurance proceeds received when her husband died and a personal residence with an estimated market value of $40,000 in early 1975.

This case presents an interesting conflict of objectives. Jane Edwards needs as much income as possible given the assets she has, but her additional life expectancy is in the neighborhood of thirty years. With inflation likely to be a continuing problem, some asset growth is desirable. In addition, since she is unlikely to obtain many additional assets, safety of principal is an important objective. Even if Jane returns to the labor force, the assets she presently has should be well managed. Liquidity should be provided consistent with the other portfolio objectives.

Specific comments: Jane's son has one additional year to go in college. It is uncertain at the moment whether her daughter will want to receive an education beyond high school. Jane's husband had made payments to the Social Security System at the maximum earnings level each year from 1956 to 1974. Jane has never owned a stock or bond and has no formal training in investment management. Consequently, the recently received $60,000 life insurance proceeds have been invested in a passbook savings account at an interest rate of 5 percent.

Analysis: The two critical elements in this situation are the benefits to be received from the survivors provision of the Social Security System and the manner in which the insurance proceeds are reinvested. Although Jane is not wealthy by any means, a modest standard of living is possible with careful financial asset management.

Since her husband paid at the maximum earnings level set for Social Security since 1956, one need only add the yearly figures shown in the appendix for the years from 1956 through 1974 as the first step in the determination of the average monthly wage. The years from 1951 to 1955 would be dropped as allowed by law since they are the years with the lowest earnings. This procedure results in an average monthly wage of $542.11. The benefits payable on the basis of this average monthly wage are $619.90 for a widow and two children, $512.60 for a widow and one child, and $244.40 for a widow at the age of sixty. Jane can obtain $7,438.80 for the remaining year her son has in school, and $6,151.20 for the following years until her daughter reaches age eighteen. If her daughter does not continue in school, Jane receives nothing until she reaches the age of sixty in thirteen more years. If her daughter remains in school, Jane would receive $6,151.20 annually for up to four years. This would reduce her benefitless years to nine.

While the Social Security income is adequate for the next two to six years, the insurance proceeds should be reinvested, because her present portfolio is inefficient in a portfolio theory context. She needs to obtain a larger income for her benefitless years and to supplement Social Security widow's benefits that become available at age sixty. While going back to work is a possibility, we will proceed on the basis of no earned income. Since Jane presently has a low taxable income and three personal exemptions, it would seem a good time to redeem the Series E bonds and pay any tax on the $1,750 of accrued but unrealized interest income. Redemption results in a total of $66,500 available for reinvestment, counting the $61,000 presently in savings accounts and the $5,500 from the redemption of the Series E bonds.

How should this $66,500 be reinvested? Consistent with the objectives of reasonable income, safety of principal, and modest growth possibilities, a portfolio of high quality corporate bonds and stocks is reasonable. The stocks would need to have attractive dividend yields from well-secured dividends. She ought to be able to earn a yield of 8 percent without sacrificing much safety of principal. This would give her an annual investment income of $5,320. Since Jane presently has Social Security benefits, the investment income should be reinvested. Assuming reinvestment for two years, the size of the portfolio becomes $77,566, which would produce investment income of $6,205 annually at a return of 8 percent.

Since Jane may not require a $40,000 house, she should consider its sale. Adding the estimated equity of $25,000 in the house to her $66,500 produces an investment fund of $91,500. At an 8 percent annual return, investment income is $7,320. If this income can be reinvested for two years, the value of the portfolio becomes $106,726. This portfolio would have an income of $8,538 at an 8 percent return. Since she is inexperienced in investment matters, she should seek well-qualified financial counsel. Because her standard of living is at stake, any money spent for sound investment advice would be a wise "investment."

Attention must also be given to her insurance program. Since Jane effectively has no dependents at the present time and also has a modest size estate, life insurance does not seem necessary. She should purchase health insurance in the nature of a Blue Cross/Blue Shield policy, and she should consider a major medical policy. The automobile insurance appears adequate. The homeowner's insurance, if she decides not to sell the house, should be increased to at least $32,000 and an inflation adjustment provision added to the policy.

Summary of recommendations:

1. Purchase health insurance and possibly a major medical policy.
2. Increase the homeowner's insurance coverage and add an inflation adjustment provision.
3. Redeem the Series E bonds.
4. Reinvest the portfolio assets in good quality stocks and bonds producing adequate income consistent with safety of principal. In the selection of stocks, give minor consideration to possible growth of principal.
5. Seek competent investment advice to accomplish recommendation 4.

Case Three

General comments: Donald Ryan, a fifty-five-year-old business executive, is well established financially. He has a good measure of financial independence and should now start considering the management of his assets with retirement in mind. The $35,000 income, shown in Exhibit 25–1, is salary and does not include any investment income. Important investment objectives include liquidity, safety of principal, and adequate income. It is still prudent to invest in good quality growth situations and, given Donald's financial strength, an occasional speculative investment would be acceptable.

Specific comments: His pension plan is fully vested and allows early retirement starting at age fifty-five. Pension benefits are determined by the following benefit formula: 40 percent of the average of the highest three years earnings if retirement occurs from age fifty-five to age fifty-nine and 45 percent of the average of the highest three years earnings if retirement occurs at age sixty or later. Retirement is normally expected at age sixty-five unless a special waiver is granted by the company. The $35,000 salary has remained constant for the past three years.

Social Security retirement benefits will be available at retirement in accordance with the provisions of the Social Security System. Donald has participated in the system since 1947 and has paid in the maximum amount each year since then.

In the life insurance area, the $35,000 group life policy decreases in value by $3,000 yearly. At age sixty-five, the employee obtains a $5,000 paid up policy from the company. Retirement prior to age sixty-five allows the employee to obtain $5,000 of coverage in the form of a paid up policy granted at the time of retirement. The $30,000 ordinary whole life policy was purchased many years ago and presently has a cash value of $15,000. No borrowing has occurred under the provisions of this policy, although the policyholder may borrow the cash value at an interest rate of 5 percent.

Exhibit 25–2 shows the investments that make up the other assets. These consist of the savings account, the common stock portfolio, and the corporate bond portfolio.

Analysis: Donald could retire at the present time and receive $14,000 annually from the pension plan. Combined with investment income of $10,628 from dividends ($3,824 from dividends, $5,223 in corporate bond interest, and $1,581 from the savings account and the Series E bonds), his total retirement income would be $24,628. Social Security retirement benefits would be available at age 62 to supplement the pension plan and investment income. Retirement certainly appears financially possible at this time.

The common stock and corporate bond portfolios seem to have been constructed with conflicting objectives. This could be the main reason that the market value is less than cost in both situations. The corporate bond portfolio is generally of only fair quality and high income seems to have been the main objective in this situation. It might be wise to sell some of the low rated bonds to realize a capital loss for tax purposes and reinvest the proceeds in higher quality bonds. Donald's taxable income is unknown, but a realistic range of $36,000 to $38,000 would mean a 45 percent marginal tax bracket. Given this high marginal tax bracket, Donald should consider the purchase of good quality municipal bonds. According to Exhibit 19–2, a taxable income of $36,000 to $40,000 would produce a taxable equivalent yield of 10.91 percent if 6 percent municipal bonds are purchased. This gives no consideration to potential benefits from a reduction in state income taxes from the purchase of municipals issued by state and local government units in Donald's state.

The common stock portfolio is of fairly good quality and has some growth potential. As with the bond portfolio, some of the poorer quality

EXHIBIT 25–2
Case Three—Investment Portfolio

Savings account:
$2,500 in daily interest 5¼% account
5,000 in two-year 6½% certificate of deposit
5,000 in four-year 7½% certificate of deposit
(Both certificates are one year old)

Common stocks:

Description	*Market Value*	*Cost*	*Income Received*
500 shares Alza Corporation	$ 12,500	$ 5,000	$ 0
400 shares American Telephone & Telegraph	20,000	24,000	1,360
200 shares Georgia Pacific	9,000	10,000	160
100 shares IBM	21,000	10,000	600
2,000 shares Kampgrounds of America	10,000	15,000	0
2,000 shares Ozark Airlines	6,000	10,000	100
200 shares Polaroid	7,200	15,000	64
1,100 shares Southern Company	14,300	18,000	1,540
	$100,000	$107,000	$3,824

Corporate Bonds*			
$10,000 Chrysler, 8⅞, 1995 (A)	$ 7,200	$10,000	$ 888
10,000 Cleveland Electric, 9.85, 2010 (AA)	10,400	10,000	985
10,000 Consolidated Edison, 5, 1987, (BB)	6,000	8,000	500
15,000 LTV, 5, 1988 (CCC)	7,300	11,000	750
10,000 Occidental Petroleum, 11, 1982 (BBB)	10,200	10,000	1,100
10,000 TWA, 10, 1985 (BB)	8,900	10,000	1,000
	$50,000	$59,000	$5,223

*Par value, name, coupon rate, maturity (S&P rating).

stocks or those with somewhat questionable growth prospects could be sold and the proceeds reinvested in better quality growth stocks such as Eastman Kodak, 3M, or Xerox. In general, however, only slight changes appear necessary in the common stock portfolio, although common stocks as a percentage of total assets might gradually be reduced during the next ten to fifteen years.

Some changes appear desirable in his insurance. The amount of coverage of the homeowner's policy should be increased to at least 80 percent of the replacement value of the home. The $30,000 ordinary whole life policy is not really needed given the total assets under Donald's control. The policy could be cancelled and the $15,000 cash value invested or the $15,000 cash value could be borrowed at 5 percent. Borrowing the cash value at 5 percent and investing this money in top quality corporate bonds yielding 8 percent would increase income by $450 with almost no increase in risk. The automobile liability limits might be increased to $300,000/$500,000, considering the assets that could be taken in the event of a high judgment resulting from an accident.

The Series E bonds could be retained as they are. There is no reason to redeem them since they are earning a 6 percent rate of return that is being tax deferred. In addition, they amount to a relatively small portion (about 5 percent) of the total assets being managed if one includes the equity in the home.

Summary of recommendations:

1. Purchase additional automobile liability coverage.
2. Increase the coverage on the homeowner's policy to at least $56,000 and add an inflation adjustment feature.
3. Consider selling some of the lower quality bonds at a capital loss and upgrading the quality of the bond portfolio.
4. Investigate the purchase of municipal bonds since the marginal tax bracket is 45 percent.
5. Make minor changes in the common stock portfolio and concentrate on high quality growth stocks in the future.
6. Do not redeem the Series E bonds, but wait until the income level drops at retirement.

SUMMARY

This chapter attempted to integrate many of the topics previously discussed. We looked at the lifetime portfolio approach, noting that the investor needs to formulate carefully those investment objectives most appropriate for his or her age, income and wealth level, marital status, and risk preference. Although general investment objective guidelines were presented and three case studies were examined, the answers given should not be considered as the only correct answers or even as entirely appropriate under the circumstances. In many instances, it is necessary only to arrive at "ballpark" figures, given the uncertainties involved in forecasting, to manage one's assets well. However, the reader should have developed an appreciation of the manner in which such diverse elements as life and health insurance, pension plan participation, and direct investments can be integrated to form a logical, comprehensive plan for financial asset management.

We observed that pension plans including Social Security have a profound impact on other investment decisions. The survivors benefit under Social Security is extremely important in the decision to purchase private life insurance for a young family. Since many people may belong to a private pension plan as well as the Social Security System, the need to set aside additional funds for retirement purposes may be drastically diminished.

Hence, the investment program of the individual could seek a relatively high rate of return by accepting more risk than would be true in the absence of these institutionally provided arrangements.

We do not suggest that the forming and implementing of an integrated financial plan is easy. It requires not only a careful analysis of each person's situation, but also considerable knowledge of the various investment alternatives available. A working knowledge of the tax laws is also a useful ingredient in financial asset planning. Although the task is not easy, a person may derive great financial and personal satisfaction from a sound financial management program.

QUESTIONS

1. What considerations should be integrated into the lifetime portfolio approach for personal characteristics and for the individual's financial condition?
2. How should the objective of growth of capital ideally vary over a person's lifetime?
3. Of what significance to the investor is the vesting provision in the pension plan provided by the employer?
4. Some pension plans have a death benefit provision and/or a disability waiver provision. In addition, a disability waiver of premium provision is available for most life insurance policies. Of what significance are these provisions to the investor?
5. What are the basic types of benefits provided by the Social Security System?
6. Of the benefits provided by the Social Security System, which are the most important to:
   a) A twenty-five-year-old unmarried person?
   b) A twenty-five-year-old married man with one child?
   c) A sixty-year-old widow.
7. Why is the acquisition of adequate life, health (including disability), and casualty insurance important for the investor?
8. What is dollar cost averaging? What problem(s) does it solve for the investor?
9. Describe in general terms the advantages of purchasing term insurance as opposed to whole life insurance.

PROBLEMS

1. Warren Hennis graduated from Southeastern University two years ago. He is presently twenty-three years of age and works for a medium-size company in Columbus, Georgia. His annual salary is $12,500 and he is

unmarried. He pays a Georgia state income tax equal to 3 percent of his gross income and Social Security taxes take another 5.85 percent. He rents an apartment for $195 a month with utilities taking another $40 per month. His employer's pension plan vests after ten years of service and does not carry a death benefit provision. He is covered by Social Security. His employer provides Blue Cross/Blue Shield coverage in addition to a major medical policy. Warren owns a late model automobile with current market value of $4,000 on which payments of $135 per month are due for the next 36 months. He carries automobile liability insurance of $25,000/$50,000 and has collision coverage with a $100 deductible. He has no homeowner's insurance coverage. His employer provides a group life insurance policy of $15,000. Warren's only other asset is $800 in a savings account. He has learned that you are taking a course in investments and wonders if you have any comments regarding his present financial situation. He is also interested in establishing some form of investment program to increase his assets for those years when he is no longer "free and reckless."

2. David Bartow, one of Professor Philips' students, approached her after class one day and wondered if she had a few minutes to talk about the financial situation facing his seventy-seven-year-old grandmother. David explained that his grandmother was a widow and received $180 a month in Social Security benefits after deductions for Medicare premiums. She lived alone in a modest apartment, but this still required expenditures of $120 a month for rent and utilities. Other living expenses brought to $300 the monthly expenditures required. David's grandmother had $20,000 in a 5 percent savings account. She used the income from this account to supplement her Social Security check. Even with this interest income, David's grandmother was using her capital since her living expenses were $35 to $40 a month greater than her income. David said she was concerned about this since she did not want to outlive her capital. In addition, she would really like to have the principal remain constant so that she could leave a "little something" to her grandchildren, as she put it. David explained that his grandmother had never owned a stock or bond in her life and was somewhat afraid of the idea of buying securities. David wondered if Professor Philips could talk to his grandmother for a few minutes since she lived in the same city and make some suggestions regarding her financial situation. If you were Philips, what would you recommend?

SUGGESTED READINGS

Apilado, Vincent P. "Pension Funds, Personal Savings and Economic Growth." *Journal of Risk and Insurance,* September 1972, pp. 397–404.

Bauman, W. Scott. *Performance Objectives of Investors.* Occasional Paper Number

2. Charlottesville, Va.: The Financial Analysts Research Foundation, 1975, pp. 59–68.

Gregg, Davis W. and Vane B. Lucas, eds. *Life and Health Insurance Handbook.* 3rd ed. Homewood, Illinois: Dow Jones-Irwin, 1973.

Klemkosky, Robert C. and David F. Scott, Jr. "Pension Funds: Prevailing Issues." *MSU Business Topics,* Winter 1974, pp. 15–27.

Okner, Benjamin A. "The Social Security Payroll Tax, Some Alternatives for Reform." *Journal of Finance,* May 1975, pp. 567–78.

"Pension Reform's Expensive Ricochet." *Business Week,* March 24, 1975, pp. 144–55.

Smith, Keith V. "The Major Asset Mix Problem of the Individual Investor." *Journal of Contemporary Business,* Winter 1974, pp. 49–62.

Stone, Gary K. "Life Insurance Sales Practices on the College Campus." *Journal of Risk and Insurance,* June 1973, pp. 167–79.

"Term Insurance vs. Whole Life." *Forbes,* March 15, 1975, pp. 45–50.

The Consumers Union Report on Life Insurance. Mount Vernon, N.Y.: Consumers Union, 1972.

Appendix

Outline of Social Security Program Benefits*

I. Eligibility—must qualify by personal status and by insured status (A and B below)
   A. By personal status
      1. Age of retired
         a. over 65 for full benefits
         b. 62 for reduced benefits
         c. 72 whether retired or not
      2. Dependents of retired
         a. wife over 65 (reduced benefits at age 62)
         b. children
            1) under 18
            2) over 18 if disabled before age 22
            3) between 18 and 22 if attending school and unmarried

*This outline is adapted from material organized by Michael Murray, Associate Professor of Insurance at the University of Iowa, and used with his permission.

c. former wives (divorced), if married 20 years and retiree has contributed to support, may receive benefits at age 62
3. Those paying last expenses for deceased (lump sum)
4. Survivors of deceased
   a. widow
      1) age 62 (60 with reduced benefits)
      2) regardless of age if caring for child (under 18 or disabled)
      3) age 50 if disabled receives reduced benefits
   b. widower age 65 (50, if disabled, receives reduced benefits)
   c. former wife
      1) over 62
      2) with eligible child (same as widow)
   d. dependent parents over 62
   e. children
      1) under 18
      2) over 18 if:
         a) disabled before 22
         b) under 22 and attending school and unmarried
5. Disabled—both a and b below
   a. total—unable to engage in any kind of substantial gainful employment which exists in the economy
   b. permanent—has lasted more than 5 months
6. Dependents of disabled—essentially the same as deceased
7. Aged incurring hospital bills (Medicare—Part I)
8. Aged incurring doctor bills (Medicare—Part II)

B. By insured status
   1. Meaning of terms
      a. quarter—earnings of $50 or more in covered employment in a calendar quarter
      b. insured
         1) fully insured requires 1 quarter of coverage for every 4 since 1950 or since age 21 and until becoming deceased, disabled, or 65.
         2) currently insured requires 6 of the last 13 quarters
         3) "disability" insured requires 20 of the last 40 quarters except if under age 31; one-half of the quarters since age 21 with a minimum of 1½ years
   2. Status required to qualify for benefits—fully insured qualifies for all benefits except disability. Even if not fully insured, some benefits are available if currently insured

II. Amount of Benefit
   A. Calculation of Average Monthly Wage (AMW)
      1. Determine number of years to use
         a. all those since 1950 or age 21 (less five years)
         b. minimum: five years for retirement and two years for disability or survivors benefits

2. List *all* year's earnings
3. Reduce any years which are above the maximum eligible wages
   a. 1951–1954 $3,600
   b. 1955–1958 4,200
   c. 1959–1965 4,800
   d. 1966–1967 6,600
   e. 1968–1971 7,800
   f. 1972 9,000
   g. 1973 10,800
   h. 1974 13,200
   i. 1975 14,100
4. Cross off years of "disability freeze"—those years in which you were eligible for disability benefits
5. Cross off from the remaining number of years the years of lowest earnings until the number of years equals the number in II.A.1. above
6. Total the remaining yearly earnings and divide by the number of years and then by 12 to obtain AMW

B. Use benefit table to estimate the benefit to be received
C. Retirement Test for those between date of retirement and age 72 requires loss of one dollar in Social Security benefits for each two dollars earned over $2,520 yearly. Determinations are made on monthly basis and earned income does not include interest, dividends, rent, or other pension plan benefits.

A–1

Social Security Benefit Schedule

	Monthly Benefits			
		Survivor's		
Average Monthly Wage	Retirement (old age) at 65	Widow at 60	Mother + 1 child	Maximum Family
$ 400	$279.80	$200.10	$419.80	$510.50
500	323.40	231.30	485.20	593.30
600	371.50	265.70	557.40	657.30
700	410.70	293.70	616.20	718.70
800	437.00	312.50	655.60	764.80
900	461.00	329.70	691.60	806.80
1000	485.00	346.80	727.60	848.70
1100	506.60	362.30	760.00	886.50

*

Author Index

*

Subject Index

N

O

P

Q

R

S

T

†